# PRAISE FOR *EXPLORING THE U.S. CENSUS: YOUR GUIDE TO AMERICA'S DATA*

D0165883

The most comprehensive source book on the subject that will be invaluable for anyone doing research using census data.

—A. Victor Ferreros, Florida State University

This book is interesting and easy to read, and it compiles information that I often have a hard time gathering before covering the census in my course. I feel much more prepared just having read it. I teach geography, and students make extensive use of census data but don't have a good understanding of where it comes from and its possibilities and limitations. While reading the book, I was considering teaching our census data class that has been on the shelf for a while. I was inspired by the text to offer it!

—Anne M. Mahar, Arcadia University

*Exploring the U.S. Census* provides an excellent overview of many parts of the U.S. Census Bureau's work. It is a timely reference for anyone interested in using their current and historic data.

—David S. Lamb, University of South Florida

This book integrates material that is difficult for new users of census data to find, as it is spread across dozens of technical manuals for different years and different data products. The attentive reader will skip years of novice traps and false starts. There is no comparable product on the market today.

—Dr. Stephanie Deitrick, Arizona State University

This is a much-needed text that will help students, researchers, and practitioners understand and properly use census data.

—Lee Hachadoorian, Temple University

This text is a welcome, comprehensive introduction to working with and understanding census data.

—Hugh Bartling, DePaul University

This is the most comprehensive guidebook to the use of the census. The author's experience is invaluable.

—Elizabeth C. Delmelle, University of North Carolina at Charlotte

# Exploring the U.S. Census

## Your Guide to America's Data

Sara Miller McCune founded SAGE Publishing in 1965 to support the dissemination of usable knowledge and educate a global community. SAGE publishes more than 1000 journals and over 800 new books each year, spanning a wide range of subject areas. Our growing selection of library products includes archives, data, case studies and video. SAGE remains majority owned by our founder and after her lifetime will become owned by a charitable trust that secures the company's continued independence.

Los Angeles | London | New Delhi | Singapore | Washington DC | Melbourne

# Exploring the U.S. Census

## Your Guide to America's Data

**Frank Donnelly**
*Baruch College CUNY*

Los Angeles | London | New Delhi
Singapore | Washington DC | Melbourne

**FOR INFORMATION:**

SAGE Publications, Inc.

2455 Teller Road

Thousand Oaks, California 91320

E-mail: order@sagepub.com

SAGE Publications Ltd.

1 Oliver's Yard

55 City Road

London, EC1Y 1SP

United Kingdom

SAGE Publications India Pvt. Ltd.

B 1/I 1 Mohan Cooperative Industrial Area

Mathura Road, New Delhi 110 044

India

SAGE Publications Asia-Pacific Pte. Ltd.

18 Cross Street #10-10/11/12

China Square Central

Singapore 048423

Acquisitions Editor: Leah Fargotstein

Editorial Assistant: Claire Laminen

Content Development Editor: Chelsea Neve

Production Editor: Rebecca Lee

Copy Editor: QuADS Prepress Pvt. Ltd.

Typesetter: Integra

Proofreader: Ellen Brink

Indexer: Will Ragsdale

Cover Designer: Candice Harman

Marketing Manager: Shari Countryman

Printed in the United States of America

*Library of Congress Cataloging-in-Publication Data*

Names: Donnelly, Frank (Francis P.), author.

Title: Exploring the U.S. census : your guide to America's data / Frank Donnelly, Baruch College.

Description: Los Angeles : SAGE, [2020] | Includes bibliographical references and index.

Identifiers: LCCN 2019029185 | ISBN 978-1-5443-5542-9 (paperback ; alk. paper) | ISBN 978-1-5443-5543-6 (epub) | ISBN 978-1-5443-5544-3 (epub) | ISBN 978-1-5443-5545-0 (adobe pdf)

Subjects: LCSH: United States. Census. | United States—Census. | United States—Population—Statistical methods. | United States—Population—Statistics.

Classification: LCC HA181 .D66 2019 | DDC 317.3—dc23

LC record available at https://lccn.loc.gov/2019029185

This book is printed on acid-free paper.

SFI label applies to text stock

19  20  21  22  23  10  9  8  7  6  5  4  3  2  1

# BRIEF CONTENTS

# DETAILED CONTENTS

# PREFACE

The census, meaning the array of demographic and socioeconomic datasets produced by the U.S. Census Bureau, is an incredibly valuable and freely available resource for students, researchers, policy makers, and practitioners in many fields. In spite of this, in my 12 years of working as an academic librarian, I've discovered that this resource is either unknown or impenetrable to many. The sheer number of datasets, the unfamiliar terminology, difficult search interfaces, or conversely too many websites and tools to choose from, and the diffused nature of resources for learning about the census are formidable. Once I help students overcome these barriers, a new set typically emerges: Now that I have this data, what do I do with it? How do I study, manipulate, process, visualize, and integrate it into my work?

This book was designed to gather and organize all the essential information about the census in one place and to cover the basic geographic and subject-based concepts and the most important datasets in conjunction with tools and exercises that illustrate how to work with the data. I wrote it to appeal to the broadest possible audience, so that it doesn't focus on details that are relevant to only one or two specific fields. It's a hybrid of an academic text and a computer technology guidebook. Like the techie guidebooks, this book assumes that you learn best by doing, with practical step-by-step examples that all users will need to perform when working with the census. Like the academic texts, this book provides you with the necessary background and context needed for understanding, interpreting, and applying the statistics.

Given this broad audience, I chose to employ free and open source tools: spreadsheets, relational databases, GIS, and freely accessible websites to guarantee that anyone who reads this book will have ready access to both the data and applications. If you're a techie novice, you'll learn a lot about census data while simultaneously learning these tools. If you're already a tech expert and a seasoned analyst, but your knowledge of the census is limited, you'll learn a lot about these datasets and how to interpret and work with them properly. This book does not focus on statistical analysis, as the audience for this topic is narrower and there are already countless books devoted to learning it.

This book is divided into three parts. Part I is designed to provide essential context and background information that will apply to all the datasets that we cover: the role and function of census data, the primary interface used for obtaining data, and geographic and subject terminology used for organizing it. This part also provides initial exposure to several datasets that are explored in earnest in the second part. In Part II, each chapter covers a specific dataset in detail with exercises geared to common data-processing tasks. Part III covers advanced topics that will be valuable to many researchers.

The first six chapters should be read in order. If you skip Chapters 3 and 4 that discuss how the data is organized geographically and by subject, the subsequent chapters will make little sense. If you skip Chapter 2, you won't learn the basics of navigating and downloading data from the Census Bureau's website. Since downloading the data every time would be tedious, exercise data for this book can be downloaded in one package from the publisher's website. Chapters 5 and 6 cover the decennial census and American Community Survey, respectively, and should be covered in that order as the latter is based on the former. Chapters 4 through 6 also introduce the basics of working with spreadsheets and SQL, and in subsequent chapters, knowledge of these tools is presumed. The remaining chapters from 7 to 12 can be covered in any order based on the reader's individual research interests. These include additional population and business datasets (Chapters 7 and 8), integrating census data into research (Chapter 9), mapping and GIS (Chapter 10), creating derivatives for analysis (Chapter 11), and historical research and microdata (Chapter 12).

As I received questions from students and faculty throughout the most recent semester, I kept wishing that this book was finished so I could refer them back to specific chapters or sections that would answer their questions—and so I could remember the details too! My hope is that this book will initially be your key to unlocking the census, and then, it will become your indispensable reference once you have.

# ACKNOWLEDGMENTS

While writing is a solitary endeavor, the process of creating a book certainly is not, and I'd like to thank a number of people who helped make it happen. Thanks to Laura Horne-Popp, Stephen Francoeur, and Jason Haremza, who graciously agreed to review the proposal. Special thanks to Jean Yaremchuk, Jessie Braden, and Hannah Gurman, who reviewed it and met with me to strategize; Laura, Jessie, Steve Romalewski, and Joel Alvarez, who agreed to serve as references; my graduate students, past and present: Ryan Lennon, Abigail Andrews, and Chris Kim, who reviewed the exercises and took them for a test run; Anastasia Clark for her Python advice; and Janine Billadello for keeping the lab up and running while I was off writing.

Having a yearlong sabbatical is truly a privilege (thanks to the faculty of Baruch College who approved my fellowship leave), but after the first solitary month sitting in your one-bedroom New York City apartment, it becomes slightly dreary. So I'm grateful for many people who provided other places for releasing my creativity: the staff at the New York Public Library for the Performing Arts at Lincoln Center, Jane Huerta and Pastor John Flack for their coworking space at Our Savior's Atonement Lutheran Church in Washington Heights, and Jean-Paul Gheleyns and Jacqueline Degallaix for loaning us their place in Etel, Brittany, for one lovely month (where the one-bedroom apartments have views of the sea and a constant supply of fresh baguettes nearby).

Many thanks to the staff at SAGE, especially to my encouraging and patient editor Leah Fargotstein, and to all the reviewers of this book:

Hugh Bartling, *DePaul University*

Richard F. Bieker, *Delaware State University*

Courtney Broscious, *Eastern Connecticut State University*

Perry L. Carter, *Texas Tech University*

Dr. Stephanie Deitrick, *Arizona State University*

Elizabeth C. Delmelle, *University of North Carolina at Charlotte*

Rustu Deryol, *University of South Florida Sarasota-Manatee*

A. Victor Ferreros, *Florida State University*

Lee Hachadoorian, *Temple University*

David S. Lamb, *University of South Florida*
Anne M. Mahar, *Arcadia University*

Thanks to my mother and father for their lifelong support. Last but not least, thanks to my wife, Julie Poncelet, for simply everything.

# ABOUT THE AUTHOR

Frank Donnelly is a geospatial information professional whose practice blends the service-based and organizational skills of an academic librarian with the subject knowledge and analytical methods of a researcher. He has served as the Geospatial Data Librarian at Baruch College, CUNY, in midtown Manhattan since 2007, where he helps members of his university navigate geospatial and census data sources. He holds the rank of associate professor in the library and manages a GIS lab, where he and his graduate students provide research consultations, teach workshops, process and create data, and maintain a repository of GIS data. He was an early proponent of free and open source GIS software in academia and has introduced hundreds of people to GIS through his workshops and tutorial manual. He has written several academic articles, technical papers, and reports that utilize census data to study socioeconomic and demographic trends and provide information to researchers and policy makers. Prior to becoming a librarian, he worked as a planner and data analyst in the government and nonprofit sectors. He holds master's degrees in library and information science from the University of Washington and in geography from the University of Toronto. You can follow him at his blog **At These Coordinates: https://atcoordinates.info/**.

# INTRODUCTION

## 1  INTRODUCING THE CENSUS

When most Americans think of the census, they think of the form they fill out every 10 years that's used to count the nation's population. Or they think of the Census Bureau, which is the agency that conducts the census. This book will demonstrate that the census is more than just a basic 10-year counting exercise; it is actually a rich collection of public datasets that are updated on an ongoing basis. The census plays an essential role within the government, as it is used for reapportioning seats in Congress between the states and redrawing legislative districts. It is also used to distribute hundreds of billions of dollars in federal funds to states and local governments to support education, transportation infrastructure, and social services.

Beyond simply counting the number of people and houses, the census includes data on educational attainment, commute time to work, home values, internet access, components of population change (births, deaths, migration), types and numbers of businesses, and much more. The data is summarized by age, sex, race, income brackets, occupations, and industries for large geographic areas like states, metropolitan areas, and counties as well as small areas like ZIP Codes and census tracts that can be used to study neighborhoods. The Census Bureau uses consistent methods and definitions across datasets and, to the extent possible, across time periods.

This high-quality, geographically detailed data is in the public domain and, thus, is freely available for anyone to use for any purpose. Census data is used by researchers, policy makers, urban and regional planners, academics, activists, journalists, entrepreneurs, data scientists, nonprofits, businesses, and federal, state, and local governments to study and understand society, identify markets, solve problems, provide services, and create profiles, maps, charts, reports, and web applications.

There is a learning curve in working with census data. There are many datasets to choose from, there is unfamiliar terminology, and there is a dizzying array of websites of varying complexity where the data can be accessed and downloaded. Some of the datasets require a degree of technical knowledge to interpret and use them properly, and you will need some technical skills to effectively process and summarize the data in order to use it to meet your needs. This book is your guide for exploring, understanding, and mastering the essentials of working with census summary data and will do the following:

- Demonstrate how to access and obtain census data from several sources, in varying quantities.

- Introduce the terminology and concepts that are used across all census datasets as they relate to subjects and geography.

- Cover each of the primary census datasets in detail: their purpose, how they're constructed, and what data is available.

- Demonstrate basic techniques for processing and summarizing data using spreadsheets.

- Demonstrate how to create derived data and how to work with essential census formulas.

- Show you how census data can be applied in different use cases.

- Illustrate advanced techniques like storing and querying data in a relational database and mapping data with geographic information systems (GIS).

This book is an introductory guide aimed at researchers and practitioners in many fields. It was designed as a hybrid between an academic text and a technology-oriented guidebook based on the fundamental principle that you learn best by doing, and you will work through examples with relevant tools rather than having concepts explained to you without a meaningful application. If you are new to the census and know absolutely nothing about the datasets except that you want to use them for your research, and your technical skills are limited to copying and pasting values in spreadsheets, this is the perfect book for you. At the beginning, we will use basic tools like spreadsheets and web applications and will gradually introduce more advanced techniques. You won't be able to fully learn tools like relational databases or GIS here, but I will illustrate the basics of each and how you can apply them to the census to plant the seeds of what's possible in your mind and prepare you to go off and learn more.

On the other hand, if you are a census novice but possess good technical skills, this book is also a good fit for you. You will learn all the census fundamentals, so you can work with the data confidently and correctly. You will be able to move more quickly through the technical basics and will appreciate the advanced techniques introduced in later chapters. You will be able to readily draw from the book's examples and apply them.

Now that we covered what's in the book, let's discuss what this book is *not* about:

- *Working with individual, case-level data.* This book focuses on census summary data, which has been aggregated by population groups and geographic areas. The individual responses to the census forms are not publicly available and are kept confidential for 72 years. While the census does release some sample data of individual responses that we will cover in Chapter 12, it is not the primary focus of this text.

- *Genealogy.* This book is not going to show you how to research your family history. We will focus largely on summary data that is contemporary. While Chapter 12 covers historical census data, the focus is on working with data that is summarized by places and groups and not on retrieving historic records of individuals.

- *Learning statistics.* This book is not a primer for statistical analysis, so if you want to learn how to do linear regression, this is not the book for you. This book covers plain data analysis: obtaining, processing, summarizing, creating derivatives, and understanding what the data represents, so you can use it to support research or create new information.

- *Summarizing everything on the Census Bureau's website.* The Census Bureau publishes a ton of datasets, applications, and reports. Instead of covering them all, we focus on essential datasets that are widely used by most researchers and on a selection of the most salient and useful tools.

## 2    ROADMAP OF TOPICS

This book is divided into three sections. The chapters in Part I (Census Fundamentals) cover the essential information that applies to all the datasets included in the book. Chapter 1 provides a summary of what the census is with examples of how you can use it for research, and places the census within the context of U.S. society and the world of data. In Chapter 2, we will take a crash course in using the new data.census.gov, which is the primary portal for accessing all of the Census Bureau's datasets. By 2020, it will fully supplant the veritable American Factfinder, which had served as the previous portal for 20 years. In navigating data.census.gov, you will gain exposure to the different datasets we will explore throughout the book. One of the best aspects of working with the various census datasets is that they all employ the same concepts and terminology. In Chapters 3 and 4, we explore the two principal means by which census data is summarized: geography and population categories that are known as universes. We will navigate the census geographic hierarchy, which goes from the nation down to individual census blocks, and will explore the fundamental categories of race, ethnicity, households and families, and the labor force.

In Part II (The Primary Datasets), we will tackle each of the major census datasets in turn. Each chapter includes a discussion of the purpose, collection methods, variables, and use cases for each dataset and addresses how each one fits into the larger census canon, while highlighting when you should use one relative to another dataset. In these chapters, we'll also explore a number of different sources for accessing census data in varying quantities. Chapter 5 focuses on the decennial census, which is the foundation of all census datasets. We will discuss how the 2010 census was a break from the past and what the 2020 census will look like. Chapter 6 covers the American Community Survey (ACS), which is the chief source for annual, geographically detailed data on the socioeconomic characteristics of the nation. A detailed exploration of the ACS methodology will give you a solid understanding for how to use and interpret the estimates. Chapter 7 introduces the Population Estimates Program, which is a compact and easy to use dataset for studying annual population growth. Chapter 8 pivots away from population and housing to businesses with the introduction of the County Business Patterns and the Economic Census and concepts such as the North American Industrial Classification System that are essential for studying businesses. Once each dataset has been covered, Chapter 9 illustrates how you can integrate census data into your writing and research and provides useful background information on geographic considerations and historical trends that influence research findings.

Each of the chapters in Parts I and II include hands-on exercises that use online tools, spreadsheets, and relational databases to explore, process, and analyze data. We will begin using spreadsheets in Chapter 2 and will introduce relational databases and SQL in Chapter 5. Part III (Advanced Topics) is devoted to more advanced topics: types of analyses we haven't covered in the first two sections, datasets that are important but not as commonly used as the primary ones, and advanced tools like GIS that allow you to geographically visualize and analyze data.

Chapter 10 introduces the different geographic products that the Census Bureau produces that can be used with GIS. You will get a crash course in GIS, so that you can use these products and make your own maps of census data. Chapter 11 focuses on creating derivative data, everything from simple aggregates of geographies to population distribution measures. This chapter consists of a series of vignettes that demonstrate different measures and techniques that can be implemented in spreadsheets, databases, and GIS.

Chapter 12 concludes with two advanced topics. The first is analyzing historic census summary data and coping with changes in subjects and geographic boundaries over time. The second is working with census microdata, which are samples of individual responses to census questions. This chapter will introduce the Current Population Survey and will use tools from the Minnesota Population Center for accessing both historical census data (the NHGIS) and microdata (IPUMS).

## 3    DATA AND SOFTWARE

We will be doing exercises throughout the book, and you will learn how to navigate the Census Bureau's website and a few other resources, such as the Missouri Census Data Center and the Minnesota Population Center, to access data. Since it would be tedious to have to download each and every data table we need, most of them are bundled together and can be downloaded from the publisher's website at **study.sagepub.com/census**. The data is organized in folders by chapter and exercise number. Each of the data tables and sources are listed prior to beginning each exercise, so if you prefer to download them from the original source you could. Some exercises are not included in this book but exist as supplementary material on the website. They consist of more specialized material that will be of interest to some readers and to others who would like more practice working with the data.

You will need to download some software in order to complete the exercises and learn the concepts. Since the census is a free and open dataset, we are going to use free and open source software to work with it. The packages listed below are freely available, are easy to install, and will run on any operating system: MS Windows, Mac, or Linux. They are well-established products that are stable and widely used. Links for downloading the software are below each title; we will start using Calc in Chapter 2 and SQLite$^®$ in Chapter 5 but won't get to QGIS until Chapter 10. Several of the exercises will use web-based resources and tools, and you are free to use your favorite web browser with the caveat that the rendering of websites and the mechanics of downloading files may vary between browsers. Mozilla Firefox was used for the examples and exercises in this book.

### Spreadsheet: LibreOffice$^®$ Calc 6

`https://www.libreoffice.org/`

The spreadsheet is still the Swiss Army Knife of the data world, and given its ubiquity and familiarity, it will be our first tool of choice. LibreOffice$^®$ is a free and open source office suite that includes all the standard office tools: a word processor, a slide presentation program, a spreadsheet, and so on. Originally a proprietary package, it was relaunched as the open source OpenOffice suite and then subsequently branched into LibreOffice in 2010, so that development could continue via an independent open source team. In this book, we will be using LibreOffice version 6.

The LibreOffice spreadsheet is called Calc, and it looks and behaves just like any other spreadsheet package. If you are familiar with MS Excel or Mac Numbers, you can easily pick up Calc. Most of the formulas in Calc are identical to formulas used in Excel, and in Calc, you can open and save files in either the modern (.xlsx) or old (.xls) Excel format in addition to the open office format (.ods). Compared with Excel, Calc has much better support for working with CSV and text-delimited files, although its graphing functions are not as slick.

If you are a die-hard Excel user, you can still follow most of the examples in this book with Excel; the primary differences will be with the interfaces for accessing various tools and the charting functionality. I will mention some of the significant differences between the two packages as we move through the exercises.

## Database: SQLite

`http://sqlitebrowser.org/`

While a spreadsheet offers flexibility and ease of use, it's less effective when you need to tie related but separate tables of data together, or when you need to group or summarize data. Relational databases give you the power to easily organize, summarize, and relate data because they offer structure and integrity over flexibility, and they don't mix formatting and presentation of data with organization and storage.

In this book, you will get a brief introduction to databases and the structured query language (SQL) using SQLite. While you may have never heard of SQLite, you probably use it everyday. It is a small, public domain database that is embedded in just about everything for storing information, such as your web browser (for storing bookmarks), phone (for storing contacts), and millions of websites. While it's commonly used as an embedded database within software, it can also be employed as a simple desktop database where each database is stored in a single file.

The SQLite developers provide the core program as well as a basic command-line interface for interacting with the database. Since the project is in the public domain, many independent developers have built graphical interfaces that make the database easier to use. In this book, we will use the DB Browser for SQLite. Of all the possible options, it has a clean and simple design and can easily be downloaded and installed on any operating system.

## Geographic Information Systems: QGIS 3

`https://www.qgis.org/en/site/`

GIS are used to organize, process, and study spatial data, which is data that is tied to a specific location or place. Census data is inherently geographic, as each record represents a place and each column contains attributes that describe that place. We can use GIS to tie census data together, do geographic analysis, and make maps. GIS software works with special kinds of data files that incorporate the geometry and location of features so that they can be displayed graphically. The Census Bureau produces boundary files for every single geography that it tabulates data for. It also publishes features that it uses for creating its boundaries, such as roads, railroads, water, and other landmarks. If we have census boundaries for areas like counties, and we have census data for those counties in a table, we can join the table to the boundary file based on the common geographic code that they share and voila, that data is now visual and we can map it!

QGIS has emerged as one of the most popular free and open source GIS packages. It has a large number of developers and contributors, and updates are rolled out on a regularly scheduled basis. It has solid tools for both visualization and mapping as well as analysis and is highly extensible. Compared with other packages, there is a lot more user documentation devoted to it, and it's now commonly deployed in academia, the geospatial tech sector, nonprofits, and increasingly in government. In this book, we will use QGIS version 3.4.

If you have never used GIS, this book will introduce enough of the basics, as well as the common stumbling blocks, so that you can see the power of using it to work with census data. But when it is time to work on your own projects, you will need to learn more on your own. I'll offer suggestions on resources that you can turn to.

# 4   CONVENTIONS

Before we get started, some notes about terminology. When we talk about "the census," we could be referring to many things: the decennial census, the Census Bureau, or the census in the general sense referring to the collection of all census datasets and products. To keep things straight, I will refer to the 10-year count as the decennial census or will reference the specifc decennial census such as the 2020 census. I will refer to the agency as the Census Bureau, or simply as the Bureau, and will use the term *census* to generically reference all datasets and products.

When referring to "the census," the word is seldom capitalized. According to the Government Printing Office, you capitalize "census" only when you are referring to the agency itself (either in full as the Census Bureau or in part when referring to the agency as "the Census" or "the Bureau") or when referring to an official title of a product (U.S. Census 2020, the Twenty-Third Decennial Census, 2012 Census of Agriculture). You would not capitalize "census" if you are referring to a product generally (2020 census, the decennial census, the census of agriculture). Throughout this book, I am going to avoid official titles and will stick with general references.

Naturally, when you work with government information, you are going to encounter a lot of acronyms. Here are the most common ones that we will use throughout:

ACS:   American Community Survey (a census dataset)

BLS:   The Bureau of Labor Statistics (a federal statistical agency)

CBP:   County Business Patterns (a census dataset)

CPS:   Current Population Survey (a census dataset)

GIS:   geographic information systems (a type of software)

MCDC:   Missouri Census Data Center (a data provider)

MOE:   margin of error (statistical concept used with ACS data)

NAICS:   North American Industrial Classification System (a classification system)

NHGIS:   National Historic Geographic Information System (a census data repository)

OMB:   Office of Management and Budget (a federal agency)

PEP:   Population Estimates Program (a census dataset)

PUMA:   Public Use Microdata Area (a census geography)

USDA:   U.S. Department of Agriculture (a federal agency)

ZBP:   ZIP Code Business Patterns (a census dataset)

ZCTA:   ZIP Code Tabulation Area (a census geography)

> **Supplementary Digital Content:** Find datasets and supplemental exercises at the companion website at `http://study.sagepub.com/census`.

# CENSUS FUNDAMENTALS

# PART I

# PLACING THE CENSUS IN CONTEXT

This chapter provides an introduction to the census in the broadest sense: as a series of datasets, a statistical agency, and a social and political concept. We begin with a summary of the fundamental datasets that are covered in this book and explore how you can use census data in your research with some examples. In doing so, we will touch on concepts that we will cover throughout the text. While this book is primarily a practitioner's guide to working with census data, this chapter provides essential background information so you can better understand and appreciate the importance and value of the census. We will discuss the roles the census plays within American society and how census data fits within the context of the ever-expanding universe of data that includes the federal statistical system, the open data movement, and big data.

## 1.1   WHAT IS CENSUS DATA?

We can think of the U.S. Census as a collection of datasets about population, housing units, and businesses that is created by the Census Bureau, which is part of the U.S. Department of Commerce. Census data is collected at regular intervals using methodologies such as total counts, sample surveys, and administrative records. After it is collected or generated, census data is summarized to represent counts or estimates of groups of people for different geographic areas. Census geographies, categories, and terminologies are relatively consistent across the different census datasets, and we will explore them in Chapters 3 and 4. A comparative summary of the datasets covered in this book is provided in Table 1.1.

| TABLE 1.1 ● COMPARISON OF CENSUS DATASETS COVERED IN THIS BOOK | | | | | |
|---|---|---|---|---|---|
| Dataset | Method | Frequency | Subjects | Geographies | Variables |
| Decennial Census | 100% Count | 10 years | Population, housing | Many | Several |
| American Community Survey | Sample survey 3.5 million addresses | Annual | Population, housing | Many | Many |
| Population Estimates Program | Administrative records | Annual | Population | Several | Few |
| Current Population Survey | Sample survey 60k households | Monthly | Population | Few | Many |
| Business Patterns | Administrative records | Annual | Businesses | Several | Few |
| Economic Census | 100% count and sample survey | 5 years | Businesses | Several | Several |

When most Americans think of the census, they think of the 10-year or decennial census that is used to gather basic data about the total population. The decennial census is an actual count of people and housing units, and it serves as the baseline for measuring and generating other census datasets. Demographers refer to data that is collected from total counts as enumerations, or simply as populations. The American Community Survey (ACS) and the Current Population Survey (CPS) are ongoing sample surveys of the population that collect detailed demographic and socioeconomic characteristics. Sample surveys collect information from just a small subset of the population, either randomly or from targeted groups, which is used to estimate what the total population is. The size of the sample is carefully determined, so that the sample data can be used to estimate the total population for a given geographic area with a reasonable level of precision. The ACS is a large survey that is published annually for large and small geographic areas, while the CPS is a smaller survey that is published monthly and is summarized for the nation as a whole or for the states. The Population Estimates Program (PEP) is produced from administrative records and other census datasets to create annual estimates for areas like states, counties, and municipalities. The Census Bureau produces data for businesses via the Economic Census, which is a 5-year count of most types of businesses and a sample of other types, and the County and ZIP Code Business Patterns (ZBP), which is created from administrative records on an annual basis.

Who is counted in the census? It varies based on the dataset, and we will cover the specific details about the different methodologies that are used and the variables that are collected in Part II of this book. For now, the short answer is "everyone." The decennial census counts all people residing in the United States on census day: citizens and permanent residents; documented and undocumented immigrants; people living in households; people living in institutionalized settings like college dormitories, military bases, prisons, and hospitals; and the homeless.

The ACS and CPS are primarily sample surveys of residential addresses, so they do not capture the full spectrum of the population that the decennial census captures. The ACS does sample people living in group quarters (institutionalized settings), but the sample is small enough that it is able to publish coarse estimates only for large areas like states. The PEP is derived from the decennial census and administrative records that include birth and death certificates, so in theory it captures everyone. The business datasets capture most businesses, with some exceptions.

Census data is captured from households, institutions, and businesses through paper and online forms and, when necessary, through on-site visits and canvassing. One of the reasons that the Census Bureau is able to produce reasonably accurate and geographically detailed counts and estimates of the population is that it is a government agency that is backed by law. People are required to fill out and return their census forms. The Census Bureau sends out a series of reminders to nonrespondents, and if a household still does not respond, the Bureau sends an actual enumerator out to interview them for the decennial census and follows up with a sample of nonrespondents in person or on the phone for the ACS. In contrast, private polling agencies would never be able to accomplish a count or survey at the same scale due to the cost of conducting it and their inability to compel people to respond.

## 1.2    APPLICATIONS OF CENSUS DATA

What can you use census data for? At the simplest level, you may want to look up information for your town, city, or state to get some basic facts to support a story you are writing or research you are doing. The Census Bureau publishes profiles that contain a broad swath of data for one place. With the Bureau's new data discovery platform, **data.census.gov** (Figure 1.1), a simple place name search will provide you with quick facts, charts, and maps. We will explore this platform in Chapter 2.

Alternatively, you might want to compare one variable for many places in order to see which cities are growing fastest or which areas have the highest income or most unemployment. The Census Bureau publishes comparison tables that you can search through, modify, and download. Or maybe you need to gather many census variables for many places for a research project where you are creating new data, maybe even with data from other sources. The Census Bureau allows you to download data

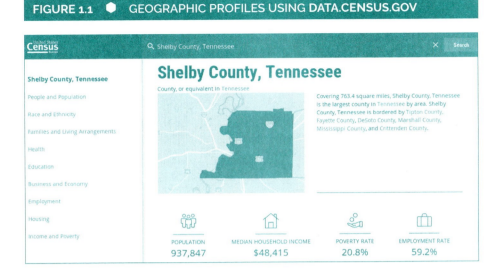

**FIGURE 1.1 ● GEOGRAPHIC PROFILES USING DATA.CENSUS.GOV**

in bulk or to access it via a computer program or script using an API (application programming interface).

Or perhaps, you need to visualize census data. You can do this using a number of online tools, or you can download the data and visualize it on your desktop using spreadsheets or geographic information systems (GIS). In this book, we will demonstrate several of these methods to create charts and maps like the examples in Figure 1.2 that depict commuting data for the Northeast Corridor and New York City from the ACS.

As an academic librarian who specializes in geographic datasets, I have helped hundreds of people find, process, and interpret census data for their projects to support arguments in their research and to create new information. This is the kind of data analysis that professor Gary Klass describes in his book *Just Plain Data Analysis* and that we will cover in this text. Klass makes a distinction between "plain data analysis" as processing, presenting, and evaluating statistics to support social and political research as opposed to statistical analysis, which focuses on the testing of hypotheses (Klass, 2012). Here are a few examples that illustrate the kinds of research you can do with census data and what you will learn from reading this book.

- Each semester, I help journalism students with neighborhood reporting projects in New York City. The Census Bureau does not collect data for "neighborhoods" like Midtown, Chelsea, or Harlem, as these are areas that are defined locally. I assist them with translating the Census Bureau's geographies

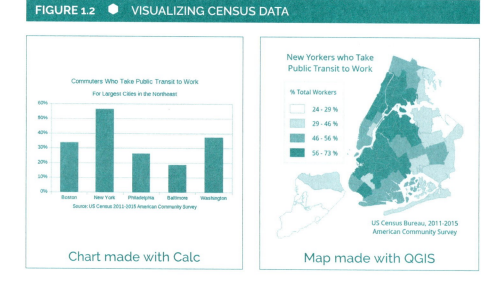

**FIGURE 1.2 ●   VISUALIZING CENSUS DATA**

Chart made with Calc

Map made with QGIS

like census tracts or Public Use Microdata Areas into what we consider to be neighborhoods, and we walk through a number of different online sources for census data where they can get profiles. We will cover sources for data in Chapter 2, geography in Chapter 3, creating aggregates for neighborhoods in Chapter 6, and integrating census data into writing in Chapter 9.

- I worked with two journalism professors to combine ACS data and presidential election results in order to identify counties that had low median income, high unemployment, and high poverty compared with the U.S. average and that had switched to voting for the Republicans in 2016 after having voted for the Democrats in the previous two presidential elections. I gathered and loaded the variables into a database, so that we could select counties that met the criteria. The professors combined the results of this analysis with other data to select a county that would serve as a field trip destination for an investigative reporting class. We will cover population groups in Chapter 4 and the ACS in Chapter 6 and will introduce databases in Chapter 5.

- A PhD student was doing research on heat waves, heat-related death, and poverty. She was working with county-level data from many sources from the 1970s to the early 2010s. We not only dove into the historical census files to obtain population and poverty data but also discovered another important variable she could use: From 1960 to 1980, the census asked people whether they had air conditioning in their homes. She was able to use this data for older decades and then created estimates for recent decades using data from the Department of Energy. We will explore historical census data in Chapter 12.

- Our lab advised the New York City Comptroller's Office in creating a series of statistical profiles on the economy of each of the city's Community Districts (New York City Comptroller's Office, 2017). It took data from the ZBP and summed it to ZIP Code Tabulation Areas so the data could be related and assigned to the districts. They collated the ZBP, ACS, and decennial census data into a concise and attractive report and web-based interface. We will cover census geography in Chapter 3, business datasets in Chapter 8, and creating derivatives and relating different geographies in Chapter 11.

- As part of a workshop I teach on GIS, I incorporate an example where we use demographic data from the census, TIGER geographic boundary files, and other geographic data such as the location of subway stations and coffee shops to identify possible locations for opening a new neighborhood coffee shop. We will cover GIS and the Bureau's geographic products in Chapter 10.

## 1.3 ROLE OF THE CENSUS IN AMERICAN SOCIETY

In this section, we will consider how census data and the Census Bureau fit within the context of American society. In doing so, we will also touch on various aspects of the Census Bureau's history. For a fuller historical treatment, Margo Anderson's *The American Census: A Social History* (2015) is a definitive account, and the history portion of the Census Bureau's website at `https://www.census.gov/history/` is quite comprehensive.

The census has played a vital role in American democracy since the country's founding. The United States was the first country to institute a population census for the purpose of assigning representatives to a democratically elected legislature (Emigh, Riley, & Ahmed, 2016a). Article I, Section 2, of the U.S. Constitution provides the original, legal basis for the census:

> Representatives and direct Taxes shall be apportioned among the several states which may be included in this Union, according to their respective Numbers. . . . The actual Enumeration shall be made within three Years after the first Meeting of the Congress of the United States, and within every subsequent Term of ten Years, in such Manner as they shall by Law direct.

The first census was taken as stipulated in 1790 and has been conducted every 10 years since. The decennial census is used to reapportion seats in Congress based on the differential growth in population between the states, and the data is subsequently used to redraw legislative districts in states that either gained or lost seats. Other provisions in the Constitution provide justification for a federal statistical system. Article I, Section 9, requires that federal appropriations have legal authorization and that the government provides regular statements of its accounts, and Article II, Section 3, stipulates that the president must give Congress an annual update on the state of the union. Statistics were seen as one method for fulfilling these obligations and measuring the nation's progress (Anderson, 2010).

Outside the Constitution, a large body of federal law requires that specific census variables be collected. The statutory uses of each variable that will be collected in the 2020 census and the future iterations of the ACS are published in a report that the Census Bureau submitted to Congress (U.S. Census Bureau, 2017h). For example, the Civil Rights and Voting Rights Acts require data on age, sex, race, employment, and disabilities to evaluate whether civil rights are being protected. Census data is used for allocating hundreds of billions of dollars of funding for federal assistance programs to states and local governments, such as Medicaid, Highway Planning and Construction, Title I Education grants, Temporary Aid for Needy Families, Community Development Block Grants, and more (U.S. Government Accountability Office, 2009). In fiscal year 2016, approximately 320 federal programs used census data to allocate more than $880 billion in federal funds, primarily to state and local governments but also to individuals through direct assistance programs (Reamer, 2017, 2018).

The original decennial census was conducted by U.S. Marshalls, who fanned out across the country on horseback and counted people based on instructions from Congress. As the country grew in size and population and demands for census data increased, the mechanisms for collecting, tabulating, and presenting data grew in complexity and sophistication to meet the demands. Beginning in 1850, a temporary Census Office was established prior to each census to direct operations and tabulate the results (Anderson, 2015, pp. 41–58), and by 1880, this office, staffed with professional statisticians, took control over all census operations (Anderson, 2015, pp. 89–101). In 1902, Congress established the Census Bureau as a permanent office under the Department of Commerce and Labor that remained in operation year-round, and it became one of the chief statistical agencies within the expanding federal government. The number of questions on the census grew from the mid-19th to early 20th century at the instigation of stakeholder groups that included professional statistical societies and business interests. From the mid- to late 20th century, the needs of the federal government for allocating funding and directing policy became the driving force behind the addition and standardization of questions.

Placed squarely in the middle of America's political mechanisms, the census is a strongly debated and contested issue. In their two-volume, comparative, historical study of censuses in the United Kingdom, the United States, and Italy, Emigh et al. (2016a, 2016b) conclude that this intense interaction around the U.S. Census ensures that it remains a vibrant social institution, whereas in other countries, population counting is seen as either a bureaucratic or symbolic exercise since it is disconnected from political outcomes. In the United States, there are fierce debates and lawsuits over how the census is conducted, what questions are asked, how categories for race and ethnicity are defined, and whether the census is accurate or not. Undercounting specific areas or population groups can result in the loss of federal aid and political power for these places or groups.

There are two peculiarities of American government vis-à-vis the census that help ensure that it remains relevant to society at large. First, since it is stipulated as part of the Constitution, it is reasonably assured that the census will be conducted every 10 years in a manner that's relatively consistent. Many other countries have abandoned doing actual counts of the population in favor of using annual sample surveys, estimates based on administrative data, or population registers (Baffour, King, & Valente, 2013). Following years of controversy and lawsuits against the Census Bureau concerning population undercounts in the 1980 and 1990 census, the Supreme Court ruled that the decennial census must be an actual count: It cannot be based on a sample and the count cannot be adjusted using statistical means in any way (Anderson, 2015, pp. 228–247). The Census Bureau can create and adopt new innovations like the ACS, but it must continue to do an actual 10-year count for apportionment purposes.

Second, according to U.S. copyright law (Title 17, Section 105), all works produced by the U.S. government, with few exceptions, are automatically released into the public domain and can be used by anyone for any purpose. This makes the census widely available and accessible, and throughout history, public, private, academic, and nonprofit agencies have employed census data for their own purposes. Stakeholder and interest groups throughout society lobby for changes in the census to meet their needs and also lobby on behalf of the Census Bureau to keep programs funded. In contrast, many other countries copyright their census data and limit what is available. With few exceptions, the United States is rather unique for having a large and established ecosystem of census data users.

Given the accessibility and quality of the census, it is employed for many purposes throughout American society. The Economics and Statistics Administration published a study on the value of the ACS with the subtitle: *Smart Government, Competitive Businesses, and Informed Citizens* (2015) that contains detailed statistics and vignettes on how census data is used. Examples include Kroger supermarkets creating sales projections and siting new stores and academic researchers and governments in Hawaii creating disaster management plans to cope with volcanic eruptions and lava flows.

State and local governments have always been heavy users of census data, because they can use it to study their own communities and create appropriate policies for urban and regional planning, social assistance, public services, and economic development. Within academia, the census serves as a foundational dataset within the social sciences. Compared with many other datasets, the census is geographically detailed, rich in its breadth of variables, relatively consistent, longitudinal, relatively accurate, and well documented. In academic research, the census is used to provide context and a frame of reference for describing places and population groups, can be used as criteria for selecting areas of study, can help define sampling strategies, and serves as the basis for new and derived estimates (Dickason, 2012). For example, census data is particularly important in the field of public health, where it is used as the basis for studying different populations in relation to risk and exposure to public health threats (Wilson et al., 2017).

In the private sector, there are two types of business that routinely use census data: (1) those who use it to make business decisions and (2) information brokers who use it as a commodity. Census data is used extensively within the fields of marketing and real estate. Marketers use it to identify populations and areas that would be good targets for their products and services, while real estate agents use census data to supplement their own information in order to understand housing markets and characterize neighborhoods. Information brokers gather data from many different sources, aggregate it, and use it to produce intelligence that they can sell to third parties, while others create web-based products that can be used for doing research.

Census data plays a key role within American representative democracy for apportioning political power and the resources of the U.S. government. Over time, it has become a vital piece of the nation's infrastructure that is similar to other public goods and services, in that it provides a piece of the foundation on which the country's society and economy rest through the basic yet essential information it provides. Based on the definition of public goods as described by political philosopher Angela Kallhoff in her book *Why Democracy Needs Public Goods* (2011), census data fits the definition as it is nonrival (each individual can use it without affecting someone else's use) and nonexcludable (it is free for all to share). Census data helps generate a public sphere by providing reliable information that creates mutual awareness of others in our society, and it serves as a focal point for debate over issues of common concern.

## 1.4    CRITICISM OF THE CENSUS

The census is not without flaws or critics. In this section, we'll summarize some of the philosophical and political objections to the census (we will cover issues related to methodology such as undercounting and sample sizes as we discuss each dataset in later chapters). The first and certainly the most earnest concern is the confidentiality and privacy of an individual's responses to the census questionnaires. Throughout the 20th century, federal law stipulated that the Census Bureau would not publish or share records of individual responses to census questionnaires (U.S. Census Bureau, 2009). The current law, established in the 1950s and amended in the 1970s, prohibits the disclosure of individual-level census information for 72 years from the date the census was conducted. Despite these laws, there is a general and growing suspicion of government surveillance (fanned by controversies such as the National Security Agency's PRISM system) and government data-gathering programs from all sides of the political spectrum. Census confidentiality statues were rescinded during the First and Second World Wars under emergency security measures (Anderson, 2015; Aratani, 2018), so there are concerns that it could happen again given some future emergency.

While there is reason for concern, it is important to consider the environment in which the Census Bureau operates. The federal government is composed of hundreds of agencies that operate according to their own missions, needs, and interests and that compete for resources. What's in the best interest of one agency may not be in the best interest of another. The Census Bureau's goal is to create the most accurate population statistics that it possibly can. To achieve this, it must establish a high level of trust with the American people and ensure that each individual's responses will be held in confidence according to the law. Therefore, it is not in the Census Bureau's best interest to share information with other government agencies as it will erode the public's trust and jeopardize the accuracy of the statistics, if people refuse to respond out of fear for their privacy.

In Margo Anderson's (2015) account of the Census Bureau's history, she describes how the Bureau fought to maintain its independence within the federal statistical system so that it could fulfill its mission of generating accurate statistics. In particular, the Bureau successfully resisted every attempt to tie its statistical-gathering activities to other branches of the government that specialized in regulatory enforcement, so that it could reassure individuals and businesses that their data would be used only for the purpose of generating summary statistics.

The Bureau continues with this struggle today. In late 2017 and early 2018, the Justice Department lobbied the Census Bureau to include a question on citizenship on the 2020 census form, which they deemed necessary for upholding the Voting Rights Act and fighting voter fraud (Baumgaertner, 2018; H. L. Wang, 2018h). Given the bitter partisan debates over immigration and the uncertainty and fear among immigrant groups (both legal and undocumented) about their status, the Census Bureau and its supporters (including the two previous secretaries of Commerce under the Obama and Bush administrations; Pritzker & Gutierrez, 2018) strenuously objected to this suggestion. All residents, regardless of their status, are counted in the decennial census. Given deepening suspicion of the government's motives, it's likely that many would refuse to participate and thus would jeopardize the accuracy of the count and all the programs that depend on it. In June 2019 the Supreme Court ruled against the addition of a citizenship question to the 2020 census.

Some members of Congress have suggested that since the census is used for apportioning seats in Congress, either people who can legally vote or only U.S. citizens should be counted. This would be contrary to the intentions of the Founding Fathers and the 220-year history of the census, which has always counted every single person as it was deemed to be the simplest and fairest method for conducting the count. Children cannot vote, but there are approximately 74 million children in the United States and they depend on basic government services like schools. Legal permanent residents cannot vote and are not citizens, but they pay taxes and contribute to society. Politicians are elected to represent all members of their districts, and the Supreme Court agrees. The Court reconsidered the practice of counting every person as opposed to counting eligible voters during the drafting of the Fourteenth Amendment after the Civil War and decided to uphold the population count as the simplest and fairest approach. Since then, the Court has upheld this opinion on several occasions, most recently in 2015, when they ruled that states may count all residents, regardless of whether they are eligible to vote, when drawing legislative districts (Liptak, 2016).

Beyond the issue of confidentiality is a simpler issue of personal privacy that can be summarized as follows: "Why is the government asking me all these questions? It's none of their business!" In this view, the Constitution says that there must be a 10-year count and says nothing about asking other questions or running additional surveys like the ACS. Therefore, some believe that most of the questions are unconstitutional and people have a right to refuse to answer them. However, as discussed in the previous section, there are several sections of the Constitution that provide a basis for establishing a federal statistical system. There are also federal laws and court decisions that require the government to collect statistics in order to fulfill many obligations. The Census Bureau cannot ask questions simply because they might be novel or interesting; every single question is asked because it has some basis in the law.

The Census Bureau explicitly ties each question to the law that requires it and presents this information to Congress (U.S. Census Bureau, 2017h).

In terms of privacy, the image of the government as a 1984 Big Brother that's gathering information about every citizen through coercion seems less plausible given life in the early 21st century. Every day, millions of Americans freely share information about themselves (knowingly and unknowingly) on social media and the internet that is infinitely more personal and potentially compromising than anything they share on a census form. This information is held by technology companies, credit agencies, and data brokers, many of whom sell it to third parties. By and large, these companies are completely unaccountable, and we cannot even know or request what data has been collected about us (Kitchin, 2014). Concerns about the Census Bureau's collection of basic demographic information seems minor in comparison.

The economics of the census is another issue that's frequently raised by fiscal conservatives. The census has been criticized as a waste of tax payer dollars, and it has been suggested that the private sector could do a better job. In reality, the federal statistical agencies' share of federal budget resources represented about 0.04% of gross domestic product in 2016 (Executive Office of the President, 2017), a trifling amount compared with the budgets for defense, Social Security, and Medicare. The private sector cannot compel people to fill out census forms and could not possibly conduct a count or survey of the same scope and detail. Businesses rely on census data the same way they rely on other public goods, such as roads, mass transit, and schools, as fundamental pieces of infrastructure that the economy is built on. When census programs are threatened by budget cuts, business leaders and trade groups are among the first to lobby against them. For example, when the American Community Survey was threatened with cuts in 2012, the Target Corporation collaborated with the Census Bureau to produce a YouTube video that showcased how Target uses census data to tailor its stores and products to different markets (U.S. Census Bureau, 2012b). Many fiscal critics fail to measure the cost of the census against the benefits that it provides (Wilson et al., 2017).

There are good reasons to scrutinize the census. It is important to debate the census questions and categories to ensure that they reflect the changing nature, interests, and needs of our society. It is necessary to highlight issues with methodology that could result in unforeseen consequences regarding the accuracy of statistics. Given the creeping amount of surveillance in our society and the growing number of data breaches, confidentiality must be of utmost concern. But like every other political or public policy issue, it is important to study the underlying arguments to determine whether they are rooted in facts or opinions, either informed or uninformed. The ability to have reliable information for the purpose of checking facts is one of the reasons why we create census data to begin with.

## 1.5   THE CENSUS WITHIN THE DATA UNIVERSE

Where does the census fit into our data-saturated world? In this section, we'll situate census data within this context. The census datasets exist as part of a larger federal system of data collecting and publishing activities. The census can also be considered as part of the growing open data movement with some caveats, while it is largely distinct and separate from what most people think of as big data.

### The Federal Statistical System

The census is part of the U.S. Federal Statistical System, whose mission is to provide evidence-building functions, which the government describes as "the collection, compilation, processing, analysis, and dissemination of data to create general purpose, policy- and program-specific, and research-oriented statistics and datasets. They also include program evaluation, performance measurement, and public health surveillance" (Executive Office of the President, 2017). The Census Bureau is one of the 13 principal statistical agencies whose primary mission is the production and analysis of statistics, and it receives the largest share of the statistical program's budget ($1.4 billion out of $7.2 billion in 2016).

Given the Census Bureau's size and the depth and breadth of its knowledge for creating statistics, it supports many other federal and state agencies in gathering and creating data. It has a long history of innovation in this field. In the late 19th century, it pioneered the use of mechanical punch card technology for tabulating data (Figure 1.3 shows women reading entries from 1940 census enumerator forms to create punch cards, which would be fed into machines to tabulate results). The Census Bureau was in the forefront of developing statistical sampling methods in the 1930s, which were envisioned as efficient ways for collecting timely data on an ongoing basis (Anderson, 2015, pp.  176–179). Sample survey methods and the Bureau's early adoption of digital computer technology in the mid-20th century allowed for the expansion and growth of data collection and tabulation. In the late 20th century, the Census Bureau helped spread the adoption of GIS in the United States through the creation and distribution of TIGER, a database of geographic boundary files. They were also one of the earliest agencies to publish data on the internet.

> **FIGURE 1.3** ● CARD PUNCH OPERATORS CREATING POPULATION CARDS FOR THE 1940 CENSUS

*Source:* National Archives https://catalog.archives.gov/id/7741405

Many of the statistical agencies specialize in providing data that is specific to their departments and missions. The Bureau of Transportation Statistics focuses on transportation-related data while the National Center for Education Statistics focuses on education-specific data. The Census Bureau is unique in that its datasets appeal to a broad range of fields and interests; there are questions on commuting, education, the labor force, disabilities, and housing. It is also distinct in its ability to provide detailed data for small geographies that is uniform and comparative; almost all of the other datasets published by the government are not tabulated below the state or county level (Hartnett, Sevetson, & Forte, 2016).

Datasets can be classified into three categories based on how they are created: (1) statistical, (2) administrative, and (3) derived. Most of the Census Bureau's datasets are statistical datasets, while the majority of the other agencies produce data from administrative sources. Statistical datasets are created for the specific purpose of having data to answer specific questions. Statistical datasets can be generated from a total count, like the decennial census, or from sample surveys, like the ACS. In contrast, administrative datasets are created as a by-product of some process. For example, the primary function of the (IRS) is to collect taxes to raise revenue for the federal government, and it uses forms like the 1040 to gather this information. The purpose is to collect taxes, not to produce data. As a by-product, the IRS creates datasets that are used to measure migration between states and counties, based on whether a person's address changed from one year to the next. Derived datasets are data created from other data. The Census Population Estimates Program is a derived dataset that uses data from the decennial census, the ACS, the IRS, the Medicare Enrollment Program, and the National Center for Health Statistics to estimate the annual population for states, counties, and metropolitan areas.

## Open Data

Over the past decade, there has been increasing interest around the concept of open data. In the most basic sense, data is considered open if it's free to use, reuse, and redistribute with minimal requirements. The open data movement seeks to build collaboration and participation around free datasets that can be used to study and improve public services and to spur economic growth (Goldtstein & Dyson, 2013). Open data should meet a number of technical requirements that are intended to ensure that it is as accessible as possible. Data should be complete, primary (not summarized), timely, well-documented, and machine readable in nonproprietary data formats, so it can be easily processed without restrictions or expensive tools (Kitchin, 2014).

In many ways, the census could be considered as the original open dataset, as it has been well-documented, widely distributed, and publicly available since its inception in 1790. It falls within the public domain and can be used by anyone for any purpose. It is highly accessible as it can be discovered via several different web interfaces. The data is stored in machine-readable formats (CSV, text-delimited, spreadsheets, database tables, XML), which are formats that have a suitable organization and structure that allows data to be directly retrieved and manipulated. Given the number of datasets and their size and complexity, search engines cannot always crawl and index them directly, but in many instances, users can get persistent URLs to tables so that data can be linked to and cited. It is well-structured and indexable; every record represents a piece of American geography, and that geography is assigned a unique ID code (called a GEOID) that is relatively consistent within and across datasets and years. Census data stored in separate tables can be related and tied together using these identifiers.

One of the challenges for both description and accessibility is the sheer size and complexity of the datasets, which makes them confusing for new and even seasoned users to understand and navigate. The Census Bureau invests a lot of effort in providing tools to cater to many users, and the process for creating datasets is transparent. Each of the Bureau's data discovery tools includes links to glossaries with definitions and terminology, and each of the individual statistical program websites (the decennial census, the ACS, the Economic Census, etc.) includes detailed and frequently updated information that describes the methodology used for collecting and processing the data.

The census is not "complete" in the sense that it's not a primary or secondary dataset. Primary data is data that's collected by an individual or organization for their own use, secondary data is primary data that's distributed for use by outside researchers for their own purposes, and tertiary data is derived data: data that's been aggregated and summarized from the primary set. The Census Bureau's primary data, records of individual responses to census questionnaires, is subject to confidentiality regulations that protect individual's privacy. An individual's responses to the census are kept confidential for 72 years before they can be released, and until then, the data cannot be shared with anyone, including other branches of the government. The Census Bureau provides samples of individual responses with personal identifying information removed in public use microdata files, but not the complete datasets. Most of the data is summarized by population groups and geographic areas, some of which are quite small in size.

Whether the census is timely is a matter of opinion. It is more timely than it used to be, as the detailed socioeconomic characteristics of the population are provided annually as part of the ACS, rather than just every 10 years with the decennial census. The Population Estimates Program and the County Business Patterns are published on an annual basis, and the Current Population Survey is published monthly. But in the big data world where data is provided in real time, the census is not considered timely. It is published at set intervals, and there is a time lag from the time the data is collected to the time it is processed and released.

Given their transparency, accessibility, documentation, structure, and geographic detail, the census datasets do serve as foundational layers in the open data universe. From the open data perspective, they cannot be considered primary or timely, and on these points, we can contrast the census with "big" datasets.

## Big Data

In the colloquial sense, the census is quite large, but in the technical sense, it is not big data. Big data is captured in real time and has a granular level of detail, representing a specific person or event at a specific geographic location. Cameras and sensors that constantly monitor the environment are capturing big data, as are websites monitoring clicks, social media sites registering every comment and post, and online forms like 311 requests that are capturing individual complaints. In his book *The Data Revolution*, Rob Kitchin (2014) contrasts big data with small data, and he characterizes the latter as traditional datasets that are produced in a tightly controlled manner with limited scope, size, and time frame. Census data is a prime example of a small dataset: The size and scope are limited to a specific number of questions: if the data is sample based, it is limited to a certain number of respondents, and the time frame ranges from 1 to 10 years. Because of confidentiality reasons, the data is often coarse, summarized by groups and by places. The design is also inflexible; once a count or survey begins, the methods cannot be changed without compromising the dataset and generating great expense.

In contrast, big data seeks to be exhaustive and finely detailed, and is flexible and scalable in production. Kitchin describes big data as being high in velocity (the speed in which it is produced) and volume (the sheer amount that is produced). The allure of big data is the notion that we can simply collect as much information as possible and analyze it in the hope of uncovering trends and making connections and predictions that were previously impossible to conceive without access to modern resources like machine learning and infinite disk space. So why bother with small data like the census when we have big data?

Big data captures what's easy to capture and whatever is openly expressed. It is often represented at face value by technology enthusiasts, even though the data is often not designed to answer specific research questions it's being applied to and is often dirty or unprocessed. While limited in volume and velocity, small data has a long development history with established practices and a design that seeks to answer specific research questions. Kitchin uses the analogy of gold mining; small data studies look for gold in narrow seams while big data studies attempt to extract nuggets from large-scale open pit mining. The principal difference is in investing resources to collect data to answer specific, targeted questions versus searching through tons of big data and hoping it tells us something (Kitchin, 2014). Ultimately, big data has the same limitations as small data; it is merely a representation of reality that is influenced and biased by the context in which it's created. Despite the hype generated around big data, it is not the objective, exhaustive, perfect, and sole solution for answering all of the world's questions.

Let's look at two recent examples that illustrate the limitations of big data versus the value of census data. In 2017, Facebook was touting its strengths to advertisers and investors by saying that its social media platform had the ability to reach 41 million adults in the United States between the ages of 18 and 24, and 60 million adults between the ages of 25 and 34. This sounded pretty impressive, until an analyst at an investment firm checked Facebook's numbers against the latest census data and found that there are only 31 million adults in the United States aged 18 to 24 and 35 million aged 25 to 34 (Hem, 2017; Swant, 2017). When presented with these discrepancies, Facebook responded that their data was designed to estimate how many people in a given area are eligible to see an advertisement that a business might run. Their estimates were derived based on Facebook user behavior, user demographics, and location data from devices and were not designed to match population or census estimates. They concluded by saying that they are always working to improve their estimates.

There are three lessons we can draw from this example. First, big data suffers from the same limitations as small data. The Facebook data was never cleaned or processed to estimate the actual population; it was simply taken at face value and accepted as is. Their statistics can be inflated because people misrepresent their age, have multiple or fake accounts, and because the location services capture people who are in a given area but don't necessarily live there, such as tourists. The census suffers from these same issues; people can be undercounted or overcounted, and there are challenges determining what a person's residence is (people with vacation homes, military personnel overseas, the homeless). The Census Bureau has an advantage relative to Facebook regarding data accuracy, as a person has more to gain by having multiple accounts or lying about their age on a social media platform versus a government form that most people fill out once every 10 years. More important, the Census Bureau has experience with addressing these issues and has methodologies for coping with missing and possibly false information.

This leads to the second lesson. Because the census is in the public domain, the process is transparent. We can go on the census website and freely access the data and all the documentation that's associated with collecting, processing, and disseminating it. People who disagree with the data can lobby the Census Bureau and Congress to try to force changes. While this might be difficult to achieve, you still have the right to do it and have the information at your disposal to create meaningful arguments. In sharp contrast, the Facebook data is in a black box. We can only guess and make assumptions about how it is created. While tech companies constantly push and pull us to freely give them data about ourselves, they resist any attempt to share the data they collect about us with us, or even disclose what they do with it. Many of the big datasets, especially the data generated from social media, suffer from this lack of transparency.

Last, this example illustrates one of the important use cases of census data: The census can serve as a baseline that we can check other datasets against. It can be used for fact checking, as the analyst used it in checking Facebook's claims, and for benchmarking, calibrating, and adjusting population estimates that are generated from other sources, which is what Facebook failed to do.

Meanwhile, *The Washington Post* reported in 2017 that scientists were now able to estimate what the demographic characteristics of different neighborhoods were based on the cars that are parked in the neighborhood (Ingraham, 2017). The researchers collected Google Street View images from 200 U.S. cities, created a schema that correlated the makes and models of thousands of cars with cars in the images, and used this data to build a model that predicts the race, income, and voting characteristics of the population in small census areas. The researchers compared their findings with the ACS data and found a high correlation between their estimates and the actual census data. They suggested that their method could be used to provide more data that is just as accurate as the ACS but could do so in a timely fashion at a fraction of the cost (Gebru et al., 2017).

There are a number of lessons that can be drawn here. Like many experiments that take place in Silicon Valley, the results are novel and interesting, but the exercise takes place in a moral vacuum. Instead of asking a person to identify themselves on a government census form with information that describes how the data will be used, a private company takes pictures of a neighborhood and a third party uses this information to estimate who lives there. Is it just or fair to estimate what a neighborhood's population is like by photographing the cars parked on its streets? The ACS is used to allocate federal funds for everything from transportation projects, to programs for schools, to assistance for needy families. Would it be ethical to use the car-based data to allocate this money, instead of the ACS? Or what if another third party uses this data instead of the ACS to make decisions on whom to give a home loan? While the researchers never explicitly claim that their method should be used to replace the ACS, they implicitly point in this direction as they emphasize how expensive and untimely the ACS data is.

As part of its mission, one of the Census Bureau's goals is to ensure that everyone in the United States is counted as part of the decennial census and that a representative sample of the entire population is included in all their sample-based products. Furthermore, the categories that are used for tabulating the data must represent the entire U.S. population, and the census data itself must be accessible to everyone as a public good.

This mission cannot be fulfilled by the private interests in any one of the examples just described. Researchers in the car study state that they were unable to reliably estimate the presence of children or people employed as farmers, as children don't drive cars and the study omitted rural areas. In the Facebook example, even though a large percentage of the population uses Facebook, there are groups of people that tend to use social media less than others. In the United States, about 7 in 10 Americans used social media in 2018, and people who were older, lower income, or living in rural areas used it less than people who were younger, higher income, and urban (Pew Research Center, 2018). In essence, the big datasets that seek to be exhaustive are not truly exhaustive, but suffer from selection bias based on their context and, in some cases, by conscious decisions made by the people who shape how the data is created.

This does not mean that big data should be dismissed entirely, but it should not be considered as a holy grail. "Small" datasets like the census continue to play a valuable role as high-quality open datasets that are designed to answer targeted questions regarding the demographic and socioeconomic characteristics of the United States. As a public good, the census is transparent, accessible, representative of the entire population, and accountable to the public in ways that private or proprietary datasets cannot be.

## 1.6   CONCLUSION AND NEXT STEPS

This chapter was designed to give you an overview of the census, so you can understand its legal justification, see the various roles it plays in U.S. society, and place it within the context of a broader data universe. The rest of this book is devoted to teaching you the practical concerns of understanding, finding, retrieving, processing, analyzing, and interpreting census data. As we address these concerns and learn about the different geographies, subjects, and datasets, we will touch on some of the contextual and ethical issues that we covered in this chapter. While many of our concerns will seem practical (How do I represent these racial categories? How can I combine these areas to study a neighborhood? What threshold should I use for establishing some criteria?), decisions made in creating and using data will always have social, political, economic, or ethical consequences.

In the next chapter, we'll get moving right away: We'll go directly to the main source for census data and start exploring the different datasets and tables, and then we'll step back in Chapters 3 and 4 to understand how this data is summarized and organized geographically and categorically.

# DIVE INTO THE DATA

## 2.1   INTRODUCING DATA.CENSUS.GOV

In this chapter, we dive right into **data.census.gov**, the Census Bureau's primary tool for exploring and accessing its datasets. You will gain exposure to the scope and depth of the data that is available and will be introduced to census concepts and datasets that we will cover in closer detail throughout the book. This will be your first opportunity to use the search interface and to download and import data into a spreadsheet, so it's essential that you follow along and complete the steps to prepare for the subsequent exercises in the book.

We will begin with an overview of **data.census.gov**, how it fits within the Census Bureau's website, and a description of how census data is organized so you can learn how to effectively search across datasets. We will then cover the data search tool in four parts:

1. We begin with a topic-based search to illustrate the basic layout and functions of the tool.

2. We learn how to search for geographic profiles, which provide a wide variety of data for a specific place.

3. We establish a clear path for finding detailed data tables that allows you to compare variables for many places using the advanced search features. In doing so, you will learn about the different kinds of tables the Census Bureau provides and how to download and open the data in a spreadsheet.

4. Once we have fully explored this approach, we will repeat it using concise steps without a lot of narration to ensure that the method is clear.

Once our tour of **data.census.gov** is complete, we will summarize some alternate sources of data outside the Census Bureau. All these sources allow you to look up and download individual statistics, profiles for places, and detailed comparison tables. We conclude with a brief introduction to the Census Bureau's library of research papers and technical reports, if you are interested in written summaries of the latest trends and published research as opposed to individual stats or data tables.

## A New Way to Explore the Census

**data.census.gov** was designed as a modern search-based gateway to provide one point of access to all the Census Bureau's datasets, replacing the multiapplication approach used previously. Charts and maps are now coupled with the data discovery and access features in this new tool, enhancing the overall user experience. Older tools such as the American Factfinder and Census Quickfacts, which have survived in various iterations for nearly 20 years, will be phased out by the time the 2020 census is released.

This is not simply an interface redesign but is a complete overhaul of the underlying architecture. All the Census Bureau's data has been consolidated on one platform where data is pushed out to various services using the Bureau's API (application programming interface, a method for making data directly available through scripts or software). While this platform will be used by the Census Bureau to publish its own applications and content, the same platform will also be available to third parties for creating their own content and services.

**data.census.gov** will be your tool of choice if you want basic profiles or if you need to download a couple or even a dozen tables for projects you are working on. We will cover tools for downloading data in bulk in the exercises in Chapters 5 and 6.

## The Census Bureau's Website

The main website for the Census Bureau, `https://www.census.gov/`, serves many purposes beyond providing access to data. It provides information about the Census Bureau's mission and history, details about all the Bureau's programs and products, access to reference materials and research publications, and news about the Bureau's activities and data releases.

Within the Census Bureau's website are pages for individual programs: the 2010 census and 2020 census, the American Community Survey (ACS), the Economic Census, and so on. The goal of these pages is to provide the same type of information for these programs that the home page provides for the Bureau in general. You will find useful documentation on methodology, reference guides, timelines on data collection and release, and updates on activities. In some cases, you may find summary data, but with few exceptions, these program pages are not the places you would visit to access data. The primary data portal is `https://data.census.gov/`.

## Data Tables

Before we begin searching **data.census.gov**, it is important to understand exactly what we will be searching through. The principal unit of organization for all census datasets is a table. Variables are grouped into tables by topic, and each table has an ID number that is unique within a dataset for a particular year. When possible the Census Bureau uses the same table ID number across years, so that a table ID in the 2017 5-year ACS is the same number used in the 2017 1-year ACS, and the same used in 2016, 2015, and so on. In some cases, an ID may change if a new table is created, dropped, or significantly modified.

There are a few different kinds of tables. Profile and subject tables are designed to provide a broad swath of data about a particular topic, while a detailed table is designed to provide just the most focused and detailed information. Variables will usually appear in more than one table. For example, median household income appears in several subject and detailed tables. For the detailed tables, there will always be one table that provides the most basic information, such as the value for median household income and nothing else. Median household income also appears in additional tables that are cross tabulations of population groups by sex, age, race, and so on. As we move through the examples in this chapter, you will learn how to identify and view the different types of tables.

When you are searching for data, you will have to decide whether you want a broad or narrow swath of information, and whether you want cross tabulations or not. Ultimately, you will be viewing and downloading individual tables that contain data of interest and not choosing individual variables to construct your own tables. One aspect of working with these datasets is that you will often need to download several tables that contain what you need, and then you will use a spreadsheet to collate and reorganize the data and eliminate what you do not want.

## 2.2   FIRST STEPS IN DATA EXPLORATION

Let's get started! Launch your favorite web browser so that you can follow along. Be aware that what you see on your screen may appear differently from the examples printed in this chapter, as **data.census.gov** is configured to display the most current data that is available. When this chapter was written, the 2017 ACS was the most recent dataset. Feel free to follow along with whatever dataset is most current.

## Tool Overview and Topical Search

One of the strengths of the platform is its ability to perform keyword searches, which was something that was quite limited in earlier tools. Searching **data.census.gov** is a bit different from using a commercial search engine such as Google, Bing, or DuckDuckGo. The Census Bureau uses specific terminology for describing its topics and concepts, and familiarity with this terminology will increase your odds of finding what you need.

The good news is that the tool can give you suggestions. Go to `https://data.census.gov/`. Let's say, we are interested in knowing the number of children who are enrolled in school. Instead of searching for that exact phrase, start typing the word "school" in the search box. As you do, underneath the box a number of search suggestions appear that include "Type of School," "School Enrollment," and a number of places that contain the letters "school" (Figure 2.1). Click on the "School Enrollment" suggestion.

Doing so brings us to the summary results page. Let's take a moment to examine this page's layout, which is divided into three parts: (1) tables, (2) maps, and (3) pages. In the tables section, the tool returns a portion of the first table that it thinks is the best match based on our query, and then the titles of a few additional tables that may also be good candidates. In this example, the first table returned is School Enrollment, Table S1401 (Figure 2.2). In our search, we did not specify a geographic

**FIGURE 2.1 ◆ SEARCHING FOR SCHOOL ENROLLMENT DATA**

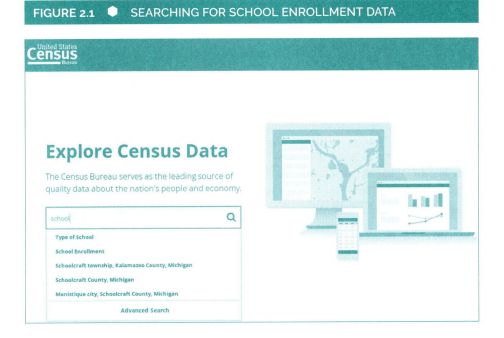

## FIGURE 2.2  ●  SCHOOL ENROLLMENT SEARCH RESULTS

area, so data for the entire United States is returned by default. If we scroll down a little further, we see links to some sample maps and web pages that are related to school enrollment. We will return to maps in Chapter 10; the pages are often useful for pointing us to methodology, research reports, and, in some cases, other data applications on census.gov that contain information of interest related to our search.

Scroll back up to the table results section. Click on the school enrollment table to view it. This takes us away from the summary results page and into the table view page (Figure 2.3). We're shown a list of the most relevant tables on the left and the details and data in the School Enrollment Table S1401 on the right.

The filter link above the list of tables allows you to apply parameters to modify the results that are returned, while the Customize Table button above the table allows you to change settings for that particular table, which in turn are applied to the other results. Click the Customize Table button. Beside the School Enrollment title, hit the blue drop-down arrow. The options on the left allow you to modify the geography

FIGURE 2.3 ● THE TABLE VIEW WINDOW

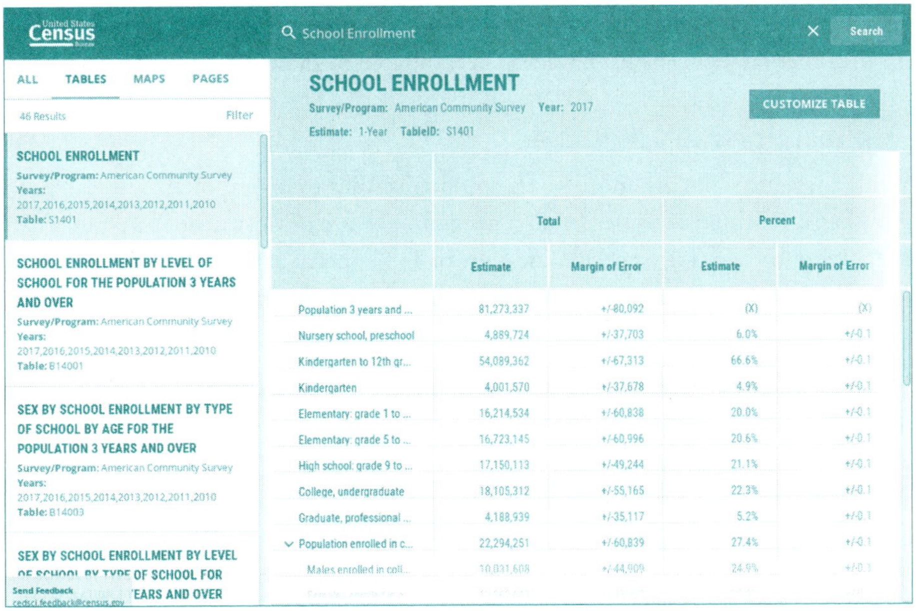

FIGURE 2.4 ● CUSTOMIZE TABLE OPTIONS

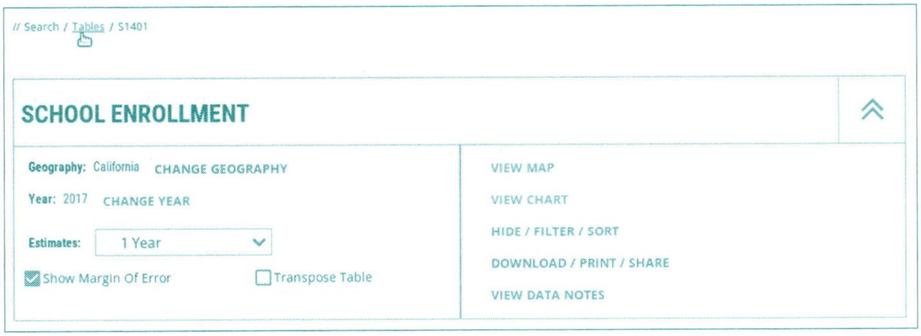

and year, and the period estimate for the ACS (we'll cover the different period estimates in detail in Chapter 6). Options on the right allow you to download the table and modify its contents (Figure 2.4).

Let's change the geography to view data for California instead of the entire United States. Select the Change Geography option. This opens a filter menu. Select Geography, 040—State, and California. Click the up arrow to close the filter menu. The table below now displays results for the State of California. In the upper left-hand corner is a series of links called breadcrumbs, which can lead us back to earlier parts of the search process. Click the Tables link in the breadcrumbs to return to the tables listing. All the other tables in the list have also been filtered to show data for California.

## Profiles: Portraits of Places

While there are some instances where you might want to do a topic-based search, in most cases, it would be easier to do a geographic search. Most people are interested in looking for data for a specific location or for a specific type of geography. With a geographic search, we can narrow down the options and find a lot of information about a particular place.

Let's say, we are interested in learning some basic facts about California. Go back to the home page for **data.census.gov**. Type "California" in the search box. As you type, notice that some tips appear below the search box (Figure 2.5). There's an info box that gives us a profile about California and some other California-related options: all counties in California, all places in California, and so on.

| FIGURE 2.5  ●   SEARCH FOR CALIFORNIA |
| --- |

**Explore Census Data**

The Census Bureau is the leading source of quality data about the nation's people and economy.

| California | × | Search |

**California Profile**

California has a total area of 155,751.4 square miles, including 7,900.2 square miles of water, making it the 3rd-largest state by area.

All places in California

All counties in California

All AIA/ANA/HHL in California

Advanced Search

Let's select the Profile option first. Profiles are available for several geographies and are special reports that give us a broad overview of a specific place with some nice graphics. Click on the profile suggestion under the search box. The profile page provides a short geographic description of California and a location map. Below it are a number of facts such as the total population and median household income.

As you scroll down the page, you will see a series of charts and maps that highlight various facts about the population. For example, the first statistic is for median age

**FIGURE 2.6 ● AGE CHART FOR CALIFORNIA**

**People and Population**

**Age and Sex**
**36.5** +/- 0.2
Median age in California

**38.1** +/- 0.1
Median age in the United States

Table: DP05
Table Survey/Program: 2017
American Community Survey
1-Year Estimates

**Population by Age Range in California**

Under 5 years - 6.2%

18 years and older - 77.1%

65 years and older - 13.9%

0    10    20    30    40    50    60    70    80

⬤ Margin of Error          Share / Export    Customize Chart

(Figure 2.6). The median is the midpoint value; if we were to line every Californian up from the youngest to the oldest and pick out the person in the middle of the line, that person's age represents the median of the age distribution. The median in this example is 36.5 years ± 0.2 years; the subscript text indicates that this is a margin of error for this estimate (so the true value could be as low as 36.3 or as high as 36.7). By default, **data.census.gov** gives us the latest statistic that is available; in this case, we see it's from the 2017 ACS 1-year estimates.

Take a moment and scroll through the profile to get a sense of the kind of data that's available. The profile incorporates data from many datasets: the decennial census, the ACS 1- and 5-year averages, the Business Patterns dataset, and more. These profiles are a nice feature, but they are available only for certain geographies: states, counties, cities, and towns. What if you want a profile for a different place, like a metropolitan area or a census tract? Or perhaps, you want a data table that neatly captures much of this information?

We could return to the main search screen, search for California, and hit the enter key rather than selecting the profile. This would return us to the tables/maps/pages screen that we saw in the previous section, where we could access a list of all tables that are related to California. Let's take a shortcut instead. Scroll back to the Age and

**FIGURE 2.7 ● ACS DEMOGRAPHIC PROFILE TABLE DP05**

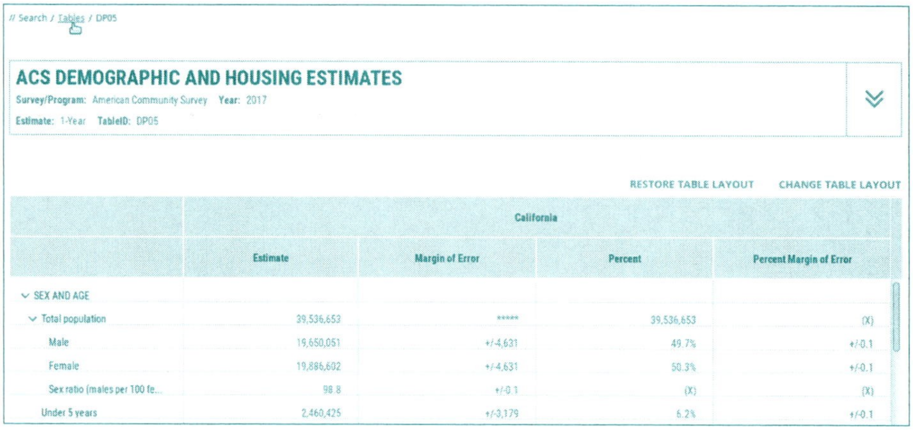

Sex chart at the top of the page, to the statistic for median age. Below the statistic is a link to the table it was drawn from, DP05. Click on the link for that table, which takes us out of the search view and into the table view.

The table view shows us ACS Demographic and Housing Estimates Table ID DP05, from the latest 1-year estimates of the ACS (Figure 2.7). The table begins with data for Sex and Age, and if you scroll down, you will get a broad overview of the demographic variables collected in the ACS: age, sex, race, and Hispanic or Latino ethnicity.

All the Census Bureau's data is organized in a series of tables that have unique identifiers within each dataset. So when you are searching for a particular value such as age or income, you will retrieve a series of tables where that kind of data is stored. For this table, DP is shorthand for Data Profile table. There are four of these tables in the ACS datasets, DP02 through DP05, that by design give you a broad swath of the most common census variables.

How can we see the other profiles? Above the title of the table, click the middle breadcrumb to return to the Tables view. Click the Filter link above the list of tables (Figure 2.8). When the filter options menu appears on the right, choose the option for Surveys. Check the box near the top for the ACS 1-Year Estimates Data Profiles. Close the filter menu by clicking the downward arrow button. Now look at the table options on your left. You will see each of the four profile tables: (1) Selected demographic, (2) social, (3) economic, and (4) housing characteristics. Take a few moments to explore what's in each table, to see the different variables that are collected in the ACS.

**FIGURE 2.8 ●   FILTER RESULTS TO SEE DATA PROFILES**

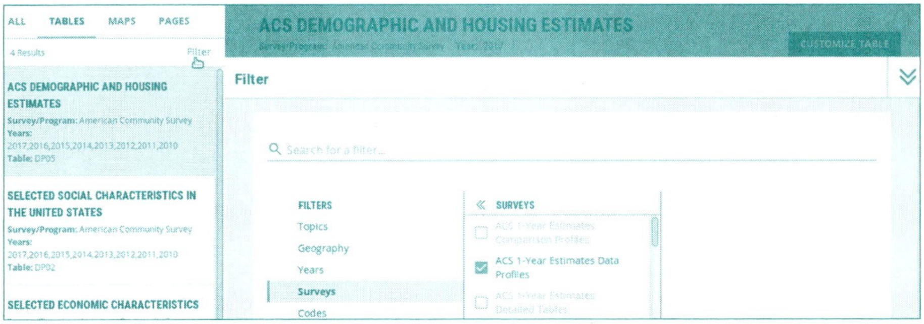

## 2.3   CHART A CLEAR PATH WITH ADVANCED SEARCH

**data.census.gov** is an open-ended tool, which is well-suited for users who want to casually search and browse around for data. Retrieving geographic profiles is pretty straightforward. But if you are interested in finding several, specific detailed comparison tables (showing limited numbers of variables for many places), and you want to know what all the possibilities are before making an informed choice, the open-ended nature of the tool can be frustrating. It would be helpful if there was a set path you could follow. There are many paths we can take, but this is the one I recommend: Use the advanced search tool and choose your survey, year, geography, and topics, and then browse through the resulting tables. It is much easier to apply these filters at the outset to narrow down the list of possible tables, rather than browsing or searching across all of them.

### Advanced Search and Table Types

In this example, we will use the advanced search interface and explore the various types of tables used for packaging census data. Let's say we are interested in getting educational attainment data for all counties in Nevada. Return to the main page for **data.census.gov**. Click in the search box, and then click on Advanced Search when the box appears underneath.

At the top of the Advanced Search screen is a keyword search box, and underneath is a filters section. Scroll down to the filters and click on Surveys. This will display the different datasets that the Census Bureau produces (Figure 2.9). I always recommend that you choose the dataset first, as in most cases, you are not going to want to mix and match data from different datasets and this will help filter out a

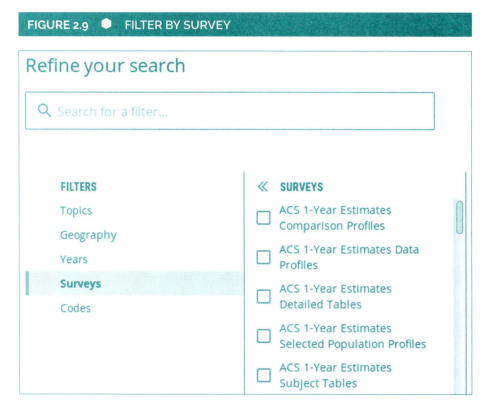

**FIGURE 2.9  ●  FILTER BY SURVEY**

lot of tables. How do you know which one to select? That's what this book is designed for! Once you familiarize yourself with the datasets, you can make an informed choice.

As we will learn in Chapter 6, educational attainment data is collected only as part of the ACS, and 1-year ACS data is published only for places that have at least 65,000 people. Since there are many rural counties in Nevada that have fewer than this number, the 5-year ACS would be our choice. You will see that there are different collections of ACS data: comparison profiles, data profiles, detailed tables, and subject tables. Because I want to demonstrate the differences between each one, we are going to skip this filter for now and we will not select a survey.

Select the Years filter, and choose 2017. Then select the Geography filter (Figure 2.10). Choose the option for County, then choose Nevada for the state, and then choose the option for all counties in Nevada. Then go to Topics. You can select Education, and in the next menu, select Educational Attainment. Or just above, there is a search box that says "Enter text to filter." You can start typing Educational attainment and then check the box when it appears in the filter results.

FIGURE 2.10 ● FILTER BY GEOGRAPHY

Now that we have applied all our filters, scroll to the bottom of the screen and click the View All Results button. The results page shows us all tables, maps, and pages related to educational attainment for the counties in Nevada for 2017. Click on the first table in the list, Educational Attainment Table S1501.

The first table displayed on the tables page and previewed on the right is Educational Attainment, Table S1501 from the ACS. As you look through this table, you will see that it contains a variety of variables. There are records for educational attainment for different age brackets by race, by poverty status, and by income. There are values representing the actual estimates as well as percent totals. This particular table is a Census Subject table; our clue is that it begins with the letter S. A subject table is always going to have a summary of cross-tabulated data with percent totals for each value.

Scroll down through the tables on the left (and if needed, load more) until you see Educational Attainment for the Population 25 Years and Over, Table ID B15003. You will see that this table does not contain the same variety of variables (Figure 2.11). Each row represents just the estimates of attainment at a specific grade level without percent totals. Any table that starts with a B or a C is a detailed table, which means that it contains the most specific level of information without the extra summaries that are included in the S tables.

What's the difference between B and C? The "B" is short for base table, while "C" stands for collapsed table. Scroll down and load more tables until you find Educational Attainment for the Population 25 Years and Over, ID C15003. Select this table to preview it, and you will see the difference (Figure 2.12). There are fewer rows in Table C, as the attributes are aggregated. Instead of listing each individual grade as in Table B, Table C has combined Nursery School to fourth grade in one category, fifth and sixth grades in another category, and so on. The Census Bureau publishes C tables when the margins of error for individual categories are unacceptably high in the 1-year dataset. Aggregating the data into fewer categories increases the size of the sample on which the estimate is based and lowers the margin of error.

**FIGURE 2.11 ⬡ DETAILED B TABLE FOR EDUCATIONAL ATTAINMENT**

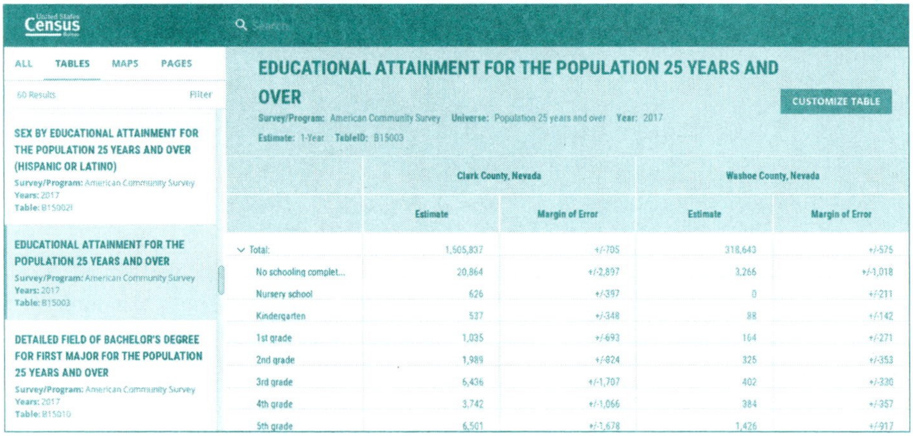

**FIGURE 2.12 ⬡ DETAILED C TABLE FOR EDUCATIONAL ATTAINMENT**

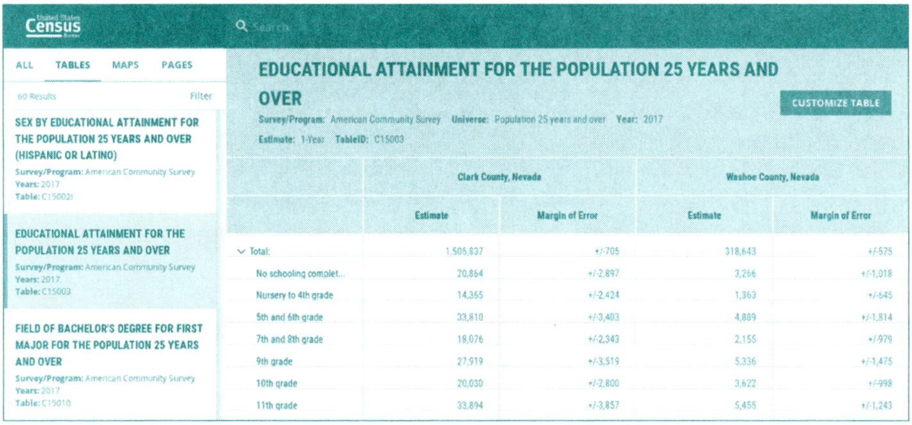

If you scroll further down and load additional tables, you will eventually see the general data profile, Selected Social Characteristics in the United States DP02, that we saw in the previous section as educational attainment appears in this table along with many other variables. There is also a table called Comparative Social Statistics (CP02); these CP tables compare one 5-year ACS period with an earlier nonoverlapping 5-year-period. There is one CP table for each DP table.

So which one of these tables do you choose? The subject S tables are useful if you are doing broad-based research where you are going to cite or visualize a lot of different statistics. They are also convenient because percent totals have been calculated for each value. Alternatively, if you just need specific, detailed variables without a lot of the extras, then the detailed tables are the best choice as you won't have to spend extra time filtering out or deleting attributes that you are not interested in.

Table 2.1 summarizes the most common table prefix codes. The codes we have discussed so far all pertain to the ACS. The decennial census uses a different numbering system; there is a general data profile table called DP01, decennial subject tables are called quick tables and begin with the letters QT, and detailed tables are assigned a letter P or H based on whether the data represents people or housing units. We will discuss these codes in more detail when we study the individual datasets in Part II of the book.

Let's filter by dataset, so we can see just the detailed tables for the 5-year ACS. Scroll to the top of the tables results on the left, and hit Filter option. Choose Surveys, and in the options that appear, choose ACS 5-Year Estimates Detailed Tables. Then hit the blue arrow to close the filter screen. On the left, you should see fewer table results, as we have just the detailed tables.

## Downloading and Importing Data

Select the Educational Attainment Table B15003. Hit the Customize Table button. Hit the blue down arrow to see the options. Select the option to Download the table.

| TABLE 2.1 ● MOST COMMON PREFIXES FOR CENSUS TABLES | | |
|---|---|---|
| | **ACS** | **Decennial Census** |
| Data profiles | DP02 through DP05 | DP 1 |
| Comparative profiles (historical) | CP02 through CP05 | not available |
| Summary tables | S subject table | QT quick table |
| Detailed tables | B base table<br>C collapsed table<br>K special supplemental table | P population subject<br>H housing subject<br>CT not available below census tract level |
| Geographic comparison | GCT limited to specific geographies | |
| Narrative profiles (textual) | NP limited to specific geographies | |

*Note.* Suffixes PR is a particular table for Puerto Rico, letters A through I indicate tabulation for a specific race or ethnic group.

FIGURE 2.13   ●   DOWNLOADING DATA

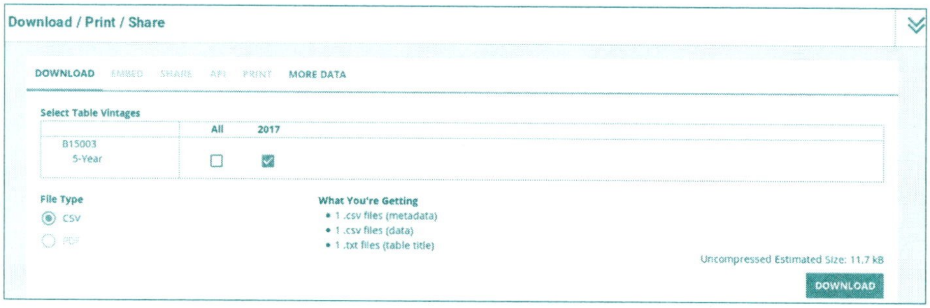

On the download screen, keep the CSV file option (Figure 2.13) The application will zip up the data and create a file to download. When prompted by your web browser, choose the download option.

The file's download location will vary based on your browser configuration and your operating system. Most browsers give you the option to go directly into the folder where a file is downloaded, often from a button located on the browser's main toolbar. The most likely download location would be a downloads folder, your desktop, or a user name folder. Go to the location where your file was downloaded, and unzip the file. On most operating systems, this is as simple as selecting, right-clicking, and choosing the option to unzip or uncompress.

The data is stored in a comma separated value or CSV format. CSV files are stored as plain text, where each row represents a record, and values for different attributes are separated by commas. CSV files are commonly used for distributing and exchanging data, as they are a simple format that can be viewed or imported into any number of programs.

Once the file is unzipped, you should see three text files: the first one is a CSV file that contains the actual data and has the word "data" in the filename, the second CSV has the word "metadata" in the filename and contains a description of all the columns, and the third one is a text file that contains a description of the table and dataset.

Depending on how your operating system is configured, double-clicking on the CSV will open it in a default program, usually a spreadsheet package. We are using Libre-Office Calc throughout this book as our spreadsheet, but you can also use Excel. You can double-click on the file to see if your spreadsheet package will open it. Alternatively, you can launch your spreadsheet package, go to File—Open, browse through your folders, and select the data file, which contains the word "data" in the filename.

**FIGURE 2.14 ● IMPORTING CSV DATA WITH LIBREOFFICE CALC**

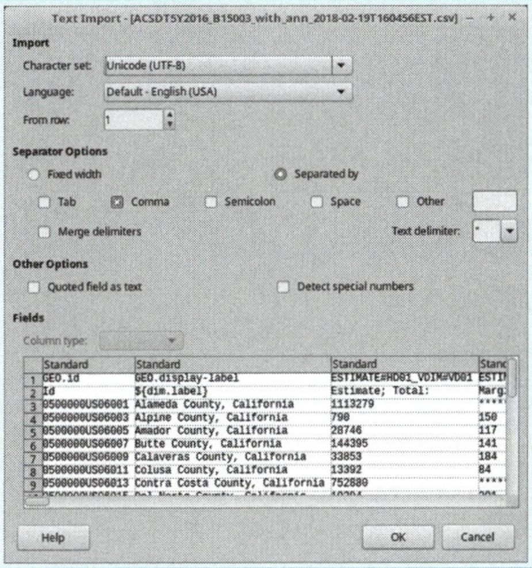

LibreOffice Calc prompts you with a Text Import menu (Figure 2.14). When opening a CSV file, spreadsheets have to parse each attribute into separate columns using the commas and determine whether a particular column should be designated as a number or text. Calc always gives you the option to set the column types yourself before parsing and displaying the file, while Excel only does this if you launch Excel first and then open the file within Excel; if you simply double-click on the file to open it, Excel will take its best guess for what the column types should be. In this example, we have nothing to worry about, so click OK.

That's it! You will see that there are two header rows, one with a unique ID for the column names and another with a descriptive name (Figure 2.15). If you were planning on importing this data into a database, statistical package, or geographic information system (GIS), you would need to delete the descriptive header row; most packages will only accept one header row and column names must be brief. Remember you have a metadata file that you can use as a reference for relating the column ID numbers with descriptive names. You also need to watch out for footnotes embedded in the data, usually indicated with a series ofx asterisks.

The GEO_id column uniquely identifies each row, which represents an individual geography. The first set of digits up to the letters US represent summary codes that the Census Bureau uses to designate geographic levels. The digits after the letters US are the ANSI-FIPS codes; 32 represents the State of Nevada, while the last three digits are unique to the county within the state. We will learn more about these codes in the next chapter.

FIGURE 2.15 ● VIEWING DATA IN LIBREOFFICE CALC

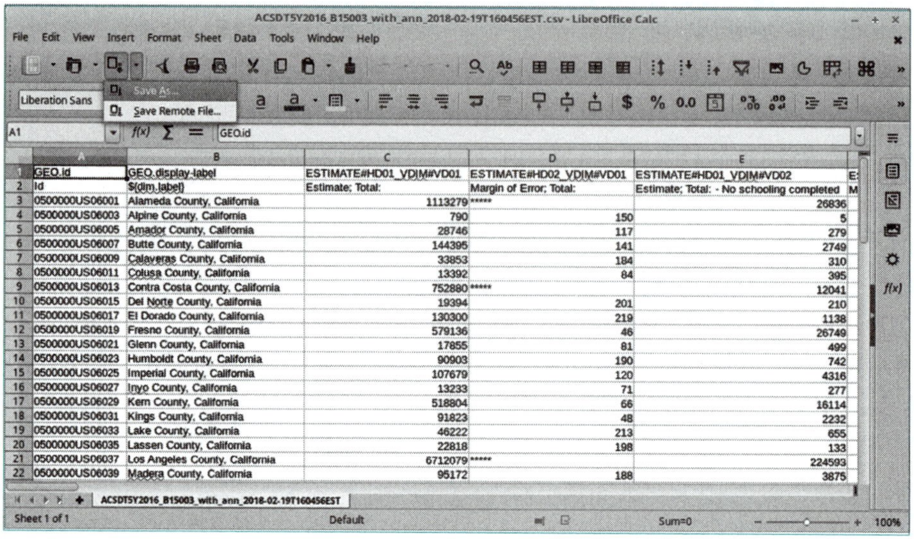

If you hit the Save button, Calc will ask you whether you want to save the file in a spreadsheet format, or if you want to keep it in the original text CSV format. By default, Calc uses the Open Document Format, .ods. If you go to File—Save As, you can choose another format, such as Excel's .xlsx format. If you are going to manipulate, analyze, or visualize this data, it's best to save it in a spreadsheet format that can support formatting, formulas, and graphs; text-based formats such as CSV are used only for storing and exchanging data.

## Follow the Path for Advanced Search

We have established a clear path for navigating an advanced search by using the filters to choose: your survey/dataset, year, geography, and topic. Let's follow this path step by step without digression to get some practice. In this example, let's download the total population for all counties in the United States from the 2010 census. If your goal is to download one or more tables because you want to work with this data in a spreadsheet, or you eventually want to import it into a database, stats package, or GIS software, these are the steps you will take.

1. Go to **data.census.gov**, click in the search box, and choose the Advanced Search option.

2. Scroll down to the filters, select Surveys, and choose Decennial Census Summary File 1.

✔ **INFOBOX 2.1 ALTERNATE SEARCH STRATEGY: SEARCH BY TABLE ID**

Another effective strategy for finding census data is a known-item search, where you search for data based on the table's ID number. For example, if you know that the table number for Educational Attainment for the Population 25 Years and Over from the ACS is B15003, you can type B15003 in the initial search box. It will appear in the pop-up window below the box, and you can select it. By default, you'll get the latest ACS table for the United States, but then you can start applying filters for year and geography to get the data you want.

How would you know what the table ID number is? You can search through the appropriate technical documentation on the Census Bureau's website for that specific dataset. In the documentation (usually a large PDF file), there will be a complete table list. Some of the other resources that we will mention provide lists of tables in their own documentation. For example, The Census Reporter has good documentation for the tables included in the ACS: `https://censusreporter.org/topics/table-codes/`. We will discuss how the datasets are organized and labeled throughout Part II of the book.

You will also learn what the table ID numbers are through experience. As you spend more time working with census data, you will start to recognize and remember the tables that are most relevant to your work. Once you do, a known-item search will be the quickest way to retrieve them.

3. Select Years, and choose 2010.

4. Select Geography, choose County, then choose the option for All counties within the US.

5. Select Topics. Choose Populations and People, Counts Estimates and Projections, and Population Total.

6. At the bottom of the screen, hit the View All Results button.

7. In the results page, select Total Population ID P1.

8. In the table view page, select P1 and hit the Customize Table button.

9. Hit the drop-down arrow, and download the table.

10. Go to the location where the file is stored, unzip it, and open it in a spreadsheet.

Filtering the data using the advanced search is always a better strategy for finding detailed data tables compared with keyword searching or browsing across everything stored on the census data server. Once you gain enough experience working with census data, a known-item search becomes another sound strategy (see InfoBox 2.1).

## 2.4    OTHER SOURCES FOR CENSUS DATA

Since census data is in the public domain, many organizations take the data and create their own portals for exploring and accessing it. These portals add value by limiting the focus to specific datasets or geographic areas (thus making the data easier to search through) or by creating different tools for searching and visualizing the data, or both. Depending on your needs, these sources may make accessing the data easier or may provide tools or formats that you like. We'll look at some of the best, free alternatives in this section.

### Missouri Census Data Center

`https://census.missouri.edu/`

Don't let the name fool you; the Missouri Census Data Center (MCDC) is a repository that contains census data for the entire country. The MCDC provides a number of useful tools for relating geographies as well as the Dexter tool for downloading census data in bulk (we will cover this tool in Chapter 6). It has several applications for creating profiles, which are available directly on its home page in the menu on the right-hand side (Figure 2.16). There are applications for generating profile and

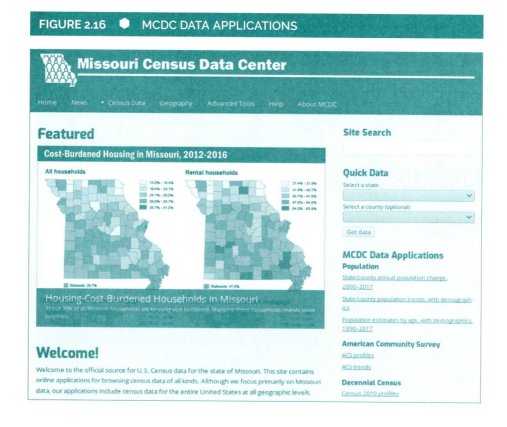

**FIGURE 2.16  ●  MCDC DATA APPLICATIONS**

trends reports from the Population Estimates Program, the ACS, and the decennial census. The profiles are a derivative of the data profile tables that we explored, DP02 to DP05 from the ACS and DP01 from the decennial census. Using their clean and simple interface, you can create a profile (with charts) that compares up to four geographies with just a few clicks. We will explore several of these applications in detail in subsequent chapters.

You can also create historical trends reports from all three census programs using applications that share the same basic design as the profile reports. These historical profiles are particularly valuable because the Census Bureau does not focus on creating historical comparative data, and thus, you can save yourself the time and trouble of pulling disparate years of data together for making basic comparisons.

Data from the profiles and trends applications can be exported to Excel for doing your own analysis or as PDF files if you want a presentation-style report. Graphs can be printed or saved as image files. The website is also a valuable resource for documentation about datasets, topics, and geographies.

## The Census Reporter

`https://censusreporter.org/`

The Census Reporter was designed to make census data easier to access, visualize, and use. It was created as part of a Knight News Challenge–funded project, specifically so that journalists could have easy access to data for supporting stories. The website emphasizes data visualization, with graphs, charts, and maps accompanying many of the facts and tables (Figure 2.17). In many ways, the capabilities of the Census Reporter foreshadowed the features in **data.census.gov**.

### FIGURE 2.17 ◆ A GRAPHIC PROFILE FROM THE CENSUS REPORTER

**Households**

**105,249** ±1,864
Number of households

the Anchorage, AK Metro Area: 135,554 ±2,050
Alaska: 248,468 ±2,841

**2.8**
Persons per household

a little less than the figure in the Anchorage, AK Metro Area: 2.9

a little less than the figure in Alaska: 2.9

Population by household type

Married couples **59%**

■ Married couples
■ Male householder
■ Female householder
■ Non-family

Hide data / Embed

Population by household type (Table B11002)   View table

| Column | Anchorage | | | Anchorage, AK Metro Area | | | Alaska | | | | |
|---|---|---|---|---|---|---|---|---|---|---|---|
| Married couples | 59.4% | ±2.9% | 172,654 | ±8,520 | 62% | ±2.2% | 243,545 | ±9,811 | 60.4% | ±1.5% | 431,087 | ±10,927 |
| Male householder | 7.9%[†] | ±2% | 23,047 | ±5,897 | 7.2%[†] | ±1.5% | 28,411 | ±5,911 | 7.7%[†] | ±0.9% | 54,716 | ±6,534 |
| Female householder | 15%[†] | ±2.1% | 43,469 | ±5,977 | 14.2%[†] | ±1.5% | 55,893 | ±5,838 | 14.7% | ±1.1% | 105,063 | ±8,173 |
| Non-family | 17.7% | ±1.3% | 51,364 | ±3,824 | 16.6% | ±1% | 65,243 | ±4,019 | 17.3% | ±1% | 123,202 | ±8,921 |

Hide data

A key distinction is that the Census Reporter focuses on just one dataset: all the data is from the most recent release of the ACS. The application provides 1-year data when possible and 5-year data for geographies that do not meet the 1-year threshold.

The Census Reporter offers users two pathways for finding data: (1) pick a place to get a profile and (2) explore by topic via a table or column name. The website makes it relatively easy to move from one topic to the next or between different but related geographies. Data can be downloaded in a number of formats, including text, CSV, spreadsheets, and shapefiles. The website is particularly notable for the strength of its user documentation, with clear descriptions of topics and direct links to related tables.

## National Historical Geograhic Information System

`https://www.nhgis.org/`

The National Historical Geographic Information System (NHGIS) is one of several data repositories maintained by the Minnesota Population Center at the University of Minnesota. As the name implies, the NHGIS is a historical repository that contains all census summary data and geographic boundary files going back to the original census in 1790. It is the go-to source if you need historical census data, as the Census Bureau stores only contemporary data in **data.census.gov**.

Since the repository is continuously updated with new data, many researchers choose to access contemporary as well as historical datasets through this portal. We will cover the NHGIS in detail when we explore historical census data in Chapter 12. Unlike the other sources mentioned here, you must register to use it, but registration is free and the site is noncommercial.

## State and Local Governments

State, county, and municipal governments often gather census data for their jurisdictions for internal use and republish it as a public service for their citizens. Many agencies simply compile summary reports and provide basic spreadsheets, but in some cases, local governments provide sophisticated platforms for visualizing and analyzing data. Local governments make the data for their areas more accessible by simply filtering out the rest of the data from the United States, and many add significant value to the data by aggregating it into neighborhoods, wards, and districts that are locally defined and are of interest to their constituents.

For example, the New York City (NYC) Department of City Planning's Population Division publishes spreadsheets and reports from the decennial census and the ACS that they draw from the Census Bureau's data profile tables. The Population Division has created special geographies called Neighborhood Tabulation Areas, which are aggregates of census tracts that were designed for producing more reliable neighborhood-level estimates (as the margins of error for tract-level ACS data can be quite large) and to provide named areas that are more familiar to New Yorkers.

NYC also created a map-based application called the NYC Population Factfinder at `https://popfactfinder.planning.nyc.gov`, which allows users to see demographic profiles for tracts, the neighborhood areas, and Public Use Microdata Areas. Users can also aggregate geographies to build their own neighborhoods (Figure 2.18), and in doing so, the application calculates a new margin of error for each ACS estimate; a challenging feat that many other applications simply ignore. Data can be downloaded in CSV format, and the profiles (even custom-built ones) can be shared and returned to via a unique link.

About 100 miles to the south, the Delaware Valley Regional Planning Commission coordinates regional transportation planning for the Philadelphia Metropolitan Area, which includes nine counties in two states. One of its priorities is ensuring that the hundreds of municipalities in its area have easy access to census data. They created a Municipal Data Navigator at `https://www.dvrpc.org/asp/DataNavigator/`, which provides basic ACS,

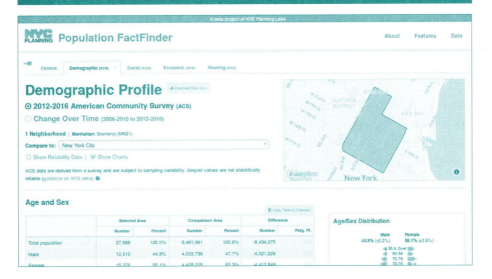

**FIGURE 2.18  ●  NYC DEPARTMENT OF CITY PLANNING'S NYC CENSUS FACTFINDER**

decennial, and population estimates for counties and municipalities. With a few clicks, you generate a location map, chart, and table that can be downloaded.

To see if local governments in your area provide census extracts or applications, start with a basic web search. You could use `https://www.usa.gov/` instead of a commercial search engine, as it indexes only government websites. The most common government offices that work with census data include state data centers, regional and city planning, economic development, labor, and information technology.

## 2.5    CENSUS RESEARCH REPORTS

In this chapter, we covered where you can access census data to obtain the numbers—either an individual statistic or data tables that you can download for doing your own analysis. But what if you are not interested in doing your own analysis? Perhaps, you simply want to know what the trends are so you can cite them in your research, or you want to provide some context for your own findings.

If that's the case, you will want to visit the Census Bureau's library at `https://www.census.gov/library.html`. Researchers at the Census Bureau write concise reports where they analyze the latest data and summarize the findings, study historical trends, and provide insight into different topics of interest. Examples of recent publications include Quarterly Summary of State and Local Government Tax Revenues, Small Area Income and Poverty Estimates, Americans with Disabilities, Characteristics of Voters in the Presidential Election of 2016, and The Population 65 Years and Older in the United States.

You can search through the reports by topic, census program, and year of publication. The library also contains case studies, infographics, and photos. Like the data itself, everything in the library is freely available and in the public domain.

Beyond the Census Bureau, there are a number of nonprofit think tanks that study census data, and they publish everything from summary blog posts to in-depth technical reports. The Brookings Institute, the Pew Research Center, and the Population Reference Bureau are noteworthy examples.

This chapter has given you a crash course in finding and accessing census data. The next two chapters in this part cover the fundamental organizing principles of the census: geography and subject characteristics of the population. An understanding of these concepts will help you make informed decisions when finding and accessing data and will prepare you for studying the individual datasets in detail in Part II of the book.

## 2.6   REVIEW QUESTIONS AND PRACTICE EXERCISES

1.  Use `data.census.gov` to retrieve a geographic profile for your state. Based on the latest data, what is the total population, median age, and percentage of the population who are foreign born?

2.  Pull up the four data profile tables (DP02 to DP05) from the latest ACS for an area of your choosing. Which one contains data on marital status?

3.  Summarize the kinds of information that are available in the data profile table for Selected Economic Characteristics.

4.  Do an advanced search to generate a data table that contains a count of all housing units for all counties in the United States from the latest decennial census. Download the data and load it into a spreadsheet.

5.  Use the MCDC's ACS Profile application at `https://census.missouri.edu/` to generate a comparison table for three counties in your state, using the demographic profile table for Selected Housing Characteristics from the most recent 5-year ACS.

# CENSUS GEOGRAPHY

## 3.1 GEOGRAPHY MATTERS

Census data describes people in places. This chapter is your guide to the types of places that are included in the census, which are called census geographies. Census geographies exist within a nested hierarchy called summary levels, and while different datasets will include different collections of geographies, geographic definitions are standardized and are the same across all the census datasets. We will begin with studying this basic framework before discussing the central geographies in the hierarchy, followed by a detailed overview of other geographies that you will likely use. We will use the Census Bureau's TIGERweb application to visualize and explore them.

The choice of geography is an important one. As we saw in Chapter 2, one of the principal filters that you apply when narrowing your search for census data tables is geography. In some cases, the geographies will be familiar to you and the decision for which to choose will be obvious. If you want population data for your state or several states, it is a simple matter of selecting states as your geographic option. So why do we need to spend time studying geography?

In many cases, the option for which geography to choose will not be clear until you have some experience working with census data. For example, many people are confused when they go to search for data about their town but cannot find an option for cities or towns. In the census, these areas are known as *places*, which seems like a generic term to us but it's a technical term in the census that refers to incorporated cities and towns as well as informal but concentrated settlements of people. Likewise, we may think of urban areas and metropolitan areas as being the same, but in the census, these areas are quite different in definition and scope. An urban area is any concentration of people over a given threshold, while metropolitan areas are large areas composed of counties that have strong demographic and economic linkages.

There are also geographies that you have likely never heard of, like census tracts and census block groups, which are of paramount interest if you are interested in studying neighborhoods or local areas. The Census Bureau does not create boundaries or tabulate data for areas like neighborhoods, as these are informal places that are locally defined. If you are interested in studying data at this level, you will need to identify and use a census geography to approximate the neighborhood.

Once you understand these geographic concepts, you need to make a choice as to which type is suitable for studying your area of interest. If you were doing a national study of educational attainment, would you use states or counties? If you wanted to identify markets for targeting a product, would you use metropolitan areas or places (i.e., cities and towns)? The choice will be driven by your study. If you were trying to target a market, metropolitan areas would be a logical choice as these areas have a common labor market and shared cultural and social institutions. They represent logical groupings of counties based on population settlement and economic patterns, and there are a workable number of them: 366 metropolitan areas and 576 smaller micropolitan areas. In contrast, there are more than 29,000 places that vary tremendously in size, shape, and population, and there are large swaths of the United States that are not part of a place.

In other cases, the choice of geography is driven by what is available, and you will be forced to compromise. Some datasets such as the Population Estimates Program (PEP) include a limited number of geographies, and none for small areas. The American Community Survey (ACS) includes data for small areas like census tracts, but the data may have a large margin of error. You could opt for high geographic detail and a less precise estimate, or you could choose a larger area like a Public Use Microdata Area (PUMA) or county and get a more precise estimate in exchange for less detailed geography. The ACS also includes different period estimates for 1-year and 5-year data, and any geography, regardless of its type, is included in the 1-year ACS only if it has more than 65,000 people.

In short, geography matters. Understanding this terminology is essential for ensuring that you are looking at data that describes your area of interest and is appropriate for your research.

## 3.2   CENSUS GEOGRAPHY HIERARCHY

Census geography includes both legal areas and statistical areas. Legal areas in the United States include geographies like states, counties, cities, and towns that have elected governments and boundaries that are codified by law. Statistical areas are created by the Census Bureau for the sole purpose of tabulating and presenting statistics. Legal areas change over time as new counties are created from existing ones, or as towns incorporate, annex land, or unincorporate. The annual Boundary and Annexation Survey (`https://www.census.gov/programs-surveys/bas.html`) tracks all of the changes in legal boundaries in the United States, so that the Census Bureau can tabulate new data based on the most current definitions. In contrast, statistical areas are updated every 10 years in conjunction with the decennial census. Since many of the statistical areas are defined by a population threshold, they are redrawn as their populations grow or decline.

All census geography, whether legal or statistical, is designed so that smaller geographies representing the more basic units fit or nest within larger geographies. Figure 3.1 illustrates how all these pieces fit. The smallest unit of geography is the census block, which is the geographic building block used for constructing all the other geographies in the hierarchy. For statistical areas, the blocks are combined into larger block groups, which in turn are combined into census tracts, based on specific population thresholds and physical as well as legal boundaries. The process is not entirely driven from the bottom up; legal areas such as states and counties exist as a matter of course, and so the smaller statistical areas are constrained to fit within these boundaries.

We can see in Figure 3.1 that there is one primary "trunk" that appears as a straight line going from census blocks at the bottom to the nation at the top. Census blocks fit within block groups, which fit inside census tracts, which fit inside counties, inside states, inside divisions, inside regions, inside the United States. Based on this diagram, we know that a census tract will not cross county boundaries or the boundaries of any geography directly above it. The geographies outside this central trunk have a different nesting structure. For example, there is a direct line from census blocks to places, followed by a line from places to states. This indicates that places may indeed cross census tract and county boundaries but nest within states and never cross state boundaries.

This hierarchy enforces a logical structure that ensures that all census geography is built from the same basic blocks to avoid arbitrary overlapping or double counting of areas. It allows us to see how data can be aggregated by geography or not. For example, we could easily aggregate tract data to the county level if we need to, but

**FIGURE 3.1  ●   CENSUS BUREAU GEOGRAPHIES**

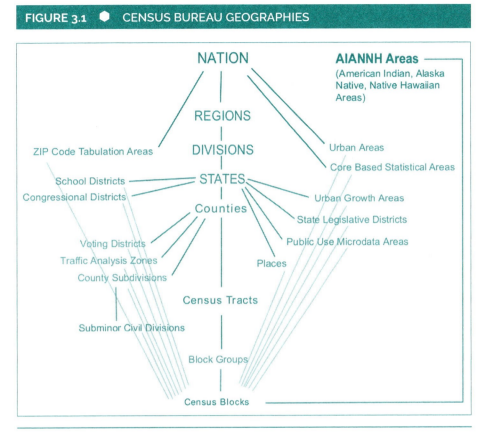

*Source:* https://www.census.gov/programs-surveys/geography/guidance/hierarchy.html

there will be discrepancies if we tried to aggregate tracts to places as they do not nest. In that instance, we could not do a simple aggregation but would need to invent a scheme for apportioning data across the boundaries (covered in Chapter 11). The hierarchy diagram also aids us when searching for data; if we try to download all the places within a county, we will need to specify whether we want places that are located entirely in the county or partially within it, since places do not nest with counties.

Every piece of census geography in the United States has a unique identifier that is generally referred to as a GEOID. The GEOID allows us to relate geographies across tables and even across datasets. Unique identifiers are important for ensuring that records are not mistakenly duplicated and to facilitate the joining of data across tables. Names are not reliable for this purpose because they are duplicated across the country. Think of how many Washington, Jefferson, and Lincoln counties there are in the United States.

| TABLE 3.1 ⬢ A PORTION OF SUMMARY LEVELS FOR STATE FILES |
|---|
| **040**  State |
| **050**  State–County |
| **060**  State–County–County Subdivision |
| **067**  State–County–County Subdivision–Subminor Civil Division |
| **070**  State–County–County Subdivision–Place/Remainder |
| **140**  State–County–Census Tract |
| **150**  State–County–Census Tract–Block Group |
| **155**  State–Place–County |
| **160**  State–Place |

The Census Bureau uses two systems of ID codes for uniquely identifying an individual piece of geography and its location within the geographic hierarchy. ANSI Federal Information Processing Series (FIPS) codes are used for identifying individual geographies and can be assembled to form unique GEOIDs. Summary-level codes indicate the type of geography *and* where it nests within the hierarchy. FIPS codes can be appended to the summary-level codes to form an even longer GEOID.

Table 3.1 illustrates a portion of the summary levels published under the state files for the 5-year ACS. You can see how individual codes nest under others: counties below states, county subdivisions below counties, and so on. When the Census Bureau packages raw data files together, they create a series of files for each individual state with levels that nest under the state and create a national file for levels that generally do not nest under the states but fit under the nation. Exceptions are made to the nesting rules by providing subdivided areas. In Table 3.1, places are listed multiple times. Places nest within states and are captured in summary level 160. However, it may be useful to retrieve a list of places within counties and county subdivisions, even though they do not nest. Summary level 070 reports data for all places that fall within a county or subdivision in two parts: (1) the population for the place that falls within the area and (2) the remainder that falls outside.

In Chapter 2, we downloaded data on educational attainment for each of the counties in Nevada from the ACS. Let's deconstruct the GEOID for the first record in the results, Churchill County:

0500000US32001

The first three digits represent the summary level; in this case, 050 means that this is a state-county summary level. The next two digits, 00, represent something called a variant code, and the following two digits, 00, represent the component code. In most cases, these codes will be zeros. The variant codes are used for congressional districts and voting areas to indicate which session of Congress or legislative chamber the geography is for, while the component code is used in national summary files to indicate whether a piece of geography is a part of an urban or a rural area, or a metropolitan or a micropolitan area.

The letters "US" always separate this first set of codes for summary levels from the FIPS codes that uniquely identify the actual geographic area. While the summary codes have a fixed length of seven digits, the FIPS codes vary in length based on the summary level. For a state-county summary level, the FIPS codes are five digits long: two for the state and three for the county. The two-digit 06 code is the FIPS for California, and within Nevada, 001 is the FIPS for Churchill County. To uniquely identify a geographic record, you can use the full summary level/FIPS GEOID 0500000US32001, but in many cases, you could simply use the FIPS GEOID 32001. You can browse and look up the ANSI/FIPS codes and GEOIDs for the most common geographies using the Missouri Census Data Center's Geographic Codes Lookup application at `https://census.missouri.edu/geocodes/`.

## 3.3  THE PRIMARY TRUNK

The primary trunk of census geography is fundamental to all the other geographies in the hierarchy and is widely used. All these geographies are coterminous and contiguous; they cover the United States in its entirety, so that every square foot of land and water is included within each of these areas. Data for the three small statistical areas (blocks, block groups, and tracts) has been available for all parts of the United States since the 1990 census, and tracts or some corollary were available for portions of the country (mostly urban areas) back to the 1940 census. Table 3.2 lists the geographies in the trunk from the largest to the smallest with their summary level codes. Let's start at the top and work our way down.

### Nation

This may seem obvious that the nation is the United States, but this bears some scrutiny. Are the U.S. territories part of the United States? When the Census Bureau publishes totals that represent the United States, these totals represent the sum of the population for the 50 states plus the District of Columbia. However, if you were to download data for all of the individual states, counties, or places, you

| TABLE 3.2 ◆ PRIMARY TRUNK OF CENSUS GEOGRAPHIES | | |
| --- | --- | --- |
| **Summary Level** | **Geography** | **Type** |
| 010 | Nation | Legal |
| 020 | Region | Statistical |
| 030 | Division | Statistical |
| 040 | State | Legal |
| 050 | County | Legal |
| 140 | Census tract | Statistical |
| 150 | Census block group | Statistical |
| 101 | Census block | Statistical |

would find that records for Puerto Rico are included in the dataset. Given Puerto Rico's special status with the United States and its size (with 3.7 million people, it is larger than many states), it is included in all of the Census Bureau's programs and is treated like a state. Data for Puerto Rico is not folded into any population totals for the United States, and it is not included as part of a census region or division.

The other territories of the United States—the U.S. Virgin Islands, the Northern Marianas, Guam, and American Samoa—are collectively referred to as the Island Areas. They are treated as being equivalent to states but are not included in any census tables for the United States. During the decennial census, a special tabulation is conducted for these areas and the data is published in a series of separate datasets. The territories are not included in the ACS or PEP, but some of them are included in the business datasets. The U.S. Minor Outlying Islands consist of eight small islands or atolls in the Pacific Ocean and one in the Caribbean. They are unorganized territories with no permanent population and are not included in the modern census.

## Regions and Divisions

Census regions and divisions are statistical areas that consist of groups of states. There are four regions (Northeast, Midwest, South, and West) and nine divisions that are subdivisions of the regions (see Figure 3.2). The current structure of the regions was introduced in 1880 and has not changed significantly since 1950. The main criterion was to create areas that consisted of adjacent states that shared similar socioeconomic characteristics and a common historical and cultural background

**FIGURE 3.2 ● CENSUS REGIONS AND DIVISIONS**

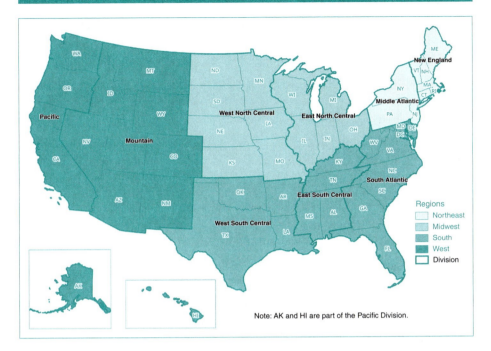

Note: AK and HI are part of the Pacific Division.

(U.S. Census Bureau, 1994). The Census Bureau uses the regions and divisions in their research reports to provide regional summaries of national trends.

The general concept of regions is a subjective one, and many people would disagree over what constitutes the South or West or would argue over whether certain states belong to one region or another. Other federal agencies, such as The Bureau of Economic Analysis, have created their own regions for publishing and analyzing data for states that focus on other characteristics. The Census Bureau's regions and divisions are simply one option for summarizing national statistical data. If you wanted or needed to use a different regional structure, you could simply aggregate state-level census data.

Each census region has a code numbered from 1 to 4, and each division is numbered from 1 to 9. Regional and division codes are used solely for identifying these areas and are never incorporated into the GEOID codes for smaller areas like states or counties.

## States

States are the primary subdivisions of the United States and consist of the 50 states plus the District of Columbia. As legal entities, states hold a considerable degree of autonomy; any powers that are not explicitly vested to the federal government are considered to be within the purview of the states. As such, the socioeconomic characteristics of states vary to some degree based on the outcomes of the various political and administrative structures and policies in each place. Given these differences, comparing the demographic or socioeconomic characteristics between the different states can be meaningful. On the other hand, using states to study the distribution of populations is less meaningful, given the large variation in size, shape, and total population of the states. State-level data can often mask distinct trends within the states.

For example, if we studied the percentage of each state's population that is Asian, it would be meaningful to say that California has a large Asian population compared with other states for social, economic, and historical reasons. This state-level data is useful for comparing the population of the states. However, if we are interested in studying the distribution of the Asian population across the country, states would be a poor choice given their variance in size and population. While California has a large Asian population, county-level data reveals that most of the state's Asian population is clustered in a few counties near the largest cities.

State-level data is widely available; it's published in every census dataset and in most other federal statistical datasets. It is one of the few geographies that is included in its entirety in the 1-year ACS.

Each state and territory is assigned a unique two-digit FIPS code as shown in Table 3.3. The names of the states are sorted alphabetically and the numbers run from 01 to 56, *not* from 01 to 51 as some numbers are intentionally skipped (if one of the territories became a state, it could be renumbered and inserted in the correct alphabetical order). States are also commonly identified in census datasets with their two-letter postal abbreviation.

## Counties

Counties are the secondary subdivisions of the United States. As legal subdivisions of states, most counties exercise some degree of governmental authority. Counties vary widely in total population, but their variance in geographic area is much smaller than the variance between states. They are a popular choice for studying and mapping data for the United States as there is a good number of them relative to the size of the country, and their variance in geographic area is not too great. There is also a lot of data available for them, both inside and outside the census. Data for counties is published in the decennial census, ACS, PEP, and all the business datasets.

Variance in population size is one of the major limits of using county-level data. Approximately 80% of the U.S. population lives in 20% of the counties. National county-level thematic maps of census data can appear distorted unless the data

## TABLE 3.3 ● CODES FOR STATES AND TERRITORIES

| Name | USPS | ANSI/FIPS | Name | USPS | ANSI/FIPS |
|------|------|-----------|------|------|-----------|
| Alabama | AL | 01 | New Hampshire | NH | 33 |
| Alaska | AK | 02 | New Jersey | NJ | 34 |
| Arizona | AZ | 04 | New Mexico | NM | 35 |
| Arkansas | AR | 05 | New York | NY | 36 |
| California | CA | 06 | North Carolina | NC | 37 |
| Colorado | CO | 08 | North Dakota | ND | 38 |
| Connecticut | CT | 09 | Ohio | OH | 39 |
| Delaware | DE | 10 | Oklahoma | OK | 40 |
| District of Columbia | DC | 11 | Oregon | OR | 41 |
| Florida | FL | 12 | Pennsylvania | PA | 42 |
| Georgia | GA | 13 | Rhode Island | RI | 44 |
| Hawaii | HI | 15 | South Carolina | SC | 45 |
| Idaho | ID | 16 | South Dakota | SD | 46 |
| Illinois | IL | 17 | Tennessee | TN | 47 |
| Indiana | IN | 18 | Texas | TX | 48 |
| Iowa | IA | 19 | Utah | UT | 49 |
| Kansas | KS | 20 | Vermont | VT | 50 |
| Kentucky | KY | 21 | Virginia | VA | 51 |
| Louisiana | LA | 22 | Washington | WA | 53 |
| Maine | ME | 23 | West Virginia | WV | 54 |
| Maryland | MD | 24 | Wisconsin | WI | 55 |
| Massachusetts | MA | 25 | Wyoming | WY | 56 |
| Michigan | MI | 26 | | | |
| Minnesota | MN | 27 | American Samoa | AS | 60 |
| Mississippi | MS | 28 | Guam | GU | 66 |
| Missouri | MO | 29 | Northern Mariana Is. | MP | 69 |
| Montana | MT | 30 | Puerto Rico | PR | 72 |
| Nebraska | NE | 31 | U.S. Minor Outlying Is. | UM | 74 |
| Nevada | NV | 32 | U.S. Virgin Is. | VI | 78 |

*Source:* https://www.census.gov/library/reference/code-lists/ansi.html

*Note:* ANSI = American National Standards Institute; FIPS = Federal Information Processing Series; USPS = U.S. Postal Service.

is normalized (showing a mean, median, or percent total) and even then, small population values in many counties can skew results.

Another challenge is the variety of local exceptions as to what constitutes a county. The Census Bureau refers to counties as "Counties or Statistically Equivalent Entities" to capture these differences. For example, Louisiana has parishes instead of counties, Alaska has no counties but has entities such as cities and towns that serve as an equivalent, and four states have one or more incorporated cities that function as counties. InfoBox 3.1 summarizes the major exceptions to the rules, which you will encounter if you work with county-level data on a regular basis.

Counties are identified with a three-digit code that begins with 001 and usually increments in odd numbers (003, 005, etc.). The county code by itself is only unique within the state; when working with a dataset of counties from multiple states, you would need a GEOID with both the state and county codes in order for the id to be unique. For example, there is a county 001 in every state; in Alabama it's Autauga County and in Arizona it's Apache County. We would uniquely identify the county by combining the state and county FIPS code: 01001 for Autauga, AL, and 04001 for Apache, AZ.

## Census Tracts

Census tracts have long been the geography of choice for researchers who are interested in studying data below the county level, particularly within urban and suburban areas. Census tracts are designed to be relatively permanent statistical divisions of counties; each county must have at least one census tract. Tracts are designed to have an optimal size of 4,000 residents, within a range of 1,200 to 8,000. This equivalency in population allows researchers to study areas of equal population size while largely eliminating the possibility that any differences between areas are due to differences in the number of people. Since they are defined by population, tracts vary widely in geographic area. In urban areas, they are small enough to represent portions of neighborhoods; in suburban and some rural areas, they represent subdivisions of counties; and in really rural areas, there is one tract that coincides with the county boundary.

The Census Bureau delineates census tracts in consultation with state and local officials. While the intent is to keep the tracts relatively permanent to make historical comparisons possible, tracts must be divided, combined, or redrawn as the population increases or decreases every 10 years to maintain the optimal threshold for population size. Of the 73k census tracts with land area that were drawn for the 2010 census, 31% had boundary adjustments relative to the 2000 census that resulted in population being shifted from one tract to another (Logan, Xu, & Stults, 2014).

## ✔ INFOBOX 3.1 COUNTY EXCEPTIONS AND QUIRKS

Alaska has no counties. Its equivalent entities include legal areas such as boroughs, cities, and municipalities and statistical areas called census areas, which are jointly delineated by the state and the Census Bureau. The boundaries for these census areas are often modified, as populations grow large enough to create incorporated places. Alaska is one of two states that usually has county boundary changes between decennial censuses.

District of Columbia is considered to be both a state and a county.

Hawaii Kalawao County sits on a tiny peninsula on the island of Molokai and was the Islands' leper colony from the mid-19th to the mid-20th century. It is the nation's smallest county; it is administered by the state health department, and the only residents are the remaining patients who chose to live there. Given these special circumstances, some researchers will either exclude or aggregate data for the county into surrounding Maui County.

Independent Cities are incorporated places that are independent of any county and represent primary subdivisions of their state. They have a county FIPS designation of 510 and are not sorted alphabetically among the counties within their state. They are Baltimore City, Maryland; St. Louis, Missouri; and Carson City, Nevada.

Louisiana has parishes instead of counties, as a result of the state's unique history as a former French and Spanish colony. As local governments, their functions are similar to counties.

New England States of Connecticut and Rhode Island no longer have functioning legal governments at the county level, as do 9 of Massachusetts's 14 counties. The Bureau continues to publish data for these areas to provide comparable units for data analysis.

U.S. Territories have their own subdivisions that are considered equivalent to counties. These include municipios in Puerto Rico, districts and islands in American Samoa, municipalities in the Northern Marianas, and islands in the U.S. Virgin Islands. Guam has no subdivisions, but it is considered to be both a territory and a county.

Virginia has many incorporated places that are equivalent to counties. They are sorted alphabetically with the regular counties and have standard FIPS codes. Since they are small in area and many have declining populations, it is not uncommon that they unincorporate and dissolve into the surrounding county. Virginia is the other state that usually has county boundary changes between decennial censuses. For statistical purposes, some researchers will aggregate data for the city counties with the larger surrounding counties.

Tracts are also drawn to isolate areas that have no residential population (large parks, industrial areas, airports, mountains, wasteland, etc.) and to encapsulate large facilities that house group quarters populations (prisons, military bases, college dormitories, etc.) so that these areas can be excluded or studied separately from the residential population. Given the nesting structure of census geography, tracts may include land and water as their boundaries must coincide with legal boundaries for counties and states. Some large bodies of water are designated as their own census tracts.

Tract-level data is available in the decennial census and, functionally, is the smallest geographic unit available in the 5-year ACS. For all intents and purposes, census tracts are the smallest level of geography for which the most detailed socioeconomic characteristics of the population are available. As such, and given that there are only 76k census tracts in the United States, it is one of the most popular geographies used for demographic and geographic analyses. Many state and local agencies use census tracts as building blocks for creating both legal and statistical geographies of local interest.

As we will discuss in Chapter 6, the introduction of the ACS and the discontinuation of the detailed decennial census long form have created serious limitations to working with tract-level data. The margins of error for 5-year ACS tract-level data can be quite large, particularly for small population groups (Salvo, Lobo, Willett, & Alvarez, 2007; Spielman, Folch, & Nagle, 2014). Researchers have responded by ignoring the margin of error (a terrible idea) or by creating larger, locally defined geographies by aggregating census tracts. Using tracts to study or build neighborhoods can be challenging, as the idea of a neighborhood is locally and contextually driven and tract boundaries are not drawn to fit these conceptions (Sperling, 2012). The next-largest official statistical area with a consistent population size that is available for the entire United States is the PUMA, which has a much higher population threshold of 100k. We will wrestle with the concept of neighborhoods in the first exercise in Chapter 6.

Census tracts are numbered with a six-digit code, with up to four digits to the left of the decimal place and an optional two to the right. In maps and publications, a tract number is commonly referenced with the least number of digits, such as Tract 1 or Tract 2.01. When used as a unique identifier in a data table, the numbers are padded with zeros to bring the number of digits up to six places, so 1 becomes 000100 and 2.01 becomes 000201. Some tract numbers identify special land-use characteristics; for example, tracts numbered in the 9900s cover large bodies of water. The suffix (numbers to the right of the decimal place) indicates whether a tract has been split in the past. For example, if Census Tract 2 has grown significantly in population since the 2010 census, it might be split into two tracts numbered 2.01 and 2.02 in 2020. Census tract numbers are only unique within the county where they are located. When comparing tracts across counties or states, you would need the full GEOID code for them to be unique. For example, 04001000100 is Census Tract 1 (000100) in Apache County (001), Arizona (04).

## Census Block Groups

As the name suggests, block groups are aggregates of census blocks. Like census tracts, the Census Bureau delineates block groups in consultation with state and local officials. Block groups are designed to have a population between 600 and 3,000 people and must cover a contiguous area. Each census tract must contain at least one block group. Block groups are assigned a single-digit number from 1 to 9, and this number is only unique within a specific tract.

Block group data is published in the decennial census and in the 5-year ACS. While it is the smallest geography available in the ACS, its utility is limited by the large margins of error at this scale, which make the data too unreliable for most applications. There were approximately 300k block groups in the 2010 census. When working with decennial census data, the smaller number of block groups makes it a more practical option for studying small areas compared with census blocks, while offering more geographic detail than census tracts.

## Census Blocks

The census block is the smallest statistical area created by the Census Bureau and is the fundamental building block for all of the other census geographies. While the term *block* was derived from the Bureau's early attempts to tabulate data for major cities by block (U.S. Census Bureau, 1994), census blocks are not always synonymous with city blocks; they can be larger or smaller in area and are delineated in both urban and rural areas. Census blocks tend to be small in geographic area, and their boundaries are created based on visible features such as streets, railroads, and waterways and invisible features such as property lines and legal boundaries for municipalities, counties, and states.

Block data is published only for the decennial census, and the number of variables is limited to basic tabulations of age, race, sex, ethnicity, household and family status, and housing unit occupancy and tenure. Besides its role as the geographic building block, block data is used for congressional redistricting following the decennial census, and blocks are used for conducting the actual enumeration (i.e., the decennial population count). You will need to use a scripting language, database software, or a statistical package to effectively work with block-level data, given the sheer number of blocks (11 million in 2010). Unless you have a pressing need for basic demographic data at superfine resolution, you probably won't work with block data. Block groups and tracts are more practical choices.

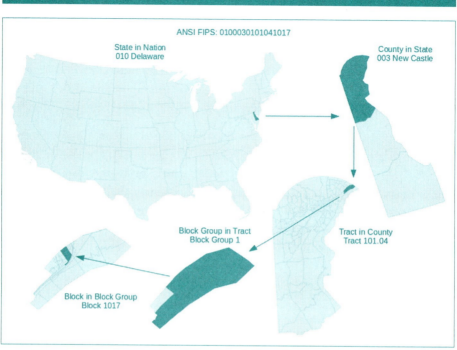

**FIGURE 3.3 ● CENSUS GEOGRAPHY HIERARCHY AND NESTING**

Census blocks are assigned a four-digit number, where the first number represents the block group. This is an exception to the rules we have seen thus far, in that the block group number is *part* of the block number and is *not* an addition to it. So 040010001001000 would be Block number 1,000, which is in Block Group 1, within Census Tract 1, in Apache County, Arizona. While census tract numbers are designed to be relatively stable from one decennial census to the next, block group and block numbers are *not* stable and may be completely renumbered.

## Fitting the Pieces Together

Figure 3.3 illustrates the hierarchy and nesting of the central trunk geographies that we just explored, from nation to state, to county, to census tract, to census block group, to census block, and how the FIPS ID codes are used to identify each level (regions and divisions are often omitted from diagrams like this, as their codes are not a component of the levels below them). Notice the relative size and number of the small statistical geographies and how they fit together. In the next section, we will explore this particular example interactively using TIGERweb.

## 3.4    EXPLORING CENSUS GEOGRAPHY WITH TIGERWEB

TIGER is the collection of digital geographic base files that the Census Bureau uses to delineate census geography. The Census Bureau uses the TIGER data to create maps for enumerating the census as well as for tabulating data and publishing the results. It is designed to ensure that the hierarchical integrity of each location is maintained, so that tract boundaries nest within and never cross county boundaries, and county boundaries nest within and never cross state boundaries, and so on. We will look at how we can use these boundary files to make our own maps in Chapter 10.

The TIGERweb application illustrates the different geographies and demonstrates how they relate to one another. Let's use it to explore the census geographies we have just discussed. Launch your favorite web browser and go to TIGERweb, and follow the steps below:

`https://tigerweb.geo.census.gov/tigerweb/`

1. On the right is a map of the United States, and on the left is a control panel for the map (Figure 3.4). The default menu option in the panel is Layers, which indicates the current layers that are active on the map. At the top is a

**FIGURE 3.4  ⬡    TIGERWEB APPLICATION**

drop down called Vintage. The current vintage represents whatever the most current geography is. Other vintages include what was used in the latest ACS and the 2010 census. Remember, statistical areas such as tracts and blocks rarely change once the decennial census is conducted, but legal areas such as counties or places (towns, cities) can change each year.

2.  Leave the vintage option as Current. Check the box for Transportation (Roads and Railroads) to give us some additional context, and check the box for Census Tracts and Blocks. Nothing will change on the map just yet, because there are too many of these features to display at a national scale.

3.  Above the map in the right-hand corner of the screen is a search box. Let's enter an address here to zoom to a specific location. Type 3600 Philadelphia Pike, Claymont DE 19703, and hit Enter. Once you do, a little tip appears below the search box to confirm the location. Click on it, and that zooms us in to the area where I went to high school. On the left, the menu option will switch from Layers to Task Results, and it shows you the address and its longitude and latitude coordinates (Figure 3.5).

4.  To the right of the address search box in the upper right-hand corner is a button with the letter i inside a blue circle. This is the identifier tool. Click that button to make it active, and then click on the screen near the location of my high school, to the east (right) of Manor Ave and below Philadelphia Pike.

## FIGURE 3.5  ●  TIGERWEB ADDRESS SEARCH RESULTS

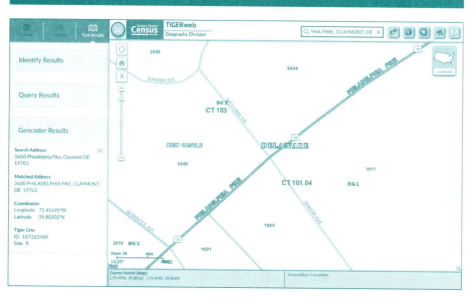

**FIGURE 3.6** ● **RESULTS FOR DELAWARE AND INFORMATION WINDOW**

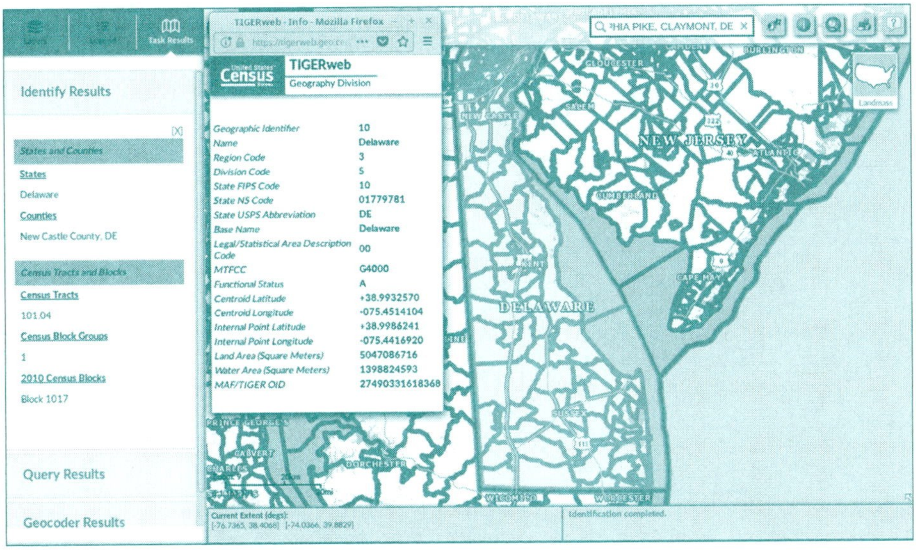

On the left, the Task Results will update and display where this geography is located: state, county, tract, block group, and block.

5.  To get a better sense of where you are, under States click on the link for Delaware. This does two things. First, the map zooms out to show you all of Delaware (Figure 3.6). The thick blue lines are census tract boundaries (to verify this, you could click on the middle Legend button in the control panel to see the colors for the features). Second, it launches a pop-up window (if your web browser stops it from opening, give it permission to do so and try again). The pop-up window gives us some basic metadata about Delaware; its geographic identifier (FIPS code) is 10.

6.  In the menu on the left, click New Castle County. This highlights the county (the northernmost one in the state) and zooms us in closer. You can move the map around by simply hovering the cursor over the map, holding down the left mouse button, and then dragging the mouse across the screen. Another pop-up window tells us the geographic identifier is 10003; the FIPS for Delaware is 10 and within Delaware the code for New Castle County is 003.

7.  In the menu on the left, click on the Census Tract Number 101.04. This zooms us in much closer and outlines the tract in a yellowish color (Figure 3.7). The bold letters on the map indicate the tract number: CT 101.04, CT 103, CT 101.01, and so on. Since Tracts 101.01 and 101.04 have the same prefix (101)

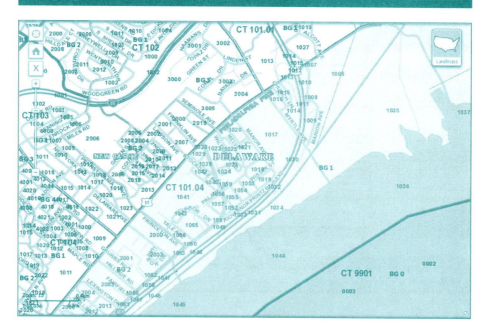

**FIGURE 3.7    ●    DETAILED MAP OF CENSUS TRACTS**

but different suffixes (.01 vs. .04), this is a clue that these tracts were once part of a larger one that has since been broken apart. The pop-up box shows us that the geographic identifier is 10003010104; Tract 101.04 is coded as 010104.

8.  In the menu, click on the block group number. This highlights Block Group 1 in this tract, and unlights the only other block group in this tract, Block Group 2 to the south. Why is 1 so much larger than 2? Remember that block groups and tracts are delineated so that areas have a relatively equal number of people (600–3,000 for a block group, 1,200–8,000 for a tract). At the top of Block Group 1, it looks like there is a lot more open space, as there are few roads. This northern part consists of an industrial area with no housing, and my high school, which occupies a large lot. Most of the housing in Block Group 1 is in the south. In contrast, Block Group 2 is covered in roads and is entirely residential; so just as many people, but in a smaller space.

9.  Last, in the menu on the left, click on Block 1017. This zooms you in pretty close. We can clearly see that this block is delineated using significant features: an interstate highway to the south, a U.S. highway to the north, and smaller roads east and west (Figure 3.8). Move the map around, and you can see that the other blocks are similarly drawn based on the location of roads, railroads, and water. Since roads are often used to delineate boundaries, this means that houses (and people) on opposite sides of the street will be counted in separate

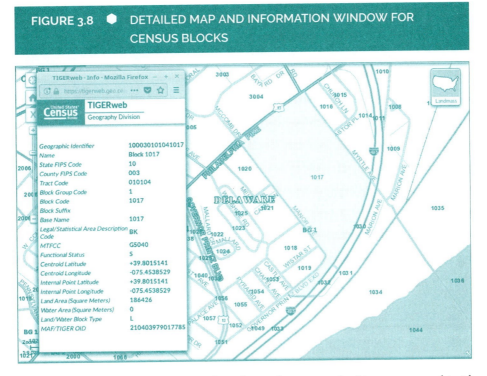

**FIGURE 3.8 ● DETAILED MAP AND INFORMATION WINDOW FOR CENSUS BLOCKS**

blocks. The last pop-up window shows that we are looking at geographic id 100030101041017. From back to front, we can break this down to Block 1017 (in Block Group 1), Tract 101.04 (from 010104), in New Castle County (003), Delaware (10).

So there you have it, census geography from the primary building blocks up to the nation. Try typing in an address you are familiar with in the search box and explore your own area.

## 3.5  OTHER GEOGRAPHIES: THE BRANCHES

In the previous section, we covered the primary trunk of census geography, but there are several other branches to explore. We are not going to cover them all here, but will explore the ones that you are most likely to use. There are three key differences between these geographies and the ones we have just explored. First, many of these other geographies do not completely cover the United States. Some portions of the country are part of a place or a metropolitan area, while other portions fall outside these areas, so the sum of these parts will not equal the whole. Second, many of these geographies will contain a hybrid of place types that vary from state to state,

| TABLE 3.4    ⬡    ESSENTIAL BRANCHES OF CENSUS GEOGRAPHY | | | |
|---|---|---|---|
| Summary Level* | Geography | Subdivisions | Type |
| 060 | County subdivision | Municipal civil divisions and census county subdivisions | Legal/Statistical |
| 160 | Place | Incorporated places and census-designated places | Legal/Statistical |
| 860 | ZIP Code Tabulation Area (ZCTA) | | Statistical |
| 861 | USPS ZIP Code | | Statistical |
| 795 | Public use microdata area (PUMA) | | Statistical |
| 400 | Urban area | Urban Areas and Urban Clusters | Statistical |
| 310 | Metropolitan areas | Several | Statistical |
| 500 | Congressional district | | Legal |
| 250 | Native American lands (AIANNH) | Several | Legal/Statistical |

*Indicates top-level summary codes for the nation. Some geographies have additional summary codes to indicate whole or partial geographies within states and counties.
*Note:* AIANNH = American Indian, Alsaka Native, Native Hawaiian

whereas the trunk geographies shared the same basic, uniform rules in terms of either their legal status or how they were constructed. Last, since these geographies do not nest within the trunk, they are assigned several different summary-level codes to indicate whole or partial nesting within states, counties, and other areas. The geographies we will cover and their top-level summary codes are listed in Table 3.4. The Census Bureau provides additional background information for many of these other geographies at `https://www.census.gov/programs-surveys/geography/guidance/geo-areas.html`.

## Places and County Subdivisions

The new **data.census.gov** makes the process of finding your town easier, as you can simply type the name and find the data. The confusion comes in when you want to compare towns; you go to look at the types of geography, and neither city nor town is an option. In census jargon, you have two types of geographies to consider: you can look at places or at county subdivisions.

Census places are concentrated settlements of people and are divided into two categories: (1) incorporated places and (2) census-designated places (CDPs). An incorporated place is a legal area with a governing body (e.g., a mayor or city council) that is elected by local residents to administer services that are specific to that jurisdiction. Incorporated places have fixed, legal boundaries that are recognized by the state. In contrast, a CDP is a settled concentration of people that is identifiable by name, but it is not a legal entity. It is not incorporated by law, and it doesn't have a government or set boundaries. CDPs are statistical areas created by the Census Bureau in consultation with local officials for the purpose of publishing data for these settlements.

Within the geographic hierarchy, places are created from blocks and nest within states. This means that a place can cross both county and census tract boundaries. Incorporated place boundaries are often irregular and circuitous, given the unique history and laws governing annexation and incorporation in the United States (The Economist, 2018). Places are assigned a five-digit code that's created by alphabetizing the list of places in a state. A place code is only unique within a state; for national comparisons, you add the two-digit state code to the front of the place code. The letters "CDP" appear after a place's name to distinguish these statistical areas from the legal incorporated places.

County subdivisions are a second option for studying local communities. Like places, county subdivisions consist of two types: minor civil divisions (MCDs) and census county divisions (CCDs). An MCD is a legal area that exists below the county level and is recognized by state government as having fixed boundaries for providing administrative or governmental functions. The types of functions MCDs provide vary widely between states; there are 29 states that have MCDs, and in 12 of them, the MCD provides enough services that it functions similar to an incorporated place. In nine states where MCD's do not cover the entire state, the Census Bureau creates statistical areas to cover the unogranized territory. In 20 states where MCDs do not exist, the Census Bureau creates CCDs in consultation with local officials. These areas have no legal or administrative purpose and exist solely for publishing data below the county level. Alaska has areas that are similar to CCDs while the District of Columbia has no subdivisions. Table 3.5 summarizes the status of county subdivisions by state.

There are two major differences between county subdivisions and places. First, county subdivisons cover the states and the nation in their entirety; there is not a piece of land that is not part of a county subdivision. In contrast, places are an either or scenario—an area is a place or isn't. Second, county subdivisions are built from

| TABLE 3.5 ⬥ COUNTY SUBDIVISION TYPES BY STATE | | | | | | | | | |
|---|---|---|---|---|---|---|---|---|---|
| | CCD | MCD | MCD Qualifier | | | CCD | MCD | MCD Qualifier | |
| | | | Local Government | Unorganized Territory | | | | Local Government | Unorganized Territory |
| Alabama | o | | | | Montana | o | | | |
| Alaska[a] | o | | | | Nebraska | | x | | |
| Arizona | o | | | | Nevada | o | | | |
| Arkansas | | x | | x | New Hampshire | | x | x | |
| California | o | | | | New Jersey | | x | x | |
| Colorado | o | | | | New Mexico | o | | | |
| Connecticut | | x | x | | New York | | x | x | x |
| Delaware | o | | | | North Carolina | | x | | x |
| Florida | o | | | | North Dakota | | x | | x |
| Georgia | o | | | | Ohio | | x | | |
| Hawaii | o | | | | Oklahoma | o | | | |
| Idaho | o | | | | Oregon | o | | | |
| Illinois | | x | | | Pennsylvania | | x | x | |
| Indiana | | x | | x | Rhode Island | | x | x | |
| Iowa | | x | | x | South Carolina | o | | | |
| Kansas | | x | | | South Dakota | | x | | x |
| Kentucky | o | | | | Tennesse | | x | | |
| Louisiana | | x | | | Texas | o | | | |
| Maine | | x | x | x | Utah | o | | | |
| Maryland | | x | | | Vermont | | x | x | |
| Massachusetts | | x | x | | Virginia | | x | | |
| Michigan | | x | x | | Washington | o | | | |
| Minnesota | | x | x | x | West Virginia | | x | | |
| Mississippi | | x | | | Wisconsin | | x | x | |
| Missouri | | x | | | Wyoming | o | | | |

[a]Alaska has census subareas, which are statistical areas similar to CCDs.

*Note:* CCD = census county division; MCD = minor civil division.

blocks and nest within counties, as opposed to places that nest within states. The geographic identifiers for county subdivisions are five digits long and are assigned alphabetically, but to be unique, they must be prefixed with both the state and county codes.

Let's look at an example to understand these differences better. New Jersey is a state that has MCDs. Every square foot of the state is carved into municipalities, and they have relatively strong governmental powers relative to the counties. The MCDs have different forms of government; the more concentrated settlements are designated as cities, towns, or boroughs, while suburban and rural areas have township governments. If we downloaded data for New Jersey's county subdivisions, data for all 565 MCDs would be included. In contrast, the census places for New Jersey only include the concentrated settlements; those that use a city, town, or borough government. In addition to these incorporated places are a number of CDPs. These are not legal areas but are concentrated settlements that are identifiable by name that exist within the state's townships.

Across the river and bay to the west, Delaware does not have MCDs. Compared with New Jersey, county governments in Delaware are stronger and hold the authority that the municipalities in New Jersey would exercise. Delaware has places that are incorporated as cities and towns, but any areas outside of those cities and towns are governed by the county. Since Delaware has no MCDs, its county subdivisions are CCDs that were created by the Census Bureau in consultation with local officials. These divisions are statistical areas used simply for publishing data and were named based on historic property divisions. Delaware's census places consist of all its incorporated cities and towns, plus some CDPs.

The choice of using either places or county subdivisions is going to vary based on your research needs. Census places are important for local policy, planning, and economic development as they represent concentrations of people. Incorporated places in particular are the geography of choice when studying local government across the United States. At a national level, places are usually studied for signs of trends, that is, which places are growing or shrinking the fastest. Places are a poor choice for geographical comparisons and mapping given their irregular boundaries and because they don't cover the entire United States; county subdivisions are a better choice for these applications. County subdivisions carry extra meaning in states like New Jersey, where municipal civil divisions are legal authorities with a direct impact on people's daily lives. While places are included in all census datasets, outside the decennial census and the ACS county subdivision, data is only provided for MCDs in the12 states where they serve as general-purpose governments.

## ZIP Codes, ZCTAs, and PUMAs

ZIP Codes are U.S. postal codes and are a popular choice for studying local areas as they are a geography that all Americans are familiar with. The Zone Improvement Plan (ZIP) was introduced by the U.S. Postal Service (USPS) in the 1960s to improve the efficiency of mail delivery (Hayter, 2015). A ZIP Code has five digits: the first digit indicates the state, the second and third digits represent a large sectional center facility for processing and distributing mail, and the last two are specific to a village, town, or section of a large urban area. In the 1980s, an optional four-digit suffix was added to indicate more detailed geographic segments such as a city block, group of apartments, or cluster of post office boxes.

Since the ZIP Code is a part of all U.S. addresses, it is commonly used for aggregating and summarizing address data. However, contrary to popular belief, ZIP Codes are *not* geographic areas with formally delineated boundaries. They are simply numbers that are assigned to addresses along streets in a large flat-file database system. Marketing companies and tech firms like Google purchase this address data from the USPS and create geographic boundaries for ZIP Codes by grouping addresses that share the same ZIP Code number together. So when you search for a ZIP Code and see the boundary on Google Maps, this boundary is something that Google has created based on the underlying USPS address data.

The Census Bureau also takes the USPS data and uses it to construct ZIP Codes, but unlike Google, its process is transparent and it uses census blocks as a base geography. The Census Bureau counts the number of addresses that fall within each census block and sums the number of different ZIP Codes. The census block is assigned the ZIP Code number that appears most frequently. After all census blocks have been assigned a ZIP number, they are aggregated to form areas, and then these areas are modified to create areas that are largely contiguous so that an area does not consist of large numbers of disconnected blocks.

These resulting areas are called ZIP Code Tabulation Areas (ZCTAs, pronounced zicktas). ZCTAs are identified with the same five-digit numbers that are used for ZIP Codes, but they are not strictly equivalent to ZIP Codes for a few reasons. In some cases, there may be addresses in a ZCTA that actually belong to a different ZIP Code, but were assigned to that ZCTA because the majority of addresses within their census block shared that ZCTA's number. Some ZIP Codes are never aggregated to form a ZCTA with the same number, because the number of addresses with that ZIP Code are too few. The USPS assigns ZIP Codes to large clusters of post office boxes and to large organizations that process a lot of mail. These ZIP Codes are not captured and turned into ZCTAs because they do not cover a sufficiently large geographic area. As a result, there are more ZIP Codes than there are ZCTAs, and some ZIP Codes do not have a ZCTA counterpart.

The Census Bureau introduced ZCTAs as a geography in the 2000 census based on feedback from user groups and stakeholders. ZCTA data is tabulated for the decennial census and the 5-year ACS. The process for creating ZCTAs has changed over time. For the 2000 census, the Census Bureau assigned special ZCTA numbers to unpopulated areas such as mountain ranges and bodies of water that lacked addresses and streets. It discontinued this practice for the 2010 census, so that any area that is unpopulated is simply not assigned to a ZCTA. The Census Bureau only updates ZCTAs every 10 years when the new decennial census is taken.

While having ZCTA-level data is convenient, ZCTAs pose a number of problems for researchers (Grubesic, 2008). The underlying ZIP Code system on which they are based was never designed for tabulating and studying population data and, thus, does not follow a logical set of rules for delineation. ZCTAs vary tremendously in size, shape, and population and do not nest or correlate with any other census geography; they are built from census blocks and nest within the nation. While ZIP Codes are assigned a city name based on the name of the post office that serves them, this name usually does not correspond to the legal municipal entity where the post office is located (Stevens, 2006). The Census Bureau does not assign place names to ZCTAs.

To add to the confusion, while decennial census and ACS data is tabulated using ZCTAs, the census business datasets (the Economic Census and the Business Patterns) use actual ZIP Codes. In the business datasets, the ZIP Code is simply captured from the address of each business and the data is aggregated using the ZIP numbers. As a statistical area, the ZCTA has serious limitations, but it is popular given people's familiarity with ZIP Codes and the amount of outside data that's available for them. In Chapter 11, we will discuss how to relate ZIP Code and ZCTA-level data.

A lesser known statistical area that is actually quite valuable is the PUMA. As the name suggests, PUMAs were created so that census microdata (samples of individual responses to the decennial census and ACS) can be summarized and aggregated to a geographic level that would protect the anonymity of the respondents. PUMAs are built from census blocks and nest within states and are designed to have an ideal population size of 100k people.

PUMAs were subsequently adopted as a geography for publishing summary-level ACS data, as there were no census geographies that could be reported in their entirety below the state level in the 1-year dataset. A particular geography must have

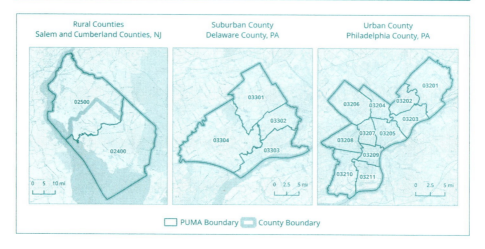

**FIGURE 3.9  ●  COMPARISON OF PUMA BOUNDARIES BY COUNTY TYPE**

at least 65k people to be included, and thus data is not available for all counties as many do not meet this threshold. Since PUMAs were designed to have 100k people, they all meet the minimum threshold, and the Census Bureau began publishing summary data for them in the 1-year and 5-year ACS. PUMAs serve as the "super-sized" equivalent to census tracts, as they are both statistical areas designed to have an equal population size.

PUMAs are assigned a five-digit number that is unique within each state and are unique across states if the two-digit state FIPS is added as a prefix. After the 2010 census, PUMAs were assigned names based on suggestions from local authorities to increase their usability. Since PUMAs are delineated by population, they vary in geographic area. In urban areas, they can be used to represent clusters of neighborhoods or large city districts and have been named to indicate this. In suburban areas, PUMAs represent subdivisions of counties, and in rural areas, a PUMA can consist of multiple counties (e.g., see Figure 3.9).

One oddity is that PUMA-level data is not published in the decennial census but only in the ACS. New PUMA geography is not released alongside other statistical areas like tracts and ZCTAs but is released a couple of years following the decennial census.

## Urban/Rural Status and Metropolitan Areas

In 2010, approximately 81% of the U.S. population was urban and about 85% of the total population lived in metropolitan areas. The issues and needs of people who live

**FIGURE 3.10    ⬡    CENSUS URBAN AREAS**

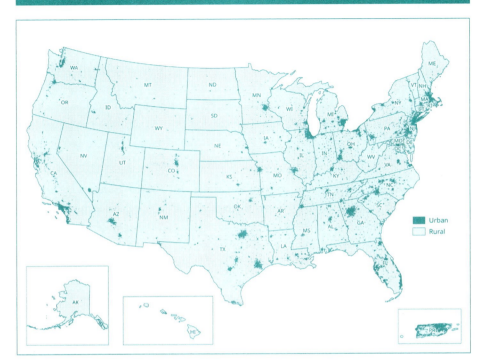

in urban and rural areas are often quite different, and the socioeconomic characteristics and trends are distinct. The Census Bureau uses two approaches for measuring urbanity: (1) an ecological approach called urban/rural status and (2) a functional approach that defines metropolitan areas (M. Wang, Kleit, Cover, & Fowler, 2012).

The concept of urban/rural status is an ecological one, in that it relates to the physical footprint of development on the landscape (see the map in Figure 3.10). It measures whether people are living together in a densely populated, tightly clustered area or not. The Census Bureau has two levels of urbanity. An urbanized area (UA) is a densely developed territory that contains 50k or more people and is used to distinguish urban and rural territory near large places. An urban cluster (UC) is a densely populated territory that has at least 2,500 people but less than 50k people. It is used to provide a consistent measure of urban population throughout the United States. Both types of areas are assigned a state code and a five-digit sequential code, as well as a general name that indicates where the area or cluster is located. The urban/rural concept is useful for researchers who need to study the actual footprint of urbanity on the landscape for regional planning, emergency management, and environmental studies.

The process for delineating urban areas and clusters has evolved over time to incorporate greater complexity. Early measures were restricted to simply using thresholds for total population and density. From the 2010 census onward, census blocks have been assembled into urban areas and clusters using an iterative process based on population density of the block, land use, and distance (Ratcliffe, Burd, Holder, & Fields, 2016). For land use, unpopulated areas that have urban characteristics (factory complexes, commercial areas, airports) are counted as urban, and the distance measurement captures urban uses that may be separated from other urban areas by short distances due to the presence of green space areas (parks, farms, cemeteries) or as the result of suburban sprawl.

Beyond its role as a geography, urban/rural status is also a variable that is reported in the decennial census and the ACS. For any geographic area, you can see the percentage that is urban and rural, and in some cases, variables such as age, sex, and race are cross tabulated based on urban/rural status. Unlike the other geographies, urban and rural status are represented not by a three-digit summary-level code in the state-level summary files but by the two-digit component code in a GEOID: 01 for urban and 43 for rural. In the national summary files, the summary code for urban areas is 400.

The second concept of metropolitan areas is familiar to a wider audience of researchers. Metropolitan areas are functional concepts that incorporate both population measures and economic ties. Metro areas consist of one or more adjacent counties that meet certain population thresholds for total population, density, and commuting patterns. Since they are county based, they will contain a mixture of urban areas, urban clusters, and rural areas. In some places, large areas of a particular metropolitan county may be quite rural. What is important is that the county has a core urban area or urban cluster that meets the threshold, and it has enough interaction with a larger neighboring area so that it can be classified as metropolitan.

Specifically, if a county has at least 50% of its population in urban areas with at least 10k people, and at least 5k are located in a single urban area of at least 10k people, then that county can qualify as a central metro county. Adjacent, outlying counties can be included in a metro area if at least 25% of their workers work in the central county or its associated counties, or if 25% of the county's employment consists of workers from those areas. A county cannot belong to multiple areas: If it qualifies as being a central county and as an outlying county of another metro, it is classified as a central county within its own metro. If it is classified as being an outlying county for multiple metros, then it is classified with the metro where it has the strongest commuting ties (Office of the Federal Register, 2010). The map in Figure 3.11 illustrates which counties are classified as metropolitan areas, smaller micropolitan areas, or nonmetropolitan areas.

**FIGURE 3.11   ●   COUNTIES BY METROPOLITAN STATUS**

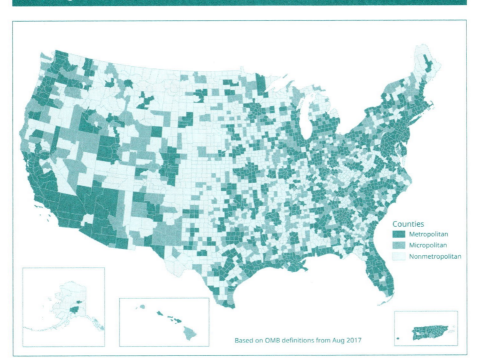

Counties
- Metropolitan
- Micropolitan
- Nonmetropolitan

Based on OMB definitions from Aug 2017

Metropolitan areas were introduced in the 1950s, and rules for defining them have changed over time. Given changes in methodology and actual changes in demographic and economic patterns, it is not uncommon for counties to be included in a particular metro area in one iteration of the metro definitions and then drop out in another iteration either to become an independent metro or to become assigned to a neighboring metro. There are a number of different terms and groupings of these areas that are intended to give users flexibility in choosing what is appropriate for their studies. The term *metropolitan area* is often used in a general sense to refer to all of these areas, but technically, it refers to just one subset of the types. *Core-Based Statistical Area* (CBSA) is the technical term for "metro areas" that includes "metropolitan areas" as well as smaller ones called "micropolitan areas." The current terminology is shown in Table 3.6.

For a detailed example of these concepts, Utah's five metropolitan and four micropolitan areas are shown in Figure 3.12. All CBSAs are named after their principal cities, which are the largest settlements in the area. Some CBSAs, like Ogden-Clearfield and Provo-Orem, consist of multiple counties, while others like Cedar City and St. George consist of a single county. The Logan metropolitan area extends across

| TABLE 3.6 ● METROPOLITAN CONCEPTS | |
|---|---|
| **Core-Based Statistical Area—310** | An umbrella term that includes both metropolitan statistical areas and micropolitan statistical areas (CBSA). |
| **Metropolitan Statistical Area** | Has at least one urbanized area of at least 50k people in a county that contains this core, plus adjacent counties that have a high degree of social and economic integration with the central county. |
| **Micropolitan Statistical Area** | Has at least one urban cluster with a population of at least 10k but less than 50k, plus adjacent counties that have a high degree of social and economic integration with the central county. |
| **Principal City—312** | Identifies the largest census places in the CBSA that represent the nuclei for the entire area. Includes the largest places, plus additional places that meet certain population or employment thresholds. |
| **Metropolitan Division—314** | Smaller groupings of counties within a larger metro area (population of at least 2.5 million) that have close economic ties. |
| **Combined Statistical Area—330** | Consists of two or more adjacent CBSAs that have substantial employment interchange (CSA). |
| **New England City and Town Area—350** | An alternative set of geographic entities that is similar in concept to CBSAs. NECTAs are based on county subdivisions in the New England states. This concept also includes divisions and combined areas. |

*Note:* Indicates top-level summary codes for the nation. CBSAs have additional summary codes to indicate geographies within states.

state lines to include a county in neighboring Idaho. Three of Utah's metro areas and two of its micro areas share enough economic and social ties that warrant grouping them into one, larger consolidated statistical area (CSA) called Salt Lake City-Provo-Orem, Utah.

Many researchers who work with metro geography use just the basic units of the CBSAs: the metropolitan and micropolitan statistical areas, and in some cases, just the metropolitan areas. In other cases, it may be useful to use the larger CSAs for all counties that fall within a CSA and the metro and micro areas for counties that do not. The metropolitan areas are useful as units of study because they capture areas that have distinct economic markets and cultural identities, and since they are county based, there is a wealth of data available for them.

**FIGURE 3.12 ⬡ CORE-BASED STATISTICAL AREAS IN UTAH**

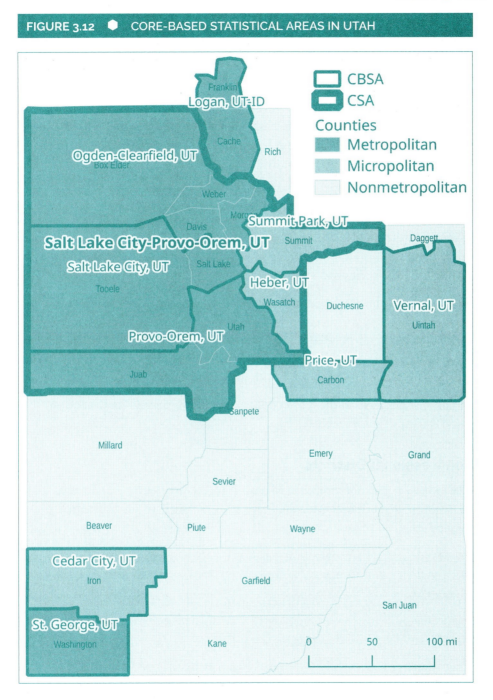

The metro geographies are created by the Office of Management and Budget (OMB) in consultation with the Census Bureau, and not by the Bureau itself as they are widely used by many federal agencies. As such, metro areas are delineated out of step with the other census geographies and are updated a few times each decade, with major updates occurring a few years after a decennial census. Metro areas and their different combinations are assigned a variety of ID codes that can change over time, making historical comparison difficult. Fortunately, since they are county based, it is easy to aggregate county-level data to fit current or former boundaries.

The urban/rural concept and the CBSAs are both created by using criteria that define what it means to be urban, and by default, whatever is not urban is considered rural. But what if you were specifically interested in studying rural areas? Just as there are gradations in what it means to be considered urban, there are also gradations in what it means to be rural that are defined by number of people, density, and land use (Ratcliffe et al., 2016). Parts of southern New Jersey, the plains of Kansas, and the Alaskan frontier could all be considered rural based on low population and an orientation toward agricultural and mining activities, but they are quite different from one another based on their population totals and density.

The U.S. Department of Agriculture (USDA) has created a series of codes for classifying the degree to which a county is urban and rural that include the urban–rural continuum codes, urban influence codes, and economic typology codes. County-level census data can be aggregated to fit these categories to obtain more finely grained measures of ruralness. We will work with these codes in two exercises in Chapter 5:

```
https://www.ers.usda.gov/topics/rural-economy-population/
rural-classifications/
```

## Congressional Districts

The primary purpose of the decennial census is to reapportion seats in the U.S. House of Representatives among the states every 10 years based on the differential growth in population. For states that gain or lose seats, the decennial census is used to redistrict or redraw congressional district boundaries. Every congressional district should contain approximately the same number of people, and areas should be contiguous and compact. Based on the size of the U.S. population and the fixed number of seats, each district is designed to ideally serve approximately 711,000 people. The actual population of districts varies, since every state is guaranteed to have at least one seat regardless of population.

The redistricting process can be abused by the political party that holds control of the state legislature, governors office, or both. Gerrymandering is the process of creating districts that concentrate certain types of voters into specific districts for the purpose of ensuring control of the highest possible number of districts in a state, at the expense of creating districts that have compact and common-sense boundaries. The degree of gerrymandering varies as states have different laws and processes for redrawing districts. Some states use committees of legislators, others use independent commissions, and some may rely on outside advisers to varying degrees (Brennan Center for Justice, 2017).

In the latter half of the 2010s, there has been increased interest in gerrymandering and courts have overturned some of the most egregious cases while upholding others. The utility of congressional districts for demographic or geographic analysis is quite limited. Unless you are studying voting patterns or political matters, you probably will not use these areas. If a congressional district is redrawn due to legal action, new data is published for any newly redrawn areas. Otherwise, the districts remain the same until the next decennial census.

## Native American Lands

Geographies for Native American lands, known collectively as American Indian, Alaska Native, and Native Hawaiian (AIANNH) areas, are created via a separate process in consultation with the different tribes. Like the other geographies, they are generated from census blocks and contain a mix of legal and statistical areas. These areas are not created *instead* of the standard block groups, tracts, and county designations, but they are created *in addition* to these areas for use by tribal leaders and organizations, as well as for researchers who study Native American government and lands.

Legal divisions are the formal boundaries of reservations and include Alaska Native regional corporations, American Indian reservations established under federal and state law, Hawaiian home lands, joint-use areas that are governed by more than one tribe, and off-reservation trusts lands. There are also American Indian tribal subdivisions that represent administrative areas, communities, or districts and a variety of statistical areas that function similar to CDPs, as they represent concentrated communities that can be identified with a common name but lack an organized local government.

# 3.6   REVISITING TIGERWEB

Let's return to TIGERweb at `https://tigerweb.geo.census.gov/tigerweb/` to explore some of these additional geographies.

1.  In the menu on the left, check the box for Places and County Subdivisions. In the address search bar in the upper right-hand corner, let's return to my old high school at this address: 3600 Philadelphia Pike, Claymont, DE, 19703.

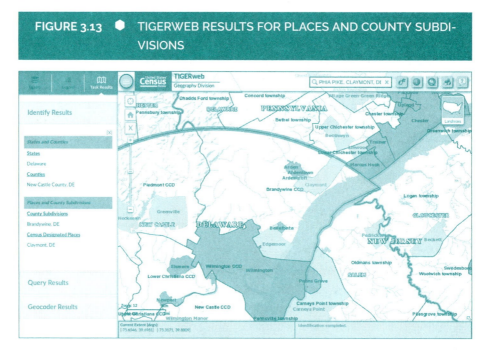

FIGURE 3.13  ●  TIGERWEB RESULTS FOR PLACES AND COUNTY SUBDI-
                VISIONS

2.  On the left, we will see the address and coordinates returned. Click on the information tool (circular i button beside the address search) and click on the map in the area near the address. That will change our Identify Results window to show us the geography we selected: We are in a CDP called Claymont and a County Subdivision called Brandywine.

3.  Click on Claymont, DE, in the menu. This zooms us out a little further, so we can see the Claymont CDP in its entirety. Use the slider bar on the left to zoom out a little further so you can see more of the surrounding area (Figure 3.13). Notice the areas that are a light orange color, like Claymont. These are CDPs, which are concentrated settlements that are recognizable by name, but they lack a local government and formal boundaries. The purple areas are incorporated places. They are formal, legal areas that have a government and are recognized by the state. Notice that neither type of place covers the state in its entirety; there are blank areas that fall outside of all places.

4.  The boundaries that are shown in black with black lettering are county subdivisions. Click on Brandywine, DE, in the menu on the left to highlight this subdivision. You can see that these areas are much larger, and they cover the entire state. Notice the label for the subdivision says that this is the Brandywine CCD. Delaware does not have formal subdivisions, so the Census Bureau

creates them. In contrast, across the river in New Jersey, the subdivisions have names that end in "Township." New Jersey has legal subdivisions called municipal civil divisions that have an actual government.

5.  In the control panel on the left, click on the Layers menu. Uncheck Places and County Subdivisions. Check PUMAs, UGAs (Urban Growth Areas), and ZCTAs. This will look like spaghetti on our map, so hit the little plus symbol beside the layer to see its individual components. Check just one of them at a time, and explore the differences between ZCTAs and PUMAs. The ZCTAs vary widely in size and shape, while the PUMA boundaries are more regular and vary based on the population of a given area, as they are designed to contain 100k residents.

6.  Take a few moments to explore these geographies by typing in an address you are familiar with. You can also zoom out to a national scale to explore Congressional Districts, metropolitan and micropolitan statistical areas, and AIANNH lands.

## 3.7   GEOGRAPHIC REFERENCE

The Census Bureau has a dedicated geography division that is charged with drawing and maintaining geographic definitions, boundary files, and maps. The division provides a variety of reference materials on its home page at `https://www.census.gov/programs-surveys/geography.html` that include the following:

Documentation: A guide to state and local geography that summarizes the different kinds of geography available for each state, with details on the peculiarities of different places. The *Geographic Area Reference Manual* is useful for getting a historical overview of each geography type.

Historical changes: There is a list of recent incorporations, annexations, and mergers from the annual Boundary and Annexation Survey and a list of changes to county boundaries from 1970 to present.

Identifiers: There are tools for looking up individual FIPS codes for states and counties and files with lists of GEOIDs for other places.

Features: The gazetteer is a directory of all individual pieces of geography in the United States with GEOID codes, longitude and latitude coordinates, and areas for land and water. The Population Centers files contain coordinates that represent the midpoint of a population's distribution for states, counties, tracts, and block groups.

These files are also convenient for quickly obtaining total decennial population with areal measurements.

The geography division produces boundary reference maps in PDF and JPG formats and provides tallies on the number of census geographies, if you wanted to know how many ZCTAs there are or how many tracts were there in a particular state. We will cover the TIGER geographic boundary files they provide for GIS users in Chapter 10 and their geocoder for obtaining coordinates for addresses in Chapter 11.

Finally, if you need to look up or browse FIPS and GEOID codes for the most common geographies, consult the Missouri Census Data Center's Geographic Codes Lookup application at `https://census.missouri.edu/geocodes/`.

## 3.8   REVIEW QUESTIONS AND PRACTICE EXERCISES

1. What is the difference between a legal area and a statistical area? Provide some examples of both types.

2. Using the current geography vintage at TIGERweb at `https://tigerweb.geo.census.gov/tigerweb/`, enter the address for the Transamerica Pyramid: 600 Montgomery Street San Francisco, CA 94111. What is the full FIPS code for the area where the building is located, down to the block level? Provide the specific geography that each part of the FIPS code refers to.

3. The Florida Keys are a long chain of islands that stretch from the south of Florida into the Caribbean Sea. Using TIGERweb, zoom into this area, and turn on the Places and County Subdivisions layer. In the southernmost islands, in the Key West CCD, what are the names of the three census places located there? Which ones are incorporated and which ones are census designated?

4. Using TIGERweb, zoom into northern Utah and create a map of metropolitan areas around the Salt Lake CSA similar to the one shown in Figure 3.12. Make sure to turn on the labels in the legend. To save the map, hit the Print button in the toolbar in the upper right-hand corner, and save the map as a portrait format with legend and scale bar as either a PDF or PNG file.

5. What is the difference between an urban area and a metropolitan area? Why would you choose to use one over the other?

# SUBJECT CHARACTERISTICS

## 4.1    THE CENSUS UNIVERSE

In this chapter, we will discuss the major subject categories that are used to summarize data by groups of people. The technical term for this is *census universes*, and these categories are applied uniformly throughout the census datasets covered in this book. The major characteristics of population and housing include age and sex, race and Hispanic or Latino origin, households and families, living quarters, housing characteristics, and the labor force. We will discuss each of these, in turn, to provide a foundation for exploring the datasets in detail in subsequent chapters.

As with the geography summary levels, it's important to differentiate between terms that we use in everyday speech and the technical terms the Census Bureau uses, so we can choose the best variable for our research and avoid assumptions that can lead to mistakes. We all have different ideas about what constitutes a "family," but according to the Census Bureau, a family is a group of people living in a household who are related by birth, marriage, or adoption. If a person is living alone or is living with an unmarried partner, they are not considered to be a family unless there is at least one other person in the household who is related to one of the householders.

An understanding of these terms is important for presenting and interpreting census data correctly. Many people are surprised to learn that the Census Bureau does not count Hispanics and Latinos as a race, but as a separate ethnicity. If you are creating a table or chart illustrating the percentage of the population by race, most Hispanics are grouped into either the white or the other category. You would need to decide how to address the "missing" Hispanic data, either with a footnote or with a different compilation of data that summarizes race by Hispanic ethnicity. Or perhaps, you are writing a short article about the declining unemployment rate as people are increasingly finding jobs. On closer inspection of the data, the unemployment rate may be going down not because more people are finding jobs but because they have given up looking for work and have dropped out of the labor force.

With the exception of the labor force, these subject characteristics represent most of the variables that are collected in the decennial census, which focuses just on capturing basic demographic characteristics. While we will explore the decennial census fully in the next chapter, we will address how these fundamental subject categories will change between the 2010 and 2020 census in this chapter, as these changes will also affect future iterations of the American Community Survey (ACS), Population Estimates Program (PEP), and Current Population Survey (CPS). The Census Bureau has published the list of subjects (U.S. Census Bureau, 2017h) and the specific questions (U.S. Census Bureau, 2018b) that will be asked in 2020 and future versions of the ACS (2020–2029) in reports submitted to Congress. Reporters at National Public Radio (NPR) and correspondent Hansi Lo Wang, in particular, have done a thorough job in providing clear summaries on how each of these questions will (or will not) change, and I reference their articles throughout.

You can find brief definitions for all the subject characteristics and concepts in the Census Bureau's glossary at `https://www.census.gov/glossary/`. For more detailed explanations, consult the appendices in the technical documentation for the 2010 census (U.S. Census Bureau, 2012a) and the subject definitions published for each ACS (U.S. Census Bureau, 2016a).

At the end of the chapter, we will do a number of exercises to create basic summaries and estimates using several of these characteristics. Beyond introducing you to working with this data, these exercises will serve as your introduction to the Calc spreadsheet package that we will use throughout the book.

Before we begin, we need to address the concept of residency as this concept *does* vary between different datasets, and it determines who gets counted where.

## 4.2  RESIDENCY

The concept of residency is used to determine whether a person lives in a particular place and should be counted there, and unlike the subject characteristics, this concept differs between datasets. When individuals fill out the decennial census form, they are asked to indicate their "usual residence," which is defined as the place where the person lives and sleeps most of the time as of the census day on

April 1. This may differ from the person's voting or legal residence. If a person owns a second home, they must indicate which one is their usual residence. College students and military personnel would indicate their usual residence as their dormitory or their off-campus or off-base housing, whatever the case may be. The census form asks additional questions regarding whether any person in the household occasionally lives somewhere else, like a dorm or a barrack, as a safety check to avoid double-counting. If a person does not have a usual residence, for example, if they are homeless, they are counted in the location where they happen to be when the census is conducted.

In contrast, the ACS is based on a large sample of addresses and its goal is to measure the characteristics of society as opposed to creating exact counts. When people fill out the ACS, they are asked to indicate their "current residence." If they are staying at the address being sampled for at least 2 months, that address is considered as their current address. The ACS does not capture people without an address and focuses primarily on people living in a residential setting. People living in a group quarters setting, like a college dorm or a military barrack, are included in the ACS but are captured in a different sample frame.

The PEP uses the decennial census as its base and gathers and summarizes administrative data to create estimates, so in theory, it aims to incorporate the entire population. Records for births and deaths are pretty universal, although there can be difficulties in making a distinction between the location where a person was born or died versus the location where they will, or did, live. The CPS is like the ACS in that it is a sample survey for measuring population characteristics, but its sample frame is limited to just occupied households.

The issue of residency reveals that the process of counting people is more complicated than it may initially seem. This concept has real implications for many communities; remember that the decennial census is used for reapportioning political power and the ACS is used for distributing billions of dollars in funding, and these decisions are made based on where people live and, in some cases, where people with specific characteristics are concentrated. Should people in prison be counted where the prison is located or counted at their residence prior to their incarceration? Where should military personnel who have been temporarily deployed overseas be counted? The Census Bureau has reconsidered how they count these populations for the upcoming 2020 census (H. L. Wang, 2018b).

Currently, the incarcerated population is counted at the location where they are incarcerated, which has the effect of increasing the population of rural areas where many large prisons are located. Urban communities have argued that this deprives them of the funding and political representation that they need for preventing and fighting crime. The Census Bureau has decided to keep the current policy for counting prisoners in prisons, arguing that the prison represents their usual residence. In contrast, the Census Bureau decided to change how it counts military personnel. In 2010, if they were temporarily deployed overseas they were counted at the home address they provided when they enlisted. Beginning in 2020, military personnel will be counted at the home base where they are officially stationed prior to deployment. This will increase the population in areas that are home to bases, which also tend to be in rural areas.

The residency concept also has a strong impact on communities that are primarily resort areas with seasonal populations (Van Auken, Hammer, Voss, & Veroff, 2006). These areas typically have a large number of housing units and a sizable physical infrastructure for supporting a peak population at certain times of the year. During the off-peak season, the population declines, and much of the housing and infrastructure is unused or underutilized. The decennial census captures usual residence as of April 1, which typically does not capture the high-season populations of winter or summer resort areas. The ACS captures this population if a housing unit in these areas is surveyed during the high season and seasonal residents are staying for more than 2 months. Since ACS data is aggregated into 12- and 60-month time periods, these estimates represent an average of the high and low seasons. We will talk more about measuring this population when we discuss housing units, and our second exercise will focus on creating estimates for these areas.

## 4.3   POPULATION CHARACTERISTICS

The characteristics that we will discuss in this section are the principal ones for summarizing people. Which people? All individuals are counted in the census whether they are U.S. citizens, legal residents, or undocumented aliens. Citizens include people born in the United States as well as naturalized citizens. Legal residents include permanent legal residents (green card holders) or people living in the United States with work or student visas. The only people who are not counted are visitors, tourists, and people on particular visas that limit their stay in the United States to a short period of time. The 2010 census did not capture these details on citizenship or residency status, and there is currently a fierce debate over adding this question to the 2020 census (which we will discuss in the next chapter). The ACS and CPS ask questions that relate to citizenship. As we discussed in Chapter 1, a person's voting eligibility, citizenship status, and legality of residence have never been used as a basis for whether someone should be counted in a census dataset or not.

## Age and Sex

Age and sex are the two most fundamental variables of demography. They are necessary for estimating the current population and predicting future populations. People of different ages and sex have different social and health needs and requirements, and they face different legal obligations and barriers. There are social and economic disparities between various age-groups and between the sexes. Given the importance of these characteristics, most census data is cross tabulated by age and sex.

On the decennial census and the ACS, people are asked to state their age and to enter their date of birth (these two questions are compared with each other as a quality control measure). Data for age is presented in tables for 1-year, 5-year, and varying cohorts (i.e., age brackets) and is also cross tabulated by sex. The census also summarizes data by age-groups that have some social or legal meaning in society, such as the population under 18, under 21, and over 64. Age is frequently used to create logical subdivisions of the population when reporting different characteristics. For example, the population enrolled in school is reported for people who are 3 years old and over, as it does not make sense to report data for small children who would never be in school.

When studying any characteristic, it is important to consider what population that characteristic should be measured against; in other words, what is the denominator (population) versus the numerator (population with the characteristic). If we were studying the percentage of the population who were veterans, it would only make sense to measure the number of veterans (numerator) against the civilian population 18 and over (denominator). The total population is not used as a denominator as it includes juveniles who are too young to serve and active members of the military who are not considered veterans until they leave active service. So when the ACS indicates that 7.4% of Americans were veterans in 2016, this percentage is not calculated based on the total population but just on the subset who are civilians 18 years and over.

In journalism, marketing, and some social research, it is common to discuss age-groups in terms of generations: the Baby Boomers, Generation X, Millennials, and so on. There are few firm definitions on what constitutes the boundaries between these categories. The Census Bureau takes no official stance and does not use generations for classifying or summarizing data. If you wanted generational data, you would have to take population data that is subdivided by age and then aggregate the age-groups into categories based on a given definition. The Pew Research Center (2015) defines generations as follows: Greatest Generation (1901–1927), Silent Generation (1928–1945), Baby Boomers (1946–1964), Generation X (1965–1980), and Millennials (1981–1997). The boundary between Millennials and the as-of-yet unnamed generation behind them is still relatively undefined and stretches from 1997 to 2004. Take these categories with a grain of salt. At the end of this chapter, we will do an exercise on aggregating age data by generation.

Data for sex is divided into two categories: male and female. The Census Bureau has made a conscious decision to use the word "sex" and not the word "gender" in its forms and data tables. The term *sex* is interpreted strictly as a biological concept associated with chromosomes, anatomy, and hormones, whereas *gender* is a social construct associated with a person's identity. Over the course of the 2010s, the Census Bureau investigated whether to add questions about sexual orientation and gender identity to the 2020 Census and future iterations of the ACS. Ultimately the Bureau decided not to cover this topic, stating that there was no federal data need or legislative mandate that made the questions necessary (H. L. Wang, 2018j).

The arguments in favor of adding these questions focus on the issue of civil rights. As the lesbian, gay, bisexual, transgender, and queer (LGBTQ) population faces discrimination and a denial of rights, many argue that there is legal justification for adding these questions to the census based on the Civil Rights Act, for the same reasons that questions are asked about race, sex, and disabilities: to verify and ensure that people's rights are not being denied on the basis of who they are. While some opposition to adding these questions comes from people who are morally or religiously opposed to homosexuality, the issue is more complex. There are homosexuals, heterosexuals, and people from both sides of the political spectrum who feel that such questions are an invasion of privacy. Should the government have the right to ask people about their sexual orientation? This issue differs from other privacy arguments over questions about a person's income or whether they have recently had children, as these are easily identifiable facts. A person's gender identity and their sexual expression is much more personal, difficult to identify, and has long been outside the purview of the government.

While there has been no "official" way to count or estimate the number of LGBTQ people in the census, there is an unofficial way of estimating the number of households that are made up of same-sex partners, and from the 2020 census onward, a question on same-sex partners and marriage will be asked. We will explore this further in the section on households and relationships.

## Race and Ethnicity

A society's divisions are usually reflected in its census data (Emigh et al., 2016a, 2016b). While the chief social divisions in many societies are based on social class, ancestry, language, religion, or place, the primary social divider in the United States without a doubt is race. In the first and simplest census in 1790, the only questions were "How many people are in the household?" "How many are women and children?" and "Are the occupants white?" The question on whether people were white was necessary for distinguishing free persons from slaves, who were only counted as partial people for the sake of enumerating the population for apportioning Congress (based on the notorious three-fifths compromise in the Constitution). Within a few decades, specific questions and categories were added to identify whether a person was white, a free person of color, or a slave (Anderson, 2015).

As the 19th century progressed, additional racial categories were added as the country grew more diverse with immigrants from Europe and Asia. Native Americans also began to be counted as U.S. residents; they were initially excluded as they were viewed as living outside of America's boundaries and society. When black slaves were freed and counted as whole people after the Civil War, a whole series of questions were added to the census based on pseudo-scientific and racist concepts to quantify the degree to which black people were of mixed race based on the "purity of their blood." The most outrageous categories disappeared by the end of the 19th century, and the last of these questions was dropped in 1930. From 1930 to 1960, the so-called one-drop rule was employed, where a person was counted as white if both parents were white, otherwise they were counted as being the race of the nonwhite parent (Humes & Hogan, 2009).

The racial categories that we have today have their origins in the 1960 and 1970 census, which marked a major turning point in data collection methods, how society viewed race, and the rationale used for gathering racial data. Prior to 1960, census takers visited homes to interview people for the census, which naturally had an impact on how the questions were answered and recorded. In 1960, many people received their forms by mail for the first time, and a census taker came to verify and pick them up. The 1970 census was the first census that was conducted entirely by mail, where people filled the forms out themselves and mailed them back. While each form did contain explanations of the categories with instructions, individuals could choose how to identify themselves without interacting with a government official (Anderson, 2015).

The Census Bureau was not immune to the social movements of the 1960s, where racial identity transitioned from being a source of stigma and control to a source of pride and identity. The civil rights and voting rights acts of the mid-1960s sought to guarantee equal rights for all races under the law, and data on race would be crucial for ensuring that people's rights were being upheld. Beginning with the 1970 census, the Census Bureau conducted outreach to community and ethnic groups for feedback on the racial categories and how the questions should be worded.

The federal government issued Directive 15 in 1977 to codify and standardize the collection of racial data across statistical agencies to ensure that data would be comparable. The directive specified four racial categories: (1) white, (2) black, (3) Asian or Pacific Islander, and (4) American Indian or Alaskan Native. These were the categories used in the 1970 census, and they were applied again in 1980 and 1990. Directive 15 was modified in 1997 to split Asians and Hawaiian or Pacific Islanders into two separate categories (so there are now five races) and to allow people to identify themselves as multiracial by selecting more than one racial category (Office of the Federal Register, 1997). These changes were implemented and applied in 2000 and 2010 and have been used in every ACS since 2005.

The Census Bureau began tabulating racial data using three different approaches in the 2000 census to accommodate the addition of the multiracial option. There are data tables that count the number of people who identified as one race (referred to as race alone), which includes a final category that sums people who identified as multiracial. The sum of these categories equals the total population. There are a separate set of tables that count the number of races that people identified with—that is, the sum of all people who marked white, the sum of all people who marked black, and so on. These numbers do not sum to the total population, as people are double-counted in different categories if they are multiracial. Last, there are a couple of tables that count every possible combination of race.

You will notice that these five races do not include Hispanics or Latinos. Up until the mid-20th century, Hispanics or Latinos were not counted as a separate category or race and were primarily identified as being white. This was largely because Hispanics were considered as originating from Spain, a European country that was considered to be white. As the 20th century progressed, this distinction no longer seemed to fit reality, as an increasing number of Mexicans, Puerto Ricans, Cubans, and others began immigrating to the United States. The Census Bureau made some efforts at tabulating this population in specific states based on Spanish surnames submitted on census forms and added a sample question on Hispanic ethnicity on one of the sample forms for the 1970 census, but this proved to be inadequate for measuring this distinct and rapidly growing population (Humes & Hogan, 2009; Anderson, 2015).

The federal government created a separate *ethnic* category for Hispanics and Latinos in Directive 15 of 1977 instead of a *racial* one. While there was clearly a need and desire to count Hispanic people, there was a lack of consensus on whether to classify this group as a race. As a compromise, and a logical extension to the separate sample question asked in 1970, it became a separate category and question on the form. So a person would identify whether they were Hispanic or not in one question and would choose one of the racial categories (or one or many from 2000 onward) in a separate question. A person could be Hispanic and white, Hispanic and black, non-Hispanic and white, and so on. This practice was instituted for the 1980 census and has been used ever since for the decennial census and the ACS. Hispanics and Latinos were also given the option to designate a national origin such as Mexican, Puerto Rican, or Cuban.

Figure 4.1 illustrates what the Hispanic ethnicity and race questions looked like on the 2010 census form, and Table 4.1 provides a short description of each category. Current forms for the ACS (2010–2019) are similar. The form's Hispanic ethnicity and race questions are separate and distinct. People who identify as Asians or Pacific Islanders choose a specific ethnicity or national origin such as Chinese, Japanese, Hawaiian, and so on, or they write in their ethnicity. The Census Bureau subsequently summarizes these nationalities into an Asian or Pacific Islander category based on the responses. Prior to Directive 15, these nationalities were tabulated as individual races in the census, and in interviews with the Census Bureau, most Asian communities wanted the ability to continue to identify with their nationality as opposed to an umbrella term for all Asians.

While these changes allowed respondents to express their identity more freely and explicitly than in the past, it also created conundrums for summarizing and using racial data. In U.S. society, it is common to present Hispanics and Latinos as a separate race when presenting racial data, but this is difficult to do as Hispanics are not counted as a race in census data. The situation gets murkier when you consider that the Census Bureau includes a miscellaneous category for Other race, for people who choose not to identify with one of the categories. If you look at the description for the Some Other Race category in Table 4.1, it includes all responses that do not fall within one of the five racial categories. If someone writes in that they are Irish or Haitian instead of checking the box for white or black, the Bureau recodes those responses to white and black, respectively. But if a person writes that they are multiracial (instead of checking several race boxes) or they report that they are Hispanic, Latino, or one of the Hispanic nationalities, then they are counted as being Some Other Race.

Studies have shown that the majority of people who are Hispanic or Latino identify their race as white or as the Some Other Race category. This suggests that many Hispanic and Latinos think of their race as Hispanic and choose Other as a race, since Hispanic is not an option for the race question (Terry & Fond, 2013). In 2010, 53% of Hispanics who indicated a single race said that they were white, and 37% indicated Some Other Race (Humes, Jones, & Ramirez, 2011).

Data users typically approach this problem in one of two ways. For the first approach, data that's published in Table P3 for the decennial census or Table B02001 for the

**FIGURE 4.1   ⬣   HISPANIC AND RACE QUESTIONS ON THE 2010 CENSUS FORM**

➡ **NOTE: Please answer BOTH Question 8 about Hispanic origin and Question 9 about race. For this census, Hispanic origins are not races.**

**8. Is Person 1 of Hispanic, Latino, or Spanish origin?**

☐ **No,** not of Hispanic, Latino, or Spanish origin
☐ Yes, Mexican, Mexican Am., Chicano
☐ Yes, Puerto Rican
☐ Yes, Cuban
☐ Yes, another Hispanic, Latino, or Spanish origin — *Print origin, for example, Argentinean, Colombian, Dominican, Nicaraguan, Salvadoran, Spaniard, and so on.* ↘

```
[                                                      ]
```

**9. What is Person 1's race?** *Mark* ☒ *one or more boxes.*

☐ White
☐ Black, African Am., or Negro
☐ American Indian or Alaska Native — *Print name of enrolled or principal tribe.* ↘

```
[                                                      ]
```

☐ Asian Indian      ☐ Japanese      ☐ Native Hawaiian
☐ Chinese           ☐ Korean        ☐ Guamanian or Chamorro
☐ Filipino          ☐ Vietnamese    ☐ Samoan
☐ Other Asian — *Print race, for example, Hmong, Laotian, Thai, Pakistani, Cambodian, and so on.* ↘      ☐ Other Pacific Islander — *Print race, for example, Fijian, Tongan, and so on.* ↘

```
[                                                      ]
```

☐ Some other race — *Print race.* ↘

```
[                                                      ]
```

ACS for Race Alone is presented for the five racial groups, along with the additional categories of Some Other Race and Multiracial. In parts of the country where the Hawaiian and Pacific Islander population is quite small, this population is often grouped with the Asian population. A footnote is added that says that $X$ percentage of the population is Hispanic or Latino. Data for the footnote is drawn from Table P4 or B03003 (Hispanic or Latino origin).

| TABLE 4.1 ● CENSUS HISPANIC ETHNICITY AND RACE CATEGORIES | |
|---|---|
| **Hispanic or Latino** | A person of Cuban, Mexican, Puerto Rican, South or Central American, or other Spanish culture or origin regardless of race. |
| **White** | A person having origins in any of the original peoples of Europe, the Middle East, or North Africa. It includes people who indicated their race(s) as "White" or reported entries such as Irish, German, Italian, Lebanese, Arab, Moroccan, or Caucasian. |
| **Black or African American** | A person having origins in any of the Black racial groups of Africa. It includes people who indicated their race(s) as "Black, African Am., or Negro" or reported entries such as African American, Kenyan, Nigerian, or Haitian. |
| **American Indian or Alaska Native** | A person having origins in any of the original peoples of North and South America (including Central America) and who maintains tribal affiliation or community attachment. This category includes people who indicated their race(s) as "American Indian or Alaska Native" or reported their enrolled or principal tribe, such as Navajo, Blackfeet, Inupiat, Yup'ik, or Central American Indian groups or South American Indian groups. |
| **Asian** | A person having origins in any of the original peoples of the Far East, Southeast Asia, or the Indian subcontinent, including, for example, Cambodia, China, India, Japan, Korea, Malaysia, Pakistan, the Philippine Islands, Thailand, and Vietnam. It includes people who indicated their race(s) as "Asian" or reported entries such as "Asian Indian," "Chinese," "Filipino," "Korean," "Japanese," "Vietnamese," and "Other Asian" or provided other detailed Asian responses. |
| **Native Hawaiian or Other Pacific Islander** | A person having origins in any of the original peoples of Hawaii, Guam, Samoa, or other Pacific Islands. It includes people who indicated their race(s) as "Pacific Islander" or reported entries such as "Native Hawaiian," "Guamanian or Chamorro," "Samoan," and "Other Pacific Islander" or provided other detailed Pacific Islander responses. |
| **Some Other Race** | Includes all other responses not included in the White, Black or African American, American Indian or Alaska Native, Asian, and Native Hawaiian or Other Pacific Islander race categories described above. Respondents reporting entries such as multiracial, mixed, interracial, or a Hispanic or Latino group (e.g., Mexican, Puerto Rican, Cuban, or Spanish) in response to the race question are included in this category. |

*Source:* As published in Humes et al. (2011)

For the second approach, census tables for Hispanic or Latino origin that are subdivided by race (P5 in the decennial census, B03002 in the ACS) can be modified and used to identify Hispanic as a separate race. To accomplish this, every person

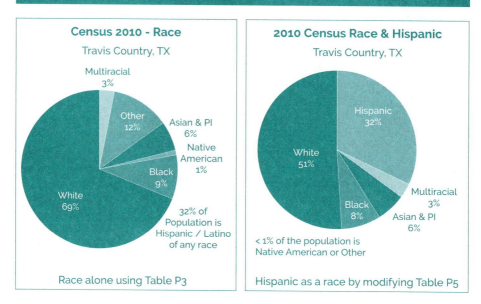

**FIGURE 4.2  ●  REPRESENTING RACE AND HISPANIC DATA**

**Census 2010 - Race**
Travis Country, TX

Multiracial 3%
Other 12%
Asian & PI 6%
Native American 1%
Black 9%
White 69%
32% of Population is Hispanic / Latino of any race

Race alone using Table P3

**2010 Census Race & Hispanic**
Travis Country, TX

Hispanic 32%
White 51%
Multiracial 3%
Black 8%
Asian & PI 6%
< 1% of the population is Native American or Other

Hispanic as a race by modifying Table P5

who identified as Hispanic or Latino regardless of their race is counted as Hispanic, and every person who is not Hispanic or Latino is counted based on the race they identified. One exception is that people who identified as multiracial are counted as multiracial regardless of whether they are Hispanic or not.

Figure 4.2 illustrates these first two approaches for Travis County, Texas, which is home to the state capital of Austin. Using the first approach, the majority of the population (69%) is white and a footnote indicates that 32% of the population is Hispanic or Latino, but we don't know of what race. Using the second approach, the Hispanic population appears within the chart. The white population is now a slim majority (51%), and the Other Race population is tiny, shrinking from 12% to 0.2%, as most Hispanics identify as either white or other. The Native American population declines from 1% to 0.3%. Of all racial groups, Native Americans are the most likely to report multiple races, and in certain areas like the Southwest, many identify as Hispanic given a shared cultural heritage and geographic proximity.

Which approach is best? This is a matter of interpretation. The chart using Table P3 faithfully reports the race data but not what most Americans would consider as race since Hispanics are not counted separately. The chart generated by manipulating the data from Table P5 is often used in the media and in research studies. Some would criticize this approach as misrepresenting the data, as you are taking people who identified as a specific race, are discarding their response, and are counting their Hispanic

| TABLE 4.2 ● TABLE ID SUFFIXES FOR DETAILED RACE TABLES | |
|---|---|
| **Suffix** | **Category** |
| A | White Alone |
| B | Black or African American Alone |
| C | American Indian and Alaska Native Alone |
| D | Asian Alone |
| E | Native Hawaiian and Other Pacific Islander Alone |
| F | Some Other Race Alone |
| G | Two or More Races |
| H | White Alone, Not Hispanic or Latino |
| I | Hispanic or Latino |

*Note:* Used in the decennial census and the ACS.

response as their race. The counterargument is that the majority of Hispanics would choose Hispanic as a race if it were listed as a racial option. You could opt to show two charts, one for Hispanics and one for non-Hispanics by race using Table P5. This approach would represent the data faithfully but makes it more difficult to conceptualize what the overall population of Travis County (and other places) is really like. Ultimately, one must attempt to balance faithful representation of the data with the intended audience's likely expectations and interpretations.

Since white is the most common racial category chosen by Hispanics and Latinos, and some researchers (in public health for example) need to separate Hispanics from European or Caucasian whites, the Census Bureau tabulates many data tables for individual races, including a non-Hispanic white category. The ID numbers of these tables (in the decennial census and ACS) have suffixes that range from letter "a" to letter "i" (see Table 4.2). The first seven are for the standard racial categories, and the last two are for non-Hispanic whites and Hispanic or Latino of any race. For example, in the decennial census, Table P12 is Sex by Age and Tables P12A through P12I are Sex by Age for each one of these groups. These tables are suitable for studying an individual race, as opposed to comparing them (as the data is split across nine tables).

After a decade of research, the U.S. Census Bureau (2017a) proposed modifying the form for the 2020 census to change the Hispanic ethnicity question and make Hispanic and Latino a race instead of an ethnicity. They also proposed adding a new racial category for people of Middle Eastern and North African (MENA) descent, as this group is currently counted as being white. These changes require approval from the Office of Management and Budget (OMB), as they would require updating Directive 15, which applies to all federal statistical agencies. In early 2018, the OMB chose to take no action on the proposal (H. L. Wang, 2018c, 2018i). As a result, the racial and Hispanic/Latino ethnicity questions that were used in 2010 will be used again in the 2020 census and in subsequent versions of the ACS. The only noteworthy change will be that white (H. L. Wang, 2018f) and black (H. L. Wang, 2018e) Americans will be able to write in a specific national identity or ancestry under their race, just as people of other races have been able to do.

Race will always be an evolving and contentious issue in American society, and these categories will continue to change as America changes. Some argue for the ability to exercise greater self-expression, and even to do away with fixed racial categories altogether in favor of submitting free-form answers. Others have argued for the elimination of the race question as the number of categories has grown so unwieldy and American society has become so racially intermixed that the categories are no longer useful or applicable (Connerly & Gonzalez, 2018). In his book on race and the census, former Census Bureau director Kenneth Prewitt argued that the government, by officially measuring race using artificial and outdated concepts, hardens the concepts of race in society and makes them real, thus increasing social and political divisions. He argues for a complete reform of the system, eliminating race and ethnicity questions from the decennial census while keeping them in the ACS in a modified form (Prewitt, 2013).

On the other hand, many data users and policy makers argue that as long as there are differential outcomes in society in terms of economics, criminal justice, and health based on race, and as long as we have laws that require that we collect, study, and apply this data to policy and law, racial categories are absolutely necessary (T. P. Johnson & Tourangeau, 2018). The categories must have some degree of uniformity, otherwise the data would be incomparable and useless.

## Households, Families, and Relationships

All people, regardless of age, sex, race, or ethnicity, fall within a series of groups and subgroups based on their living arrangements. The top category (see Figure 4.3) consists of households and group quarters; we will look at households in this section and will consider group quarters in the following section. Households are subdivided into family households and nonfamily households.

A household includes people who live in a housing unit, which is an individual residential living setting that includes single-family homes, condos, apartments, mobile homes, or even a group of rooms or a single room. A key aspect of a housing unit is

**FIGURE 4.3  ●  POPULATION SUBDIVISIONS BY LIVING ARRANGEMENTS**

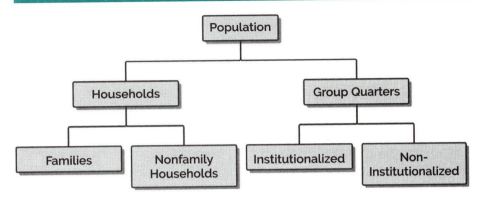

that the occupants have separate living quarters, in which they live apart from other people in the building. Occupants have direct access to their own living quarters either through a front door or common hallway. We can distinguish a household from a group quarters setting like a dormitory, barrack, or prison, where unrelated people live together in a nonresidential setting in a shared common space.

Each household has a householder, who is generally the person whose name appears on the mortgage or lease, or is simply the person who filled out the census form on behalf of other members of the household. If the householder lives with one or more people who are related to him or her, then that household is classified as a family household, or family for short. The decennial, ACS, and CPS forms ask for the name of every person in the household and for their relationship with the householder. The relationships include spouse, child, and other relatives. Each of these characteristics can be further subdivided; Figure 4.4 illustrates the various relationships listed on the 2010 census form and also applies to recent versions of the ACS (2010–2019).

The Census Bureau uses this data to create cross tabulations of different kinds of family types: husband–wife families and other families (male householder, no wife present, female householder, no husband present). It also creates cross tabulations of relatives to indicate families that do and don't have children, single-parent families, grandparent-headed families that include their grandchildren, and so on.

If a householder lives alone, or lives with people whom he or she is not related to, then this is a nonfamily household. Relations between the householder and other occupants of a nonfamily household include roomers or boarders, roommates, and unmarried partners. This is an important distinction for many reasons, as there are

FIGURE 4.4 ● RELATIONSHIP QUESTION ON THE 2010 CENSUS FORM

**1. Print name of Person 2**

Last Name

First Name                                    MI

**2. How is this person related to Person 1?** *Mark* X *ONE box.*

☐ Husband or wife              ☐ Parent-in-law
☐ Biological son or daughter   ☐ Son-in-law or daughter-in-law
☐ Adopted son or daughter      ☐ Other relative
☐ Stepson or stepdaughter      ☐ Roomer or boarder
☐ Brother or sister            ☐ Housemate or roommate
☐ Father or mother             ☐ Unmarried partner
☐ Grandchild                   ☐ Other nonrelative

several trends that have led to an increase in unmarried-partner households: couples who cohabitate prior to marriage, couples who live in common law as if they were husband and wife but never marry, and same-sex couples whose marriages were not recognized under federal law prior to 2015. While many of us may consider these groups to be families in the colloquial sense, under the Census Bureau's technical definitions, they are counted as nonfamily households.

Why are these distinctions important? There is a great deal of social research on household and family relations (Coontz, 2010), and trends over the past several decades illustrate that single-person households, unmarried-partner households, same-sex unions, single-parent households, and households headed by grandparents have all increased (Iceland, 2014, pp. 38–60). Household and family relationships can be good indicators of present social trends and good predictors of future population growth. Single-parent households or grandparent-headed households that include grandchildren face more financial burdens than dual-parent households. An increase in the number of older children who continue living with their parents and increases in the number of elderly people who move back in with their adult children are both growing trends in an economy with stagnant wages and an unaffordable health care system. A decline in the number of families and a rise in the number of one-person households may reflect a desire for growing individualism and independence, but it can also be a sign of increasing social isolation.

For purely practical purposes, it is important to recognize the differences between a household and a family when choosing indicators. In their broad survey of using social science datasets for research, Maier and Imazeki (2013) stress the inappropriateness of using family data when household data would be a better fit. While 80% of households were married-couple families in 1950, only 50% were in 2010, as nonfamily arrangements like unmarried partners and people living alone have become more common (pp. 25–27). In most cases, family indicators are going to be of narrow interest to researchers who specifically study families, while household indicators are applicable to broader research questions as they capture a larger swath of the population.

In addition to counting the number of households and families, the census also tabulates the total number of people who are in households and in families, so you can choose the appropriate numerator or denominator for a particular characteristic. If you wanted to know the percentage of owner-occupied households, the denominator would be the number of households, and the numerator would be the number of households that were occupied. If you wanted to know the percentage of people living in a residential setting, the denominator would be the total population, and the numerator would be the number of people living in households.

As mentioned earlier, the census does not ask questions about the LGBTQ population, but prior to the 2020 census, it did offer a roundabout way for measuring same-sex partnerships via the relationship question that pertains to unmarried-partner households (U.S. Census Bureau, 2016b). An unmarried partner is an adult who is not related or married to the householder but shares living quarters and a close personal relationship with the householder. If the unmarried partner was the same sex as the householder, they were classified as an unmarried same-sex couple household. Paradoxically, if the householder reported that they were married, and their spouse is of the same sex, the Census Bureau reclassified them as being an unmarried same-sex partner household. The Census Bureau began reporting this information with the 2005 ACS and applied significant methodological refinements in the 2008 ACS. This data was tabulated in the decennial census for the first time in 2010.

Now that same-sex marriage is recognized by federal law, and many stakeholders have petitioned the Census Bureau for greater clarity on this issue, the Bureau decided to add explicit choices under the relationship question for how each person is related to the householder on the 2020 Census and subsequent versions of the ACS (H. L. Wang, 2018d). The four options will include the following: opposite-sex husband/wife/spouse, opposite-sex unmarried partner, same-sex husband/wife/spouse, and same-sex unmarried partner. While this represents an improvement in data collection, it's important to recognize that the data for same-sex spouses and partners captures only a slice of the LGBTQ population, since it measures only people who are in a relationship and living together.

## Group Quarters

The group quarters population includes all people who do not live in a household. Group quarters are managed by an organization that provides housing and specific services to residents who live in a common space. Typically, the people living in group quarters are not related to one another but live together because of a shared mission or a need for specific services. Data for group quarters is collected in the decennial census, the ACS, and the PEP but is available for only small geographies with a sufficient degree of detail in the decennial census.

Group quarters are divided into two types of quarters: (1) institutional and (2) non-institutional. Colloquially, you may think of the term *institutional* as applying to all these settings, as they represent institutions and not residences. In the technical census sense, "institutional" is really referring to "institutionalized," where occupants have been committed to these places by others. Noninstitutional refers to group settings where occupants have entered of their own free will and can leave if they wish.

The institutional group quarters population includes people who are unable, ineligible, or unlikely to participate in the labor force. In many cases, they are held in group quarters against their will and are not able to leave without special permission and supervision. Institutional group quarters include the following: correctional facilities for adults and juveniles that include state and federal penitentiaries as well as local jails, group homes, or residential treatment facilities for juveniles, nursing homes, mental or psychiatric hospitals, inpatient hospice facilities, and residential schools for people with disabilities.

Housing for the elderly has become increasingly diverse and falls into a variety of categories. A nursing home is a facility where nurses are available to provide 24-hour care 7 days a week for people who require long-term care, and residents may not come and go as they please. Thus, a nursing home is classified as an institutionalized group quarters setting. In contrast, assisted-living facilities where seniors live more or less independently are not classified as group quarters at all, but as households if the building meets the criteria of a housing unit: a structure where people have independent access to their living space and live separately from one another. If seniors are living in a communal setting that's not a housing unit but can come and go as they please, then they're considered to be living in noninstitutional group quarters.

The noninstitutional group quarters population includes people who are able, eligible, and likely to participate in the labor force and who are free to come and go as they please. These quarters include the following: college dormitories, military barracks, homeless shelters, group homes or residential treatment facilities for adults, maritime vessels, workers' living quarters (typically for migrant agricultural workers), natural disaster shelters, and religious quarters (like a monastery or convent).

If you are conducting a study in a small geographic area or a sparsely populated place, it is important to take the group quarters population into consideration. For instance, the Wikipedia entry for Maurice River Township in southern New Jersey says the population was 7,976 in 2010. The article subsequently mentions that the township is home to two state penitentiaries. If we consult decennial census Table P42 Group Quarters for the township, it says 4,405 people live in correctional facilities—over half the population of the municipality! If you were using census data to measure accessibility to the local public library, or you want to see how many customers your small town coffee shop could attract, your study would need to account for this population.

Just as the census counts the number of households and families as well as the number of people within each group, it also counts the number of people who are in both institutional and noninstitutional group quarters settings. In the example above, you would subtract the institutional group quarters population from the total population to measure the population that can actually be reached and served: people who live in households and people who live in noninstitutional group quarters. In geographical studies, it's often possible to identify and eliminate the largest group quarters settings (regardless of the type), as census tracts are often drawn to enclose these areas to separate them from the rest of the population.

Group quarters populations can have a large impact on population change for small communities and rural counties. If a large expansion is built for a prison, or a military base downsizes or closes, the population for that area could change dramatically. Any interpretation of this population change would need to account for the group quarters. Conversely, if you were studying heavily populated areas or larger regions, this population will have a minimal impact on the overall findings, given its small size relative to the total.

## 4.4   HOUSING UNIT CHARACTERISTICS

A housing unit is a living space where the occupant or occupants live separately from one another and have independent access to their home from either outside the building or through a common hallway. It can be a single-family home, an apartment, a condominium, a mobile home, even a tent, recreational vehicle, or boat. Certain types of fixed units are always counted as housing units regardless of whether someone lives there or not. This includes single-family homes, apartments, condos, and mobile homes if they are at a fixed location. Other types of units are counted as housing units only if someone is living there when the census is taken. This includes vehicles of any kind and places like hotel or motel rooms that are being used as longer term living quarters.

A housing unit is distinct from a structure, which is a building that holds one or many units. For example, an individual apartment or condo is a housing unit, while the apartment building is a structure. There are separate counts for structures and for the number of units located in structures. The census also categorizes housing units by types. For instance, a single detached home is a home whose four walls do not touch another building, while an attached home is a house that touches neighboring buildings (a townhouse or rowhouse). The ACS includes additional details on housing units not captured in the decennial census, such as the number and type of rooms in a unit.

Housing units that are being constructed are not counted as units until they reach a livable state—typically, when windows and exterior doors have been installed and the unit has usable floors. Conversely, housing units that are in ruins where the roof, walls, windows, and doors no longer protect the unit from the elements are not counted as housing units. Units that are scheduled to be condemned or demolished are also excluded.

## Occupancy

Housing units are divided into occupied and vacant units (see Figure 4.5). A unit is classified as occupied if the person filling in the census form indicates that it is their usual place of residence as of the census day (for the decennial census) or if it is their current residence if they are living there for longer than 2 months (for the ACS).

Housing units are classified as vacant if no one is living there on census day or when a survey is sent (unless the person is temporarily absent), or if someone is there, but they indicate that it is not their usual (decennial census) or current (ACS) residence. Given these distinctions, a vacant housing unit captures a number of different use cases: units that are empty because they are for sale or rent, units that have been sold or rented but have not been occupied yet, and units that are for seasonal, recreational, or occasional use. An Other vacant category captures a variety of miscellaneous cases, such as homes that are under repair or renovation or homes that are owned and unoccupied but the owner does not wish to sell or rent them.

FIGURE 4.5 ● HOUSING UNIT SUBDIVISIONS BY STATUS

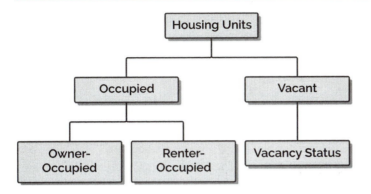

Counting the true population of seasonal or resort communities can be challenging because their populations fluctuate throughout the year. While the total population represents the number of permanent residents who make those communities their home, the number of housing units can be used to estimate, from an infrastructure stand point, the physical size or footprint of the community. Statistics for vacant housing units that are classified for seasonal or recreational use are often used as baseline numbers for calculating what the maximum seasonal population is. As we will see in our second exercise, this data can be used in conjunction with average household size and the number of bedrooms per unit (measured in the ACS) to create seasonal estimates.

## Tenure

Occupied housing units can be further subdivided based on whether the unit is owned or rented. In census jargon, this concept is referred to as tenure. A housing unit is owner-occupied if the owner or co-owner lives in the unit, regardless of whether it is mortgaged or fully paid for. All housing units that are not occupied by an owner or co-owner are counted as renter-occupied, regardless of whether the tenant pays rent or lives there freely. Obviously, this data is fundamental for studying the U.S. housing market, specifically the prevalence and distribution of homeowners versus renters who have different needs and require different services. The decennial census simply counts the number of owner-occupied and renter-occupied housing units. Surveys like the ACS and CPS provide additional detailed variables about each: home value, mortgage status, homeowner expenses, and various methods for measuring rent for renters.

## 4.5 THE LABOR FORCE

The concept of the labor force describes a person's employment status, and like all Census Bureau definitions, the terminology is quite specific. The labor force consists of all people 16 years of age or older who are working (employed), are not working but are actively seeking work (unemployed), or are members of the U.S. Armed Forces (on active duty in the Army, Air Force, Navy, Marines, or Coast Guard). This is important to understand: Members of the military are part of the labor force but are neither employed nor unemployed, they exist in their own separate category. Economists who do not want to factor in the military look at the civilian labor force, which consists of just the employed and the unemployed. The Census Bureau indents descriptions in its tables to indicate whether a category is a subgroup of another category. Notice in Figure 4.6 how both the civilian labor force and armed forces are indented under "In Labor Force" indicating that both are part of the labor force, while employed and unemployed are indented as subcategories under civilian labor force.

Within the civilian labor force, people are counted as employed if they were either at work during the reference frame for the survey or held a job but were not at work during the reference period due to a temporary absence (illness, vacation, union action, or personal reasons). A person is counted as employed if they did any work during the reference period as a paid employee, worked in their own business or profession (including farming), or worked 15 or more unpaid hours a week as part of a

---

**FIGURE 4.6 ●  EMPLOYMENT STATUS FOR THE UNITED STATES IN THE 1-YEAR 2017 ACS**

### « SELECTED ECONOMIC CHARACTERISTICS

| | United States | | | |
|---|---|---|---|---|
| | Estimate | Margin of Error | Percent | Percent Margin of Error |
| **EMPLOYMENT STATUS** | | | | |
| Population 16 years and over | 257,950,721 | +/- 46,662 | 257,950,721 | (X) |
| In labor force | 162,892,043 | +/- 128,219 | 63.1% | +/- 0.1 |
| Civilian labor force | 161,879,627 | +/- 124,848 | 62.8% | +/- 0.1 |
| Employed | 152,571,041 | +/- 138,252 | 59.1% | +/- 0.1 |
| Unemployed | 9,308,586 | +/- 49,229 | 3.6% | +/- 0.1 |
| Armed Forces | 1,012,416 | +/- 15,973 | 0.4% | +/- 0.1 |
| Not in labor force | 95,058,678 | +/- 113,918 | 36.9% | +/- 0.1 |
| Civilian labor force | 161,879,627 | +/- 124,848 | 161,879,627 | (X) |
| Unemployment Rate | (X) | (X) | 5.8% | +/- 0.1 |

family business or farm. Persons who engage in unpaid volunteer work and personal housework or home repairs are not counted as being employed.

Within the civilian labor force, people are counted as unemployed if they want a job, are actively seeking work, and are available to start working, but they currently do not have a job. Examples of job-seeking activities that would verify a person's status as unemployed include registering at an unemployment office, going to job interviews, and submitting job applications and résumés. The unemployed also include people who were laid off from a job temporarily and are waiting to be called back and people who could work but have a temporary illness that precludes them from holding a job. The unemployment rate represents the number of unemployed people divided by the total civilian labor force (the sum of the civilian employed and unemployed). Military personnel are never factored into the unemployment rate; they are part of the labor force but not the civilian labor force.

Outside of the labor force (civilians and military) are people who are not in the labor force. People not in the labor force include full-time students, stay-at-home parents, retirees, unpaid volunteers, institutionalized people (in prison, nursing homes, pyschiatric hospitals), people doing less than 15 hours a week of unpaid family work (for a business or farm), seasonal workers who are interviewed during an off-season when they are not working, *and* anyone else who is simply not employed and not looking for work. There is a big distinction between people who have no job and are not looking for work and the unemployed population, who *are* part of the labor force because they are actively seeking work.

The labor force participation rate represents the percentage of the population 16 years and older who are in the labor force. This consists of everyone in the labor force (employed, unemployed, and military) divided by the total population 16 years and older. The labor force participation rate measures how active society is in the working world. A low participation rate indicates that a smaller segment of the population must work to support a larger segment that isn't working.

When we read stories in our news feed about how the unemployment rate is going down, we have to interpret these numbers with caution. For example, the unemployment rate can go down either because people have found jobs or because people have left the labor force. The first case is good news, while the second case may or may not be. People leave the labor force because they are able to retire, or they leave due to injury or simply because they have given up looking for a job because it is too hard to find. Conversely, the unemployment rate can go up either because people have lost their jobs, or because more people have suddenly joined the labor force to look for work. The first case is bad news, while the second case could be good or bad. The economy may be strong enough that people are more confident that they can find work, or then again maybe people are forced to go to work because they can't afford not to.

The decennial census does not ask questions on labor force status. The ACS, CPS, and a number of surveys from the Bureau of Labor Statistics (BLS) employ these labor force concepts and measure additional characteristics on occupation, industry, and whether work is full-time or part-time. The ACS is appropriate for getting a broad picture of the labor force for geographic areas large and small. The CPS and BLS are better for more up-to-date statistics that cover large geographic areas.

The population-centered census datasets focus on the resident labor force, which are the members of the labor force who live in a particular place. This is quite different from measuring the labor force where they actually work. The ACS does ask some questions on residency by place of work, and the business-focused datasets (the Business Patterns and the Economic Census) count the number of businesses by location, including the number of employees and wages. Labor force and business data are usually divided into specific sectors and industries that describe the primary type of work that is being performed. We will discuss the North American Industrial Classification System codes with the business datasets in Chapter 8.

## 4.6   DERIVED MEASURES

For all of its datasets, the Census Bureau provides actual counts or estimates that represent the number of people or housing units within a specific geographic area that describe a particular characteristic. These counts or estimates tell us "how many." But in many instances, we need to know "how many in relation to what." It is useful to know that 65 million Americans have a bachelor's degree, but it would be more useful to know that 30% of Americans have a bachelor's degree. The percentage provides us with context.

It's particularly important to have this context when we are comparing places. Florida has more people with a college degree than Georgia, but that's simply because Florida has twice as many people. Based on the 2016 ACS, 30.5% of people 25 years of age and older have a bachelor's degree in Georgia versus 28.6% in Florida. In cases where we are comparing geographies that have an equal number of people by design (like a census tract), charting or mapping the total number of people would be irrelevant; we would need to use percentages or averages to make meaningful comparisons.

Averages and percentages are known as derivatives; they are statistics that are derived from counts and estimates. The Census Bureau conveniently tabulates a

> ### ✔ INFOBOX 4.1 DERIVED MEASURES IN THE CENSUS
>
> Mean: represents an arithmetic average of a set of values. It is derived by dividing the sum (or aggregate) of a group of numerical items by the total number of items in that group. For example, average family size is obtained by dividing the number of people in families by the total number of families.
>
> Median: represents the middle value (if *n* is odd) or the average of the two middle values (if *n* is even) in an ordered list of *n* data values. The median divides the total frequency distribution into two equal parts: one half of the cases falling below the median and the other half above the median.
>
> Percentage: calculated by taking the number of items in a group possessing a characteristic of interest and dividing by the total number of items in that group and then multiplying by 100.
>
> Rate: a measure of occurrences in a given period of time divided by the possible number of occurrences during that period. For example, the homeowner vacancy rate is calculated by dividing the number of vacant units "for sale only" by the sum of owner-occupied units, vacant units that are "for sale only," and vacant units that have been sold but not yet occupied, and then multiplying by 100. Rates are sometimes presented as percentages.

*Source:* As published in Summary File 1 Technical Documentation (U.S. Census Bureau, 2012a).
*Note:* The Census Bureau usually employs rates as percentages but sometimes uses rates normalized by a constant—that is, the number of births in past 12 months for every 1,000 unmarried women = (unmarried women aged 15 to 50 who gave birth/all women aged 15 to 50 who gave birth) × 1,000.

number of derivatives for us: means, medians, percentages, and rates (summarized in InfoBox 4.1). Percent totals are provided in the data profiles, subject (ACS), and quick (decennial) tables but not in the detailed tables (you would need to make your own calculations).

Calculating your own means and medians can be difficult or not possible depending on the variable. Most census data is summarized in classes or intervals (i.e., age brackets, income brackets) and by geography. You need to have the sum of all values to calculate a mean; in some cases, the Census Bureau provides sums (e.g., aggregate income is the sum of all incomes) or it may be something you can derive (the sum of all ages if single-age brackets are available), but in other cases, it won't be possible. To calculate medians, you would need the actual individual records, which are not publicly available. In these cases, you would have to use summary data to interpolate or derive what the median is (see Chapter 11). In short, whenever possible, use the published means (averages) and medians calculated by the Census Bureau.

When given a choice between a mean or median for a census variable, the median is usually the better summary measure as the mean is susceptible to being skewed by outliers. For instance, mean household income takes the sum of all income and divides it by the number of households in an area. If a particular town consists largely of middle-income earners but includes a small number of multimillionaires, the millionaires will skew the mean household income by pushing it higher. In contrast, median household income is calculated by sorting the income of individual households from the lowest to the highest and selecting the household that falls in the middle of the distribution. The income value would be drawn from the middle earners who form the bulk of the population, muting the impact of the millionaires at the end of the scale.

## 4.7    EXERCISES

Now that we've covered the primary subject characteristics in the census datasets, we'll explore some of them in more detail in two exercises using the LibreOffice Calc spreadsheet. These exercises will introduce you to spreadsheet basics that we'll return to throughout the book. A brief description of LibreOffice and a link for downloading this free and open source package is in the Introduction of the book. You may use Excel or another program if you choose, but be aware that the names of certain tools and buttons will be different. The basic functions and formulas we are using will mostly be the same.

Remember that you can visit the publisher's website at **study.sagepub.com/census** to easily download all the data you need for doing the exercises. The exercise data is structured with a folder for each chapter, with subfolders labeled with the exercise numbers. Alternatively, you can download each of the tables from `https://data.census.gov/`:

PCT12 Sex by Age: 2010 Decennial Census, Summary File 1, United States (nation)

B25002 Occupancy Status: 2012–2016 American Community Survey, Lewes Delaware (place)

B25004 Vacancy Status: 2012–2016 American Community Survey, Lewes Delaware (place)

B25041 Bedrooms: 2012–2016 American Community Survey, Lewes Delaware (place)

# Exercise 1: Generational Categories and Introduction to the Calc Spreadsheet

In this exercise, we will aggregate census data on age for the entire United States into the generational categories used by Pew Research Center (2015). This first example is designed to give you basic practice working with spreadsheets to reorganize data, aggregate categories, and create percent totals. Since this is our first exercise, the instructions for working in the spreadsheet will be pretty detailed. The level of detail (i.e., click in this cell, do a single right-click, and choose X option) will decline in subsequent exercises as you become more familiar with the environment.

Table PCT12 Sex by Age from the 2010 decennial census counts the number of men and women in single-year age brackets. The prefix "PCT" indicates that this is population data that is available down to the census tract level. If we wanted sex and age data for block groups and blocks, we would need to use Table P12, which aggregates the ages into brackets that vary from 1 to 5 years.

1. **Open the file**. Open the file for Chapter 4 Exercise 1 in LibreOffice Calc, either by going to the folder, selecting the file, right-clicking, and choosing open with Calc or by launching Calc and going to File—Open and then navigating to the file's location. We are looking for this file: DecennialSF12010_PCT12_with_ann.csv.

2. **View the data**. On the import screen, you will get a preview of the file's contents. We don't need to do anything in this case, so click OK. That opens the file in our spreadsheet. You should see three rows: two header rows and the record for the United States (Figure 4.7).

3. **Save as a spreadsheet**. Before we begin modifying the data, we need to save it in a spreadsheet format, instead of modifying the CSV. Go to File—Save As, name the file exercise1 and save it in the same folder as the CSV. Under Formats, change the type to ODF Spreadsheet, which is the open document spreadsheet format ODS. Notice that you could also save the file in the Excel .xlsx format. Hit the Save button.

**FIGURE 4.7 ● AGE DATA AFTER IMPORTING**

| | A | B | C | D | E | F | G | |
|---|---|---|---|---|---|---|---|---|
| | GEO.id | GEO.display-label | D001 | D002 | D003 | D004 | D005 | |
| 2 | Geographic identifier code | Geographic area name | Total: | Total: - Male: | Total: - Male: - Under 1 year | Total: - Male: - 1 year | Total: - Male: - 2 years | |
| 3 | 0100000US | United States | 308745538 | 151781326 | 2014276 | 2030853 | 2092198 | |

4.   **Copy, paste special, transpose**. By default, data downloaded from the Census Bureau is saved so that each row is a piece of geography and each column is an attribute. This is ideal when working with several geographies, but in this case, it makes working with the data clumsy as we have only one row of geography and many attributes. Let's transpose the data. Select all three rows by clicking on the first row number, hold down the shift key, and then click the last row. Right-click on one of the three rows to expose the edit menu, and choose the copy option. At the bottom of the spreadsheet beside the long name of our current sheet, hit the plus symbol to add a new sheet, which appears as sheet2. Click on the tab for sheet2 to open it. Click in the first empty cell, A1, to select it, then right-click and choose the Paste Special option. In this box, leave the options for Text, Numbers, and Dates checked, and near the bottom, check the Transpose box (Figure 4.8). Then hit OK. Transpose switches the rows to columns. Choosing text, numbers, and dates (known collectively as values) just copies our data over and nothing else: no formatting or formulas. Throughout this book, this latter operation will be referred to in short as copy—paste special—values, and it is a common step that you'll perform over and over again (Figure 4.9). Transposing is an option that only needs to be performed in limited circumstances. Go to File—Save, or hit the Save button on the toolbar.

**FIGURE 4.8   ●   PASTE SPECIAL MENU**

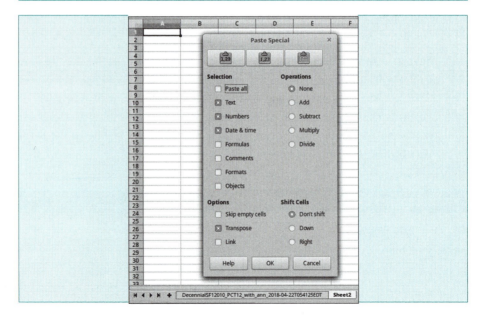

**FIGURE 4.9  ●  DATA TRANSPOSED**

| | A | B | C | D |
|---|---|---|---|---|
| 1 | GEO.id | Geographic i⬦ | 0100000US | |
| 2 | GEO.display⬦ | Geographic a⬦ | United States | |
| 3 | D001 | Total: | 308745538 | |
| 4 | D002 | Total: - Male: | 151781326 | |
| 5 | D003 | Total: - Male:▸ | 2014276 | |
| 6 | D004 | Total: - Male:▸ | 2030853 | |
| 7 | D005 | Total: - Male:▸ | 2092198 | |
| 8 | D006 | Total: - Male:▸ | 2104550 | |
| 9 | D007 | Total: - Male:▸ | 2077550 | |
| 10 | D008 | Total: - Male:▸ | 2072094 | |
| 11 | D009 | Total: - Male:▸ | 2075319 | |
| 12 | D010 | Total: - Male:▸ | 2057076 | |
| 13 | D011 | Total: - Male:▸ | 2065453 | |
| 14 | D012 | Total: - Male:▸ | 2119696 | |
| 15 | D013 | Total: - Male:▸ | 2135996 | |

5. **Rearrange data to place male and female data side by side**. Hover your cursor between the heading cells for columns B and C so you see the sideways arrow appear, then double-click. This extends the width of column B, so we can read the labels clearly. Select row 1 by clicking on the row number, right-click, and choose Delete Rows. Now we have just one header row. Do the same thing for row 2, labeled D001, which contains the total population, and delete that row. Next, scroll down until you see the female population, beginning with D106—total female. Click on the cell that contains the value for D106, and while holding down the left mouse button, move your cursor over to highlight the cells to the right that contain the label and actual values (Figure 4.10). Keep holding the button down, and drag your cursor down the length of all the cells until you get to the last row, then release the mouse button. You just highlighted all the records for age brackets for females (Figure 4.11). Do a single right-click on any one of the highlighted cells and choose the Cut option. Scroll back to the top of the screen, click in the empty cell in row D2, right-click, and choose Paste. Make sure that the records line up correctly, so the total for men and total for women appear in the same row (Figure 4.12).

**FIGURE 4.10  ●  FIRST RECORD FOR FEMALE AGE BRACKETS**

| 104 | D104 | Total: - Male: - 105 to 109 years | 736 |
| 105 | D105 | Total: - Male: - 110 years and over | 131 |
| 106 | D106 | Total: - Female: | 156964212 |
| 107 | D107 | Total: - Female: - Under 1 year | 1929877 |
| 108 | D108 | Total: - Female: - 1 year | 1947217 |
| 109 | D109 | Total: - Female: - 2 years | 2004731 |
| 110 | D110 | Total: - Female: - 3 years | 2014490 |

**FIGURE 4.11  ●  SELECT AND CUT FEMALE AGE DATA**

| | A | B | C | D | E |
|---|---|---|---|---|---|
| 202 | D202 | Total: - Female: - 95 years | 98766 | | |
| 203 | D203 | Total: - Female: - 96 years | 73799 | | |
| 204 | D204 | Total: - Female: - 97 years | 53582 | | |
| 205 | D205 | Total: - Female: - 98 years | 36641 | | |
| 206 | D206 | Total: - Female: - 99 years | 26193 | | |
| 207 | D207 | Total: - Female: - 100 to 104 years | 40846 | | |
| 208 | D208 | Total: - Female: - 105 to 109 years | 3157 | | |
| 209 | D209 | Total: - Female: - 110 years and over | | | |
| 210 | | | | ✂ Cut | |
| 211 | | | | 🗐 Copy | |
| 212 | | | | 🗋 Paste | |
| 213 | | | | | |

**FIGURE 4.12  ●  PASTE FEMALE AGE DATA BESIDE MALE DATA**

| | A | B | C | D | E | F |
|---|---|---|---|---|---|---|
| 1 | GEO.display▸ | Geographic area name | United States | | | |
| 2 | D002 | Total: - Male: | 151781326 | D106 | Total: - Fema▸ | 156964212 |
| 3 | D003 | Total: - Male: - Under 1 year | 2014276 | D107 | Total: - Fema▸ | 1929877 |
| 4 | D004 | Total: - Male: - 1 year | 2030853 | D108 | Total: - Fema▸ | 1947217 |
| 5 | D005 | Total: - Male: - 2 years | 2092198 | D109 | Total: - Fema▸ | 2004731 |
| 6 | D006 | Total: - Male: - 3 years | 2104550 | D110 | Total: - Fema▸ | 2014490 |
| 7 | D007 | Total: - Male: - 4 years | 2077550 | D111 | Total: - Fema▸ | 1985620 |
| 8 | D008 | Total: - Male: - 5 years | 2072094 | D112 | Total: - Fema▸ | 1984764 |
| 9 | D009 | Total: - Male: - 6 years | 2075319 | D113 | Total: - Fema▸ | 1991062 |

6.  **Clean up data to prepare for calculating totals**. Select column A that contains the ID codes for men by clicking on the column letter, right-click, and choose Delete Columns. Then delete the columns with the female codes and the female labels. In the header row in the cell that contains "United States,"

**FIGURE 4.13 ● FIND AND REPLACE TO MODIFY AGE LABELS**

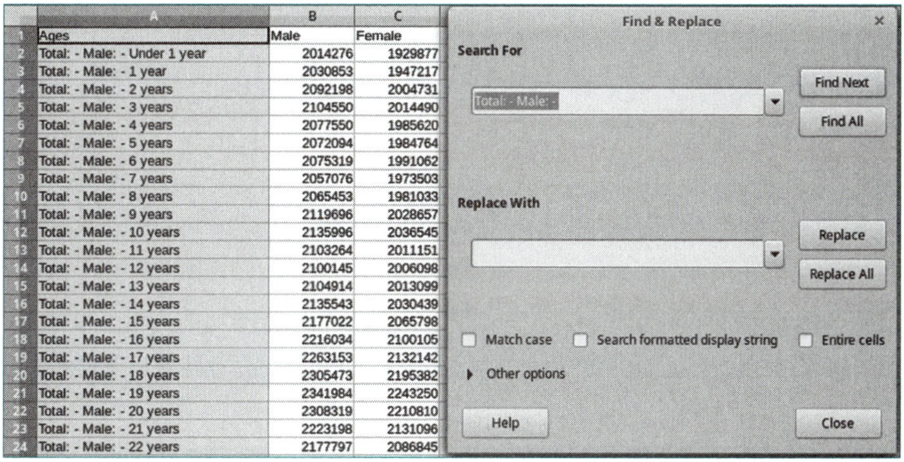

double-click on the cell, erase the words, and replace them with "Male." In the adjacent blank cell, double-click to enter the cell and type "Female." Now in cell A1, replace the existing text with "Ages." Select row 2, which contains the total for men and women, right-click and delete the row. Now click on column A to highlight it. Go up to the Edit menu and choose Find and Replace. In the Search for box type "Total: - Male: - " (without the quotes, and make sure you leave a space after the second dash). Leave the Replace All box blank and hit the Replace All button (Figure 4.13). If prompted with another window detailing the changes hit close, and close the Find and Replace button. Your sheet should look like Figure 4.14. Save your work.

7. **Calculate totals, first formulas**. In cell D1, type "Total." In cell D2, enter this formula: =B2+C2. Formulas always begin with an equals sign. When you hit Enter, the cell populates with the result of the formula. But if you click on the cell, the formula (not the resulting value) will appear in the input line above the column headings (Figure 4.15). With cell D2 selected, it will be outlined in black with a little black box in the lower right-hand corner. Now double-click on the little box, and that will paste your formula all the way down the column while updating the formula by one row value: If you click on cell D3, you will see that the formula was updated to add B3 and C3 together. This copy/paste shortcut works to carry formulas all the way down as long as there are no blank values in the cell that is to the left of the formula. If we stop at this point, the formula will be dynamic and will change if the values in column B or C change.

## FIGURE 4.14 ● CLEAN AND FORMATTED AGE DATA

| | A | B | C |
|---|---|---|---|
| 1 | Ages | Male | Female |
| 2 | Under 1 year | 2014276 | 1929877 |
| 3 | 1 year | 2030853 | 1947217 |
| 4 | 2 years | 2092198 | 2004731 |
| 5 | 3 years | 2104550 | 2014490 |
| 6 | 4 years | 2077550 | 1985620 |
| 7 | 5 years | 2072094 | 1984764 |
| 8 | 6 years | 2075319 | 1991062 |
| 9 | 7 years | 2057076 | 1973503 |

## FIGURE 4.15 ● INSERT FORMULA TO CALCULATE TOTAL

D2 ▾   f(x)  Σ  =   =B2+C2

| | A | B | C | D |
|---|---|---|---|---|
| 1 | Ages | Male | Female | Total |
| 2 | Under 1 year | 2014276 | 1929877 | 3944153 |
| 3 | 1 year | 2030853 | 1947217 | |

8. **Make formula results values**. Alternatively, we can make the values permanent. Select column D to highlight it. Right-click on the column header (letter D) and choose Copy. Then right-click on the column again and choose Paste Special (Figure 4.16). In the Paste Special box, uncheck Transpose, and make sure that only Text, Numbers, and Dates are checked. Hit OK. Now click in cell D2. You will see that the cell contains the actual total value, and the formula is gone. With this paste special values trick, we copied all the formulas in the column and replaced them with their values. Save your work.

9. **Quick summaries**. Select column D. In the lower right-hand corner of the spreadsheet window, beside the slider zoom bar, either an average or a total summation is displayed. Right-click on that number, and you will see all the options there are for getting quick summations: Average, Count, CountA (i.e., count text values), Sum, and so on. Choosing one of those options and then highlighting a row, column, or selection of cells will give you the outcome of that operation. Choose Sum, and then select column D. The total should be

**FIGURE 4.16** ● COPY AND PASTE SPECIAL TO REPLACE FORMULAS WITH VALUES

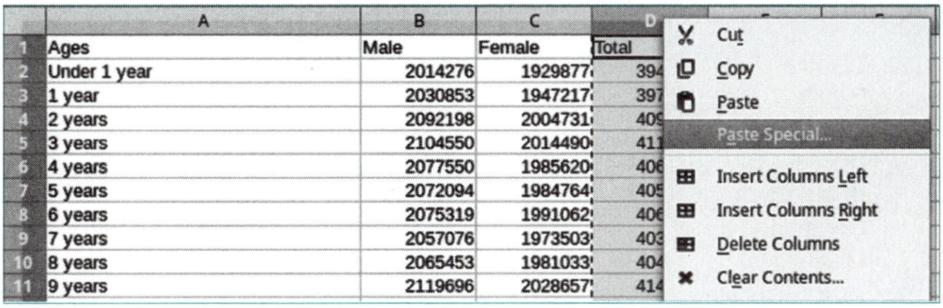

| | A | B | C | D | | |
|---|---|---|---|---|---|---|
| 1 | Ages | Male | Female | Total | ✂ | Cut |
| 2 | Under 1 year | 2014276 | 1929877 | 394 | ▢ | Copy |
| 3 | 1 year | 2030853 | 1947217 | 397 | ▯ | Paste |
| 4 | 2 years | 2092198 | 2004731 | 409 | | Paste Special... |
| 5 | 3 years | 2104550 | 2014490 | 411 | | |
| 6 | 4 years | 2077550 | 1985620 | 406 | ⊞ | Insert Columns Left |
| 7 | 5 years | 2072094 | 1984764 | 405 | ⊞ | Insert Columns Right |
| 8 | 6 years | 2075319 | 1991062 | 406 | | |
| 9 | 7 years | 2057076 | 1973503 | 403 | ⊞ | Delete Columns |
| 10 | 8 years | 2065453 | 1981033 | 404 | ✖ | Clear Contents... |
| 11 | 9 years | 2119696 | 2028657 | 414 | | |

**FIGURE 4.17** ● GENERATIONS' START AND END POINTS BY YEAR

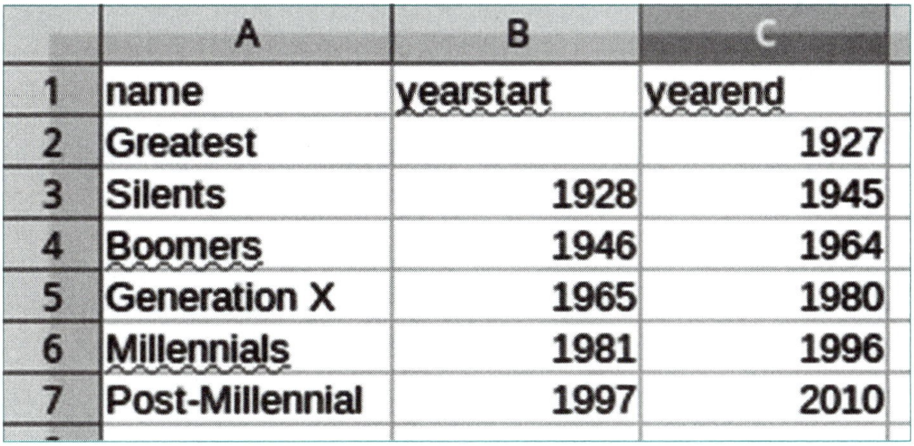

| | A | B | C |
|---|---|---|---|
| 1 | name | yearstart | yearend |
| 2 | Greatest | | 1927 |
| 3 | Silents | 1928 | 1945 |
| 4 | Boomers | 1946 | 1964 |
| 5 | Generation X | 1965 | 1980 |
| 6 | Millennials | 1981 | 1996 |
| 7 | Post-Millennial | 1997 | 2010 |

308,745,538. Now select Columns B and C together (click on B, keep holding down the left mouse button, move over to click on C, and release). The total of the male and female columns should match the totals column.

10. **Create generational table**. Add a new sheet to a workbook called sheet3 (hit the little plus symbol at the bottom of the screen, beside our existing sheets). Click on sheet3. Use Figure 4.17 as your guide for creating this table from scratch. The three columns will contain the generation names, the year the generation begins, and the year it ends. Note that the unnamed post-Millennial generation does not have an end year (at least not yet). Since our data is from 2010, we will set that as our end year.

**FIGURE 4.18  ⬢  GENERATIONS' START AND END POINTS BY AGE**

| E3 | ▼ | *f(x)* Σ  = | =2010-B3 | |
|---|---|---|---|---|

| | A | B | C | D | E |
|---|---|---|---|---|---|
| 1 | name | yearstart | yearend | youngest | oldest |
| 2 | Greatest | | 1927 | 83 | |
| 3 | Silents | 1928 | 1945 | 65 | 82 |
| 4 | Boomers | 1946 | 1964 | 46 | 64 |
| 5 | Generation X | 1965 | 1980 | 30 | 45 |
| 6 | Millennials | 1981 | 1996 | 14 | 29 |
| 7 | Post-Millennial | 1997 | 2010 | 0 | 13 |

11. **Calculate generational breakpoints**. We need to determine which ages fall within what generation by relating the ages to year of birth. To do that, we subtract the year that the data was published from each of the breakpoints. So first, create two additional columns, one called the youngest and the other called the oldest. In the youngest column, in cell D2, enter the formula: =2010-C2. This tells us that the youngest member of the Greatest Generation in 2010 was 83 years old. With that cell highlighted, double-click the little black box to paste the formula all the way down to get the youngest possible age for each group. In the oldest column, click on cell E3 for the Silent generation and enter the formula: =2010-B3. Then copy and paste that formula down to get the oldest members of each group (Figure 4.18). We do not calculate an oldest year for the Greatest Generation, as the age of the oldest living person represents the end of that generation and we can simply apply all of the age categories from 83 and above.

12. **Summing population by generation**. There are a couple of ways to achieve this. The simplest approach is the most labor-intensive, but it is feasible as there aren't too many categories. The youngest member of the Greatest Generation in 2010 was 83 years old. Flip over to sheet2, scroll down and find the row that has 83-year-olds. It's in row 85, and the top-level age-group is 110 years and over in row 104. The totals column is D, so our range is D85 to D104. Flip back to sheet3 and create a column in F called total. Click on cell F2, then on the toolbar, hit the Functions button *f(x)* or go to Insert—Function. In the list of functions, scroll down and select SUM, then hit Next. The next screen provides a list of possible arguments to give the function (Figure 4.19). Click in the box for number 1. Hit the select button to shrink the box. Hop back to sheet2, click on cell D85, and drag the purple box down to

**FIGURE 4.19** ⬡ FUNCTION WIZARD SUM FUNCTIONS

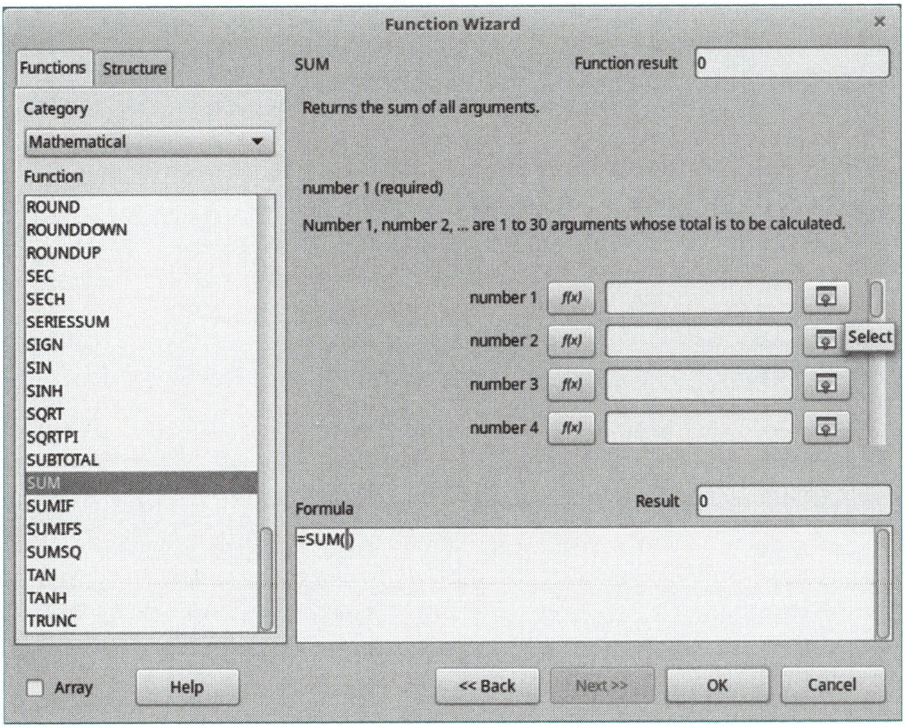

the last cell in D104. This populates the selection window with the range (Figure 4.20). Hit the selection button again to return to the wizard, then hit OK. Back in sheet3, we should see the total number of people in this generation (Figure 4.21).

13. **Sum the other generations**. Click on cell F2 and look at the formula in the display box. It reads =SUM(Sheet2.D85:D104). The arguments for functions always go in parentheses, if the data we are referencing is in a different sheet, we reference the sheet first, and then a period separates it from the range. The range of cells is separated with a colon. Now that we know the formula, we don't need to go back to the wizard; we can type it from scratch or just copy/paste and change the range values. Copy cell F2 and paste it into cell F3 for the Silents. This generation goes from age 65 to 82 in 2010. Flip over to sheet2 and identify this range: D67 to D84. Flip back and modify the function in cell F3 to fit this range; just double-click in the cell and type to modify it. Repeat this process for the remaining generations. When you are finished, do a summary on the column to make sure it totals to 308,745,538.

## FIGURE 4.20 ● SELECTING RANGE OF AGE DATA FOR GREATEST GENERATION

| | | | | |
|---|---|---|---|---|
| 80 | 78 y | Function Wizard - SUM( number 1; ... )  × | | 123 |
| 81 | 79 y | | | 195 |
| 82 | 80 y | Sheet2.D85:D104 | | 511 |
| 83 | 81 years | | | 865 |
| 84 | 82 years | 462983 | 698438 | 1161421 |
| 85 | 83 years | 419831 | 654978 | 1074809 |
| 86 | 84 years | 373131 | 612590 | 985721 |
| 87 | 85 years | 336819 | 577904 | 914723 |
| 88 | 86 years | 293120 | 521091 | 814211 |
| 89 | 87 years | 249803 | 463105 | 712908 |
| 90 | 88 years | 217436 | 423183 | 640619 |
| 91 | 89 years | 176689 | 361309 | 537998 |
| 92 | 90 years | 136948 | 298615 | 435563 |
| 93 | 91 years | 103799 | 241188 | 344987 |
| 94 | 92 years | 81072 | 200317 | 281389 |
| 95 | 93 years | 59037 | 157941 | 216978 |
| 96 | 94 years | 43531 | 125918 | 169449 |
| 97 | 95 years | 30951 | 98766 | 129717 |
| 98 | 96 years | 21424 | 73799 | 95223 |
| 99 | 97 years | 14556 | 53582 | 68138 |
| 100 | 98 years | 9259 | 36641 | 45900 |
| 101 | 99 years | 6073 | 26193 | 32266 |
| 102 | 100 to 104 years | 8295 | 40846 | 49141 |
| 103 | 105 to 109 years | 736 | 3157 | 3893 |
| 104 | 110 years and over | 131 | 199 | 330 |

## FIGURE 4.21 ● SUMMING THE AGE DATA FOR THE GREATEST GENERATION

F2 ▾  f(x)  Σ  =  =SUM(Sheet2.D85:D104)

| | A | B | C | D | E | F |
|---|---|---|---|---|---|---|
| 1 | name | yearstart | yearend | youngest | oldest | total |
| 2 | Greatest | | 1927 | 83 | | 7553963 |
| 3 | Silents | 1928 | 1945 | 65 | 82 | |
| 4 | Boomers | 1946 | 1964 | 46 | 64 | |
| 5 | Generation X | 1965 | 1980 | 30 | 45 | |
| 6 | Millennials | 1981 | 1996 | 14 | 29 | |
| 7 | Post-Millennial | 1997 | 2010 | 0 | 13 | |

14. **Calculate percent totals and round**. In column G, add a new header called ptotal. In cell G2, enter this formula: =(F2/(SUM(F2:F7)) * 100. First, we

divide the members of the Greatest Generation by the total population (the sum of all generations) and then multiply by 100 to get a percentage of 2.44666, and so on. The parentheses indicate that the summing and division must come before the multiplication (order of operations). Next, use the ROUND function and modify the formula to round the percentage to a whole number: =ROUND((F2/SUM(F2:F7)) * 100,0). Here, ROUND takes the outcome of our formula as the first parameter, and the number of decimal places as the second parameter; the two are separated by a comma.

15. **Distinction between rounding and formatting**. When we multiply by 100 and use ROUND, we are changing the actual outcome of the formula. Alternatively, if we wanted to leave the output of the formula as a fraction (0.024666), we could skip multiplying by 100, open the formatting window for the column (by selecting the column, right-clicking, and choosing Format Cells), and specify that the column represents a percentage. If we use this formatting option, we apply "window dressing" to the cells; the values do not actually change, the spreadsheet just displays them to us a particular way.

16. **Locking cells**. If we copy and paste the formula down the column for the other generations, Calc will update the value ranges by one increment, as we saw previously. While we want that to happen for the numerator (which has the one generation), we do *not* want the range that we are summing (the cells for all generations) to increment; we want it to remain fixed. In spreadsheet formulas, the dollar sign "$" is used for locking ranges so they do not change:

    * F2: is unlocked
    * F$2: locks the row, 2
    * $F2: locks the column, F
    * $F$2: locks the cell, F2

    We want to lock row values so they do not increment. In cell G2, modify the formula to lock the rows for the sum total: =ROUND((F2/SUM(F$2:F$7)) * 100,0). Then paste the formula down the column (highlight cell G2 and double-click the black box in the lower right-hand corner) (Figure 4.22). Save your work.

We can see that the Greatest Generation has almost passed on by 2010, while the Silent Generation is also relatively small. The Baby Boomers represent the largest chunk, while Generation X and the Millennials are roughly equivalent in size. If we

### FIGURE 4.22  ◆  PERCENT TOTAL FORMULA WITH LOCKED ROWS

| G2:G7 | ▾ | $f(x)$ | Σ | = | =ROUND((F2/SUM(F$2:F$7))*100,0) |

| | A | B | C | D | E | F | G |
|---|---|---|---|---|---|---|---|
| 1 | name | yearstart | yearend | youngest | oldest | total | ptotal |
| 2 | Greatest | | 1927 | 83 | | 7553963 | 2 |
| 3 | Silents | 1928 | 1945 | 65 | 82 | 32714021 | 11 |
| 4 | Boomers | 1946 | 1964 | 46 | 64 | 76980577 | 25 |
| 5 | Generation X | 1965 | 1980 | 30 | 45 | 65541573 | 21 |
| 6 | Millennials | 1981 | 1996 | 14 | 29 | 68894173 | 22 |
| 7 | Post-Millennial | 1997 | 2010 | 0 | 13 | 57061231 | 18 |

wanted to use more recent data, estimates for age and sex are also available from the ACS and the PEP. The PEP is the better choice, as it's easier to work with (we'll cover the ACS in Chapter 6 and the PEP in Chapter 7).

If this was your first foray in using spreadsheets, see the tips in InfoBox 4.2 that will help you navigate through large amounts of data. Instead of aggregating age data into categories manually, we could automate this process with the use of conditional statements like IF, COUNTIF, and SUMIF. View the online supplemental material for this chapter at **study.sagepub.com/census** to learn more. The steps we took in this exercise are the ones you will perform over and over again as you work with census data. We will cover a few more essentials in the following exercise.

## Exercise 2: Estimating Seasonal Populations and Basic Modeling With Calc

In this exercise, we will study the impact that vacant housing units have on the size of resort communities and learn how to create different estimates to measure seasonal populations using ACS data in Calc. This exercise serves as a basic introduction to modeling. A model is an attempt to represent or estimate existing conditions or predict future ones based on reasonable assumptions and available data. We do not have firm statistics on what the seasonal population is, but given the data available to us, we can make a series of assumptions to produce a number of estimates that we can evaluate.

Lewes, Delaware, is an incorporated place in southern Delaware that faces the Delaware Bay and a cape that separates it from the Atlantic Ocean. It has a small, old town center that is populated throughout the year and has a mix of older and newer housing along the beach that includes many seasonal vacation homes. Since Lewes is a small city, ACS data is only available for it in the 5-year dataset. The population of Lewes was 2,955 people between 2012 and 2016, plus or minus 23

## ✓ INFOBOX 4.2 TIPS FOR NAVIGATING LARGE SPREADSHEETS

As you start working with larger datasets that have thousands of rows and dozens of columns, it can be easy to get lost. You can waste a lot of time scrolling around to find things, and the likelihood of making a mistake increases. The following tools can help you quickly locate and identify values you need. These instructions are specifically for Calc, but Excel has the same features.

Freezing rows or columns: View—Freeze Cells. As you are scrolling down a sheet, you can forget what each of the columns represents. Freezing the first row locks it in the view, so as you scroll down, you can see the column headers. Similarly, you can freeze the first column so you can see the identifier for the record as you scroll across.

Optimal width for columns: Select—right-click—Optimal Width. This makes the width of the column wide enough based on the longest value in a column's cell, so you can read the whole value. This can backfire for really long values; you can right-click and choose Column Width to set a fixed width.

Hiding rows and columns: Select—right-click—Hide or Show. If you have a bunch of columns or rows that you don't need and they are impeding your ability to see what's important, you can simply hide them (instead of deleting them). You can tell when something is hidden because you will see gaps in the sequence of column letters or row numbers.

Finding values: Edit—Find. Opens a search box where you can search for specific values. The view will jump to the first found value, and you can iterate through them.

Highlighting: Select—right-click—Format, or Styles toolbar buttons. If you want to mark a particular column, record, or value, you can quickly change the color of the font or the background color of the cells by clicking on the appropriate button on the toolbar. A drop-down menu beside each button lets you choose colors.

Conditional formatting: Format—Conditional Formatting—Manage. If you want to highlight cells (change their font or background color) when the value meets a specific condition, you select the column and apply the criteria you want. For example, make the font red if the value is negative, make the cell yellow if the value is greater than 1,000, or make the font bold if the value equals "Midwest."

people. Based on these estimates, we are 90% confident that the population was between 2,932 and 2,978 during this time period (we will cover these details about the ACS in Chapter 6).

1.  **Open the first file and save.** Open the file for the first table on occupancy status (Table B25002), labeled ACSDT5Y2016_B25002_with_ann.csv in Chapter 4 Exercise 2 folder, in Calc. Click OK to get through the import screen. Once you see the data, go to File—Save As and save the data in an ODF spreadsheet format called exercise2.ods.

| FIGURE 4.23 ● | ACS DATA FOR HOUSING OCCUPANCY |
| --- | --- |

| | A | B | C | D | E | F |
| --- | --- | --- | --- | --- | --- | --- |
| 1 | GEO.id | GEO.display-label | ESTIMATE#HD01_VDIM#VD01 | ESTIMATE#HD02_VDIM#VD01 | ESTIMATE#HD01_VDIM#V | ESTIMATE#HD02_VDIM#VD02 | E |
| 2 | Id | $(dim.label) | Estimate; Total: | Margin of Error; Total: | Estimate; Total: - Occupied | Margin of Error; Total: - Occupied | E |
| 3 | 1600000US1041830 | Lewes city, Delaware | 2781 | 242 | 1632 | 141 | |
| 4 | | | | | | | |

2. **Examine the data**. Columns for ACS data always come in pairs, with one column for the estimate followed by its margin of error (MOE). We can see that Lewes has 2,781 housing units, plus or minus 242. Of these, 1,632 are occupied (±141) and 1,149 are vacant (±197) (Figure 4.23). The number of housing units is almost equal to the number of residents, and almost 60% of Lewes' housing units are vacant. These are both clues that Lewes is a seasonal resort community.

3. **Import the second file in a new sheet**. Rather then opening our second table into a new workbook, we want to insert it into our current workbook as a new sheet. Go to Sheet—Insert Sheet From File. Browse and select Table B25004 (Vacancy Status) that's named ACSDT5Y2016_B25004_with_ann.csv. Click OK on the Import Screen and OK again to import the sheet.

4. **Examine the data**. Since we are working with a very small area and population, the MOEs for these estimates are quite high. For example, the number of vacant units that are for rent is 108, plus or minus 114! Fortunately, the precision of the estimate we are interested in is much better; scroll over until you see the estimate for seasonal, recreational, or occasional use. The estimate is 879 units, plus or minus 193 (so it could be as low as 686 units or as high as 1,072). So approximately 77% of the vacant units in Lewes are seasonal units, which means that in the summer season these units will be populated with vacationers, swelling the city's population. How many extra people could there be?

5. **Gather additional facts**. We could multiply the average household or family size of the occupied units by the number of seasonal units to create a basic, low-end estimate of what the total population could be. Instead of downloading and importing a lot of additional tables, we can simply look up these statistics. The data that we need is basic, so we can look at the ACS Data Profile Tables (DP02 to DP05) that we explored in Chapter 2. While we could use **data.census.gov**, we'll introduce the Missouri Census Data Center's application instead as it will allow us to obtain the data more quickly. Go to https://census.missouri.edu/. In the Data Applications menu on the right, click ACS Profiles. In the Menu under Select period, choose 2012–2016 under the 5-year ACS. Then choose Places under area type, Delaware as the state, and Lewes city, Delaware, as the area. Since the concept of household

FIGURE 4.24 ● CREATING ACS PROFILES AT THE MISSOURI CENSUS DATA CENTER

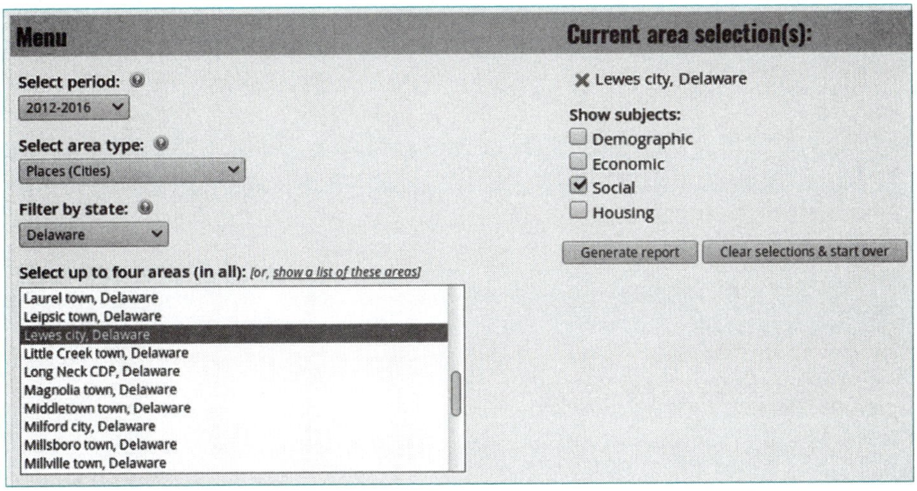

pertains to how people living together are related (or not), it is considered a social indicator. Check just the Social profile on the right, and generate the report (Figure 4.24).

6. **Consult the social profile**. The first section of the report, S1 Households by Type, summarizes the number of families and nonfamily households, which is about a 50–50 split in Lewes (Figure 4.25). If you hover your cursor over each value, a little tooltip appears that indicates what the MOE is, expressed as a percentage of the total and a range of values. We can see the average size of all households (1.71 people per household, ±0) and family households (2.25 ± 0.3). The range for the latter is 1.95 to 2.55; subtract one from the other and we obtain a MOE of ±0.3. We can use these numbers as our multipliers.

7. **Create estimates sheet**. Return to Calc, and add a new sheet. Instead of keeping the generic name of sheet2 or sheet3, and so on, double-click on the new sheet tab and rename it "estimates." Consult Figure 4.26 and manually enter the labels and data for total population (2,955), seasonal units (879), and the seasonal MOE (193) in cells A1 to B3. In cell A6, type Multiplier, and type 1.71 in cell B6 and 2.25 in cell C6. Just above these numbers, type AHS and AFS to indicate what the multipliers are (average household size and average family size). Last, in cells A8, A9, and A10, type labels for High Season Pop, Difference, and High Season MOE.

## FIGURE 4.25  ●  SOCIAL PROFILE TABLE MISSOURI CENSUS DATA CENTER

| Subject | Lewes city, Delaware Number | Percent |
|---|---|---|
| **S1. HOUSEHOLDS BY TYPE** | | |
| Universe: Total households | | |
| Reference tables: B11001 B11003 B11005 B11010 B11007 B11002 B19001 | | |
| Total households | 1,632 | |
| Family households | 789 | 48.3 |
| With own children under 18 years | 96 | 5.9 |
| Married-couple families | 649 | 39.8 |
| With own children under 18 years | 13 | 0.8 |
| Male householder, no wife present | 28 | 1.7 |
| With own children under 18 years | - | |
| Female householder, no husband present | 112 | 6.9 |
| With own children under 18 years | 83 | 5.1 |
| Nonfamily households | 843 | 51.7 |
| Householder living alone | 694 | 82.3 |
| 65 years and over living alone | 471 | 55.9 |
| Households with one or more people under 18 years | 108 | 6.6 |
| Households with one or more people 65 years and over | 1,054 | 64.6 |
| Average household size | 1.71 | |
| Average family size | 2.25 | |
| **S2. PERSONS BY HOUSEHOLD TYPE / GROUP QUARTERS** | +/- 13.33% (1.95, 2.55) | |
| Universe: Total population | | |

## FIGURE 4.26  ●  ESTIMATES SHEET FOR SEASONAL UNITS

| B8 | ▼ | f(x)  Σ  = | =ROUND(($B2*B6)+$B1) |

| | A | B | C | D |
|---|---|---|---|---|
| 1 | Total Population | 2955 | | |
| 2 | Seasonal Units | 879 | | |
| 3 | Seasonal MOE | 193 | | |
| 4 | | | | |
| 5 | | AHS | AFS | |
| 6 | Multiplier | 1.71 | 2.25 | |
| 7 | | | | |
| 8 | High Season Pop | 4458 | 4933 | |
| 9 | Difference | 1503 | 1978 | |
| 10 | High Season MOE | 330 | 434 | |

8. **Enter formulas**. For High Season Pop in cell B8, enter this formula: =ROUND(($B2*B6)+$B1). This multiplies the seasonal units by the AHS to get an estimate for seasonal population and then adds the long-term resident

population to get a total. Then for Difference in cell B9, enter =B8-$B1 to subtract the long-term population from this new estimate to see what the increase in population is. Then, in High Season MOE in cell B10, enter =ROUND($B3*B6). This multiplies the seasonal units' MOE by the multiplier to give us a MOE for the seasonal population. Last, copy the three cells from B8 to B10 and paste them into C8 to C10 (Figure 4.26). Since we added a "$" to lock the columns for our constants, the formulas recompute the values using the AFS.

9. **Study the result and expand**. If we use AHS as the multiplier, our most conservative estimate for the seasonal population is 1,503 people (±330 people) higher than the total population. If we want to argue that people who go on vacation usually go in groups (regardless of whether they go to a seasonal home they own or they rent a home for a week or two), then we can use the higher AFS multiplier that increases the size by a few hundred people. The AFS does have a MOE of 0.3, and to account for this, we could create two additional estimates for low and high family size (1.95 as the low end and 2.55 at the high end). We'll keep our example simple for now but will return to this issue in Chapter 6.

10. **Import data for bedrooms**. We could argue for an even higher estimate, if we assume that many vacationers who rent go as large groups to cover the high price of the rental and that many seasonal homeowners invite family and friends to join them (or they rent their home for part of the season). Go to Sheet—Insert Sheet From File. Browse and select Table B25041 (Bedrooms) that's named ACSDT5Y2016_B25041_with_ann.csv. Click OK on the Import Screen and OK again to import the sheet. To see this data more clearly, create a new sheet called bedrooms, and do a copy/paste special—transpose to paste this data into the new sheet.

11. **Calculate number of bedrooms**. This table shows the number of housing units by the number of bedrooms it has. For example, there are 268 housing units that have one bedroom (±161 units). Unfortunately, there is no cross tabulation for bedrooms by occupancy status, so these estimates are for all housing units, occupied and vacant. We need to calculate how many bedrooms there are, and how many there are in the seasonal units. We will assume that the distribution of bedrooms for the seasonal units is the same for all housing units. In cell D2, add a label for bedrooms. In cell D7, for one bedroom, enter =C7. If each unit has one bedroom, the number of bedrooms equals the number of units. In cell D9, for two bedrooms, type =C9*2. There are 467 units

**FIGURE 4.27** ● CALCULATING AND APPORTIONING BEDROOMS TO SEASONAL UNITS

| | A | B | C | D | E |
|---|---|---|---|---|---|
| 1 | GEO.id | id | 1600000US1041830 | | |
| 2 | GEO.display-label | ${dim.label} | Lewes city, Delaware | bedrooms | seasonal bedrooms |
| 3 | ESTIMATE#HD01_VDIM#VD01 | Estimate; Total: | 2781 | | 2645 |
| 4 | ESTIMATE#HD02_VDIM#VD01 | Margin of Error; Total: | 242 | | |
| 5 | ESTIMATE#HD01_VDIM#VD02 | Estimate; Total: - No bedroom | 0 | | |
| 6 | ESTIMATE#HD02_VDIM#VD02 | Margin of Error; Total: - No bedroom | 11 | | |
| 7 | ESTIMATE#HD01_VDIM#VD03 | Estimate; Total: - 1 bedroom | 268 | 268 | 84.688 |
| 8 | ESTIMATE#HD02_VDIM#VD03 | Margin of Error; Total: - 1 bedroom | 161 | | |
| 9 | ESTIMATE#HD01_VDIM#VD04 | Estimate; Total: - 2 bedrooms | 467 | 934 | 295.144 |
| 10 | ESTIMATE#HD02_VDIM#VD04 | Margin of Error; Total: - 2 bedrooms | 158 | | |
| 11 | ESTIMATE#HD01_VDIM#VD05 | Estimate; Total: - 3 bedrooms | 1242 | 3726 | 1177.416 |
| 12 | ESTIMATE#HD02_VDIM#VD05 | Margin of Error; Total: - 3 bedrooms | 252 | | |
| 13 | ESTIMATE#HD01_VDIM#VD06 | Estimate; Total: - 4 bedrooms | 578 | 2312 | 730.592 |
| 14 | ESTIMATE#HD02_VDIM#VD06 | Margin of Error; Total: - 4 bedrooms | 142 | | |
| 15 | ESTIMATE#HD01_VDIM#VD07 | Estimate; Total: - 5 or more bedrooms | 226 | 1130 | 357.08 |
| 16 | ESTIMATE#HD02_VDIM#VD07 | Margin of Error; Total: - 5 or more bedrooms | 140 | | |

with two bedrooms, so multiply by 2 to get the total bedrooms. Do the same for cells C11, C13, and C15 multiplying by 3, 4, and 5, respectively.

12. **Apportion bedrooms**. Now that we know how many bedrooms there are in total, we have to calculate how many are in the seasonal units. There are 2,781 housing units and 879 are seasonal, so seasonal units represent 31.6% of the total. In cell E2, add a label for seasonal bedrooms, and in cell E7, type =D7*.316. Then go to E9, and type =D9*.316. Repeat this for the other categories to calculate the number of bedrooms for each type. Last, at the top in cell E3, type =ROUND(SUM(E7:E15)) to calculate the total bedrooms in the seasonal units. Your sheet should resemble Figure 4.27.

13. **New estimate using bedrooms**. Flip back to the summary sheet, and add labels for the following: By bedrooms in A12, Difference in A13, and High Season MOE in A14. In cell B12, type =ROUND(bedrooms.$E3*B6)+$B1 to multiply the bedrooms in the bedroom sheet by the AHS multiplier, and add the total population. In cell B13, type =B12-$B1 to calculate the difference between the total and seasonal populations. In cell B14, type =ROUND(((bedrooms.$E3/$B2) ∗ $B3) ∗ B6) to get a MOE. This divides the total number of seasonal bedrooms by the total number of all seasonal units to get the average number of bedrooms per unit (about 3). This average is multiplied by the MOE for the seasonal units and last by the multiplier to see the possible range of people. When you are finished, you can copy and paste the formulas across to the AFS column (Figure 4.28).

14. **Evaluation**. Applying the multipliers to the number of bedrooms as opposed to the number of seasonal units yields even higher estimates. At the low end, there could be an additional 3,530 people (4,523 − 993) and at the high

| FIGURE 4.28 ⬢ | SEASONAL ESTIMATES USING AVERAGE HOUSEHOLD AND FAMILY SIZE BY BEDROOMS |
|---|---|

**B14**     ▼   $f_x$  Σ  =  =ROUND(((bedrooms.$E3/$B2)*$B3)*B6)

| | A | B | C | D | E |
|---|---|---|---|---|---|
| 1 | Total Population | 2955 | | | |
| 2 | Seasonal Units | 879 | | | |
| 3 | Seasonal MOE | 193 | | | |
| 4 | | | | | |
| 5 | | AHS | AFS | | |
| 6 | Multiplier | 1.71 | 2.25 | | |
| 7 | | | | | |
| 8 | High Season Pop | 4458 | 4933 | | |
| 9 | Difference | 1503 | 1978 | | |
| 10 | High Season MOE | 330 | 434 | | |
| 11 | | | | | |
| 12 | By Bedrooms | 7478 | 8906 | | |
| 13 | Difference | 4523 | 5951 | | |
| 14 | High Season MOE | 993 | 1307 | | |

end 7,258 more people (5,951 + 1,307). Alternatively, we could also apply a commonsense multiplier like two people per bedroom. What matters here is that we regard each of these outcomes as estimates with a range of values and acknowledge that the estimates can change based on the assumptions and variables you add to your model.

A professional working in local or state government would likely present a range of estimates and then through dialog narrow down which ones are best based on shared assumptions. For example, in Lewes, would it be more reasonable to apply AHS or AFS against either units or bedrooms? Furthermore, was our assumption that the number of bedrooms in vacant seasonal units is the same as the distribution for all units a reasonable one? Local observations, surveys, other data sources, and institutional community knowledge could help narrow down the assumptions. Some models rely on administrative data, such as utility records on water and sewer usage or transportation statistics like traffic counts, either in addition to or instead of census data. For an example of a case study that accounts for many factors, see *Northwest Michigan Seasonal Population* (MSU Land Policy Institute, 2014).

Lewes does not have a large number of hotels and motels. This is important, because commercial establishments are not captured in the decennial or ACS statistics. If we were looking at a resort community that had a large number of commercial establishments, we would have to use local and possibly proprietary data sources outside of the census to factor in the additional population from these places. Arguably, given the small size of Lewes and the fact that a typical motel could have up to a hundred rooms, we probably should factor in the half-dozen hotels and motels to get a better estimate.

Last, it's important to recognize that the MOEs for the ACS can be high for small areas. In our exercise, we did not regard the errors that existed for housing units classified by number of bedrooms but used a simpler approach to factor in the MOE for all seasonal units to at least provide some basic error measurement. If the occupancy and vacancy status estimates are too imprecise, you could check them against the decennial census, particularly in the earlier parts of a decade when the decennial data is still relatively current.

This chapter has provided you with an overview of the fundamental subject categories used in the census datasets and a crash course in using spreadsheets to work with census data. This first part of the book has laid the foundation for understanding the census, by covering the main subjects and geography, the official portal for accessing census data, and context for how the census is situated within U.S. society. We will build on this foundation in the next part as we explore each of the primary census datasets in detail.

## 4.8  REVIEW QUESTIONS AND PRACTICE EXERCISES

1. Summarize the differences between the questions on race and Hispanic/Latino origin and how these differences affect the presentation of data.

2. What is the difference between a household and a family? How are they related to one another?

3. Visit `https://data.census.gov/` and look up Table H14 Tenure by Race of Householder in the 2010 decennial census for the entire United States. Download the table, open it in a spreadsheet, reformat it, and calculate the percentage of the population who are homeowners versus renters for each race. Then download Table H15 Tenure by Hispanic or Latino Origin, and calculate the same percentage for the Hispanic population.

4. Explain what the different components of the labor force are, and what the distinction is between people who are in the labor force and people who are not.

5. Return to Exercise 2, add a "commonsense" multiplier to the estimate sheet for two people (2.0), and apply it to both the seasonal units and seasonal bedrooms to create additional estimates.

---

**Supplementary Digital Content:** Find datasets and supplemental exercises at the companion website at `http://study.sagepub.com/census`.

# THE PRIMARY DATASETS

PART II

# THE DECENNIAL CENSUS

## 5.1  INTRODUCTION

The decennial census is the original and foundational census dataset. As discussed in Chapter 1, its legal basis is in Article I Section 2 of the Constitution, which stipulates that a 10-year count of the population be taken to reapportion seats in the U.S. House of Representatives between the states and in other constitutional clauses that support the gathering of federal statistics. Each question is asked because it is required to satisfy specific federal laws. The decennial census is also used to redistrict congressional boundaries for states that gain or lose seats and by states to redraw their own assembly and legislative districts. The decennial census is crucial for providing geographically detailed baseline statistics that are used to create or benchmark other census products, such as the American Community Survey (ACS) and Population Estimates Program (PEP), as well as countless other datasets, estimates, and projections created in both the public and private sectors.

We considered the role of the census in American society in Chapter 1 and covered some of the Census Bureau's history there. We will begin this chapter with contemporary comparisons between the 2000, 2010, and the upcoming 2020 censuses. We will cover how the decennial census is conducted from start to finish and will address issues regarding how accurate it is. Then we will dig into the data itself, looking at the different summary files that the Census Bureau packages and what geographies and subjects they include. All the subjects that we covered in Chapter 4 are the basis for the decennial census, with the exception of the labor force. The exercises in this chapter demonstrate how you can pull separate data tables together in a spreadsheet and how you can use a relational database to relate and aggregate data. Once we complete a crash course in databases, you will be able to use them to store and manipulate data in bulk. A supplemental online exercise for this chapter demonstrates how to use the Census Bureau's File Transfer Protocol (FTP) site to download, parse, and load an entire summary file for a particular state into a database.

The Census Bureau's website is subdivided so that each statistical program or division has its own series of pages. These pages provide you with basic information about the program and the dataset, detailed technical documentation, release timelines, press releases, promotional materials, data visualizations, and in some cases links to actual data. To access the full series of data, you would need to use **data.census.gov**, the FTP site, or the API. The link for all the decennial census program pages is

```
https://www.census.gov/programs-surveys/decennial-census.html
```

## When Do You Use the Decennial Census?

The decennial census is a 100% count of basic population and housing variables that is available down to the smallest level of census geography—census blocks. When should you use the decennial census relative to another dataset? When:

- you need detailed counts of the population down to the smallest level of geography;

- all you require are basic demographic variables such as total population, age, sex, race, relationships, housing units, housing occupancy, and housing tenure;

- you need a precise count rather than an estimate;

- looking for baseline numbers to create estimates or projections;

- studying small population groups that are not available in other datasets;

- it is the beginning of the decade, and the data is still recent enough to represent contemporary patterns; and

- making historical comparisons with previous decennial censuses.

The decennial census will *not* be your first choice if you need

- broader socioeconomic characteristics of the population (use the ACS or CPS instead);

- data that is more current or recent (use the ACS, CPS, or PEP instead); and

- to study basic demographic variables on an annual basis (use the PEP instead).

## 5.2　THE CENSUS IN THE 21ST CENTURY

Since the 2010 census represented a major break from the recent past, we will explore the principal differences between it and the 2000 census. The 2020 census is just over the horizon, and while it will be cast in the same mold as 2010, there are a few important differences. We will discuss what those differences are, and when we can expect the 2020 data to be released.

### The Recent Past: 2000 Versus 2010

The decennial census from 1970 to 2000 is often regarded as a set that can be readily studied for historical research. While census geography has been redrawn each decade and questions have changed, the overall collection methods and variables remained fairly consistent during this period. The decennial census consisted of a short form that collected basic demographic variables from 100% of the population, and a long form that captured a wide range of socioeconomic and housing variables from a 1 in 6 sample of the population. This sample was large enough that the estimates were often treated as if they were counts.

The 2010 census represented a major break from the past. It consisted of just the 100% short form, which had only 10 questions that covered the basics (age, sex, race, relationships for people, occupancy and tenure for housing), and no long form. In 2005, the ACS was launched as a more cost-effective and timely alternative to the long form to provide ongoing statistics to characterize the socioeconomic status of the population. We will discuss the rationale for creating the ACS more fully in Chapter 6.

There were several practical implications of this change that affected everyone who relies on census data. First, the decennial census is no longer the sole and chief source for the nation's population statistics. This role is now divided between the decennial census and the ACS, and users must choose which one to use for a given purpose. Second, the ACS is a more complex dataset to work with, as it is released in a series of different period estimates with margins of error. We will discuss these challenges in Chapter 6. Last, making historical comparisons between the 2010 census and previous decennial censuses has become more difficult, as the majority of the variables that were in the decennial census of the past are no longer in the contemporary count. For example, if you wanted to compare median household income or educational attainment, these variables appeared in the 2000 and previous censuses but not in 2010. You would need to use the ACS instead, and since its methodology is quite different, the variables are not strictly comparable.

| TABLE 5.1 ● CHANGES APPROVED AND DISREGARDED FOR THE 2020 CENSUS | |
|---|---|
| **Items that are changing** | |
| Same-sex households | People can explicitly state if they have a same-sex or opposite-sex spouse or unmarried partner. Previously, there was no question about same-sex households; the data was computed based on other responses on the form. |
| Black and white ethnicity | People who identify their race as black or white can write in an optional ethnicity or nationality. Previously, this option was available for other races but not for blacks and whites. |
| Military residency | Members of the armed forces temporarily deployed overseas will now be counted at their home military base, instead of the address they provided at the time of their enlistment. |
| **Items that are *not* changing** | |
| Prison residency | Prison inmates will still be counted at the location where they are incarcerated and not at the address they had prior to their incarceration. |
| Hispanic and Latino | This category will remain as an ethnicity question that is separate from the race question. |
| MENA race | People of Middle Eastern or North African origin will continue to be counted as white and not as a separate race. |
| Gender identity | There will be no question on gender, sexual identity, or sexual preference. The question on sex continues to be based strictly on male/female biology (chromosomes, anatomy, hormones) and not on gender or identity. |
| Citizenship | There will be no question on citizenship status. This data will continue to be collected as part of the ACS. |

## The Near Future: 2010 Versus 2020

The upcoming 2020 census will be similar to 2010, in that it will consist of a short form that 100% of the population completes that asks the same basic questions. Since the decennial census captures the primary subject characteristics that are collected across most census datasets, we covered whether the questions were going to change or not in the previous chapter. This information is summarized in Table 5.1. The primary changes that are being made for the 2020 census are that military personnel who are temporarily deployed overseas will be counted at their home military base instead of the home address they filed at enlistment, white and black respondents will be able to write in an ethnicity or nationality for the first time, and same-sex couples will be able to explicitly identify whether they are unmarried partners.

We did not address citizenship in the previous chapter because it is not one of the primary subject characteristics, but it is one of many questions that was traditionally asked on the decennial census long form (from 1960 to 2000) and now on the ACS (from 2005 to present). The last time citizenship was asked as part of the decennial census was in 1950 (Keith, 2018). Adding a citizenship question to the 2020 census was controversial, and in June 2019 the Supreme Court ruled that the question could, not be added, given that it could not be justified by the rationale the Department of Commerce provided.

Federal agencies can submit requests to the Census Bureau to add new questions to the decennial census and future versions of the ACS in order to obtain data they need to fulfill specific legal obligations that their agency is charged with. In late 2017, the Department of Justice requested that the Census Bureau add a question on citizenship to the 2020 census to have better data on voting-age citizens in order to protect against discrimination of racial and language minorities under the Voting Rights Act.

The request was unusual because the Department of Justice presented no evidence to demonstrate how a question on citizenship was related to protecting minorities, nor did they present any analysis to demonstrate how the ACS data was insufficient for their needs. Further investigation revealed that this request actually did not originate from the Department of Justice, but it came from the Secretary of Commerce and was politically motivated. At the time this book was written, several state and local governments filed lawsuits against the Department of Commerce, and cases were winding their way through the courts. The Supreme Court ruled that the Commerce Department's justification for adding the question was contrived, and the administration decided to drop the matter. (Kendall & Adamy, 2019; H. L. Wang, 2019).

Opposition to adding the question was fierce. The two previous Secretaries of Commerce and the six previous Directors of the Census Bureau who served under both Republican and Democratic administrations have voiced strong objections (Pritzker & Gutierrez, 2018). The Census Bureau's primary mission is to ensure that the count is as accurate as possible. To achieve this, they must give the public assurance and confidence that their individual, personal responses will not be published or shared with anyone (including other branches of the government), that the data will only be summarized by groups and geographies for statistical purposes, and that the Census Bureau has no obligation to support other agencies that have regulatory enforcement powers.

In the early 21st century, trust in government institutions is at an all-time low. Census experts and policy makers believed that many immigrants would refuse to fill out the form out of fear that their responses would be used against them by regulatory agencies (H. L. Wang, 2018h). This could result in an undercount that would influence how Congress is apportioned, how federal dollars are allocated, and how accurate the hundreds (if not thousands) of datasets derived from the decennial census would be. Some members of Congress who favored adding the question incorrectly claimed that citizenship data should be taken into account when apportioning seats and redistricting, even though there are 220 years of history and several Supreme Court cases that emphasize that the census must be a count of the total population, not the voting population or the citizen population or the legal population. State and local government officials argue that they must provide services to everyone who lives in their jurisdiction regardless of what their status is, and therefore, every person who lives in their jurisdiction must be counted (H. L. Wang, 2018a, 2018g).

## 5.3    THE DATA COLLECTION PROCESS

In its operational plan, the Bureau states that "the goal of the 2020 Census is to count everyone once, only once, and in the right place" (U.S. Census Bureau, 2018a). While the goal is straightforward, achieving it requires a large and complex series of tasks that involves many departments, agencies, and stakeholders. The work begins shortly after the last census is conducted and is not complete until a few years after the count is taken. Figure 5.1 illustrates the primary operational components for conducting the census, but there are some operations that come before and after this process. In this section, we will examine the process from start to finish.

### Leading Up to the Count

In the decade leading up to a decennial census, the Census Bureau conducts tests to experiment with data-gathering and -processing procedures to determine whether and how the next census should change. They create different versions of census forms and test different questions to see how they affect responses. They also experiment with their own processes, such as the best approaches for following up with people who do not respond. After years of testing, they summarize the results and create internal proposals by mid-decade, so that final proposals on subjects and questions can be presented to Congress a few years prior to census day. The Bureau conducts a dry run of the final procedures in one or more test locations a couple of years prior to the census to identify any unforeseen problems.

Once testing is complete, the operational plan takes shape and the items in Figure 5.1 can be addressed. The first step is establishing where to count. The Census Bureau

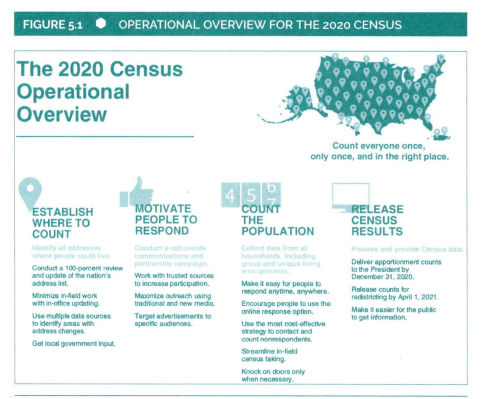

*Source:* U.S. Census Bureau (2018a).

maintains a Master Address File (MAF) of all addresses in the United States. This file is a crucial component of the decennial census that is used for mailing out census forms and keeping track of every household and group quarters institution that has (and has not) returned its form. By the time the count is complete, every address in the file must be accounted for and marked as submitted, not submitted, or invalid address. Census enumerators use the MAF to go out into the field to contact hard-to-count locations that are not contacted by mail and to follow up personally with nonresponders. The Census Bureau updates the MAF on an ongoing basis using administrative records from local government officials, building permit data for new homes, and data from the U.S. Postal Service. The Local Update of Census Address Operations (LUCA) is a program that launches about 3 years prior to the decennial census that encourages state, local, and tribal officials to work with the Bureau in updating addresses for their areas.

There are two additional operations that are part of the process for updating census geography. The Boundary and Annexation Survey (BAS) is conducted on annual basis to record changes for all legal geographies: states, counties, incorporated places, municipal civil divisions, and certain tribal areas. Since the survey is annual, changes for these areas are incorporated into each version of the ACS and ultimately into the next decennial census. The Participant Statistical Areas Program (PSAP) is charged with updating the boundaries of all the census statistical areas, which happens only once every 10 years just prior to the decennial census. The Census Bureau updates the census block boundaries and then drafts a proposal with updated boundaries for census tracts, block groups, census-designated places, and census county divisions. Members of state, local, and tribal governments as well as regional planning organizations are invited to join the program, where they can review and propose changes to the boundaries. The program begins about 2 years prior to the census and concludes at the end of the census year.

The Census Bureau lays the groundwork for a public relations campaign a few years before the decennial census. The Bureau advertises through traditional mass media and social media platforms, but a large aspect of the public relations campaign are the Census Bureau's partnering programs. The Bureau has six regional offices that coordinate outreach to individual states, counties, and communities. They offer educational programs and sponsor events and work with local stakeholders such as local governments, nonprofits, schools, universities, and community groups to help them reach individual communities and neighborhoods. The PR campaign emphasizes that everyone counts and must be counted to ensure that your community is represented, the census is key to the functioning of our government and the distribution of federal funds, and your personal information is kept confidential.

## The Counting Process

The decennial census has always been conducted in the first year of each decade (ending in zero) and April 1 has been the official census day since 1930. In reality, this date is just a reference point for filling in the form; the count itself is conducted over a period of several weeks. The census has been conducted through the mail since 1970, but for the first time households will be able to respond over the internet in 2020. The Census Bureau has had a few years to perfect the platform as households have had the option to respond to the ACS online. Households can elect to fill out and submit a paper form or go online using a code that is sent in the mail. The paper and electronic forms are available in a variety of languages to help ensure that non-English speakers and ESL (English as second language) speakers can respond.

All households are required by law to submit the census. If a household does not respond, they are sent another form and may receive a phone call. If there is still no response, the Census Bureau may send a census taker out to the household to conduct the count in person. In the year leading up to the census, the Census Bureau hires and trains hundreds of thousands of temporary workers who go out into the field to assist with outreach, to update the MAF based on visual inspection, and to knock on doors and follow up with households that do not respond. Obviously, this increases the cost of the census to a large degree. Based on outside recommendations, in 2020, the Census Bureau will attempt to decrease the cost associated with nonresponse follow-up by focusing more energy on improving the MAF and relying on administrative records such as tax returns, Medicaid applications, and public utility records to "fill in the blanks" for households that do not respond (Cook, Norwood, & Cork, 2011).

The Center for Urban Research at the Graduate Center for the City University of New York (CUNY) created web mapping applications for the 2010 and 2020 census that depict hard-to-count areas at the census tract level. The 2020 maps illustrate the mail return rate, which is the percentage of households that responded to the census by mail (Figure 5.2). The map shades census tracts that were in the bottom 20% of return rates, where less than 74% of the tract's households responded by mail. The application also provides data for measuring other risks of a low count such as low internet connectivity rates (as 2020 will be the first decennial census that can be submitted over the internet) and the percentage of the population who are minorities (who tend to be undercounted). The map is useful for identifying communities that had a low response rate, so that stakeholders and census partners can target public relations in these areas and provide assistance to help increase the response rate.

**FIGURE 5.2  ●  HARD-TO-COUNT MAP FOR 2020 CENSUS**

*Source:* City Universityof New York Mapping Service at the Center for Urban Research, CUNY Graduate Center. https://www.censushardtocountmaps2020.us/

## INFOBOX 5.1 THE HOMELESS POPULATION

The decennial census must count everyone residing in the United States, including the homeless. Since the census is designed to tabulate people by address within residences, counting this population is particularly difficult and requires that census enumerators go out into the field and work with service-based organizations to identify and count people who are homeless. This specific program is called the Service-Based Enumeration Operation.

For the 2010 census, this program was conducted over 3 days from March 29 to 31, and each day focused on counting the homeless in three distinct places: (1) emergency and transitional shelters for people experiencing homelessness, (2) soup kitchens and regularly scheduled food vans, and (3) nonsheltered outdoor locations. The shelters were distinguished from other types of emergency shelters that are used in the event of natural disasters, and the nonsheltered outdoor locations included vehicles, public parks, tent encampments, and any location where people experiencing homelessness live without having to pay. These locations are counted as different types of noninstitutional group quarters facilities.

While the Census Bureau counts homeless people, it does not publish data tables or even summary totals of the homeless population. There is no standard definition or consensus as to what constitutes homelessness, and the Census Bureau acknowledges that the complexity of this group makes it likely that they are missing people in the service-based count. It is also likely that people who are homeless may be counted within different segments of the population outside of this service-based group; for example, someone who has no home and is temporarily staying with a friend or relative.

The Census Bureau does tabulate the emergency and transitional shelters for people experiencing homelessness as a specific group quarters type in Table PCT20, and it published a summary report on this segment of the population (A. S. Smith, Holmberg, & Jones-Puthoff, 2012) that included 209,325 people in 2010. Specific counts for the soup kitchen and nonsheltered locations are not available, as they are aggregated into a summary category for Other noninstitutional facilities that includes group quarters types that are not related to homelessness.

If you are working with small-level geography like census tracts within large cities, and discover some nonresidential areas that have small population counts, it is possible that these counts include the soup kitchen or nonsheltered populations (the other possibility would be a housing unit mistakenly assigned to the tract). For example, Census Tract 1 in New York County, New York, encompasses all of Central Park in Manhattan. In 2010, the tract had 25 people but no housing units or households. All 25 people were counted as being in noninstitutional group quarters.

Not all households receive a form. Census tracts that are particularly difficult to count use a special Update/Leave method, where census enumerators go into the field and distribute census forms by hand. The Update/Leave areas are a mixed group that includes seasonal areas that have a large number of vacant units, rural areas and Native American areas where addresses and streets are not well marked, and areas with large seasonal migrant worker populations. Unconventional housing units, such as cars, recreational vehicles, boats, and hotels and motels are captured over a fixed period of time through address canvasing. These types of units are counted only if they are occupied and the people living there count this as their usual place of residence when the census is taken.

The group quarters population is handled separately. Addresses in the MAF are marked to indicate whether they are group quarters dwellings, and this list has to be updated and verified on a regular basis. The administrator of the group quarters dwelling is contacted in advance to remind him or her that the census is approaching. Administrators may distribute the forms to individuals and collect them for submission to the Census Bureau, or they may use their own records to complete the questionnaire on behalf of the residents. In the case of service-based organizations (soup kitchens, homeless shelters), the Census Bureau takes a more direct role in visiting the quarters to count people in person (InfoBox 5.1).

Completed paper forms are scanned and entered into a system along with data captured directly via the internet. As data enters the system, addresses from the MAF are marked as complete, while nonrespondents are flagged for follow-up and addresses identified as invalid are marked for removal. Each address must be registered as being occupied, vacant, or nonexistent. The Bureau reconciles duplicates for addresses that have submitted more than one form.

At some point, the Census Bureau decides to cease nonresponse follow-up and scrutinizes the data it has collected. For forms that were not submitted, that were partially filled out, or that contain conflicting information (a birth date and an age that don't match, the total number of individuals recorded does not match the number of individuals listed on the form, a race written in as "Some Other Race" that could be classified under one of the specific categories) the Bureau uses a series of procedures called imputation. Imputation has three distinct components: (1) assignments, (2) allocations, (3) and substitutions. Assignments are made on an item-by-item basis for individual characteristics, when one item for a person is inconsistent with another item. The inconsistent item is assigned an appropriate value based on other information on the form (e.g., the age and birth date) or even from characteristics submitted for a matched person record in the previous decennial census or the ACS. Allocation is used to impute data for missing person or housing characteristics. In this case, responses are derived based on responses from a person with similar characteristics who lives in the same geographic area. Substitution is used to derive a full set of characteristics for an entire household (instead of just one person). If there is some indication that a household contains several people but no occupants are listed, or they are listed but no characteristics are given, then another household in the same area that is of similar size is duplicated and used as a substitute for the missing household.

While the Census Bureau strives to get a 100% count, it is simply not possible to get a response from every single person in a country as large and complex as the United States. The final mail participation rate was 74% for all households in both the 2010 and 2000 censuses, which required costly field visits to the remaining 26%. The number of allocations and substitutions for every geographic area are published as part of each decennial census (assignments are not). Of the total population in 2010, 1.9% of the population was substituted, and for the population that was not substituted, 8.4% had one or more items allocated. In the 2010 census, the Bureau published substitution numbers for the total population and occupied housing units in Tables P44 and H20, respectively, and substitution numbers for specific characteristics in Tables P45 to P51 for population and H21 and H22 for housing units.

The final step in the operational plan is to release and publish the results. We will discuss this in detail in the next section on data. Before we do, let's address the issue of accuracy.

## Postcensus Activities and Accuracy

How accurate is the decennial census? While the U.S. Census is arguably one of the most accurate population counts in the world, it is inevitable that some percentage of the population will be missed and that some degree of undercounting (missing people) and overcounting (counting people more than once) will occur. Following each decennial census, the Bureau conducts a series of tests to determine how accurate it was. There are two different approaches for creating coverage estimates, which measure how accurately different populations were covered.

The first approach uses postenumeration surveys. A survey that asks similar questions to the decennial census is sent to a sample of the population, and the individuals who respond to this survey are matched to their decennial census response to determine whether people were missed or counted twice. The second approach is called demographic analysis, which relies on data from the PEP. Administrative data for births, deaths, and migration is compared with the decennial census count to identify discrepancies by age, sex, and race.

Based on analyses from postenumeration surveys, the decennial census slightly overcounted the total U.S. population by 0.01% ($\pm$0.14) in 2010 and by 0.49% ($\pm$0.20) in 2000. In contrast, the 1990 census undercounted the population by 1.61% ($\pm$0.20). It is important to remember that these estimates represent net differences; some people are duplicated, while others are missed. The analysis estimated that there were 10 million erroneous enumerations in 2010, of which 8.5 million were duplicates, and 16 million omissions, of which only 6 million were captured by imputation (Mule, 2012).

The fact that undercounts and overcounts are differential is a major issue. Some population groups and parts of the country tend to be undercounted (minorities, urban areas, renters), while others tend to be overcounted (whites, suburban areas, homeowners). The census began conducting postenumeration surveys in 1940, but it was not until 1970 that the issue garnered a lot of public attention. Net and differential undercounts after the 1980 and 1990 censuses led to decades of controversy and lawsuits, as many cities, states, and stakeholder suits sued the Bureau over the results of the count (Anderson, 2015). As discussed previously, the Supreme Court ruled against statistically adjusting the census to account for the differentials and against replacing the count with a survey. Because of these controversies, the Census Bureau did increase its efforts to get a better count through public relations, the creation and ongoing maintenance of the MAF file, and improvements in nonresponse follow-up and imputation.

While there have been improvements and the net undercounts have been replaced with overcounts, problems remain. In 1990, the black population was undercounted by 4.6%; in 2000 and 2010, the undercount was reduced to around 2%. In contrast, the non-Hispanic white population went from an undercount of approximately 0.7% in 1990 to an overcount of about 1% in 2010. About 1.5% of all Hispanic people were missed in 2010, down from 5% in 1990, and about 5% of Native Americans who lived on reservations were missed in 2010, down from a shockingly high 12% in 1990 (Mule, 2012).

Once the Census Bureau publishes the official numbers, they are difficult to change. The original numbers that are released are used in the apportionment process, so they are never removed or revised. In recent decades, there have been count resolution programs, where state, local, and tribal officials may challenge their jurisdictions' census counts. The name for the program in 2010 was the Census Count Question Resolution (CQR) Program. Jurisdictions are able to submit challenges for their counts within a fixed period of time following the census. If the Census Bureau accepts a challenge, it issues official revised counts to those governments and incorporates these changes into subsequent population estimates for that community in the PEP. An errata document is published and footnotes are added to the appropriate tables that are available via **data.census.gov**.

## 5.4   DECENNIAL CENSUS DATA

In the not too distant past, publishing the decennial census required several series of books that numbered in the thousands and took up several aisles of shelves in a library. The Census Bureau provided machine-readable data in a number of formats

**FIGURE 5.3** ● THE CENSUS BUREAU'S FIRST WEBSITE

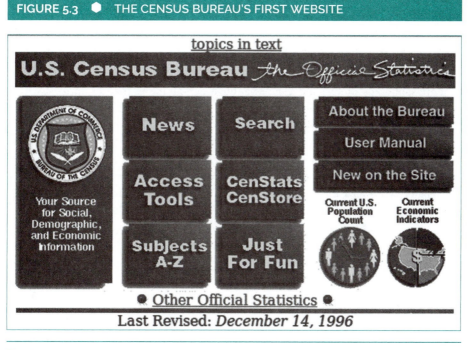

Source: Internet Archive https://web.archive.org/web/19961227012639/http://www.census.gov/

(punch cards, data tape, disks, and CDs) that computer users could access by visiting a library or research lab. The internet changed all of this, allowing individuals to look up facts or download as much data as they want. The 2000 census was the last time that the data was published in bulk in physical and print products.

The Census Bureau launched its first website in the mid-1990s (Figure 5.3) and immediately began to make its data accessible through applications like Quick Facts and the American Factfinder, which was launched before the 2000 census. The Factfinder went through a significant overhaul prior to the 2010 census, and it and many other applications are being replaced with **data.census.gov** just in time for the 2020 census.

As we have seen, the data is published via many channels: in part, through the decennial census program web page and in full via **data.census.gov**, the Census Bureau's FTP site (for bulk downloads), through appilcation programming interfaces (for access via scripts and programs). There is also a series of research reports that summarize the major characteristics of the population that is distributed through the Census Bureau's online library.

While there have been changes in platforms and technology, the fundamental structure and grouping of the data releases has remained consistent for the past several decades. The Census Bureau summarizes the individual responses by characteristics and geographies into a series of tables for population and housing, and these tables are bundled into collections called summary files. The summary files are broken down into a series of individual state-based files (all 50 states, District of Columbia, and Puerto Rico) that contain geographies that nest within states (and a few geographies that are split across states) and a national file for geographies that do not nest within states. Data for the U.S. territories other than Puerto Rico are collected as part of the Island Areas Census (InfoBox 5.2).

It takes about 3 years from census day on April 1 for all of the decennial summary data to be released, but most of the data that's of the broadest interest to researchers is available within 18 months. For the 2020 census, redistricting data will be published in April 2011, and the bulk of the summary file data will be released between May 2021 and September 2022. All 2020 census data products will be released by April 2023.

In the next sections, we look at each of the summary products in order of their release.

---

✔ **INFOBOX 5.2 U.S. TERRITORIES AND THE ISLAND AREA CENSUS**

The decennial census includes all 50 states, the District of Columbia, Puerto Rico, and U.S. civilians and the military who are living abroad. It does not include residents of the other populated U.S. territories: American Samoa, the Northern Marianas, Guam, and the U.S. Virgin Islands. The populations of these territories are counted as part of the Island Areas Census (IAC), which is conducted concurrently with the decennial census. Data for each territory is released individually in its own summary file named for the territory.

There are three key differences between the decennial census and the IAC. First, since the territories do not vote in federal elections, their population totals are not used for apportionment (as they have no seats in Congress), but they can use the data for reapportioning their own local legislatures (data is provided for tracts, block groups, and blocks). Second, the census is not conducted by mail. Enumerators visit each residence to do the count in person, or they drop off forms for the household to fill out and return to pick them up. Third, all residents of the island areas (not just a sample) fill out a census long form that captures detailed socioeconomic and housing characteristics. The form for 2020 will be similar to the ACS questionnaire, with adjustments that match the residency and time frame concepts used in the decennial census. The reason for this is that the Island Areas are not included in the ACS, so this is the only opportunity to capture detailed data for them.

Even though Puerto Rico is a territory and has no federal representation in Congress (and thus is not part of the apportionment process), it *is* included in both the regular decennial census and in the ACS, and it is essentially treated like a state. Its population is not included in total population counts of the United States.

## PL 94-171

Under Title 13 of the U.S. Code (which is the body of federal law under which the Census Bureau is governed), the Bureau is required to present population totals for each of the states to the president before the end of December of the census year. These are the counts that are used to launch the process of reapportioning seats in Congress (InfoBox 5.3). The next milestone is the release of data for legislative redistricting. Public Law (PL) 94-171 was passed in 1975 and stipulates that geographically detailed data for redistricting must be delivered to Congress within 1 year of the decennial census (April 1, 2021, for the 2020 census).

---

✔ **INFOBOX 5.3 APPORTIONMENT**

The first statistics that are published from the decennial census are the total population counts for each of the states, which are used for reapportioning seats in the U.S. House of Representatives. The totals and apportionment results must be presented to the president by Deccember 31 of the census year.

There are 435 seats in the House. Each state is guaranteed to have at least one seat, so that these seats are assigned to each state and the remaining 385 seats are apportioned. Apportionment is conducted using the method of equal proportions, which was adopted in 1941. A priority value (PV) is calculated for all possible seats in every single state, where the state's total population is divided by the geometric mean of its current $(n-1)$ and next $(n)$ potential seat number. Since there are 50 states and 385 seats, you could calculate a list of all 19,250 values, but in general, it's sufficient to calculate enough values to account for the largest number of seats in a particular state. Since California has the most seats (53), we could calculate 60 priority values for each state to safely account for all possible seats (Burnett, 2011).

For example, the second and third seats (the first seat is never calculated, as it's assigned before the formula is applied) for Alabama is calculated as follows:

$$PV \text{ (second seat AL)} = \frac{4,802,982}{\sqrt{2*1}} = 3,396,221$$

$$PV \text{ (third seat AL)} = \frac{4,802,982}{\sqrt{3*2}} = 1,960,809$$

These calculations are repeated for the 60 potential seats in Alabama and then repeated 60 times for the other states. Once the priority values have been calculated, they are combined into a single list and ranked from the highest to the lowest, and seats are distributed one by one to each state based on where their priority values appear.

Once Congress receives the apportionment results, it informs the governors of each of the states. States that gain or lose seats must redraw their Congressional Districts using the redistricting data provided by the Census Bureau in PL 94-171. Redistricting must be completed in time for the elections for the next Congress, 2 years following the census. Once the new boundaries are drawn, the Census Bureau updates Summary File 1 by tabulating data for the new districts.

PL 94-171 is the first of the major census datasets to be released and, thus, it provides the first glimpse as to how America has changed since the last decennial census. In 2010, the dataset contained just five tables:

P1:   Race

P2:   Hispanic or Latino and not Hispanic or Latino by Race

P3:   Race for the Population 18 Years and Over

P4:   Hispanic or Latino and not Hispanic or Latino by Race for the Population 18 Years and Over

H1:   Occupancy Status (Housing)

Data in PL 94-171 is provided down to the smallest level, census blocks, so that officials have the most detailed data possible for redrawing congressional districts and state and local assembly districts. Most state officials participate in a voluntary program to have data tabulated for voting districts and other state-specific areas. In addition to voting and congressional districts, the state-based files include counties, county subdivisions, places, census tracts, block groups, blocks, school districts, and some Native American areas. A month or so after the state-based files are released, a national file is published that includes regions, divisions, states, and other Native American areas.

PL 94-171 is the smallest and the most manageable of the data releases, and since it is the first release, it receives a lot of attention. The general usefulness of PL 94-171 diminishes once Summary File 1 is published, and at that point, it is typically used just by researchers who are interested in voting and redistricting.

## Summary File 1

Summary File 1 (SF1) is the primary dataset that most researchers who work with decennial census data use. SF1 for the 2010 census consisted of 333 tables available down to the census block or census tract level, and in a few instances down to just the county level. In 2010, the earliest releases of this data occurred between late spring 2011 and summer 2011, when the demographic profile tables (DP01) were released. SF1 for each of the states was released on a rolling basis throughout the summer of 2011, and the national file was released in mid-fall 2011. The addition of the urban and rural population and data for new congressional districts were the final elements released a year later in the fall of 2012.

| TABLE 5.2 ● VARIABLES IN THE 2010 CENSUS | |
| --- | --- |
| **Population (P Tables)** | **Housing (H Tables)** |
| Population | Housing units |
| Urban/rural status | Occupancy status |
| Race | Vacancy status |
| Hispanic or Latino | Tenure (owners/renters) |
| Sex | |
| Age | |
| Households | |
| Families | |
| Relationships | |
| Group quarters | |

The variables that are included in the 2010 census are listed in Table 5.2 and include all the major subject characteristics that we covered in Chapter 4 (with the exception of labor force status). Many of these variables appear in multiple tables where they are cross tabulated by each other. These same variables will be included in the 2020 census, with the possible addition of citizenship. If the citizenship question is asked, it will ask whether respondents are citizens born in the United States, born in the U.S. territories, born abroad of U.S. citizen parent or parents, by naturalization (with year naturalized), or not a citizen. The question will not ask noncitizens about their visa (permanent or temporary) or legal status.

While many of the tables in SF1 are available down to the block level, because of the small size of some populations, the Bureau tabulates detailed data for certain tables only down to tracts and in a few instances to counties. So in some cases, you will see tables that have the same name or title but different ID numbers, because the tables offer different levels of detail.

For example, Table P42 Group Quarters Population by Group Quarters Type summarizes the group quarters population by type for the institutionalized and non-institutionalized population down to the block level, but there are a limited number of subcategories (Table 5.3). There is a tally for all correctional facilities for adults but not for specific types of correctional facilities. Table PCT20 Group Quarters Population by Group Quarters Type summarizes this same population down to the census tract level but provides several additional subcategories. For correctional facilities for

| TABLE 5.3    ●    2010 CENSUS TABLE P42 GROUP QUARTERS (GQ) POPULATION BY GQ TYPE |
| --- |
| **U.S. Total:** 7,987,323 |
| **Institutionalized population:** 3,993,659 |
| **Correctional facilities for adults:** 2,263,602 |
| **Juvenile facilities:** 151,315 |
| **Nursing facilities/skilled-nursing facilities:** 1,502,264 |
| **Other institutional facilities:** 76,478 |
| **Noninstitutionalized population:** 3,993,664 |
| **College/university student housing:** 2,521,090 |
| **Military quarters:** 338,191 |
| **Other noninstitutional facilities:** 1,134,383 |

adults, you can see divisions by federal detention centers, federal prisons, state prisons, local jails, correctional residential facilities, and military jails. Tables PCT20A through PCT20I provide the same summaries but for individual race and Hispanic categories. There are also tables summarizing the group quarters population by age and sex (P43 and PCT21) using the same division levels as the total count tables, but the age brackets are limited to three groups: (1) under 18, (2) 18 to 64, and (3) 65 and over. More detailed age data in 5-year cohorts is only available for certain types of facilities at the county level, in Tables PCO1 to PCO10.

Remember that variables are published in more than one table, so it pays to browse around. Table P42 contains the details about the group quarters population, but the total group quarters population subdivided by institutionalized and noninstitutionalized is also published in Table P29, Household Type by Relationship, which includes summaries of the total population, the population within households and families, and population by various relationships. Table P42 is useful for giving you the details about the group quarters population, while P29 is useful for context and comparisons (for calculating percent totals or creating an adjusted population count that removes the institutionalized population—we will do this in our first exercise).

If you want the definitive list of all the subjects, tables, and variables included in SF1, view the Technical Documentation for Summary File 1, which is available online (U.S. Census Bureau, 2012a).

## Summary File 2

SF2 is a smaller dataset that provides additional, detailed cross tabulations of data published in SF1 by 331 different combinations of race and Hispanic and Latino ethnicity categories. In the 2010 census, it contained 71 tables that go down to either the census tract or county level. SF2 was published in the spring of 2012, about 2 years after the actual count was conducted. Unless you are a researcher who specifically studies race in America, or you are interested in studying detailed elements of the multiracial population that are not captured elsewhere, you probably will not use SF2.

## Summary Files 3 and 4

These files are no longer tabulated as part of the decennial census; the last time they were used was in the 2000 census. They contained the detailed socioeconomic characteristics of the population (SF3) and their cross-tabulation by detailed racial groups (SF4). The data that was collected in SF3 is now captured in the ACS. Data that was captured in SF4 is largely unavailable given the small sample sizes used in the ACS.

# 5.5   EXERCISES

These exercises will give you exposure to working with decennial census data and will cover some of the specific issues we addressed in this chapter. It's likely that you will often need to download data that's contained in multiple census tables and bring specific variables from those tables together in order to summarize and analyze them. In these two exercises, we will demonstrate how you can do this in a spreadsheet and a relational database for individual tables. A third, supplemental online exercise demonstrates how you can download tables in bulk using the FTP site. We will be using LibreOffice Calc again, as well as the DB Browser for SQLite. A brief description of SQLite and a link for downloading this free and open source software is available in the Introduction of the book.

Remember that you can visit the publisher's website to easily download all the data you need for doing the exercises. Alternatively, you can download each of the datasets from the sources listed below:

P29 Household Type by Relationship Sex:  2010 Decennial Census, Summary File 1, Colorado (all counties in state)—https://data.census.gov/

Rural–Urban Continuum Codes: UDSA, RUCC 2013 edition, United States (nation)—https://www.ers.usda.gov/data-products/rural-urban-continuum-codes.aspx

## Exercise 1: Relating Group Quarters and Rural Categories With Calc

In this exercise, you will learn how to tie data from two different sources together in a spreadsheet. We will cover how to reformat ID codes in order to form a relationship and how to relate them using VLOOKUP. We will also learn how to summarize data by categories using a pivot table.

As we discussed in this chapter and the previous one, the institutional group quarters population can inflate the total population of rural places. This population includes people in penitentiaries and psychiatric hospitals who are not free to come and go as they please. If we were trying to measure access to a good or service, or wanted to distribute funds for a program, we might want to remove this population as members are unlikely to participate. In this example, we will adjust the total population of all the counties in Colorado to remove this population and see what impact this has on the population ranking of the counties. Then, we will assign each county to its rural–urban continuum code (RUCC), so that we can create summaries of this adjusted population by these areas. If you recall from Chapter 3, RUCC was created by the USDA's Economic Research Service so that researchers can study the populations of rural counties in greater detail.

Since we covered the nitty-gritty details of navigating spreadsheets in the exercises in Chapter 4, we won't be going into as much detail with these steps. Refer back to the earlier exercises to refresh your memory on copying and pasting, selecting ranges, and using formulas.

1. **Open the RUCC file**. In the folder for Chapter 5 Exercise 1, open the Excel file called ruralurbancodes2013.xls in Calc. The workbook contains two sheets: one has the codes for each county, sorted by county and state, and the other has documentation (Figure 5.4).

2. **Import the households table**. Go to Sheet—Insert Sheet from File, and in the Exercise 1 folder select the file called DecennialSF12010_P29_with_ann.csv. On the Import screen, select OK, and hit OK again on the Insert screen. In the tab for the sheet, double-click on the long name and rename the tab P29. This table has data on Households by Relationship Status for the counties of Colorado. We can see the total population, the population in households, followed by columns that provide subtotals of families and relationships (Figure 5.5).

## FIGURE 5.4 ◆ USDA RURAL–URBAN CONTINUUM CODES

| | A | B | C | D | E | F |
|---|---|---|---|---|---|---|
| 1 | FIPS | State | County_Name | Population_2010 | RUCC_2013 | Description |
| 2 | 01001 | AL | Autauga County | 54,571 | 2 | Metro - Counties in metro areas of 250,000 to 1 million population |
| 3 | 01003 | AL | Baldwin County | 182,265 | 3 | Metro - Counties in metro areas of fewer than 250,000 population |
| 4 | 01005 | AL | Barbour County | 27,457 | 6 | Nonmetro - Urban population of 2,500 to 19,999, adjacent to a metro area |
| 5 | 01007 | AL | Bibb County | 22,915 | 1 | Metro - Counties in metro areas of 1 million population or more |
| 6 | 01009 | AL | Blount County | 57,322 | 1 | Metro - Counties in metro areas of 1 million population or more |
| 7 | 01011 | AL | Bullock County | 10,914 | 6 | Nonmetro - Urban population of 2,500 to 19,999, adjacent to a metro area |
| 8 | 01013 | AL | Butler County | 20,947 | 6 | Nonmetro - Urban population of 2,500 to 19,999, adjacent to a metro area |
| 9 | 01015 | AL | Calhoun County | 118,572 | 3 | Metro - Counties in metro areas of fewer than 250,000 population |
| 10 | 01017 | AL | Chambers County | 34,215 | 6 | Nonmetro - Urban population of 2,500 to 19,999, adjacent to a metro area |
| 11 | 01019 | AL | Cherokee County | 25,989 | 6 | Nonmetro - Urban population of 2,500 to 19,999, adjacent to a metro area |

## FIGURE 5.5 ◆ TABLE P29 HOUSEHOLDS BY HOUSEHOLD TYPE

| | A | B | C | D | E |
|---|---|---|---|---|---|
| 1 | GEO.id | GEO.display-label | D001 | D002 | D003 |
| 2 | Geographic identifier code | Geographic area name | Total: | Total: - In households: | Total: - In households: - In family households: |
| 3 | 0500000US08001 | Adams County | 441603 | 437576 | 378879 |
| 4 | 0500000US08003 | Alamosa County | 15445 | 14705 | 11976 |
| 5 | 0500000US08005 | Arapahoe County | 572003 | 567083 | 470646 |
| 6 | 0500000US08007 | Archuleta County | 12084 | 11955 | 9911 |
| 7 | 0500000US08009 | Baca County | 3788 | 3706 | 3001 |
| 8 | 0500000US08011 | Bent County | 6499 | 4291 | 3573 |
| 9 | 0500000US08013 | Boulder County | 294567 | 285618 | 212053 |
| 10 | 0500000US08014 | Broomfield County | 55889 | 55607 | 47235 |
| 11 | 0500000US08015 | Chaffee County | 17809 | 16373 | 13073 |

The last three columns in the sheet contain the groups quarters population, institutionalized and noninstitutionalized. Save the workbook—when prompted, you can keep the file in the current .xls format.

3. **Delete columns**. The workbook has a lot of columns we don't need. If we think we might use them later, we could simply select a range of columns, right-click, and choose the option to hide them. In this case, we will delete them. Select all columns from D to AB, right-click, and choose Delete columns. Then scroll over and delete the last column (E, noninstitutionalized population). Your worksheet should have just four columns: geoid, geoname, total population, and institutionalized population. Save your work.

4. **Fix header rows**. Select the first row, right-click, and delete rows. Rename the headers to the following: geoid, county, totpop, instpop.

5. **Calculate percent total and sort**. In cell E1, type pct_inst as a label. In cell E2, enter the formula =ROUND((D2/C2)*100). Then with cell E2 selected, double-click on the small black box to paste the formula all the way down the column. Select all the columns from A to E and go to Data—Sort. Go to the Options tab and make sure the box that says Range Includes Labels is checked. Flip back to the Sort Criteria tab, and under Sort Key 1, choose pct_inst as the sort column and select Descending for the sort order, and click OK. We can see

| FIGURE 5.6 | ● | FIXED HEADERS AND CALCULATED PERCENT TOTALS |
|---|---|---|

| E2 | ▼ | f(x) | Σ | = | =ROUND((D2/C2)*100) |
|---|---|---|---|---|---|

| | A | B | C | D | E |
|---|---|---|---|---|---|
| 1 | geoid | county | totpop | instpop | pct_inst |
| 2 | 0500000US08025 | Crowley County | 5823 | 2682 | 46 |
| 3 | 0500000US08011 | Bent County | 6499 | 2149 | 33 |
| 4 | 0500000US08043 | Fremont County | 46824 | 8664 | 19 |
| 5 | 0500000US08073 | Lincoln County | 5467 | 1030 | 19 |
| 6 | 0500000US08075 | Logan County | 22709 | 3459 | 15 |
| 7 | 0500000US08063 | Kit Carson County | 8270 | 1054 | 13 |
| 8 | 0500000US08015 | Chaffee County | 17809 | 1389 | 8 |

that there are seven counties where a large percentage of the population (from 8% to 46%) is in institutional group quarters (Figure 5.6). Save your work.

6. **Calculate adjusted population**. In cell F1, add a label called adjpop (for adjusted population). In cell F2, enter the formula =C2-D2. This subtracts the institutionalized population from the total population. Copy and paste the formula all the way down.

7. **Calculate ranks**. In cell G1, add the label ranktot. In cell G2, enter the formula =RANK(C2,C$2:C$65). Copy and paste the formula all the way down. This ranks the counties by total population (remember the "$" is used to lock values, in this case the row ranges, as we don't want this to increment as we paste the formulas down). Now in cell H1, type the label rankadj. In H2, enter the formula =RANK(F2,F$2:F$65). Copy and paste the formula all the way down to rank the counties by adjusted population. Last, in cell I1, enter the label rankchange. In cell I2, enter the formula =G2-H2. Copy and paste the formula all the way down (Figure 5.7). This shows us how a county's population rank changes if its adjusted population is used instead of its total population. In Crowley County, almost half of the population is institutionalized. If we rank counties using their "free" population, Crowley's population rank falls eight positions from 48 to 56. Rural counties of similar population to Crowley but that lack a large institutionalized population, like Washington, Gilpin, and Ouray counties, increase their ranks by three positions. Save your work.

8. **Modify GEOID codes**. To relate the counties to the RUCC codes, each table needs to use the same ID codes. The RUCC table uses the Federal Information Processing Series (FIPS) code: two digits for the state and three for the county.

## FIGURE 5.7 ● CALCULATE ADJUSTED POPULATION AND CREATE RANKS

| G2 | ▼ | f(x) Σ = | =RANK(C2,C$2:C$65) |

| | A | B | C | D | E | F | G | H | I |
|---|---|---|---|---|---|---|---|---|---|
| 1 | geoid | county | totpop | instpop | pct_inst | adjpop | ranktot | rankadj | rankchange |
| 2 | 0500000US08025 | Crowley County | 5823 | 2682 | 46 | 3141 | 48 | 56 | -8 |
| 3 | 0500000US08011 | Bent County | 6499 | 2149 | 33 | 4350 | 46 | 52 | -6 |
| 4 | 0500000US08043 | Fremont County | 46824 | 8664 | 19 | 38160 | 16 | 17 | -1 |
| 5 | 0500000US08073 | Lincoln County | 5467 | 1030 | 19 | 4437 | 49 | 49 | 0 |
| 6 | 0500000US08075 | Logan County | 22709 | 3459 | 15 | 19250 | 25 | 25 | 0 |
| 7 | 0500000US08063 | Kit Carson County | 8270 | 1054 | 13 | 7216 | 40 | 43 | -3 |
| 8 | 0500000US08015 | Chaffee County | 17809 | 1389 | 8 | 16420 | 27 | 28 | -1 |
| 9 | 0500000US08027 | Custer County | 4255 | 150 | 4 | 4105 | 54 | 53 | 1 |
| 10 | 0500000US08071 | Las Animas County | 15507 | 601 | 4 | 14906 | 30 | 32 | -2 |
| 11 | 0500000US08121 | Washington County | 4814 | 184 | 4 | 4630 | 51 | 48 | 3 |

## FIGURE 5.8 ● MODIFY GEOID CODES

| A2 | ▼ | f(x) Σ = | =RIGHT(B2,5) |

| | A | B | C |
|---|---|---|---|
| 1 | fipsid | geoid | county |
| 2 | 08025 | 0500000US08025 | Crowley County |
| 3 | 08011 | 0500000US08011 | Bent County |
| 4 | 08043 | 0500000US08043 | Fremont County |
| 5 | 08073 | 0500000US08073 | Lincoln County |
| 6 | 08075 | 0500000US08075 | Logan County |
| 7 | 08063 | 0500000US08063 | Kit Carson County |
| 8 | 08015 | 0500000US08015 | Chaffee County |
| 9 | 08027 | 0500000US08027 | Custer County |
| 10 | 08071 | 0500000US08071 | Las Animas County |
| 11 | 08121 | 0500000US08121 | Washington County |

The census table uses a longer GEOID that includes the summary-level codes and the FIPS. We will need to modify these codes. In the P29 worksheet, select column A, right-click, and choose Insert Column Left. In cell A1, type the label fipsid. In cell A2, type the formula =RIGHT(B2,5). Copy and paste the formula all the way down (Figure 5.8). The formula reads the code in cell B2 and returns the text from the first five positions starting from the right side of the value. RIGHT is a function for working with text values; similar formulas include LEFT to go from the other direction and MID to read from the middle. Select column A, and do a copy–paste special for values (do *not* transpose) to replace the formulas for the fipsid with the actual values. Save your work.

9. **Tie the GQ population and RUCC codes together with VLOOKUP.** Select cell K1, and type ruccid. Select cell K2. Then on the formula bar, launch the Function Wizard—the $f(x)$ button. Scroll toward the bottom of the functions, select VLOOKUP, and hit Next. In the search criterion box, type A2 (our first fipsid). In the array box, hit the select button beside the box, navigate over to the RUCC worksheet, and select all the cells in the sheet for all columns from the first row down to the row for the District of Columbia. Hit the Select button to return to the wizard. In the Index box, type 5—this is the column number (counting from 1 in Column A to 5 in Column E) that contains the value that we want to look up. In the sort order box, we leave it blank if the array is sorted in ascending order—since the RUCC codes are sorted by FIPS, this is true (Figure 5.9). Click OK, and the value of 8 is printed in cell K2—this is the RUCC code for Crowley County.

10. **How did this work?** In the formula, we indicated that we are using the ID code in cell A2, to look up a value that's in the array in the RUCC table. Calc

FIGURE 5.9 ● FUNCTION WIZARD FOR VLOOKUP

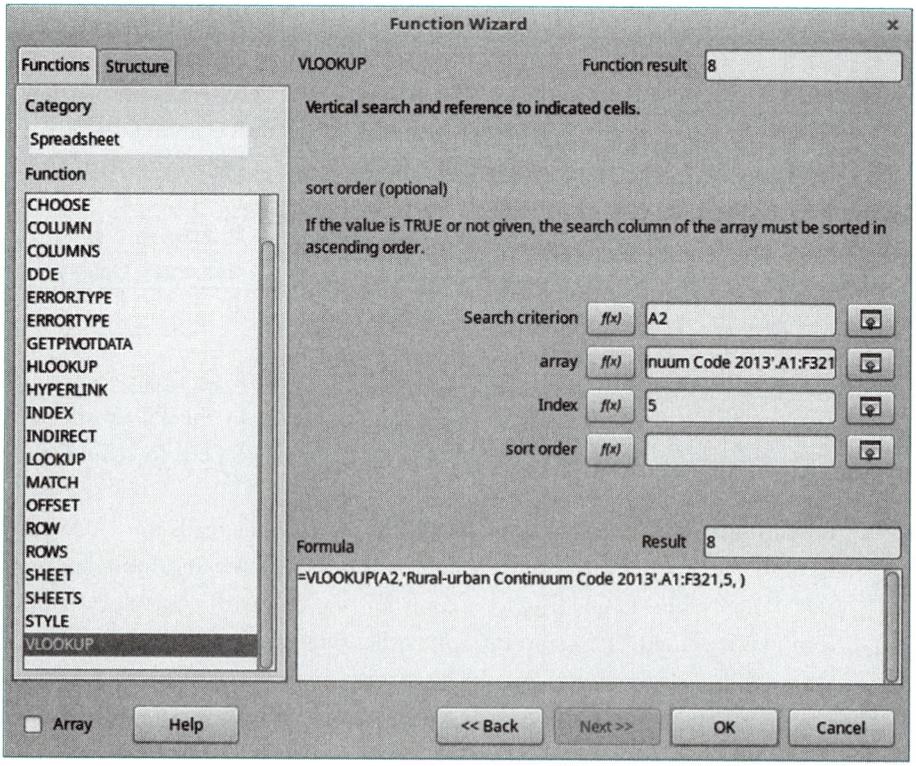

takes the value of cell A2 and looks for it in the first column of our array (so for VLOOKUP to work, the first column in the array *must* have the matching ID that we are using as a search criteria). Since the RUCC sheet is sorted by state and county, we took a shortcut and didn't select everything in the sheet but just went down to the record for DC, since we know all of Colorado is included before it. Once VLOOKUP finds the matching ID, it moves across the row to the position we specify (the RUCC ID is in Column E, the fifth column) and returns it.

11. **Modify the formula to lock cells**. Click in cell K2, and modify the formula to lock cells: =VLOOKUP($A2,'Rural-urban Continuum Code 2013'.$A$1:$F$321,5, ). Putting the dollar sign in front of cell A2 locks column A, which will allow us to paste the formula to the adjacent column without incrementing. Putting dollar signs on both sides of the column references in the array allows us to paste values down rows and across columns without the values changing. Copy the formula all the way down Column K (Figure 5.10). Save your work.

12. **Look up label values**. In cell L1, type the label: ruccname. Copy the formula from cell K2 and paste it in cell L2. In cell L2, change the formula's position value from 5 to 6. Copy and paste the formula in cell L2 all the way down the column. Save your work and spot-check one of the values to make sure the formulas are correct—our sheet says Lincoln County is ruccid 8, "Nonmetro—completely rural or less than 2,500 urban population." Go into the RUCC sheet and manually identify this county to make sure the record matches.

13. **Create pivot table**. Pivot tables are useful for summarizing data by categories and for flipping data so that a value stored in a row can become a column heading. Let's summarize Colorado's counties by RUCC category. Select Columns A through L in the P29 sheet, and go to Insert—Pivot Table. Click OK to work with the current selection. Under available fields, drag the ruccid and

---

**FIGURE 5.10** ◆ **COMPLETE VLOOKUP FORMULA**

Σ = =VLOOKUP($A2,'Rural-urban Continuum Code 2013'.$A$1:$F$321,5, )

| C county | D totpop | E instpop | F pct_inst | G adjpop | H ranktot | I rankadj | J rankchange | K ruccid | L ruccname | M | N |
|---|---|---|---|---|---|---|---|---|---|---|---|
| Crowley County | 5823 | 2682 | 46 | 3141 | 48 | 56 | -8 | 8 | Nonmetro - Completely rural or less than | | |
| Bent County | 6499 | 2149 | 33 | 4350 | 46 | 52 | -6 | 7 | Nonmetro - Urban population of 2,500 to | | |
| Fremont County | 46824 | 8664 | 19 | 38160 | 16 | 17 | -1 | 4 | Nonmetro - Urban population of 20,000 o | | |
| Lincoln County | 5467 | 1030 | 19 | 4437 | 49 | 49 | 0 | 8 | Nonmetro - Completely rural or less than | | |
| Logan County | 22709 | 3459 | 15 | 19250 | 25 | 25 | 0 | 7 | Nonmetro - Urban population of 2,500 to | | |
| Kit Carson County | 8270 | 1054 | 13 | 7216 | 40 | 43 | -3 | 7 | Nonmetro - Urban population of 2,500 to | | |
| Chaffee County | 17809 | 1389 | 8 | 16420 | 27 | 28 | -1 | 7 | Nonmetro - Urban population of 2,500 to | | |
| Custer County | 4255 | 150 | 4 | 4105 | 54 | 53 | 1 | 8 | Nonmetro - Completely rural or less than | | |
| Las Animas County | 15507 | 601 | 4 | 14906 | 30 | 32 | -2 | 7 | Nonmetro - Urban population of 2,500 to | | |
| Washington County | 4814 | 184 | 4 | 4630 | 51 | 48 | 3 | 9 | Nonmetro - Completely rural or less than | | |

**FIGURE 5.11 ● PIVOT TABLE LAYOUT MENU**

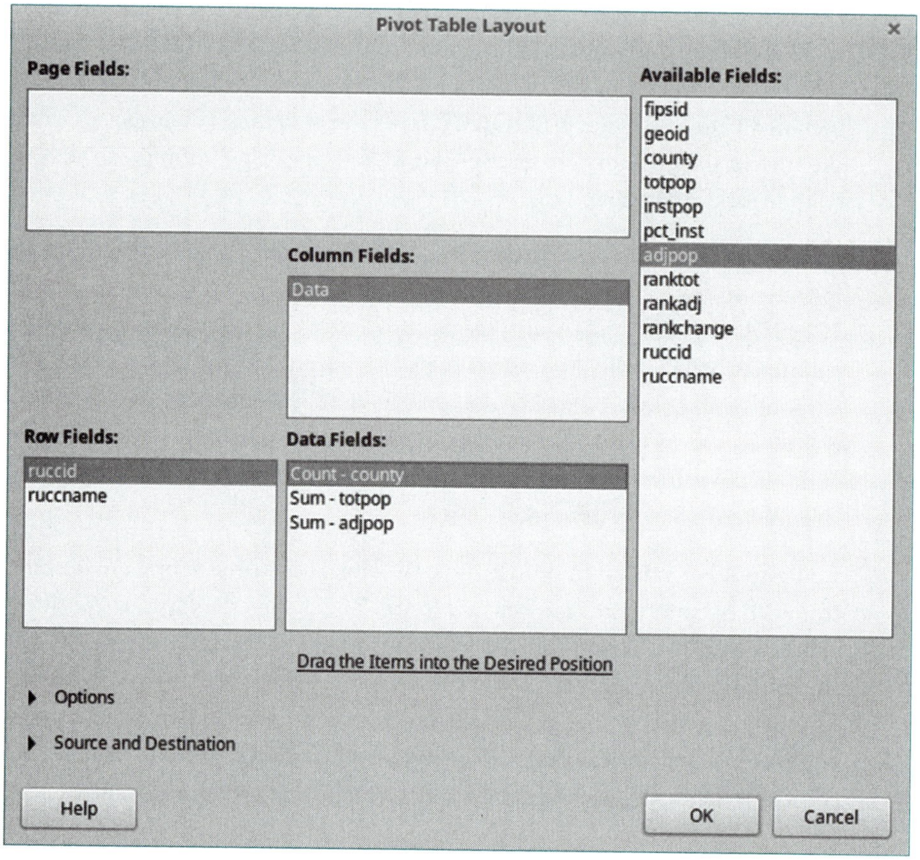

ruccname into the Row Fields box (Figure 5.11). Then drag county, totpop, and adjpop into the Data Fields box. Double-click on Sum—county in the Data Fields, select the Count function, and hit OK. Back in the Pivot Table Layout, notice there are Options at the bottom that you can modify; we will keep the defaults, so we get summaries of rows and columns. Hit OK. Calc creates the pivot table in a new sheet. For every RUCC category, we can see the number of counties in each (under the count) and the sum of both the total and adjusted population for each category (Figure 5.12). Save your work.

This example has demonstrated how you can tie two separate tables in a spreadsheet together using common ID codes and VLOOKUP and how a large group quarters populations can influence total population values for rural places.

**FIGURE 5.12 ⬡ PIVOT TABLE SUMMARIZING POPULATION BY RUCC**

| ruccid | ruccname | Count - county | Sum - totpop | Sum - adjpop |
|---|---|---|---|---|
| | | Data | | |
| 1 | Metro - Counties in metro areas of 1 million population or more | 10 | 2543482 | 2523154 |
| 2 | Metro - Counties in metro areas of 250,000 to 1 million population | 5 | 1492635 | 1481717 |
| 3 | Metro - Counties in metro areas of fewer than 250,000 population | 2 | 305786 | 301238 |
| 4 | Nonmetro - Urban population of 20,000 or more, adjacent to a metro area | 3 | 139434 | 130081 |
| 5 | Nonmetro - Urban population of 20,000 or more, not adjacent to a metro area | 3 | 136580 | 135949 |
| 6 | Nonmetro - Urban population of 2,500 to 19,999, adjacent to a metro area | 6 | 117498 | 115756 |
| 7 | Nonmetro - Urban population of 2,500 to 19,999, not adjacent to a metro area | 15 | 217518 | 207823 |
| 8 | Nonmetro - Completely rural or less than 2,500 urban population, adjacent to a metro area | 3 | 15545 | 11683 |
| 9 | Nonmetro - Completely rural or less than 2,500 urban population, not adjacent to a metro area | 17 | 60718 | 60204 |
| Total Result | | 64 | 5029196 | 4967605 |

## Exercise 2: Relating Group Quarters and Rural Categories With SQLite

In this exercise, we will use the data from our last example to accomplish the same tasks, but this time, we'll use a database to do it.

The flexibility that spreadsheets provide is great for cleaning data, moving small chunks of it around, and doing quick summaries and visualizations. But when you need to work with large amounts of data and require the ability to quickly tie related pieces of information together, spreadsheets come up short. This is because spreadsheets lack structure; they are flat files that allow you to copy and paste data anywhere you please, but this doesn't lend itself to organizing, storing, and relating large datasets. Spreadsheets can store a limited number of rows, and storing several dozen tables in different tabs and relating them with VLOOKUP is not practical. Spreadsheets also mix the formatting and presentation of data with its organization, which inhibits you from creating a solid structure.

This is where relational databases come in. In a database, data are stored in a series of tables, where a row represents the basic unit of information and the columns contain attributes that describe that unit. Each column has a data type that limits the kind of data that can be stored in it, such as text, integers, or decimal numbers. Databases give you the ability to enforce additional constraints on columns, such as specifying a range of allowable values or requiring that there be no duplicate or no null (blank) values. Ideally, each table should have a column that is designated as a primary key, which is a unique identifier that allows data to be sorted quickly and can enable two tables to be related to one another. The formal structure of a database gives the data integrity, helping ensure that the data doesn't become corrupted with duplicates or values that don't belong, and allows tables to be related to one another based on values they share in common. Databases don't focus on presentation: The order of rows and columns never matters, and there is no extemporaneous information or documentation embedded in the data.

You can interact with all traditional relational databases using the Structured Query Language, or SQL for short. SQL is a standard that is common across all databases, with some variations. The language consists of simple declarative commands in English for creating, updating, and querying data. If you learn how to use SQL, you will be able to use just about any relational database package.

We are using SQLite, which is a file-based database that's typically embedded in software applications but can also be used as a stand-alone, file-based database. SQLite is open source, and the developers create the core database program and a Command Line Interface (CLI) for interacting with it. We will be using a graphical user interface (GUI) called the Database Browser for SQLite that makes it easy to visualize and interact with our data. A full treatment of databases and the SQL language is beyond the scope of this book, but we will introduce just enough to get you started and will work with several examples throughout. For a fuller treatment of SQLite, see this tutorial at Zetcode: `http://zetcode.com/db/sqlite/` and Jay Kreibich's book *Using SQLite* (2010).

Since SQLite is a "light" database, it does not implement the full range of SQL commands. For a list of SQL commands and supported functions, visit `https://sqlite.org/lang.html`. SQLite also has a limited range of data types for columns: TEXT, INTEGER for whole numbers, REAL for decimal numbers, and BLOB for large binary objects.

1. **Rules for database tables**. Instead of using the data we created in Exercise 1, we'll go back to the beginning and start fresh. In the folder for Chapter 5 Exercise 2, open the Excel file ruralurbancodes2013.xls in Calc. To import data into a database, the data must be in a clean state, where each row represents a unit of data and each column contains the attributes. There must be only one header row, and the headings must follow these rules: They should be short, must start with a letter (not a number), must not contain spaces (use the underscore "_" character instead), and must not contain any punctuation. The columns should contain one type of data (text or numbers) and not a mixture, and there can be no formulas, no titles or footnotes, and no total or subtotal rows. Our spreadsheet must contain a column that can serve as a unique ID column. The good news is that the RUCC spreadsheet is well formatted and meets all these criteria.

2. **Save the RUCC file as a CSV**. To import the data into SQLite (and into most DB packages), we need to save the file as a CSV. Go to File— Save As and choose the option for Text CSV (.csv). Keep the file name (ruralurbancodes2013) the same. Make sure you save the file in the Exercise

FIGURE 5.13 ● EXPORT TEXT FILE MENU IN CALC

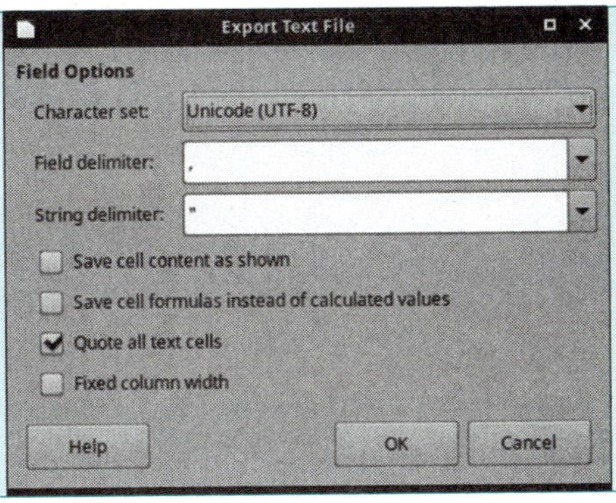

2 folder. When prompted by Calc, select the Use Text CSV Format button. When the Export Text screen appears, uncheck the box that says Save cell content as shown and check the box that says Quote all text cells (Figure 5.13). Hit OK. The file is now saved as a CSV, so we can close it.

Note: Checking the box to quote all text cells is important for two reasons. First, it ensures that any values that have a comma embedded as part of the value are "escaped," so that they are not treated as delimiters. Second, when you import CSVs into other software programs, the quoted values send a signal to that program that the data saved in them should be saved as text and not as numbers. We'll return to this in a moment.

3. **Launch SQLite and create a database**. Launch the DB Browser for SQLite. First, we need to create a new database file to serve as a container for holding our data. Click on the button for new database, browse to Chapter 5 Exercise 2 folder, and save it as exercise2.sqlite. Once we do, a dialog box pops up that asks whether we would like to create a blank table. Hit Cancel.

4. **Import the RUCC data as a table**. Go to File—Import—Table from CSV File. Browse to where the ruralurbancodes2013.csv file is stored and select it. Once we do, we'll get a preview of what the table will look like. Change the table name to rucc and check the box that says Column names in first line. Make sure your screen looks like the screen in Figure 5.14. If your version of the DB Browser for SQLite contains an options menu for autodetecting values, turn autodetect off. Then hit OK, and once the import is complete, hit OK again. In the database window on the Database Structure tab, we'll see our new table called rucc. Select the table, and hit the little down arrow beside it. This allows us to see all the columns in the table and the decisions the database made in assigning the column types.

FIGURE 5.14 ● IMPORT RUCC CSV INTO SQLITE BROWSER

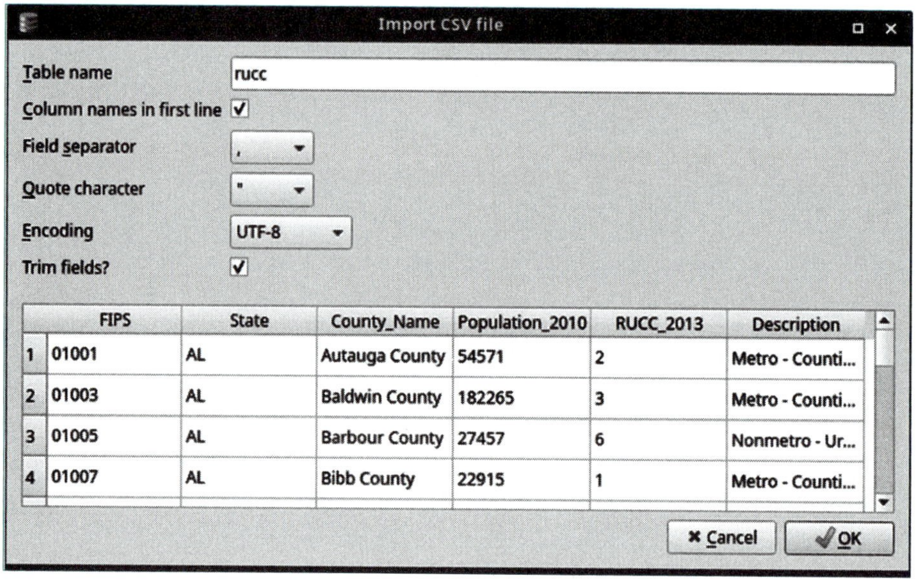

Old versions of the DB Browser for SQLite would automatically import all columns as text, which then requires the user to modify the column's data types after import. The newer version of the software has an autodetect feature that attempts to assign the most appropriate data type to each column. This feature can be switched off under the options menu. It is important that you study your data when deciding whether to turn this feature on or off. If you have any ID codes that consist solely of numbers and have leading zeros, like FIPS or ZIP codes, these codes will be saved as integers and the leading zeros will be dropped, rendering the codes useless. To avoid this, you should turn autodetect off as we did in this case. On the other hand, if your data does not contain any codes like this—say your data uses the full GEOID that has a mix of alphanumeric characters—then it's better to leave autodetect on to save yourself the time and trouble of changing the types manually.

You also need to be careful when modifying data types, as there is a possibility that data can be lost. For example, if a column contains decimal numbers and you assign it an integer type, the numbers will be rounded off and you will lose everything to the right of the decimal place.

Since we turned autodetect off, we must assign the types ourselves. Select the table, hit the modify table button, and then assign the right types. Every column should be saved as text except the RUCC codes and population columns, which should be saved as integers. You can also designate constraints, such as indicating a primary key column (unique identifier) or requiring that a column contain no null values (blanks). Designate the FIPS column as the primary key by checking the PK box (Figure 5.15).

5. **Explore the interface**. Hit the Browse Data tab, and with the rucc table selected in the top drop-down menu, you'll see the actual data (Figure 5.16). Note that you can use the GUI to do a number of operations: Clicking on a column name sorts the table by that column, and if you click in a cell you can edit it in the Edit Database Cell window on the right. In the lower right-hand window, change the tab to DB Schema, and you will be able to see the database structure and the actual table view simultaneously. Table 5.4 summarizes the functions of the menus and tabs in the DB Browser.

6. **Save your work**. Hit the Write Changes button to save your work. In a traditional database, any action you perform is executed and saved the second you do it. The DB Browser has this additional saving mechanism as a safety feature; you can use Revert Changes if you need to undo something you did.

7. **First SQL statements—basic SELECT**. Hit the Execute SQL tab, and in the lower right-hand corner, select the DB Schema tab. This is an ideal configuration that let's us see our database structure while we write statements (in the

**FIGURE 5.15 ● TABLE BROWSER AND MODIFYING TABLE DEFINITIONS**

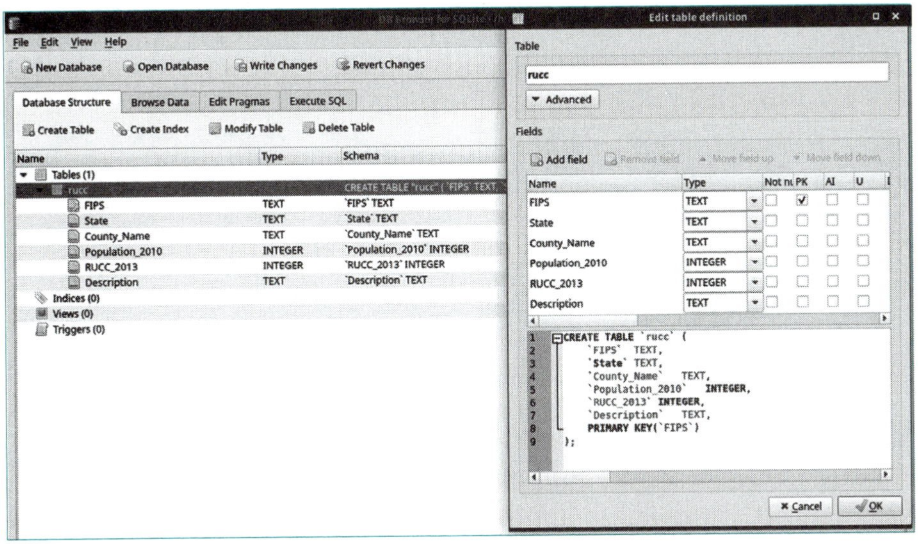

## FIGURE 5.16 ● SQLITE BROWSER INTERFACE: BROWSE DATA TABLE

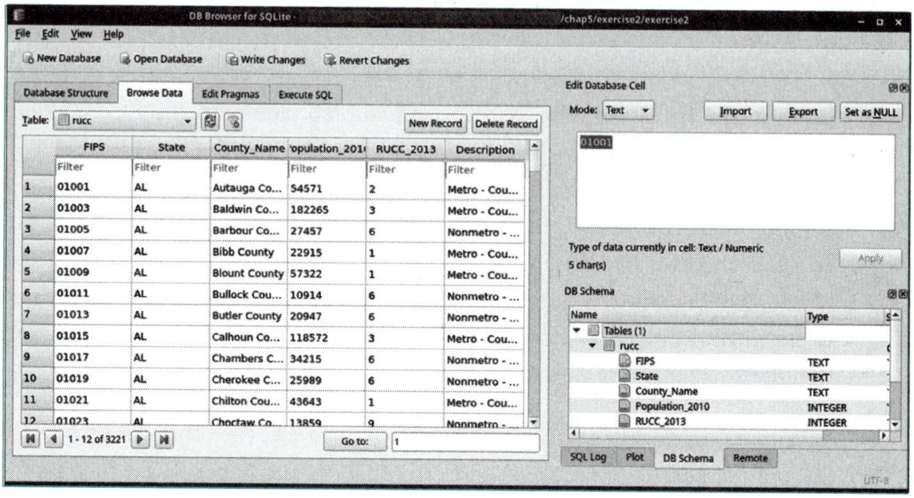

## FIGURE 5.17 ● WRITING AND EXECUTING SQL STATEMENTS

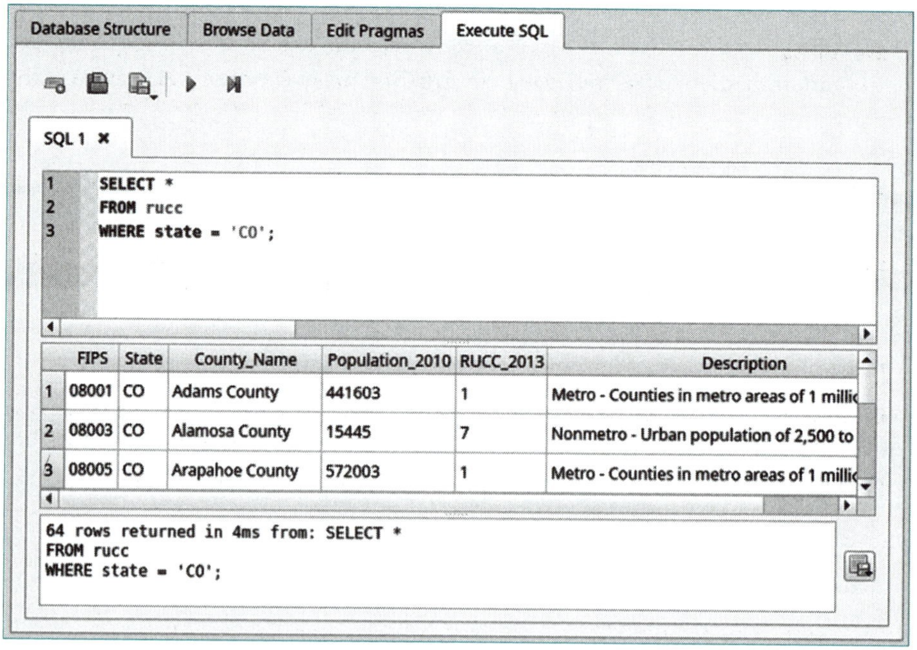

DB Schema, you can hit the down arrow beside the table name to see the individual column names). Let's select all the RUCC codes that are in Colorado. The most basic SQL statement is the SELECT statement, where you SELECT

| TABLE 5.4 ⬡ INTERFACE FOR THE DB BROWSER FOR SQLITE | |
|---|---|
| **Menus** | |
| **File:** | For creating databases, opening and closing them, saving or undoing changes, importing data, quitting the program. Some buttons appear below as shortcuts. |
| **Edit:** | Repeat of some of the buttons in the Database Structure tab. |
| **View:** | For opening a window or menu (if you accidentally closed it). Also modify preferences like font type, size, and color. |
| **Help:** | Access online documentation. |
| **Tabs** | |
| **Database Structure:** | Lists all objects (tables, views), statements used for creating them, column names and types. Use this screen to create, modify, or delete tables or views. |
| **Browse Data:** | Use this to see the actual values in a table and view. You can sort data, manually add or delete records, and modify them using the Edit Database Cell window. |
| **Edit Pragmas:** | Change internal settings in the database. Don't modify this unless you know what you are doing! |
| **Execute SQL:** | For writing SQL statements to query objects or to create, modify, or delete objects. Top window is for typing and running statements, middle window shows the result, and bottom window provides summary of what was returned or error messages if the statement is invalid. |
| **Edit Database Cell:** | If the Browse Data tab is selected, you can use this window to edit values. |
| **SQL Log:** | A list of every statement that's been executed; includes statements you typed or imported, and any statements generated through interaction with the GUI. |
| **Plot:** | Allows you to create basic graphs of data. |
| **DB Schema:** | Duplicate of the Database Structure window. Convenient to have this window open when you are browsing data or writing SQL statements. |
| **Remote:** | Info for connecting to a remote database (not stored on your computer). |

some columns FROM some tables WHERE some criteria is met. Type the following statement in the SQL 1 window (Figure 5.17), and then hit the Run button (single blue arrow above the SQL window) to execute it:

```
SELECT *
FROM rucc
WHERE state='CO';
```

In this statement, the asterisk is shorthand for selecting all columns. In SQL, it is conventional to place each clause on a separate line and capitalize the name of the command. You don't have to do this, but it makes your statements easier to read (and to debug if there is a problem). The names of columns and tables are not case sensitive. When we specify criteria in the WHERE clause, we are saying return all records where the value CO appears in the STATE column. When referencing text values, we must put the values in quotes and values *are* case sensitive: 'CO' and 'co' would be treated as two different values. You can use single or double quotes. If we were referencing numeric values, we could just type the numbers without quotes. SQL is very strict; if the syntax is slightly off, you'll get an error message printed at the bottom, which you can use for troubleshooting your statement. Ending statements with a semicolon ";" is also a SQL convention that you should follow.

8. **SELECT specific columns and sort**. If we want a subset of the columns, we can list the ones we want in the SELECT clause, separated by commas. Never put a comma after the last column name (otherwise you'll get a syntax error). The order of *records* in a database never matters, so if we want the results sorted, we must specify that with ORDER BY. The order of *clauses* always matters in a SQL statement; ORDER BY always goes at the end, WHERE always follows FROM, and so on. In this example, select all the columns except the population column, and sort by RUCC code and then FIPS. Modify your previous query and replace it with this one:

```
SELECT fips, state, county_name, rucc_2013, description
FROM rucc
WHERE state='CO'
ORDER BY rucc_2013, fips;
```

We should have 64 records in the results, as there are 64 counties in Colorado.

9. **Aggregate and count**. Databases are great at aggregating data by categories. Let's say we want to count the number of counties in Colorado that are in each RUCC category. Here's how we do that:

```
SELECT rucc_2013, description, COUNT(rucc_2013) AS total
FROM rucc
WHERE state='CO'
GROUP BY rucc_2013, description
ORDER BY rucc_2013;
```

The result should have nine rows, one for each category. To aggregate data, we specify *only* the columns that we want to use in the summary, and then we use an aggregate function like COUNT, SUM, or AVERAGE to calculate the summary; the function comes first and the column that gets summarized follows in parentheses. The summary will appear in a new column, and the AS clause assigns an alias or name to the column. The GROUP BY clause does the aggregation, and it must include *all* the columns that appear in the SELECT statement *except* for the aggregate function. This is important: We cannot include columns that cannot be summarized. For example, we can't include the fips or county_name columns in this statement if we want to summarize by RUCC codes, because they are unique values that cannot be collapsed into smaller categories.

10. **Saving your statements—create a view**. To save the results of our statement, the simplest thing to do is to create a view. A view is a stored SQL statement that appears as an object in our database. Clicking on a view runs the statement and displays the result. Creating a view is easy, you just add a preface to your select statement:

```
CREATE VIEW co_rucc_count AS
SELECT rucc_2013, description, COUNT(rucc_2013) AS total
FROM rucc
WHERE state='CO'
GROUP BY rucc_2013, description
ORDER BY rucc_2013;
```

To see the view, go back to the Browse Data tab and select it as you would a table, in the drop-down menu at the top (Figure 5.18). If we flip to the Database Structure tab, we will see it listed under Views. Views are dependent on the underlying tables in the statement; if data in the table changes, the results of the view will also change. If we want to get the results out of the database, we could go to File—Export and save our view as a CSV. Views are good if we know we simply want to retrieve the result and we don't want to clutter up our database with lots of additional tables. But if this result will be integral to our database, we could opt to save our query as a new table (we'll demonstrate this a little later). Last, when creating a view, it's always best to compose the SELECT statement first and tinker with it until you get it right. Once it's perfected, you can insert CREATE VIEW at the beginning to save it.

11. **GUI tools—deleting a column**. The SELECT statements that we've just written are part of a subset of the SQL language called the Data Manipulation Language (DML), which is used for retrieving and modifying data in a database. The other commands in the DML include INSERT, DELETE, and

| FIGURE 5.18 ● VIEW SUMMARIZING COLORADO COUNTIES BY RUCC |
|---|

Database Structure | Browse Data | Edit Pragmas | Execute SQL

Table: co_rucc_count

| | RUCC_2013 | Description | total |
|---|---|---|---|
| | Filter | Filter | Filter |
| 1 | 1 | Metro - Counties in metro areas of 1 million population or more | 10 |
| 2 | 2 | Metro - Counties in metro areas of 250,000 to 1 million population | 5 |
| 3 | 3 | Metro - Counties in metro areas of fewer than 250,000 population | 2 |
| 4 | 4 | Nonmetro - Urban population of 20,000 or more, adjacent to a metro area | 3 |
| 5 | 5 | Nonmetro - Urban population of 20,000 or more, not adjacent to a metro area | 3 |
| 6 | 6 | Nonmetro - Urban population of 2,500 to 19,999, adjacent to a metro area | 6 |
| 7 | 7 | Nonmetro - Urban population of 2,500 to 19,999, not adjacent to a metro area | 15 |
| 8 | 8 | Nonmetro - Completely rural or less than 2,500 urban population, adjacent to a metro area | 3 |
| 9 | 9 | Nonmetro - Completely rural or less than 2,500 urban population, not adjacent to a metro area | 17 |

UPDATE for modifying records. A second subset of the language is the Data Definition Language (DDL), which is used for creating and modifying objects in the database and includes commands such as CREATE, DROP, and ALTER. Many of these DDL commands can be executed by simply interacting with the DB Browser's menus and controls. For example, let's delete the population column by flipping to the Database Structure tab, selecting the rucc table, selecting Modify table, selecting population_2010, clicking the button to Remove field, and hitting OK. Save your work (Write Changes button).

12. **Prepare the P29 table for import**. Minimize (don't exit) the database for now. Open Calc, and import the P29 CSV (DecennialSF12010_P29_with_ann.csv) that's in Chapter 5 Exercise 2 folder into a spreadsheet using Sheet—Insert Sheet From File. We can keep this data in CSV format, since we'll be importing it into the database. Select all columns from D to AB, right-click, and choose Delete columns. Scroll over, and delete the last column (E, noninstitutionalized population). Your worksheet should have just four columns: geoid, geoname, total population, and institutionalized population. Then select the first row, right-click, and delete it. We are not allowed to have more than one header row in a database table, so this step is essential. Rename the headers to the following: geoid, county, totpop, instpop. Go to File—Save As and save the file as p29co.csv, as a Text CSV file. When saving, choose the option to quote all text cells.

13. **Import the P29 table**. Go back to the database, go to File—Import—Import Table from CSV file, select the p29co table, and import it. Keep the table name as p29co, check the box for Column names in the first line (Figure 5.19). You can keep the autodetect feature on, since we do not have any numeric IDs

with leading zeros. Once imported, select the table in the Database Structure tab and choose Modify Table. Check the PK box to make geoid the primary key. Make sure that totpop and instpop are integers. Select the Browse tab to make sure the table looks good. Save the changes.

14. **Create new ID for P29 table**. Remember, to relate the rucc table to the P29 table, we need to change the GEOIDs in P29 so they represent five-digit FIPS codes. We could have done this in the spreadsheet before importing it, but we'll do it in the database to demonstrate how it works. Go to the Execute SQL tab, erase your previous statement, and write this one to add a column to hold the new code:

```
ALTER TABLE p29co
ADD COLUMN fips TEXT;
```

Whenever you execute a statement that is *not* a SELECT statement, you won't get a visual result in the middle window but will get a statement in the bottom window indicating whether the statement was executed successfully or not. This statement added a new column to the p29co table called fips and designated it as a text field. Next, we populate this new column like this:

```
UPDATE p29co
SET fips=SUBSTR(geoid,-5);
```

This updates table p29co by setting the value of the empty fips column to the last five places of the value of the geoid column. The function substr stands for substring, or portion of text. This is the same as the RIGHT function in Calc. If we wanted to read from the LEFT, we would leave the minus sign off of the second argument, and if we wanted to read from the middle, we would add a third argument that specifies how many places we want to read. Browse the table and verify that it looks correct (Figure 5.20).

FIGURE 5.20 ● ADDED AND UPDATED COLUMN WITH FIPS CODE

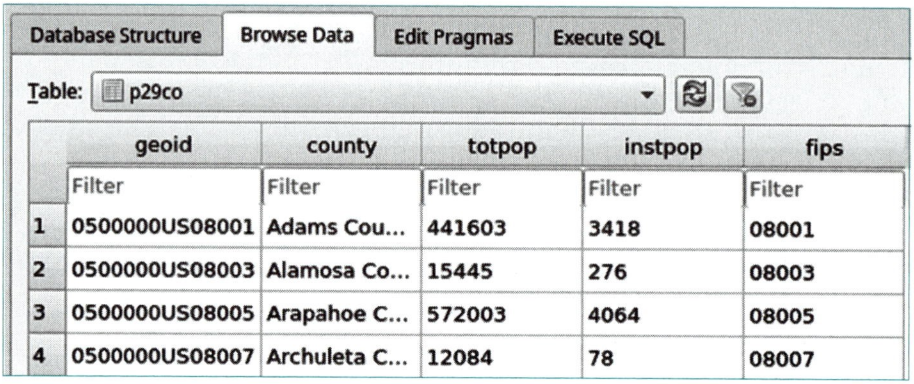
Database Structure
Browse Data
Edit Pragmas
Execute SQL
Table: p29co
geoid county totpop instpop fips
Filter Filter Filter Filter Filter
1 0500000US08001 Adams Cou... 441603 3418 08001
2 0500000US08003 Alamosa Co... 15445 276 08003
3 0500000US08005 Arapahoe C... 572003 4064 08005
4 0500000US08007 Archuleta C... 12084 78 08007

15. **Join two tables**. Joining two tables together is straightforward. Flip back to the Execute SQL tab. To join the rucc table to the p29co table, we do this:

```
SELECT p.fips, p.county, p.totpop, p.instpop, r.rucc_2013,
  r.description
FROM p29co p
INNER JOIN rucc r ON (r.fips=p.fips);
```

When joining two tables together, we need to indicate what columns belong to each table using the syntax tablename.columnname. Since it's tedious to type the entire table name each time, we provide a short alias for the table in the FROM clause. So p29co is aliased as "p" and rucc is aliased as "r" (when aliasing table names, we can leave out the word AS). To do the actual join, the first table is provided in the FROM clause, the second table following INNER JOIN, and after ON we specify where the ID of one table equals the ID of the other table. This matches the data row by row based on the ID they share in common. This type of join is known as an inner join, where matching records for each table are included in the set, and any nonmatching records from both tables fall away. Since table p29co only has records for Colorado, the records for the rest of the United States in the rucc table fall out of the result (Figure 5.21).

16. **Calculate adjusted population**. There are a number of ways we can calculate the adjusted population (removing institutionalized groups quarters from the total). We could add a column to p29co and use UPDATE—SET to permanently add the column to the table, or do a SELECT statement on p29co where we calculate the new value on the fly:

```
SELECT p.fips, p.county, p.totpop, p.instpop,
  (p.totpop - p.instpop) AS adjpop, r.rucc_2013,
```

## FIGURE 5.21 ● JOINING TWO TABLES TOGETHER

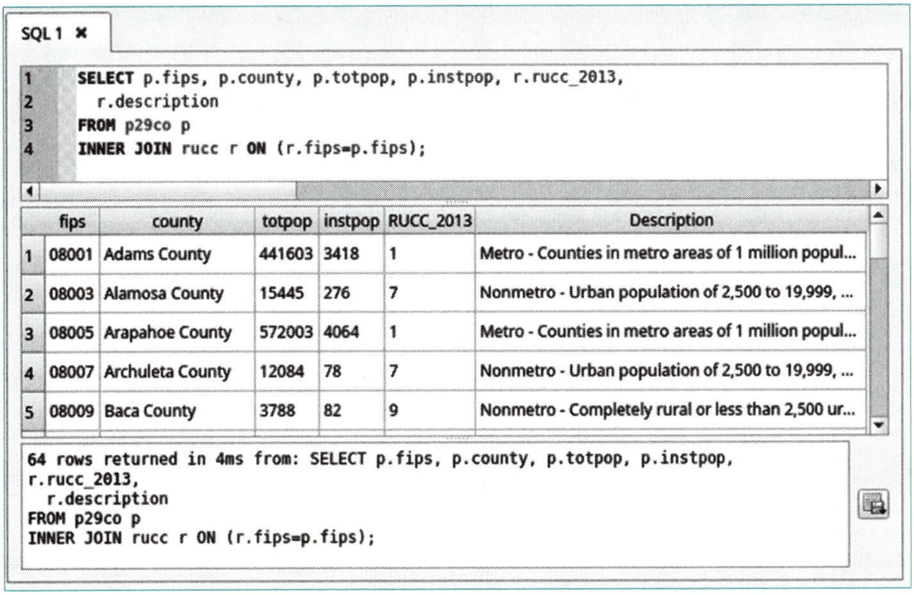

```
SQL 1 ✕

1    SELECT p.fips, p.county, p.totpop, p.instpop, r.rucc_2013,
2       r.description
3    FROM p29co p
4    INNER JOIN rucc r ON (r.fips=p.fips);
```

| | fips | county | totpop | instpop | RUCC_2013 | Description |
|---|------|--------|--------|---------|-----------|-------------|
| 1 | 08001 | Adams County | 441603 | 3418 | 1 | Metro - Counties in metro areas of 1 million popul... |
| 2 | 08003 | Alamosa County | 15445 | 276 | 7 | Nonmetro - Urban population of 2,500 to 19,999, ... |
| 3 | 08005 | Arapahoe County | 572003 | 4064 | 1 | Metro - Counties in metro areas of 1 million popul... |
| 4 | 08007 | Archuleta County | 12084 | 78 | 7 | Nonmetro - Urban population of 2,500 to 19,999, ... |
| 5 | 08009 | Baca County | 3788 | 82 | 9 | Nonmetro - Completely rural or less than 2,500 ur... |

```
64 rows returned in 4ms from: SELECT p.fips, p.county, p.totpop, p.instpop,
r.rucc_2013,
   r.description
FROM p29co p
INNER JOIN rucc r ON (r.fips=p.fips);
```

## FIGURE 5.22 ● RESULT OF JOINED TABLES WITH A CALCULATED FIELD

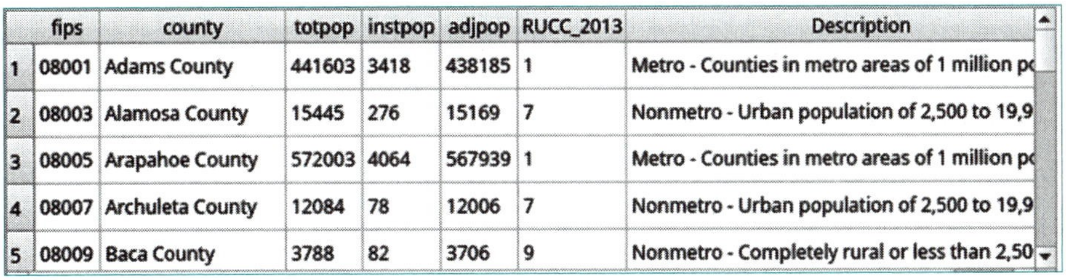

| | fips | county | totpop | instpop | adjpop | RUCC_2013 | Description |
|---|------|--------|--------|---------|--------|-----------|-------------|
| 1 | 08001 | Adams County | 441603 | 3418 | 438185 | 1 | Metro - Counties in metro areas of 1 million p |
| 2 | 08003 | Alamosa County | 15445 | 276 | 15169 | 7 | Nonmetro - Urban population of 2,500 to 19,9 |
| 3 | 08005 | Arapahoe County | 572003 | 4064 | 567939 | 1 | Metro - Counties in metro areas of 1 million p |
| 4 | 08007 | Archuleta County | 12084 | 78 | 12006 | 7 | Nonmetro - Urban population of 2,500 to 19,9 |
| 5 | 08009 | Baca County | 3788 | 82 | 3706 | 9 | Nonmetro - Completely rural or less than 2,50 |

```
   r.description
FROM p29co p
INNER JOIN rucc r ON (p.fips=r.fips);
```

To create the adjusted population, we simply subtract one field from the other and provide an alias for the new column (Figure 5.22): This is called a calculated field. Note that when doing this, we're *not* using an aggregate function like SUM or COUNT; the aggregate functions are only for doing calculations *across rows*. For calculations *across columns*, you simply do the math: subtraction, addition, division, and so on.

| FIGURE 5.23 | ● | RESULT OF JOINED TABLES WITH AN AGGREGATED AND CALCULATED FIELD |
| --- | --- | --- |

| | RUCC_2013 | Description | totpop | instpop | adjpop |
| --- | --- | --- | --- | --- | --- |
| 1 | 1 | Metro - Counties in metro areas of 1 million popul... | 2543482 | 20328 | 2523154 |
| 2 | 2 | Metro - Counties in metro areas of 250,000 to 1 mi... | 1492635 | 10918 | 1481717 |
| 3 | 3 | Metro - Counties in metro areas of fewer than 250... | 305786 | 4548 | 301238 |
| 4 | 4 | Nonmetro - Urban population of 20,000 or more, ... | 139434 | 9353 | 130081 |
| 5 | 5 | Nonmetro - Urban population of 20,000 or more, ... | 136580 | 631 | 135949 |

17. **Create population summaries by categories**. To create population summaries by RUCC code, we incorporate a GROUP BY statement and the aggregate function SUM to aggregate across rows:

```
SELECT r.rucc_2013, r.description, SUM(p.totpop) AS totpop,
  SUM(p.instpop) AS instpop,
  (SUM(p.totpop) - SUM(p.instpop)) AS adjpop
FROM p29co p
INNER JOIN rucc r ON (p.fips=r.fips)
GROUP BY r.rucc_2013, r.description
ORDER BY r.rucc_2013;
```

Notice that we have to sum the populations across the rows first, and then we can subtract one summed result from the other across columns (Figure 5.23).

18. **Save data in a new table**. As we saw previously, we can save our statement as a view so we can easily call it up again. But what if we wanted to make this a permanent table? In SQLite, it's a two-step process. First, we create the empty table that will hold our data where we assign column names, types, and constraints. We'll specify rucc as the primary key since it will be unique, and we'll indicate that the description should never be blank (NOT NULL). Type this is the SQL window:

```
CREATE TABLE colorado_rucc (
  rucc INTEGER PRIMARY KEY,
  description TEXT NOT NULL,
  totpop INTEGER,
  instpop INTEGER,
  adjpop INTEGER);
```

For a CREATE TABLE statement, you specify the table name first, open parentheses, and on each line provide a column name, data type, and constraint. The line for each column ends with a comma, and you close parentheses at the end of the statement.

Next, we can insert the results of our query directly into this empty table. In the INSERT clause, we specify which columns are going to hold the data indicated in the SELECT statement. Order matters: The first column in INSERT will hold the first column listed in SELECT, and so on. The names of the columns don't have to be the same, but the number and order of the columns must match:

```
INSERT INTO colorado_rucc (rucc,description,totpop,
 instpop, adjpop)
SELECT r.rucc_2013, r.description, SUM(p.totpop) AS totpop,
 SUM(p.instpop) AS instpop, (SUM(p.totpop) - SUM(p.instpop))
 AS adjpop
FROM p29co p,
INNER JOIN rucc r ON (p.fips=r.fips)
GROUP BY r.rucc_2013, r.description
ORDER BY r.rucc_2013;
```

Be careful when running INSERT statements; if you execute the statement more than once, you could insert the data into the table multiple times, creating duplicates. In this case, since we designated a primary key the database will prevent us from doing this, because a primary key must be unique. Try running the insert again, and you will receive the error message "UNIQUE constraint failed." Once the insert is done, you can go to the Browse tab and verify that the records were inserted correctly. Save your work.

Since this was a small example, you could choose whether to do this in a spreadsheet or a database. For larger datasets and for projects that will expand in size and scope over time, a database will win over a spreadsheet hands down when it comes to organization, storage, and creating relationships to generate new information. See InfoBox 5.4 for more examples of criteria that you can specify in a WHERE clause.

Instead of having twos separate tables for the codes and the population, why not store all of this data in one table? This would be OK for small projects or as a quick means

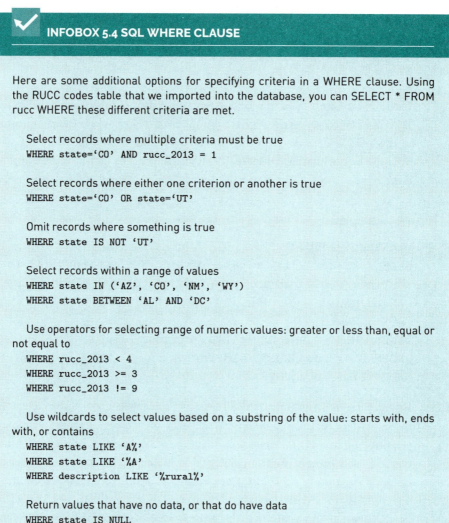

**INFOBOX 5.4 SQL WHERE CLAUSE**

Here are some additional options for specifying criteria in a WHERE clause. Using the RUCC codes table that we imported into the database, you can SELECT * FROM rucc WHERE these different criteria are met.

Select records where multiple criteria must be true
```
WHERE state='CO' AND rucc_2013 = 1
```

Select records where either one criterion or another is true
```
WHERE state='CO' OR state='UT'
```

Omit records where something is true
```
WHERE state IS NOT 'UT'
```

Select records within a range of values
```
WHERE state IN ('AZ', 'CO', 'NM', 'WY')
WHERE state BETWEEN 'AL' AND 'DC'
```

Use operators for selecting range of numeric values: greater or less than, equal or not equal to
```
WHERE rucc_2013 < 4
WHERE rucc_2013 >= 3
WHERE rucc_2013 != 9
```

Use wildcards to select values based on a substring of the value: starts with, ends with, or contains
```
WHERE state LIKE 'A%'
WHERE state LIKE '%A'
WHERE description LIKE '%rural%'
```

Return values that have no data, or that do have data
```
WHERE state IS NULL
WHERE state IS NOT NULL
```

to an end, but for larger projects, it's better to keep them separate. In good database design, individual tables should hold attributes that are strongly tied to the entities that they are describing. In this case, the RUCC codes are created independently of the census by the USDA. What if we need to modify these codes or replace them with updated ones? If the data is stored in separate tables, we can safely modify or update the codes without modifying the census data and then join the two. This is easier, and from a data integrity standpoint safer, than storing everything in one large table that has to be modified.

### Supplemental Exercise: Accessing Data in Bulk via FTP

While **data.census.gov** is the destination for most users who want to look up census statistics or download a few tables, it will not be your destination if you need to download data in bulk. There are a few alternatives that you can use, and the census FTP site at `https://www2.census.gov/` is the place to go if you really want all data for all geographies for a particular state for a specific dataset. The site is organized similarly to a file system on a computer or local network: There are folders for census programs with subfolders for specific datasets. You navigate through the folders until you find what you're looking for, and you download what you need in a large zip file. Given the size of these files and the way they are constructed, using a database is infinitely preferable to using a spreadsheet.

Visit the publishers website at **study.sagepub.com/census** to follow this supplemental exercise, where we'll examine how Summary File 1 from the 2010 census is constructed and how you can load this data into SQLite. We'll parse and load several tables for the State of Hawaii and write some SQL code to tie them together. The structure for the 2020 summary files will likely be similar, and we will also briefly address how the ACS is structured on the FTP site.

The FTP site is really intended for getting all data one state at a time, or for the die-hard researcher who needs absolutely everything and plans to download and stitch it all together. If this seems like overkill for your needs, we'll demonstrate the Dexter tool in the next chapter, which is useful for creating customized extracts in bulk. In terms of complexity, customization, and volume of data, it sits inbetween **data.census.gov** and the FTP site.

## 5.6   REVIEW QUESTIONS AND PRACTICE EXERCISES

1.  What are the primary differences between the 2010 and 2020 census, and why are the differences relevant?

2.  Summarize the principal summary files that are used for packaging decennial census data and describe what they contain.

3.  In what circumstances would you want to adjust the total population of an area by removing the institutionalized group quarters population?

4.  In the extras folder, there is a subfolder with data from Table H4 Tenure for all the counties in Colorado. Using Exercise 1 as a guide, import the CSV into

a spreadsheet. Use VLOOKUP to tie this data to the RUCC codes and create a pivot table summarizing data on homeowners and renters by RUCC.

5. Using Table H4, create a table for it in the database that you created in Exercise 2. Load the data from the CSV into the table. Write one SQL statement where you join the tenure data to the RUCC table to display county-level results, and write a second statement where you group the tenure data and summarize it by RUCC codes.

---

**Supplementary Digital Content:** Find datasets and supplemental exercises at the companion website at `http://study.sagepub.com/census`.

# THE AMERICAN COMMUNITY SURVEY

## 6.1   INTRODUCTION

The American Community Survey (ACS) is going to be your primary source for current, detailed socioeconomic characteristics of the population and the nation's housing units. Formally launched in 2005, it replaced the decennial census long form so that this data could be produced annually at a lesser cost. All the basic demographic variables that are published in the decennial census are included in the ACS, plus educational enrollment and attainment, veteran status, income, marital status, labor force status, place of origin and birth, commuting time to work, housing costs, detailed physical characteristics of housing units, and more. Each question in the ACS satisfies some requirement in federal law, and the data is used for distributing federal aid to state and local governments and individuals. Like the decennial census, ACS data is published for most legal and statistical areas in the country.

The ACS is a sample survey, and the statistics are estimates published with a range of possible values. With the decennial census, we can say that 5,716 people lived in Taos, New Mexico, on April 1, 2010. With the ACS, we can say that we are 90% confident that 5,735 people (plus or minus 249 people) lived in Taos between 2012 and 2016. The estimates are more challenging to interpret and work with, and the margin of error (MOE) can be high enough that estimates for small population groups or small geographies can be too unreliable for practical use. Creating derivatives like aggregates and percent totals is more laborious, as recomputing the MOE requires formulas that may seem complex to new users. Some researchers and the media simply ignore the error margins and present the estimates as if they are counts, which is a terribly misleading and inappropriate use of the data.

We begin this chapter with a brief discussion of how and why the ACS was created, followed by a detailed overview of how it differs from the decennial census, and what the benefits and challenges of using it are. There are a lot of variables in the ACS, and we will cover the major categories and how you can identify the different subjects. Understanding how to interpret the estimates and create derivatives is crucial for working with this dataset, so in the exercises, we will cover the formulas for recalculating MOEs in great detail.

The program page for the ACS is continuously updated. With every new period-estimate release, there is new documentation on subjects, variables, and methodology. Compared with the other datasets, more documentation is devoted to using and interpreting the data: `https://www.census.gov/programs-surveys/acs/`

## When Do You Use the ACS?

The ACS is a sample survey of 3.5 million addresses that is published annually as 1-year- and 5-year-period estimates. Estimates are published at a 90% confidence interval with MOEs provided for each value. Functionally useful data is available down to the census tract level for the 5-year dataset and for any geography that has at least 65k people in the 1-year dataset. When should you use the ACS relative to another dataset? When

- you need broad and detailed socioeconomic characteristics of the population;

- you need the most recent data that's available for these characteristics;

- you need data for small geographies like census tracts, Zip Code Tabulation Areas (ZCTAs), and subcounty divisions that is not available from other federal statistical sources; or

- you want a data source that includes many different variables that are collected using the same methodology and time frame.

The ACS will *not* be your first choice if you need the following:

- Actual counts of the population (use the decennial census instead)

- Actual counts of socioeconomic characteristics at the state or county level (search for administrative data sources from other federal agencies)

- Data for the smallest census geographies like blocks and block groups (use the decennial census instead)

- To study basic demographic variables on an annual basis (use the Population Estimates Program [PEP] instead)

- National data on a monthly basis (use the Current Population Survey [CPS] instead)

## 6.2  FUNDAMENTALS OF THE ACS

In this section, we'll discuss the origins of the ACS, the basics of how the survey is conducted, and the fundamentals for understanding how this dataset of sample-based estimates differs from the basic decennial census count. We will see how to interpret the estimates and MOEs and decide when to use one period estimate versus the other. Last, we will grapple with the challenges and shortcomings of the ACS, so that you can learn to interpret and use the data correctly.

### Origins of the ACS

In the early 1990s, against a backdrop of undercounting controversies and a desire to shrink costs, Congress passed a bill that mandated that the Census Bureau investigate ways to improve census taking. The Census Bureau began experimenting with the continuous rolling sample method. The idea was that data could be collected from sample surveys on a monthly basis and then could be rolled up to create a pool of samples for generating different period estimates. Estimates for large geographies and heavily populated areas could be created annually from 12 months of sample data. For smaller areas, you could accumulate a larger pool of samples over a longer time period and publish estimates for the longer interval. These intervals could be updated each year by refreshing the sample pool, dropping out an older period of data while adding a newer period. Eventually, the entire population would be sampled using this process.

Experiments were conducted throughout the 1990s using the continuous rolling sample concept, and test data was compared with the 2000 census count. The Bureau and stakeholders liked the results of the tests, and Congress authorized funds to expand the ACS in the early 2000s. The first official ACS numbers were published in 2005 for geographies that had at least 65k people. In 2007, data was published in 3-year intervals for geographies that had at least 20k people, and by 2009, 5-year data was published for all geographies down to the census tract level. By the time the

2010 census was conducted, there was enough ACS data to publish detailed 5-year estimates on an annual basis, and the decennial long form was discontinued.

There are a number of factors that led to the creation and adoption of the ACS (Hayslett & Kellam, 2010; Herman, 2008). The first was the expense that was involved in conducting the decennial census. Every decade, there was a large ramp up in hiring and costs followed by a large ramp down once the census was complete. By conducting a survey on an ongoing basis, the Census Bureau could hire a smaller number of full-time experts to keep the program going, which was less expensive than hiring, training, and letting go a large body of people. The ACS also uses a much smaller sample; it captures about two to three people out of a 100, whereas the decennial long form captured an enormous one in six people. The smaller sample size alone would generate savings as there are fewer people to survey and follow up with.

Second, placing the collection of detailed socioeconomic statistics into a separate program allowed the decennial census to focus more on its original mission and temporarily satisfied concerns from conservative members in Congress that the census had become too burdensome as it asked too many questions. With the ACS, fewer people would be surveyed over a longer period of time.

Third, it satisfied the needs of many stakeholders and census data users who argued that the value of the decennial census decreased as the decade wore on, as the data became less useful for studying contemporary issues. The other census data sources were either too limited in the scope of their variables (the PEP) or in their level of geographic detail (the CPS) to serve as replacements. The ACS provided detailed variables and geography on an ongoing basis and used a similar definitional framework as the decennial census for subjects and geography.

## Sampling and Estimate Creation

The ACS is a continuous rolling sample survey of approximately 292,000 residential addresses a month, adding up to 3.5 million addresses a year. The sample is stratified (broken into groups) to decrease variability in the sample selection (U.S. Census Bureau, 2017c, 2017d). The sample is assembled in stages. In the first stage, any housing units that were already sampled in the past 4 years are excluded, and 20% of all addresses that are included in the sample are "new" addresses that have never appeared in a previous extract. In the second stage, 16 strata or groupings are applied based on geographic size. The strata are sorted by the number of addresses in each county by stratum and geographic order, including tract, block, street name, and house number. A census block is assigned to a stratum proportionately based on information about the set of geographic entities that contain the block. These entities include counties, incorporated places, minor civil divisions with functioning governments, Native American Areas, urban/rural status, and a few others. The purpose of this is to prevent creating a sample that happens to be concentrated in one part of the country—for example, a sample of addresses that is largely concentrated in California and Texas without any households from Alaska and Wyoming. In addition, approximately 2.5% of all group quarters addresses are sampled in a year and are divided into a small and large group quarters stratum based on the size of the quarters.

The questions that appear on the ACS form are largely fixed at the beginning of the decade, when subjects and questions for both the decennial census and ACS are approved. Households and group quarters that are included in a given sample are notified by mail, and they have the option of submitting a paper form or filling it out online. Completing the ACS is required by law, but in contrast to the decennial census, the Census Bureau follows up only with a sample of nonrespondents. In 2016, out of the 3,527,047 addresses that were included in the survey, only 2,229,872 (63%) were used as the base for generating the estimates. This is referred to as the coverage rate and is published in every ACS dataset in Table B98011.

After a year's worth of responses have been received, the Census Bureau uses this sample pool to create population estimates for each characteristic and geography. Similar to the decennial census, the Census Bureau uses imputation techniques to assign and allocate responses that are in error or are missing. Allocations for each characteristic are published in tables that begin with B98 and B99. The actual number of persons and housing units that are in the sample are published in Tables B00001 and B00002, respectively. This is referred to as the unweighted sample.

The Bureau assigns weights to each sample to quantify the number of people in the total population who are represented by a sampled household or individual. In their thorough review of sources of error and uncertainty in the ACS, Spielman and colleagues (2014) use the example of an Asian male who earns a certain amount of income. If that category were assigned a weight of 50, then the population for an area that includes one Asian man in that bracket in the sample would equal 50 Asian men in the same income bracket for the total population. Naturally, a good method for estimating survey weights is necessary for creating the estimates, and the process is a complex one that must be constantly updated. In 2016, weighting areas were built from collections of whole counties with similar demographic and social characteristics using data from the 2010 Census and the 2007–2011 ACS (U.S. Census Bureau, 2017c, 2017d). Additionally, the Census Bureau uses estimates from the PEP by age, sex, race, and Hispanic origin as controls for what the total population should be.

This ensures that the ACS estimates for counties, incorporated places, and minor civil divisons do not exceed these population thresholds.

## Interpreting Period Estimates

Because the ACS sample size is much smaller than the old decennial long form, all ACS estimates are published as intervals at a 90% confidence level. The MOE describes the precision of an estimate at the given level of confidence—that is, the likelihood that the sample estimate is within a certain distance from the population value. The confidence level is the degree of certainty that the interval defined by the MOE contains the actual value of the characteristic. Essentially, ACS values represent likely distributions: The MOEs represent the spread of the distribution, the estimate is the center of the spread, and the confidence level indicates the likelihood that the actual population falls within the estimated distribution.

For example, we are 90% confident that the population of South Dakota's largest city, Sioux Falls, was 174,350 in 2016, ±38. The MOE of 38 people means that the actual population could be as low as 174,312 or as high as 174,388. The Census Bureau publishes estimates with MOEs as $174,350 \pm 38$. Alternatively, if the actual range of possible values is presented (174,312 174,388), this is referred to as the confidence *interval*. The confidence *level* means that there is a 90% chance that the true estimate lies within this interval and a 10% chance that it lies outside the interval.

The MOE measures the variation in the random samples due to chance, and its size is affected by three factors. First, the MOE increases as the size of a sample decreases. With a smaller sample, we cannot estimate what the true population is at the same level of precision. If we wanted a more precise estimate, we would need a bigger sample. Second, increasing the confidence level (to say 95% or 99%) while keeping the sample size the same would also increase the MOE. We would be more certain that the true population values fall within the interval, but the range of the interval would be greater. Last, the amount of variability in the population can also increase the size of the MOE. The more variable a population is, the harder it is to estimate. To decrease the MOE, we would need to increase the sample size or decrease the level of confidence. Decreasing the level of confidence is not desirable; in statistics, a confidence level of 90% is typically the lowest acceptable threshold.

Given the size of the ACS sample and a confidence level of 90%, the Census Bureau cannot estimate the population for small areas on an annual basis with an acceptable level of precision. So each year, they release two different period estimates: (1) a 1-year estimate for geographies that have a population of at least 65k and (2) a 5-year estimate for all geographies down to the census block group level. By

| TABLE 6.1  ● COMPARISON OF ACS ESTIMATES FOR SOUTH DAKOTA CITIES | Sioux Falls | Rapid City | Pierre |
|---|---|---|---|
| **2016, 1-Year** | | | |
| Total population | 174,350 ± 38 | 74,050 ± 26 | NA |
| Population 16 and over | 133,814 ± 1,414 | 58,144 ± 1,279 | NA |
| Civilian labor force | 99,531 ± 2,462 | 36,222 ± 1,802 | NA |
| **2012–2016, 5-Year** | | | |
| Total population | 167,884 ± 45 | 72,441 ± 103 | 13,959 ± 25 |
| Population 16 and over | 130,318 ± 490 | 57,021 ± 388 | 11,231 ± 126 |
| Civilian labor force | 96,330 ± 1,030 | 37,059 ± 765 | 7,795 ± 262 |

publishing 5-year estimates, the Census Bureau is able to use a much larger sample (60 months of data instead of 12), which it can use to more reliably estimate the population for these smaller areas. With a larger sample, the MOEs will be lower and will be acceptable for most (but not all) applications, depending on the size of the geography and population group.

The Bureau used to publish 3-year estimates (36 months) for any geographies that had at least 20k people, but they dropped this alternative beginning with the 2014 ACS and replaced it with 1-year supplemental estimates. This supplemental 1-year data is provided for all geographies that have at least 20k people and uses larger subject and interval groupings so that the MOEs are not unacceptably large. There are a smaller number of tables in this series, and their table ID numbers are prefaced with the letter "K."

Table 6.1 illustrates the differences between different ACS periods and population subgroups for the two largest cities in South Dakota and the state capital. Since Sioux Falls and Rapid City have populations above the 65k threshold, they are included in both the 1-year- and 5-year-period estimates, while Pierre falls below the threshold and is only available in the 5-year ACS. Notice that the MOEs for the total populations for all cities is pretty small for both period estimates. This is because total population for counties and incorporated places is controlled in the ACS using PEP data, so the values do not exceed those estimates by a large degree. The MOEs become much larger once you start looking at subgroups of the population. As we move

| TABLE 6.2  ●  DISTINGUISHING FEATURES BETWEEN ACS PERIOD ESTIMATES | | |
|---|---|---|
| **1-Year Estimates** | **1-Year Supplemental Estimates** | **5-Year Estimates** |
| 12 months of data | 12 months of data | 60 months of data |
| Data for areas with populations of 65,000+ | Data for areas with populations of 20,000+ | Data for all areas down to block groups |
| Smallest sample size | Smallest sample size | Largest sample size |
| Less reliable than 5-year | Less reliable than 5-year | Most reliable |
| Most current data | Most current data | Least current data |
| Released 2005–present | Released 2014–present | Released 2009–present |
| Use when currency is more important than precision, analyzing large populations | Use when currency is more important than precision, analyzing smaller populations, examining smaller geographies not available in the standard 1-year estimates | Use when precision is more important than currency, analyzing very small populations, and examining tracts and other smaller geographies not available in the 1-year estimates |

*Source:* Derived from `https://www.census.gov/programs-surveys/acs/guidance/estimates.html`
*Note:* When comparing geographies, use a period estimate that includes them all.

from the total population, to the population that's over 16, to the population over 16 in the civilian labor force, the MOEs increase. If we look at the same characteristic in two different period estimates, there is a big difference in the size of the intervals. In 2016, the civilian labor force for Sioux Falls was estimated to be 99,531 ± 2,462, but in 2012–2016, the estimate was 96,330 ± 1,030. Since the 5-year data is based on a larger sample, we can get an estimate that has a lower MOE.

When should you use the 1-year estimate versus the 5-year estimate? If you were making comparisons between places and not all the places were included in the 1-year dataset, then it's better to use the 5-year dataset as mixing and matching places from two different periods is not ideal. If we were comparing all three of these cities, we should use the 5-year dataset, as Pierre is not included in the 1-year dataset. What if we were comparing just Sioux Falls and Rapid City? Then we would have a choice. If we wanted our estimate to be more precise in terms of the size of the interval, we would use the 5-year period as the MOE is much lower. If we want our estimate to be more precise in terms of the time frame (we want data that's most current), then we would use the 1-year estimate. Table 6.2 provides guidance on which period estimate to choose.

Every year, the Census Bureau releases new 1-year-period estimates at the beginning of the fall and new 5-year-period estimates at the end of the fall. There is a lag of about 9 months between the time data collection for a year ends and the time data is published; data collection for 2016 was finished by January 2017, and the estimates were released in September 2017, while the 5-year 2012–2016 data was released in December 2017.

For the 5-year estimates, the estimate is recomputed by dropping the oldest year of data from the sample and adding the latest year. Geographies that cross the threshold of 65k will appear in the 1-year estimates for the year they cross the threshold, and geographies that fall below the threshold will be dropped. The statistical geographies for the ACS are based on the decennial census geographies that were current during the latest year of the estimate. All ACS data from 2010 to 2019 is based on the 2010 census tracts, block groups, ZCTAs, census-designated places, and so on (Public Use Microdata Areas [PUMAs] are a notable exception, as they are delineated a couple of years after the decennial census). For 5-year estimates, the samples are recalculated to fit the latest statistical geography: While the 2015–2019 ACS will use 2010 census geography, the 2016–2020 ACS will use 2020 geography. Legal areas (states, counties, incorporated places) are different, in that ACS data is tabulated based on the latest boundaries from the Boundary and Annexation Survey. Dollar values in the 5-year ACS are based on the Consumer Price Index for the most recent year in the sample.

## Challenges and Caveats

While the ACS offers a number of benefits over the decennial long form (it's more timely, less expensive to conduct), there are also a number of disadvantages. These challenges include greater complexity in interpreting, understanding, and working with the estimates and less reliability in the precision of the statistics, especially for small geographies and population groups. Many of these issues and approaches for addressing them were identified soon after the release of the first ACS datasets (National Research Council, 2007).

Table 6.3 shows the 2010 census count and the 5-year 2008–2012 ACS population estimates by race for a census tract in midtown Manhattan. The population for the tract was 7,614 people on April 1, 2010, and was between 5,566 and 7,200 (with 90% confidence) during the period from 2008 to 2012. The difference between these two values is rather stark, in the first case, we have a simple total for a single point in time, and in the second case, we have a fuzzier range of values over a longer period. The ACS estimate may be lower than the actual count simply due to the methodological differences between the count and the survey or due to a longer time range (before or after 2010) when the population may have been lower. This underscores

**TABLE 6.3 ●    COMPARISON OF 2010 CENSUS AND ACS ESTIMATE FOR CENSUS TRACT 68, NEW YORK COUNTY**

|  | 2010 Census | 2008–2012 ACS |
|---|---|---|
| **Total population** | 7,614 | 6,383 ± 817 |
| **White** | 5,414 | 4,716 ± 735 |
| **Black** | 330 | 297 ± 187 |
| **Native American** | 9 | 0 ± 17 |
| **Asian** | 1,080 | 725 ± 295 |
| **Pacific Islander** | 3 | 0 ± 17 |
| **Some Other Race** | 30 | 85 ± 137 |
| **Multiracial** | 188 | 91 ± 75 |
| **Hispanic/Latino** | 560 | 469 ± 186 |

*Note:* Data by race is presented for people of that race alone who are not Hispanic, while Hispanic / Latino includes all Hispanics regardless of their race.

that the decennial census is designed to get an actual count, while the ACS attempts to generally characterize an area over a period of time.

The size of the MOE is a big problem for the smaller population groups. Since white people represent a majority of this census tract and their overall population is high, the MOE for this group is lower. There are 4,716 whites, within a range of 3,981 and 5,451. The MOE for black people is much higher relative to the estimate: The estimate is 297 but could be 110 or 484. The MOE for Some Other Race is actually higher than the estimate itself, so the true value could be zero! A statistic called the coefficient of variation measures the relative amount of sampling error associated with an estimate and is typically used to determine whether a particular estimate is reliable enough to use. You can compute the coefficient of variation (CV) for an ACS estimate with this formula (which we will do in the exercises):

$$CV = \frac{MOE/1.645}{ACS\ Estimate} * 100$$

What is an acceptable CV? Opinions vary. In a national study, the Census Bureau examined CVs at the county level for key ACS variables and grouped the findings into three categories: (1) estimates with CVs of 0 to 12 were highly reliable, (2) 12 to 34 were of medium reliability, and (3) 35 and above were of low reliability (Heimel, 2014). In its web applications and published tables, the Population Division of the New York City (NYC) Department of City Planning flags all estimates with a CV higher than 20 as unreliable. For this particular census tract, the only reliable estimates based on any standard would be the total and the white populations that have a CV of 8 and 10, respectively. The CV for the Hispanic population is 24, the Asian population is 25, and the black population is 38.

What can you do when estimates are unreliable? The solution is to increase the size of the sample. For end users working with published census data, this means either aggregating categories into larger groups or geographies into larger areas. In some cases, aggregating groups is acceptable; for instance, the number of households classified by income brackets can be grouped into a smaller number of brackets with larger intervals. In this example, our options are limited. We could aggregate the smaller racial groups into another category if we were studying this one census tract, but census tracts are seldom studied individually. If we were studying all of Manhattan or NYC, there would be areas where the black and Hispanic populations are higher and the white and Asian populations are lower, so we can't aggregate these groups if we want to make comparisons. The other option would be to aggregate the census tracts into larger areas (which we will do in our first exercise) or use a larger statistical geography like PUMAs. This would increase the accuracy of the estimate by reducing the MOE, but the trade-off is that the geography is less detailed.

For example, in 2008–2012, neighboring Census Tract 64 had a total population of $7,439 \pm 621$ with a CV of 5. If we combine its population with Census Tract 68, we have a total population of 13,822. To calculate the new MOE, we take the square root of the sum of the squares for each of the MOEs:

$$MOE = \sqrt{MOE1^2 + MOE2^2}$$

This gives us a total population of $13,822 \pm 1,026$. The CV for this new estimate is 4.5, which is a little lower than the CVs for the total population for each individual tract (8 for Tract 68 and 5 for Tract 64). We can get an even better estimate if we aggregate additional tracts.

NYC's Population Division has created aggregates of census tracts called neighborhood tabulation areas to facilitate the use of ACS data. However, the aggregation of tracts in smaller cities and towns may not make sense for local planners and policy makers, as tracts can cross the town's boundaries and jurisdictional areas (Salvo & Lobo, 2010). Even within large cities, aggregating tract-level data can mask small subgroups of the population that researchers are trying to study. For researchers who are studying marginalized populations and poverty, this data may be visible at the tract level but becomes diluted if you look at a larger area like a ZCTA or PUMA, as this smaller population gets combined with a larger population with different characteristics (Bazuin & Fraser, 2013).

The amount of uncertainty in the ACS relative to the old census long form has exceeded the Census Bureau's expectations (Spielman et al., 2014). MOEs in the ACS are higher due to the smaller sample size, the decision to follow up with only a sample of nonresponding households, and the use of population controls that are not collected in conjunction with the ACS. In their review of the patterns and causes of uncertainty in the ACS, Spielman and colleagues (2014) state that block group and tract-level data in the ACS "fail to meet even the loosest standards of data quality" (p. 147). The sample sizes of the ACS simply aren't large enough to provide reasonable certainty for estimating the characteristics of census tracts (Salvo et al., 2007). To some degree, this is because the sample itself is too small, but it's also due to the degree of variability that exists for several demographic characteristics at that scale. Samples of the same size can yield different estimates based on variations in the composition of populations in census tracts.

Bazuin and Fraser (2013) conducted a case study of a largely black census tract in Nashville, Tennessee, whose poverty declined sharply between the 2000 census and 2005–2009 ACS. They administered their own survey of the area and compared their results with the 2000 decennial census count and with estimates from the ACS. They discovered that the small sample size, the variability in characteristics of the tract, and nonresponse rates were skewing the poverty rate lower. The ACS was capturing both the elderly black population—homeowners who were more likely to be retired, be home during the day, own landline telephones, and respond to surveys—and a small younger group of more affluent whites. It was missing poorer black renters who had children and was overestimating the number of vacant homes and underestimating average household size.

The U.S. Government Accountability Office (2016) found that there is a lack of data for measuring income for small communities, as the ACS is either unreliable at that scale or is tabulated for geographic areas that do not conform to the project area's boundaries. The greater complexity of interpreting the ACS has created barriers to applying it correctly. A survey of three federal agencies that use ACS data to fulfill regulatory requirements for distributing funds found that none of them take the MOE into account when using the data (Nesse & Rahe, 2015). Regulators were concerned about the complexity of incorporating calculations to account for the MOE and were worried that stakeholders would be confused by what it was.

The Census Bureau has taken steps to improve the accuracy of the ACS, with better nonresponse follow-up, adjustments in creating weights, and more publicity to encourage people to respond. The sample size was originally fixed at 3 million addresses, but as the U.S. population grew, the sample represented a smaller portion of the population. The sample size was increased to 3.5 million beginning with the 2012 ACS and has increased slightly each year. In 2016, 3.54 million addresses were included in the sample, but it's important to remember that this number represents the addresses that were selected for inclusion. The actual number that was finally interviewed excludes the following addresses: determined to be nonexistent or commercial, not selected in the subsample for personal visit follow-up, and not interviewed due to refusals or other reasons. In 2016, 2.23 million addresses were used to actually compute the estimates. For the group quarters population, just over 200k people are included in the initial sample and about 160k are used to create the estimates. The Census Bureau is transparent about the ACS methodology, which you can read in detail at `https://www.census.gov/programs-surveys/acs/methodology.html`.

Continuous improvements to the Master Address File should boost the number of addresses that make it to the final interview. However, without a substantive increase in the sample size, reliability issues with the smallest geographies will remain. Data at the block group level is so poor that users should disregard it entirely. Data at the census tract level varies in quality, and you should scrutinize the MOE and calculate CVs to determine reliability. Despite these challenges, the ACS is still a valuable dataset that is broad in scope and geographically detailed. In the exercises, we will cover how you can assess the quality of the estimates and use formulas to create aggregates. InfoBox 6.1 contains suggestions for tools that you can use to make your work with ACS formulas a bit easier for either automating the process or checking your work.

## 6.3   ACS VARIABLES

The ACS has a wealth of variables compared with the current decennial census. It includes all the questions asked in the current decennial census, most of the questions asked on the old decennial long form last used in 2000, and new questions on topics such as computer and internet access and health insurance coverage that were added due to new federal laws.

There are a few key conceptual differences between the decennial census and ACS. First, the concept of residency for the ACS is based on "current residence," which is where the respondents are currently living at the time they receive the ACS questionnaire. If they are living there at that time and intend to stay there for at least

## ✓ INFOBOX 6.1 TOOLS FOR WORKING WITH ACS FORMULAS

Cornell PAD ACS Calculator: One calculator for comparing two values to test for significant difference and another for computing a new value (estimate and MOE) for two estimates. Great for checking your own work. `https://pad.human.cornell.edu/acscalc/`

Census Bureau's Statistical Testing Tool: A spreadsheet that allows you to compare estimates for more than 3,000 pairs of values to determine whether they are significantly different or not. `https://census.gov/programs-surveys/acs/guidance/statistical-testing-tool.html`

Fairfax County VA ACS Tools: As part of their Research Tools, the county has developed individual spreadsheets for calculating specific formulas like CVs, statistical difference, percent change, percent total, and aggregates. `https://www.fairfaxcounty.gov/demographics/research-tools`

The American Community Survey Statistical Analyzer: Created at the University of South Florida, this spreadsheet is a sophisticated collection of macros and formulas that includes formulas not only for the published ACS estimates but also for ACS PUMS (Public Use Microdata Sample) and Census Transportation Planning Products. It goes beyond the basics and includes formulas for calculating other derivatives like means, medians, and frequencies. `http://www.nctr.usf.edu/abstracts/abs77802.htm`

Map Reliability Calculator: Developed by the Population Division of NYC City Planning, this spreadsheet calculator is designed for thematic mappers of ACS data who want to measure the reliability of classification schemes. `http://www1.nyc.gov/site/planning/data-maps/nyc-population/geographic-reference.page`

acs-R: A package for the open source statistical programing language R that includes specific modules and functions for working with ACS data. `https://cran.r-project.org/web/packages/acs/index.html`

tidycensus: Another R package for working with ACS and decennial census data. `https://walkerke.github.io/tidycensus/`

---

the next 2 months, then that address counts as their current residence. In contrast, the decennial census employs the concept of "usual residence," which is the place where the household lives and sleeps most of the time as of April 1 of the census year.

Second, the concept of time in the ACS is not constant for all people who are filling out the form, since the ACS is a rolling sample and a couple of hundred thousand addresses are receiving the form each month. Questions like "Last month what was the cost of electricity in this house?" and "Did this person live in this house or apartment a year ago?" are going to have different points of reference for households who filled the form out in February versus August. The ACS is used to provide general characteristics of the population over a given time period, not precise measurements at a fixed point in time.

The Census Bureau publishes its list of subjects for the ACS each year (U.S. Census Bureau, 2017b) and categorizes them into four groups for Social, Economic, Housing, and Demographic topics (see Table 6.4). As you recall, the ACS publishes data profile tables for each of these categories (DP02 through DP05), which are convenient for seeing what's included in the ACS at a glance. As we saw in Chapter 2, each of the tables has its own ID code with the following prefixes: S for subject (collections and summaries of data), B for base, and C for collapsed (detailed tables focused on a narrow subject), followed by a numeric ID. The first two digits of the numeric ID for the detailed tables indicates what the table's subject is (Table 6.5).

### TABLE 6.4 ● SUBJECTS INCLUDED IN THE ACS

| Social | Housing |
| --- | --- |
| Ancestry | Bedrooms |
| Citizenship status | Computer and internet use |
| Disability status | House heating fuel |
| Educational attainment | Kitchen facilities |
| Fertility | Occupancy/vacancy status |
| Grandparents as caregivers | Occupants per room |
| Language spoken at home | Plumbing facilities |
| Marital history | Rent |
| Marital status | Rooms |
| Migration/residence 1 year ago | Selected monthly owner costs |
| Place of birth | Telephone service available |
| School enrollment | Tenure (owner/renter) |
| Undergraduate field of degree | Units in structure |
| Veteran status; period of military service | Value of home |
| Year of entry | Vehicles available |
| **Economic** | Year householder moved into unit |
| Class of worker | Year structure built |

| TABLE 6.4 ● CONTINUED | |
|---|---|
| Commuting and place of work | **Demographic** |
| Employment status | Age; sex |
| Supplemental Nutrition Assistance Program (SNAP) | Group quarters population |
| Health insurance coverage | Hispanic or Latino origin |
| Income and earnings | Race |
| Industry and occupation | Relationship to householder |
| Poverty status | Total population |
| Work status last year | |

| TABLE 6.5 ● ACS TABLE SUBJECTS AND ID CODES | |
|---|---|
| 00 | Unweighted Count (of the Sample) |
| 01 | Age and Sex |
| 02 | Race |
| 03 | Hispanic Origin |
| 04 | Ancestry |
| 05 | Foreign Born; Citizenship; Year or Entry; Nativity |
| 06 | Place of Birth |
| 07 | Residence 1 Year Ago; Migration |
| 08 | Journey to Work; Workers' Characteristics; Commuting |
| 09 | Children; Household Relationship |
| 10 | Grandparents; Grandchildren |
| 11 | Household Type; Family Type; Subfamilies |
| 12 | Marital Status and History |
| 13 | Fertility |
| 14 | School Enrollment |
| 15 | Educational Attainment |
| 16 | Language Spoken at Home and Ability to Speak English |
| 17 | Poverty |

| TABLE 6.5 ● CONTINUED | |
|---|---|
| 18 | Disability |
| 19 | Income (Households and Families) |
| 20 | Earnings (Individuals) |
| 21 | Veteran Status |
| 22 | Transfer Programs (Public Assistance) |
| 23 | Employment Status; Work Experience; Labor Force |
| 24 | Industry; Occupation; Class of Worker |
| 25 | Housing Characteristics |
| 26 | Group Quarters |
| 27 | Health Insurance |
| 98 | (Data) Quality Measures |
| 99 | Imputations |

The way data is presented varies based on the subject. Most of the estimates are published as total values that are subdivided into other categories and cross tabulated with basic subject characteristics like age, sex, race, Hispanic origin, household and family status, occupancy, and tenure. As we have seen, some of the estimates are calculated as subsets of the population; that is, educational attainment is measured for people 18 and over and 25 and over, veteran status is measured for civilians who are 18 and over, and so on.

Interval variables like income, earnings, home value, and rent are presented as estimates for households, families, and individuals who are divided into brackets for a certain range of values. The last value in the bracket is always top-coded, measuring items of a certain value to some unspecified upper limit. The Census Bureau also provides summary measures for interval data such as a mean, median, per capita value, and aggregate value (i.e., the sum of all rents or incomes). The aggregate value is useful if you need to combine subject groups or geographies and need to compute new summary measures.

Like the decennial census, variables in the ACS may appear in several tables, presented in different ways. For example, Table 6.6 shows gross rent in Charlotte, North Carolina, from the 2012–2016 ACS, as published in the data profile table DP04 for housing. Gross rent is the amount of contract rent plus the estimated average monthly cost of utilities and fuels if these are paid for by the renter. In the data profile table,

| TABLE 6.6 ● GROSS RENT IN CHARLOTTE, NORTH CAROLINA, 2012–2016 | | | | |
|---|---|---|---|---|
| | Estimate | Margin of Error | Percent | Percent Margin of Error |
| Occupied units paying rent | 141,768 | ± 1,973 | 141,768 | (X) |
| Less than $500 | 7,070 | ± 561 | 5.0% | ± 0.4 |
| $500 to $999 | 69,911 | ± 1,447 | 49.3% | ± 0.9 |
| $1,000 to $1,499 | 50,009 | ± 1,476 | 35.3% | ± 0.9 |
| $1,500 to $1,999 | 11,125 | ± 733 | 7.8% | ± 0.5 |
| $2,000 to $2,499 | 2,189 | ± 341 | 1.5% | ± 0.2 |
| $2,500 to $2,999 | 524 | ± 145 | 0.4% | ± 0.1 |
| $3,000 or more | 940 | ± 203 | 0.7% | ± 0.1 |
| Median (dollars) | $966 | ± 7 | (X) | (X) |
| No rent paid | 3,084 | ± 373 | (X) | (X) |

*Source:* Data Profile Table DP04 2012–2016 ACS.

occupied housing units that pay rent are summarized: in rent brackets with a range of $500 and a top-coded value of $3,000 or more, by median rent, and with an estimate of those paying no rent. In the detailed tables, Gross Rent (B25063), Median Gross Rent (B25064), and Aggregate Gross Rent (B25065) are published separately. The detailed gross rent table provides estimates of households in smaller brackets that range from $50 at lower values to $500 at higher values, with a top-coded value of $3,500 or more. The trade-off is that the MOEs are higher, since the brackets are smaller interval ranges. Gross rent and median gross rent are cross tabulated in other tables with number of bedrooms, year structure built, and as a percentage of household income, and the components of gross rent (contract rent, costs of utilities and fuel) are published in separate tables.

Some of the variables are derived from user responses and defined based on specific measurement criteria. For example, the ACS does not ask whether or not a person is in poverty. The ACS includes questions on income and earnings and on the relationship status of every person in the household. The Census Bureau uses this data and follows the Office of Management and Budget's Statistical Policy Directive 14 to determine whether or not a household or family is in poverty based on family size, composition, and a set of money income thresholds. The official poverty definition uses money income before taxes and does not include capital gains (from selling stocks or bonds) or noncash benefits (e.g., public housing, Medicaid, and food stamps). The poverty thresholds are updated for inflation using the Consumer Price Index and are published annually. The thresholds vary based on size of the household, number of children, and age above or below 65. In 2016, the threshold for four people of whom two are children was $24,339.

Some poverty researchers argue that the thresholds are too low and that the methodology is outdated (Klass, 2012, pp. 157–170). The Census Bureau and the Bureau of Labor Statistics produce a Supplemental Poverty Measure that expands the definitions beyond families, accounts for a wider array of expenditures, adjusts for geography and different housing costs, and uses a different mix of income. This data is derived from the CPS and is published annually at the national and state level with an accompanying report (Fox, 2017).

Many of the economic variables on occupation, industry, and the labor force are classified into industries using the North American Industrial Classification System. We will explore this classification system in Chapter 8 when we cover data for businesses. Variables on migration and commuting are also available in special tabulations in different formats that allow users to examine the flows of people from one place to another:

Migration: `https://www.census.gov/topics/population/migration.html`

Commuting: `https://www.census.gov/topics/employment/commuting.html`

While the ACS captures many characteristics, it doesn't capture everything. InfoBox 6.2 provides a sample of what's not available in any census datasets. The Census Bureau conducts a number of smaller sample surveys that are of interest to researchers in specific fields, such as the American Housing Survey and the Survey of Income and Program Participation. These surveys ask more detailed questions related to their subject matter but can only be summarized for large geographic areas like states and metropolitan areas. We will provide a summary of these in Chapter 12 when we discuss the CPS.

## 6.4   EXERCISES

Working with ACS data requires you to interpret how reliable the estimates are and to calculate the MOE for any new derivatives you create, such as aggregates or percent totals. In these exercises, you will learn several of the formulas for measuring

> ✓ **INFOBOX 6.2 WHAT'S NOT IN THE CENSUS**
>
> While the census covers a lot of ground, it doesn't include the three topics that you should avoid discussing with your family during holidays, plus other information that has nothing to do with people, houses, or businesses.
>
> Sex:    As we saw in Chapter 4, the census does not include questions on gender identity or sexual preference, other than asking whether someone is in a same-sex partnership or marriage. Public sources for this data are scattered across a number of federal and local datasets. A professor from Drexel University has compiled a list at http://www.lgbtdata.com/.
>
> Politics:    The census does not provide data on election results, party affiliation, or campaign donations. The Federal Election Commission provides a detailed database on donations and woefully inadequate data on election results (compiled at the state level). Elections in the United States are local affairs, and detailed data are kept at the state level. The Census Bureau does publish national and state-level data on voter eligibility, participation, and registration every 2 years following a federal election in the CPS and tabulates the number of people who are eligible to vote in the ACS.
>
> Religion:    During the 19th century, religious bodies were counted in the decennial census, but in the early 20th century, these questions were moved to a separate survey that was defunded in the 1950s. During the 1970s, Congress amended the laws governing the census and prohibited any mandatory questions on religion citing a separation of church and state. The Association of Religion Data Archives publishes a decennial census of religion that counts adherents at the state and county level: http://www.thearda.com/.
>
> Miscellaneous:    The Census Bureau primarily counts people, housing units, and businesses. If you are looking for data on point incidents (crime, traffic accidents, home sales, air travel, pollution, the weather), visit the federal agency responsible for collecting that data. While the Census Bureau collects some health-related data (insurance and recent births in the ACS, births and deaths in the PEP), it does not specialize in this area. The National Center for Health Statistics at the Centers for Disease Control and Prevention is the primary source. The 500 Cities Project provides detailed health data for small areas: https://www.cdc.gov/500cities/. There are some federal agencies that provide alternate sources to some census variables (i.e., the Department of Education publishes data on education). This data tends to be from administrative sources and is usually published at the state and county level. See *The Reference Guide to Data Sources* for suggestions (Bauder, 2014).

reliability and creating estimates. The Census Bureau explains these formulas in the annual technical documentation they release for each period estimate (U.S. Census

Bureau, 2017c, 2017d), and they published a guidebook for researchers with many examples (U.S. Census Bureau, 2018c). We will use Calc to translate these formulas from statistical notation into spreadsheet formulas.

In the first exercise, we'll cover many of these formulas as we aggregate data for a neighborhood. In the second exercise, we will learn how to use the MCDC's Dexter tool to build customized extracts of ACS data. In terms of complexity and flexibility, this tool sits inbetween what we have covered thus far, as it's a bit more powerful than **data.census.gov** and less involved than downloading data in bulk from the FTP (File Transfer Protocol) site. At the end of the exercise, we'll return to SQLite with some brief examples of writing queries that account for the fuzziness of ACS estimates. There's also an online supplemental exercise that demonstrates additional formulas and the potential impact that interpreting estimates has on policy decisions.

Visit the publisher's website for the data we will be using, or download it from the source:

**B07204 Geographical Mobility In The Past Year For Current Residence:** 2012–2016 ACS, Cincinnati city, Ohio (place in state) and Census Tracts 9, 10, 16, and 17, Hamilton County, Ohio (census tracts)—https://data.census.gov/

## Exercise 1: Aggregating Tract-level Estimates to Neighborhoods With Calc

The reliability of ACS data at the tract level can be quite low. In this exercise, we'll calculate CVs to quantify reliability, and then we'll aggregate tracts into a larger area to get a better estimate. We'll also compute percent totals for each category. For the aggregate and the percentages, we'll calculate new MOEs and will assess how the estimates have improved as a result of aggregating them.

When aggregating small geographies like tracts into larger ones, you must establish some criteria so that you are not arbitrarily grouping areas together. You could create areas that have an equal population size or that have similar demographic characteristics. Better yet, you could combine the tracts to approximate areas that have some existing social, economic, or political meaning. Neighborhoods are areas that are defined locally and are a historic product of the physical, social, and political landscape. Ideally, they are defined by the people who live there, but neighborhoods are also contested spaces where outsiders may seek to influence what the neighborhood is to suit their own purposes. For example, real estate agents or developers may try to "re-brand" neighborhoods to make them more attractive to affluent home buyers, often in opposition to current residents.

The question of what constitutes a neighborhood is fraught with issues (Nicotera, 2007; Sperling, 2012), and there are few official "definitions" that you can apply and certainly none that are national in scope. Do some research on the internet for your area of study and see what exists. In particular, look at the local city and regional planning agencies, neighborhood organizations, universities, and the local open data movement. Some cities have taken census tracts and combined them either to create or approximate neighborhoods that local residents would recognize or to create statistical areas for studying communities, or both. Some cities have areas like districts, wards, or community planning areas that fulfill some legal or administrative function. These might be related or constructed from census geographies, or they might not. If they are related, you can use their data to identify which census tracts were used for constructing the area, and then you can reconstruct it using the same tracts. If they are not related, you may have to compare resources like local maps to the census geography (e.g., in TIGERweb) to approximate the areas using census tracts. Geographic information system (GIS; covered in Chapter 10) can be used to help make these decisions.

In this example, we will look at four census tracts that make up the Over the Rhine neighborhood, which is just north of downtown Cincinnati, Ohio (Figure 6.1). Originally a working class neighborhood, the area has a large concentration of historic buildings and has recently become more gentrified. Like many city planning agencies, the Department of City Planning in Cincinnati has a section of its website dedicated to Plans, Maps, and Data, and another section dedicated to Census and Demographics. The department has aggregated census tracts and, in some cases, block groups to create Statistical Neighborhood Approximations: https://www.cincinnati-oh.gov/planning/reports-data/census-demographics/. The city publishes reports with detailed maps displaying the boundaries along with 2010 census and 2006–2010 ACS data. They do not publish the MOEs for the ACS data for either the individual tracts or the aggregated values.

We will look at Table B07204: Geographical Mobility in the Past Year for Current Residence–State, County and Place Level. This data shows us how many people lived in their current homes during the past year. For residents who didn't, we can see if they previously lived in a different city, county, state, or outside the United States. This data is useful for illustrating residential stability versus dynamism: Have most people lived in the neighborhood for a long time, or is there a large influx of newcomers?

**FIGURE 6.1 ● CENSUS TRACTS IN THE OVER THE RHINE NEIGHBORHOOD, CINCINNATI, OHIO**

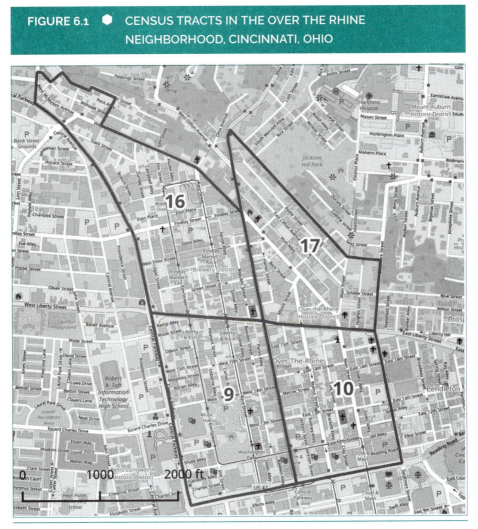

*Source:* Base map is from the OpenStreetMap: https://www.openstreetmap.org/

Interpreting this requires a point of reference, so we will compare the neighborhood's data with the entire city.

Before we begin to work with the formulas, we will need to sift through all the variables in this table and whittle them down to just the ones we need. Given the large number of variables in the ACS, it's important to distinguish what represents a category versus a subcategory versus a subsubcategory in order to ensure that you are comparing apples with apples. We will spend some time dissecting the mobility and residency table to understand how the pieces fit.

1.  **Import the residency table and save.** Launch Calc, go to Sheet—Insert Sheet From File, and from Chapter 6 Exercise 1 folder import the file ACSDT5Y2016_B07204_with_ann.csv. Hit OK to get through the import screen. Save the file as a Calc spreadsheet in Chapter 6 Exercise 1 folder. As you look at this file, you'll see there are five rows of data, one for the City of Cincinnati and four for each of the census tracts that are part of the Over the Rhine neighborhood (Figure 6.2). There are a lot of columns: In ACS tables, columns always come in pairs, one for the estimate and one for the MOE for that estimate.

2.  **Transpose the data and study the attributes.** Add a new worksheet and name it OTR (for Over the Rhine). Copy the data in the original sheet and do a Paste Special—Transpose into this new sheet, so that the attribute names are now rows and the geographies are in columns. This will make it easier for us to analyze. Make the attribute column wider so you can read the labels. Save your work. The data in this table is broken down into a number of subcategories or facets, and the facets are indicated with repeating labels for the upper category followed by a dash and the label for the subcategory (Figure 6.3). At the top is the total estimate and its MOE, which for this dataset is the population aged 1 year and over. Under that is the number of people who lived in the Same House 1 year ago and its MOE. This category has no additional facets. But for the number who lived in a Different house in the United States 1 year ago, there are

**FIGURE 6.2  ●  RESIDENTIAL MOBILITY FOR CINCINNATI AND OVER THE RHINE CENSUS TRACTS**

| | A | B | C | D | E |
|---|---|---|---|---|---|
| 1 | GEO.id | GEO.display-label | ESTIMATE#HD01_VDIM#VD01 | ESTIMATE#HD02_VDIM#VD01 | ESTIMATE#HD01_VDIM#VD02 |
| 2 | Id | $(dim.label) | Estimate; Total: | Margin of Error; Total: | Estimate; Total: - Same house 1 year ago |
| 3 | 0600000US3906115000 | Cincinnati city, Hamilton County, Ohio | 293772 | 451 | |
| 4 | 1400000US39061000900 | Census Tract 9, Hamilton County, Oh | 1588 | 246 | 220219 |
| 5 | 1400000US39061001000 | Census Tract 10, Hamilton County, Oh | 1399 | 225 | 1033 |
| 6 | 1400000US39061001600 | Census Tract 16, Hamilton County, Oh | 1004 | 196 | 975 |
| 7 | 1400000US39061001700 | Census Tract 17, Hamilton County, Oh | 1074 | 142 | 677 |
| | | | | | 759 |

**FIGURE 6.3  ●  TABLE TRANSPOSED, FACETING OF VARIABLES**

| | A | B | C | D | E | F | G |
|---|---|---|---|---|---|---|---|
| 1 | GEO.id | Id | 0600000US39 | 1400000US3 | 1400000US3 | 1400000US3 | 1400000US390 |
| 2 | GEO.display | $(dim.label) | Cincinnati cit | Census Tract | Census Tract | Census Tract | Census Tract 17 |
| 3 | ESTIMATE# | Estimate; Total: | 293772 | 1588 | 1399 | 1004 | 1074 |
| 4 | ESTIMATE# | Margin of Error; Total: | 451 | 246 | 225 | 196 | 142 |
| 5 | ESTIMATE# | Estimate; Total: - Same house 1 year ago | 220219 | 1033 | 975 | 677 | 759 |
| 6 | ESTIMATE# | Margin of Error; Total: - Same house 1 year ago | 2593 | 202 | 165 | 167 | 188 |
| 7 | ESTIMATE# | Estimate; Total: - Different house in United States 1 year ago: | 71169 | 555 | 419 | 327 | 315 |
| 8 | ESTIMATE# | Margin of Error; Total: - Different house in United States 1 year ago: | 2501 | 150 | 203 | 97 | 143 |
| 9 | ESTIMATE# | Estimate; Total: - Different house in United States 1 year ago: - Same city or town: | 41198 | 332 | 211 | 253 | 207 |
| 10 | ESTIMATE# | Margin of Error; Total: - Different house in United States 1 year ago: - Same city or town: | 2226 | 116 | 110 | 77 | 125 |
| 11 | ESTIMATE# | Estimate; Total: - Different house in United States 1 year ago: - Same city or town: - Same county | 41198 | 332 | 211 | 253 | 207 |
| 12 | ESTIMATE# | Margin of Error; Total: - Different house in United States 1 year ago: - Same city or town: - Same county | 2226 | 116 | 110 | 77 | 125 |

several facets: Different house—Same City or town, then Different House—Same City or town—same county, and so on. It's important to interpret this correctly to make proper comparisons without double counting or omitting values that we need.

You can view a more human-readable version of this table in **data.census.gov** or view the table structure either in the Census Bureau's technical documentation or on an alternative site like the Census Reporter `https://censusreporter.org/`, where you can type the table ID number into the Explore Box and get the table structure as a result (Figure 6.4). Based on the indentation, we can clearly see that under the Total the top level categories are "Same house 1 year ago," "Different house in the United States 1 year ago," and "Abroad 1 year ago." If we add up these three values, we would get the total value. If we summed the subcategories for Same city or town and Elsewhere, we would get the total for Different house in United States 1 year ago. Alternatively, if we summed Same city or town with Same county and Different county under Elsewhere, we would also get the total for Different house. Paying attention to the indentation or faceting is the key to understanding the relationship between the variables.

In deciding which variables to include in our summary, we want to make sure our data will sum to the total and that we can capture enough essential or interesting information about residency and migration. We would omit subcategories where the values are too small to be reliable or are not meaningful for the place we are studying.

3. **Delete attributes**. Starting from the bottom and working our way up, delete the following rows:

   (a) Rows 35 to 40, abroad subcategories. These values are too small to be meaningful for our area.

   (b) Rows 25 to 32, different state regional subcategories. These values are also too small for our area.

   (c) Rows 19 to 20, elsewhere—different county. We'll keep the subcategories for this total instead.

   (d) Rows 15 to 16, elsewhere. We're keeping several subcategories of this category.

   (e) Rows 11 to 14, same city or town subcategories. These don't apply to our area, since Cincinnati does not cross county boundaries.

   (f) Rows 7 to 8, different house in United States. We're keeping several subcategories of this category.

**FIGURE 6.4    ●    READABLE TABLE STRUCTURE FOR ACS TABLE B07204**

**Table universe:** Population 1 Year and Over in the United States

**Colums in this table**

Total:

   Same house 1 year ago

   Different house in United States 1 year ago:

     Same city or town:

       Same county

       Different county (same state)

     Elsewhere:

       Same county

       Different county:

         Same state

         Different state:

           Northeast

           Midwest

           South

           West

 Abroad 1 year ago:

   Puerto Rico

   U.S. Island Areas

   Foregin country

*Source:* The Census Reporter https://censusreporter.org/tables/B07204/

When you are finished, we should have 16 rows remaining (Figure 6.5). We have enough variables to indicate whether residents live in the same house, or in a different house in the same city, outside the city but in the same county, in a different county in the same state, in a different state, or abroad. Pick a row for one of the tracts, and verify that each of the estimates sums to the total to ensure that you've saved the right columns. Save your work.

4. **Clean up**. Delete column A (contains variable IDs) and delete row 1 (contains geographic IDs). Give the variables and the geographies the shorter names

**FIGURE 6.5  ●  COLUMNS REMAINING IN TABLE B07204 AFTER DELETIONS**

| | A | B | C | D | E | F | G |
|---|---|---|---|---|---|---|---|
| 1 | GEO.id | Id | 0600000US3▶ | 1400000US3▶ | 1400000US3▶ | 1400000US3▶ | 1400000US390 |
| 2 | GEO.display | $(dim.label) | Cincinnati cit▶ | Census Tract▶ | Census Tract▶ | Census Tract▶ | Census Tract 1 |
| 3 | ESTIMATE# | Estimate; Total: | 293772 | 1588 | 1399 | 1004 | 1074 |
| 4 | ESTIMATE# | Margin of Error; Total: | 451 | 246 | 225 | 196 | 142 |
| 5 | ESTIMATE# | Estimate; Total: - Same house 1 year ago | 220219 | 1033 | 975 | 677 | 759 |
| 6 | ESTIMATE# | Margin of Error; Total: - Same house 1 year ago | 2593 | 202 | 165 | 167 | 188 |
| 7 | ESTIMATE# | Estimate; Total: - Different house in United States 1 year ago: - Same city or town: | 41198 | 332 | 211 | 253 | 207 |
| 8 | ESTIMATE# | Margin of Error; Total: - Different house in United States 1 year ago: - Same city or town: | 2226 | 116 | 110 | 77 | 125 |
| 9 | ESTIMATE# | Estimate; Total: - Different house in United States 1 year ago: - Elsewhere: - Same county | 9618 | 32 | 100 | 9 | 31 |
| 10 | ESTIMATE# | Margin of Error; Total: - Different house in United States 1 year ago: - Elsewhere: - Same county | 1056 | 28 | 155 | 10 | 42 |
| 11 | ESTIMATE# | Estimate; Total: - Different house in United States 1 year ago: - Elsewhere: - Different county: - Same sta▶ | 10525 | 91 | 33 | 23 | 36 |
| 12 | ESTIMATE# | Margin of Error; Total: - Different house in United States 1 year ago: - Elsewhere: - Different county: - Sar▶ | 676 | 72 | 21 | 22 | 43 |
| 13 | ESTIMATE# | Estimate; Total: - Different house in United States 1 year ago: - Elsewhere: - Different county: - Different ▶ | 9828 | 100 | 75 | 42 | 41 |
| 14 | ESTIMATE# | Margin of Error; Total: - Different house in United States 1 year ago: - Elsewhere: - Different county: - Diff▶ | 902 | 44 | 43 | 46 | 34 |
| 15 | ESTIMATE# | Estimate; Total: - Abroad 1 year ago: | 2384 | 0 | 5 | 0 | 0 |
| 16 | ESTIMATE# | Margin of Error; Total: - Abroad 1 year ago: | 455 | 11 | 8 | 11 | 11 |

**FIGURE 6.6  ●  RENAME ROWS AND COLUMNS IN TABLE B07204**

| | A | B | C | D | E | F |
|---|---|---|---|---|---|---|
| 1 | Geography | Cincinnati | Tract 9 | Tract 10 | Tract 16 | Tract 17 |
| 2 | Total Residents | 293772 | 1588 | 1399 | 1004 | 1074 |
| 3 | TR MOE | 451 | 246 | 225 | 196 | 142 |
| 4 | Same house | 220219 | 1033 | 975 | 677 | 759 |
| 5 | SH MOE | 2593 | 202 | 165 | 167 | 188 |
| 6 | Dif House Same City | 41198 | 332 | 211 | 253 | 207 |
| 7 | DHSC MOE | 2226 | 116 | 110 | 77 | 125 |
| 8 | Dif House Dif City Same County | 9618 | 32 | 100 | 9 | 31 |
| 9 | DHDCSC MOE | 1056 | 28 | 155 | 10 | 42 |
| 10 | Dif House Dif County Same State | 10525 | 91 | 33 | 23 | 36 |
| 11 | DHDCSS MOE | 676 | 72 | 21 | 22 | 43 |
| 12 | Dif House Dif State | 9828 | 100 | 75 | 42 | 41 |
| 13 | DHDS MOE | 902 | 44 | 43 | 46 | 34 |
| 14 | Abroad | 2384 | 0 | 5 | 0 | 0 |
| 15 | A MOE | 455 | 11 | 8 | 11 | 11 |

that appear in Figure 6.6. Since we are just working with this small amount of data in a spreadsheet, we can use human-readable names with spaces. If this were a larger dataset, or we were importing this data into a database or GIS, we would need to use shorter, cryptic names without spaces or simply keep the original variable ID numbers and use a lookup table for the names. Save your work.

5. **Copy and paste special—transpose**. Select all the data cells, copy, click in cell G1 and do paste special—transpose. Then delete columns A through F. This gets our finished and formatted data back to the original structure, where the geographies are in rows (Figure 6.7). This simply makes the data easier to read, as you can see the MOE beside each value. Save your work.

6. **Calculate CVs for total residents**. The MOEs for many of the tract values look high. For example, in Tract 17, 207 people ±125 lived in a different

FIGURE 6.7  ●  TRANSPOSE CLEANED DATA BACK TO THE ORIGINAL STRUCTURE

| | A | B | C | D | E | F | G | |
|---|---|---|---|---|---|---|---|---|
| 1 | Geography | Total Resider | TR MOE | Same house | SH MOE | Dif House Sa | DHSC MOE | D |
| 2 | Cincinnati | 293772 | 451 | 220219 | 2593 | 41198 | 2226 | |
| 3 | Tract 9 | 1588 | 246 | 1033 | 202 | 332 | 116 | |
| 4 | Tract 10 | 1399 | 225 | 975 | 165 | 211 | 110 | |
| 5 | Tract 16 | 1004 | 196 | 677 | 167 | 253 | 77 | |
| 6 | Tract 17 | 1074 | 142 | 759 | 188 | 207 | 125 | |

FIGURE 6.8  ●  CALCULATE COEFFICIENT OF VARIATION (CV) FOR TOTAL RESIDENTS

D2    ▼  $f_x$  Σ  =    =ROUND(((C2/1.65)/B2)*100)

| | A | B | C | D | E |
|---|---|---|---|---|---|
| 1 | Geography | Total Resider | TR MOE | TR CV | Same house |
| 2 | Cincinnati | 293772 | 451 | 0 | 220219 |
| 3 | Tract 9 | 1588 | 246 | 9 | 1033 |
| 4 | Tract 10 | 1399 | 225 | 10 | 975 |
| 5 | Tract 16 | 1004 | 196 | 12 | 677 |
| 6 | Tract 17 | 1074 | 142 | 8 | 759 |

house in the same city a year ago. Let's calculate CVs for each variable. The formula is as follows:

$$CV = \frac{MOE/1.645}{ACS\ estimate} * 100$$

We divide the MOE by the $Z$ value, then divide that result by the estimate, then multiply by 100. In statistics, $Z$ values are constants that represent the critical value for the specific confidence interval being used. Since all ACS estimates are published at a 90% confidence interval, the $Z$ value will always be 1.645.

Select column C, right-click, and Insert Column Right. In cell D1, type the label TR CV. In cell D2, type the formula =ROUND(((C2/1.65)/B3)*100). Paste the formula down the column. The CVs for total population are pretty low, so these estimates are of high reliability (Figure 6.8). Remember that the definition of reliability varies; we could say 0 to 15 is low, 16 to 34 is medium,

FIGURE 6.9 ● CALCULATE COEFFECIENT OF VARIATION (CV) FOR OTHER VARIABLES

| | Geography | Total Residen | TR MOE | TR CV | Same house | SH MOE | SH CV | Dif House Sa | DHSC MOE | DHSC CV | |
|---|---|---|---|---|---|---|---|---|---|---|---|
| J2 | | | $f_x$ $\Sigma$ = | =ROUND(((I2/1.65)/H2)*100) | | | | | | | |
| 1 | Geography | Total Residen | TR MOE | TR CV | Same house | SH MOE | SH CV | Dif House Sa | DHSC MOE | DHSC CV | |
| 2 | Cincinnati | 293772 | 451 | 0 | 220219 | 2593 | 1 | 41198 | 2226 | 3 | |
| 3 | Tract 9 | 1588 | 246 | 9 | 1033 | 202 | 12 | 332 | 116 | 21 | |
| 4 | Tract 10 | 1399 | 225 | 10 | 975 | 165 | 10 | 211 | 110 | 32 | |
| 5 | Tract 16 | 1004 | 196 | 12 | 677 | 167 | 15 | 253 | 77 | 18 | |
| 6 | Tract 17 | 1074 | 142 | 8 | 759 | 188 | 15 | 207 | 125 | 37 | |

and 35 and above is high. Or we could say anything below 20 is acceptable and everything above is not.

7. **Calculate CVs for remaining values.** Insert columns to the right of each of the MOE columns. In the first cell of each of these columns, enter a label for the column that mimics the label for the MOE column. For example, for Same house, the MOE column is SH MOE. Name the CV column SH CV. Then copy the five formulas in column D and paste them into each of the new CV columns. The formulas will auto increment, so they draw values from the estimates and MOE columns that are to their immediate left (Figure 6.9). In the final column for Abroad, you will get some error messages; this is normal because the estimates are zero, and you cannot divide zero by another number. The CVs for the census tracts are extremely high for many of the variables. For different house, same city (DHSC), most of the values are of medium reliability (16–34) except for Tract 17, which is of low reliability ($\geq$ 35). The values for different house, different city, same county (DHDCSC) are wholly unreliable, with CVs between 53 and 94. It's clear that we should aggregate to increase reliability. Save your work.

8. **Calculate sum and MOE for total residents**. In cell A7, type the label Over the Rhine. In cell B7, type the formula =SUM(B3:B6). This returns the total population of the neighborhood by combining the four tracts: 5,065. To calculate the MOE for a sum, you take the square root of the sum of the squares for each MOE:

$$MOE = \sqrt{MOE1^2 + MOE2^2}$$

In cell C7, type the formula =ROUND(SQRT(SUMSQ(C3:C6))). The SUMSQ function is convenient because we can give it an array of values, instead of having to square each individual value and sum it. The MOE for the neighborhood is 412 (Figure 6.10). Last, copy the CV formula in cell D6 and paste it into cell D7. The CV for the Over the Rhine estimate of total

### FIGURE 6.10 ● CALCULATE MARGIN OF ERROR FOR POPULATION OF OVER THE RHINE

| C7 | | ▼ | $f_x$ Σ = | =ROUND(SQRT(SUMSQ(C3:C6))) | |
|---|---|---|---|---|---|

| | A | B | C | D | E |
|---|---|---|---|---|---|
| 1 | Geography | Total Resider TR MOE | | TR CV | Same house |
| 2 | Cincinnati | 293772 | 451 | 0 | 220219 |
| 3 | Tract 9 | 1588 | 246 | 9 | 1033 |
| 4 | Tract 10 | 1399 | 225 | 10 | 975 |
| 5 | Tract 16 | 1004 | 196 | 12 | 677 |
| 6 | Tract 17 | 1074 | 142 | 8 | 759 |
| 7 | Over the Rhine | 5065 | 412 | 5 | |

residents is 5. This is a good improvement; the CVs for the individual tracts ranged from 8 to 12. Save your work.

9. **Calculate the summaries for the other variables**. Select the three values in cells B7 to cell D7 by selecting cell B7 and dragging your mouse to cell D7. Right-click and copy. With the cells highlighted, click on the black box in the lower right-hand corner of cell D7, and drag it slowly to the right. As you do this, a purple outline appears around the cells. Drag the box until you reach the last cell V7 and then release. You just copied these three formulas across the row as a set. Spot check the formulas and values to verify they are correct. Values for Same House in Over the Rhine should be 3,444 residents with an MOE of 362 and a CV of 6. Residents who were previously in a different house but in the same city are $1,003 \pm 217$ with a CV of 13. By aggregating the values for this category, we now have an estimate that's highly reliable compared with the individual tracts that had estimates of medium reliability. In most cases, the improvements are good, but in some, the values are still too small to produce reliable estimates. The neighborhood estimate for Different house, different city, same county has a high CV of 57. Save your work.

10. **Adjust the formulas for estimates of zero**. Scroll over to the last variable, residents who lived abroad a year ago. For three of the tracts the estimate is zero, but there's still a MOE that suggests the value could be $0 \pm 11$. When summing estimates that include values of zero, we only incorporate the largest MOE for the zero values *once*. Click in cell U7, and modify the formula to this: =ROUND(SQRT(SUMSQ(U3:U4))). This incorporates the MOE of

just one of the zero values (Tract 9) and the one tract that had a nonzero value (Tract 10). Once you modify the formula, the MOE decreases from 21 to 14, and the CV value will decline as well.

11. **Calculate percent totals**. We'll calculate percent totals for the city and the neighborhood. In cell A9, add a label for Cincinnati, and in cell A10, one for Over the Rhine. In cell E9, enter the formula =E2/$B$2. In cell E10, enter the formula =E7/$B$7. This calculates the percentage of Cincinnati's and Over the Rhine's residents who lived in the same house a year ago. It's important that we don't multiply the result by 100 to get whole values; the MOE formula depends on the value being represented as a fractional proportion. So we can read the values more easily, select rows 9 and 10, right-click, choose Format Cells, and under Category select the option for Percent.

12. **Calculate MOE for percent totals**. Calculating the MOE for the percent total is more involved: You square the percent total and the MOE for the total population, multiply them, subtract that result from the square of the MOE for the subset population (the numerator), take the square root of that result and divide it by the total population (the denominator):

$$MOE = \frac{\sqrt{MOE\,subset^2 - (PCT\,total^2 * MOE\,total^2)}}{Total}$$

In cell F9, type the formula =(SQRT(F2^2 - (E9^2*$C$2^2)))/$B$2. In cell F10, type the formula =(SQRT(F7^2 - (E10^2*$C$7^2)))/$B$7.

We use dollar signs to lock the total resident estimate and MOE in place, since this will be the base for all our percentages. About 75% ± .88% of Cincinnati's residents lived in their homes a year ago compared with 68% ± 4.53% of Over the Rhine's residents, suggesting that there is more housing turnover in the neighborhood compared with the city as a whole. Pay attention to your cell references and the order of parentheses, as it's easy to make a mistake. After you enter a formula, if you double-click in the formula cell, all the cells you are referencing will be highlighted (Figure 6.11). To exit this feature, hit the escape key (don't click in another cell, otherwise you'll be modifying your formula). Save your work.

13. **Check your work**. To verify that your formula is correct, visit the ACS calculator at the Program for Applied Demographics at Cornell University: `https://pad.human.cornell.edu/acscalc/`. Scroll down

**FIGURE 6.11** ● CALCULATING THE MARGIN OF ERROR FOR PERCENT TOTALS FOR THE CITY AND NEIGHBORHOOD

| ROUND | | | fx | ✗ | ✓ | =(SQRT(F7^2-(E10^2*$C$7^2)))/$B$7 | | |
|---|---|---|---|---|---|---|---|---|
| | A | B | C | D | E | F | G | H |
| 1 | Geography | Total Residen | TR MOE | TR CV | Same house | SH MOE | SH CV | Dif House Sa |
| 2 | Cincinnati | 293772 | 451 | 0 | 220219 | 2593 | 1 | 41198 |
| 3 | Tract 9 | 1588 | 246 | 9 | 1033 | 202 | 12 | 332 |
| 4 | Tract 10 | 1399 | 225 | 10 | 975 | 165 | 10 | 211 |
| 5 | Tract 16 | 1004 | 196 | 12 | 677 | 167 | 15 | 253 |
| 6 | Tract 17 | 1074 | 142 | 8 | 759 | 188 | 15 | 207 |
| 7 | Over the Rhine | 5065 | 412 | 5 | 3444 | 362 | 6 | 1003 |
| 8 | | | | | | | | |
| 9 | Cincinnati | | | | 74.96% | 0.88% | | |
| 10 | Over the Rhine | | | | 68.00% | =(SQRT(F7^2-(E10^2*$C$7^2)))/$B$7 | | |

to the second calculator for "Computing a new value from two existing values." For the first value, enter the estimate and MOE for Over the Rhine's Same house: 3,444 and 362. For the second value, enter the total residents: 5,065 and 412 (Figure 6.12). Hit the proportion button, and the result is calculated below. You're on the right track if this result matches yours.

14. **Apply formulas to other values**. Select cells 9 and 10 in columns E, F, *and* G: the four formulas *and* the two blank cells to the right of them. As we did earlier, copy these cells, drag across to the end, and release to paste. The references for the subset MOE and percentage should auto increment, while the two total values should be locked in place with the dollar signs. The value for different house, same city should be 14.02% ± 0.76% for the city and 19.80% ± 3.97% for the county (Figure 6.13). Save your work.

15. **Are the differences between values significant?** Based on these estimates, a higher percentage of the city's residents lived in the same house a year ago compared with Over the Rhine's residents (75% vs. 68%), and a higher percentage of Over the Rhine's residents lived in a different house in Cincinnati a year ago compared with citywide residents as a whole (almost 20% vs. 14%). This suggests that there's been a small influx of new residents to Over the Rhine, as people are moving from other parts of the city to the neighborhood (to measure change over time, see InfoBox 6.3).

It's important to remember that these are estimates that fall within a range of values; 19.8% of Over the Rhine residents lived in a different house in Cincinnati a year ago, ± 3.97%. The actual percentage could be as low as 16% or as high as 24%, and there's a 10% chance that the true value could fall outside this range. Is the value for the neighborhood significantly different from the city's?

## FIGURE 6.12 ● CORNELL PAD ACS CALCULATOR

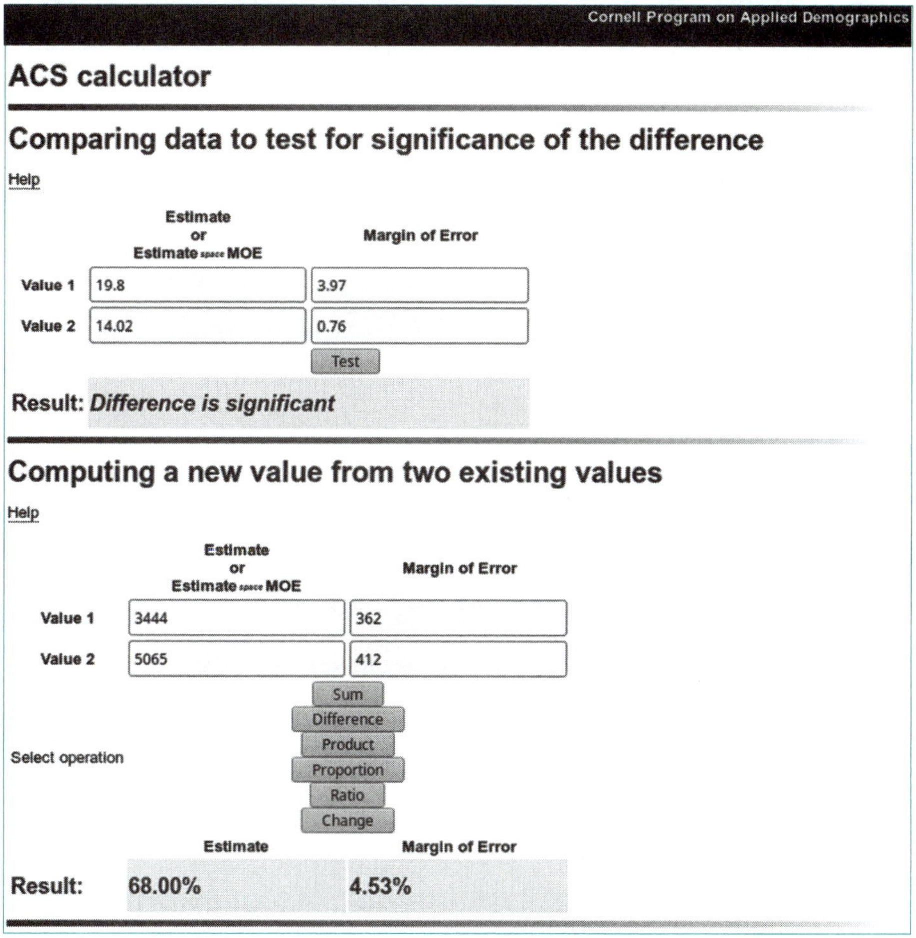

Cornell Program on Applied Demographics

### ACS calculator

## Comparing data to test for significance of the difference

Help

| | Estimate<br>or<br>Estimate *space* MOE | Margin of Error |
|---|---|---|
| Value 1 | 19.8 | 3.97 |
| Value 2 | 14.02 | 0.76 |

Test

Result: *Difference is significant*

## Computing a new value from two existing values

Help

| | Estimate<br>or<br>Estimate *space* MOE | Margin of Error |
|---|---|---|
| Value 1 | 3444 | 362 |
| Value 2 | 5065 | 412 |

Select operation

Sum
Difference
Product
Proportion
Ratio
Change

| | Estimate | Margin of Error |
|---|---|---|
| Result: | 68.00% | 4.53% |

## FIGURE 6.13 ● CALCULATE PERCENT TOTALS AND MARGINS OF ERROR FOR REMAINING VARIABLES

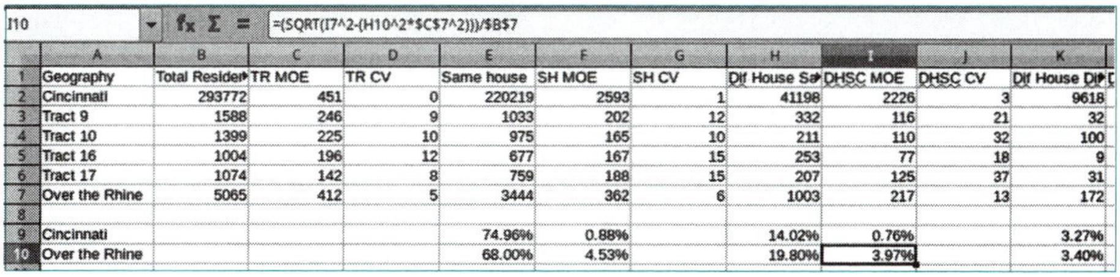

I10    fx Σ =    =(SQRT(I7^2-(H10^2*$C$7^2)))/$B$7

| | A | B | C | D | E | F | G | H | I | J | K |
|---|---|---|---|---|---|---|---|---|---|---|---|
| 1 | Geography | Total Resider | TR MOE | TR CV | Same house | SH MOE | SH CV | Dif House Sa | DHSC MOE | DHSC CV | Dif House Dif D |
| 2 | Cincinnati | 293772 | 451 | 0 | 220219 | 2593 | 1 | 41198 | 2226 | 3 | 9618 |
| 3 | Tract 9 | 1588 | 246 | 9 | 1033 | 202 | 12 | 332 | 116 | 21 | 32 |
| 4 | Tract 10 | 1399 | 225 | 10 | 975 | 165 | 10 | 211 | 110 | 32 | 100 |
| 5 | Tract 16 | 1004 | 196 | 12 | 677 | 167 | 15 | 253 | 77 | 18 | 9 |
| 6 | Tract 17 | 1074 | 142 | 8 | 759 | 188 | 15 | 207 | 125 | 37 | 31 |
| 7 | Over the Rhine | 5065 | 412 | 5 | 3444 | 362 | 6 | 1003 | 217 | 13 | 172 |
| 8 | | | | | | | | | | | |
| 9 | Cincinnati | | | | 74.96% | 0.88% | | 14.02% | 0.76% | | 3.27% |
| 10 | Over the Rhine | | | | 68.00% | 4.53% | | 19.80% | 3.97% | | 3.40% |

## ✔ INFOBOX 6.3 CALCULATING CHANGE OVER TIME

There are two issues to bear in mind when using ACS estimates to measure change over time. First, if you are using a 5-year-period estimate, you should only compare estimates that cover nonoverlapping periods of time. For example, you could compare 2012–2016 with 2007–2011 because these estimates were generated from two different sample pools. It would not make sense to compare 2012–2016 with 2011–2015 because these two periods have significant overlap; four fifths of these estimates were generated from the same pool of samples.

Second, if you are using 1-year-period estimates, it may not make sense to calculate annual change or to compare changes from one year with the next. With the exception of rapidly growing or declining places, any change from one year to the next is likely due to sampling variability. If you want to study population change over time in total or by gender, age, or race, it's better to use data from the PEP.

The population for Over the Rhine was $3,163 \pm 510$ in 2007–2011 and $5,065 \pm 412$ in 2012–2016, an increase of 1,902. The formula for calculating change (difference) is the same one used for calculating aggregates (sums):

$$MOE = \sqrt{510^2 + 412^2} = 656$$

The population growth rate for Over the Rhine for this time period was 60.1% (1,902/3,163). The formula for calculating percent change is the same one used for calculating a ratio. It incorporates the MOE for the most recent population estimate, the ratio between the most recent and oldest estimate, the MOE from the oldest estimate, and the oldest estimate. Be careful and make sure that your parentheses in the spreadsheet formula are correct.

$$MOE = \frac{\sqrt{MOE\,newpop^2 + (ratio^2 * MOE\,oldpop^2)}}{oldpop}$$

$$MOE = \frac{\sqrt{412^2 + ((5065/3163)^2 * 510^2)}}{3163} = .290$$

Spreadsheet: =(SQRT(412^2+((5065/3163)^2*510^2)))/3163

This is a rapidly growing neighborhood. The Population of Over the Rhine grew by $1,902 \pm 656$ between 2007–2011 and 2012–2016, a growth rate of $60.1\% \pm 29.0\%$.

Let's go back to Cornell's ACS calculator. In the top calculator, "Comparing data to test for significance of the difference," enter the neighborhood's percentage and MOE as Value 1: 19.8 and 3.97. Enter the city's as Value 2: 14.02 and 0.76 (refer back to Figure 6.12). Hit test. The result is a significant difference, so we can say that these two estimates are indeed different from each other. If we looked at some of the other variables to the right in our spread-sheet, it's likely that many of the differences would not be significant, as the estimates are closer to one another and many of the intervals (indicated by the MOE) overlap. In those cases, any difference in the estimate may be the result of random chance.

Instead of using the Cornell calculator, you can calculate statistical difference yourself using this formula:

$$SD = \left| \frac{EST1 - EST2}{\sqrt{SE1^2 + SE2^2}} \right|$$

You subtract the second estimate from the first estimate and divide it by the square root of the sum of squares for the standard errors of each estimate, and take the absolute value of the result. The standard error is a measure of the variability of the sample mean. We calculate it by dividing the MOE by the $Z$ value for the 90% confidence level, 1.645. If the test value (the result of this formula) is greater than the $Z$ value of 1.645, then the differences between the values is significant. Otherwise, if the result is lower than 1.645, the difference is not significant. Here's what the formula looks like in Calc, with values from the last step of the exercise hard coded in =ABS(19.8-14.02)/SQRT((3.97/1.645)^2+(0.76/1.645)^2)

The result is 2.352, indicating significant difference since the value is higher than 1.645. If you want practice using this formula, try the supplemental online exercise at the end of this chapter.

There are two important caveats to the exercise we just did. First, in some circumstances, it is possible that the formula for calculating the MOE for the percent total will fail. This happens when the value under the square root is negative (you can't take the square root of a negative number). In this instance, and for those specific values, you would use the formula for calculating a ratio instead of a proportion. The ratio (in this case) is the total population divided by the subset (as opposed to the subset divided by the total for a proportion), and it gets added under the square root instead of subtracted:

$$MOE = \frac{\sqrt{MOE\ subset^2 + (Ratio^2 * MOE\ total^2)}}{Total}$$

Since it would be cumbersome to compute all the ratios in advance (like we did the proportions), we would do the ratio calculation as part of the formula. In our example, the formula would look like this: =(SQRT(F7^2 + (($B$7/E7)^2*$C$7^2)))/$B$7, where ($B$7/E7) is the ratio calculation.

Second, the placement of data and formulas in the spreadsheet should vary based on how you intend to use it. If you are working with a small amount of data and your goal is presentation, then you can do what we did in this exercise and place the percentages on their own rows in the same sheet. You could even place them in a separate worksheet and rearrange the end result so it's more readable. On the other hand, if this was a large dataset or one that was eventually going into a database, stats package, or GIS, you would need to follow strict rules of keeping geography in rows and attributes in columns. You could arrange the columns in sets of four: (1) estimate, (2) MOE, (3) percent total, and (4) MOE for percent total. You might even include the CVs. This format makes it harder to read, but the idea is you would be using those other packages to pull and analyze the data.

## Exercise 2: Creating Custom Extracts With Dexter and Using ACS Data in SQLite

This exercise demonstrates how to access the MCDC's Public Data Archive using the Uexplore Dexter tool. This tool allows you to create customized data extracts and to download data in bulk. After creating and downloading an extract, we'll briefly summarize how to process the data in order to prepare it for loading into a database. Since we have covered this material in the last exercise, we will not go into step-by-step detail for this part. We'll conclude with considerations and examples of querying ACS data in SQLite. SQL queries of ACS data have to be constructed to account for the fact that ACS estimates represent intervals, and some values may not be statistically different from other values.

### MCDC's Uexplore/Dexter for Creating Extracts

In this exercise, we'll use the Dexter tool at the MCDC to create a customized extract. The MCDC has loaded all the summary files into its databases and has created an extract program where users specify criteria in a series of web forms to pull data. Using this tool requires familiarity with how the summary files are structured, working knowledge of summary levels and GEOID codes, and knowledge of what's available in the census. While the tool may look daunting at first glance, it's really not difficult to use *if* you are familiar with how census data is structured. It requires just a few inputs, as much of the form is optional. The MCDC provides a quick start guide as well as a video and detailed instructions at http://mcdc.missouri.edu/help/uexplore-dexter/. Our exercise will cover the basics.

Data on voter identification shows that areas tend to identify with one political party versus the other based on certain socioeconomic characteristics (Pew Research Center,

2018). Let's say, we are interested in studying voting patterns and we want to identify all the counties in the United States that have less than 250k population and are below the national average for median income and the percentage of the population with a bachelor's degree. Once we locate these counties, we also want to know what the median age is. Dexter will allow us to select just the variables we need in a single extract.

1. **Scan through the data profiles**. Since the data profiles contain a broad cross section of data, it makes sense to look there first to see if we can obtain our variables from there instead of the individual detailed tables. The MCDC creates its own customized versions of the DP02 to DP05 profile tables with some additions and deletions. We've looked at these profiles in earlier chapters. Go to the ACS profiles menu at `https://census.missouri.edu/acs/profiles/`. Select 2012–2016 as the period and counties as the type. Choose any state and any county. Generate the report for all four subjects, and browse or search through it to find our variables. It just so happens that all of them are included in these profiles, so we can get our data from this source.

2. **Launch Dexter**. Now that we have identified the variables, launch Uexplore Dexter at `http://mcdc.missouri.edu/applications/uexplore.html`. First, we select the dataset: At the top under American Community Survey Data, click 2016, then choose acs2016—American Community Survey Data, 2016 vintage. On the next page, we choose whether we want the base tables for the 1-year or 5-year ACS at the top, or one of the MCDC profiles. This list allows us to filter by geography at the outset, or we can simply select an option with all geographies and filter later. Remember, we want data on counties, and many counties are not in the 1-year ACS as their population is less than 65k people. So click on the link for usmcdcprofiles5yr.sas7bdat, Period estimates (2012–2016 5-year) for all U.S. geographies above tract, regardless of population (Figure 6.14).

3. **Enter Dexter criteria in Sections I and II**. At the top of the page, we see there are almost 580k rows in this dataset (for every piece of geography for which a profile is published) and more than 1,000 columns. We'll use Dexter to narrow that down. Section I in the tool allows you to choose a variety of output formats that include data-friendly (delimited files and database files) and presentation-friendly (listing/reports in PDF or HTML) formats. Choose CSV. Section II is where we apply filters to the rows. Under Variable/Column in the first box, we'll select SumLev, under the Operator, we'll choose Equal to (=), and in the Value box we'll type 050, which is the summary-level code for counties (see Chapter 3). The other options in the drop-down

**FIGURE 6.14   ●   MCDC UEXPLORE MENU FOR 2016 ACS DATA**

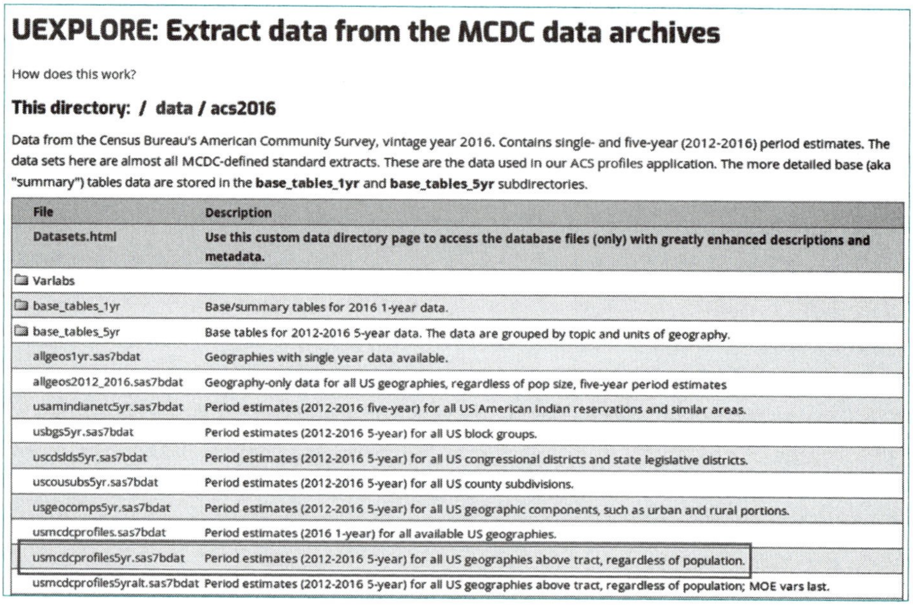

menu include column names, which would allow you to eliminate rows using criteria-based extracts. For our purposes, we'll take all the data and make those decisions later.

In the second Variable/Column box, change the value from None to State. Under Operator, select the radio button for And, and in the drop-down menu, choose Not Equal to (≠). In the Value box, we'll type 72 (Figure 6.15). This is the FIPS (Federal Information Processing Series) code for Puerto Rico; Puerto Rico is always included in all national data extracts, but since they don't participate in federal elections, we'll remove them from our extract (review Chapter 3 or visit `https://census.missouri.edu/geocodes/` to look up geographic codes).

4. **Choose columns in Section III**. Section III is where we select the specific columns/variables we want. We need to select our identifiers on the left and our variables/numerics on the right. When selecting multiple variables in each menu, you need to hold down the Control key (Ctrl) while making the selections. If you select something, take your finger off the Ctrl key, and select something else, you will undo your previous selection. For the Identifiers, select geoid and AreaName. There's no need to select county, as we're filtering for counties and they will appear in the geoid and area name. Under Numerics,

**FIGURE 6.15 ●  MCDC DEXTER DATA EXTRACTOR: CHOOSE OUTPUT FORMATS AND ROWS**

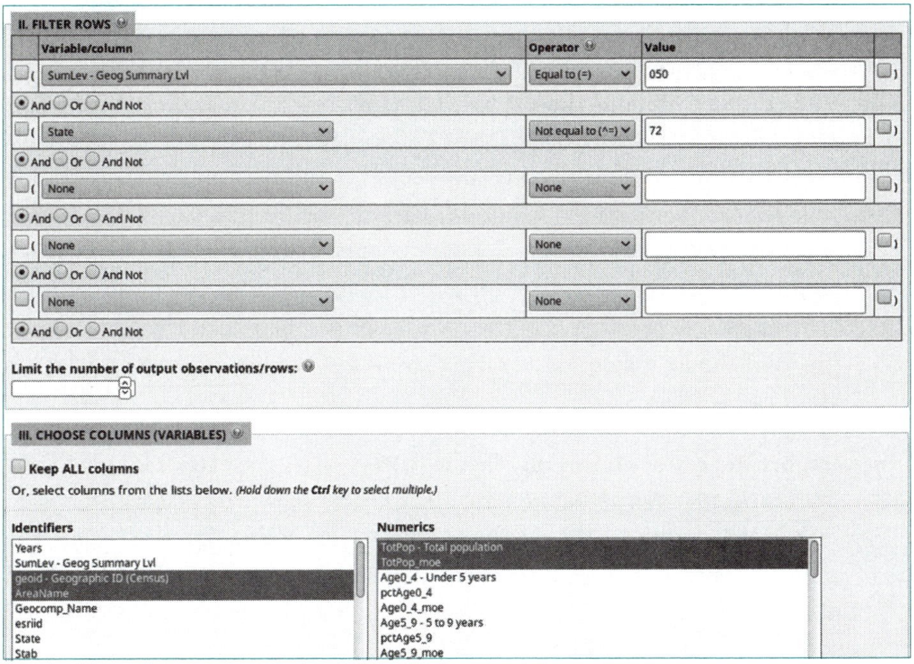

the columns are designated with names created by the MCDC for their profile tables, and they are listed in approximately the order in which they appear in the profiles. Each variable appears in twos (estimate, MOE) and in some cases threes (percentage) if the value is not a total. Scroll through and select *all* the relevant columns (estimate, MOE, and percentage when available) for each of these variables (the number in parentheses represents whether there are 2 or 3 columns):

- TotPop—Total Population (2)
- Median Age—Median Age in Years (2)
- Over25—25 years and over (3)
- MedianHHInc—Median Household Income (2)
- Bachelorsormore—Bachelor degree or higher (3)

We need to take the over-25 population, as this is the population from which the Bachelor's or more population is measured. Once you've made the selections, hit the Extract Data button at the bottom of Section III. Be patient while the application creates the extract; it could take a few seconds or a few minutes depending on how big the extract is. Eventually, you'll be presented with a Data Extraction Output screen where you can view a summary log of the request and the actual delimited file.

5. **View the log file and the extract.** Click on the Summary log. In the log, verify that you selected 16 variables (2 identifiers and 14 numerics) and scrutinize the list; if you're missing anything, hit the back button and modify your request (don't worry—you don't have to start from scratch). You should have 3,142 observations, one for each county. If the summary looks good, click the Delimited file link. This either prompts you to download it (if so, save the file), or it opens it in the browser (if so, right-click anywhere on the page and choose the option to save). Save it in Chapter 6 Exercise 3 folder as xtract.csv.

6. **Import the extract into Calc.** Figure 6.16 displays the extract in calc. Some processing is required before you can use this data in a database or GIS, such as deleting the extra header row. Any dollar values like median income are saved as text because a dollar sign is embedded in the value. You would need to use the Calc VALUE function to create a numeric value in a new column in order to work with this variable as a number. Note that all percent totals lack an MOE. You would need to calculate these yourself using the percent total formula, or, in cases where the formula fails, the ratio formula, as demonstrated in this chapter's first exercise. Save the extract as a Calc spreadsheet.

**FIGURE 6.16 ● MCDC EXTRACT RESULT IN CALC**

| | A | B | C | D | E | F |
|---|---|---|---|---|---|---|
| 1 | geoid | AreaName | TotPop | TotPop_moe | MedianAge | MedianAge_moe |
| 2 | Geographic ID (Census) | | Total population | TotPop_moe | Median age in years | MedianAge_moe |
| 3 | 05000US01001 | Autauga County, Alabama | 55049 | 0 | 37.8 | 0.5 |
| 4 | 05000US01003 | Baldwin County, Alabama | 199510 | 0 | 42.3 | 0.2999999523 |
| 5 | 05000US01005 | Barbour County, Alabama | 26614 | 0 | 38.7 | 0.5999999046 |
| 6 | 05000US01007 | Bibb County, Alabama | 22572 | 0 | 40.2 | 0.8999996185 |
| 7 | 05000US01009 | Blount County, Alabama | 57704 | 0 | 40.8 | 0.3999998569 |
| 8 | 05000US01011 | Bullock County, Alabama | 10552 | 0 | 39.2 | 1.6999998093 |
| 9 | 05000US01013 | Butler County, Alabama | 20280 | 0 | 40.6 | 0.3999998569 |
| 10 | 05000US01015 | Calhoun County, Alabama | 115883 | 0 | 39.1 | 0.3999998569 |
| 11 | 05000US01017 | Chambers County, Alabama | 34018 | 0 | 43.1 | 0.2999999523 |
| 12 | 05000US01019 | Cherokee County, Alabama | 25897 | 0 | 45.7 | 0.3999998569 |
| 13 | 05000US01021 | Chilton County, Alabama | 43817 | 0 | 38.7 | 0.6999998093 |
| 14 | 05000US01023 | Choctaw County, Alabama | 13287 | 0 | 45.1 | 0.0999999642 |
| 15 | 05000US01025 | Clarke County, Alabama | 24847 | 0 | 42 | 0.8999996185 |
| 16 | 05000US01027 | Clay County, Alabama | 13483 | 0 | 43.7 | 0.5 |

For the sake of demonstration, let's see what would be involved in getting detailed tables through Dexter, as opposed to the data profiles. Go back to `http://mcdc.missouri.edu/applications/uexplore.html`. Click 2016 under American Community Survey, then choose acs2016/American Community Survey Data, 2016 vintage. On the next page, choose the link for base_tables_5yr. The following page displays how the summary files are divided: There are separate files for different types of geography. Within these groups, the ACS tables are split across several files that contain sequences of tables, and then estimates are stored in one file and MOEs in another. The files at the top of this list (Table Shells and Table Number Lookup) can be used for identifying table subjects and variables.

For example, if we wanted data on citizenship status by county, we can find the table number and variables in the documentation—it's B05001. This table is located in usstcnty00_07.sas7bdat, which contains base tables from B00001 to B07413 for all states and counties. We can tell based on the file name: 00 to 07 includes all tables within this range of table prefixes, while stcnty indicates the geography. We would click on this file and go through the same interface as before and then would go back to mostcnty00_07.sas7bvew to get the MOEs for our estimates. Variable names and descriptions are stored in a series of metadata files at the bottom of the file listing.

It's not worth using the Dexter application if we just need a couple of variables from one table for one type of geography (**data.census.gov** is easier to use for that purpose), but it is invaluable if we need to create a selection of many variables from many different tables for one or more types of geography.

## Working With ACS Estimates in a Database

The fact that ACS estimates are fuzzy intervals introduces uncertainty when comparing statistics and ranking variables. In this part, we will see how to account for this when writing SQL queries. Rather than following a step-by-step exercise, we will simply demonstrate how to construct some sample queries based on the data we extracted from the MCDC. For a SQL refresher, refer back to the exercises in Chapter 5.

Before you can load the MCDC extract into SQLite, you will need to perform some basic processing in Calc. You can practice making these edits yourself on the extract you've downloaded or use a cleaned version called county_xtract.csv that's stored in Chapter 6 Exercise 2 folder. Since SQLite is a "light" database, it doesn't include a lot of advanced mathematical functions, such as calculating a square root. Use Calc to calculate MOEs for the percent totals, alter these formulas to calculate ratios for MOEs in the event the percent total calculation fails, convert median income to a numeric value, round all values to a sensible number of decimal places, delete the extra header row, and, if you wish, modify column names and the order in which they appear.

In querying county values that are above or below a national threshold, we also want to calculate whether the value for a particular county is statistically different from the national value. If it's not, we will want to exclude it from our results. In Calc, we would calculate statistical difference for income and the population with a bachelor's degree or higher using the statistical difference formula introduced in this chapter's first exercise and covered in more detail in the online supplemental exercise. We would incorporate the national values into the formula:

Median Income:  $55,322 \pm 120$

Population Over 25 With Bachelor's Degree or Higher:  $30.3\% \pm 0.1\%$

Import the finalized extract (saved as a CSV) into a new SQLite database. For column data types, the geoid and name would be text values, median age, all percentages, and the scores from the statistical difference formula would be reals (as they are decimal numbers), and all other values would be integers. After import, we would modify the table so geoid is designated as the primary key.

For readability, I've modified the names of the original variables in the MCDC extract. A basic query that selects counties with fewer than a quarter of a million people and with median income and college attainment lower than the national average would look like this:

```
SELECT geoid, areaname, totpop, totpop_moe, medinc,
medinc_moe, pctbach, pctbach_moe
FROM county_xtract
WHERE totpop < 250000 AND medinc < 55322
AND pctbach < 30.3
ORDER BY totpop DESC;
```

This query would return 2,277 counties out of 3,142. By adding the DESC qualifier to ORDER BY, we sort the population values from the largest to the smallest. This query fails to account for the fact that the estimates are intervals that have a possible range of values. Median household income in the United States could be $120 higher or lower than $55,322, and of course, each county estimate also has a MOE. To account for this, we subtract the MOE from each county estimate to get the *bottom* threshold for the estimate and compare it with the *top* threshold for the nation. By doing so, we ensure that we are returning all counties whose possible values fall below the highest possible values for the United States:

```
SELECT geoid, areaname, totpop, totpop_moe, medinc,
medinc_moe, pctbach, pctbach_moe
FROM county_xtract
WHERE (totpop - totpop_moe) < 250000
AND (medinc - medinc_moe) < (55322 + 120)
AND (pctbach - pctbach_moe) < (30.3 + 0.1)
ORDER BY totpop DESC;
```

This returns 2,445 records. We have more results now that we're including the full, possible range of values. What if a county value meets the criteria of being lower than the national value, but its estimate is really not statistically different from the national estimate? We omit these records from our results by selecting only counties where the statistical difference score is greater than the $Z$ value of 1.645:

```
SELECT geoid, areaname, totpop, totpop_moe,
medinc, medinc_moe,
pctbach, pctbach_moe
FROM county_xtract
WHERE (totpop - totpop_moe) < 250000
AND (medinc - medinc_moe) < (55322 + 120)
AND (pctbach - pctbach_moe)< (30.3 + 0.1)
AND sd_medinc > 1.645 AND sd_bach > 1.645
ORDER BY totpop DESC;
```

This drops the result down to 2,013 rows. By incorporating statistical difference, we have omitted more than 400 counties whose estimates are not statistically different from the national estimate.

Now that we have a final result set, we can add additional variables of interest to the query like median age (since we weren't using median age as a filter or for interpretation, we omitted it from previous queries). Then add this line to the top of the statement and execute it to save it as a view:

```
CREATE VIEW county_below_us_avg AS
```

If we added additional variables to our criteria and those variables were strongly correlated with one another (i.e., low income, high unemployment, and high poverty), we probably would need a different approach where we count the number of variables that are statistically different from the national average and use that count as criteria, otherwise our result set might become too small. Ultimately, the rationale is to find counties that fit the general criteria; since the estimates are fuzzy, our criteria may also need to be a bit fuzzy.

We could also take the extra step of calculating CVs. Each estimate could have a CV in a dedicated column, and we could use that criteria to omit unreliable estimates (i.e., only includes values where the CV is less than 35). Since the CV formula involves basic arithmetic, we could do that calculation either in the database or beforehand in a spreadsheet.

### Supplemental Exercise: Ranking ACS Data and Testing for Statistical Difference

Census data is commonly used to categorize and rank places, often for the purpose of distributing state or federal aid to communities. In their case study of three federal programs, Nesse and Rahe (2015) found that none of the programs incorporated the MOE for ACS estimates into their calculations. In this supplemental exercise, we will explore the impact the MOE has on rankings, and we will get some more practice with aggregating values. We will use the U.S. Department of Agriculture's Supplemental Nutrition Assistance Program as an example, as it was one of the programs included in that study. Visit **study.sagepub.com/census** to do this additional exercise.

## 6.5   REVIEW QUESTIONS AND PRACTICE EXERCISES

1.  Describe the various components of ACS estimates—the estimate, MOE, and confidence level—and explain how these estimates are different from the decennial census count.

2.  When would you use a 5-year-period estimate instead of a 1-year-period estimate?

3.  Use **data.census.gov** to download housing units by tenure for the four census tracts in the Over the Rhine neighborhood and the city of Cincinnati, Ohio (Hamilton County), from the 2012–2016 ACS. Similar to what we did in Exercise 1, calculate the CV for the city and each of the four tracts for these three variables: (1) total housing units, (2) owner-occupied units, and (3) renter-occupied units.

4.  Using the data from Question 3, aggregate the housing data for the four tracts, calculate percent totals, and calculate new MOEs for the total and percent totals.

5. Use the UExplore Dexter tool to create an extract for all PUMAs—summary level 795 in Wisconsin. Use the 5-year 2012–2016 ACS MCDC data profiles just as we did in Exercise 2. Select the following estimates and MOEs: renter-occupied units, median rent, and rental vacancy rate. Import the extract into Calc and do the following: Convert the median rent values from text to values, calculate CVs for median rent and rental vacancy rate, and calculate statistical difference for median rent and the vacancy rate against the *state's* 5-year values (look them up using the MCDC ACS Profile tool).

---

**Supplementary Digital Content:** Find datasets and supplemental exercises at the companion website at `http://study.sagepub.com/census`.

# POPULATION ESTIMATES PROGRAM

## 7.1   INTRODUCTION

Many researchers are less familiar with the data generated from the Population Estimates Program (PEP), but this small dataset plays a vital role in several census programs. It's used to estimate coverage rates for the decennial census, it's employed for controlling estimates in the American Community Survey (ACS) and Current Population Survey (CPS), it's a key dataset used for studying migration, and it's often the basis for creating short-term population projections (estimates of what the population will be in the future). It was the only source of geographically detailed annual population data prior to the ACS, and it is still used in instances where better precision is needed for studying annual change for basic demographic variables such as age, sex, and race. It's smaller and easier to use relative to the decennial census and ACS, as much of the data for a specific type of geography can fit in a single spreadsheet.

While the decennial census and the ACS are statistical datasets created from counting or sample surveying, respectively, the PEP is an administrative dataset. County-level vital statistics collated by the National Center for Health Statistics (NCHS) are combined with data from the Internal Revenue Service (IRS) and the Social Security Administration to measure annual population change based on births, deaths, and migration, using the decennial census as the initial baseline. The Census Bureau publishes the data for these components of change so we can see which places are growing or declining due to natural increase or immigration/emigration. Population totals are published by age, sex, race, and Hispanic origin for states, counties, incorporated places and municipal civil divisions, and metropolitan areas.

In this chapter, we will see how population estimates are created, explore the various components that are used to generate them, and look at several applications for the data. Since this is a smaller dataset, the Census Bureau publishes the data in ready-made CSV files that can be downloaded directly from the PEP program page, in addition to the tables published in **data.census.gov**:

```
https://www.census.gov/programs-surveys/popest.html
```

## When Do You Use the PEP?

Population estimates are an administrative dataset that is published annually. When a new year of data is published, it is bundled with revised estimates from the previous years that go back to the last decennial census. Once a new decennial census is conducted, the estimates from the prior decade are revised for a final time to more accurately reflect population change over that period. Each annual release is called a vintage estimate, and each 10-year revision is known as an intercensal estimate. When should you use the PEP data relative to another dataset? You can use it when

- you are studying annual population change;

- you need basic, recent demographic variables;

- you need to study components of population change (births, deaths, migration);

- you only need data for large geographies like states, counties, places, and metro areas; and

- you want a small and simple dataset to work with.

The PEP will *not* be your first choice if you need the following:

- Detailed socioeconomic characteristics of the population (use the ACS instead)

- Actual population counts (use the decennial census instead)

- Data for small geographies like census tracts and Zip Code Tabulation Areas (use the decennial census or ACS instead)

- Housing-related variables beyond a simple estimate of total housing units (use the decennial census or ACS instead)

## 7.2    PEP FUNDAMENTALS

The Census Bureau publishes detailed explanations of its methodology for producing population estimates each year (U.S. Census Bureau, 2017g). In this section, we summarize the essentials. The estimates are created in different stages so that the sum of all totals and characteristics is consistent, that is, the sum of a state's county values equals the state totals, and the sum of the states equals the national totals.

The last decennial census is used for creating the baseline estimate from which all subsequent annual estimates are based. The decennial census count is adjusted to account for revisions stemming from challenges from state and local communities over the accuracy of their count via the count resolution program (see Chapter 5), adjustments to racial categories to reassign people who chose Some Other Race to one of the five official racial categories in accordance with Directive 15 from the Office of Management and Budget (see Chapter 4), and subsequent changes in legal boundaries that affect what the total population is in a given area. This adjusted value is called the estimate base. Using this base, the first estimate for the decade is produced for July 1 of the decennial census year, and it reflects what happened in the 4-month period between April 1 and July 1. From that point onward, estimates are created each year with July 1 as the reference date.

The estimates are created using the cohort component method, which is a fundamental approach in demography for creating population estimates and projections. The initial base population is summed in 1-year age brackets. In the following year, the number of people in each bracket is advanced 1 year: The number of people who died are subtracted from each bracket, migration is accounted for by adding and subtracting the number of people who moved in and out of the particular area, and the number of babies that were born are added to the first bracket (less than 1 year of age). The basic equation is

$$\text{Estimate} = \text{Population base} + \text{Births} - \text{Deaths} + \text{Migration}$$

Instead of using one dataset for the entire population and applying the changes to it, different sets are created by sex, race, and Hispanic origin, and the process is carried out in stages at different geographic levels. The actual factors that go into each equation vary based on geographic scale; for example, at the national level, births and deaths are studied on a monthly basis and there's no need to account for domestic (internal) migration, while at the county level, data is employed on an annual basis and domestic migration between counties is accounted for.

Population totals and characteristics by age, sex, race, and Hispanic origin for the United States are generated first using the cohort component method, and the Census Bureau takes special measures to estimate the civilian versus military population and the household versus group quarters population. Population totals for counties are generated second using a simpler approach that looks at just three age brackets—0 to 17, 18 to 64, and 65 plus—and accounts for domestic migration between counties. The data for the counties is controlled so that the sum of their totals does not exceed the national sum, and then the county totals are summed to the state level. The characteristics of the county and state populations are generated third using an iterative process. The process uses the same approach as the national one: adding births, subtracting deaths, accounting for domestic and international migration, and aging the population forward in single-year age cohorts. State characteristics are controlled to national characteristics and the state total is controlled to the sum of its county's totals, while county characteristics are controlled to state characteristics and to the county's total. The end result ensures that the totals and all the characteristics sum to the same national total.

Last, the county-level data for population totals and components of change is aggregated for metropolitan, micropolitan, and consolidated statistical areas using the latest definitions from the Office of Management and Budget. The Census Bureau does not publish characteristics for the metro areas, but since metro areas are simple aggregations of counties, you can easily sum county-level data to the metro level if necessary.

Birth and death data are known collectively as vital statistics. In the United States, this data is generated at the county level by county health departments and is collated by the NCHS and the Federal-State Cooperative for Population Estimates. Data for migration comes from several sources. Data on domestic migration (movement within the United States) is collected from the IRS for all people under 65. The IRS compares individual names listed on tax returns and generates data based on the number of people whose address changed between filing years. If a person's address has changed, they are counted as having moved. Domestic migration data for the population 65 years and older is generated from Medicare enrollment data from the Centers for Medicare and Medicaid, because coverage rates for seniors in this dataset is higher than the IRS dataset. Address changes in enrollment are also the basis for counting moves.

Foreign migration is estimated in several parts: immigration of the foreign born, emigration of the foreign born, net migration between the United States and Puerto Rico, net migration of the native born to and from the United States, and the net movement of armed forces personnel to and from the United States. Data for the foreign born and Puerto Rican migration is captured from the ACS question on residency 1 year ago, while the movement of the armed forces is collected from the Department of Defense. The movement of native-born U.S. residents is hardest to track,

> ### ✓  INFOBOX 7.1 ESTIMATES AND PROJECTIONS FOR OTHER COUNTRIES
>
> The Census Bureau creates population estimates and projections for other countries and provides this data via its International Data Base:
>    `https://www.census.gov/programs-surveys/international-programs/about/idb.html`.
>    The simple interface allows you to retrieve country-level data by sex and age together with measures of fertility, mortality, and migration. You can retrieve data for individual countries, for predefined regions, or you can aggregate countries to form your own regions. You can make comparisons between countries and regions, and data can be downloaded in Excel or CSV format.
>    Detailed documentation on the methodology is provided on the website. These statistics are *not* the official statistics published by the census or statistical agencies of the respective countries but are generated by the U.S. Census Bureau. The United Nations would be an alternate source: `http://data.un.org/`.

as the federal government does not have an established protocol for counting Americans who move overseas. Data from more than 80 countries is used to estimate this population (InfoBox 7.1).

An entirely different and separate process is used to create estimates for cities and towns (U.S. Census Bureau, 2017f), which are actually a mix of places and county subdivisions. The Census Bureau publishes estimates for the legal areas within these two geographies: (1) incorporated places in all states and (2) municipal civil divisions in the 20 states that have them. To create these estimates, the Census Bureau generates an estimate of housing units first (U.S. Census Bureau, 2017e). Using the last decennial census as a base, they annually estimate new construction based on building permits issued and completed, and demolitions or abandonment based on data from the American Housing Survey. These housing unit estimates are used as controls for the ACS and as inputs for estimating city and town population in the PEP. The housing unit estimate is multiplied by the last decennial census housing occupancy rate and number of people per household to produce an uncontrolled population estimate. These estimates are then controlled to the county level, so they do not exceed the county's total.

## 7.3    PEP DATASETS AND VARIABLES

Estimates are released on a rolling basis for geographies and characteristics, and there is about a 1-year delay between the reference period of the estimate and the initial release of data. For example, the first estimates for July 1, 2017, were released in spring 2018, and the release of different tables continued throughout the summer. Data for population totals and components is released first, followed by data for characteristics.

The structure of the PEP variables and tables differs from the other census datasets, in that the release of a new series of estimates supersedes the previous release and contains revisions of all the previous data plus the newest estimates. Each year of data that's released is known as a vintage estimate, and that vintage contains estimates for the latest year plus revised estimates for all previous years going back to the last decennial census. For example, the 2017 vintage estimates contain estimates for 2017 that were just released, plus revised estimates for all previous years back to the 2010 census. If we compared the estimates for the year 2016 in vintage 2017 with vintage 2016, the estimates would be slightly different. The Census Bureau adjusts previous estimates based on improvements in methodology, count resolution challenges, the discovery of errors, and changes in legal boundaries. If a boundary change occurs in a given year, the vintage population estimates for that year (the latest year and all previous years in the vintage) will account for it. So if you were working with PEP data on an ongoing basis, you would want to wholly replace last year's vintage with this year's.

Once we reach the next decennial census, the base for the subsequent vintages will change from 2010 to 2020. At that point, the Census Bureau will go back and revise the estimates for the 2010 decade a final time to smooth out the data to reflect what really happened between 2010 and 2020. This estimate is called an intercensal estimate. If we are studying historic population change, we will want to use the intercensal estimates for all the past decades and the most recent vintage estimates for the decade we are in. The intercensal estimates are calculated for the nation, states, counties, and Puerto Rico. Data for geographies that are not adjusted (cities and towns) are grouped into decadal tables called postcensal estimates.

As illustrated in Table 7.1, the level of detail that's available varies with geography. The most detail is available at the national level and the least at the city/town level. Data for race and Hispanic origin is reported as race alone and as race in combination with another race. Data for age is summarized in 5-year cohorts and for some geographies in 1-year cohorts, and median age is usually reported. Puerto Rico is the only U.S. territory included in this dataset, and some tables are published for its primary subdivisions (municipos).

Unlike the decennial census and the ACS, tables in the PEP do not follow a numbering scheme but are named with abbreviations based on the variables they contain. Some tables include annual estimates with values published for each year, while others contain just cumulative estimates with the most recent year and the sum of

| TABLE 7.1 ● AVAILABILITY OF POPULATION ESTIMATES BY GEOGRAPHY | | | | | | | |
|---|---|---|---|---|---|---|---|
| | Nation | Metros | States | Counties | Places | Puerto Rico | Municipos |
| Total resident population | X | X | X | X | X | X | X |
| Components of change | X | X | X | X | | X | X |
| By age and sex | X | | X | X | | X | X |
| By age, sex, race, and Hispanic origin | X | | X | X | | | |
| By 1-year age cohorts and sex | X | | X | | | X | |
| By group quarters | X | | | X | | | |
| By households/group quarters and civilians/military | X | | | | | | |
| Monthly population estimates | X | | | | | | |
| Total housing units | X | | X | X | | | |

*Note:* Data is reported annually and ages are reported in 5-year cohorts unless noted otherwise.

previous years. Since this dataset is typically used to study annual change, there are a series of ranking tables with ranks based on total population or fastest growing places; in particular, there are dedicated ranking tables for fastest growing counties and cities/towns.

The variables and field names for the population characteristics are self-explanatory. The field names for the component of change tables are similar for each of the geographic files and are summarized in Table 7.2. The first few columns include geographic identifiers for the records, and the name and number of these columns differ based on the geographic file. The actual population count from the decennial census appears first, followed by the ESTIMATESBASE, which is the adjusted decennial count on which all the subsequent estimates are based. The reference date for both is April 1.

POPESTIMATE is the total estimate for that year as of July 1, while NPOPCHG is the net population change between one year and the next. The next sets of columns are the vital statistics from the NCHS: the actual number of births and deaths, followed by the difference between the two identified as NATURALINC for natural

| TABLE 7.2 ● VARIABLES AND FIELD NAMES IN THE COMPONENTS OF CHANGE FILES |
| --- |
| **geographic identifiers:** the names and number of fields vary between different files |
| **CENSUS2010POP:** the official count from the decennial census |
| **ESTIMATESBASE:** adjusted decennial count on which all the subsequent estimates are based |
| **POPESTIMATE:** resident total population estimate as of July 1 of that year |
| **NPOPCHG:** total population change between estimates |
| **BIRTHS:** births that occurred between estimates |
| **DEATHS:** deaths that occurred between estimates |
| **NATURALINC:** natural increase—the difference between births and deaths |
| **INTERNATIONALMIG:** net international migration—the difference between in-migration and out-migration between the United States and U.S. territories/foreign countries |
| **DOMESTICMIG:** net domestic migration—the difference between in-migration and out-migration within the United States between different geographies |
| **NETMIG:** net migration—the difference between net international and net domestic migration |
| **RESIDUAL:** adjustments to the estimates that are made after the components are applied to ensure that the sum of estimates for smaller areas (parts) equals the total estimate for the larger area (whole) |
| **GQESTIMATESBASE:** adjusted decennial count of the group quarters population on which all subsequent estimates are based. This field is only published in the county tables |
| **GQESTIMATES:** total group quarters population estimate as of July 1 of that year. This field is only published in the county tables |
| **fields beginning with "R":** are rates that are calculated for each of the components. These fields are not published in the metropolitan area tables |

*Note:* Names that appear in bold are the actual field names. In the data files, each name is followed by the year for the estimate—that is, POPESTIMATE2011.

increase. This term is still used even if the value represents a decrease. This is followed by international net migration and domestic net migration. Domestic migration covers movement within and among the 50 states and the District of Columbia, while international migration includes movement between the United States and Puerto Rico, the other U.S. territories, and foreign countries. Note that these values are net values: the difference between people who immigrated and emigrated from abroad and who immigrated and emigrated within the nation. The PEP does not provide values on total in-migrants and out-migrants for each category. NETMIG is the difference between net international and net domestic migration.

The final set of columns are the residuals or adjustments that were made to the estimates for each year. As described previously, the residuals are calculated and applied to smooth out the estimates, so that the sum of estimates for smaller places is equal to the larger place of which it is part. The county file also includes specific estimates for the group quarters population (which is a part of the total resident population), and all the files, except the metropolitan areas file, contain rates for each of the components.

There are a number of places where you can access PEP data. Like the other datasets, you can access tables from **data.census.gov** and from the FTP (File Transfer Protocol) site. Unlike the other datasets, you can browse through and download most of the data directly from the PEP's program page at `https://www.census.gov/programs-surveys/popest.html`. From this page, you can click on Tables and the option to view all tables, and then see all tables published in a particular year classified by type (total estimates or characteristics) and by geography (Figure 7.1). Each page contains a description of the datasets and the technical documentation that describes the methodology and layout of the fields. The PEP program page and **data.census.gov** are designed to provide you with data from the latest vintage, so if you click on 2015, you will get 2015 estimates from the latest vintage and *not* from vintage 2015. Data from the two most recent vintages are provided, while older vintages are archived on the FTP site. Selecting a decennial census year (2010, 2000) or any year that falls between two decennial censuses will yield the intercensal and postcensal estimates for the decade in which that year falls.

The Missouri Census Data Center provides a number of applications for producing summaries and charts of PEP data for the nation, states, and counties from their population estimates page at `https://census.missouri.edu/population-estimates/`. The annual population trends application lets you generate a table and chart displaying population change and net migration back to the 2000 census, like the example shown for the District of Columbia in Figure 7.2. The population trends report allows you to generate data on characteristics, while the estimates by age report lets you generate reports with your own age cohorts and characteristics.

## 7.4   APPLICATIONS FOR PEP DATA

PEP data is often used in both mass and social media to identify and rank the fastest-growing states and cities in the country, often for the simple purpose of identifying "winners" and "losers." More nuanced studies seek to uncover trends in the nation's migration patterns. Visuals like the chart shown in Figure 7.3 illustrate that there is differential growth in population based on settlement size and region: Larger areas are

### FIGURE 7.1 ● NAVIGATING THROUGH THE POPULATION ESTIMATES WEBSITE TO ACCESS DATA

**Population and Housing Unit Estimates**

| | |
|---|---|
| About this Section | **Population and Housing Unit Estimates Tables** |
| **Data** | The population and housing unit estimates are released on a flow basis throughout each year. Each new series of data (called vintages) incorporates the latest administrative record data, geographic boundaries, and methodology. Therefore, the entire time series of estimates beginning with the most recent decennial census is revised annually, and estimates from different vintages of data may not be consistent across geography and characteristics detail. When multiple vintages of data are available, the most recent vintage is the preferred data. |
| Datasets | |
| Data Tools | |
| **Tables** | |
| Errata Notes | The vintage year (e.g., V2017) refers to the final year of the time series. The reference date for all estimates is July 1, unless otherwise specified. |
| Special Tabulation Program | |
| Geographies | Additional estimates files are available in the Datasets section and via the Census Bureau application programming interface (API). |
| Guidance for Data Users | Information on the Population and Housing Unit Estimates Special Tabulation Program is available here. |
| Guidance for Geographies Users | |
| Library | |
| News | |
| Technical Documentation | |

All | 2017 | 2016 | 2015 | 2014 | ▶

City and Town Population Totals: 2010-2017
This page features Vintage 2017 population estimates totals.

County Population Totals and Components of Change: 2010-2017
This page features Vintage 2017 population estimates totals.

Metropolitan and Micropolitan Statistical Areas Totals: 2010-2017
This page features Vintage 2017 population estimates totals.

### FIGURE 7.2 ● CHART GENERATED FROM THE MISSOURI CENSUS DATA CENTER'S POPULATION TRENDS APPLICATION

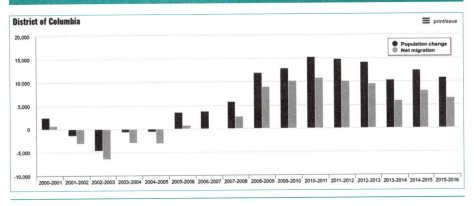

*Source:* https://census.missouri.edu/population/

growing larger while smaller areas are declining, and the West and South are growing more rapidly than the Northeast and Midwest.

Researchers typically use PEP data for studying annual change in population and basic demographic characteristics over time, studying migration, comparing basic counts

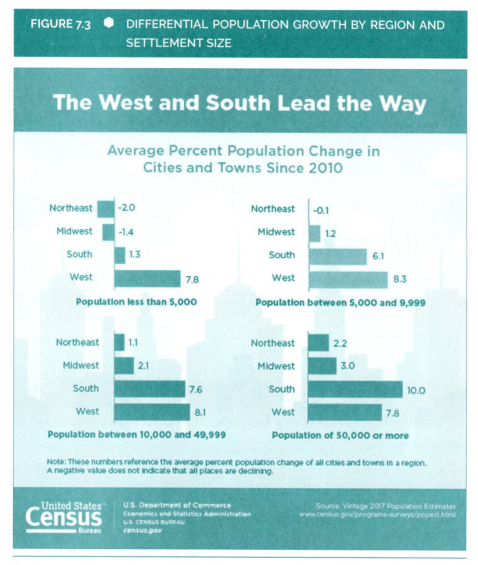

**FIGURE 7.3 ⬡ DIFFERENTIAL POPULATION GROWTH BY REGION AND SETTLEMENT SIZE**

*Source:* https://www.census.gov/library/visualizations/2018/comm/subcounty-estimates.html

against administrative data, creating population projections (forecasts of what the future population could be), and using it as baseline for other estimates in cases where the ACS is too complex and when the decennial census becomes too outdated for studying contemporary patterns.

The PEP is a fundamental source for studying and comparing the components of population change for different places. While PEP data gives us the end result of where people are migrating (the net change), it cannot tell us anything about the flow between places—that is, where are people moving to and from. For this reason,

PEP data is often studied in conjunction with other datasets. Both the ACS and the IRS publish annual data on the domestic flow of populations between states and counties, and the county data can be used for studying metro flows. Studying foreign flows is more complicated; the ACS can be used for studying people immigrating to the United States, but detailed data on emigration is harder to come by. Researchers at the real estate firm Zillow have weighed the pros and cons of using the PEP, IRS, ACS summary data and ACS microdata for studying domestic migration flows (Terrazas, 2016), and recent case studies on New York (Donnelly, Clark, & Billadello, 2018), Washington, D.C. (Chapman, 2017), and Philadelphia (Eichel & Schmitt, 2016) illustrate how these datasets can be applied to studying population change.

PEP data is less fuzzy than the ACS, as the estimates represent a specific value at a point in time rather than intervals at a specific confidence level over an average period. However, it's important to remember that population estimates are still *estimates*: reasonable attempts to measure what the total population is based on certain assumptions, methods, and available data sources. PEP data tends to decrease in reliability as the estimates move further away in time from the base decennial year. Dynamic places that are growing or declining rapidly, or that experience large inflows and outflows of people can be harder to estimate, and sudden events can have an impact on a population's trajectory that can overturn the assumptions on which the estimates are based. For example, estimates for 2007 demonstrated that Phoenix had surpassed Philadelphia to become the nation's fifth-largest city, but when the 2010 census was taken, this finding was overturned. It's likely that the housing boom in Phoenix had inflated the estimates to some degree, while the bust during the Great Recession applied the brakes on growth. In contrast, Philadelphia's housing market was more stable and the city registered population growth for the first time since 1950.

Estimates are useful for approximating what the total population and its characteristics are presently or were in the recent past. Estimates can also be used for creating short-term projections of what the future population might be. Simple approaches to predicting future population include extending the trend line of past estimates into the future or apportioning existing projections for larger areas to sub-areas based on some reasonable criteria such as the proportion of current population or past growth or a constraining factor like the amount of vacant developable land. The Census Bureau only publishes national projections, but state and local governments often produce projections for their own areas. The most likely departments that would produce projections include labor, economic development, and state or regional planning.

More sophisticated approaches employ the cohort component method. Such a model would look at a base population for a given year, drawn from either the PEP or decennial census. In its simplest form, the data would be divided into 5-year cohorts of males and females, and parameters from a series of modules would be applied to project each cohort into the future. For each cohort, the population would be advanced 5 years based on the number of people who survive to live an additional 5 years, the number of people who migrate into and out of the given area, and the number of babies born. Mortality or survivability is estimated for each cohort using survivability ratios, which are computed from life tables published annually by the NCHS (Arias, Heron, & Xu, 2017). The NCHS is also the source for data on nativity, so for each cohort of women of childbearing age, you can calculate the number of babies likely to be born (Martin, Hamilton, Osterman, Driscoll, & Drake, 2018). Migration is always the toughest variable to estimate; some combination of the PEP and the ACS is typically used. For a full explanation of approaches, considerations, and data sources, see *A Practitioner's Guide to State and Local Population Projections* (S. K. Smith, Tayman, & Swanson, 2013).

## 7.5   EXERCISES

PEP data is divided into two groups: (1) tables with total population estimates and the components of change (births, deaths, net domestic migration, net international migration) and (2) tables that provide estimates of the characteristics of the population (age, sex, race, Hispanic origin). In this exercise, we will use Calc to work with the first set of tables to study how components of change influence population growth in the nation's largest metropolitan areas.

Visit the publisher's website for the data we will be using, or download it from the source (if vintage 2017 data is no longer available from the source, you can use the latest vintage).

**Metropolitan and micropolitan statistical area population and estimated components of change** April 1, 2010, to July 1, 2017: CBSA-EST2017-alldata, All Metro and Micro areas in the United States—https://www.census.gov/data/tables/time-series/demo/popest/2010s-total-metro-and-micro-statistical-areas.html.

### Exercise 1: Studying Components of Change With Charts in Calc

In this exercise, we will identify the 10 largest metropolitan areas in the country, compute their cumulative population change between 2010 and 2017, and study how the populations of these areas have grown relative to each other by creating a stacked bar chart showing the components of change. This exercise illustrates how metropolitan area and components of change files are structured and provides you first opportunity for learning how to create charts in Calc.

1. **Launch Calc and import the data**. Open Calc, browse to Chapter 7 Exercise 1 folder, and open the file cbsa-est2017-alldata.csv. Be careful on the import screen—many of the ID codes in this file have leading zeros that we don't want to lose. Click on the first column (CBSA [Core-Based Statistical Area]) in the import screen, and in the column type drop-down, change the type from Standard to Text. Do the same thing for the second (MDIV [metropolitan division]) and third (STCOU [state and county FIPS code]) columns (Figure 7.4). Then click OK. Once the file is loaded, save it as new Calc spreadsheet file (not as a CSV) using the same file name.

2. **Examine the file**. The file is sorted alphabetically by CBSA, but the records represent different components of the CBSA (refer back to Chapter 3 for explanations of the metropolitan terminology). The first CBSA 10180 is Abilene, TX (Figure 7.5). The three records below it are the individual counties that are part of that CBSA. How can we tell? The CBSA-level record for Abilene has a CBSA ID number but does not have a code for MDIV or STCOU. The records for Callahan, Jones, and Taylor counties have the same CBSA number (10180) but also have values for STCOU. Column E (LSAD [Legal/Statistical

**FIGURE 7.4 ● IMPORT MENU: IMPORT ID CODES AS TEXT TYPE**

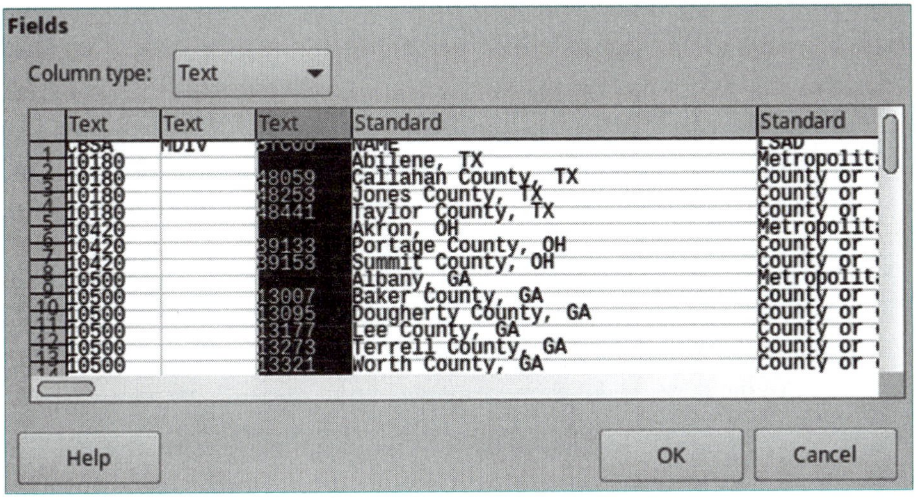

FIGURE 7.5 ● ORGANIZATION OF THE METROPOLITAN AREA FILE BY CBSA AND CONSTITUENT COUNTIES

| | A | B | C | D | E | F |
|---|---|---|---|---|---|---|
| 1 | CBSA | MDIV | STCOU | NAME | LSAD | CENSUS2010POP |
| 2 | 10180 | | | Abilene, TX | Metropolitan Statistical Area | 165252 |
| 3 | 10180 | | 48059 | Callahan County, TX | County or equivalent | 13544 |
| 4 | 10180 | | 48253 | Jones County, TX | County or equivalent | 20202 |
| 5 | 10180 | | 48441 | Taylor County, TX | County or equivalent | 131506 |
| 6 | 10420 | | | Akron, OH | Metropolitan Statistical Area | 703200 |
| 7 | 10420 | | 39133 | Portage County, OH | County or equivalent | 161419 |
| 8 | 10420 | | 39153 | Summit County, OH | County or equivalent | 541781 |

FIGURE 7.6 ● TEN LARGEST METROPOLITAN AREAS IN 2017

| | A | B | C | D | E | F |
|---|---|---|---|---|---|---|
| 1 | CBSA | MDIV | STCOU | NAME | LSAD | CENSUS2010▶ |
| 2 | 35620 | | | New York-Newark-Jersey City, NY-NJ-PA | Metropolitan ▶ | 19567410 |
| 3 | 31080 | | | Los Angeles-Long Beach-Anaheim, CA | Metropolitan ▶ | 12828837 |
| 4 | 16980 | | | Chicago-Naperville-Elgin, IL-IN-WI | Metropolitan ▶ | 9461105 |
| 5 | 19100 | | | Dallas-Fort Worth-Arlington, TX | Metropolitan ▶ | 6426214 |
| 6 | 26420 | | | Houston-The Woodlands-Sugar Land, TX | Metropolitan ▶ | 5920416 |
| 7 | 47900 | | | Washington-Arlington-Alexandria, DC-VA-MD-WV | Metropolitan ▶ | 5636232 |
| 8 | 33100 | | | Miami-Fort Lauderdale-West Palm Beach, FL | Metropolitan ▶ | 5564635 |
| 9 | 37980 | | | Philadelphia-Camden-Wilmington, PA-NJ-DE-MD | Metropolitan ▶ | 5965343 |
| 10 | 12060 | | | Atlanta-Sandy Springs-Roswell, GA | Metropolitan ▶ | 5286728 |
| 11 | 14460 | | | Boston-Cambridge-Newton, MA-NH | Metropolitan ▶ | 4552402 |

Area Description]) indicates what type of geography the record represents. The entire file is arranged sequentially in this manner so you can see the pieces that make up each metro or micro area, but you can sort and pull out data for the categories and subcategories based on the presence or lack of the different identifiers. While scrolling across the columns, you can refer back to Table 7.2 to identify what the field names refer to.

3. **Pull records for the 10 largest metro areas**. Add a new sheet to the workbook and name it big10. Copy the first row (the column headers) from the original sheet and paste it into the first row in big10. In the original sheet, sort the data by LSAD in ascending order and by POPESTIMATE2017 in descending order. Scroll down through the records until you get to the beginning of the Metropolitan Statistical Areas: CBSA 35620 New York–Newark–Jersey City will be the first of these records. Select the rows for the first 10 metros (from New York to Boston). Copy these records, flip over to the big10 sheet, select cell A2 and paste (Figure 7.6). Save your work.

4. **Calculate cumulative change**. Let's calculate the total change in population between 2010 and 2017 and the percent change. Since columns B and C are null, let's repurpose them. Replace the existing labels in cells B1 and C1 with the labels CHANGE and PCT, respectively. When measuring change,

## FIGURE 7.7 ◆ CALCULATING CUMULATIVE POPULATION GROWTH FOR THE LARGEST METROS

| | A | B | C | D | E | F | G |
|---|---|---|---|---|---|---|---|
| C2 | | | fx Σ = | =ROUND((B2/G2)*100,1) | | | |
| 1 | CBSA | CHANGE | PCT | NAME | LSAD | CENSUS2010 | ESTIMATESP F |
| 2 | 35620 | 754396 | 3.9 | New York-Newark-Jersey City, NY-NJ-PA | Metropolitan ▶ | 19567410 | 19566480 |
| 3 | 31080 | 524946 | 4.1 | Los Angeles-Long Beach-Anaheim, CA | Metropolitan ▶ | 12828837 | 12828961 |
| 4 | 16980 | 71499 | 0.8 | Chicago-Naperville-Elgin, IL-IN-WI | Metropolitan ▶ | 9461105 | 9461541 |
| 5 | 19100 | 973431 | 15.1 | Dallas-Fort Worth-Arlington, TX | Metropolitan ▶ | 6426214 | 6426231 |
| 6 | 26420 | 971941 | 16.4 | Houston-The Woodlands-Sugar Land, TX | Metropolitan ▶ | 5920416 | 5920486 |
| 7 | 47900 | 580228 | 10.3 | Washington-Arlington-Alexandria, DC-VA-MD-WV | Metropolitan ▶ | 5636232 | 5636361 |
| 8 | 33100 | 592525 | 10.6 | Miami-Fort Lauderdale-West Palm Beach, FL | Metropolitan ▶ | 5564635 | 5566299 |
| 9 | 37980 | 130427 | 2.2 | Philadelphia-Camden-Wilmington, PA-NJ-DE-MD | Metropolitan ▶ | 5965343 | 5965693 |
| 10 | 12060 | 597993 | 11.3 | Atlanta-Sandy Springs-Roswell, GA | Metropolitan ▶ | 5286728 | 5286743 |
| 11 | 14460 | 283935 | 6.2 | Boston-Cambridge-Newton, MA-NH | Metropolitan ▶ | 4552402 | 4552596 |

we need to use the estimates base and not the actual decennial count. Enter the formula =SUM(P2:W2) in cell B2 to sum the net change in population for each year. In cell C2, enter =ROUND((B2/G2)*100,1) to calculate the percent change from the estimate base. Copy and paste both formulas down the columns (Figure 7.7). We can see that Houston was the fastest-growing big metro, growing by more than 16% over these 7 years, while Chicago had the slowest growth rate at less than 1%. Save your work.

5. **Calculate cumulative components of change**. Let's see how each of the metros grew over this period. When creating a chart, it's usually easier to group and isolate the specific values that you're going to use first, and then select them as the data source for the chart prior to inserting it. Type these headers in cells A13 to D13: Metro, Domestic Migration, Foreign Migration, Natural Increase. In column A, from cells 14 to 23, enter short labels for the metro areas that we'll use as labels in the chart; refer to Figure 7.8 for details. You can scroll across the sheet and identify the range for the domestic, international, and natural increase columns. In cell B14 (domestic), type the formula =SUM(BD2:BK2). In cell C14 (foreign), enter =SUM(AV2:BC2). In cell D14 (natural increase), type =SUM(AN2:AU2). Copy and paste each formula down the columns. Save your work.

6. **Check your work**. Right-click in the lower right-hand corner of Calc to make sure that the quick summary function is enabled. Then select the net domestic, foreign, and natural increase values you calculated for New York City (NYC). The quick summary tells us that the sum of these values is 754,919. But in cell B2, the net change for NYC is 754,396. Why are our calculations off? Scroll all the way to the right of the sheet, and select all the residual values for

**FIGURE 7.8 ◆ CALCULATING CUMULATIVE COMPONENTS OF POPULATION CHANGE**

| | B14 | ▼ | $f_x$ Σ = | =SUM(BD2:BK2) | |
|---|---|---|---|---|---|

| | A | B | C | D | |
|---|---|---|---|---|---|
| 1 | CBSA | CHANGE | PCT | NAME | |
| 2 | 35620 | 754396 | 3.9 | New York-Newark-Jersey City, NY-NJ-PA | |
| 3 | 31080 | 524946 | 4.1 | Los Angeles-Long Beach-Anaheim, CA | |
| 4 | 16980 | 71499 | 0.8 | Chicago-Naperville-Elgin, IL-IN-WI | |
| 5 | 19100 | 973431 | 15.1 | Dallas-Fort Worth-Arlington, TX | |
| 6 | 26420 | 971941 | 16.4 | Houston-The Woodlands-Sugar Land, TX | |
| 7 | 47900 | 580228 | 10.3 | Washington-Arlington-Alexandria, DC-VA-MD-WV | |
| 8 | 33100 | 592525 | 10.6 | Miami-Fort Lauderdale-West Palm Beach, FL | |
| 9 | 37980 | 130427 | 2.2 | Philadelphia-Camden-Wilmington, PA-NJ-DE-MD | |
| 10 | 12060 | 597993 | 11.3 | Atlanta-Sandy Springs-Roswell, GA | |
| 11 | 14460 | 283935 | 6.2 | Boston-Cambridge-Newton, MA-NH | |
| 12 | | | | | |
| 13 | Label | Domestic ▶ | Foreign ▶ | Natural Increase | |
| 14 | NYC | -1089495 | 1067992 | | 776422 |
| 15 | LA | -502545 | 408586 | | 623365 |
| 16 | CHI | -479482 | 183162 | | 367709 |
| 17 | DAL | 369622 | 185964 | | 415968 |
| 18 | HOU | 273005 | 260385 | | 436331 |
| 19 | DC | -66116 | 301884 | | 342413 |
| 20 | MIA | -63639 | 513783 | | 142462 |
| 21 | PHL | -147001 | 149902 | | 130620 |
| 22 | ATL | 188169 | 130807 | | 278251 |
| 23 | BOS | -55710 | 226725 | | 116075 |

NYC, in cells BT2 through CA2. The sum of the residuals is −523. If we subtract this number from our component summary, we get the net change value of 754,396. After taking all the components into account, the Census Bureau adjusts its numeric change columns (and thus the total estimate) by these residuals, so the sum of the counties won't exceed state totals. Since these residuals are small relative to the total population for our areas and we're abstracting the data for use in a chart, we can set the discrepancies aside.

7. **Insert chart.** Click in cell A13 and drag to draw a box around all of our summary data from cells A13 to D23, then go up to Insert—Chart. In Step 1 for Chart Type, select Bar as the type, and select the middle option to get a stacked bar chart (Figure 7.9). Click Next. The options for Step 2 Data Range should already be established, since we selected the range before inserting the chart.

**FIGURE 7.9 ● CHOOSING THE OPTION TO INSERT A STACKED BAR CHART**

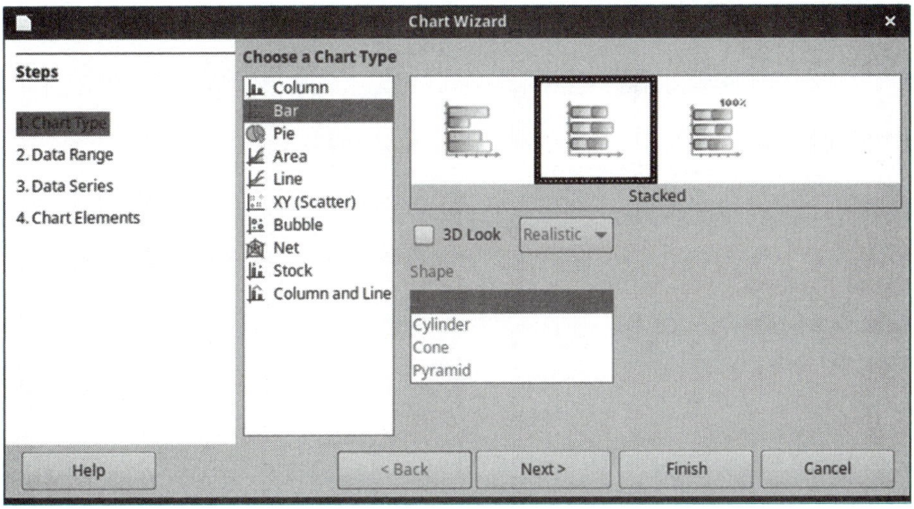

The data series is in columns, and first row and first column labels should be checked. Hit Next. Likewise, in Step 3 Data Series, the defaults are correct because we formatted and selected our chart data in advance. Click Next. Under Step 4 Chart Elements for the title, enter Components of Population Change 2010 - 2017. For Subtitle, enter Ten Largest Metro Areas. For the Display Legend option on the right, check the radio button that says Bottom (this will free up some vital real estate on our chart). Click Finish. Your chart should resemble Figure 7.10.

8. **Clean up the chart**. Let's modify some elements to improve the design of the chart. You can click on a chart to activate it, and then you'll be able to right-click and modify properties of the chart as a whole. If you click on a specific element of the chart, like a value, an axis, or a label, you can then right-click and modify specific values of that element. Alternatively, instead of right-clicking, if you have some element of the chart selected, the chart toolbar becomes active at the top of the screen, and you can select a specific element from the drop-down menu and select properties to modify. It does take a little practice.

Select the chart by clicking on it, and then click on the *y*-axis, the gray line running horizontally at the bottom of the chart. Once selected, right-click and choose Format Axis. On the Numbers tab, uncheck the Source format box on the right, and then under the options, check the box for Thousands separator

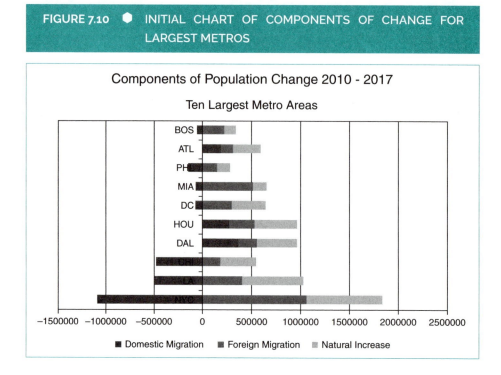

**FIGURE 7.10 ●    INITIAL CHART OF COMPONENTS OF CHANGE FOR LARGEST METROS**

Components of Population Change 2010 - 2017

Ten Largest Metro Areas

■ Domestic Migration    ■ Foreign Migration    ▨ Natural Increase

(Figure 7.11). Then flip over to the Scale tab, uncheck the Automatic box beside the Maximum value, and change the value to 2000000. Click OK. Next, with the chart selected, select the *x*-axis (the gray vertical line in the middle of the chart representing the 0 value). Once selected, right-click and choose Format Axis. On the Positioning tab, change the drop down for Place labels from Near axis to Outside start. Hit OK. Last, select the chart, hover over the small blue box at the bottom center of the chart, and click and drag to make the chart a little taller. Your chart should look like Figure 7.12. Save your work.

9. **Format colors**. Let's change the default colors. When choosing colors, you need to avoid anything garish or that makes variables difficult to distinguish from one another. In this case, it would be ideal to make the migration variables different shades of the same color as they are related. It's also important to remember that some portion of the population is color blind and may not be able to distinguish between certain colors, particularly red and green. You can avoid the simultaneous use of these colors, or make sure that one is a dark shade and the other is light. For a brief explanation of color blindness vis-à-vis graphic design, see Shaffer (2016). While designed for creating maps, the Color Brewer tool at http://colorbrewer2.org/

**FIGURE 7.11** ● MODIFYING THE *Y*-AXIS TO ADD THOUSANDS SEPARATOR (COMMAS) FOR LABELS

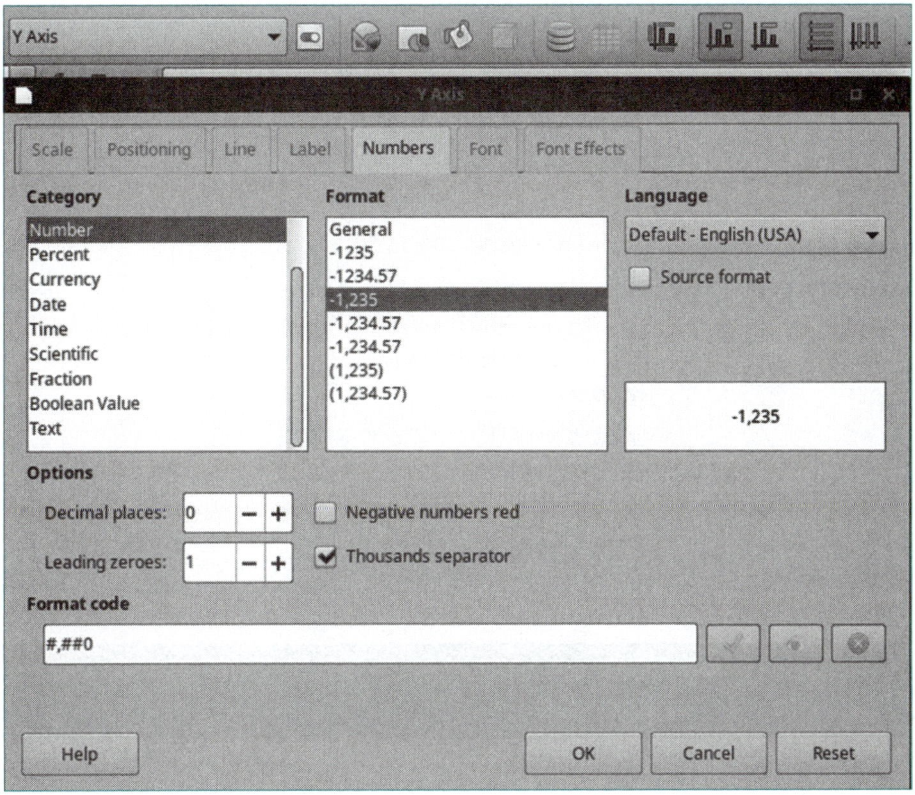

can also be used to choose good color schemes for charts, including color blind–friendly palettes. The following color choices are based on one of their suggestions.

Activate the chart, and click on the blue domestic migration bars on the left side of the graph. Right-click, and choose Format Data Series. On the Area tab, under the New Color option on the right, type the following values into each box: R—236, G—231, B—242 (Figure 7.13). Hit OK. These RGB codes (red, green, blue) are frequently used in web and graphic design for modeling colors. Repeat these steps for the other two series: For foreign migration (middle bars), enter values 166, 189, 219, and for natural increase (right bars), enter 43, 140, 190. Save your work.

10. **Study your chart**. Your final chart should resemble Figure 7.14. The growth patterns for America's largest metro areas are quite distinct. The fastest growing

**FIGURE 7.12 ●  REVISED CHART OF COMPONENTS OF CHANGE FOR LARGEST METROS**

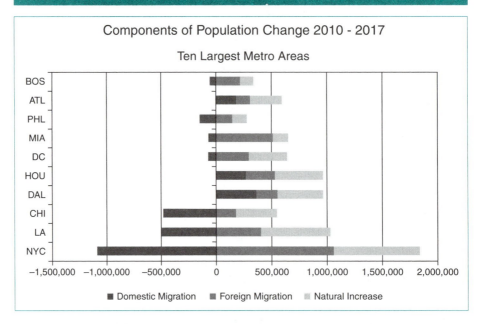

**FIGURE 7.13 ●  CHANGING THE COLORS FOR A DATA SERIES: ENTERING HEX CODES**

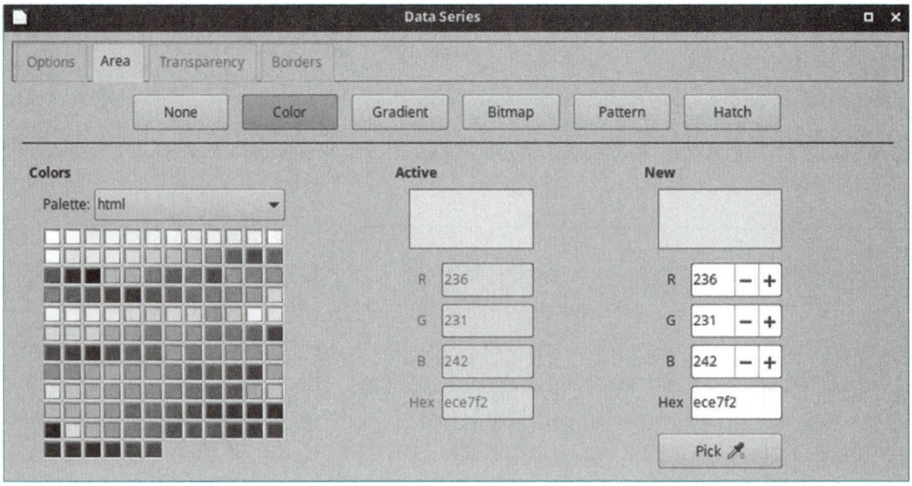

**FIGURE 7.14** ⬢ FINAL CHART OF COMPONENTS OF CHANGE FOR LARGEST METRO AREAS

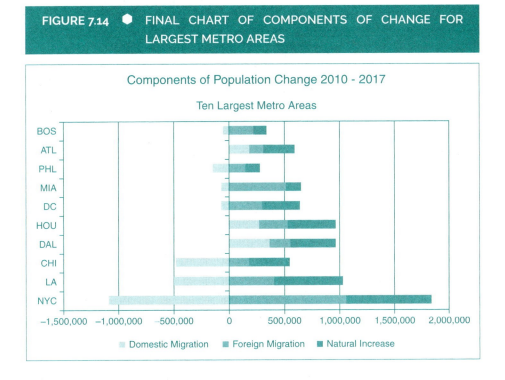

metros (Houston, Dallas, and Atlanta) are also the only metros that have positive net domestic migration. In contrast, the nation's three largest metros (New York, Los Angeles, and Chicago) depend on high net foreign migration to offset large losses in domestic migration. Negative domestic migration in New York is offset by an equal amount of positive foreign migration, so ultimately, natural increase accounts for its population growth. In Los Angeles, there's more natural increase relative to foreign migration, which helps offset domestic loss. In Chicago, negative domestic migration is offset by foreign migration and natural increase combined, so the metro experiences little net growth. While the Chicago metro has only grown by 71,000 people between 2010 and 2017 (0.8%), that does not mean that the population isn't changing: Net domestic out-migration was approximately 479,000 people, new foreign in-migration was 183,000, and natural increase was 367,709.

11. **Export your chart.** If you need to insert your chart into a report, web page, or slide presentation, click on the chart to select it, right-click, and choose Export as Image. You can select from a variety of image types in the All Formats drop down in the lower right-hand corner. TIFF files are best if you need to preserve the full resolution of the image, but these files will be large. PNG files are good

for most purposes and are a better alternative to JPEGs for saving gradations in color without appearing too blurry. PDF is an option for stand-alone documents, while SVG is best if you plan on editing the chart in a graphic design package like Illustrator or Inkscape.

Studying the components of change helps us understand the factors that influence growth or decline in different places and can help us anticipate what could happen in the future. Falling birth rates, a tight housing market, restrictions on foreign immigration, and macrolevel changes in the economy can have a disproportionate impact on different areas depending on what drives their population growth. The components also illustrate the degree to which populations are changing. The net change for an area could be small because the population is relatively stable, or it could be small if there are large but equal shifts in the components that are canceling each other out.

Our stacked bar chart worked well for this particular example, as all of these metros had positive net foreign migration and positive natural increase, which guaranteed that we could show domestic net migration as either positive or negative since it was on the left side of our chart. But what if this wasn't the case? How could we depict areas that had negative foreign migration or natural decrease? For example, there are several rapidly growing metro areas in Florida that have negative natural increase (i.e., decrease) because growth in these areas is driven by retiring senior citizens, whose deaths outnumber births from the smaller cohorts of younger people.

One approach would be to split natural increase into its constituent parts: deaths and births. Deaths will always be negative, so we could place them on the far left of the graph, and births are always positive, so they can go on the far right. Up until this point in recent history, domestic migration is the component that's most likely to be split between positive and negative values, so it would be safest to keep it to the left of the chart. International migration at the state and metro scales is seldom negative. So an ideal arrangement from left to right would be deaths, domestic migration, foreign migration, and births. Alternatively, we could choose a different type of chart, like a normal (nonstacked) bar chart where each component is a separate bar displayed side by side.

The default color schemes for charts in most spreadsheet packages are usually poor, and you should always consider modifying them. As a general rule, when charting positive quantitative data, use shades of a single color that go from light to dark. If you have a mix of negative and positive values, you can use a diverging color scheme. Don't use a garish fruit salad of colors, avoid gimmicky options like 3D charts, and be mindful of both the audience (color blindness, subject expertise) and the final medium in which the chart will be displayed. For graphic design advice, *The Wall Street Journal Guide to Information Graphics* (Wong, 2010) is a good place to start. If you want examples that are spreadsheet specific, consult Stephanie Evergreen's *Effective Data Visualization* (2017) for guidance. Even though it's written for MS Excel, much of the content transcends any specific software package, and many of the Excel examples can be adapted to Calc.

# 7.6  REVIEW QUESTIONS AND PRACTICE EXERCISES

1.  Describe each of the components of a population estimate.

2.  Download the latest vintage estimates for states from the PEP website, and identify the five states that had the largest year-to-year change relative to the previous year and the five that had the largest percent change over the previous year.

3.  Use the Missouri Census Data Center's State/County Annual Population Change application at `https://census.missouri.edu/population/` to create a table and chart of annual population change for a county of your choice.

4.  Based on what we did in Exercise 1, use Calc to create a stacked bar chart that displays the cumulative components of change from 2010 to 2017 for the six largest metropolitan areas in California: (1) Los Angeles, (2) San Francisco, (3) Riverside, (4) San Diego, (5) Sacramento, and (6) San Jose. Describe how differences in the components drive population growth in each of the areas.

5.  Describe some common applications for population estimates, and explain what the difference is between a population estimate and a population projection.

> **Supplementary Digital Content:** Find datasets and supplemental exercises at the companion website at `http://study.sagepub.com/census`.

# BUSINESS DATASETS

## 8.1   INTRODUCTION

The Census Bureau has been gathering and publishing data on businesses almost as long as it has been counting people. Some of the first questions added to the decennial census at the beginning of the 19th century were designed to count businesses and measure productivity and trade. Over time, these business-focused questions were separated from the decennial census and became separate statistical programs and products. Like the demographic datasets, the business datasets don't provide data on individual businesses but summarize data by geography and industry, as the data is covered by the same privacy and confidentiality regulations.

In this chapter, we will explore two of the Census Bureau's primary business datasets. The Business Patterns is an administrative source that provides an annual measure of the number of employees, establishments, and wages for most industries in the nation. It is divided into the County Business Patterns (CBP) and ZIP Code Business Patterns (ZBP), which also supply data for states, metropolitan areas, and Congressional Districts. The Economic Census is conducted every 5 years in years ending with 2 and 7, and it provides a more comprehensive but less timely picture of the nation's economy. The Economic Census employs a mix of full counting and sample surveying to capture the variables included in the Business Patterns, while also including data on production and sales for various industries and additional summary levels (incorporated places and municipalities).

The Bureau of Labor Statistics (BLS) also produces a variety of business-related datasets that are less geographically detailed but are more timely, being released quarterly or even monthly. They also collect data on employment, wages and salaries, and occupation by industry. We'll briefly cover these datasets at the end of the chapter to see what they capture and how they differ from the census datasets.

Persons and housing units are the primary units of data collection in the decennial census and American Community Survey (ACS). For most of the business datasets that we'll cover here, the primary unit is a business establishment, which is a single physical location where business is conducted or where services or industrial operations are performed. While some of these datasets include statistics on multiunit establishments (companies and firms), these are exceptions and not the rule.

Because the business datasets count or survey establishments, they are summarizing data geographically based on where people *work*. This is fundamentally different from the demographic datasets we've covered, which primarily summarize population and labor force characteristics based on where people *live*. Our discussion of the BLS datasets at the end of the chapter will also include the labor force statistics generated from the Current Population Survey (CPS) and the ACS. Since these datasets are surveys of households and people, they are able to capture additional statistics like unemployment and labor force participation.

Using any of these datasets requires an understanding of how businesses are classified into industries. An industry is a group of businesses that produce similar products or provide similar services. The North American Industrial Classification System (NAICS—pronounced "nakes") is a hierarchical system of categories that is used to classify business establishments and the labor force in broad groups and detailed subdivisions that describe what industries produce. We'll begin this chapter with an introduction to the NAICS codes and will cover issues that are pertinent to working with all datasets that are classified using this system. Then we'll explore the Business Patterns and Economic Census and will discuss the variables and issues that are unique to each and how this data can be used to study local economies. We'll summarize the BLS datasets at the end of the chapter, and the exercise will give you the opportunity to work with industry data classified using NAICS.

## When Do You Use the Business Datasets?

The Census Bureau and the BLS publish a variety of datasets that count business establishments and measure the labor force, often by industry. A business establishment is a single physical location where business is conducted, and an industry is a group of businesses that produce similar products or provide similar services. These datasets are useful for measuring the geographic distribution of businesses and comparing the economies of different places. The data can also be used in a nongeographic sense to study specific industries as a whole or to measure broad trends in the national economy.

Use the Business Patterns when

- you want annual data on establishments, employment, and wages by industry for large geographies and

- you need business data for ZIP Codes or Congressional Districts (not collected elsewhere).

Use the Economic Census when

- doing research that is more long term, where timeliness is less important;

- doing either geographic or nongeographic industrial research;

- you need data for production and sales for certain industries; and

- you need data for incorporated places or minor civil divisions (not collected elsewhere).

Use the BLS datasets when

- you need timely data that's produced monthly, quarterly, or annually;

- you want to look at historical trends without having to do a lot of data processing; and

- geographical detail is not important: few datasets below the state level, no datasets below the county level.

Use the CPS labor force data when

- you need timely data on unemployment and labor force participation.

Use the ACS labor force data when

- you need data for small geographies like tracts and Zip Code Tabulation Areas (ZCTA);

- you are already working with other ACS variables and want to use data from the same source; and

- you can live with fuzzier estimates that generally characterize an area rather than precisely measure it.

## 8.2   NAVIGATING INDUSTRIES WITH NAICS

`https://www.census.gov/eos/www/naics/`

The NAICS is a hierarchical system of codes used to classify business establishments and employment into industries, which are groups of businesses that produce similar products or provide similar services. The NAICS system was introduced for the 1997 Economic Census. As part of the North American Free Trade Agreement (NAFTA), Canada, the United States, and Mexico wanted to establish a common system for classifying industries to standardize measurement and facilitate the exchange of this data. The codes were also designed to replace the older Standard Industrial Classification (SIC) system, which was designed to measure an older manufacturing-centered economy that no longer reflected the reality of a late-20th-century service-based economy.

The codes were designed so that industries could be described in an increasing level of detail from broad sectors of the economy down to very specific groups of businesses. Table 8.1 lists the two-digit sector-level codes that represent the most general level of classification. These sectors capture many related businesses under broad headings like construction, manufacturing, and retail trade. Some sectors capture a wider group of activities, while others are a bit narrower. Sector 21 captures anything related to resource extraction from the earth (mining, quarrying, oil and gas extraction), while Sector 52 is specific to finance and insurance businesses. Services are broken across many different sectors dedicated to professional and scientific services, educational services, accommodation and food services, and so on.

Sectors are divided and subdivided into groups that describe industrial activity in narrower detail. Table 8.2 illustrates this nested hierarchy for Sector 22 Utilities, which is the smallest sector in terms of the number of subdivisions. The Utilities sector includes establishments engaged in providing electric power, natural gas, steam supply, water supply, and sewage removal. Subdivisions of a sector are identified with the addition of extra digits to the sector code. The three-digit level is called a subsector, which is pretty simple in the case of Utilities as there is only one. A broader sector like 11 Agriculture, Forestry, Fishing and Hunting has several subsectors. The four-digit level is called the industry group level. With Utilities, this is broken down into industries that are engaged with electric power (2211), natural gas (2212), and water and sewage systems (2213).

You can see the logic in the divisions as you drill further down. The five-digit code is the industry level. For electric power, this is subdivided into Electric Power Generation (22111) and Electric Power Transmission (22112). The six-digit codes are the most specific and are called U.S. industry-level codes (at this level, each of the

| Sector | Description |
|---|---|
| **TABLE 8.1 ⬡  NORTH AMERICAN INDUSTRIAL CLASSIFICATION SYSTEM SECTORS** | |
| 11 | Agriculture, Forestry, Fishing and Hunting |
| 21 | Mining, Quarrying, and Oil and Gas Extraction |
| 22 | Utilities |
| 23 | Construction |
| 31–33 | Manufacturing |
| 42 | Wholesale Trade |
| 44–45 | Retail Trade |
| 48–49 | Transportation and Warehousing |
| 51 | Information |
| 52 | Finance and Insurance |
| 53 | Real Estate and Rental and Leasing |
| 54 | Professional, Scientific, and Technical Services |
| 55 | Management of Companies and Enterprises |
| 56 | Administrative and Support and Waste Management and Remediation Services |
| 61 | Educational Services |
| 62 | Health Care and Social Assistance |
| 71 | Arts, Entertainment, and Recreation |
| 72 | Accommodation and Food Services |
| 81 | Other Services (except Public Administration) |
| 92 | Public Administration |

three countries in NAFTA can create their own categories). Electric Power Generation is subdivided into the means by which the power is generated: hydroelectric, fossil fuel, nuclear, and so on. Other industries that have a narrower focus have fewer or no subdivisions. For example, Natural Gas Distribution is not subdivided any further, and the four-, five-, and six-digit codes refer to the same collection of industries.

The NAICS codes are available online at `https://www.census.gov/eos/www/naics/`, where you can browse through the hierarchy by clicking on sectors to

## TABLE 8.2 ● NAICS LEVELS FOR THE UTILITIES SECTOR

**22** Utilities (*sector level*)

**221** Utilities (*subsector level*)

**2211** Electric Power Generation, Transmission and Distribution (*industry group level*)

**22111** Electric Power Generation (*industry level*)

**221111** Hydroelectric Power Generation (*U.S. industry level*)

**221112** Fossil Fuel Electric Power Generation

**221113** Nuclear Electric Power Generation

**221114** Solar Electric Power Generation

**221115** Wind Electric Power Generation

**221116** Geothermal Electric Power Generation

**221117** Biomass Electric Power Generation

**221118** Other Electric Power Generation

**22112** Electric Power Transmission, Control, and Distribution

**221121** Electric Bulk Power Transmission and Control

**221122** Electric Power Distribution

**2212** Natural Gas Distribution

**22121** Natural Gas Distribution

**221210** Natural Gas Distribution

**2213** Water, Sewage and Other Systems

**22131** Water Supply and Irrigation Systems

**221310** Water Supply and Irrigation Systems

**22132** Sewage Treatment Facilities

**221320** Sewage Treatment Facilities

**22133** Steam and Air-Conditioning Supply

**221330** Steam and Air-Conditioning Supply

*Note:* NAICS = North American Industrial Classification System.

navigate down the system, or you can search by keyword. The website is invaluable for understanding how the codes are structured and what the definitions are. For example, if you were to drill down in the utilities sector and chose the six-digit code 221117 Biomass Electric Power Generation, you would see the entry in Table 8.3. The entry

**TABLE 8.3  ●  2012 NAICS DEFINITION FOR BIOMASS ELECTRIC POWER GENERATION**

**221117 Biomass Electric Power Generation**

This U.S. industry comprises establishments primarily engaged in operating biomass electric power generation facilities. These facilities use biomass (e.g., wood, waste, alcohol fuels) to produce electric energy. The electric energy produced in these establishments is provided to electric power transmission systems or to electric power distribution systems.

Cross-References

- Establishments primarily engaged in operating trash disposal incinerators that also generate electricity are classified in U.S. Industry 562213, Solid Waste Combustors and Incinerators.

| 2002 NAICS | 2007 NAICS | 2012 NAICS | Corresponding Index Entries |
|------------|------------|------------|------------------------------|
| 221119 | 221119 | 221117 | Biomass electric power generation |
| 221119 | 221119 | 221117 | Electric power generation, biomass |
| 221119 | 221119 | 221117 | Power generation, biomass |

*Source:* https://www.census.gov/cgi-bin/sssd/naics/naicsrch?chart=2012

provides a specific definition of what's included in the industry and what it produces. Below the definition are two important pieces of information: cross-references to related industries and changes to the classification over time. Let's address each of these issues in turn.

The cross-references are used to distinguish an industry from an industry that may be related to it but is classified elsewhere. In this example, businesses that operate trash disposal incinerators that also generate electricity are not classified as biomass utilities but as 562213 Solid Waste Combustors and Incinerators, which falls under Sector 56 Administrative and Support and Waste Management and Remediation Services. What's the difference? Biomass utilities are *primarily* engaged in burning wood, waste, and alcohol fuels for the purpose of generating electricity, which they sell to customers. In contrast, solid waste incinerators focus *primarily* on providing services for burning trash, although they may generate some income by generating electricity from it.

In the census and BLS summary datasets, all businesses are classified into one industry based on the activities they primarily engage in. When studying any industry, or trying to identify which businesses fall into a specific industry, you need to consider all the possible categories that could apply. How is the decision to classify a business made? For example, under Accommodation and Food Services, there are four-digit industry group codes for Drinking Places that Serve Alcoholic Beverages (7224) and Restaurants and Other Eating Places (7225). How would a restaurant that has a bar be classified? In the census and BLS datasets, this is typically up to the owner of the establishment, who is asked to identify the primary activity of their business. They can base their decision on physical space devoted to each activity, where the majority of their revenue comes from, or simply from their perception of what they think their business is. In some cases, the Census Bureau or BLS will classify or reclassify a business based on information submitted in a survey or from administrative records.

For certain kinds of research, particularly geographic research below the county level that attempts to measure accessibility to specific types of activities, this classification of businesses can be problematic. Since we don't have access to individual business-level information, we don't know how a specific business was classified, and the relevant activities being studied may be split across several categories or combined into categories with nonrelevant activities.

For instance, the study of food deserts, which are defined as concentrated areas of poverty that lack access to affordable sources of healthy food or more generally to supermarkets, has been an intense area of research in public health, geography, and sociology for many decades (Beaulac, Kristjansson, & Cummins, 2009; Charreire et al., 2009). Supermarkets (445110) are classified as a retail industry that specifically excludes convenience stores, which are classified separately as Convenience Stores (445120) and Gasoline Stations with Convenience Stores (447110). Food desert researchers typically exclude convenience stores, as the food tends to be more expensive and the options are less healthy. However, while large stores like Wal-Mart and Target don't specialize in groceries, they have large sections of their stores dedicated to them. In terms of floor space, the size of these sections rivals that of small supermarkets. Wal-Mart and Target could be classified as department stores, discount department stores, or warehouse clubs and supercenters, which may lump them in with businesses unrelated to groceries.

For this type of research, it's often necessary to go beyond the summary census data and look at proprietary databases that provide lists of individual businesses in an area. Examples include ReferenceUSA by InfoUSA and Dun and Bradstreet's Million Dollar Directory. These sources allow you to search for individual business by primary and secondary NAICS codes to create extracts. These products are proprietary and subscription based, so you would need to access them from your college, university, or public library. Unlike the census datasets, you would need to consider these sources as raw data that would have to be checked and verified for completeness.

Ultimately, the specific subject of study and the geographic scale would determine whether you would need to consult these resources or simply use the summarized census data. For example, a study on the concentration of alcohol outlets on college campuses in 10 states found that using summary ZBP data was just as good (based on statistical correlation) as using data aggregated from lists of individual businesses that were obtained from proprietary databases or state government sources (Matthews, McCarthy, & Rafail, 2011). The authors did take special care in defining what an alcohol outlet was; beyond liquor stores and bars, it is legal to buy alcohol at supermarkets, convenience stores, and gas stations in certain states. They also decided to include full-service restaurants (restaurants with table service) as they would be the most likely restaurants to have bars, while excluding other types of restaurants (limited service, where you order at a counter) that were less likely to serve alcohol.

In short, when you are researching a specific type of activity, you need to carefully consider the NAICS definitions and cross-references to understand how these activities are classified, so you can select the industries or groups that most accurately capture what you are trying to study. Some activities and industries will be easier to target and study than others.

Let's return to Table 8.3 and consider the second issue, which is change over time. NAICS codes are revised every 5 years in conjunction with the Economic Census to reflect the evolving nature of the economy. In our biomass electric power example, this industry was classified as 221117 Biomass Elecetric Power Generation in the 2012 NAICS but was classified as 221119 Other Electric Power Generation in earlier series (2002 and 2007). In the older series, solar, wind, hydroelectric, and biomass were lumped together into this catchall category. Since these activities have increased in size and importance, they were broken up into dedicated categories in 2012.

These kinds of changes are the most common in the NAICS: An activity either grows enough in importance that it splits from an existing category or moves out of the miscellaneous other category (which is present in most subdivsions) into its own dedicated category. Conversely, if an activity declines in importance, it may lose its distinct category. When studying industries over time for four- to six-digit activities, you need to be aware of these changes so you're not comparing unrelated activities, or in the case of the biomass power industry, you would need to modify the past categories. The census publishes a series of concordances or crosswalks on the NAICS website for relating current codes with older ones, so you can account for the changes and make modifications.

You also need to identify the specific version of NAICS that a given dataset is using. The Economic Census is straightforward, as the year of the census reflects the version of NAICS that was used—that is, the 2017 Economic Census will use 2017 NAICS codes. Currently, the Business Patterns dataset applies NAICS codes based on their year of introduction. For example, 2012 NAICS codes were used from 2012 to 2016. The 2017 NAICS will be used from 2017 to 2021. Earlier Business Patterns datasets had a 1-year delay before the codes were applied (i.e., 2008–2011 data used 2007 NAICS). The Census Bureau does *not* revise or modify earlier years of data once new codes are published.

Now that we have a basic understanding of how businesses are classified into industries using NAICS and what some of the considerations are, we can begin to explore the datasets that use this classification.

## 8.3   DATA FOR BUSINESS ESTABLISHMENTS

### County and ZBPs

```
https://www.census.gov/programs-surveys/cbp.html
```

The CBP is an administrative dataset generated annually from the Business Register, a large relational database that includes every business establishment in the United States and the U.S. territories that has paid employees. The Business Register is updated on an ongoing basis by many federal agencies, particularly the Internal Revenue Service, the BLS, and the Census Bureau. Major updates are made every 5 years based on the counts and larger sample surveys conducted for the Economic Census. Data is released about 16 months after the time it is generated and is published in the spring. For example, data for the 2016 CBP was published in spring 2018.

Despite the name, data is also published for a number of other geographic areas such as states, metropolitan areas, and Congressional Districts. Below the county level, data is tabulated for ZIP Codes as part of the ZIP Code Business Patterns. Unlike the decennial census and ACS, the ZIP Codes in the ZBP are actual ZIP Codes and not ZCTAs (see Chapter 3). The Census Bureau simply aggregates the data using the ZIP Code that's part of each establishment's address. As such, you cannot directly relate ZBP data to ZCTA-level demographic data, but we'll discuss a method of crosswalking them in Chapter 11.

The data in the CBP/ZBP is relatively straightforward. There are estimates of the number of employees, establishments, annual payroll, and first quarter payroll with a reference period of mid-March. This data is summarized by NAICS codes for the sum of all sectors (indicated with the code 00) down to the smallest six-digit U.S. industries in one table. There is a separate table that counts the number of establishments by employment size class with a given range of categories, so you can study small businesses versus large businesses by industry and geography. The CBP (but not the ZBP) includes a third table that summarizes businesses by type of legal establishment such as corporation, sole proprietorship, nonprofit, and so on. A limited amount of data is summarized for multiunit firms, which are establishments owned by the same company. Industries in the CBP/ZBP are primarily classified based on responses from the Economic Census, or in cases where this is unknown, they are classified by the Census Bureau based on administrative records or imputation techniques.

The CBP and ZBP do *not* include data on self-employed individuals, employees of private households, railroad employees, agricultural production employees, and most government employees. The following industries are excluded: Crop and Animal Production (NAICS 111, 112), Rail Transportation (482), Postal Service (491), Pension, Health, Welfare, and Vacation Funds (525110, 525120, 525190), Trusts, Estates, and Agency Accounts (525920), Private Households (814), and Public Administration (92). There are a few exceptions to these rules—for example, hospitals that are run by government agencies are included under Hospitals (622). Employers that don't have a fixed address or where the county is unknown are assigned to a generic statewide classification.

Data for the self-employed population is available through the Nonemployer Statistics program. This administrative dataset is also generated annually from the Business Register. Records for businesses that list no paid employees are flagged and scrutinized to determine whether they should be classified as nonemployers. The Census Bureau uses records from the Internal Revenue Service to update the database. Data is classified by industry and published for states, metro areas, and counties:

```
https://www.census.gov/programs-surveys/nonemployer-
statistics.html
```

## The Economic Census

```
https://www.census.gov/programs-surveys/economic-census.html
```

The Economic Census is a much larger undertaking relative to the CBP, in that it's an actual count or a large sample survey (depending on the industry) of all business establishments in the United States and territories that's taken every 5 years. Economic statistics from businesses had been collected as part of the decennial census all the way back to 1810, but it wasn't until the mid-20th century that this dataset was decoupled from the 10-year count and conducted in 5-year increments. The practice of doing the survey in years ending with 2 or 7 began with the 1967 Economic Census and continues to the present (Micarelli, 1998).

There are some similarities between the Economic Census and the CBP in that both use the business establishment as the unit of measurement and both count establishments, employment, and wages by industry down to the six-digit NAICS level. Both of them provide geographic summaries for metropolitan areas, states, counties, and ZIP Codes; the Economic Census also tabulates data for incorporated places and minor civil divisions but not for Congressional Districts. The type and amount of data that's available varies by geography and industry.

There are several important differences. Since the Economic Census is based on total counts and large sample surveys, it is used to adjust and update the Business Register that's used to produce the CBP. Similar to the decennial census and the ACS, responses to the Economic Census are required by law. Businesses submit responses online and the Census Bureau conducts a certain number of follow-ups and has procedures for imputing values for nonresponders. The Economic Census also collects information on production and sales that are not included in the CBP. Since the Economic Census is broader in scope and more in depth, data is summarized and published in separate geography and subject series, where the subject series is focused on particular industries. For example, in the subject series for retail trade, there are dedicated data tables on product lines, summaries by employment size and sales size, summary statistics for single-unit and multiunit firms, data on firm concentration, and even statistics on floor space.

The Economic Census excludes a larger number of industries compared with the CBP. Given the differences in coverage and methodology, comparing Economic Census data directly with the CBP is not advisable. With a few exceptions (e.g., hospitals and federal reserve banks), the Economic Census excludes all government-owned establishments: public administration, public utilities, public transit systems, public libraries, and more. Data for government establishments is captured in the Census of Governments, which takes place concurrently with the Economic Census. All industries in Sector 11, Agriculture, Forestry, Fishing and Hunting are also excluded. This information is collected by the U.S. Department of Agriculture (USDA) in the Census of Agriculture, which is also conducted concurrently (see InfoBox 8.1). Table 8.4 summarizes the data that is not collected and references alternative sources. Data for some industries like religious organizations can be found entirely in the CBP, while data for other industries like schools and colleges are partially available (for private schools). The Census of Governments would be the source for data on public schools and universities, which are included under NAICS Sector 61.

> ✓ **INFOBOX 8.1 CENSUS OF GOVERNMENTS, CENSUS OF AGRICULTURE**
>
> The Census of Governments and the Census of Agriculture capture data for these industries that are excluded entirely from the Economic Census and included partially in the Business Patterns. Both programs are conducted concurrently with the Economic Census in years that end in 2 and 7. With the exception of Puerto Rico in the Census of Agriculture, the U.S. territories are not included in these programs.
>
> The Census of Governments is conducted by the Census Bureau and captures information on local, state, and federal government organization, finance, and employment. In addition to establishments, employees, and wages, data is collected on taxation, expenditures, debts, and assets. The Census Bureau maintains a directory of all government establishments that it updates using an annual sample survey. The 5-year census is sent to all 89k establishments listed in the directory. Data on employment is released about a year after the census is conducted, and data on government finances is released about 6 months later. Data is published at the state level and is available from **data.census.gov**, the FTP (File Transfer Protocol) site, and the dedicated program page: `https://www.census.gov/programs-surveys/cog.html`
>
> The Census of Agriculture is conducted by the USDA and is a complete count of all farms, ranches, and fisheries. Any individual operation or place is included if more than $1,000 of fruits, vegetables, flowers, or farm animals were raised and sold during the census year. Data is captured on size of land, yields, values, and sales for types of crops and animals, employment, wages, and demographic characteristics about the owners/operators. There are special subject series on horticulture, aquaculture, forestry, and more. Responses to the Census of Agriculture fall under the same confidentiality regulations as the Economic Census.
>
> Data is collected in December of the census year and is published a little over a year later for states, Congressional Districts, and counties. This data is not available through the Census Bureau's applications or web pages but is provided directly from the USDA: `https://agcensus.usda.gov/index.php`

While the Economic Census is far more detailed than the CBP, it is a lot less timely. Once data collection is finished, it takes almost 2 years for the first data extracts to be released and an additional year for all the data to be released in its entirety. The geographic area series is published first, followed by the subject series.

## Accessing Data, Confidentiality, and Disclosure

In this section, we'll demonstrate how to access the CBP, and in doing so, we'll learn how confidentiality regulations affect the data. Like the other census datasets, the CBP, ZBP, and Economic Census can be downloaded from **data.census.gov** and from the FTP site. The Census Bureau also provides access to the CBP and ZBP files from the CBP program page at

| TABLE 8.4 ● INDUSTRIES NOT INCLUDED IN THE ECONOMIC CENSUS | | |
|---|---|---|
| **NAICS** | **Description** | **Coverage Elsewhere** |
| 11 | Agriculture, Forestry, Fishing and Hunting | CBP (except 111,112), USDA |
| 482 | Rail Transportation | |
| 491 | Postal Service | |
| 525 | Funds, Trusts, and Other Financial Vehicles | CBP (except 5251) |
| 6111 | Elementary and Secondary Schools | CBP (private schools only) |
| 6112 | Junior Colleges | CBP (private schools only) |
| 6113 | Colleges, Universities, and Professional Schools | CBP (private schools only) |
| 8131 | Religious Organizations | CBP |
| 81393 | Labor Unions and Similar Labor Organizations | CBP |
| 81394 | Political Organizations | CBP |
| 814 | Private Households | |
| 92 | Public Administration | |

*Source:* https://census.gov/programs-surveys/economic-census/guidance/understanding-naics.html
*Note:* Data for government-owned establishments is included in the Census of Governments. Data for the self-employed is included in the Nonemployer Statistics.

https://www.census.gov/programs-surveys/cbp.html. By clicking on the tab for data and CBP datasets, you can click on a specific year and get all the data for a particular level of geography in one ZIP file.

If you recall from Chapter 2, going to the advanced search of **data.census.gov** allows you to filter by selecting a survey, year, geography, and topic. You can also filter by industries using the NAICS codes. For example, if we wanted to select all the 2016 CBP data for electric power generation facilities at the six-digit level in Oregon, we would select our survey, year, and geography and then would click on the Industries filter, click through each level of NAICS to browse down to the area we want, and check all the relevant codes (Figure 8.1). We can select a mixture of levels, such as all of the six-digit power generation industries plus the five-digit Electric Power Generation category that sums them. Clicking on the tables button at the bottom of the screen displays the three tables available from the CBP at the state level: (1) the basic geographic area report that sums employees, establishments, and wages; (2) the summary series on establishments by employment size; and (3) the summary series by legal form (count of corporations, nonprofits, etc.).

FIGURE 8.1 ● FILTERING BY NAICS CODE UNDER ADVANCED SEARCH IN DATA.CENSUS.GOV

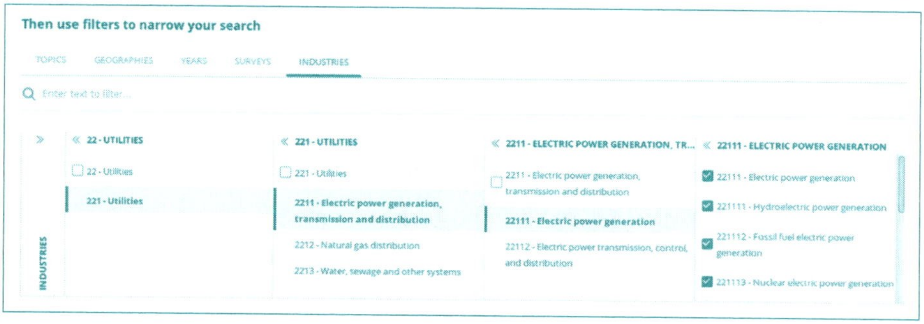

TABLE 8.5 ● POWER GENERATION IN OREGON

| NAICS | Description | Employment | Establishments | Annual Payroll ($1,000s) |
|-------|-------------|------------|----------------|--------------------------|
| 22111 | Electric power generation | 990 | 42 | 112,892 |
| 221111 | Hydroelectric power | 208 | 8 | 17,564 |
| 221112 | Fossil fuel electric power | 306 | 6 | 35,041 |
| 221114 | Solar electric power | a | 1 | D |
| 221115 | Wind electric power | 327 | 13 | 50,565 |
| 221117 | Biomass electric power | 93 | 6 | 5,775 |
| 221118 | Other electric power | b | 8 | D |

*Source:* Census 2016 County Business Patterns.

A portion of the geographic area table is shown in Table 8.5. There are a few details we need to examine. First, not all the six-digit NAICS industries that we selected for Oregon power generation appear in the results: There are no records for Nuclear Power (221113) or Geothermal Power (221116). When this occurs, it could mean that the value for those records is zero (if Oregon does not have any establishments in those industries), or data for those industries is not included in the CBP (because they are publicly owned). Second, in the CBP and Economic Census, dollar values are always abbreviated in thousands of dollars, so the annual payroll of $5,775 reported for the Biomass Electric Power Industry is really $5,775,000.

For several records, you'll notice that we don't have an actual value, but there is a letter inserted in its place. The business datasets fall under the same confidentiality regulations as the demographic ones, in that records for individual businesses are confidential and cannot be disclosed for 72 years. The Census Bureau must take extra precautions to prevent businesses from being identified individually in the summary data, as this is much easier to do as there are fewer businesses than there are people. In instances where there are only a couple of businesses within a specific industry or geography, or when there are one or two large businesses that dominate the market in an industry or area, the Census Bureau employs one of three suppression techniques in the CBP and Economic Census for employment, wages, and sales.

The first option is to suppress or not disclose the data, and the second option is to provide a range of possible values instead of the precise value. In Table 8.5, Solar Electric Power (221114) has only one establishment in the state. The capital letter "D" in the payroll field indicates that the payroll is not being disclosed, as there is only one business. The lowercase letter "a" is an employment size range footnote and indicates that there are between 1 and 19 employees in that industry. Similarly, for Other Electric Power (221118), the employment range for letter "b" is 20 to 99 employees and the payroll is also suppressed. Since there are eight establishments, it's possible that one or two of them dominate the market, necessitating data suppression.

The third option is that the Census Bureau can inject "noise" into a data value by adjusting it by a small percentage. Although it's not displayed in Table 8.5, if you downloaded the data and examined the CSV, there are separate noise range columns for employment and each of the payroll fields. There are four possibilities indicated with a footnote: (1) low, (2) medium, (3) high noise, or (4) the data is withheld completely to avoid disclosing data for individual companies. The footnotes for employment size ranges and noise are printed in Table 8.6. In this example, the annual payroll for the biomass industry was injected with medium noise, so that the actual value of the payroll is 2% to 5% higher or lower than the reported value. Payroll for the other six-digit sectors was injected with high noise or not disclosed, while the five-digit category for total electric power was subjected to low noise.

In employing these methods, the Census Bureau attempts to balance protection of confidentiality with providing useful data. When possible, the least invasive strategy of noise is used, followed by replacing values with size ranges and not disclosing values as a last resort. The footnotes published in Table 8.6 apply to both the Business Patterns and the Economic Census.

These procedures create several practical implications for using these datasets. The first is that the sum of the parts is seldom going to equal the whole. In this example, the sum of employment for the six-digit industries where we have precise values does not equal the five-digit summary value (934 vs. 990 employees). This holds true

| TABLE 8.6 ● | DATA SUPPRESSION FOOTNOTES IN THE BUSINESS DATASETS |
|---|---|
| **Symbol** | **Description** |
| | **Employment ranges** |
| a | 0–19 employees |
| b | 20–99 employees |
| c | 100–249 employees |
| e | 250–499 employees |
| f | 500–999 employees |
| g | 1,000–2,499 employees |
| h | 2,500–4,999 employees |
| i | 5,000–9,999 employees |
| j | 10,000–24,999 employees |
| k | 25,000–49,999 employees |
| l | 50,000–99,999 employees |
| m | 100,000 employees or more |
| | **Noise infusion** |
| G | Low: 0% to <2% adjustment |
| H | Medium: 2% to <5% adjustment |
| J | High: >5% adjustment |
| | **Data withheld** |
| D | Withheld to avoid disclosing data |

not only for summing industries into their larger parts but also when summing geographies: The sum of all counties for an industry will probably not equal the state total. If you need summaries for a larger industry or geography, which is already published in the CBP or Economic Census, you should download the data for those larger areas in addition to the smaller areas instead of aggregating the smaller areas. If data for your industry or area is fuzzy or not disclosed, the solution would be to use a larger industry or area. Alternatively, if employee size range footnotes are provided, you can present summaries of employment as intervals with a low and high value or as an estimate using the range's midpoint. We'll look at examples of both in the exercise.

The second implication is that the insertion of footnotes into the data wreaks havoc with data processing. Databases and scripting languages operate on the basis that values in a particular column have a specific type, either a text or a numeric value. Most relational databases will reject any data that has text in a field that's designated as numeric, while functions in scripting languages for processing numbers will throw errors if they encounter text. When importing data into GIS, the software will convert any numeric column to text if it finds one nonnumeric character, which then precludes using or mapping the values as numbers. Spreadsheets allow you to put data anywhere you please, but mixing values of different types together makes it difficult to apply formulas. Simply deleting the footnotes is a mistake, as you're ignoring the data's limitations. The standard practice is to separate footnotes into their own dedicated columns, while leaving the numeric values blank or null. If you download individual tables from **data.census.gov**, you will need to separate footnotes from data values, but if you download the data in bulk, the footnotes are published in separate columns.

## Using Industry Data to Study Places

When economists and economic geographers compare the economies of two or more places, they are often interested in measuring the degree to which an economy is specialized versus diversified, identifying what the specialized industries are, and tying together separate industries that work in concert as part of a larger economic group. In this section, we'll look at how industrial-based data can be used in research.

In *The Rise and Fall of Urban Economies*, Michael Storper and his colleagues studied how the economies of Los Angeles and San Francisco evolved and diverged between 1970 and 2010. Of the many analyses they conducted, one identified the economic specializations of these metro areas and how they changed over time using employment data by industry from the CBP (Storper, Kemeny, Makarem, & Osman, 2015, pp. 29–39). To measure specialization, economists need to distinguish between tradable and nontradable industries. Tradable industries represent the portions of the economy that are specialized: These are goods or services that the region exchanges or exports to other regions. In contrast, nontradable goods and services are items that are consumed locally and are ubiquitous throughout the country. The production of software and motion pictures, hotel accommodation, and computer system design services could all be considered tradable goods. They are neither goods that are consumed wholly by the local population nor industries that are spread evenly throughout the country. In contrast, cement production, auto salvage yards, laundromats, and general doctors offices are considered nontradable goods, as they are often consumed locally and are commonplace throughout the economy.

Tradable industries usually drive a regional or metropolitan economy, while nontradable industries grow to support the tradable industries and the local population. The generation of nontradable jobs from tradable jobs is known as the multiplier effect. As a software industry grows and produces software for export to the world, other industries emerge and grow to support it. These can include other tradable industries that become part of the larger group of specialized industries, such as data processing services and computer hardware wholesalers, as well as nontradable industries that grow to support that labor force and the population more generally, such as grocery stores, doctor's offices, and home construction and repair industries.

There is no definitive source or a simple list that you can use to determine what a tradable versus a nontradable industry is, and definitions will vary based on local context. In the Los Angeles and San Francisco study, the authors applied a method used in another paper that measured the degree of concentration of service industries across the United States (Jensen & Kletzer, 2006). Industries that were highly concentrated within specific geographic areas were considered tradable. After applying this method, the authors made a number of commonsense adjustments for the two metros they were studying. The entertainment industry was classified as nontradable using the methods in the first study, as in most places, this industry consists of movie theaters or amusement parks. Since Los Angeles is home to Hollywood, the entertainment industry is quite different there and acts like a tradable industry, in that it encompasses a wider range of activities and draws people from around the world (employees and tourists) and produces goods and services that are exported everywhere.

Let's illustrate the concept of specialization with an example. We'll examine CBP data for Clark County, Nevada; Maricopa County, Arizona; and Salt Lake County, Utah, which are home to the cities of Las Vegas, Phoenix, and Salt Lake City and are the central counties of much larger metropolitan areas. Based on the 2016 CBP, these counties employed approximately 847k, 1.6m, and 581k people, respectively.

Since the two-digit sector levels are quite broad and encompass activities that you would find in most places, it's difficult to identify specialization at this scale for most counties and metro areas. Clark County's economy is unique as 32% of its employment is devoted to Sector 72 Accommodation and Food Services (in contrast to Maricopa and Salt Lake where employment in this sector is 11% and 8%, respectively). Beyond this distinction, we cannot glean a lot of information from the sector level as differences in the percentage of total employment between the three counties are not that large.

We can begin to detect levels of specialization at the smaller four-digit industry group level. Table 8.7 shows the 10 largest industry groups for each county by percentage of

| TABLE 8.7 ◆ PERCENTAGE OF TOTAL EMPLOYMENT FOR LARGEST INDUSTRY GROUPS FOR THREE WESTERN COUNTIES | | | | | |
|---|---|---|---|---|---|
| NAICS | Industry Group | % Total Employment | Rank | | |
| | | | CC | MC | SLC |
| **Clark County, Nevada** | | | | | |
| *7211* | *Traveler accommodation* | 20.4 | 1 | 12 | 16 |
| 7225 | Restaurants and other eating places | 9.9 | 2 | 1 | 1 |
| 6221 | General medical and surgical hospitals | 2.8 | 3 | 2 | 2 |
| *4481* | *Clothing stores* | 2.1 | 4 | 22 | 32 |
| 2382 | Building equipment contractors | 2.0 | 5 | 10 | 7 |
| 4451 | Grocery stores | 2.0 | 6 | 8 | 8 |
| 5511 | Management of companies and enterprises | 1.9 | 7 | 3 | 4 |
| 5617 | Services to buildings and dwellings | 1.8 | 8 | 5 | 18 |
| 5613 | Employment services | 1.5 | 9 | 4 | 6 |
| 6211 | Offices of physicians | 1.5 | 10 | 7 | 15 |
| **Maricopa County, Arizona** | | | | | |
| 7225 | Restaurants and other eating places | 8.8 | 2 | 1 | 1 |
| 6221 | General medical and surgical hospitals | 3.5 | 3 | 2 | 3 |
| 5511 | Management of companies and enterprises | 3.0 | 7 | 3 | 4 |
| 5613 | Employment services | 2.5 | 9 | 4 | 6 |
| 5617 | Services to buildings and dwellings | 2.2 | 8 | 5 | 18 |
| *5241* | *Insurance carriers* | 2.1 | 38 | 6 | 34 |
| 6211 | Offices of physicians | 2.0 | 10 | 7 | 15 |
| 4451 | Grocery stores | 2.0 | 6 | 8 | 8 |
| 5221 | Depository credit intermediation | 2.0 | 19 | 9 | 9 |
| 2382 | Building equipment contractors | 1.9 | 5 | 10 | 7 |
| **Salt Lake County, Utah** | | | | | |
| 7225 | Restaurants and other eating places | 6.5 | 2 | 1 | 1 |
| *8131* | *Religious organizations* | 3.8 | 55 | 29 | 2 |
| 6221 | General medical and surgical hospitals | 3.5 | 3 | 2 | 3 |
| 5511 | Management of companies and enterprises | 3.0 | 7 | 3 | 4 |

| NAICS | Industry Group | % Total Employment | Rank | | |
|-------|----------------|--------------------|------|------|------|
| | | | CC | MC | SLC |
| 5614 | *Business support services* | 2.2 | 26 | 24 | 5 |
| 5613 | Employment services | 2.1 | 9 | 4 | 6 |
| 2382 | Building equipment contractors | 1.8 | 5 | 10 | 7 |
| 4451 | Grocery stores | 1.6 | 6 | 8 | 8 |
| 5221 | Depository credit intermediation | 1.5 | 19 | 9 | 9 |
| 5222 | *Nondepository credit intermediation* | 1.5 | 62 | 19 | 10 |

**TABLE 8.7 ● CONTINUED**

*Source:* Census 2016 County Business Patterns.

*Note:* Industries in *italics* appear in the top 10 for only one of the three counties, indicating possible specialization.

total employment. The last columns rank the industries by total employment for each of the counties, so if an industry is ranked in the top 10 for only one or two of the counties, we can still identify its level of importance for the other places. There are six industries that appear in the top 10 for all three counties: (1) restaurants, (2) general hospitals, (3) building equipment contractors, (4) grocery stores, (5) management of companies, and (6) employment services. There are some industries like physicians offices that fall outside the top 10 (in Salt Lake County, they're ranked 15th) that are also common nontradable services that employ a lot of people and exist uniformly throughout the country.

We can detect specialization based on differences not only in the share of total employment but also in overall ranking. In Clark County, it's clear that there is specialization in traveler accommodation as 20.4% of all employment is concentrated there. This industry ranks highly for Maricopa (12th) and Salt Lake (16th), but the share of employment is nowhere near as large as Clark's. In Salt Lake County, religious organizations have the second-highest share of employment with 3.8% of the total. In contrast, the ranks for Clark and Maricopa are 55th and 29th, respectively. The Church of Latter-day Saints (Mormons) is headquartered in Salt Lake City, which accounts for this unique specialization. Business support services are also important in Salt Lake; if we consult the NAICS definitions, we see that this group includes telephone call centers, collection agencies, and credit bureaus (Discover Financial is one of the county's major employers). In Maricopa County, insurance carriers rank sixth with 2.1% of total employment, while this industry ranks in the 30s in the other two counties. If we dig through recent business news and trade journals in Arizona, there is evidence that Phoenix has attracted an increasing number of banking and insurance firms over the past decade (Sunnucks, 2017).

This example illustrates some of the ambiguity involved when researching specialization. We could think of restaurants as being nontradable as they are found everywhere and they tend to be a top employer. But given the size of the labor force and the overall population in Clark County, the restaurant business makes up a much larger share of employment at 9.9%. This is primarily because it's tied to the resort economy and supported by a large number of visitors. In this particular case, you could argue that it's a tradable good and something that the area specializes in. Maricopa and Salt Lake counties also have tourist industries that restaurants are part of, but traveler accommodation represents a much smaller share of their total employment. Restaurants in these areas probably rely more heavily on residents. Maricopa County has a slightly lower percentage of people in this industry (8.8%), but its labor force and population are twice the size of Clark's.

We could go down to the six-digit NAICS level, which would allow us to sift through and sort out industries in more detail. At this level, the distinction between activities is so fine that we would need to aggregate them into related groups. In the Los Angeles and San Francisco study, the separate six-digit industries for software publishers, custom computer programming services, computer system design services, computer and peripheral wholesales, and data processing services were all combined and studied as an information technology group (Storper et al., 2015). This approach recognizes that these separate industries are part of a larger ecosystem where they work in concert and rely on one another. If we were studying the resort industry in Clark County, we would piece together the various components of this economy that would include traveler accommodation, restaurants, and clothing stores.

This example illustrates differences *between* economies in different places. You can also study specialization *within* specific places. Within a given metropolitan area, county, or city, there are often patterns to business location. Among the nontradable industries, there are distinctions between lower-order goods that can be found in large numbers across an area (supermarkets, gas stations) and higher-order goods that the local economy can only support in limited quantities (movie theaters, hospitals). A study of retailing in Phoenix found that certain types of businesses tend to cluster together (clothing stores, car dealers, gas stations), while others tend to be more geographically dispersed (food stores, furniture stores, building materials suppliers) (O' hUallachain & Leslie, 2013).

There are a number of different approaches to studying economic specialization and diversity. For background on the concepts, theories, and applications of economic geography, see *Key Concepts in Economic Geography* (Aoyama, Murphy, & Hanson, 2011). We could look at the percentage of total payroll instead of employment to identify industries that contribute the most to the economy's wages. Instead of percentages and ranks, there are derived measures like the GINI coefficient and location quotients. We'll cover these in Chapter 11 and will calculate location quotients in our exercise in this chapter, where we'll study industry groups that have been classified as advanced industries based on their investment in research and development.

## 8.4    LABOR FORCE STATISTICS

Beyond the CBP and Economic Census, there is a dizzying array of additional datasets published by the BLS and the Census Bureau that collect data on the labor force (recall that we discussed what constitutes the labor force back in Chapter 4). At first glance, they appear to cover many of the same topics, but each one employs a different methodology and focuses on a specific set of labor force variables at varying levels of geographic detail. In this section, we'll summarize several of these additional sources so you can determine which ones meet your needs.

Generally, the BLS datasets are similar to the CBP and Economic Census in that they survey or count business establishments to measure employment and wages, and thus, this data measures activity based on where people work. This is in contrast to the Census Bureau datasets on the labor force (the CPS and the ACS) that capture information based on where people live. All the datasets employ NAICS codes for classifying the labor force by industry.

The BLS data is more timely and less geographically specific. It has a stronger orientation toward being studied as a time series, and as such, many datasets are adjusted so that past data fits current definitions for geography and NAICS, and dollar values are updated based on inflation. One decision you'll often need to make is whether you want employment data that is seasonably adjusted or not. The size and composition of the labor force fluctuates due to cyclical, seasonal factors such as the school year, harvest season, major holidays, and the weather. To measure underlying trends in the economy, the BLS uses statistical methods to adjust and smooth out these normal seasonal fluctuations.

The BLS provides access to all its datasets plus the CPS labor force statistics through their portal at `https://www.bls.gov/data/`. It provides a number of different paths for access: a data finder search tool, one screen or multiscreen point–click–retrieve applications, lists of formatted tables, and lists of raw data files for downloading data in bulk. While our focus is just on their labor force statistics, they provide a number of other data series that cover inflation, prices, spending patterns, and more. An alternate source for obtaining BLS tables and charts is FRED, an online database created by the Federal Reserve Bank of St. Louis: `https://fred.stlouisfed.org/`.

Current Employment Statistics (CES):   a monthly survey of business establishments that measures the number of workers, hours worked, and average hourly wages. The survey is based on approximately 149k businesses and government agencies representing 651k physical locations. It does not include the self-employed, agricultural workers, and a few smaller industries. Industry data is published for broad categories (not detailed NAICS levels)—for states and metropolitan areas.

Quarterly Census of Employment and Wages (QCEW):   an actual census or count of business establishments that is conducted four times a year. It captures the same data that's in the Current Employment Statistics, plus the number of establishments, total wages, and average annual pay (wages and salaries). Data is tabulated for states, metropolitan areas, and counties but is subject to the same disclosure rules and suppression techniques used in the CBP and Economic Census.

Occupational Employment Statistics (OES):   a biannual survey of 200k business establishments that measures the number of employees by occupation as opposed to industry. The BLS uses the Standard Occupational Classification (SOC) system for classifying employees by the type of job they perform. Similar to NAICS, the SOC has a series of broad categories that can be broken down into more detailed divisions and subdivisions. The codes can be browsed and searched at `https://www.bls.gov/soc/`. Data on number of workers and wages is published for 800 different occupations for states and metro areas but does not include agricultural workers.

Current Population Survey (CPS):   is covered in more detail in Chapter 12. It is a monthly survey of 60k households that is conducted by the Census Bureau in partnership with the BLS to publish labor force statistics. Since it is household based, it counts workers by where they live instead of by where they work and is primarily focused on measuring employment, unemployment, and labor force participation. The other surveys and counts of business establishments can't capture these characteristics, as they can only measure who's employed. The CPS also captures demographics of the labor force by age, sex, race, and Hispanic origin. Monthly data is only published for the nation, but microdata is published for researchers to create their own tabulations.

Local Area Unemployment Statistics (LAUS):   is designed to provide the monthly employment and unemployment data published in the CPS for states, metropolitan areas, counties, and places. The Census Bureau and BLS use a series of statistical models to create estimates for approximately 7,000 areas.

Longitudinal Employer-Household Dynamics (LEHD):   produces a series of datasets that link employer and employee data from administrative records and other census products to create both summary and microdata. It is administered by the Center for Economic Studies at the Census Bureau.

American Community Survey (ACS):   was covered in Chapter 6. It captures labor force status (employed/unemployed), occupation by SOC, and industry of employment by NAICS primarily based on where people live, but there are a few tables that tabulate data based on where people work. The ACS data is less timely compared with these other datasets as estimates represent 1-year and 5-year averages with margins of error, but it is more geographically detailed. The ACS labor force data is best used when working on a project where you're using a number of other ACS variables and want to use labor force data that's generated using the same methodology, working with geographies for which data isn't published in other sources, or you are content with generally characterizing an area rather precisely measuring it.

Beyond the datasets mentioned here, the Census Bureau publishes a wealth of other business- and economic-related series that include annual surveys of manufactures, construction, retail and wholesale trade, commodity imports and exports, job creation and destruction (business dynamics), data on building permits, residential housing construction and sales, statistics on taxation and public employee retirement systems, and more. Visit `https://www.census.gov/topics/business-economy.html` to learn more.

## 8.5   EXERCISES

This exercise will give you exposure to working with NAICS-based data and the challenges posed by the suppression techniques that are applied to several of the business datasets. At this stage in the book, most of the operations that we'll perform in Calc should be familiar to you, but we'll introduce a few new techniques such as formulas for dealing with errors and conditional formatting. We'll briefly mention how you can manage this data in SQL with SQLite.

Visit the publisher's website for the data we will be using, or download it from the source:

Geography Area Series, County Business Patterns 2016:   Totals for the United States and for the Buffalo, Rochester, and Syracuse NY Metropolitan Statistical Areas— `https://data.census.gov/`.

America's Advanced Industries:   Data and Rankings Excel file, Brookings Institute— `https://www.brookings.edu/wp-content/uploads/2015/02/AdvancedIndustryDataDownload.xlsx`.

## Exercise 1: Measuring Advanced Industries by NAICS With Calc

The Brookings Institute, a nonprofit think tank and policy center that often uses census data in its research, published a detailed study identifying advanced industries in the United States (Muro, Rothwell, Andes, Fikri, & Kulkarni, 2015). Using four-digit NAICS industry groups, they identified advanced industries as those in which spending in research and development per worker was in the top 20% of all industries, and where the share of the industry's total workers with a significant STEM (science, technology, engineering, and mathematics) background exceeded the national average.

The authors anticipate that these industries will be primary drivers of future economic growth, given their focus on innovation and their creation of high-paying jobs. Accompanying the study is an interactive website that allows viewers to identify the locations of these industries by state and metropolitan area and see how they rank relative to each other: `http://brook.gs/2bwynvV`. An updated version of the site was published in 2016 to identify recent trends: `http://brook.gs/2aDCsgu`.

In this exercise, we'll identify the prevalence of these industries by employment in three large metropolitan areas in Upstate New York: (1) Buffalo, (2) Rochester, and (3) Syracuse. These cities ranked 59th, 38th, and 49th, respectively, for employment in these advanced industries out of the 100 largest metropolitan areas in the United States. They are part of the Frost Belt or Rust Belt, which includes older Northeastern and Midwestern cities that have suffered from a loss of manufacturing jobs and population decline (relative to growing Sun Belt cities in the South and West). Despite their misfortunes, these areas still possess a skilled workforce, are home to large research universities, and have a mix of natural and built amenities.

1.  **Open the advanced industries file**. In Chapter 8 Exercise 1 folder, open the advanced_industries.xlsx file in Calc. This file was created by copying the industry columns from the appendix of the Brooking's report and doing a paste special—values into this new workbook. Study the list, and you'll see that the four-digit codes have been classified into three broader groups: (1) manufacturing, (2) energy, and (3) services.

2. **Import the CBP Data**. Go to Sheet—Insert Sheet From File to import the CBP data from the file BP_2016_00A1_with_ann.csv. On the import screen, designate the first two ID columns as text. Once imported, rename the worksheet CBP. Examine the sheet, and you'll see that each record represents a four-digit NAICS industry for a specific geography: the entire United States and each of the three upstate NY metro areas. Scroll right and you'll see the variables for establishments, employees, and first quarter payroll and annual payroll in $1,000s of dollars. Save your work; when prompted, save the file in the Calc format.

3. **Move the NAICS columns in the CBP data to the left**. We're going to use a VLOOKUP to pull data from the CBP sheet into the advanced industries sheet. To do that, the ID for the NAICS must appear in the leftmost column of the CBP sheet, as this will be the first column in the VLOOKUP array. Cut the two columns for the NAICS ID and description and insert them at the beginning of the sheet. The ID and description should be in columns A and B, the geographic identifiers in columns C and D. The employment data should appear in column H (Figure 8.2). Save your work.

4. **Add totals and modify headers in the advanced sheet**. Flip back to the advanced industries sheet. Insert a row below the header row and type the labels: 0, Total, Total for All Industries in cells A2, B2, and C2, respectively. Enter labels for the United States, Buffalo, Rochester, and Syracuse in cells D1, E1, F1, and G1, respectively.

5. **Enter the VLOOKUP formula for the United States**. We're going to look up the employment values for the United States from the CBP sheet using the matching NAICS codes in the industries sheet. Recall that we learned VLOOKUP in the first exercise in Chapter 5. Click in cell D2. If you want extra guidance, you can use the function wizard by selecting the *Fx* button on the toolbar, selecting VLOOKUP, and then entering each value in turn.

FIGURE 8.2 ● MOVE NAICS ID AND DESCRIPTION COLUMNS TO THE FRONT OF THE WORKSHEET

| A | B | C | D | E | F | G | H |
|---|---|---|---|---|---|---|---|
| NAICS.id | NAICS.display-label | GEO.id | GEO.id2 | GEO.display-label | YEAR.id ESTAB | | EMP |
| 2012 NAICS | Meaning of 2012 NAICS code | Geographic id | Id2 | Geographic area name | Year | Number of establish | Paid employees fo |
| 0 | Total for all sectors | 0100000US | | United States | 2016 | 7757807 | 126752238 |
| 1131 | Timber tract operations | 0100000US | | United States | 2016 | 480 | 4181 |
| 1132 | Forest nurseries and gathering of forest products | 0100000US | | United States | 2016 | 183 | 1357 |
| 1133 | Logging | 0100000US | | United States | 2016 | 8076 | 50188 |
| 1141 | Fishing | 0100000US | | United States | 2016 | 2449 | 5461 |
| 1142 | Hunting and trapping | 0100000US | | United States | 2016 | 358 | 1650 |
| 1151 | Support activities for crop production | 0100000US | | United States | 2016 | 4848 | 66007 |
| 1152 | Support activities for animal production | 0100000US | | United States | 2016 | 4488 | 19885 |
| 1153 | Support activities for forestry | 0100000US | | United States | 2016 | 1712 | 11682 |

**FIGURE 8.3 ● USE VLOOKUP TO LOOK UP U.S. EMPLOYMENT DATA**

| | A | B | C | D | E | F | G |
|---|---|---|---|---|---|---|---|
| D2 | | fx Σ = | =VLOOKUP(A2,$CBP.A$3:J$292,8,) | | | | |
| 1 | NAICS | Group | Description | US | Buffalo | Rochester | Syracuse |
| 2 | 0 | Total | Total for All Industries | 126752238 | | | |
| 3 | 3241 | Manufacturing | Petroleum and Coal Products | 104748 | | | |
| 4 | 3251 | Manufacturing | Basic Chemicals | 157443 | | | |
| 5 | 3252 | Manufacturing | Resins and Synthetic Rubbers, Fibers, and Filaments | 95232 | | | |
| 6 | 3253 | Manufacturing | Pesticides, Fertilizers, and Other Agr. Chemicals | 29651 | | | |
| 7 | 3254 | Manufacturing | Pharmaceuticals and Medicine | 247268 | | | |
| 8 | 3259 | Manufacturing | Other Chemical Products | 80447 | | | |
| 9 | 3271 | Manufacturing | Clay Products | 33392 | | | |
| 10 | 3279 | Manufacturing | Other Nonmetallic Mineral Products | 75786 | | | |
| 11 | 3311 | Manufacturing | Iron, Steel, and Ferroalloys | 93759 | | | |
| 12 | 3313 | Manufacturing | Aluminum Production and Processing | 57221 | | | |
| 13 | 3315 | Manufacturing | Foundries | 119032 | | | |

Or just type this formula in D2: =VLOOKUP(A2,$CBP.A$3:J$292,8,). The first argument is the NAICS code we want to look up in the current sheet. The second argument is the array that contains the relevant values: It's important that this argument *just* contains the ranges that are relevant to the United States, because the NAICS code is repeated for each geography. Instead of eyeballing the range, after you enter the first argument of "A2," you can flip over to the CBP worksheet and draw a selection box around the range for the array to get it to appear in the formula. You will need to enter the dollar signs before the start and end of the array, to lock the array values in place. The third argument "8" is the number of the column that contains the value we want to retrieve: employment. The fourth and final argument is blank, which indicates that the relevant ID values are sorted (indeed, they are sorted by NAICS). Copy and paste the formula down the column (Figure 8.3). Save your work.

6. **Look up the values for the three metros**. Perform the same operation to populate the employment columns for the three metro areas. Take care to specify the array ranges correctly to select values from just that metro area's records. They should be A$293:J$566 for Buffalo, A$567:J$835 for Rochester, and A$836:J$1089 for Syracuse. Make sure to lock the cell values by manually entering the dollar sign between the column and row value. Copy and paste the results down each column. Spot check some values for each column to ensure they are correct. Save your work.

7. **Handling footnotes, identifying value ranges**. Once you've applied VLOOKUP for all the values, you'll notice that a mix of footnotes (labeled a through g) and errors (#NA) appear in some records. Let's tackle the footnotes first. As we discussed in this chapter, the actual values are suppressed if the number of businesses is too small, or a small number dominate the market. The list of possible footnotes is included in the readme text file that

| | A | B | C | D |
|---|---|---|---|---|
| | | | | |
| 1 | Note | Low | High | Mid |
| 2 | a | 0 | 19 | 10 |
| 3 | b | 20 | 99 | 60 |
| 4 | c | 100 | 249 | 175 |
| 5 | e | 250 | 499 | 375 |
| 6 | f | 500 | 999 | 750 |
| 7 | g | 1000 | 2499 | 1750 |
| 8 | h | 2500 | 4999 | 3750 |

**FIGURE 8.4 ● EMPLOYEE SIZE RANGE CODES FOR SUPPRESSED DATA**

*Note:* The letter "d" is intentionally omitted, as it is reserved for nondisclosed values.

accompanies every CBP download. Create a new worksheet called ranges and manually enter the values shown in Figure 8.4 that illustrate the lowest and the highest possible value for each note. For the middle value, you can use a formula to calculate it =ROUND((B2+C2)/2). Notice the letter "d" is missing; it is reserved for values that are not disclosed at all. Save your work.

8. **Calculate estimates for footnotes**. We'll use the midpoint of each size range as an estimate for employment when the actual employment figure isn't provided. Flip back to the advanced industries sheet. In cells H1, I1, and J1, enter the labels Brevised, Rrevised, and Srevised, respectively. In cell H2, type the following formula:

=IF(ISNUMBER(E2),E2,VLOOKUP(E2,$range.$A$1:$D$8,4,)).

This formula combines an IF with a VLOOKUP function. If the value in E2 (Buffalo employment) is a number, then simply return the number. Otherwise, use the VLOOKUP formula to take the footnote, look it up in the ranges sheet, and return the midpoint value. By using two sets of dollar signs, we lock the column and cell values, so we can copy and paste the formula across to the other metros and down all the columns. Do so (Figure 8.5), and save your work.

9. **Handling errors**. Let's tackle the errors. NA means that value is not available or not found in the lookup table. For example, for 3346 Magnetic and Optical Media, there were no records for Syracuse. This means that either this data

**FIGURE 8.5 ● CALCULATING REVISED ESTIMATES FOR METRO AREAS BASED ON EMPLOYEE SIZE RANGES**

`=IF(ISNUMBER(E2),E2,VLOOKUP(E2,$range.$A$1:$D$8,4,))`

| Description | US | Buffalo | Rochester | Syracuse | Brevised | Rrevised | Srevised |
|---|---|---|---|---|---|---|---|
| Total for All Industries | 126752238 | 478608 | 452595 | 260468 | 478608 | 452595 | 260468 |
| Petroleum and Coal Products | 104748 | 191 | 139 | 65 | 191 | 139 | 65 |
| Basic Chemicals | 157443 | 1936 | 455 | 160 | 1936 | 455 | 160 |
| Resins and Synthetic Rubbers, Fibers, and Filaments | 95232 b | | 146 b | | 60 | 146 | 60 |
| Pesticides, Fertilizers, and Other Agr. Chemicals | 29651 | 116 | 19 a | | 116 | 19 | 10 |
| Pharmaceuticals and Medicine | 247268 | 1812 g | | 743 | 1812 | 1750 | 743 |
| Other Chemical Products | 80447 | 117 | 2483 a | | 117 | 2483 | 10 |
| Clay Products | 33392 | 233 | 180 b | | 233 | 180 | 60 |
| Other Nonmetallic Mineral Products | 75786 | 1523 | 217 | 128 | 1523 | 217 | 128 |
| Iron, Steel, and Ferroalloys | 93759 | 646 b | e | | 646 | 60 | 375 |
| Aluminum Production and Processing | 57221 a | b | f | | 10 | 60 | 750 |

was simply not reported for this industry for this area in the CBP, or the actual value is zero and thus there is no record. In cell H2, modify the VLOOKUP formula so that it reads as follows:

`=IFNA(IF(ISNUMBER(E2),E2,VLOOKUP(E2,$range.$A$1:$D$8,4,)),"")`

The IFNA formula says to return the value output from the formula, but if the output is NA, return something else. In this case, the double quotes mean apply a blank value. Alter the formulas in cells H2, I2, and J2 accordingly, and copy and paste them down the columns. The error messages should disappear. Save your work.

10. **Separate footnotes from data**. It's always a good idea to store footnotes in dedicated columns. This allows you to keep track of which values were adjusted, without mixing them into the same column with the values. In cells K1, L1, and M1, type these labels: bnote, rnote, and snote, respectively. In cell K2 for bnote, type this formula: `=IF(ISTEXT(E2),E2,"")`. This formula looks at the employment value for Buffalo. If the value is text (a footnote), print that value in the current cell. Otherwise it's not text, so print nothing. Copy the formula down the column, and apply it to the other two metros (Figure 8.6). Save your work.

11. **Calculate location quotients for Buffalo**. We've already seen examples of creating percent totals and rankings for comparing places. Let's use a different approach to identify which advanced industries these areas specialize in. A location quotient (LQ) is a derived measure that illustrates how concentrated employment is for a given industry relative to the larger economy. The basic formula is as follows:

$$LQ = \frac{\text{Local industry employment} \div \text{Total local employment}}{\text{National industry employment} \div \text{Total national employment}}$$

FIGURE 8.6 ● CREATING DEDICATED FOOTNOTE COLUMNS

| K2 | | $fx \Sigma =$ | =IF(ISTEXT(E2),E2,"") | | | | | | | | |
|---|---|---|---|---|---|---|---|---|---|---|---|
| | D | E | F | G | H | I | J | K | L | M |
| 1 | US | Buffalo | Rochester | Syracuse | Brevised | Rrevised | Srevised | Nnote | Rnote | Snote |
| 2 | 126752238 | 478608 | 452595 | 260468 | 478608 | 452595 | 260468 | | | |
| 3 | 104748 | 191 | 139 | 65 | 191 | 139 | 65 | | | |
| 4 | 157443 | 1936 | 455 | 160 | 1936 | 455 | 160 | | | |
| 5 | 95232 b | | 146 b | | 60 | 146 | 60 b | | | b |
| 6 | 29651 | 116 | 19 a | | 116 | 19 | 10 | | | a |
| 7 | 247268 | 1812 g | | 743 | 1812 | 1750 | 743 | g | | |
| 8 | 80447 | 117 | 2483 a | | 117 | 2483 | 10 | | | a |
| 9 | 33392 | 233 | 180 b | | 233 | 180 | 60 | | | b |
| 10 | 75786 | 1523 | 217 | 128 | 1523 | 217 | 128 | | | |
| 11 | 93759 | 646 b | | e | 646 | 60 | 375 | b | | e |
| 12 | 57221 a | | b | f | | 10 | 60 | 750 a | b | f |
| 13 | 119032 | 176 b | | 531 | 176 | 60 | 531 | b | | |

FIGURE 8.7 ● CALCULATING LOCATION QUOTIENTS FOR BUFFALO'S ADVANCED INDUSTRIES

| N3 | | $fx \Sigma =$ | =ROUND((H3/H$2)/($D3/$D$2),2) | | | | | | | |
|---|---|---|---|---|---|---|---|---|---|---|
| | D | H | I | J | K | L | M | N | O | P |
| 1 | US | Brevised | Rrevised | Srevised | Nnote | Rnote | Snote | BLQ | RLQ | SLQ |
| 2 | 126752238 | 478608 | 452595 | 260468 | | | | | | |
| 3 | 104748 | 191 | 139 | 65 | | | | 0.48 | | |
| 4 | 157443 | 1936 | 455 | 160 | | | | 3.26 | | |
| 5 | 95232 | 60 | 146 | 60 b | | | b | 0.17 | | |
| 6 | 29651 | 116 | 19 | 10 | | | a | 1.04 | | |
| 7 | 247268 | 1812 | 1750 | 743 | g | | | 1.94 | | |
| 8 | 80447 | 117 | 2483 | 10 | | | a | 0.39 | | |
| 9 | 33392 | 233 | 180 | 60 | | | b | 1.85 | | |
| 10 | 75786 | 1523 | 217 | 128 | | | | 5.32 | | |
| 11 | 93759 | 646 | 60 | 375 | b | | e | 1.82 | | |
| 12 | 57221 | 10 | 60 | 750 a | b | | f | 0.05 | | |

To avoid mistakes, let's hide the original data columns from the CBP. Select columns E, F, and G, right-click and select hide. In cells N1, O1, and P1, type the labels BLQ, RLQ, and SLQ, respectively. In cell N3 (*not N2*), type the formula =ROUND((H3/H$2)/($D3/$D$2),2). This divides the employees in Buffalo's petroleum and coal industry by Buffalo's total employment, divides U.S. employment in this industry by total U.S. employment, and divides Buffalo's result by the U.S. result. The judicious placement of dollar signs will allow us to copy this formula down the column and across to the other rows while locking the appropriate row (for the metro's total employment), the appropriate column (for the U.S. employment by industry), and appropriate cell (for U.S. total employment). Copy and paste the formula down the column for Buffalo (Figure 8.7).

If you need a refresher on locking cells:

- D2: is unlocked
- D$2: locks the row, 2

- $D2: locks the column, D
- $D$2: locks the cell, D2

Location quotients are usually expressed with one or two decimal places. A value of 1.0 indicates that employment in the local economy is equivalent to employment in the total economy; the distribution or concentration of employment is the same as the national distribution. The result for Buffalo's petroleum and coal industry is 0.48, which is so low that it's clear Buffalo does not specialize in this area. In contrast, its index value of 3.26 for the basic chemical industry indicates a strong specialty relative to the national economy. Save your work.

12. **Fix errors and calculate quotients for other metros**. In some cells, a #VALUE! error appears, because that employment value for Buffalo is blank or null. Modify the formula in N3 to ignore the error: =IFERROR(ROUND((H3/H$2)/($D3/$D$2),2),""). Similar to IFNA, IFERROR replaces any error value with something else, in this case, a blank. Copy and paste this formula down the column. Then copy and paste the formulas over and down for the other metros. Verify your formulas are correct: The index values for basic chemicals on row 4 should be 3.26, 0.81, and 0.49 (Figure 8.8). Save your work.

13. **Count industries and apply conditional formatting**. Let's see how many specialized industries these metros have and clearly identify values that indicate specialization. Hide the footnote columns in K through L. Enter this formula in cell N2: =COUNTIF(N3:N52,">="&1.5). This counts the number of Buffalo's industries that have a quotient greater than or equal to 1.5, which indicates a clear specialization relative to the national economy. Copy and paste this formula into O2 and P2. Next, draw a box to select all the cells that contain the location quotients. Go to Formatting—Conditional Formatting—Conditions. For condition 1, specify "Cell value is" in the first box and "greater

**FIGURE 8.8 ● MODIFY FORMULAS TO ACCOUNT FOR ERRORS**

| N3 | fx Σ = | =IFERROR(ROUND((H3/H$2)/($D3/$D$2),2),"") | | | | | | | | |
|---|---|---|---|---|---|---|---|---|---|---|
| | D | H | I | J | K | L | M | N | O | P |
| 1 | US | Brevised | Rrevised | Srevised | Nnote | Rnote | Snote | BLQ | RLQ | SLQ |
| 2 | 126752238 | 478606 | 452595 | 260468 | | | | | | |
| 3 | 104748 | 191 | 139 | 65 | | | | 0.48 | 0.37 | 0.3 |
| 4 | 157443 | 1936 | 455 | 160 | | | | 3.26 | 0.81 | 0.49 |
| 5 | 95232 | 60 | 146 | 60 b | | | b | 0.17 | 0.43 | 0.31 |
| 6 | 29651 | 116 | 19 | 10 | | | a | 1.04 | 0.18 | 0.16 |
| 7 | 247268 | 1812 | 1750 | 743 | g | | | 1.94 | 1.98 | 1.46 |
| 8 | 80447 | 117 | 2483 | 10 | | | a | 0.39 | 8.64 | 0.06 |
| 9 | 33392 | 233 | 180 | 60 | | | b | 1.85 | 1.51 | 0.87 |
| 10 | 75786 | 1523 | 217 | 128 | | | | 5.32 | 0.8 | 0.82 |
| 11 | 93759 | 646 | 60 | 375 | b | | e | 1.82 | 0.18 | 1.95 |
| 12 | 57221 | 10 | 60 | 750 a | | b | f | 0.05 | 0.29 | 6.38 |

FIGURE 8.9 ● CALC'S CONDITIONAL FORMATTING MENU

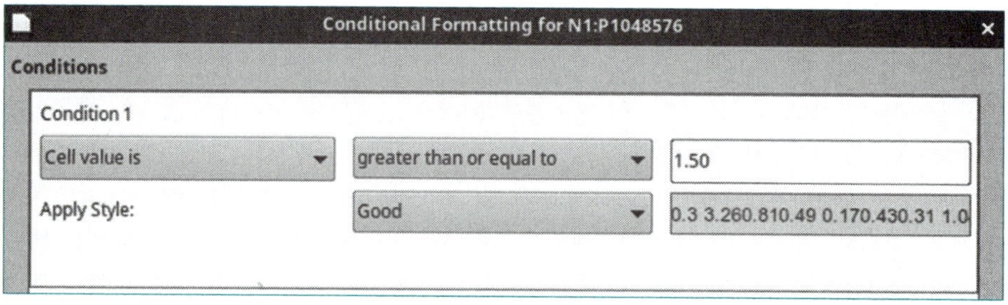

| Conditional Formatting for N1:P1048576 | ✕ |

**Conditions**

Condition 1

| Cell value is ▼ | greater than or equal to ▼ | 1.50 |

| Apply Style: | Good ▼ | 0.3 3.260.810.49 0.170.430.31 1.0 |

FIGURE 8.10 ● CONDITIONAL FORMATTING APPLIED TO HIGH LOCATION QUOTIENTS

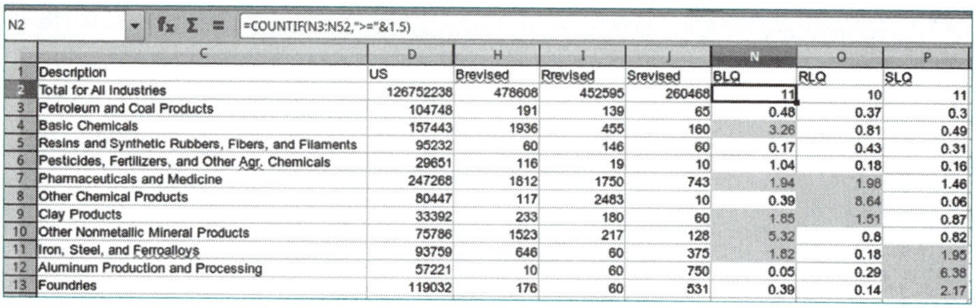

| N2 | ▼ | $f_x$ Σ = | =COUNTIF(N3:N52,">="&1.5) |

| | C | D | H | I | J | N | O | P |
|---|---|---|---|---|---|---|---|---|
| 1 | Description | US | Brevised | Rrevised | Srevised | BLQ | RLQ | SLQ |
| 2 | Total for All Industries | 126752238 | 476608 | 452595 | 260468 | 11 | 10 | 11 |
| 3 | Petroleum and Coal Products | 104748 | 191 | 139 | 65 | 0.48 | 0.37 | 0.3 |
| 4 | Basic Chemicals | 157443 | 1936 | 455 | 160 | 3.26 | 0.81 | 0.49 |
| 5 | Resins and Synthetic Rubbers, Fibers, and Filaments | 95232 | 60 | 146 | 60 | 0.17 | 0.43 | 0.31 |
| 6 | Pesticides, Fertilizers, and Other Agr. Chemicals | 29651 | 116 | 19 | 10 | 1.04 | 0.18 | 0.16 |
| 7 | Pharmaceuticals and Medicine | 247268 | 1812 | 1750 | 743 | 1.94 | 1.98 | 1.46 |
| 8 | Other Chemical Products | 80447 | 117 | 2483 | 10 | 0.39 | 8.64 | 0.06 |
| 9 | Clay Products | 33392 | 233 | 180 | 60 | 1.85 | 1.51 | 0.87 |
| 10 | Other Nonmetallic Mineral Products | 75786 | 1523 | 217 | 128 | 5.32 | 0.8 | 0.82 |
| 11 | Iron, Steel, and Ferroalloys | 93759 | 646 | 60 | 375 | 1.82 | 0.18 | 1.95 |
| 12 | Aluminum Production and Processing | 57221 | 10 | 60 | 750 | 0.05 | 0.29 | 6.38 |
| 13 | Foundries | 119032 | 176 | 60 | 531 | 0.39 | 0.14 | 2.17 |

than or equal to" in the second box (use the drop down to change the selection) and type 1.50 in the empty box beside it. In the Apply style drop down, select the "Good" option (Figure 8.9). Then hit OK. Back in our worksheet, any industry that has a high degree of specialization is marked in green font with a green background. Save your work.

14. **Examine the results**. Of the 50 industries, these upstate New York metros specialize in 10 or 11 of them, primarily in manufacturing (Figure 8.10). There is some overlap in specialization between at least two of the metros but none among all three. Rochester has some of the highest degrees of specialization, with location quotients above 8 and 9 for Other Chemical Products and Communications Equipment, respectively. None of the metros has strong specialization in energy or services, but it's important to remember that the CBP excludes most government-owned businesses. There's actually a large hydroelectric power–generating station near Niagara Falls within the Buffalo metropolitan area that's owned and operated by the New York Power Authority.

The exclusion of government entities can have a differential impact for industrial segments or geographic areas where government facilities constitute a large part of the economy. The Buffalo metropolitan area is actually a linchpin in North America's power grid, connecting the grids of Canada and the United States and generating electricity from nearby Niagara Falls. Since the utility is government owned, it doesn't appear in the CBP dataset. We would need to conduct additional research in order to see how many people are employed in the public power sector, and to determine if employment was large enough to influence our results.

Our approach for dealing with data suppression was relatively basic. This same approach could be implemented in a relational database with some caveats; see InfoBox 8.2 for an example. Alternatively, we could treat our midpoint values as if they were estimates with a margin of error. For example, the C employment range class goes from 100 to 249 with a midpoint of 175. Given that range, the true value could be $175 \pm 75$. If we factor this possible range of values into the location quotient, some industries on the margin of the 1.50 cutoff could be pushed above or below the threshold. For an entirely different approach, we could use the three-digit level NAICS that each four-digit code falls under and attempt to apportion employment or control for it using the three-digit values as a maximum.

In any analysis that involves either NAICS codes or metropolitan areas, we need to verify that the codes and areas we are using are compatible and have not changed over time:

NAICS changes:  For every edition of NAICS, the government publishes lists of changes called concordances that allow you to identify and account for changes in classifications over time. Since both the 2016 CBP and the advanced industry codes are based on the 2012 NAICS, our example is not affected by code revisions. Concordances are available at: `https://www .census.gov/eos/www/naics/concordances/concordances.html`.

Metro changes:  As discussed in Chapter 3, the Office of Management and Budget modifies the definitions of metro areas a few times each decade. The Economic Census uses whatever the current definitions are at the time of publication. The CBP uses the definitions that were used at the time of publication for the Economic Census and does not modify them until the next Economic Census is taken. So the metropolitan definitions for the 2012 through 2016 CBP are based on what was current in 2012. You can verify the specific definitions in the CBP technical documentation at `https://www.census.gov/programs-surveys/cbp/technical-documentation/reference.html`.

> ### ✔ INFOBOX 8.2 CBP AND ECONOMIC CENSUS DATA IN A RELATIONAL DATABASE
>
> Databases enforce strict rules to prevent the mixing of text and numeric values in a column designated for numbers. Most databases would reject the import of a CBP/ZBP table with footnotes embedded in the values. SQLite is a loosely typed database that would allow this, but it's still a bad practice. To avoid this problem, you can download data in bulk directly from the CBP program website, as these files are structured with footnotes in separate, dedicated columns.
>
> To calculate revised estimates for nondisclosed values using employee size ranges, create a table where each row represents a footnote and each column contains the low, high, and midpoint values for the range. Using the footnote columns, you can relate this table to the CBP table using a special join called a left outer join, which keeps all records for the left table regardless of whether there is a matching value from the right table. This prevents CBP records without footnotes from falling out of the set. The CASE clause allows you to populate a new column with an actual value if present, or the midpoint of the size range.
>
> This example selects all subdivisions for the Medical Equipment and Supplies industry for the Rochester New York metropolitan area. The employment size range table is called emprange. The emp_revised column is filled with an actual employment value if present, or else with the midpoint of the employment size range.
>
> ```sql
> SELECT c.msa, c.naics, c.est, c.emp, c.empflag, e.low, e.high,
>   CASE
>   WHEN e.mid IS NULL THEN c.emp
>   ELSE e.mid
>   END emp_revised
> FROM cbp16msa c
> LEFT JOIN emprange e ON c.empflag=e.note
> WHERE c.msa = '15380'AND c.naics LIKE '3391%';
> ```

## 8.6 REVIEW QUESTIONS AND PRACTICE EXERCISES

1. Describe what the NAICS is and how it is used to classify businesses.

2. Using the NAICS website, define what the Information sector is and list the four-digit group levels that are part of this sector.

3. Compare and contrast the County Business Patterns dataset with the Economic Census. Discuss the differences in methodology, variables, and published geographies.

4. Recall the pivot table that we created in Chapter 5 Exercise 1. Using the advanced industries workbook that we created for this chapter's exercise, create

a pivot table that summarizes total employment for the three industry groups (manufacturing, energy, services) for the three Upstate New York metro areas.

5. Download some CBP data for a particular county and all four-digit industries for a sector of your choice. Using the techniques we employed in this chapter's exercise, isolate the footnotes from the data and calculate revised estimates of employment from the employment size classes using the midpoint of each range.

---

**Supplementary Digital Content:** Find datasets and supplemental exercises at the companion website at `http://study.sagepub.com/census`.

# INTEGRATING CENSUS DATA INTO RESEARCH

## 9.1 INTRODUCTION

Now that we've covered the essentials of census data and have explored the primary datasets, we will address how to integrate census data into writing and research before moving on to more advanced topics. This chapter will cover this issue from several angles. We'll begin with best practices for writing about census data. For example, how do you convey to a reader what a statistic means and where it comes from? How do you describe a place using census data? How do you cite a census dataset in a research paper? Once we have discussed how to write about individual census statistics, we'll explore examples of how census data is used as the basis for different kinds of research.

Geographical considerations and historical patterns have a large influence on the research framework and on subsequent results, so we will explore both of these topics in more detail. Whether you are working at the national or neighborhood level, the construction of geographic areas and the selection of geographic units for analysis will frame your study. This choice involves balancing the level of geographic detail against timeliness and precision of data and can be a compromise between data availability, accuracy, and an "ideal" representation of an area. One of the most common pitfalls in contemporary research is the assumption that the patterns or findings for a local area are distinct, new, or novel, when in fact they are actually part of broader regional, national, or historic trends. We'll conclude with a brief summary of some of the major demographic and socioeconomic trends in the nation so that you can situate your work within a larger context.

## 9.2  WRITING WITH CENSUS DATA

In this section, we'll look at how census data is incorporated into writing for both a nontechnical and a technical audience. Nontechnical writing includes news stories and other forms of journalism, or any narrative that's aimed at a general audience for the purpose of telling a story. Technical writing is targeted at specialized practitioners and academic researchers and includes research reports, policy papers, academic journal articles, and books. We'll discuss how to integrate census data into your writing so that you can succinctly convey important information about the origin, timeliness, and geographic detail of data when describing places. Then we will step back to look at some examples of how census data is used in different kinds of research.

### Weaving Census Data Into Your Writing

When writing about census data, there are at least five aspects that you need to convey: (1) source (where the data is coming from), (2) currency (the year or years it refers to), (3) accuracy (is the data a count or estimate, is there a margin of error [MOE]), (4) geography (what place does the data refer to), and (5) definition (a clear explanation of technical terminology).

How you address these points and the degree to which you address them will vary based on the audience and context. In nontechnical writing, you need to strike a balance between giving the reader enough information that she needs to interpret a statistic without going into excess detail. Many news stories fail to provide enough detail about data sources or omit important details about what the data represents. In a technical sphere, it's expected that you will provide additional details about sources, definitions, and the like in the body of the paper with details about sources in footnotes or in a bibliography.

Let's begin in Chicago, Illinois, with some idealized examples of how to reference census data in nontechnical writing. We'll comment on each example to see how it addresses the five aspects and will explore how to tweak each statement to make it appropriate for technical writing. In these examples, we're assuming that the references to the census represent one small piece of a larger story that is focused on describing a place.

1. The Census Bureau estimates that the median household income of the Lake View and Lincoln Park neighborhoods was approximately $86,000 between 2012 and 2016.

2. Based on the latest figures from the Census Bureau's American Community Survey (ACS), approximately 37.7% of Cook County residents held a bachelor's degree in 2016.

3. There were 1,922 Asians living in ZIP Code 60661 in the West Loop section of Chicago according to the 2010 Census, representing 25% of the area's total population.

In the first example, by using the words *estimates* and *approximately*, we are conveying that this data is from the ACS without explicitly saying so, and we are providing the reader with clues that this is not a precise figure. Even if the reader is not familiar with the ACS and can't make this inference, the writer is attempting to faithfully represent the data as an estimate. The MOE is $1,734 or 2% of the total value. If the MOE is relatively small and we provide the warning that this is an estimate, we can omit it in narrative writing to avoid confusing nontechnical readers. In technical writing, we would explicitly reference the ACS, include the MOE in the text or a footnote, and mention that there's a 90% confidence interval. The range of years (2012–2016) is another clue that this is a data from the ACS as it's a 5-year-period estimate; it would be incorrect to say that it's from 2016 (see Chapter 6). This data is for Public Use Microdata Area (PUMA) 03502, which has the name Lake View and Lincoln Park. Since the average person wouldn't know what a PUMA is, we use its place name instead, which is also helpful for providing geographic context. In a technical paper, we would want to clearly explain what a PUMA is (see Chapter 3).

In the second example, we explicitly identify that this is data from the ACS and provide the caution of "approximately" to indicate that this is an estimate. In non-technical writing if you are indeed using the latest data, it may be acceptable to say "based on the latest figures" and the reader can use the date of publication for the article as a point of reference, although providing a date eliminates any ambiguity. In technical writing we must explicitly state that this data is from 2016, which also helps identify that this is a 1-year-period estimate. Since the MOE is low ($\pm$0.4%) we can say "approximately" without providing the MOE. In technical writing, the MOE should be provided.

In the third example, we can dispense with approximations because this is data from the 2010 census, which is an actual count. We provide a count of the number of Asians and also provide some context, saying they represent 25% of the ZIP Code's population. The Census Bureau doesn't report data by ZIP Code, but in nontechnical writing, we can simplify this so as not to confuse the reader. In technical writing, we would use the term *ZCTA* (Zip Code Tabulation Area). We provide some geographic context for where the ZIP Code is located (the West Loop), which we can obtain from OpenStreetMap or Google Maps.

Let's move down to Houston, Texas, for some additional examples.

4.  The Census Bureau defines unpaid family workers as people who work without pay for a business or farm owned by a relative. According to the American Community Survey, there were an estimated 1,555 unpaid family workers in Houston between 2012 and 2016, although the actual number could be 18% lower or higher.

5.  The City of Houston has 2.3 million people.

6.  The City of Houston had 2,312,717 people in 2017 according to Census Bureau population estimates.

In the fourth example, before presenting the statistic, we have to provide a definition of what an unpaid family worker is, as the Census Bureau is using a technical definition that people would either be unfamiliar with or would conflate with a less formal meaning. This is an ACS estimate and since the MOE is relatively high we provide this information to the reader, without going into any explanation of what a MOE is. In technical or academic writing, we would provide the actual MOE: 1,555 unpaid family workers ($\pm$273). We could have used a 1-year-period estimate for this statistic since Houston is a big city, but since the MOE is much higher (57% of the estimate), a longer time period with a lower MOE is a better choice (see Chapter 6).

The fifth example illustrates how to approach statistics that can be treated more generally. If we are providing an approximate number for something that's generally well-known, we can keep the sentence short and simple. If we are quoting a specific number as in the sixth example, providing more detail about the source is necessary.

If we were writing an article that includes several statistics from the census, a best practice would be to include a preliminary statement that summarizes the data source. For example, if we were referencing several ACS statistics throughout an article, we could preface the discussion by saying:

7.  The Census Bureau's American Community Survey is an annual sample survey of 3.5 million addresses that captures detailed demographic and socioeconomic

characteristics of the population. Estimates for small areas are published as 5-year averages that are updated each year. Since the estimates are not precise, each one is published with a MOE that indicates what the possible range of values is.

In technical writing, we would offer a more extensive description that incorporates the confidence interval (90%) and possibly even the response rate. For longer reports and articles, an extended summary of the ACS and its methodology should appear in a section dedicated to methodology or data sources.

This last example leads us to an important aspect of technical writing: citations. It's expected that the researcher provides citations in a specific format when referring to work that's not her own. Not only does this include specific quotes, but it also includes paraphrases, summaries, and any general reference to the findings of another person's work. Statistics must also be cited, with few exceptions. If we simply stated that Houston has 2.3 million people, this is not something we need to cite as we are making a generalization about a fact that's well-known and easily discoverable. If we quote a specific value like 2,312,717, then it's expected that we provide a reference for the source of this information.

There are several different citation styles, which are conventions for citing references in the body of a work and for constructing bibliographies, which are lists of all cited works that appear at the end of the paper. In the following examples, we'll use the American Psychological Association (APA) style, which is commonly used in the social sciences and public affairs. Other popular styles include the Modern Language Association (MLA) and the Chicago styles, which are typically used in the humanities. The Online Writing Lab (OWL) at Purdue University is an excellent source for guidelines on research and citations and provides examples for each of these styles: `https://owl.purdue.edu/owl/purdue_owl.html`.

While the guidelines for citing books and articles are pretty clear, the rules for government publications and electronic datasets are fuzzier due to the varied nature of these materials (Bauder, 2014). The best approach is simply to do your best. You need to provide readers with the basic elements of the data source so that they know where it's coming from and can track your reference back to the source. According to the International Association for Social Science Information Services & Technology (2012), the essential elements that you need to capture in a data citation are author, date of publication, title, publisher and/or distributor, and electronic location or identifier.

The following example illustrates how to reference a statistic within the text and how it's entry should appear in the bibliography at the end of the paper.

Houston had 2,099,451 people according to the 2010 census (U.S. Census Bureau, 2010).

Bibliography:

U.S. Census Bureau. (2010). *Table P1, Total Population* (2010 Decennial Census) [Data file]. Washington, DC. Retrieved from `https://data.census.gov/`.

In this example, we provide the specific table number, name, and dataset. The Census Bureau is considered to be the author, and the date refers to the date of the census and not the actual date the data was published (which would have been sometime in 2011). While it's preferrable to provide direct links back to the source, this is undesirable if the URL is too long, as it's cumbersome to display in a bibliography. Instead, you provide the reader with enough information so that they can follow the citation back to the source and retrieve it themselves.

Alternatively, you can cite a specific data file or provide a more general citation to an entire dataset. This is appropriate when you're citing several statistics from one dataset, or when you are using an entire dataset to conduct your research and analysis. Instead of citing statistics one by one, you provide a more general citation in the introduction of your paper, or in the section where you discuss methodology. For example,

> Data for components of population change in this study is drawn from the Census Bureau's 2017 vintage population estimates (U.S. Census Bureau, 2017).

Bibliography:

U.S. Census Bureau. (2017). *Cumulative estimates of the components of resident population change for the United States, regions, states, and Puerto Rico: April 1, 2010 to July 1, 2017 (NST-EST2017-04)* (Population Estimates Program) [Data file]. Washington, DC. Retrieved from `https://www2.census.gov/programs-surveys/popest/tables/2010-2017/state/totals/`.

Opinions vary on how you should identify the data source and the specific URL. In this example, we provided the name of the Census Bureau's program (Population Estimates Program), but you could also provide the name of the web page where the file is stored (National Population Totals and Components of Change: 2010–2017). The name of the file is used as the title, but if you weren't citing a specific file, you could use the name of the dataset instead. Since files are commonly moved over time and links become severed, a safe approach is to provide a link to the page that houses the file instead of a direct link to the file itself.

## The Census in Action: Examples in Research

Now that we have explored how to describe census data in writing at a sentence level, let's step back and look at some styles for discussing and studying census data at a document level. This section will give you a sense of how census data is used in various kinds of research.

A basic approach is to take census data, study it, and report the findings in a "just the facts" manner. Many of the technical reports and white papers published by the Census Bureau do just that. For instance, analysts at the Census Bureau compared poverty rates from the 2015 and 2016 ACS and found that nationally poverty had declined from 14.7% to 14.0% and that most states and large metropolitan areas also experienced declines (Bishaw & Benson, 2017). The report uses tables, charts, and maps to report the findings and provides a clear summary of how the Census Bureau measures poverty so that readers understand exactly what "poverty" is referring to. Another report analyzed postsecondary enrollment (education beyond high school) before, during, and after the Great Recession (2007–2009) using data from the Current Population Survey and found that enrollment increased during the recession and declined shortly thereafter (Schmidt, 2018). The author examined differences in enrollment by level of schooling (undergraduate and graduate), sex, and race to get a deeper understanding of the trends. The findings demonstrated that many people went to school when the economy was poor, partly in the hope that learning new skills would make them more competitive in the job market and partly to wait out the recession.

Many census-focused technical reports are framed around a specific issue that census data is used to address, and derivative data is often created as part of the analysis. A Brookings Institute report on population change in metropolitan areas and regions used Population Estimates Program data from 2017 to understand shifts in growth between urban, suburban, exurban (distant suburbs on the fringe of rural areas), and rural areas, particularly between 2016 and 2017 (Frey, 2018b). Brookings has its own internal definitions for what constitutes urban, suburban, and so on, and uses them to aggregate and study census data to reveal these trends. The study showed that migration to suburban and exurban areas was resuming after a lull of several years. Another Brookings study looked at housing affordability across the country using data from the ACS, where they compared the ratio of house prices with household income against historical measures that show median houses prices are roughly 2.5 to 4 times median income; with this yardstick, they identified parts of the country where housing was affordable or not (Murray & Schuetz, 2018). Researchers at the Pew Research Center used decennial census data and ACS data to measure changes in income inequality by race, and they used derivatives like the Gini coefficient and the 90:10 ratio (ratio of income in the 90th percentile of income distribution to the income at the 10th percentile) and discovered that income inequality rose most rapidly for Asian Americans (Kochhar & Cilluffo, 2018). We'll discuss Gini, the 90:10 ratio, and several other census derivatives in Chapter 11.

Each of these studies employ similar approaches. They are written in logical, plain, and objective prose. Each report provides concise definitions of terms, such as how poverty is defined and what the Gini coefficient is, and clearly discusses the approach and limitations of the data without excess detail. Each report makes ample use of tables, charts, and maps to communicate the data. All these reports take what we referred to in Chapter 1 as a "Just Plain Data Analysis" approach, as described by Gary Klass (2012) in his book of the same name. Data is summarized and presented to support policies and decision-making, the authors create derivatives like averages and indexes, they employ definitions and standards that are commonly used in their fields, and they visualize the data in a number of ways to effectively communicate it. They provide historical and regional contexts to situate their findings within broader trends.

While census data is often studied independently, in many areas of research it's used as one piece in solving a larger puzzle. In Chapter 8, we discussed how economic geographer Michael Storper and his colleagues (2015) studied data from the County Business Patterns (CBPs) to understand how the economies of Los Angeles and San Francisco diverged between 1970 and 2010 in their book *The Rise and Fall of Urban Economies*. This research involved cross walking different industrial classification systems that were used in the two eras (SIC and NAICS) and adapting and applying a method for identifying tradable industries. But this was simply one analysis in a wide-ranging book that used several datasets and approaches to address their research question. The authors also studied immigration and educational attainment using microdata from the decennial census and ACS, wages from the CBP, and other data sources such as patents, municipal expenditures, voting patterns, and election results. Beyond quantitative data, the authors also studied qualitative data: They analyzed decades of publications from regional planning agencies to identify stakeholder priorities, identified connections between industries and businesses by identifying people who served on multiple corporate boards, and studied the local economic history of each area to highlight key actors and major decisions that shaped the direction of each economy.

While many of the aspects they covered were quite technical, the book was written in a straightforward style that is accessible not only to specialized researchers but also to policy makers, politicians, and business people who would be interested in local economic development. The authors did employ some statistical analysis but placed the nitty-gritty details of these processes in the notes of the book and not the body of the text.

Sociologist Matthew Desmond (2016) makes extensive use of census data in his book *Evicted: Poverty and Profit in the American City* using a much different style. This *New York Times* bestseller tells the story of black and white renters in Milwaukee, Wisconsin, whose struggles with poverty are made worse by governments' laws and policies around eviction. It reveals how many people are stuck in a web of poverty because they are trapped in a spiral of housing evictions: They are unable to hold jobs and maintain a steady family life because they live in expensive substandard housing from which they are continually ejected. While the book is a work of nonfiction, it reads like a novel. Desmond used an ethnographic approach where he lived in the same neighborhoods as the people in his story and spent years getting to know them in order to study and understand how and why they were trapped in this cycle of eviction. The book is written as a series of stories from the perspective of black and white landlords and tenants, with Desmond as the narrator.

As each individual story unfolds, Desmond provides background and context that he ties together to create a larger narrative. He uses microdata from the ACS and the American Housing Survey, as well as data from court records and real estate sales and from his own sample survey of Milwaukee renters. Many of his studies use rigorous statistical analyses conducted by him and his colleagues or by other academic researchers. While the statistics generated from the studies appear in the text to support the narrative, the details of how these studies were conducted are contained in the endnotes. This allows the narrative to flow smoothly without interrupting the gripping stories of the renters and without confounding a nontechnical audience. He and his colleagues wrote a series of separate, academic journal articles that explored different facets of the statistical analyses in greater detail for a specialized audience of sociologists and anthropologists.

Good research for a nontechnical audience also relies on multiple data sources to tell a story. A *New York Times* piece on the shortage of workers in the fast-food industry discussed how one of the major labor pools for this industry (teenagers) are no longer interested in this type of work, as they choose to pursue other opportunities (Abrams & Gebeloff, 2018). The authors interview a number of teenagers and fast-food restaurant owners to provide color for the story, but they also spoke with experts who study the restaurant industry and they weave in statistics from over half a dozen different sources on average worker pay, the rise in fast-food establishments and jobs, the percentage of foreign-born workers, unemployment, the percentage of teenagers with a job, turnover rates, restaurant spending on labor, and cost to replace fast-food workers. Although the authors don't always mention their sources, this data is drawn from the CBP, Bureau of Labor Statistics, ACS, Current Population Survey, the Security and Exchange Commission (SEC), and proprietary data sources.

The goal of this section was to introduce you to a sample of different types of research that incorporate or focus on census data, to illustrate the range of possibilities that exist for working with the census. The best way to learn about these approaches is to read the papers and articles and use them as examples that you can follow in your own work. The next sections explore two topics that will influence the construction of your research question and the outcome of your results: (1) geographic considerations and (2) national and historical context.

# 9.3   MAKING GEOGRAPHIC DECISIONS

The choice of census variables and geography is going to have a large influence on your research findings. In Chapter 4, we described the difference between families and households where families (at least two or more people related by blood or adoption living in a residential setting) represent a subset of households (one or more people living in a residential setting). If you wanted to study general differences in income, median household income would be more appropriate than median family income in most cases, because the latter omits a large portion of the population. In Chapter 6, we saw that the choice of an ACS period estimate is a compromise between timeliness and the range of the interval. One-year data is more timely but has a larger MOE, while 5-year data has a lower MOE but represents an average of a longer time period. Furthermore, we saw that certain geographies (any with less than 65k people) are only available for 5-year periods. Alternatively, we can use precise 100% count data from the decennial census, but the number of variables is limited and it's only conducted every 10 years.

Choosing your dataset, variables, and geography involves a series of compromises in terms of precision—that is, the level of detail in terms of time period, estimate interval, and geographic scale. In this section, we'll take a closer look at geography, which possesses several unique aspects that can influence your research. These decisions are often more complex than choosing the right definition or picking the best time period. Specifically, the geographic decisions you need to consider are the selection of geographies to represent an area and the level of geographic detail necessary for studying phenomena and trends in an area.

Using census data to define and describe an area requires that we attempt to accurately portray the boundaries of that place, while making compromises based on the limitations of the census geography and data. If you recall from Chapter 6, for our neighborhood exercise in Cincinnati, we relied on official designations of neighborhoods and the aggregation of census tracts served two purposes: (1) It gave us a decent representation of the neighborhood and (2) it reduced the unacceptably high MOEs for individual census tracts. Let's explore some of the nuances of this decision-making process in closer detail.

Figure 9.1 depicts census tracts in the northern Manhattan neighborhood of Inwood in New York City. This neighborhood has relatively well-defined boundaries as it is surrounded by water on three sides. The southern boundary between Inwood and neighboring Washington Heights is often defined by locals and city officials alike

FIGURE 9.1  ●  CENSUS TRACTS IN THE INWOOD NEIGHBORHOOD, NEW YORK

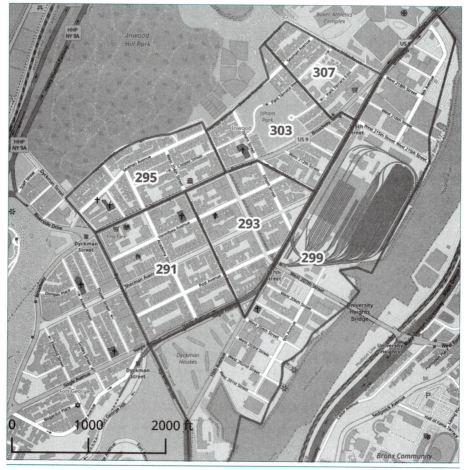

Source: Base map is from the OpenStreetMap: https://www.openstreetmap.org/

as the busy commercial corridor of Dyckman Street, although some would disagree and would include a few city blocks south of this area. If we accept this definition with Dyckman Street as the southern boundary, we could aggregate tracts above it to study the neighborhood as a whole, and if the MOEs are acceptable, we could study differences within the neighborhood at the tract level.

If the MOEs are too high, we could aggregate tracts to subdivide the neighborhood into regions. Broadway, the same street that's famous for theaters and shows, runs from the bottom of Manhattan all the way to the top and through the neighborhood before crossing over to the Bronx. It is one of Inwood's primary commercial streets, and among many residents, it constitutes a boundary line within the neighborhood. How would we discover this? We could speak with local residents, read local news sources, and examine studies from city agencies. We could also study census data between the east and west sides to identify relevant differences. Indeed, in the neighborhood there are socioeconomic and demographic differences that would justify studying them separately.

In assigning tracts to the east or west region, we would have to decide how to assign Census Tract 303 as it crosses the Broadway boundary. If we include this entire tract as part of the west side of the neighborhood, we may be mixing people whose demographic characteristics have more in common with the surrounding east side into the west, which would influence any comparisons we make. By visually inspecting some web maps, we can see that more buildings in this tract are on the west side than on the east. Additional web research reveals that one large building in the eastern half is an office building, while another is a high school. Based on these findings, placing this entire tract on the west side seems to be an acceptable compromise, as most of the tract's residents live in the west. More complex alternatives would include apportioning the population to both sides of the street using block group data. We'll discuss this assignment and apportionment process in more detail in Chapter 11.

Studying the built environment of the neighborhood reveals characteristics that can influence patterns in census data. Census Tract 299 on the east side is quite large, and the northern half consists primarily of commercial and industrial uses. Most of this tract's residents live in the south in a large public housing project called the Dyckman Houses. On the west side of the neighborhood in the middle of Tract 307, there is a large owner-occupied coopeartive called Park Terrace Gardens. Both of these communities were constructed shortly before and after World War II, and both of them concentrate renters and owners and people of low and high income in different parts of the neighborhood. Bureaucratic and market-oriented decisions made many decades ago continue to shape our contemporary built environment and communities, which are reflected directly in our current census statistics. Any detailed study of census data in a neighborhood should address this landscape. Field work, maps, and imagery can aid your decision-making when delineating areas and can also be used for understanding and interpreting findings.

Census tracts were the basis for this example because they allow us to study the neighborhood as a whole or in parts. A Zip Code Tabulation Area (ZCTA) could be used for representing the neighborhood as a whole, but ZCTAs are problematic for several reasons: They vary tremendously in area and population, they weren't drawn to represent neighborhoods, and they are difficult to study over long periods of time. There may be some instances where ZCTAs are acceptable and can be used effectively. For example, consider this description of a Bronx neighborhood that was published in the *Wall Street Journal*:

> Most of the people doing business in the Little Italy enclave—which spans about ten blocks and is concentrated on or around the main commercial arteries of Arthur Avenue and East 187th Street—come from outside the neighborhood.
>
> Even though Belmont's Little Italy reputation is strong, Italian-Americans haven't been its dominant ethnic group for decades: According to the 2010 Census, 63.8% of residents in the ZIP Code are Hispanic. (Warshawer, 2013)

This piece is a good example of how to concisely describe a neighborhood with census data. The author makes a conscious decision to use a ZIP Code (ZCTA really) for several reasons: It's easier than assembling data from many census tracts; she is describing one point in time using data from the decennial census and subsequently from the ACS, which both use ZCTAs; and she uses the ZIP Code to help orient the reader geographically and to provide a contrast between the neighborhood's Italian business district and the surrounding Hispanic residents. This piece appeared in the real estate section of the paper, and since ZIP Codes are used extensively in the real estate industry, this is a logical choice. While the author doesn't go this far, if she wanted to study the types of businesses in the neighborhood she could use the Business Patterns Dataset, which would necessitate the use of ZIP Codes since this is the smallest geography available. However, had the author used census tracts, she might have seen some of the demographic distinctions that would be visible at that scale.

The issue of geographic scale and what unit to use has a large impact on visualizing and interpreting census data. Consider the example in Figure 9.2, which illustrates

## FIGURE 9.2 ● THE EFFECTS OF GEOGRAPHIC SCALE ON DATA VISUALIZATION

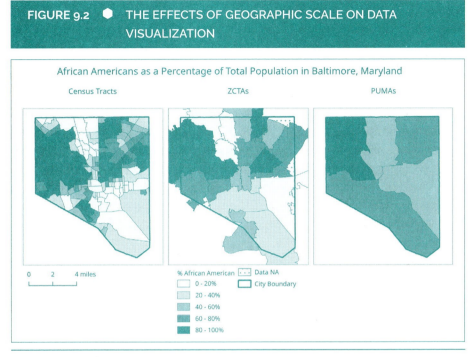

African Americans as a Percentage of Total Population in Baltimore, Maryland

Census Tracts          ZCTAs          PUMAs

0   2   4 miles

% African American    Data NA
0 - 20%               City Boundary
20 - 40%
40 - 60%
60 - 80%
80 - 100%

*Source:* 2012–2016 American Community Survey.

the percentage of the population that is black in Baltimore, Maryland, using three different geographies. At the census tract level, we can see that the black population is concentrated in the northwest and northeast corners of the city, with a smaller concentration in the south central area. African Americans represent a smaller percentage of the population in a north to south band that stretches through the middle of the city, including the downtown area. If we take this data and map it by ZCTA, this pattern is still visible but diminished; as populations are aggregated into larger areas, they are mixed in with surrounding populations, and depending on how the boundaries are drawn, a minority group suddenly may appear as a majority or may become an even smaller, less visible minority. Geographers describe this phenomenon as the Modifiable Areal Unit Problem; changing the size or shape of the areal units (geography) modifies the variables and affects the outcome of the map and the findings.

For example, notice in the ZCTA map that the downtown area has a larger percentage of African Americans relative to the tract map, and the appearance of a larger nonblack population is diminished. Conversely, the black majority in the south central portion of the city appears smaller, as it has been combined with large nonblack areas to the immediate east. The messiness of ZCTAs is also a factor, as the boundaries of many ZCTAs cross the city boundaries, including large suburban areas outside of Baltimore. If we turn to the PUMA map, the patterns here are even more generalized as we now only have five areas to view. We can still see that the northwest corner is predominantly black, while individual areas of high and low concentration have been washed out and become more generalized.

There isn't a universal answer as to which geography is best: It depends on the intent and purpose of your research. Tracts are good for showing detailed patterns and are a necessity if the population you are studying is small in a given area. It wouldn't make sense to study the distribution of Asians in Baltimore by ZCTA or PUMA because this population is too small and concentrated. ACS estimates do suffer from high MOEs at the tract level. ZCTAs may be your choice if you are studying businesses with population data, but ZCTA boundaries will often overlap other geographies. PUMAs are good for providing profiles for large subsections of the city, and are a must if you are using ACS estimates and need MOEs to be low. Using them in this map of Baltimore is a poor choice since there are only five of them, which isn't enough to show meaningful patterns (unless we were mapping the entire state). It's important to be aware of these distinctions and take them into account when choosing geography, particularly once you start using GIS (Chapter 10).

Geography can be intentionally misused to skew findings and justify misleading results. In 2017, *The Washington Post* did an investigative report on luxury high-rise developments that the firm Kushner Properties was building in Jersey City, New Jersey (Boburg, 2017). The firm wanted to take advantage of a federal program that offered developers inexpensive financing if they constructed their projects in "targeted employment areas" that have higher rates of unemployment than the national average. The developers worked with New Jersey state officials to create a map that defined the area around the 65 Bay Street site to justify that the project met the necessary requirements.

Figure 9.3 is a re-creation of the map that *The Washington Post* included in the article. Their map depicted the unemployment rates of census tracts that were included as part of the proposal area. In this version, I have included all the tracts in Jersey City to provide additional context. The map shows that the developers and state officials drew boundaries to intentionally inflate the level of unemployment around the project so that it would qualify for the program. The census tracts adjacent to the development that are actually part of the same upscale downtown neighborhood are excluded. Unemployment in those tracts is very low. Instead, the "area" stretches 4 miles to the south to include areas with high unemployment, which happen to be in the most poverty-stricken parts of the city. This proposal area does not conform to any of the commonly held neighborhood definitions in the city, as it cuts across a highway

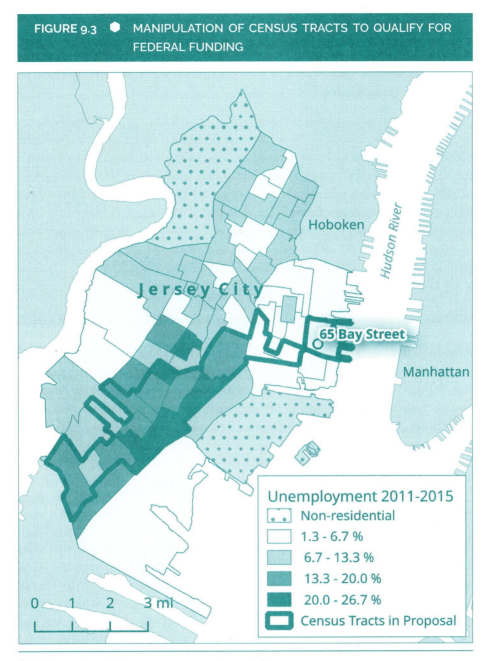

**FIGURE 9.3 ⬡ MANIPULATION OF CENSUS TRACTS TO QUALIFY FOR FEDERAL FUNDING**

*Source:* 2011–2015 ACS, *The Washington Post* (Boburg, 2017).

and many busy streets that serve as natural boundaries, and lacks the compact shape that a typical neighborhood would have. The census tract where the development is located had an unemployment rate of 2.6% and does not even share a boundary with the other tracts in the area but is connected by a single point that happens to be diagonally across an intersection.

Similar tactics have been used for drawing Congressional Districts. In some states, the party in power creates boundaries to maximize its advantage by taking voters in the opposite party and splitting them up between districts so they can't constitute a majority. This process is known as gerrymandering, where geographic data is manipulated to achieve a specific end and the aggregated areas lack any logical meaning. They do not have any administrative, psychological, or social meaning to the people who live there, and thus, they don't function as real places. Like the Jersey City example, gerrymandered districts are created as a means to an end for a predefined purpose, which is usually intended to circumvent rules and skew results.

While geography can be manipulated through aggregating data, there are also visualization tricks that can be used to alter the message without changing the data. The unemployment rates in Figure 9.3 were separated into categories using the equal intervals approach, which categorizes data so that each interval has the same range of values. It was an appropriate choice for this map, given the distribution of unemployment. If we classified the map using quantiles, where categories are created that have an equal number of data points, we would have had a more colorful map that would make the gerrymandering look even worse. We'll return to this point when we begin making maps in Chapter 10. *How to Lie With Maps* is a classic text if you wish to learn more about these practices (Monmonier, 2018).

In summary, when constructing geographic areas, use agreed-on definitions, local consensus, or logical criteria such as the existence of physical features that clearly separate places, or the objective of creating areas that have equal size or population (depending on the goal of your research). When using geography to study patterns, the selection of geographical units will be a compromise between geographic detail, estimate detail, and data availability,

## 9.4 NATIONAL TRENDS AND HISTORICAL CONTEXT

Two common mistakes that novice researchers make are that they assume that patterns or findings in their local or regional area are novel or unique and that current statistics can be used to entirely explain contemporary patterns. In reality, there are broad national trends that shape and influence what happens locally, and local findings may simply mirror those trends. Furthermore, demographic and socioeconomic trends are processes that unfold over decades that have an impact on the demographic and physical landscapes of the places we study.

An analysis of the demographic trends of the United States is beyond the scope of this book, but in this section, we'll summarize some of the most important ones so that you will have some context for your research and can pursue these topics in more detail. This summary is primarily based on four sources. Herbert Klein's (2012) *A Population History of the United States* is a definitive account of the nation's demographic trends from the colonial period up to the early 21st century. It is a chronological narrative of distinct time periods that are defined based on prevailing population trends. John Iceland's (2014) *A Portrait of America: The Demographic Perspective* primarily focuses on the postwar era (1945 to present) and is structured around themes such as family, gender, race, and economic well-being. William Frey's (2018a) *Diversity Explosion* studies recent geographic trends in the distribution of the population by race and age and discusses the impact these trends could have on future federal policies. The last source is a Census Bureau report titled *Demographic Trends in the 20th Century*, which is still relevant for providing historical context as many of the trends it documents continue into our present century (Hobbs & Stoops, 2002). A subsequent report provides details for 2000 to 2010 (Mackun & Wilson, 2011).

The United States is growing: The population of the United States has grown every decade, from the time the first decennial census was taken in 1790 up to the present. This may not seem like a groundbreaking observation unless you compare the Unites States with many other industrialized Western nations, which have experienced either low growth rates or population loss. The U.S. population growth has fluctuated based on changes in birth rates, declines in death rates, and changes to immigration policies. Population growth was at low ebb during the Great Depression of the 1930s but grew rapidly immediately after World War II (Figure 9.4). Population growth rates declined gradually from 1960 to the present, with the exception of a modest uptick during the 1990s. While the population continues to grow, the rate of growth is declining.

Some parts of the country are growing faster than others: The West and South are growing faster than the Midwest and Northeast. The westward movement of the population has been a constant theme throughout American history. While the Pacific coast was the primary destination of migrants for much of the 19th and 20th centuries, recent trends from the 1990s to the present demonstrate that the

FIGURE 9.4  ⬡  U.S. POPULATION GROWTH 1910 TO 2010

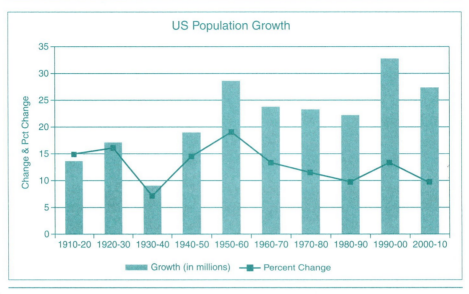

Source: Hobbs and Stoops (2002) and Mackun and Wilson (2011).

states of the Mountain West are the fastest growing, even attracting migrants from the West Coast. Migration to the South is a more recent phenomenon that began in the 1970s and continues to the present. The "Sunbelt" states of the South and West have grown because of their milder climates, lower cost of living, and lower costs for doing business, while the "Snowbelt" states have grown more slowly and continue to have out-migration to the Sunbelt. Foreign migration and natural increase have kept the Snowbelt from experiencing absolute population losses (Frey, 2018a). These regional patterns are generalizations, and there are a number of exceptions. For instance, areas of the central and Deep South have not witnessed the same growth or prosperity as Texas, Florida, or the Atlantic coastal states. The Northeast corridor that stretches from Washington, D.C., to Boston has a growing population and a revitalized economy that stands in contrast to smaller Northeastern and Midwestern cities that continue to suffer from deindustrialization and decline.

The population of the Unites States is primarily urban: Eighty-one percent of Americans lived in urban areas in 2010, and 85% lived in metropolitan areas, particularly in large metro areas. A study of the largest cities in America between 1900 and 2010 found that the nation's urban hierarchy has changed over time, as only 42 cities remained in the top 100 throughout that period (Short & Mussman, 2014). Rapidly growing and sprawling cities in the South and West have supplanted many densely populated, declining cities in the Northeast and Midwest, although many of the largest cities in these areas are rebounding. The authors classified America's cities into four types based on population change: (1) steady decline (Detroit, Buffalo, Cleveland), (2) continuous increase (San Jose, Orlando, Las Vegas), (3) growth interrupted (decline midcentury followed by a resurgence: New York, San Francisco, Atlanta), and (4) slowly resurgent (decline ended with small upward trends: Boston, Philadelphia, Washington, D.C.). Lifestyle preferences, economic transitions, the job market, and a city's ability to annex new territory are all factors that influence historical growth patterns.

There are distinct patterns of growth within metro areas: Patterns of growth within metro areas follow broad historical and national trends. While certain cities and metros have grown more than others, most of them have followed similar internal trends where downtown areas declined, suburban areas grew, and downtown areas subsequently became revitalized. During the early 20th century, population density in America's central cities was at peak levels. As the 20th century progressed, improvements in public transit, the availability of automobiles, the construction of highways, and federal housing policies encouraged the growth of suburbs. This trend began in the 1920s, was interrupted by the depression and war, and accelerated after the war. During the 1950s and 1960s, many white Americans migrated out of cities into the suburbs, and urban growth became more decentralized (Teaford, 2006). America's central cities suffered from deindustrialization, disinvestment, high crime, and population loss during the 1970s and 1980s as migration to the suburbs continued. By the 1990s and 2000s, many central cities witnessed a resurgence of growth that continues to the present. Growth in suburban areas has slowed but is still strong as minorities now follow the earlier white trend of suburbanization, while growth in exurban areas (the outer fringe between the country and city) has expanded (Frey, 2018a). Most rural areas have suffered from population decline, with the exception of areas that are close to growing metropolitan areas.

The U.S. population is becoming more diverse: The United States has always been a diverse nation. From the colonial period to the late 19th century, this diversity was driven by immigration, slavery, and territorial expansion. In the 20th and 21st centuries, it was driven solely by immigration and varying birth rates. When the U.S. Civil War ended (1861–1865), immigration resumed and exponentially increased with European immigrants arriving in large cities in the Northeast and Midwest before spreading across the country, and with Asian immigrants (largely from Japan, China, and Korea) arriving in California. As the 20th century began, the origin of European immigrants shifted from Western Europe and Ireland to Eastern and Southern Europe. World War I (1914–1918) brought immigration to a virtual halt, but when it ended and immigration resumed, anti-immigrant sentiment flared up, fueled by isolationism, nativism, and racism. A highly restrictive set of quotas and immigration laws were passed in the 1920s that sharply curtailed immigration. From the 1920s to the 1960s, immigration to the Unites States remained at historic lows, although Latin America was exempt from the laws and there was migration from Mexico, Cuba, and Puerto Rico. New immigration laws were passed in 1965 that lifted these quotas, which led to a boom in immigration in the late 20th and early 21st centuries. New immigrants came from Latin America, Asia, Africa, and countries that were formerly part of the Soviet Eastern Block (Klein, 2012). This immigration boom helped to offset lower birthrates of the native born (i.e., people born in the Unites States), which pushed population growth higher and helped older cities to revitalize.

The population is aging and birth rates are declining The population growth of the immediate postwar era (1945–1965) was fueled largely by natural increase and increasing life spans, while immigration was low due to restrictive policies. The Baby Boomer generation is named for this phenomena. The Great Depression (1929–1939) and World War II (1939–1945) created conditions that led many people to reduce or delay having children, but the end of the war and increasing material prosperity led to a boom in births. This large generation is now entering retirement age, and as it ages, the overall age of the population is increasing. This is because the generations following the Boomers (Generation X and the Millennials) are smaller and because each generation is having fewer children than the previous one. While there are different methods for measuring fertility (Livingston, 2019), most approaches show declines in the recent past, and particularly since the Great Recession (2007–2009). According to the decennial census, the median age of the nation has steadily increased from 28 in 1970 to 37 in 2010. As fertility declines and the population ages, deaths will begin to outnumber births. Recent trends show that this is already happening among the white population in half of the states (Saenz & Johnson, 2018). While Hispanics and Latinos account for the majority of U.S. population gain, birth rates among this group are declining as well (K. M. Johnson, 2019).

The concept of families is changing: While the nuclear family of husband, wife, and two or more children was the norm during the 1950s, it hasn't been the norm for quite some time. Single-parent households, households headed by grand-parents, children born outside of marriage, unmarried partners, same-sex unions, and single-person households have all increased since that time. The decennial census shows that about 80% of households had married couples in 1950 compared with approximately 50% in 2010. The factors behind these trends are complex and sharply debated but generally involve several cultural and economic transitions. Demographers often refer to the first demographic transition from agricultural to industrial societies as a decline in both birth and death rates. The second demographic transition that occurs in more developed societies often involves these shifts in family relationships and subsequent changes in childbearing (Iceland, 2014).

Income inequality is growing: In the past 40 years, the standard of living has been improving more for the wealthiest Americans and less so for everyone else. While incomes rose and poverty fell throughout the 1960s and 1970s, both have remained relatively flat for the past several decades. Adjusted for inflation, median household income hovered around $50k in 1990 and was also about the same in 2010. In the intervening years, income fell and rose by a few thousand dollars with each recession and boom. Income inequality has grown, as the wealthiest Americans have become steadily wealthier since the 1980s while the rest of society has gained relatively little. The top 1% of income-earning households own 35% of the wealth, the next 9% own 39%, and the bottom 90% own 27% (Iceland, 2014). Income inequality in the early 21st century is the highest that it's been since the 1920s, and the United States is one of the most unequal societies compared with other advanced economies. Technological innovation, demand for high-skilled workers and the decline in low-skilled jobs, globalization, the decline of unions, cuts in government services, rising salaries for CEOs, and government policies that favor the wealthy and big business are all factors behind this widening gap (Iceland, 2014).

This concludes the second part of the book, which provided you with a roadmap to all the primary census datasets and exercises that gave you practical experience in working with them. This chapter was the last logical step, demonstrating how you can refer to data in writing and providing additional insight to guide you in integrating data into your research. The next chapters focus on more advanced topics that include GIS, census data derivatives, historical data, and microdata.

## 9.5  REVIEW QUESTIONS AND PRACTICE EXERCISES

1. Visit the websites of the Census Bureau's library of publications, the Pew Research Center, and the Brookings Institution. Review some of their reports to see how they use census data in their work.

2. Take each of following statistics and incorporate them into clear sentences that address the aspects that we've discussed in Section 9.2 for conveying information about census statistics.

   a. Oklahoma County, Oklahoma, 53,840 ± 1,546 government workers, 15.0% ± 0.4% of total civilian employed population, 2012–2016 ACS, Table DP03 Selected Economic Characteristics

   b. District of Columbia, 601,723 total population, 2010 Census, 572,059 total population, 2000 census

   c. Maine, 430 establishments, 2,361 paid employees, Forestry and Logging industry (NAICS 113), 2016 Business Patterns

3. Take the first example from the previous question and rewrite it in a formal academic style with an APA citation and a bibliography entry.

4. Summarize what some of the primary considerations are when choosing census geography for doing research.

5. Search the open data page for Jersey City, New jersey, at `https://data.jerseycitynj.gov/` for wards or neighborhoods. Using these maps and the OpenStreetMap at `https://www.openstreetmap.org/`, discuss how you would aggregate census tracts to form cohesive neighborhood areas relative to the example we discussed in Section 9.3.

# ADVANCED TOPICS

# MAPPING AND GIS

## 10.1   INTRODUCTION

Maps are a natural way for visualizing and studying census data. They provide important geographic context in orienting and displaying data, so we can see where all the counties are or can understand what a census tract is. Maps also allow us to study census data in geographic space. Instead of simply listing, sorting, and ranking data on home values or unemployment in a table or summarizing distributions in a graph, we can actually see how this data is distributed across space to illustrate patterns of concentration or dispersion and to identify differences between and within places.

The Census Bureau facilitates map-making and geographic analysis via the publication of several geographic products. For every piece of census geography that the Census Bureau publishes data for, it provides precise boundary files for visualizing those areas. These files can be used in geographic information systems (GIS) to map not only census data but any dataset that can be associated with those places. In this chapter, we will explore these data sources and demonstrate how you can use these files in GIS to create your own maps and do your own analyses.

Before we address GIS, if you simply want to map census data, there are a number of free online tools that make this easy to do, and we will illustrate one of them. While these tools are simple to use, you're limited to using the data and options that are provided by the tool or website. The power of GIS is that it allows you to pull together geographic and tabular data from several sources to do many different kinds of analyses as well as create maps. After a brief overview of GIS and the Census Bureau's geographic boundary files, we'll take a whirlwind tour of QGIS, which is a popular free and open source GIS package. We'll examine public transit ridership in the Atlanta metropolitan area as a case study that will introduce several GIS basics and essentials: overlaying geographic features, creating subsets of layers, coordinating systems and projections, symbolizing features, joining data tables to GIS files to create a thematic map, selecting features that meet certain criteria based on their attributes and their geographic relationship with other features, measuring distances, and creating a finished map.

If you've never used GIS before or are only remotely familiar with it, this chapter is not going to teach you everything you need to know, but the good news is you don't need to know everything. We will cover enough material to get you started and to demonstrate the value of using GIS to work with census and geographic data. If you are familiar with GIS or are a veteran user, this chapter will be useful for illustrating the specifics of working with census data in this environment and will reveal important considerations and "gotchas" that frequently occur when mapping census data. If you are only familiar with proprietary GIS packages, this chapter will demonstrate how you can do many of the same tasks in the open source world.

Similar to Chapter 2, this entire chapter is primarily structured as one exercise. Before we begin, you should download and install QGIS as outlined in the introduction of this book. We are using QGIS version 3.4, which was the long-term service release available at the time this chapter was written. If you're generally comfortable learning new software and can adapt to minor differences, any 3.x version of QGIS will do.

## 10.2  CREATING MAPS ONLINE

If you want to make a quick map to visualize and explore data, there are a number of web mapping applications that make it easy to generate thematic maps of census data. These applications are ideal for data exploration: You can test and see what geographic patterns look like rather than downloading and processing a lot of data to discover the same thing in GIS.

As the name suggests, a thematic map is used to illustrate a theme about different places, such as public transit ridership, home sales, or population growth. Geographic features such as tracts, counties, subway stations, or businesses are depicted on maps using different colors or symbols that indicate different values for those themes. Examples of thematic maps include dot maps (dot indicates presence or absence of value), graduated symbol maps (size of symbol represents quantity), and shaded area maps (color or shade indicates quantity). In contrast, reference maps are used to display basic location for the purpose of orientation or navigation. Road atlases, wall maps of countries, Google Maps, and TIGERweb (introduced in Chapter 3) are all examples of reference maps. Our focus in this chapter is thematic maps.

The new **data.census.gov** integrates basic thematic mapping with data discovery. As we saw in Chapter 2, there are many approaches for navigating **data.census.gov**, and using it to generate a map is no different. Choose your dataset, year, geography, and filter by variable to find what you want. At the time this chapter was written, the map-making tools were still being actively developed.

To ensure that we have a working example, let's explore the map-making capabilities of the Census Reporter instead at `https://censusreporter.org/`. We mentioned the Census Reporter in Chapter 2 as an alternative to **data.census.gov** for obtaining profiles and tables from the most recent version of the American Community Survey (ACS). We also discussed it in Chapter 6 as a good source for user-friendly ACS documentation. Let's map travel time to work in Fulton County, Georgia, in preparation for our case study of the Atlanta metro.

On the Census Reporter home page, scroll down to the Topics list and select "Commute." This page gives us an overview of the Commute topic and a list of ACS tables with commuting data. Under Travel Time to Work, scroll down toward the bottom and click the link for Table B08303 Travel Time to Work. This brings us to a page dedicated to this table, which shows us all of the columns it includes. At the top is a search box that says "Start typing to pick a place." Type Fulton County and select the option for Fulton County, GA (the county where the City of Atlanta is primarily located).

This provides us with a table with the values for the county (Figure 10.1). On the left-hand side, there is a list that says "Divide Fulton County, GA into ..." and we have a number of different geographic options. Select census tracts, and the table will update to show us all the values for the tracts. In the upper right-hand corner, click on the green Map button (beside the Table button).

This opens a new window with a map of the data by tract for Fulton County. We're initially shown the first variable for Less than 5 minutes travel time to work, but by selecting the Show column drop down, we can change the variable to another option, such as 45 to 59 minutes travel time to work. This updates our map to show us these values (Figure 10.2). Notice that by default we are seeing percent totals; if we wanted to see the total estimates, we could select the Switch to totals link in the menu. We can also change the table to map a different variable at this scale pretty quickly or add more places to view all ZIP Code Tabulation Areas or all census places within this area instead. Hover over areas in the map with your mouse, and the percent total, total estimate, and margins of error (MOEs) for each value will appear in an information bubble. The data is classified into different categories and colors using the equal intervals method, where each category contains an equal range of values.

## FIGURE 10.1 ⬡ TRAVEL TIME TO WORK IN FULTON COUNTY, GEORGIA, IN THE CENSUS REPORTER

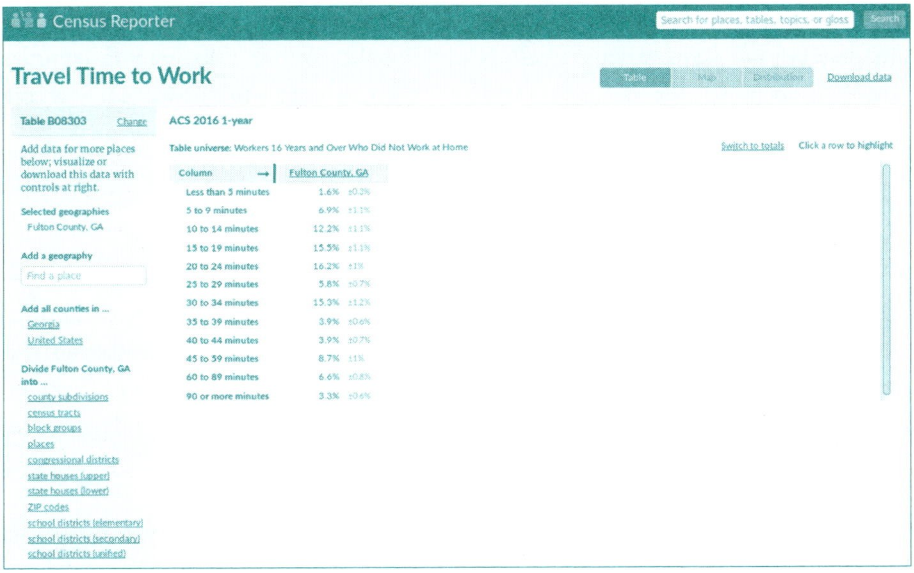

## FIGURE 10.2 ⬡ CENSUS REPORTER MAP OF TRAVEL TIME TO WORK BY CENSUS TRACT

Mapping features in the Census Reporter is straightforward, but customization is limited, and we can only map the most recent data from the ACS. The new **data.census.gov** platform will provide more customization options, and there are a number of other free and proprietary web-mapping tools that incorporate different datasets and have varying levels of functionality. While GIS is more complex and desktop based, the sky is the limit in terms of your options for analysis and visualization. The rest of this chapter is devoted to it.

## 10.3   INTRODUCTION TO GIS

This section will introduce you to the fundamentals of GIS with a conceptual overview, followed by a discussion of the geospatial data files that the Census Bureau produces for use in GIS and other mapping applications. Once we've covered this essential background information, we'll do an exercise that will provide you with hands-on experience.

### GIS Fundamentals

GIS is an integrated collection of software and data for visualizing and organizing geographic data, conducting geographic analyses, and creating maps and derived data. GIS refers not to a specific software package or data format but to any number of applications, tools, data formats, and code bases that can be used to achieve these ends. Location and place are the central concepts on which GIS is built, and the data and tools can be applied to many fields and disciplines.

In GIS, a set of related geographic features are stored in individual files or database tables that serve as layers in a project. Layers are not maps but are the raw materials that can be used for creating maps and doing analyses. For example, you can have individual layers saved in distinct files that represent train stations, roads, and census tracts that can be added to a GIS project and overlaid, so that the layers are drawn one on top of another and can be used together.

Every GIS file is georeferenced, which means that all the features in the file are tied to real locations on the earth. The features are not simple drawings that were created in a graphic design package, but drawn at a specific scale and level of detail using a specific coordinate system and map projection in the same manner that traditional paper maps were created. GIS software contains a library of these systems that allow you to overlay data files from different sources that share the same system. If the files have different systems, GIS can be used to modify or reproject the system of files so that they match and can be overlaid. We have all seen maps of the world that are drawn at different scales using different coordinate systems and map projections; each one preserves a different aspect of the earth's properties and is used for different and specific purposes. These coordinate reference systems (CRS) act as standards that allow us to share and overlay GIS datasets. In contrast, you couldn't take two drawings or images from a graphic design package and seamlessly overlay them because they have no reference points in common and may not be drawn to scale.

There are two principal methods for representing and saving real-world features as geospatial data files: vectors and rasters. In a vector format, data is stored as a series of features with discrete coordinates and surfaces that are represented as individual points, lines, or polygons (GIS jargon for areas). In a vector file of census tracts, individual tracts are saved as individual features in the file, where each node of the feature is saved as a series of coordinates that can be connected to form lines that can form enclosed areas, which can be visualized geographically. Each feature also has a record in a table that is tied to that visual feature. That attribute table contains feature information that includes identifiers such as unique ID codes and feature names, data such as area and length that can be derived from the geographic coordinates, and data that can be associated with the features such as population characteristics. Data stored in the table can be visualized as labels for the features or as values that can be depicted in a thematic map.

Given this structure, many vector files mimic the role of tables in a relational database. If we have a spreadsheet of population data for census tracts, where each record represents one tract and the columns contain population data, and we have a GIS vector file of census tracts, we can add the table to GIS and join it to the vector file using a unique ID code that they share in common, which allows us to geographically analyze and map any data that's stored in the table. This is extremely powerful, as we can take geographic data stored in any number of data formats and associate it with geospatial vector data that we can map.

This method is known as a tabular join. Alternatively, if we have a plain data file that represents point-based features that includes longitude and latitude coordinates as attributes, we can add this file to GIS and plot the locations using the coordinates to create a vector file. For example, if we have a spreadsheet of businesses with company names, addresses, number of employees, and coordinates, we can plot the coordinates to create a vector file, and then we can overlay this layer with other vector files and map the locations and employees. This method is known as plotting *XY* coordinates.

There are several different vector file formats. The most common one is a shapefile (.shp). Shapefiles were created by a company called ESRI that produces a well-known proprietary GIS package called ArcGIS. The shapefile format has been around for decades and suffers from limitations, but given its longevity and status as an open data format, it's still widely used. Geopackages are a newer vector format that's based on SQLite databases.

In this book, we will work exclusively with vector-based shapefiles, as the Census Bureau publishes its layers in this format. The other principal geospatial format is the raster file. Instead of representing individual discrete features, raster files represent a continuous surface that is divided into grid cells of equal size, and each cell has a specific value that can be symbolized. They are similar to digital photos in their construction and are often used to represent air photos and satellite imagery. Rasters can also be derived from these sources to create new raster layers to depict phenomena such as land use and land coverage or temperature grids. Raster files are georeferenced and assigned a CRS, so they can be overlayed with other GIS data. Given their construction, rasters are saved as individual tiles that cover a certain area and can be tiled or stitched together to visualize larger areas. The file formats consist of familiar types like tifs and jpegs, as well as several more obscure formats. The U.S. Geological Survey is a major distributor of raster data.

GIS software serves as a window for viewing, overlaying, and manipulating these different types of geospatial data files. While there are many different GIS software packages, most of them have developed a similar, standard interface. Each package will have a panel showing the different layers that are active in the project, which indicates how they are overlayed along with a map window that depicts the actual features. Different menus are used for viewing attribute tables; querying features to select specific criteria; symbolizing features for changing colors, lines, and labels; running different tools for summarizing or processing the data and features; and creating final, finished maps that are suitable for publication. Each package has a mechanism for coping with layers that do not share the same reference system and for converting layers from one system to another. Users can save their work in dedicated project files that save links to layers that are part of the project, symbolization, zoom, and finished map layouts. Unlike the data files, project files are not cross platform and are specific to the GIS software package.

## Census TIGER Files

https://www.census.gov/geographies/mapping-files/time-series/geo/tiger-line-file.html

The Census Bureau was a pioneer in producing and publishing geospatial data files and helped spur the adoption of GIS in academia, government, and business in the United States. GIS software does not come prepackaged with data, just as a spreadsheet program wouldn't come populated with statistics. You have to gather the data from many sources and bring it into the package in order to use it. The Census Bureau published the first TIGER Line files as part of the 1990 census and distributed them to governments and universities on physical media and through the early internet, providing a free, high-quality, and comprehensive source of spatial data files and tabular census data for desktop GIS applications. The U.S. geospatial data community and industry continues to rely on the Census Bureau as a primary source for vector GIS data.

The Census Bureau created the TIGER program and data format to make a mappable database of all the different types of census geography that met high standards of data integrity and that could link to the Master Address File to form a cohesive geographic dataset. An acronym for Topologically Integrated Geographic Encoding and Referencing, TIGER was initially a type of vector format for storing data, but over time, the name became associated with the overall program and less associated with a specific file format. The Census Bureau began releasing TIGER data in a shapefile format in 2007, and that continues to be the primary format of distribution.

TIGER was created to ensure that boundaries for census geography conform to the geographical hierarchy discussed in Chapter 3, so that there is no overlap between different geographies that are meant to nest, and there is no overlap *within* geographies, so that the boundary of one census tract doesn't cross the boundary of another. The Census Bureau uses TIGER throughout its operations, for enumerating the population, selecting households for samples, tabulating data, and publishing results. In addition to publishing data for all statistical and legal areas, the Bureau also publishes physical features that are used for delineating census blocks: rivers and bodies of water, roads and railroads, and a catchall landmarks category that includes a selection of prominent features such as parks, cemeteries, airports, industrial areas, and significant buildings.

TIGER data is updated on an ongoing basis and is released annually, but this doesn't mean that all the data is updated. Most of the statistical areas such as census blocks, block groups, and tracts are released only once in a 10-year period, so the boundaries released in 2010 are essentially the same boundaries used throughout the decade until a complete revision is conducted in 2020. The only exceptions to this rule are corrections to boundary errors, or statistical boundary changes that result from changes to legal geography. The annual updates are largely designed to capture changes in legal areas, such as places, minor civil divisions, and counties, which can happen at any time. The TIGER vintage must reflect the geography used in datasets for that year, so the 2017 TIGER files will reflect whatever is available in the 2017 ACS.

✓

**INFOBOX 10.1 GENERALIZATION AND CARTOGRAPHIC BOUNDARY SHAPEFILES**

The Census TIGER Line files are intended to accurately represent the boundaries between all legal and statistical geographies, but in cartography, precision is not always desirable. Consider Figure 10.3. The TIGER file for the State of Michigan displays the actual legal boundaries of the state, which extend into the middle of the Great Lakes where the state boundary meets the boundaries of other states and Canada. While this layer is perfect for representing the boundary of Michigan, it is not suitable for representing Michigan as a geographic feature. Looking at this shape, it's unlikely that anyone could guess that this is Michigan. We would want to display the actual land boundaries of the state. If we were mapping population data, we would also want to exclude areas that cover large bodies of water.

The Census Bureau creates a series of generalized boundary files where coastal water is removed and boundary lines are smoothed or simplified. If we were studying a small area on a large-scale map, we would need to see reasonably precise boundaries that show a high level of detail, otherwise the map would appear incorrect. If we were studying a large area on a small-scale map, this same level of detail would be unnecessary as it wouldn't be visible to the map viewer. Indeed, a high level of detail at that scale would make boundaries appear overly jagged or blurry. The Census Bureau produces three generalized versions of most of the TIGER layers that are appropriate at different scales. Looking at Figure 10.3, as we move from the least to the most generalized layer we can see that the jagged boundaries of the coastline become smoother and a number of small islands disappear. This phenomenon of generalization isn't limited to coastal areas: Any area that has boundaries with many smooth curves or jagged edges would be simplified.

Download the Cartographic Boundary Shapefiles here:

`https://www.census.gov/geographies/mapping-files/time-series/geo/carto-boundary-file.html`

TIGER shapefiles can be downloaded through a web interface or via the FTP site. The Census Bureau packages them as nation-based, state-based, or county-based coverages. This packaging is based on intended use and the overall number of features in a file. Given the way the files are packaged, you will often need to download features that cover an area that's wider than your area of interest, or you may need to download several files to cover your area. We can use GIS to create subsets of layers or stitch them together to cover a wider area, and we'll get practice doing this in the exercise.

Besides the TIGER Line shapefiles, the Census Bureau provides a number of derivative GIS products such as databases that have boundaries and related census data preassembled. The Cartographic Boundary Shapefiles (InfoBox 10.1) is one derivative that you should definitely investigate.

**FIGURE 10.3** ◆ GENERALIZATION: COMPARISON OF TIGER AND CARTOGRAPHIC BOUNDARY FILES (CBFs)

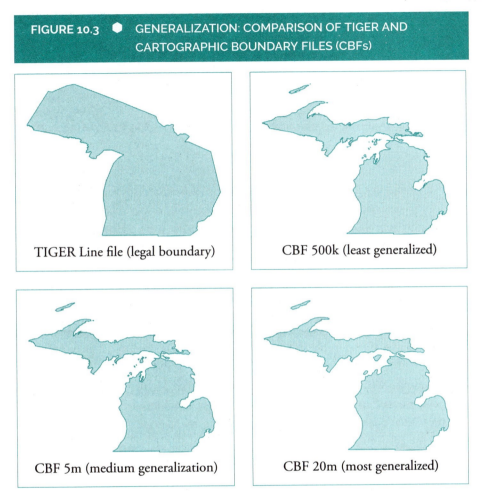

TIGER Line file (legal boundary)

CBF 500k (least generalized)

CBF 5m (medium generalization)

CBF 20m (most generalized)

## 10.4   QGIS EXERCISE

This exercise will give you a broad introduction to GIS fundamentals with census data using QGIS. We'll be using a selection of files from the 2017 TIGER Line files website, attribute data from the ACS on commuting, and a subway stations layer produced by local government agencies. Visit the publisher's website for the data we will be using, or download it from the source:

2017 TIGER Line Shapefiles: Counties for the nation, places, and census tracts for the State of Georgia—https://www.census.gov/cgi-bin/geo/shapefiles/index.php.

Transit Rail Stations shapefile:  MARTA stations layer produced by the Research & Analytics Division of the Atlanta Regional Commission and published via the Fulton County GIS Portal—`http://gisdata.fultoncountyga.gov/datasets/GARC::transit-rail-stations`.

B08301 Means of Transportation to Work:  2012–2016 ACS, all census tracts in Clayton, DeKalb, and Fulton counties in Georgia—`https://data.census.gov/`.

The ACS table in Chapter 10 folder has been preformatted so that it is readily usable for this exercise. Unlike previous exercises, we will *not* cover how to format this table step by step. If you elect to use this data from the source rather than from the publisher's website, you will need to format the table yourself based on the example provided in the text. The only variables we need from this table are estimates and MOEs for the total number of commuters and the total number who commute to work via public transit. If you take this data from Table B08301 you will also need to calculate the percentage of total commuters who take public transit and the corresponding MOE.

When searching for GIS layers of local interest, such as the subway stations, you can start by doing a web search to see if data is provided directly by the agency (MARTA) or if it is released through a city, county, or state data portal or website. Libraries or data centers at large research universities also manage portals that publish and redistribute government data.

In this example, we will study the distribution of public transit riders in the Atlanta metropolitan area and identify areas that have low transit ridership but are close to subway stations. MARTA is the metropolitan area's transit system that includes rail, streetcars, and buses. Atlanta (like many other large cities) has a reputation for traffic congestion and long commute times. The collapse of a bridge that's part of one of the city's interstate highways in 2017 led to massive traffic problems for several months. The disaster led to a spike in public transit ridership and greater interest in expanding the subway network.

Our study area consists of the three counties in the metro area that are officially part of the MARTA rail network, as they each collect sales taxes that are used to fund the system: Clayton (FIPS 063), DeKalb (089), and Fulton (121) counties in Georgia (13). The City of Atlanta is the largest and primary city in the metropolitan area. It occupies the central portion of Fulton County and a small area of adjacent DeKalb County.

The focus of this exercise is to introduce GIS and how it can be used for mapping and analyzing census data. To focus on this goal, we're going to bypass certain considerations. The primary one that we're not going to address: MOEs for ACS data. As we discussed in Chapter 6, tract-level ACS data can be unreliable, and the MOEs for public transit commuting in this example are relatively high, especially for tracts where the percentage of transit riders is small. We could address this by aggregating tracts, providing general footnotes in finished maps about data accuracy, or calculating coefficients of variation and flagging tracts with high values. There are several approaches to relaying information about uncertainty in maps, such as overlaying coefficients of variation values or statistical difference results as separate layers over actual estimates (Sun & Wong, 2010).

This exercise is longer than our previous ones, as it's designed to be comprehensive enough for GIS newcomers to learn the absolute basics while being able to reasonably complete a typical workflow from start to finish. This section is divided into subsections that represent logical components of this workflow: understanding vector shapefiles, basic orientation to a GIS interface, adding and overlaying layers, selecting attributes and creating subsets of layers, understanding and working with CRS, symbolization and labeling, joining attribute tables to layers, creating a thematic map, conducting a basic analysis using geographic selection and distance, and map layout. Important topics that are tangential or not part of this exercise are mentioned in the InfoBoxes. We'll conclude with resources that you can use to learn about GIS in greater detail.

## Vector Data in Shapefiles and CRS Basics

Before we launch QGIS, navigate to the folder for Chapter 10, and look in the folder named tiger, which contains the TIGER Line shapefiles that we'll be using in this exercise. The term *shapefile* is a bit deceiving, as one shapefile consists of multiple files that must share the same name and be stored in the same folder to function. The Census Bureau names files based on their vintage, location, and geography. tl_2017_13_place is a TIGER Line file from 2017 for the State of Georgia (FIPS code 13) for census places. We can identify how many shapefiles there are by counting the number of distinct file names. In this case, we have three: Georgia places, Georgia census tracts, and US counties.

When working with shapefiles, it is crucial that you keep all the pieces of the shapefile together in one place, and that each piece has the same filename. If you need to move the shapefile, you have to move all the pieces, otherwise it won't function. Renaming the files isn't a good idea, as you'd have to rename all the pieces and not make any mistakes. It's easier to rename data within the GIS software, as it will take care of renaming all the pieces for you.

The number of files per shapefile will vary, but at minimum, there are four that must be part of the total shapefile. Each one serves as specific purpose: (1) .shp contains the geometry, (2) .shx contains an index of the geometry, (3) .dbf is the attribute table for the features, and (4) .prj contains the CRS definition for the file. If you wanted to know what CRS the shapefile is in, you can simply open the .prj file in a text editor. The .prj files for these shapefiles contain this information:

```
GEOGCS["GCS_North_American_1983",
    DATUM["D_North_American_1983",
        SPHEROID["GRS_1980",6378137,298.257222101]],
        PRIMEM["Greenwich",0],
        UNIT["Degree",0.017453292519943295]]
```

This is a standard definition in a format called the Well Known Text Format (WKT) that tells us that this file is in the North American Datum of 1983, or NAD83 for short. This is a basic longitude, latitude CRS that all Census TIGER files use by default. Since they all share this system, you can open and immediately overlay any shapefiles from the Census Bureau in GIS. This particular definition is an ESRI format; ESRI is the company that produces the proprietary ArcGIS software package. An open source variant of WKT produced by the Open Geospatial Consortium (OGC) looks like this:

```
GEOGCS["NAD83",
    DATUM["North_American_Datum_1983",
        SPHEROID["GRS 1980",6378137,298.257222101,
            AUTHORITY["EPSG","7019"]],
        AUTHORITY["EPSG","6269"]],
    PRIMEM["Greenwich",0,
        AUTHORITY["EPSG","8901"]],
    UNIT["degree",0.01745329251994328,
        AUTHORITY["EPSG","9122"]],
    AUTHORITY["EPSG","4269"]]
```

This definition contains the same information and the files will function in the same manner. The primary difference in the OGC definitions include unique identifier codes (the EPSG codes) for each component of the system and for the entire system itself. The last code in the definition, EPSG 4269, is the unique identifier for the NAD83 CRS. These codes are a useful shorthand for referring to definitions, and QGIS relies on them. When you save new shapefiles in QGIS, they will use this OGC WKT format. See InfoBox 10.2 for a brief overview of CRS. As you work with GIS, you will become familiar with a small number of systems that you'll likely use in your work, and your two primary concerns will be ensuring that your files share the same system and that you're using an appropriate system for your area.

### INFOBOX 10.2 COORDINATE REFERENCE SYSTEMS

Also known as spatial reference systems, these systems are standards for modeling and locating objects on the earth based on geodesy (measuring and modeling the earth in three-dimensional [3D] surface) and cartography (representing the earth on a flat 2D surface). They are crucial components that underpin GIS, and all vector and raster files have a system assigned to them. Each CRS has at least three components, and some have four:

Spheroid/Elipsoid:   approximation of the earth's 3D shape as a sphere or oval.

Datum:   a set of instructions for anchoring spheroids or elipsoids to the actual surface of the earth. They can be optimized for a specific region or for the earth as a whole.

Coordinate Reference System:   a grid-like system for locating objects on the earth (this term is more specific in this context, relative to its general usage in QGIS for referencing an entire system).

Map Projection:   method for taking the 3D earth and projecting it on a 2D surface with a Cartesian *XY* coordinate system. All map projections are distortions that can preserve only one property of the earth: direction, shape, area, or distance.

Systems with the first three components are part of a family called Geographic Systems that are designed for representing the 3D earth. These systems are often used when publishing or exchanging data. Systems with all four components are known as Projected Systems, which are appropriate for representing the 2D earth when creating maps. There is no "perfect" or "correct" CRS. The one you'll use will vary with area, scale, and intended purpose. For an overview, see Radical Cartography's projection reference at `http://www.radicalcartography.net/?projectionref`.

Systems are stored in a standard format for identifying their various components. In open source GIS, all systems are assigned a unique identifier called an EPSG code. You can look up EPSG codes and definitions for different systems at Spatial Reference: `http://spatialreference.org/`. By default, all Census TIGER files are in the NAD 83 CRS, which is identified by the EPSG code 4269.

## QGIS Orientation

Launch QGIS. There are a lot of components and hundreds of tools, but don't let that overwhelm you. Eighty percent of the time you'll use 20% of the tools, and there are many tools that you'll likely never use. The main components of the interface are illustrated in Figure 10.4 and are described below:

1. **Menus:** provide access to different features and functions of the software. Some of the menus provide access to tools, while others open subcomponents of

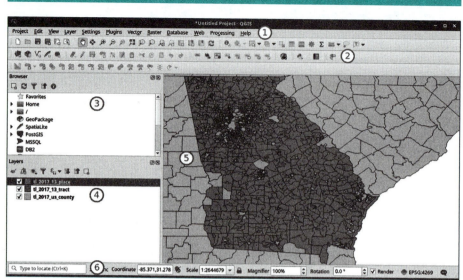

FIGURE 10.4 ● COMPONENTS OF THE QGIS INTERFACE

the software, such as the Data Source Manager for adding data and the Map Composer for creating map layouts.

2. **Toolbars:** some toolbars are simply shortcuts for features provided in the menus, while others provide the means for manipulating what you see in the Map Canvas, such as buttons for zooming in and out and for selecting and identifying features. If you hover over the left edge of a toolbar, you can click and drag it to dock it in a different location of the screen.

3. **Browser Panel:** allows you to see your file system, so you can quickly move down a folder tree and drag files directly into your project. There are also options for connecting to various databases and web mapping services.

4. **Layers panel:** displays all of the layers that are currently part of your project. The order of the layers determines how they are drawn relative to each other, and checkmarking a layer turns it on and off. Selecting a layer makes it active, so you can use the selection and identify tools on that layer. Selecting and right-clicking the layer allows you to access and modify the properties for the layer, so you can change its symbolization, turn labels on and off, and view its attribute table.

5. **Map Canvas:** the geographic display that shows all your active layers, also known as the map view. Once you have created projects in QGIS, when you initially launch the software, this area will contain a list of recent projects. You

can select a project to open it, or begin adding new layers to make the list go away and start a new project.

6. **Status Bar:** shows the current scale of the map view, the coordinates for the position where your cursor is centered over the map, and the unique identifier for the CRS for the map canvas. Hovering over the code that's displayed there will reveal the name of the system. By default, the canvas will be set to a basic system and will be updated to take the system of the first layer that you add to the project.

QGIS is highly customizable. The toolbars and panels can all be moved, resized, and even turned off. If you accidentally remove a panel or toolbar or can't find one that should be there, do a single right-click on a blank area of any toolbar. This will provide you with a list of all toolbars and panels, and you can check or uncheck an item to turn it on or off. Additional menus at the top of the screen can be added or removed if they represent optional or third-party plugins. You can add or remove certain menus by going to the Plugins menu.

## Adding and Overlaying Layers

Let's begin by adding our TIGER files to the map canvas. QGIS provides you with several paths to accomplish this goal. We can navigate through the folders in the browser panel to drag and drop files, or we can add layers via the menus at the top of the screen. Let's go to Layer—Add Layer—Add Vector Layer. In the Source area, hit the button with the three dots to begin browsing our file system (Figure 10.5). Navigate to Chapter 10 tiger folder. At the bottom of this menu, change the option from All files to ESRI shapefiles. This filters the directory contents to clearly display the three shapefiles stored there. Select the first file, hold down the shift key, and select the last file for counties, which selects all three. Hit Open, then hit the Add button in the lower right-hand corner of the vector menu. Close the menu, and you'll see the three layers in the layers menu and visually in the map canvas.

QGIS assigns a random color to each layer with dark and relatively thin borders. Data files do not contain any symbolization by default as they consist of just geographic boundaries and some attributes. It's up to you as the map maker to symbolize the layers. The canvas is adjusted to fit the layer that has the largest extent. The counties layer covers the entire United States and the territories, and since these areas extend across the date line on the far side of the world (180 degrees longitude), the zoom is global in extent. If you move your mouse across the canvas, longitude and latitude coordinates will update in the coordinates box in the status bar (bottom of the screen). If you hover over the button that says EPSG 4269 in the lower right-hand corner, it

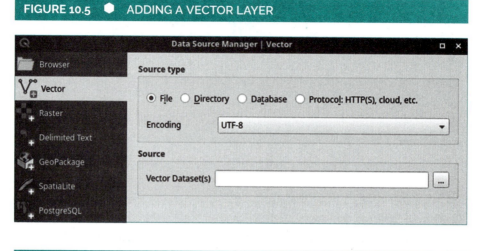

**FIGURE 10.5 ● ADDING A VECTOR LAYER**

**FIGURE 10.6 ● QGIS ZOOM BUTTONS**

tells you the map window has been set to NAD83, which is the CRS that all three of our map layers are in.

To see Georgia more clearly, select the tracts layer in the layers panel, and hit the Zoom to Layer button in the toolbar. This button is the magnifying glass in front of a gray box. If you hover your cursor over a button for a second, a tooltip will pop up that tells you what the name of the tool is (Figure 10.6). Zoom to layer recenters the map on Georgia, and we can see the tracts and places more clearly. In the layers panel, the order of the layers is places, tracts, and counties, which is the order in which we added them to the canvas. Places is drawn over top of tracts, which are drawn over top of counties. If you hit the check box for places, it turns that layer off. If you select the counties layer and drag it to the top of the layers panel, it draws the counties as the first layer and covers up the layers underneath. The order of the layers matters, as it effects the drawing order and what you can see. Restore the layers to their original order and keep them all turned on.

Experiment with the zoom tools to get comfortable with navigating the map. The magnifying glass with the plus symbol zooms in, while the one with the minus symbol zooms out. You can zoom by simply clicking the button and then clicking on the map, or with the button selected, you can use your cursor to draw a box around an area, and you will zoom in to that area. If you ever become lost, you have a few options to return to home base: the magnifying glass with the arrows extending out of it is the Zoom to Full button. It will zoom out back to the full extent of all your layers. The magnifying glasses with the left and right arrows allow you to cycle back and forth between your current and previous zooms. As we have seen, you can also select a layer in the panel and use the Zoom to Layer button to get zoom to the full extent of that layer. Last, if you don't want to change the zoom but simply want to move to another area of the map, you can use the Pan tool, the button with the white glove. Click it, and you can use the cursor to drag the map around.

## Creating Subsets of Layers, Reprojecting CRS, Saving Projects

Our ultimate goal is to map public transit ridership in the Atlanta metro area in relation to the location of MARTA subway stations. There are a number of steps we must take to process and prepare our data before we can achieve this. First, we need to take these files and create subsets of them that just contain the areas we need. The tract layer should cover just the three counties that are within MARTA's service area. The county and place layers are simply for providing points of reference, and we'll want to select just the features for the three counties and the boundary of the City of Atlanta.

Second, we will need to convert the CRS for these layers into something more suitable. The NAD83 CRS is fine for distributing national datasets, but at a local scale, there are other systems we can use that provide a better visual representation of the area. Furthermore, since we intend to measure distances, we can't use a CRS that uses longitude and latitude, as a degree is not a constant unit of measurement and typically isn't used for these purposes. Instead, we'll want to use a CRS that uses feet or meters. Last, the MARTA stations are from a different source (Fulton County GIS) and are not going to share the same CRS as the TIGER layers. We'll need to convert all our layers to the same CRS.

In the United States, the State Plane Coordinate System is typically used for mapping local areas within states. Most states are divided into one to three state plane zones (larger states have additional zones) that are designed for optimal representation of features at that scale. The most common state plane systems use a measurement grid that's in feet, but there's a complementary set that uses meters. You can search the web to identify the locations of the zones (the National Geodetic Survey is a good source `https://www.ngs.noaa.gov/SPCS/maps.shtml`) and can use the Spatial Reference website `http://spatialreference.org/` to look up the appropriate reference codes. Georgia is divided into two zones, east and west, and our study area falls in the western zone. The unique identifier for the feet-based version of the western Georgia zone is 2240.

Third, our geographic features do not contain the public transit ridership data we need. GIS boundary files seldom come with data attached; the attributes are limited to basic identifiers. We need to prepare and join an ACS data table to the census tracts using an identifier that they share in common. Once the table is joined to the tracts, we can map the data and use it as part of our analysis.

We can tackle the first two steps at the same time. Once we select the areas we need, we can reproject them as we save those areas to new layers. Let's begin with the census tracts. We can access and view various properties of the tracts layer by selecting it in the layers panel, right-clicking, and choosing an option. Choose the Open attribute table option in the middle of the menu (Figure 10.7). This table contains one record for every census tract that's part of our layer, and each record is tied to the geographic feature that it relates to. You can click on a column header to sort data in the table by that value. We can select attributes in the table to choose features, or out in the map canvas, we can select features to see what their attributes are.

The TIGER files provide unique identifiers for every feature. The GEOID column is the unique FIPS code that contains the two-digit state, three-digit county, and six-digit tract codes. These codes are also broken out into individual columns to make attribute querying simpler. There are columns with names that we can use as labels. The columns at the end of the table, such as the area of each tract that's composed of land and water in square meters, are provided for reference. Using the attribute table, we can select tracts within the three counties we're interested in using their county codes.

On the toolbar above the attribute table, hit the expression button, which is the yellow box with the Greek sigma symbol in front of it (Figure 10.8). In the Expression builder window, hit the little arrow to open the options under Fields and Values. This displays all the fields that are in the table. Select COUNTYFP and double-click it to add it to the expression on the left. Hit the equals operator button that's above the expression. Back in the middle column, with COUNTYFP selected, hit the button that says All unique and that displays all the possible county values that are in the table. Scroll down and double-click '063' to add it to the expression. Then click in the expression box and type the word OR. Then repeat the process to add the additional criteria COUNTYFP = '089' OR 'COUNTYFP = '121' (Figure 10.9)

Hit the Select features button to execute the statement. The expression builder is picky; the syntax must be absolutely correct. Fields are surrounded in double

FIGURE 10.7 ● ACCESSING LAYER PROPERTIES AND ATTRIBUTE TABLE

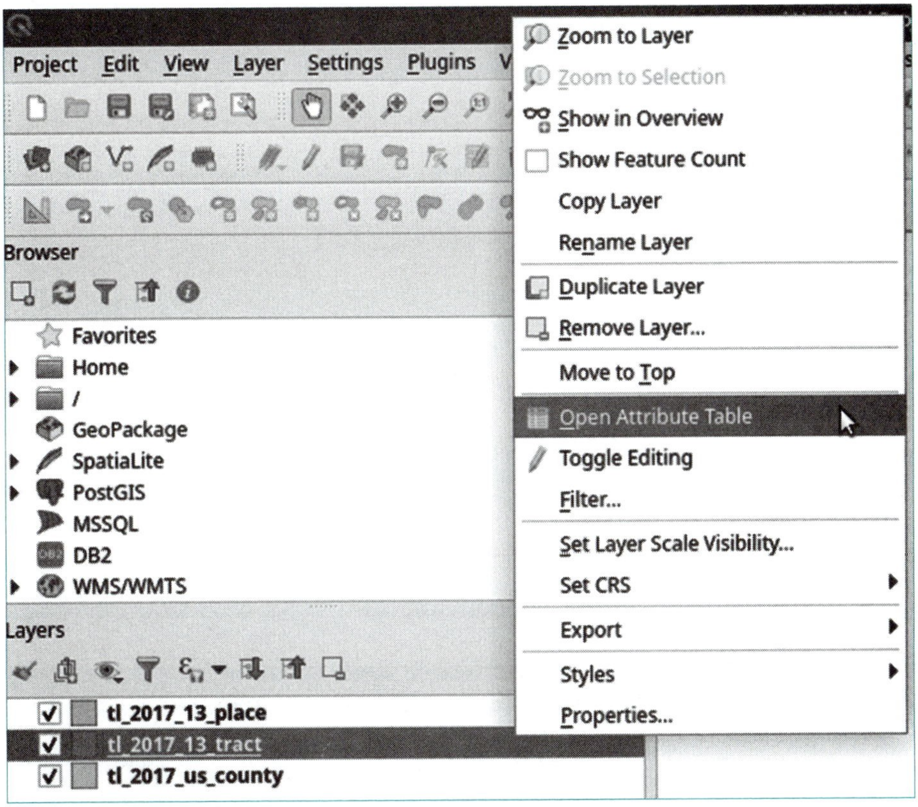


FIGURE 10.8 ● ATTRIBUTE TABLE VIEW AND LAUNCHING THE EXPRESSION BUILDER

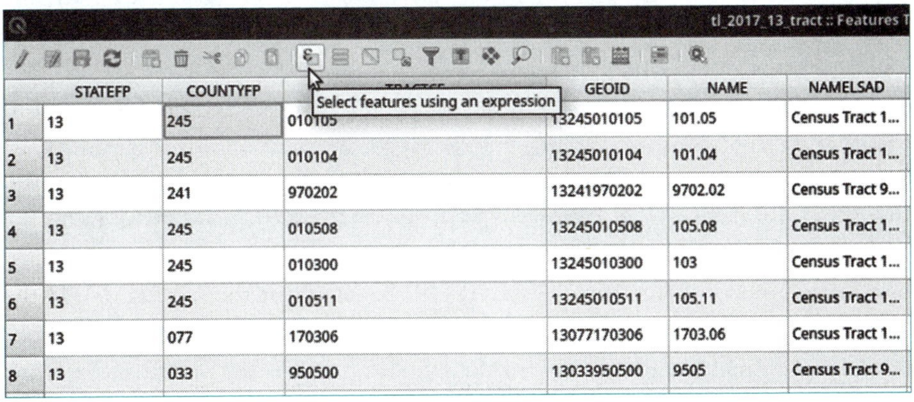

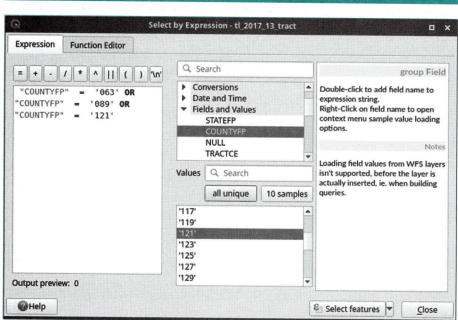

**FIGURE 10.9  ●  SELECT FEATURES USING AN EXPRESSION**

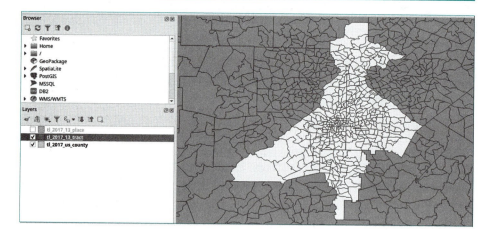

**FIGURE 10.10  ●  SELECTED FEATURES: ATLANTA METRO CENSUS TRACTS**

quotes, text values stored in the table must be surrounded with single quotes. Close the expression menu and close the attribute table. Uncheck the places layer to turn it off, and zoom in to the area with the selected tracts. Your result should look like Figure 10.10.

To save this as a new layer, select the tracts in the layers panel, right-click, and choose Export—Save Selected Features As. When saving new files, you should *always* browse to a location and save the files in the same place relative to your other project files. In the Save menu, hit the button with the dots to browse to Chapter 10 tiger folder and name the files tracts_marta. Hit Save in the browse menu. Back in the Export menu, hit the little globe button beside the CRS option. This brings up the Coordinate Reference System Selector. Type in the number 2240 in the filter menu. In the results at the bottom, you should see an option for NAD83 / Georgia West (ftUS), EPSG 2240 (Figure 10.11). Select this option, and hit OK. Back on the export screen, your menu should look like Figure 10.12. Make sure that the boxes that say Save only selected features and Add saved file to map are checked. Hit OK. The menu will

---

**FIGURE 10.12** ● SAVING SELECTED VECTOR LAYER FEATURES AS A NEW LAYER

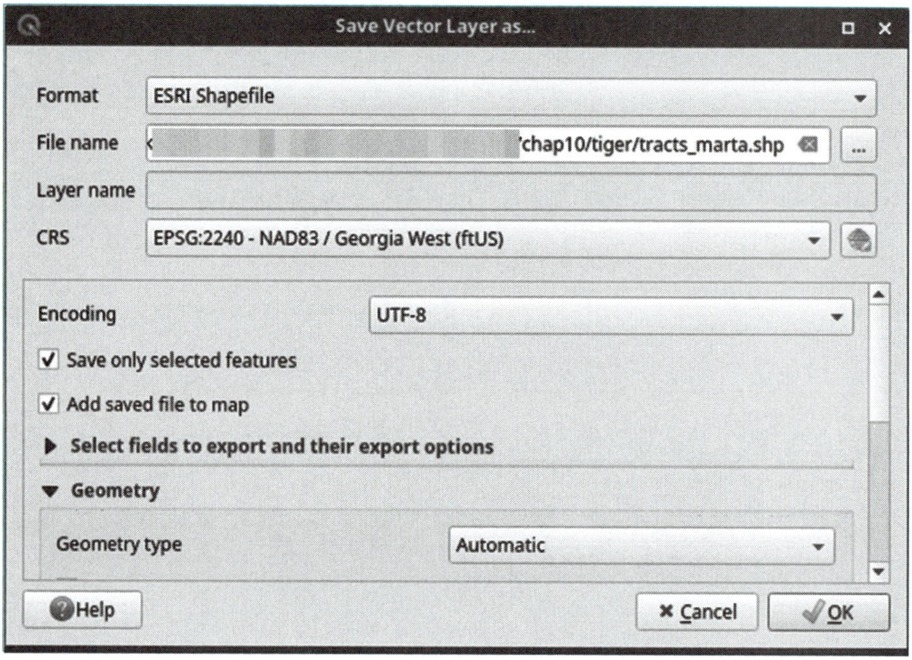

---

close, and you'll see the new tracts_marta layer that has just the tracts in the counties we're interested in added to the map canvas.

If we changed the CRS for the layer, shouldn't it look different? And why would it line up correctly with the other layers in the map if the two systems don't match? We'll return to these points in a moment. Let's create the extracts for the other two layers first. This will be easy, as we have fewer areas to select.

Activate the places layer, and make sure it is above the tracts_marta layer in the layers panel. Select the places layer to activate it. In the toolbar, select the Identify Features button, which is a blue circle with the letter "i" inside it and a white arrow. Click on the large place that's roughly in the center of our marta_census tracts. An Identify Results window pops up on the right and summarizes the attributes (taken from the table) for the feature we selected. If you clicked the right place, Atlanta should appear in the menu as the NAME attribute (Figure 10.13).

Close the Identify Results window. In the toolbar, select the Select Features Button, which is a yellow box with a white arrow beside it. With the places layer selected in

FIGURE 10.13 ● IDENTIFY FEATURES TOOL

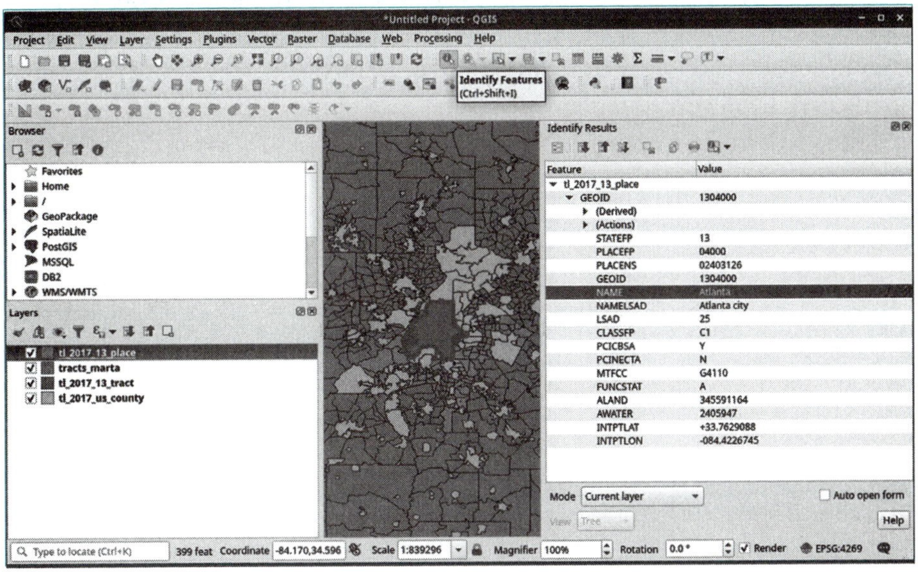

the Layers panel, click on the feature for Atlanta, which highlights it in yellow. Select the place layer in the panel, right-click, and choose Export—Save Selected Features As. Browse to Chapter 10 tiger folder and name the new file atlanta. Under CRS, if you hit the drop-down menu, you should see an option for EPSG 2240 NAD83 Georgia West, since this is a system that we used recently. Select it. Hit OK, and our new feature will be added to the map.

Turn off all the layers except the county layer, so we can see the counties more clearly. Select the counties, right-click, and choose Properties at the bottom. The properties menu is a large menu that lets us modify many different aspects of the layer. On the left-hand side, click on the tab for Labels. At the top of the labels window, choose the drop down for Single labels. Under the Label with drop down, choose the option for Name to use this attribute to label the features. Click OK. You should see the names of the counties on the map.

Hit the Select Features button. While holding down the Control key (Ctrl) on your computer, click on Clayton, DeKalb, and Fulton counties to select them, turning them yellow. The control key allows you to add additional features to your selection. If you select features without keeping this key pressed, you will undo your previous selection and can select only one feature at a time. (*Note:* If you are using a Mac, you may need to use the Command key instead.)

Once you've selected the counties, export these features as marta_counties in the tiger folder, and make sure to change the CRS to 2240. Once the counties are added to the map, rearrange the order of the layers so that atlanta is on top, marta tracts are in the middle, and marta counties are on the bottom. We no longer need any of the original layers, since we've created our extracts. Select each of the original layers, right-click, and choose the remove option.

Now, let's return to the CRS question. Why don't these layers look different since we reprojected them? There are two things going on. First, the map canvas is set to a specific CRS independent of the CRS of the specific layers. The map canvas adopts the CRS of the first layer that's added. If we add a layer that does not match the CRS of the canvas, QGIS temporarily reprojects or redraws the layer on the fly, so that it can be drawn in the canvas and will overlay properly with the other layers. The intention is to do us a favor and make all our layers work together.

In reality, this can be detrimental. Even though the layers appear to align, they are actually stored in different reference systems. If we attempt to use any of the processing or analytical tools, we will get warnings or error messages because the layers actually do not align. To see what our new layers really look like, select the atlanta layer, right-click, choose Set CRS—Set Project CRS From Layer (Figure 10.14). This resets the CRS of the map canvas to match that layer. You'll notice that three things will change: (1) the shape of the features will look different, (2) the coordinates in

**FIGURE 10.14  ●  RESETING THE PROJECT WINDOW TO MATCH LAYER CRS**

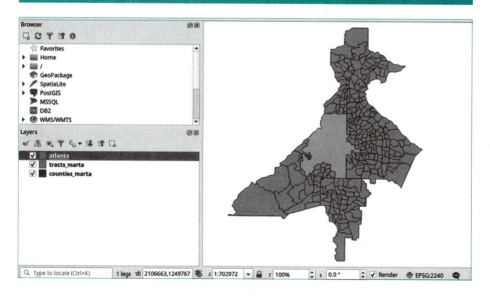

the status bar will be much larger (indicating we are not using degrees of longitude and latitude any more), and (3) the EPSG code for the project will now be 2240, indicating that our map canvas is now in the same system as the layers. How can you be sure all the layers are in the same system? If you select a layer, right-click, select properties, and go to the information tab, it will identify the CRS for the layer.

Before we go any further, we should save our project. All the extracts that we've created so far *have already been saved* as we've run processes that have created new files out in our file system. In saving this project, we'll save links to the files in our layers panel and their drawing order. Go to Project—Save As, navigate to Chapter 10 folder (*not* into the tiger folder) and save the project as transit. The project file is now linked to our data files; thus, you always have to think carefully about where the project is stored in relation to the underlying datasets. If you move a project to another location, the datasets must travel with it; otherwise, the links between the project and data become severed. If you want to share your project with someone, you have to zip the project and all the data files associated with it together and share the ZIP file. You *cannot* just give them the project file.

We still have to bring the subway stations into our project. Coordinate systems are a common source of confusion and bewilderment for new GIS users. To avoid potential problems, it's often best to modify and reproject layers that don't share the same CRS as your project's layers *outside* of the project, and then bring the layers into the project once they match.

Go to Project—New so we're working from a clean slate. Go to Layer—Add Layer—Add Vector Layer and browse to Chapter 10 marta folder. Select the rail stations, and add them to your blank project. The status bar indicates this layer is in EPSG 4326, which is a system called WGS 84. This is a very common system that uses longitude and latitude that's used throughout the world as a basic system for exchanging data. Select the stations in the layers panel, right-click, and choose Export—Save Features As. Browse to Chapter 10 marta folder and save the file as stations. Change the CRS to 2240. Once the file is added, select it, right-click, Set CRS—Set Project CRS From Layer. You'll notice that the stations will change in orientation a little bit.

Go up to Project—Open Recent, and select our transit project. When prompted to save the current project, say no. We created our newly projected stations file, and it's saved in our folder, so there's nothing else that's important to save here. Back in the transit project, add our new stations file. Make sure it's at the top of the layers panel, so it draws over top of the other layers (Figure 10.15). Hit the little blue disk button on the toolbar to save the project.

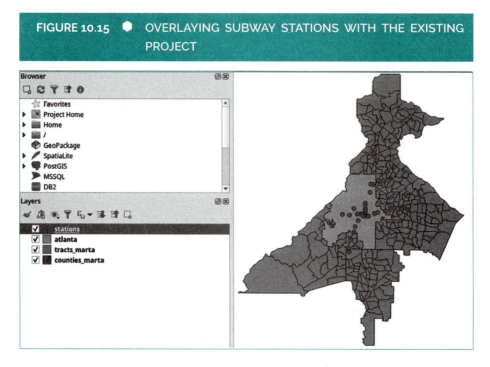

**FIGURE 10.15  ●  OVERLAYING SUBWAY STATIONS WITH THE EXISTING PROJECT**

## Symbolizing Layers

The purpose of the Atlanta and county layers is to provide some reference, but the Atlanta layer is covering up many of the tracts, and the county layer is covered by the tracts. Let's change the symbolization to make them visible simultaneously. Rearrange the layers in this order: stations, atlanta, counties, tracts.

Select atlanta in the layers panel, right-click and choose Properties. Click on the Symbology tab. In the Fill box at the top, select the Simple fill option that's directly below it. Under Fill style, change the drop down from Solid to No Brush; this makes the layer hollow. Change the stroke width to .46 by clicking the up arrow beside the value. Change the Stroke style from Solid to Dot Line (Figure 10.16). Click OK. Since the fill for the Atlanta layer is now hollow and the line is thicker and different from the tracts, both are clearly visible and distinguishable on the map.

Select the counties layer and open its properties. In the symbology tab, select Simple fill. Change the Fill style to No Brush. Change the Stroke width to .86. Click on the color in the Stroke color box. Using any one of the color palettes, change the color from black to a dull gray. Click OK in the color palette and Apply in the Symbology tab. Then select the Labels tab. Hit the top drop down to select Single Labels. Under the Label with drop down, select the NAMELSAD field (Figure 10.17). In the Text settings, change the size of the font to 8.0. Then click on the Buffer settings in the

## FIGURE 10.16  ●  LAYER PROPERTIES SYMBOLOGY WINDOW

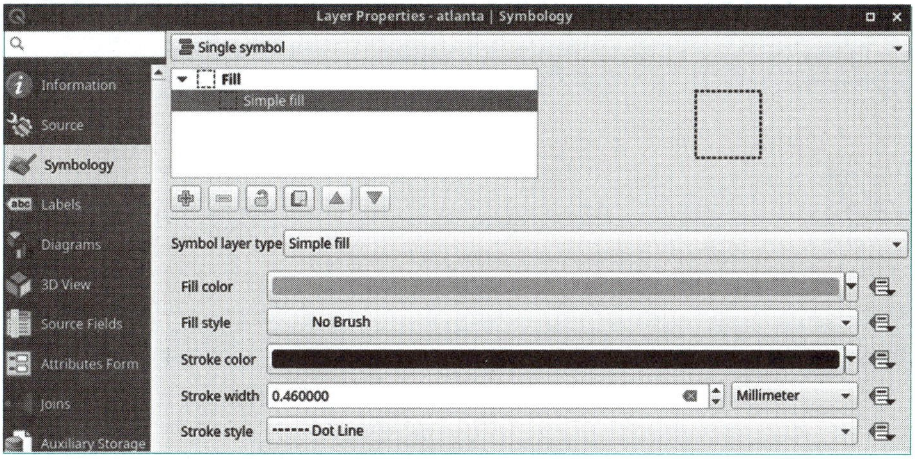

## FIGURE 10.17  ●  LAYER PROPERTIES LABELS WINDOW

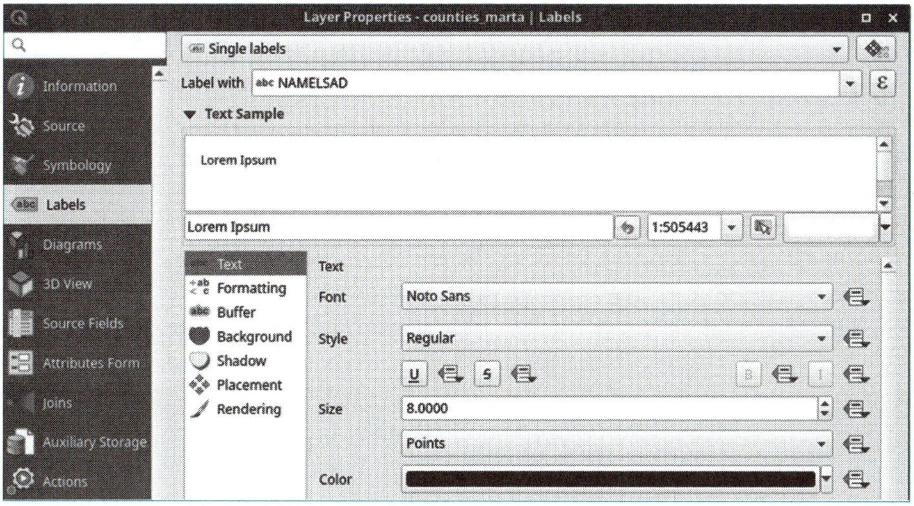

menu, and check the box that says Draw text buffer. Click OK. Now the counties are hollow, and we clearly see labels for them.

We're going to symbolize the tracts by transit ridership in the next section, so we don't need to modify their symbology yet. If your subway stations are a contrasting or garish color, go into the symbology menu and change the color to something else. Your map should resemble Figure 10.18. Save your project.

**FIGURE 10.18 ● PROJECT LAYERS RESYMBOLIZED**

## Joining Attributes and Mapping Data

The ability to join vanilla data tables to GIS features to visualize and incorporate that data into geographic analyses is one of the greatest powers of GIS. It's also one of the greatest sources of frustration for new users, because the data tables must meet strict requirements in terms of how they are structured. These requirements are essentially the same as the requirements for relational database tables that we covered in Chapter 5. Each row must represent a piece of geography, and each column contains attributes for the geography. There must be a unique ID column that will match the unique ID in the shapefile, and in your data table, your IDs should be stored as text and not numbers. Depending on the source of your census data, you may need to either concatenate or split your GEOID codes to get them to match the shapefile, using the spreadsheet functions we've demonstrated throughout the book. Your data table cannot contain multiple header rows (you can only have one), titles, footnotes, totals and subtotals, formulas, or any extraneous information. Column headings should be short, not begin with numbers, and not contain any punctuation other than under-scores. You should never mix numeric values and text values in the same column. If you ignore these rules, your joins won't work, and you won't receive any helpful error or diagnostic messages.

**FIGURE 10.19 ● ACS SPREADSHEET FOR COMMUTERS WHO USE PUBLIC TRANSIT**

B1 geoidshort

| | A | B | C | D | E | F | G | H | I | J | K |
|---|---|---|---|---|---|---|---|---|---|---|---|
| 1 | geoidlong | geoidshort | AreaName | Worker16 | Worker_moe | Commuters | Com_moe | Pubtrans | Pub_moe | Pub_pct | Pct_moe |
| 2 | 14000US13063040202 | 13063040202 | Census Tract 402.02, Clayton County, Georgia | 1079 | 177 | 1062 | 175 | 81 | 55 | 7.5 | 5 |
| 3 | 14000US13063040203 | 13063040203 | Census Tract 402.03, Clayton County, Georgia | 1503 | 269 | 1458 | 262 | 73 | 58 | 4.9 | 3.9 |
| 4 | 14000US13063040204 | 13063040204 | Census Tract 402.04, Clayton County, Georgia | 1753 | 223 | 1741 | 255 | 116 | 84 | 6.6 | 4.7 |
| 5 | 14000US13063040302 | 13063040302 | Census Tract 403.02, Clayton County, Georgia | 2089 | 297 | 1968 | 343 | 94 | 49 | 4.5 | 2.4 |
| 6 | 14000US13063040303 | 13063040303 | Census Tract 403.03, Clayton County, Georgia | 2278 | 404 | 2173 | 381 | 95 | 90 | 4.2 | 4.1 |
| 7 | 14000US13063040306 | 13063040306 | Census Tract 403.06, Clayton County, Georgia | 1578 | 272 | 1574 | 286 | 55 | 67 | 3.5 | 4.2 |
| 8 | 14000US13063040307 | 13063040307 | Census Tract 403.07, Clayton County, Georgia | 1879 | 269 | 1859 | 320 | 10 | 16 | 0.5 | 0.9 |
| 9 | 14000US13063040308 | 13063040308 | Census Tract 403.08, Clayton County, Georgia | 1819 | 273 | 1775 | 347 | 30 | 37 | 1.6 | 2.1 |
| 10 | 14000US13063040407 | 13063040407 | Census Tract 404.07, Clayton County, Georgia | 1627 | 288 | 1556 | 260 | 34 | 30 | 2.1 | 1.9 |

Minimize QGIS for the moment, navigate to Chapter 10 acs folder, and open the commuters.xlsx spreadsheet in Calc. QGIS supports spreadsheet tables in Calc and Excel formats. For table joins, it's simpler to use one of these formats and not CSV files, as it's easier to preserve data types in a spreadsheet. As mentioned at the beginning of this exercise, this data was extracted from ACS Table B08301, which you can retrieve from any of the sources we've covered in this book (you could also extract it from the data profiles from the Missouri Census Data Center Dexter tool introduced in Chapter 6, specifying 140 as the SumLev code and the five-digit FipCo values for the counties). It contains the minimum number of necessary columns along with percentage of total commuters who use public transit. These percentages are the most important values in the table, as it wouldn't make sense to map total number of riders (one tract may have more riders simply because more people live there). The names of the columns were changed to something meaningful (Figure 10.19).

This table has two GEOID columns: (1) a long one with the full summary level and fips information and (2) a short one with just the fips codes. The TIGER Line shapefiles use the latter as an ID, so the shorter code is the one we can use for the match. Close the spreadsheet.

Maximize QGIS. Go to Layer—Add Layer—Add Vector Layer. Browse to Chapter 10 acs folder, and select the commuter.xlsx spreadsheet (if you don't see any files, make sure the filter in the lower right-hand corner is set to display all files). Hit Add to add it to the project, then close the menu. The spreadsheet appears in the layer panel, but nothing appears in the map canvas. That's because spreadsheets are not actually vector files; they contain no geometry so there is nothing to visualize, but you can select the file and open its attribute table to verify it was imported correctly.

To do a join, select the *shapefile* in the layers panel that you wish to join the table to. Select the tracts and open the properties menu. Click on the tab that says Joins. In the Joins menu, click the green plus symbol at the bottom to add a new join. In the Add Vector Join, the Join layer is the data table commuters_data. The Join field is the unique ID in the table, which is geoidshort. The Target field is the matching unique ID in the shapefile, which is GEOID. At the bottom of the screen, check the Custom field name box and delete the value in the box (Figure 10.20). This will prevent QGIS from creating an ID name that's too long for our joined fields. Click OK, and then OK again in the properties menu.

Seemingly nothing has happened, but the table has been joined to the file. To verify this, select the tracts and open the attribute table. Scroll to the right of the table, and you will see that all the fields that were part of the table are now joined to the shapefile. If there were any nonmatching records, they fall out of the result. If you do *not* see the data but instead have null values, there's something wrong with the join. You may have chosen ID columns that didn't match, so you should check the join and edit if necessary. If the join still doesn't work, your data table may violate the rules somehow: Maybe your ID codes are saved as numbers or there are illegal rows or values somewhere. You'd have to undo the join and go back to your spreadsheet to verify.

At this stage, we could map the joined data. However, since we plan to go beyond mapping and use these attributes in an analysis, we'll need to take an extra step and make this join permanent. With the exception of mapping the data, other operations like measuring distance or selecting features based on the joined data won't work because the data table and shapefile are loosely coupled together within this single project, and the joined data still resides in the spreadsheet table.

We just have to save our tracts shapefile as a new shapefile, and the joined data will become a permanent part of the new file. Select the tracts layer in the panel, right-click, Export—Save Features As. Save the file as tracts_data in Chapter 10 tiger folder. Make sure the CRS is set to 2240. Hit OK to add the new file to the map. Open its attribute table and you will see the new columns on the right. Since we don't need the tracts_marta or the spreadsheet file anymore, you can select, right-click, and remove them from the project. Save the project.

Let's map the public transit data! Open the properties menu for tracts_data, and go to the Symbology tab. Select Simple fill. Change the Stroke width to .16 by manually adjusting the values. At the top of the menu, change the Single symbol drop down to Graduated. In the Column drop down, select Pub_pct, which is the percentage of commuters who ride public transit. For the Color ramp, you can change the drop down (arrow on the right) to any scheme you'd like, but make sure it is a single color that varies in hue from light to dark. Underneath the empty classes window beside Mode, change the value from Equal Interval to Natural Breaks. Hit the Classify button. This populates the Classes window with the data categories. Under this box on the far right is an option for changing the number of classes; we'll keep the default of 5 (Figure 10.21). Click OK.

You should have a thematic map of public transit ridership by census tract. In the layers panel, you can see the classification scheme for the tracts. If you would like to know how many tracts are in each category, select the tracts, right-click, and check the option that says Show Feature Count (Figure 10.22). Save your work.

We classified the data into categories using the natural breaks method. This formula determines where the largest gaps or breaks are in a given range of values and creates class divisions where these breaks occur. You can modify the data classes in the Symbology tab by changing the number of classes and the classification type under the mode drop down. Natural breaks is a good default as it is less arbitrary than other methods. Other classification options are quantile (categories that have an equal number of data points in each), equal interval (categories that have an equal range of data values in each), and manual (choose what you want the categories to be). Quantiles are useful for certain kinds of statistical and ranking analyses but can be arbitrary. Equal intervals is a good alternative, but if your data contains a number of outliers, this will skew the classes and your map will look too generalized. Manual is useful if you have outside criteria that you need to apply, or if you need to isolate certain

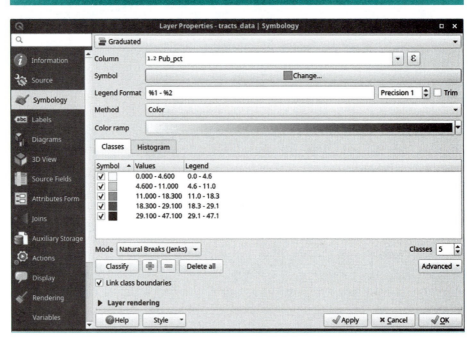

FIGURE 10.21  ●  SYMBOL PROPERTIES FOR CREATING GRADUATED MAPS

values or split positive and negative values into different categories. Experiment with the classes, and see how it effects the map.

## Geographic Analysis

We can see there are clusters where transit ridership is higher, in the southern part of Atlanta, the central portion of Fulton County, and the central portion of DeKalb County. Transit usage appears high around many stations, but there are exceptions, particularly in the northern part of the system. It's important to remember that this data measures all public transit users, which includes the subway and buses. While the ACS does break this data out into finer categories by mode of ridership, those estimates are too unreliable at the census tract level.

There are a few approaches for generating basic statistics for a variable. Select the tracts layer in the panel to make it active. On the tool bar, click on the purple sigma symbol (resembles letter "E"). With tracts selected as the layer, select Pub_pct in the drop down for the field. This provides us with basic stats such as the count, mean, median, range, sum, and a few others. The mean is 8.7%, while the median is 5.9%. This tool provides us with stats on the fly. If we wanted to save this summary in a file, we could go to Vector—Analysis Tools—Basic Statistics and run a similar process. Close the menu.

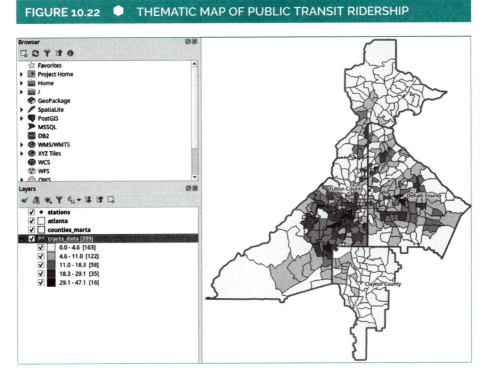

FIGURE 10.22    ●    THEMATIC MAP OF PUBLIC TRANSIT RIDERSHIP

The map illustrates that there are a number of tracts near subway stations that have low ridership. What if we wanted to select those tracts so we could study them in more detail? One option would be to use Vector—Analysis Tools—Count Points in Polygon. This will create a new layer that's identical to the tracts layer, except it will have a new column that counts the number of stations in the tracts. That would allow us to incorporate that count into a query in the expression builder in order to select tracts with stations that have low transit usage. That would be a poor technique to use in this example: If you study the map, you'll see that many stations sit on the boundary of a tract, so we would arbitrarily be counting one tract as having service and the other tract as not.

A better approach would be to select all the tracts that are within a certain distance of each station. We can achieve this with buffer tool, which allows us to draw a circle at a fixed distance around each station. We can select all the tracts that intersect the buffer and run a query to select the low ridership tracts.

Go to Vector—Geoprocessing Tools—Buffer. For the input layer, change the option to stations. For distance, change the value to 5280, which is the number of feet in a mile. Scroll down and check the box that says dissolve results (i.e., if a buffer overlaps another buffer, merge them together and don't overlap them). Click Run in background. You should see the result in Figure 10.23, where a new buffered

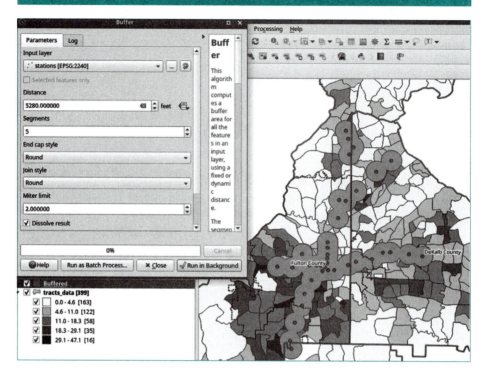

**FIGURE 10.23**    ●    BUFFER TOOL AND RESULTS

layer is added. If you place it above the tracts but below the stations, you can see how the circle extends for a mile around each station and how it overlaps with the tracts.

Next, open the attribute table for the tracts. Click on the button for the expression builder, which we used earlier for selecting tracts that were in the three counties. In the center column under Fields and Values, click on Pub_pct to add it to the expression. Then type <8.7. This is the mean value for transit ridership that we calculated in the statistics tool. Hit Select Features, then close the builder and the table. All tracts where less than 8.7% of commuters use public transit are selected in yellow.

Go up to Vector—Research Tools—Select by Location. Under "Select features from," choose tracts; check the intersect box; under "By comparing to the features from," select the Buffer layer; and "Modify current selection by" selecting within the current selection. This will select all the currently selected tracts (which have lower than average ridership) that intersect the buffer. Click Run. You should see the result in Figure 10.24 that displays these tracts. To permanently capture this selection, right-click the tracts in the layers panel, choose Export—Save Selected Features As, and save this selection in Chapter 10 tiger folder. Save your project.

**FIGURE 10.24    ⬢    SELECT BY LOCATION TOOL AND RESULTS**

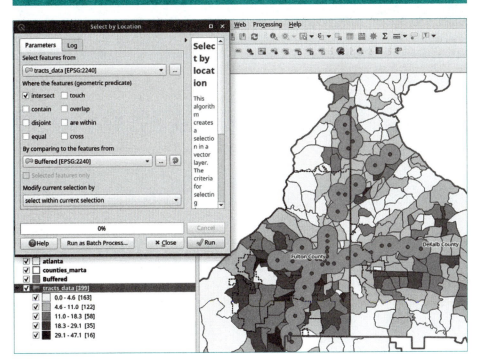

Voila! You've just performed a basic GIS analysis. You brought TIGER data, ACS data, and subway locations together to answer a research question. MARTA officials may want to survey the populations in these tracts to discover why they aren't riding the subway as much and may want to steer advertising and promotion toward those areas. To provide some context for these areas, you can enable the OpenStreetMap to see roads, buildings, green space, and water features (see InfoBox 10.3).

This represents the tip of the iceberg in terms of possible analyses. You could also measure the distance from each tract to the closest subway station to approximate how far commuters would need to travel to get to the station. You can go to Vector—Analysis Tools—Distance Matrix, and choose from a variety of options: measure all distances, closest N distances, or summary distance measures. The output will be a text file that you can import into a spreadsheet. When you're measuring distances with this tool, the distance from a polygon (area) to a point is measured from the closest edge of the area. It would be better to measure from the center, not the edge. To do this, you can use Vector—Geometry Tools—Centroids. This will take the polygon census tract layer and convert it to a point layer, where the point represents the center of the tract. Then you can measure the distance from these centroids to each of the stations.

> ✓ **INFOBOX 10.3 ADD THE OPENSTREETMAP TO YOUR MAP**
>
> If you quickly want to add a base map—an underlying reference map that provides context for the features in your thematic map—QGIS has a number of tools that allow you to connect to different web-mapping services. For example, to add the free and open source OpenStreetMap to your project, you need to do the following:
>
> 1. Make sure you have a network or wifi connection.
>
> 2. In the browser menu, select the XYZ Tiles data source, right-click and select New connection.
>
> 3. In the Name box, type OSM, and in the URL box, enter http://tile.openstreetmap.org/{z}/{x}/{y}.png.
>
> 4. Hit OK. In the browser menu, select the down arrow beside XYZ tiles to display your OSM layer. Drag it into the window to visualize the layer.
>
> 5. The default CRS for OSM is 3857 Pseudo Mercator. The project window will update to reflect this. You can select one of your existing layers and reset the project to that layer, and the OSM layer will reproject.
>
> 6. Right-click on a blank area of the toolbar, and check the Tile Scale Panel. This slider gives you finer control over the zoom of the OSM map. To use it, the project window must be set to CRS 3857.
>
> 7. In the symbol menu in the Symbology tab, you can adjust the opacity (i.e., transparency) of each of your vector layers using the slider bar. This allows you to see the OSM features under the vectors.

If you want to be even more precise, you can measure the distance from the center of the census tract's population distribution to the station. Unlike the geographic center, the population center accounts for the fact that populations may not be evenly distributed within an area. The Census Bureau publishes population centroids for several types of geography as a series of longitude and latitude coordinates (`https://www.census.gov/geographies/reference-files/2010/geo/2010-centers-population.html`). A population centroid that appears in the middle of an area indicates that the population is evenly distributed across the area, otherwise, if the centroid is offset, the distribution is concentrated more in the direction of the offset. You can convert these coordinates to a layer (InfoBox 10.4), join data to them, and measure the distances from them to the stations.

## Map Layout

Finally, let's begin to illustrate how you can create a finished map. Before we enter the map layout, zoom out to the full extent of the counties, and unselect all the selected

✓ **INFOBOX 10.4 PLOTTING COORDINATE DATA**

If you have a data file where each row represents a feature or event such as a business, a tree, a crime, or a traffic accident, and the attributes of the feature include longitude and latitude coordinates (or any type of geographic coordinate), you can plot those features in GIS using the coordinates, and then you can save the plot as a new shapefile of point features.

To plot coordinate data in QGIS, you need to do the following:

1. Store data in a plain text format like a CSV, and store each X and Y coordinate in individual columns (not as a pair in the same column).

2. It's best to plot and convert data in a blank project. Once the data is ready, you can add it to an existing project.

3. Go to Layer—Add Layer—Add Delimited Text Layer.

4. In the dialog box, indicate what delimiter is used to separate values in the file (comma, tab, etc.), which columns contain the X and Y coordinates, and what the CRS for the coordinates are. Longitude is always the X coordinate and latitude is the Y coordinate. If the data is from the Census Bureau or another U.S. government agency, the CRS is likely to be NAD 83. Otherwise, it is probably WGS 84.

5. Add the data to the map to plot it. Once plotted, select it in the layers panel, right-click, and Export the file as a new layer to save it in a vector format like a shapefile. As you're doing this, you can also reproject the layer to a new CRS if need be. This step is crucial—if you plot the coordinates but neglect to convert them to a vector format, you won't be able to use the layer in conjunction with other layers.

If you have address-based data that lacks coordinates, you can geocode the addresses to obtain them. We'll discuss geocoding in Chapter 11.

tracts (on the toolbar, there is a button with a yellow box and a red X beside it—the deselect features tool). Uncheck the buffer and the new tract selection layer to turn them off. On the tool bar, there are two buttons to the right of the Save and Save as buttons (blue disks) that are the new map layout and map composer buttons (you can also access these via the Project menu). Click the new map button, and when prompted, enter a name for your map.

This launches the map composer, a dedicated area for creating finished maps. The first thing you should do is right-click on the blank sheet and choose page properties. Change the page size from A4 to ANSI A, which is the standard $8\frac{1}{2} \times 11$ paper size used in North America. Given the orientation of our study area, change the orientation from Landscape to Portrait.

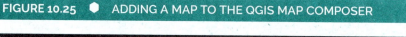

**FIGURE 10.25** ● ADDING A MAP TO THE QGIS MAP COMPOSER

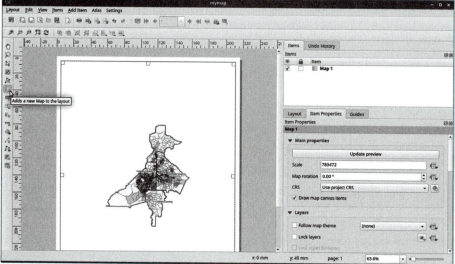

On the toolbar on the left, about halfway down the bar is a button with a blank sheet of paper and a green plus symbol. This is the add map button. Click this button, and drag and draw a box that fits just within the page layout. When you release the mouse button, whatever is currently in the map canvas will be displayed (Figure 10.25). The map is now an item that is part of the layout. If you select the white arrow button in the toolbar, you can click on different items to toggle between them. You can tell that an item is selected if it is outlined with squares appearing on each corner and side. You can resize an item by clicking on one of these squares and dragging it with the mouse. Once an item is selected, properties that are specific to that type of item become active in the menu on the right, and you can modify them if need be.

The zoom tools in the map layout do not function in the same manner as the other zoom tools. Within the map composer, the zoom buttons adjust the view of the page layout, which is analogous to holding a piece of paper closer or farther from your face. Likewise, with an item selected, you can drag the item around on the screen, but that's not going to alter the extent of the geography that's within the map item. To modify the position of the geography, you can activate the move item content button (fourth from top, blue arrows on paper), and this allows you to modify the extent. To change the zoom, you select the map item and do one of two things. If you have a mouse, you can use the mouse wheel to zoom in or out. Alternatively, in the Item Properties menu, there is a scale value that you can modify by hand. A smaller number will zoom you in, while a larger one zooms you out. Modify the

FIGURE 10.26 ● QGIS MAP COMPOSER ITEM PROPERTIES MENU FOR LEGENDS

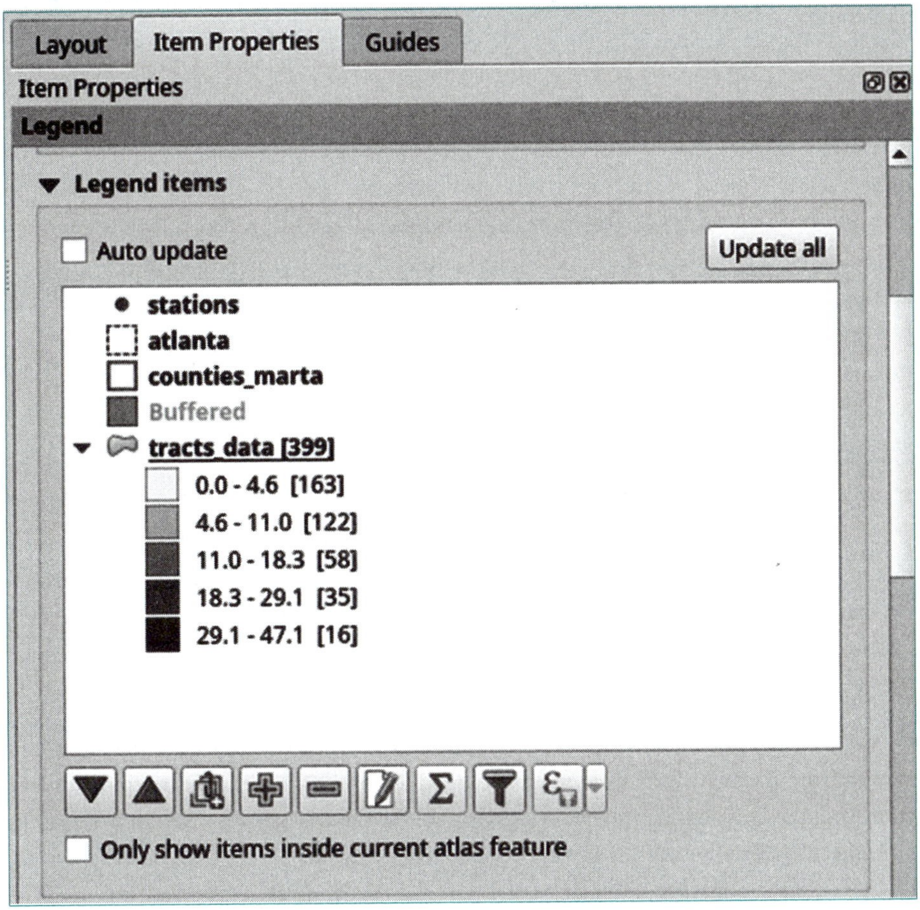

value so that your map fits nicely within the canvas. It takes a bit of practice to get it right. If you scroll down in the Item Properties menu, you can click a box to turn on a frame.

Every individual property of every item can be modified. The add legend button appears in the middle of the toolbar (it has a small series of colored boxes). Click this button, click on the map, and when prompted, hit OK. By default, the legend contains everything that was present in the primary data view. To modify it, select the legend, and in the Item Properties, scroll down to the legend items and uncheck the Auto update box (Figure 10.26). Once you do, you can modify each element: Use the arrow buttons to move a layer up or down, select a layer and hit the red minus button to remove it, select the piece of paper and pencil button to change the text for the element, and select the sigma button to remove the feature counts. Below the Legend items, you can modify the fonts for each element (type, face, size, and color), as well as the spacing and position between legend items, you can draw a frame around the legend, and so on.

There are additional buttons for adding text (for a title and source information), a scalebar, a north arrow (choose images option, under item properties open search directories menu), images, and shapes. Spend some time experimenting with the tools, and consult the QGIS documentation at `https://qgis.org/en/docs/index.html` to learn how to fully master map layout. When creating a map, you want to balance the different items on the page and provide enough clear and concise description in the title, notes, and legend that convey what the map is depicting, similar to Figure 10.27. Using the toolbar at the top, you can export your map out as an image (TIF, PNG, JPG), PDF, or SVG file. At this point, the map becomes a stand-alone non-GIS file that can be shared with anyone.

If you close the map layout and return to the primary screen, you can get back to it by pressing the map layout button (piece of paper with wrench) and choosing the map you want to open. If you make any changes in the data view, like reclassifying data or adding labels, those changes are not reflected in your map layout, unless you explicitly select the map item and in the properties click the Update preview button.

If you want to share some preliminary results with someone, but don't want to go through the process of creating a finished map, then back in the primary data view, you can go to Project—Import/Export and save the map that's in your map canvas as an image (essentially creating a screenshot).

## Next Steps

This chapter provided a whirlwind tour of mapping, the Census Bureau's geographic data files, and GIS with QGIS, so you can take your visualization and analysis of census data to the next level. There is a lot more to learn, and we could only scratch the surface here. For a fuller explanation of the features and functions of QGIS, consult the user documentation on the QGIS website. There are a number of useful technical guides such as *Learning QGIS* and *Mastering QGIS* that are devoted to covering many facets of the software and guides like *QGIS Map Design* that focus more on cartography (Graser, 2016; Graser & Peterson, 2016; Menke, Smith, Pirelli, & Van Hoesen, 2016). The Open Source Geospatial Consortium provides a searchable directory of GIS tutorials written by instructors from around the

**FIGURE 10.27  ⬡  EXAMPLE OF A FINISHED MAP: METRO ATLANTA COMMUTERS**

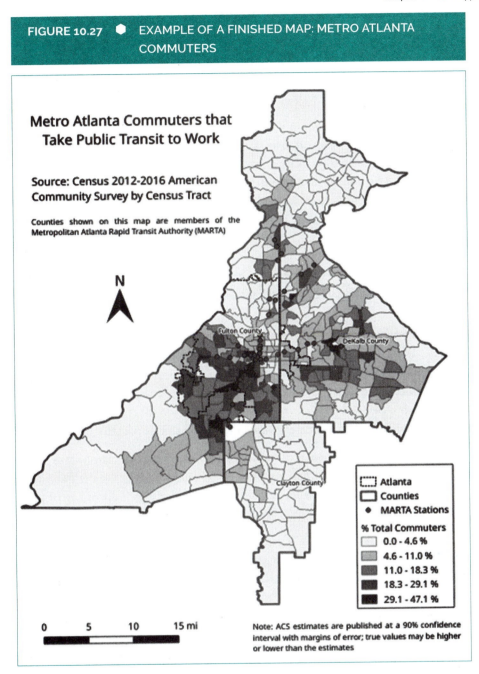

Metro Atlanta Commuters that Take Public Transit to Work

Source: Census 2012-2016 American Community Survey by Census Tract

Counties shown on this map are members of the Metropolitan Atlanta Rapid Transit Authority (MARTA)

N

Fulton County

DeKalb County

Clayton County

Legend:
- ⬚ Atlanta
- ☐ Counties
- ● MARTA Stations

% Total Commuters
- 0.0 - 4.6 %
- 4.6 - 11.0 %
- 11.0 - 18.3 %
- 18.3 - 29.1 %
- 29.1 - 47.1 %

0    5    10    15 mi

Note: ACS estimates are published at a 90% confidence interval with margins of error; true values may be higher or lower than the estimates

world: https://www.osgeo.org/resources/. If you prefer audiovisuals, there are hundreds of tutorials on YouTube. Some are part of a series that cover QGIS from beginning to end, while others focus on specific tasks.

These resources take a software-based approach and focus on covering the functionality of QGIS. Books with a software-agnostic view of GIS and mapping that offer a broader conceptual approach include *Qualitative GIS* (Cope & Elwood, 2009), *Key Concepts and Techniques in GIS* (Albrecht, 2007), *A Primer of GIS* (Harvey, 2015), and *Making Maps* (Krygier & Wood, 2016).

In Chapter 11, we will cover how you can create a number of common census derivatives, and in doing so, we will discuss some GIS-related topics for measuring the provision of services in a geographic area and for geocoding addresses (i.e., obtaining coordinates for address data so you can plot them in GIS). Since GIS is useful for studying how boundaries have changed over time, we will return to QGIS in Chapter 12, when we discuss historic census data.

## 10.5 REVIEW QUESTIONS AND PRACTICE EXERCISES

1.  Using the Census Reporter, create a map of median age by county for a state of your choice.

2.  In our GIS exercise in the Atlanta metro, redo the analysis to select all census tracts that are within a mile of a MARTA station where the total transit ridership is below the *median* value of 5.9%. How do these results compare with our original analysis where we used the mean value as the criteria?

3.  Repeat our original analysis for selecting census tracts that are within a mile of a MARTA station where the total transit ridership is below the mean value of 8.7%, but this time, only select tracts that fall within (fully or partially) the City of Atlanta.

4.  From the 2012–2016 ACS data profile table DP03 for economic characteristics, create an extract that contains the variable median travel time to work in minutes for the three counties in our study area. Prep this data in a spreadsheet, add the marta tracts layer back to the existing project, add the spreadsheet to the project, and join this data to the tracts to create a thematic map of median travel time.

5.  Describe the differences between these three map classification methods: natural breaks, quantiles, and equal intervals.

**Supplementary Digital Content:** Find datasets and supplemental exercises at the companion website at http://study.sagepub.com/census.

# CENSUS DATA DERIVATIVES

## 11.1 INTRODUCTION

Throughout this book, we have explored several census summary datasets where values are published as counts, estimates, and basic derived measures such as means, medians, and percent totals. We've covered how you can work with this published data using a number of different tools such as spreadsheets, relational databases, and geographic information systems (GIS) to study populations and places and to support different kinds of research.

This chapter will demonstrate how you can use census data to create more advanced derived measures. While census data is invaluable in and of itself for providing basic descriptive statistics, for many use cases, it also serves as raw material for creating new measures designed for studying specific aspects of society and the economy. This chapter is structured as a series of vignettes that covers some of the most common measures used in the social sciences and public policy. Each section is dedicated to a specific theme: population distribution, income and inequality, means and medians for aggregates, and geography. We'll refer to specific census datasets and tables for accessing the necessary inputs, discuss considerations and issues with each approach, and provide a formula or minimal working example that you can implement using the tools we have covered in this text.

Several of the derived measures that we cover in this chapter are indexes. An index is a compound measure that aggregates multiple values or variables to create a summary of an observation. The particular indexes presented in this chapter can be represented as whole numbers on a scale from 0 to 100 or as fractional values on a scale from 0 to 1. The choice of one over the other is a matter of preference. In these examples, as we calculate proportions such as the population of a subarea out of the total population, we will leave the proportions as fractions and will adjust the values at the end by multiplying by a whole number to get a final value of 0 to 100. Alternatively, if you calculated percent totals of 0 to 100 for the subareas, you would not have to make this adjustment at the end.

Many of the index measures require data for subunits of an area to compute the statistic for the larger area. For example, you need county-level data to calculate the Hoover Index of population concentration for states, or census tract–level data to measure segregation for a county or city. In this chapter, we will use the term *area* to refer to the entire area for which the statistic is computed, and the term *subarea* to refer to the component parts of the area that are used for creating the statistic.

As mentioned in the Preface, a background in statistics is not presumed for readers of this book. Formulas are presented using a pseudo-statistical notation so they can be readily understood by nonstatisticians. The proper statistical notation for these formulas is widely available, and you can refer to the cited references to obtain them.

## 11.2   MEASURES OF POPULATION DISTRIBUTION

### Population Density

Population density measures how many people there are by unit of area and is used for understanding how crowded a place is. To calculate it, you divide the population by the total land area:

$$\text{Population density} = \frac{\text{Population}}{\text{Land area}}$$

For example, based on the population and land area of New Jersey in 2010:

$$\frac{8,791,894}{7,352.22 \text{ (square miles)}} = 1,195.8 \text{ people per square mile}$$

New Jersey has been the most densely populated state in the country for quite some time, given its small geographic size relative to its population. In contrast, given its large size and small population, Alaska is the least densely populated state in the nation with 1.2 people per square mile.

The Census Bureau publishes data on population density but doesn't make it easy to find. Table GHT-PCT from decennial SF1 file provides population and housing unit counts, land and water areas in square miles, and population and housing unit density. Land and water areas are also published in several other places, and you can use it to calculate density yourself. These sources include the geographic header file in the FTP files (covered in the supplemental exercise for Chapter 5), the gazetteer files (mentioned at the end of Chapter 3), and as attributes in the TIGER Line shapefiles (illustrated in Chapter 10). In these sources, the attributes are labeled ALAND and AWATER, and the units are in *square meters*. To calculate results in square miles, you need to multiply the square meters by this conversion factor: 0.00000038610.

Land and water areas are remeasured for all geographies every 10 years and do change over time due to natural processes like erosion and rising sea levels and because of revisions to boundaries. Land and water areas for legal geographies such as counties and places are updated between the 10-year census if there are changes to political boundaries due to annexation, incorporation, or dissolution.

## Population Concentration

Population density is useful for measuring how crowded a place is, but it doesn't tell us anything about the distribution of the population within that place. Some areas within New Jersey and Alaska are more crowded than others, as population density is not uniform across these states. The Hoover Index is used to measure population concentration, and the statistic can be interpreted as the percentage of people that would have to move in order for the population to be evenly distributed. An index value of 0 indicates that the population is evenly distributed across an area, while a value of 100 indicates that the entire population is concentrated in one place (Rogerson & Plane, 2013).

Calculating the index for a place requires data on population and land area for that place as a whole and for all components or subareas of that place. To calculate the index for states, we can use counties as subareas. To do the calculation, calculate the proportion of the state's total population and land area that's in each county, take the absolute value of the difference between the population and land area proportions for each county, sum those county results for the state, and multiply by 50.

$$\text{Hoover index} = \text{SUM}\left(\left|\frac{\text{subarea pop}}{\text{area pop}} - \frac{\text{subarea land area}}{\text{area land area}}\right|\right) * 50$$

You can easily do this calculation in a spreadsheet. In Figure 11.1, the state's values appear in the sheet as totals that can be referenced in the formulas. The proportions of population and land area for each county are calculated first in dedicated columns (E and F), with the absolute value of the difference between them in a third column (G). An absolute value is simply the nonnegative value of any number, representing

**FIGURE 11.1 ● CALCULATING THE HOOVER INDEX IN A SPREADSHEET**

| | | | | | | |
|---|---|---|---|---|---|---|
| G2 | | $f_x$ $\Sigma$ = | =50*SUM(G3:G23) | | | |
| | A | B | C | D | E | F | G |
| 1 | GEOID | Name | Population | Land Area | | | Hoover Index |
| 2 | 34 | New Jersey | 8791894 | 7354.22 | Pop | Area | 38.6 |
| 3 | 34001 | Atlantic County | 274549 | 555.7 | 0.03 | 0.08 | 0.04 |
| 4 | 34003 | Bergen County | 905116 | 233.01 | 0.10 | 0.03 | 0.07 |
| 5 | 34005 | Burlington County | 448734 | 798.58 | 0.05 | 0.11 | 0.06 |
| 6 | 34007 | Camden County | 513657 | 221.26 | 0.06 | 0.03 | 0.03 |
| 7 | 34009 | Cape May County | 97265 | 251.42 | 0.01 | 0.03 | 0.02 |
| 8 | 34011 | Cumberland County | 156898 | 483.7 | 0.02 | 0.07 | 0.05 |
| 9 | 34013 | Essex County | 783969 | 126.21 | 0.09 | 0.02 | 0.07 |
| 10 | 34015 | Gloucester County | 288288 | 322.01 | 0.03 | 0.04 | 0.01 |
| 11 | 34017 | Hudson County | 634266 | 46.19 | 0.07 | 0.01 | 0.07 |
| 12 | 34019 | Hunterdon County | 128349 | 427.82 | 0.01 | 0.06 | 0.04 |
| 13 | 34021 | Mercer County | 366513 | 224.56 | 0.04 | 0.03 | 0.01 |
| 14 | 34023 | Middlesex County | 809858 | 308.91 | 0.09 | 0.04 | 0.05 |
| 15 | 34025 | Monmouth County | 630380 | 468.79 | 0.07 | 0.06 | 0.01 |
| 16 | 34027 | Morris County | 492276 | 460.18 | 0.06 | 0.06 | 0.01 |
| 17 | 34029 | Ocean County | 576567 | 628.78 | 0.07 | 0.09 | 0.02 |
| 18 | 34031 | Passaic County | 501226 | 184.59 | 0.06 | 0.03 | 0.03 |
| 19 | 34033 | Salem County | 66083 | 331.9 | 0.01 | 0.05 | 0.04 |
| 20 | 34035 | Somerset County | 323444 | 301.81 | 0.04 | 0.04 | 0.00 |
| 21 | 34037 | Sussex County | 149265 | 519.01 | 0.02 | 0.07 | 0.05 |
| 22 | 34039 | Union County | 536499 | 102.85 | 0.06 | 0.01 | 0.05 |
| 23 | 34041 | Warren County | 108692 | 356.92 | 0.01 | 0.05 | 0.04 |

that value's distance from zero. The spreadsheet formula ABS is used to compute it. This column is summed and multiplied by 50 to obtain the index for the state.

New Jersey has a Hoover index of 38.6, which means that the population of the state is relatively evenly distributed. About 39 out of 100 people in New Jersey would have to move from a more densely populated to a less densely populated county in order for the state's population to be equally distributed. In contrast, the index for Alaska is 73.2, which indicates that the state's population is highly concentrated in certain areas. This makes sense, as two thirds of Alaskans live in the Anchorage metropolitan area.

The choice of the subarea has a large impact on the index. For the results to be meaningful, each area should have a reasonable number of subareas, subareas must nest within the larger areas, and ideally subareas should be relatively compact and not vary too widely in geographic area. Counties are a good choice for creating a state-based index, while county subdivisions (minor civil divisions and census county divisions) may be appropriate for measuring concentration at the county level. A geography like a ZIP Code Tabulation Area (ZCTA) would be a poor choice as it violates all these rules.

## Segregation

Segregation is the degree of separation that exists between two different groups of people in a given area. If two different groups occupy completely separate and distinct subareas within an area, those groups are considered to be segregated from each other. In contrast, if the two groups overlapped and occupied the same space evenly within the area, those groups are considered to be integrated. In the United States, segregation is usually studied in a racial or ethnic context where minority groups live in neighborhoods separated from the white majority group or other minority groups. The reasons for this separation can be involuntary (coercion, racism, lack of opportunity) or voluntary (desire to live with one's ethnic group, ties to family or country of origin). Segregation is not exclusive to race and ethnicity but also occurs by age, language, income, and social class.

There are several different approaches to measuring segregation. Massey and Denton's (1988) paper *The Dimensions of Residential Segregation* is a touchstone in this field that clearly outlined 20 different measures and categorized them into five groups based on the aspect of segregation that they capture. The Census Bureau reviewed and summarized this work in a large study on late-20th-century housing segregation in the United States (Iceland, Weinberg, & Steinmetz, 2002). The five aspects of segregation are (1) evenness (the differential distribution of two groups across an area), (2) exposure (the degree of potential contact or interaction between groups), (3) concentration (relative amount of space occupied by a given group), (4) centralization (degree to which a group is located in the center of an area), and (5) clustering (the extent to which subareas inhabited by a group form compact and contiguous areas). In this summary, we'll consider three measures that cover evenness and exposure.

The index of dissimilarity is the most commonly used measure of segregation. It is an evenness measure that represents the percentage of a group's population that would have to move in order for that group to be uniformly distributed across an area relative to another group. The totals for each group in a subarea are divided by that group's total for the entire area. The result of the first group is subtracted from the result of the second, and the absolute value is taken. The results for each subarea are summed for the entire area and are multiplied by 50.

$$\text{Dissimilarity} = \text{SUM}\left(\left|\frac{\text{Group 1 pop subarea}}{\text{Group 1 pop area}} - \frac{\text{Group 2 pop subarea}}{\text{Group 2 pop area}}\right|\right) * 50$$

Figure 11.2 illustrates how the index of dissimilarity is calculated in a spreadsheet. Douglas County, Nebraska, is home to the City of Omaha, and in this example census tracts are used as subareas to measure dissimilarity between the white and black, white

**FIGURE 11.2** ● CALCULATING THE DISSIMILARITY INDEX IN A SPREADSHEET

| | G3 | | fx Σ = | =ABS((D3/SUM(D$3:D$138))-(E3/SUM(E$3:E$138))) | | | | | | |
|---|---|---|---|---|---|---|---|---|---|---|
| | A | B | | C | D | E | F | G | H | I |
| 1 | Index of Dissimilarity Douglas County, Iowa (Omaha) | | | | | | | White – Black | White – Hispanic | Black – Hispanic |
| 2 | Id2 | Geography | | Total | White | Black | Hispanic | 59.5 | 55.0 | 63.0 |
| 3 | 31055000200 | Census Tract 2, Douglas County, Nebraska | | 3759 | 2362 | 1046 | 175 | 0.0104 | 0.0045 | 0.0150 |
| 4 | 31055000300 | Census Tract 3, Douglas County, Nebraska | | 2250 | 546 | 1352 | 197 | 0.0217 | 0.0018 | 0.0199 |
| 5 | 31055000400 | Census Tract 4, Douglas County, Nebraska | | 2176 | 1330 | 129 | 635 | 0.0021 | 0.0074 | 0.0095 |
| 6 | 31055000500 | Census Tract 5, Douglas County, Nebraska | | 2328 | 1369 | 553 | 300 | 0.0051 | 0.0010 | 0.0041 |
| 7 | 31055000600 | Census Tract 6, Douglas County, Nebraska | | 1422 | 301 | 926 | 93 | 0.0151 | 0.0007 | 0.0144 |
| 8 | 31055000700 | Census Tract 7, Douglas County, Nebraska | | 1237 | 123 | 954 | 83 | 0.0162 | 0.0011 | 0.0151 |
| 9 | 31055000800 | Census Tract 8, Douglas County, Nebraska | | 1861 | 200 | 1432 | 122 | 0.0243 | 0.0016 | 0.0227 |
| 10 | 31055001100 | Census Tract 11, Douglas County, Nebraska | | 2708 | 266 | 1991 | 256 | 0.0338 | 0.0039 | 0.0299 |
| 11 | 31055001200 | Census Tract 12, Douglas County, Nebraska | | 2903 | 414 | 2119 | 198 | 0.0355 | 0.0023 | 0.0332 |
| 12 | 31055001600 | Census Tract 16, Douglas County, Nebraska | | 2577 | 2063 | 98 | 90 | 0.0051 | 0.0051 | 0.0000 |

and Hispanic, and black and Hispanic populations. In this example, there isn't a totals row for the county as a whole, so the formulas sum the values for the tracts to calculate county totals for each group. Figure 11.2 illustrates the formula for a single tract, while the value for the index is calculated in a separate formula that sums the results for the tracts and multiplies them by 50.

A value of 0 indicates total integration, while a value of 100 indicates total segregation. A value of 60 or more is considered high, as it means 60% or more of the members of one group would need to relocate to a different subarea in order for the groups to be equally distributed. Values below 30 are considered low, while values between 30 and 60 are moderate. In this example, segregation between these groups is moderate to high, and the degree of segregation between groups is relatively the same. Whites are a little more likely to live in the same areas as Hispanics (55.0) compared with blacks (59.5), while blacks and Hispanics are the least likely to live in the same area (63.0). More than half of one of the groups in each pair would need to move in order for there to be equivalency.

A variant of this index would be the measurement of one group versus the sum of all other groups in the area to calculate a more general index of segregation. While the dissimilarity index has been used for many decades and is straightforward to calculate, it suffers from limitations. Values for groups with small populations tend to be higher than large groups, and the results are scale dependent in that areas that have a larger number of subareas tend to have higher dissimilarity values versus areas with a fewer number of subareas.

Two alternate measures that gauge the potential degree of exposure between groups are the isolation and interaction indexes. The formulas for these measures are similar and examine opposite sides of the same coin: The isolation index measures the extent to which members of a group are only exposed to one another, while the interaction

**FIGURE 11.3** ● CALCULATING THE ISOLATION INDEX IN A SPREADSHEET

| | | | | | | White | Black | Hispanic |
|---|---|---|---|---|---|---|---|---|
| G3 | | | | | =(D3/SUM(D$3:D$158))*(D3/$C3) | | | |
| | A | B | C | D | E | F | G | H | I |
| 1 | Index of Isolation Douglas County, Iowa (Omaha) | | | | | | White | Black | Hispanic |
| 2 | Id2 | Geography | Total | White | Black | Hispanic | 63.0 | 37.4 | 31.9 |
| 3 | 31055000200 | Census Tract 2, Douglas County, Nebraska | 3759 | 2362 | 1046 | 175 | 0.0040 | 0.0049 | 0.0001 |
| 4 | 31055000300 | Census Tract 3, Douglas County, Nebraska | 2250 | 546 | 1352 | 197 | 0.0004 | 0.0137 | 0.0003 |
| 5 | 31055000400 | Census Tract 4, Douglas County, Nebraska | 2176 | 1330 | 129 | 635 | 0.0022 | 0.0001 | 0.0032 |
| 6 | 31055000500 | Census Tract 5, Douglas County, Nebraska | 2328 | 1369 | 553 | 300 | 0.0022 | 0.0022 | 0.0007 |
| 7 | 31055000600 | Census Tract 6, Douglas County, Nebraska | 1422 | 301 | 926 | 93 | 0.0002 | 0.0102 | 0.0001 |
| 8 | 31055000700 | Census Tract 7, Douglas County, Nebraska | 1237 | 123 | 954 | 83 | 0.0000 | 0.0124 | 0.0001 |
| 9 | 31055000800 | Census Tract 8, Douglas County, Nebraska | 1861 | 200 | 1432 | 122 | 0.0001 | 0.0186 | 0.0001 |
| 10 | 31055001100 | Census Tract 11, Douglas County, Nebraska | 2708 | 266 | 1991 | 256 | 0.0001 | 0.0247 | 0.0004 |
| 11 | 31055001200 | Census Tract 12, Douglas County, Nebraska | 2903 | 414 | 2119 | 198 | 0.0002 | 0.0261 | 0.0002 |
| 12 | 31055001600 | Census Tract 16, Douglas County, Nebraska | 2577 | 2063 | 98 | 90 | 0.0044 | 0.0001 | 0.0001 |

index measures how likely members of a group will be exposed to members of a different group.

To calculate the isolation index, for each subarea you divide the population group of the subarea by the population group for the area, divide the population group of the subarea by the total population of the area, and multiply the results together. These results are summed for all subareas and multiplied by 100. The index value ranges from 0 to 100 and represents the probability that a person in this group lives in the same area with a person from the same group.

$$\text{Isolation} = \text{SUM}\left(\frac{\text{Group pop subarea}}{\text{Group pop area}} * \frac{\text{Group pop subarea}}{\text{Total pop subarea}}\right) * 100$$

Figure 11.3 illustrates the spreadsheet calculations for isolation in Douglas County, Nebraska. The figure illustrates the formula for an individual tract, while the index value is calculated by summing the results for each tract and multiplying them by 100. Whites are the most isolated group, as the probability that a white person lives in the same area as another white person is 63%. Hispanics are the least isolated as the probability that they live in the same area with other Hispanics is 32%.

A small modification to the isolation index will yield the interaction index, which measures the likelihood that one group member will encounter or interact with a different group member living in the same area. Index values also range from 0 to 100, but the values between a pair of groups will not be the same. The probability of interaction between a white and a black person will not be the same as the probability of interaction between a black and a white person, unless these two groups form an equal proportion of the population:

$$\text{Interaction} = \text{SUM}\left(\frac{\text{Group 1 pop subarea}}{\text{Group 1 pop area}} * \frac{\text{Group 2 pop subarea}}{\text{Total pop subarea}}\right) * 100$$

A number of research programs, such as the Diversity and Disparities program of the American Communities Project at Brown University at `https://s4.ad.brown.edu/projects/diversity/` and the CensusScope project at the Social Science Data Analysis Network at the University of Michigan at `http://www.censusscope.org/`, have created websites from which you can retrieve and chart various segregation measures for cities and metropolitan areas. Most of these measures use decennial census data. While you can use American Community Survey (ACS) data to create segregation indexes, compare the results of using the ACS estimates with the decennial counts *prior* to calculating and recalculating margins of error (MOEs) for the ACS. If the values are not radically different, you can save time and effort by simply using the decennial data.

## Daytime Population

As we have seen throughout this book, the Census Bureau creates counts and estimates of the population based on where people live. When using census data in your research, you need to consider whether this is a reasonable. If you are engaged in transportation planning, emergency management, or even advertising or marketing, you may need to consider what the population of an area is during the day. The daytime population refers to the population of an area during the working day, when central business districts and areas with office parks, shopping centers, and college campuses swell with commuters while residential areas empty out.

Measuring the daytime population is trickier than counting the residential population, and there is a lot less data available. The Census Bureau suggests using ACS data tables on commuting/journey to work, which provide estimates on the number of workers within geographic areas. This does not capture all possible activities such as students traveling to school, but commuting to work is by far the largest factor that influences daytime population. They propose two methods that yield the same result; the simplest approach is adding the total resident population to the total number of workers who work in the area, and then subtracting the total resident workforce (workers who live in the area but may work inside or outside the area):

$$\text{Daytime population} = \text{Total residents} + \text{Total workers in area}$$
$$- \text{Total resident workers}$$

The ACS tables listed in Table 11.1 can be used to compute the daytime population. For example, in the 2012–2016 ACS the City of Wilmington, Delaware, had approximately 71,502 total residents (from Table B01003) and had 61,583 workers working in the city (Table B08604). There were 30,802 workers who lived in the city (Table

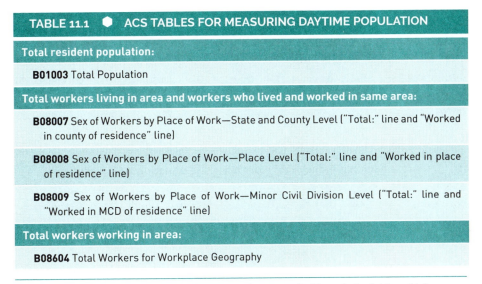

**TABLE 11.1  ●  ACS TABLES FOR MEASURING DAYTIME POPULATION**

**Total resident population:**

**B01003** Total Population

**Total workers living in area and workers who lived and worked in same area:**

**B08007** Sex of Workers by Place of Work—State and County Level ("Total:" line and "Worked in county of residence" line)

**B08008** Sex of Workers by Place of Work—Place Level ("Total:" line and "Worked in place of residence" line)

**B08009** Sex of Workers by Place of Work—Minor Civil Division Level ("Total:" line and "Worked in MCD of residence" line)

**Total workers working in area:**

**B08604** Total Workers for Workplace Geography

*Source:* `https://www.census.gov/topics/employment/commuting/guidance/calculations.html`

B08008). We add the total residents and total workers and subtract the total workers who live in the city. The subtraction allows us to avoid double counting the residents who work in the city (as they are already included in the total resident population) while omitting the residents who work outside the city (who are included in the total resident workers). The result is 71,502 + 61,583 − 30,802 = 102,283. The City of Wilmington has a daytime population that's approximately 30k people larger than its resident population. The city has a central business district that contains the offices of several large banks plus state and county government offices, and it draws many suburban commuters who work in the city but live outside.

The variables in these basic tables are also cross tabulated in other tables by age, sex, race, Hispanic origin , citizenship status, language, poverty, and tenure, so it's possible to estimate some characteristics of the daytime population. MOEs will limit the usefulness of estimates for small population groups. Data for workers living in an area who lived and worked in the same area is limited to basic geographies: states, counties, places, and minor civil divisions for states that have them.

## Location Quotient

While the previous measures are used for studying population distribution and concentration, the location quotient is used for measuring concentrations of businesses and employment. We introduced location quotients in Chapter 8, where we studied whether three metropolitan areas in upstate New York were more or less specialized than the national economy in certain advanced industries. A location quotient measures how concentrated employment is for a given industry relative to the larger economy. The result is an index where a value of 1 indicates that employment in the local area is similar to the national economy, whereas a value lower or higher than 1 indicates less or more specialization. By itself, the location quotient compares the local economy with the national one, but we can also compare location quotients (LQs) between different places to gauge their specialization. The basic formula is

$$LQ = \frac{\text{Local industry employment} \div \text{Total local employment}}{\text{National industry employment} \div \text{Total national employment}}$$

For example, we found that the City of Rochester had a high location quotient in communications equipment (NAICS 3342) in the manufacturing sector:

$$\frac{2,778 \div 452,595}{87,208 \div 126,752,238} = 8.92$$

With an LQ of 8.92, Rochester has a high specialization in this industry relative to the national economy. Syracuse also had a high LQ of 4.62, less specialized than Rochester but still much more specialized relative to the national economy. In contrast, Buffalo had a low LQ of 0.78, indicating that it's less specialized in this industry compared with the national economy and much less specialized relative to its neighbors.

While employment is typically used when calculating location quotients, wages and business establishments can also be used. Wages are useful when you want to determine which industries or sectors contribute the most or the least to an economy in dollar values. Establishments are used for nontradeable industries that deal in low-order goods, such as grocery stores or gas stations, often to determine whether there is spatial equity in the distribution of these services.

## 11.3   MEASURES OF INCOME AND INEQUALITY

### Inflation

The value of money and what it can buy changes over time. As prices increase, the amount of goods and services that a fixed amount of money can buy decreases. This loss in purchasing power is called inflation. The rate of inflation fluctuates over time due to changes in prices, wages, interest rates, and many other economic factors, and it has varied significantly in magnitude over the past 50 years (Reed, 2014). If you are comparing any variable that's measured in dollars over time, you will need to adjust for inflation in order to make meaningful comparisons. The Census Bureau reports dollar values as nominal values, which represents the value of the variable (income, rent, home value, sales, etc.) at the time the data was published. Inflation-adjusted values are referred to as real values, as they reflect what a dollar could actually purchase in today's economy.

In the 2000 census, the Census Bureau reported that U.S. median household income in 1999 was $41,994. According to the 2016 ACS, median household income was $57,617 ± 115. If we compared these nominal values, income increased by approximately $15,622. However, prices have increased over time and you could purchase more with a dollar in 1999 than you could in 2016. A dollar in 1999 had the same purchasing power as $1.43 in 2016. To adjust the 1999 median income for inflation, we multiply the value by the purchasing power of $1.43, which yields approximately $60,051. In real dollars, median income has actually declined by more than $2,400!

The Bureau of Labor Statistics (BLS) provides an inflation calculator on its website where you can calculate the purchasing power between 2 years, which you can use for creating inflation-adjusted values: `https://www.bls.gov/data/inflation_calculator.htm`. The calculator uses the Consumer Price Index, which measures the average change over time in the market-rate prices paid by urban residents for a basket of consumer goods and services. For this example, we input $1.00 and select December 1999 as the starting point and December 2016 as the end point. December represents the reference point for both of the surveys: The 2000 census asked people what their income was for the previous year (ending December 1999), while the ACS asks people on a monthly basis what their income was in the past 12 months. The Census Bureau adjusts all values for the 1-year and 5-year ACS period estimates to the CPI during the last month of the year.

When should you adjust values for inflation? There are several rules of thumb where you consider the amount of time between the start and end point of the data, and the end point of the data and the present point in time in which you are doing your research. If we were comparing data between two consecutive years, such as median income in the 2015 and 2016 ACS and were publishing our research in 2018, for *general* purposes we *usually* wouldn't adjust either value for inflation. The period of time between the data points is short, as is the period of time between the end point and the present.

If the period of time between the start and end point is larger, but the period between the end point and present is small, we would adjust the value for the starting point so that it represents the dollar values of the end point. If we were comparing median income between the 2010 and 2016 ACS in 2018, we would adjust the dollar values for 2010 so that they are represented in 2016 dollars. If the period of time between the end point and the present is large enough, then we would adjust the values of *both* the start and end point to reflect dollar values in the *present*. If we were comparing 1999 median income to 2010 median income in 2018, we would adjust both values to 2018 dollars.

## Gini Coefficient

The Gini coefficient is a common summary measure of income inequality. It is an index that ranges from 0 to 1, where 0 indicates perfect equality where there is a proportional distribution of income, and where 1 represents absolute inequality where one household owns all the wealth (although like other measures, the coefficient is sometimes represented as whole values from 0 to 100). Calculating the Gini coefficient requires data on individual persons, households, or families, which is not available from the Census Bureau's summary data. It takes a series of calculations that is rather complex (Bellu & Liberati, 2006), and some researchers use Public Use Microdata Samples microdata to calculate the coefficient for large geographic areas (we'll cover microdata in Chapter 12).

Fortunately, the Census Bureau publishes Gini coefficients for most geographies as part of the ACS in Table B19083. According to the 2016 ACS and based on household income, the Gini index for the United States was 0.482. For individual states, values ranged from a low of 0.408 for Alaska to a high of 0.542 for the District of Columbia (Guzman, 2017). The Gini index for the United States has increased by 3.9% between 2006 and 2016, which implies that there is increasing inequality. Internationally, the United States has a higher coefficient (and thus, higher inequality) relative to other Western, industrialized nations (Iceland, 2014, pp. 95–99).

## Inequality Ratios

Another approach for measuring income inequality compares wages or salary income earned by individuals in the top percentile of income earners versus the bottom percentile. There are several income inequality ratios, such as the 90:10 ratio and 80:20 ratio, where the numerator represents the top percentile (top 10% or 20% of earners) and the denominator represents the bottom percentile (bottom 10% or 20% of earners). For example, a BLS study of income inequality among metropolitan areas between 2003 and 2013 found that the 90:10 ratio for the United States grew from 4.54 to 4.86 (Cunningham, 2015). This means that households in the top 90% earned $4.86 for every $1.00 earned by households in the bottom 10% of earners.

Income inequality ratios are sensitive to the type of income used as the input values, and the outcome of the different ratios varies widely based on the percentile that's used

(Glassman, 2016). Many researchers use household after-tax income, which includes wages and salary income, self-employment income, retirement income, interests and dividends, and transfer payments (government programs such as social security and public cash assistance). Some analysts may adjust the values to remove transfer payments to reflect what people are earning in the marketplace or may simply look at salaries and wages. The former will deflate incomes at the lower percentile, while the latter will deflate incomes at both ends but primarily affects higher percentiles. The ACS provides detailed subcategories of income that make it possible to isolate and adjust for several different forms, with some notable exceptions such as capital gains, sales from real estate, and public housing subsidies (U.S. Census Bureau, 2017c, 2017d).

Statistics from the Census Bureau or BLS can be used to compute the ratio, but like the Gini coefficient, it requires data on individuals. Many researchers use sample microdata from the Public Use Microdata Samples to compute them (e.g., see Kochhar & Cilluffo, 2018). The Census Bureau does publish two summary tables that can be used for deriving ratios. Table B19082—Shares of Aggregate Household Income by Quintile—illustrates the share of all incomes earned by households in 20% increments, with a special tabulation for the top 5% of income earners (not inclusive of the quintiles). Table B19081—Mean Household Income of Quintiles—provides the mean income in dollar values for each of the quintiles and the top 5% earners. Data from both tables for the United States is shown in Table 11.2. In 2016, the top 20% of income earners made more than 50% of the total income earned in the United States, while the bottom 20% earned just over 3% of total income.

| TABLE 11.2 ● MEAN HOUSEHOLD INCOME AND SHARE OF AGGREGATE INCOME BY QUINTILE | | | | |
|---|---|---|---|---|
| Quintile | Mean Income | MOE | Share of Income | MOE |
| Lowest quintile | $12,691 | 42 | 3.12% | 0.01 |
| Second quintile | $34,089 | 69 | 8.38% | 0.02 |
| Third quintile | $57,968 | 84 | 14.25% | 0.02 |
| Fourth quintile | $92,075 | 99 | 22.64% | 0.03 |
| Highest quintile | $209,909 | 494 | 51.61% | 0.06 |
| | | | | |
| Top 5% | $378,330 | 1,568 | 23.25% | 0.07 |

*Source:* 2016 ACS Tables B19081 and B19082.

You can derive the 80:20 ratio by multiplying aggregate household income in Table B19025 by the shares of the lowest and the highest quintiles in B19082, and dividing the high income by the low income. In 2016, the aggregate household income for the United States was approximately 9.7 trillion dollars. The lowest quntile's share of this total was 3.12%, which is 0.3 trillion, while the highest qunitile's was 51.61% or 5 trillion dollars. Five trillion divided by 0.3 trillion is 16.55. The top 20% of households made $16.55 for every $1 earned by the bottom 20% of households. Once again, the type of income used as the input can have a major influence on results. Household income reported in the ACS is *before* tax income.

## 11.4   MEANS AND MEDIANS FOR AGGREGATES

In Chapter 6, we demonstrated how to create aggregates for ACS data by combining geographies and population groups. This is often necessary for creating estimates with lower MOEs, and for creating areas to conform to neighborhoods or local administrative boundaries that the Census Bureau doesn't publish data for. Our examples illustrated how you could create new count-based variables and percent totals. But what if you wanted to recompute a derived estimate like a mean or median for a larger area or group? You can't simply take the measures for the individual areas and average them together.

Recalculating a mean is relatively straightforward and requires aggregating values for both the numerator and the denominator. For example, if we wanted to combine two census tracts and calculate their mean household income we would need counts of households and the sum of all incomes for the tracts. The ACS includes a number of detailed tables for aggregates, including household and family income, detailed sources of income, gross and contract rent, home value, travel time to work, vehicles owned, and rooms in housing units. Many of these tables are cross tabulated by sex, race, and other variables. Aggregated household income was reported in Table B19025 in the 2012–2016 ACS.

Census Tracts 38 and 135 in Orleans Parish, Louisiana, are located in the French Quarter of New Orleans. In 2012–2016, they had a mean income of $115,990 (±37,218) and $133,277 (±47,081), respectively. Using the formulas in Chapter 6, if we combine these two tracts, they have 2,159 households (±201) (835 ± 126 and 1,324 ± 157) and their aggregate household income is $273.3 million (±71.0 million) (96.9 ± 35.7 million and 176.5 ± 61.4 million). We divide aggregate household income by households to get a new mean income of $126,591 (±34,946). We use the ACS ratio formula that we covered in Chapter 6 to calculate the MOE when dividing.

Calculating a new median for aggregates is more complex. Remember that the median value represents the case that falls in the center of a distribution. To calculate a new median, we would need to combine the records of individual respondents from these two census tracts, sort them, and select the middle value. This isn't possible as we only have access to summarized data. The solution is to use a method called statistical interpolation where we can derive the median from interval data, such as Table B19001 Household Income, where the number of households are counted by income brackets. The California State Data Center has published a good tutorial that demonstrates how to calculate a derived median and its associated MOE using this approach (California State Data Center, 2016). For a complete example based on this tutorial, visit Supplemental Exercise 11 on the publisher's website at **study.sagepub.com/census**.

## 11.5   GEOGRAPHIC DERIVATIVES

### Allocation and Apportionment

Crosswalking is the process of taking data that's organized and stored in one system and transferring it to a different system, while accounting for and minimizing data miscategorization or loss between systems that are not strictly compatible. In Chapter 8, we learned that the NAICS codes used for classifying businesses into industries change over time, and the Census Bureau publishes crosswalks (also called concordances) so you can modify data from the past to fit present categories, or vice versa. In a geographic sense, crosswalking is the translation of census data from one set of geographies to another, typically between geographies that do not nest. In this context, the terms *allocation* or *apportionment* are typically used, as you are either assigning or dividing data from one area to another based on the geographic intersection of land or population.

In our segregation example earlier in this chapter, we could simply select and download data for all the census tracts within Douglas County, Nebraska, and since tracts are designed to nest within counties, no allocation was necessary. But what if we were interested in studying segregation within the City of Omaha, which falls within and constitutes the majority of Douglas County? Omaha is a census place: Tracts do not nest within places, and places do not nest within counties. Using **data.census.gov** or any of the other sources, we would not be able to download data for all tracts within Omaha because they do not nest. We would have to identify the smallest possible number of geographies that completely contain Omaha, download all the tracts within those geographies, identify all the tracts that fall completely within Omaha, and then make decisions regarding what to do with tracts that cross the city boundary. We can use the Missouri Census Data Center (MCDC) Geocorr tool to help us identify these tracts and make allocation decisions.

MCDC Geocorr uses census blocks, the smallest unit of census geography, to calculate overlap between different census geographies based on land area or population. Several iterations of the Geocorr tool are available at `http://mcdc.missouri .edu/applications/geocorr.html`. Geocorr 2018 is the most recent version and is based on 2010 census geography. It also incorporates geographies that are based on 2010 boundaries that were released subsequently (like new congressional districts). Older versions of the tool are based on 2000 and 1990 census geography, which allows you to crosswalk geographies *from* those time periods, but not *between* them.

A quick web search reveals that Omaha falls completely inside Douglas County, so if we wanted to select tracts within Omaha, we would start by selecting all the tracts in Douglas. Using Gecorr, we would choose Nebraska as our state, select census tracts as our source, and places as our target (Figure 11.4). The source is the geography that you're interested in apportioning, and the target is the geography you want to apportion it to. Then we scroll down and modify the options. The weighting variable indicates how one geography should be assigned to the other, such as by land area

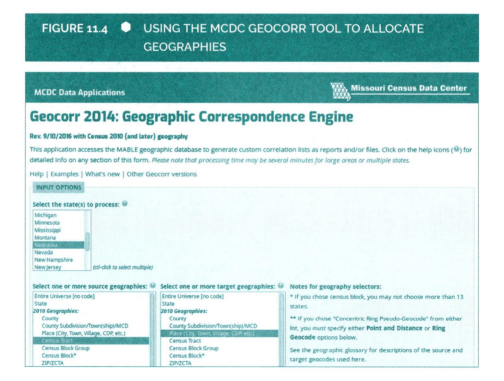

**FIGURE 11.4   ●   USING THE MCDC GEOCORR TOOL TO ALLOCATE GEOGRAPHIES**

or population. Keep population 2010 as the default. We can ignore census blocks that have a population of zero. Scroll down to the geographic filter options, and under County, enter the FIPS Code for Douglas County: 055. Instead of generating a crosswalk between all tracts and places in Nebraska, this limits the results to Douglas (if we wanted to filter for multiple counties, we would enter a list of codes separated by commas). Just above the geographic filters is a button to run the request.

This produces a HTML table we can view and a CSV we can download, where each record represents a portion of a census tract that falls within each place within the county. An output column called afact represents the allocation factor, or percentage of the total population of the tract that falls within each place. Geocorr calculates the allocation factor based on how the census blocks within one area correspond to the other area (as blocks nest within all geographies). If a record for a census tract appears only once and it has a afact value of 1, it means its population falls entirely within one place. If the place column indicates that the place is Omaha, we know it's unequivocally an Omaha census tract.

If the record for a census tract appears more than once, each record will have a different allocation factor that indicates the percentage and actual population values that are split between Omaha and other places, or between Omaha and unincorporated areas of the county (the latter appear as blank values labeled with place code 99999). For these records, we would need to make a decision to count them as part of Omaha or not. The options are as follows: exclude all tracts that are not entirely within the city, include all tracts that are partially within the city, only include tracts that have a majority of the allocation factor in the city, include tracts partially in the city that meet a certain threshold for either the allocation factor or the total population value, or keep all records that are partially in the city and use the allocation factor to proportionally split our data.

All these options except the last one are straightforward to implement, as you are making a decision to wholly include or exclude a tract from the study area. The proportional split approach is more complex as it forces you to modify the data. For example, if 65% of a tract is inside the city, then you would multiply each of your variables such as race, age groups, and labor force status by this percentage and assume the population is spread evenly across the tract. This approach is problematic for two reasons: (1) This assumption of an even distribution for all population groups may be incorrect and (2) if you're using ACS data you may be apportioning small estimates with large margins of error in a way that may not make sense, e.g., if you were apportioning 65% of 300 unemployed people ($\pm250$). The apportionment approach is less feasible with ACS data for small geographies.

| County code | County name | Tract | State code | State abbreviation | Place code | Place name | Total population (2010) | tract to placefp allocation factor |
|---|---|---|---|---|---|---|---|---|
| 31055 | Douglas NE | 0074.66 | 31 | NE | 37000 | Omaha city, NE | 5510 | 1.000 |

| County code | County name | Tract | State code | State abbreviation | Place code | Place name | Total population (2010) | tract to placefp allocation factor |
|---|---|---|---|---|---|---|---|---|
| 31055 | Douglas NE | 0074.67 | 31 | NE | 37000 | Omaha city, NE | 2889 | 0.613 |
| | | | 31 | NE | 40605 | Ralston city, NE | 692 | 0.147 |
| | | | 31 | NE | 99999 | | 1131 | 0.240 |

| County code | County name | Tract | State code | State abbreviation | Place code | Place name | Total population (2010) | tract to placefp allocation factor |
|---|---|---|---|---|---|---|---|---|
| 31055 | Douglas NE | 0074.68 | 31 | NE | 40605 | Ralston city, NE | 2398 | 1.000 |

| County code | County name | Tract | State code | State abbreviation | Place code | Place name | Total population (2010) | tract to placefp allocation factor |
|---|---|---|---|---|---|---|---|---|
| 31055 | Douglas NE | 0074.69 | 31 | NE | 37000 | Omaha city, NE | 2199 | 0.678 |
| | | | 31 | NE | 99999 | | 1043 | 0.322 |

FIGURE 11.5  ●  RESULTS FROM ALLOCATING TRACTS TO PLACES BY POPULATION

*Source:* Missouri Census Data Center Geocorr Geographic Correspondence Engine

Figure 11.5 illustrates a portion of the allocation results by population between tracts and places in Douglas County. Tract 74.66 has single record for Omaha with an allocation factor of 1.0, indicating that tract is located entirely within Omaha. Tract 74.67 has three records that indicate it is split between Omaha, Ralston City, and unincorporated parts of the county. A total of 61.3% of this tract's population is in Omaha, and we can see this equates to 2,889 people. Tract 74.68 is located entirely within Ralston City, while about two thirds of tract 74.69 is located in Omaha while the other third is located in an unincorporated part of the county. Based on this information, we would include the first tract, exclude the third one, and decide whether to include the second and fourth tracts. If we base the decision on a simple majority, we would include both. If we decide to use another criterion like a two-thirds majority, we would exclude the second one and include the fourth one.

Ultimately, the goal is to create a table that contains all the tracts that meet your criteria. After downloading the table as a CSV and identifying which tracts to include and exclude (with a new column where you designate this), you would copy and modify the allocation table so that every record represents a unique census tract with no duplicates, and you include just the tracts that you want as part of your analysis. Then you can download the demographic or socioeconomic data for your study area, which will include data for more areas than you are interested in (in this case, all the tracts in Douglas County). Using VLOOKUP in a spreadsheet or relational joins in a database, you can tie this data to your allocation table. Data for tracts that fall outside your study area will fall outside of the set, as they will have no matching value in the allocation table.

The benefit of Geocorr is that it's a readily usable tool that allows you to allocate or apportion census geographies based on population, which is better than using land area. The downside is that it has no visual component, and if you were using noncensus geographies defined by local governments (precincts, health districts, etc.), this tool can't accommodate that need. You do have the option of capturing census areas that fall within the radius of a specific point designated with longitude and latitude coordinates, but if you have many points (like the Atlanta subway stations in Chapter 10), it isn't practical.

GIS is useful for this purpose. If you have boundary files in a shapefile or vector format, you can use various spatial selection tools to select one area within another based on their geographical relationship. Figure 11.6 displays some of these possibilities using the subway buffer example in Chapter 10. Using the Select by Location tools in QGIS, you can select areas that intersect another area or are completely within that other area. Both approaches can be problematic if the tracts do not conform well to the areas; in these cases, tracts that slightly overlap the other boundary are either included or excluded. You can take the extra step of calculating the geographic center of the tracts to select ones that have their center within the other area, or you can download population centroids (`https://www.census.gov/geographies/reference-files/2010/geo/2010-centers-population.html`) to select tracts whose center of population is

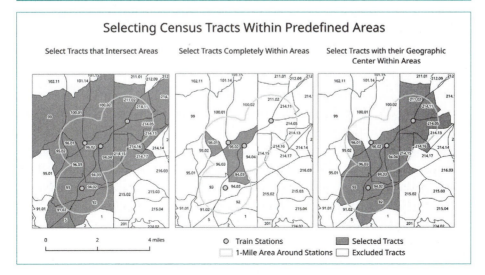

**FIGURE 11.6** ● USING GIS TO SELECT CENSUS GEOGRAPHY WITHIN NONCENSUS AREAS

### Selecting Census Tracts Within Predefined Areas

Select Tracts that Intersect Areas       Select Tracts Completely Within Areas       Select Tracts with their Geographic Center Within Areas

○ Train Stations                          ▨ Selected Tracts
▢ 1-Mile Area Around Stations             ▢ Excluded Tracts

within the other area (thus accounting for unequal population distribution within the tracts). The centroid approaches yield a better result. You can perform proportional splits using the field calculator and the union tools to calculate the percentage of a tract that falls inside and outside the area's boundary. The percentage can be used for apportioning data or as a criteria for inclusion or exclusion.

GIS is also useful for adding context that can help you make assignment or apportionment decisions. You can overlay boundaries on top of a base map to see how buildings or other features fall across a split boundary. With artful manipulation of the symbology, you can modify shades and colors to effectively see how two different geographies align. The downside of using GIS and the TIGER files for apportionment is that the process relies on the relationship between geographic areas. Population-based selections are limited to the use of centroids. It is possible to mimic the functions of Geocorr by using a census block layer to apportion two different areas, but it's a multistep and resource-intensive process.

Regardless of which tool you use, allocation works best when you are assigning a set of small geographies to a larger set of geographies. If the two geographies are equal in number or size, the accuracy of the assignment will decline. For example, if you were trying to assign ZCTAs to either Public Use Microdata Areas or counties, the result might not be viable given equivalency in the number of features and the amount of overlap between them. In cases where the population of the areas is large and they are relatively equal in number, a proportional split approach would be more viable than simple inclusion/exclusion. Ultimately, if two areas have little geographic correspondence, you should not try to relate them. Relating ZIP Codes and ZCTAs is a special challenge that's summarized in InfoBox 11.1.

## Location Analysis

Using GIS to perform location analysis is a large topic that's beyond the scope of this book, but since this type of analysis often uses census data to create derivatives, we'll provide a summary here. In this particular context, location analysis is the study of some facility and service and its surrounding population. If we wanted to measure how equitably distributed a facility or service was or how accessible it was to a surrounding population, we would measure the population as a series of generalized origin points relative to the facilities, which serve as destinations. Conversely, if we wanted to measure what the service or market area was for a facility, we would employ some method for delineating a service area around it to measure the surrounding population.

Census geography is often used for measuring origin points and for capturing or delineating what the service areas and their populations would be. For origin points,

## ✓ INFOBOX 11.1 RELATING ZIP CODES TO ZCTAS AND OTHER PLACES

As described in Chapter 3, ZIP Codes are not actual geographic areas with formal boundaries but are simply numbers assigned to addresses along street segments. The Census Bureau summarizes decennial and ACS data by ZCTAs, which are areal approximations of ZIP Codes. As mentioned in Chapter 8, the ZIP Code Business Patterns and Economic Census data are published at the ZIP Code level. Can you relate ZIP Codes to ZCTAs?

The UDS Mapper is an organization that provides resources and tools to support public health research. One of the partners of this organization, John Snow Incorporated, has created and freely provides a ZIP Code to ZCTA crosswalk table: `https://www.udsmapper.org/zcta-crosswalk.cfm`. The MCDC provides this same resource through the Dexter tool.

In this file, all ZIP Codes that cover an area are assigned to their corresponding ZCTA that shares the same five-digit number. ZIP Codes that lack area and don't have a corresponding ZCTA, such as large clusters of post office boxes or big organizations that process a lot of mail, are assigned to the ZCTA that they fall within geographically (think of them as points within areas). In a database, you can join ZIP Code level data to the UDS table using the ZIP Code number, and can write a GROUP BY statement to aggregate that data by ZCTA number. In doing so, you create a summary of the ZIP data at the ZCTA level.

The place names associated with ZIP Codes do not correspond with legal areas (Stevens, 2006), so you can't rely on the names to capture all ZIPs in an area. For example, there are dozens of ZIP Codes for Wilmington, Delaware, but only three of them cover the actual city, and they all cross the city's boundary. The remaining codes cover suburban areas and smaller towns outside the city. To capture all ZIPs within a given area, you can tie ZIPs to ZCTAs using the UDS crosswalk, and then use MCDC Geocorr to allocate ZCTAs (the source) to places or counties (the target). You will need to make allocation decisions, as ZCTAs don't nest within any other geographies.

ZIP Code → ZCTA → County or place

it's often not feasible or practical to measure distances from individual residences or buildings to a destination. The geographic or population centroids of small census geographies such as blocks, block groups, and tracts are often used as generalized, aggregate measures of a population's location. There is a trade-off between using centroids for smaller versus larger areas. Centroids for smaller areas like blocks and block groups help limit the amount of aggregation error (the degree to which a population's distribution is oversimplified, which has an impact on distance measurements [Hewko, Smoyer-Tomic, & Hodgson, 2002]), but there is a lot less data published for them relative to a larger area like a census tract. Ideally, the number of origin points should outnumber destinations by a fair margin.

When used for delineating service areas, a wider number of geographies can be used based on the context. Some public services have defined administrative or legal boundaries such as counties or cities, which can be used for counting or measuring services. Conversely, you can measure the local "effective" service areas for public goods or market areas for private goods by using smaller areas such as ZCTAs or census tracts, or by selecting a certain number of tracts, block groups, or blocks that are near the facilities or meet certain criteria.

The approaches presented here are summarized by Emily Talen (2003) in her study of neighborhoods as service providers. Each approach requires that you consider the points that we discussed in the previous section on allocation. When selecting areas that "fall within" another area, you need to decide how to select one geographic area in relation to another via intersection, centroids within, or proportional splits (Schlossberg, 2003).

Container:   When used for measuring accessibility, this is a simple count of the number of facilities contained within a given geographic area such as a tract or ZCTA. When used for understanding a service area, it is a count of the number of people in the area relative to the service. While simple to implement, the container approach suffers from several flaws, most notably from edge effects. A service could be located at the edge of a census tract for example, and that tract would be counted as having that service. Meanwhile, the adjacent tract where people could simply be living across the street would not be counted as having that service.

Coverage:   When used to measure accessibility, this represents the number of facilities within a given distance of the point of origin. When used for delineating services, it represents the number of people living within a given distance of the service. The buffering technique illustrated in Chapter 10 where circles were drawn around each subway station to measure the number of people living within a mile is an example of this approach. The size of the buffer could be fixed or variable based on some attribute. An alternative to the coverage (and container) approach would be to create Voronoi or Thiessen polygons (using QGIS) around service points and measure the population within. The polygons are created by drawing boundary lines at the midpoint between each facility and the most adjacent facilities to delineate market areas.

Minimum distance:   For accessibility, this is the distance between a point of origin and the nearest facility. Distances can be measured as Euclidean straight lines, Manhattan blocks (rectilinear), or as network distances that follow a set path of roads or transit networks. While network distance is more precise, implementing it is more time-consuming, and national studies comparing it with simple Euclidean distance show that the results correlate highly with one another (Boscoe, Henry, & Zdeb, 2012). However, the geographic context of a given place matters and will affect the degree to which you can use a simpler method over a more complicated one (Apparicio, Abdelmajid, Riva, & Shearmur, 2008). An alternative to measuring distances to the nearest facility (which is fine for accessibility but not suitable for measuring service areas) is measuring the distance between an origin and the *N* closest destinations (two, three, five, etc.).

Travel cost:  For both accessibility and service delineation, this is the average distance between a point of origin and all destinations, or vice versa, within a fixed boundary. This measure represents the overall opportunity for individuals to reach a given service. The same considerations over what type of distance measurement to use apply here. Travel time can also be calculated or derived as an alternative to measuring distance, and variables such as speed limits, traffic congestion, and the availability of public transit can be used to calculate true travel time.

Gravity model:  This approach encompasses a variety of different methods and variations, but in its simplest form, it is an index where the sum of all services or facilities is weighted by size and divided by the frictional impact of distance. Such an approach would consider that services offered at different facilities vary in terms of size, quality, or hours of operation while also considering that people are less likely to use facilities that are farther away but may travel the extra distance if a given facility is larger or of better quality and has greater "pull." A method called the two-point floating catchment area is often employed in public health and can be implemented in a series of steps using a relational database or GIS (F. Wang & Luo, 2005).

## Address Geocoding

```
https://geocoding.geo.census.gov/geocoder/
```

Address geocoding is the process of obtaining a series of geographic coordinates for an address. Traditionally, this is achieved by taking an address and matching it against a database of streets, where each street segment is a record in a database that has a range of addresses assigned to it. The address is matched against the database, a matching road segment is selected, the address is interpolated or assigned to the segment based on where it would fall along the range, and coordinates are returned. The geocoding process is often imprecise given the variable nature of addresses, so many geocoders return a match score that indicates how accurate a match is.

The Census Bureau provides a free online geocoder that is based on the TIGER Line street files and the Master Address File (MAF). The geocoder determines the approximate location of each address offset from a street's centerline. Interpolated longitude and latitude coordinates in the NAD 83 CRS are returned along with the address range on that particular stretch of road. An address can be input on a single line, or you can type the components of the address in separate fields for street, city, state, and ZIP.

The greatest strength of the geocoder over other web-based alternatives is that it allows you to do batch address matching without having to register or create an account. You can store up to 10,000 addresses in a CSV file, upload it through the batch interface, and download the results. The batch geocoder is very particular about the structure of the data: It must be in a CSV file, there can be no header row (i.e., no column names), and the data file must contain these five attributes: (1) a unique ID, (2) house number and street name, (3) city, (4) state, and (5) ZIP Code. The file cannot contain *any* additional fields; if it does, the geocoder will simply reject it. Here's an example of a CSV file in an acceptable format:

```
1,233 S Wacker Dr,Chicago,IL,60606
2,633 W Fifth St,Los Angeles,CA,90071
3,123 Main St,Metropolis,NV,89835
4,50 23rd St,New York,NY,10010
5,151 25th St,New York,NY,10010
```

After uploading it to the Find Location batch geocoder, this is the resulting CSV file:

```
"2","633 W Fifth St, Los Angeles, CA, 90071","Match","Exact",
   "633 W 5TH ST, LOS ANGELES, CA, 90071","-118.254395,
   34.050484","638700397","R"
"1","233 S Wacker Dr, Chicago, IL, 60606","Match","Exact",
   "233 S WACKER DR, CHICAGO, IL, 60606","-87.636665,
   41.878513","112050003","L"
"5","151 25th St, New York, NY, 10010","Match","Non_Exact",
   "151 E 25TH ST, NEW YORK, NY, 10010","-73.982735,
   40.74034","639380232","L"
"4","50 23rd St, New York, NY, 10010","Tie"
"3","123 Main St, Metropolis, NV, 89835","No_Match"
```

Records 1 and 2 are addresses for famous skyscrapers, and we received an exact match for both. The geocoder returns the ID and address that we submitted, the status of the match, the address our address was matched to (in capital letters), the longitude and latitude coordinates, a unique ID for the matching TIGER street segment, and the side of the street the address is on. Record 5 was matched but the result is nonexact, while Record 4 was returned as a tie with no data. In Manhattan, New York City, addresses along streets must be prefixed with an East or West qualifier, because addresses repeat on opposite sides of Broadway. Since there is an E 50 23rd and W 50

23rd Street address within the same ZIP Code, the geocoder found both entries and returned a tie. Apparently, there is only one 151 25th Street in that ZIP Code and it's E 151 25th St, so the Geocoder returned that address as the result and marked it as a partial match. There was no match for Record 3 as it's fictitious (Metropolis, Nevada, is a ghost town).

Using the geocoder requires that you do some work before and after the geocoding operation. It's likely that your address data will contain additional fields that are relevant to you. If you are using a spreadsheet, you'll need to copy just the address fields out of your sheet and paste them into a separate sheet, excluding the header row. If your data lacks a unique ID, you should assign that to your *original* sheet first, before creating the extract. Once you have your geocoded results, you will need to tie them back to your original data using that unique ID (with VLOOKUP), so you can associate the coordinates or geographic identifiers for the records back to your original data. If you have more than 10,000 records to match, you will have to divide your spreadsheet into separate sheets of 10k records each that you will export out to individual CSVs. If you are using a relational database, you can run queries to isolate just the five attribute fields you need in batches of 10k records that can be exported out to CSVs. The geocoded results could be imported back into the database, and a series of joins or update statements could be used to tie the coordinates back to the original data.

You will probably need to clean your data before and after the process. The geocoder does not return coordinates for partial matches, nor can it handle addresses that are post office boxes. Once you obtain the results from the geocoder, you may want to improve the addresses to eliminate partials, ties, and nonmatching records.

Addresses with coordinates can be plotted in GIS and converted into a GIS layer; see Chapter 10 for details. If you have a large batch of addresses to geocode and know a scripting language, the Census Geocoder has an API that you can use. You can connect to it through Python or another language, pass addresses from a file through the script, store the results in the program, and then write them out to a file.

## 11.6    REVIEW QUESTIONS AND PRACTICE EXERCISES

1.  Explain the difference between population density and population concentration, and describe how to calculate both.

2.  Download Table P5 Hispanic or Latino Origin by Race from the 2010 census for all census tracts in Miami-Dade County (FIPS 086), Florida. Calculate

the dissimilarity index of segregation between the non-Hispanic white, non-Hispanic black, and Hispanic/Latino populations.

3. Use the Geocorr tool to create a crosswalk table between census tracts and all places within Miami-Dade County, Florida, using population as the allocation factor. Bring the crosswalk into a spreadsheet, and identify all census tracts where 50% or more of the population lives within the City of Miami. Use your finished crosswalk table to identify all the tracts in the P5 table from Question 2 that fall within Miami.

4. Download tables B19013 Median Household Income from the 1-year 2010 and 2016 ACS for all four census regions (Northeast, Midwest, South, and West). Bring the data together into one spreadsheet, and calculate the change in income between those 2 years. Use the BLS calculator to adjust the values for inflation to 2016 dollars.

5. Summarize some of the different approaches for location analysis.

---

**Supplementary Digital Content:** Find datasets and supplemental exercises at the companion website at `http://study.sagepub.com/census`.

# HISTORICAL DATA
# AND MICRODATA

## 12.1   INTRODUCTION

Our focus in this book has been on census data that's summarized for population groups and places for the present and recent past. In this final chapter, we will discuss historic summary data and microdata, the latter referring to datasets that consist of individual responses to census questionnaires. These two topics are paired together in this chapter because the primary source we'll cover for accessing both is the IPUMS project at the Minnesota Population Center at the University of Minnesota.

IPUMS is an acronym for Integrated Public Use Microdata Samples and refers to the umbrella organization that manages several different datasets that consist primarily of microdata. The project provides value to these datasets by integrating data from many different sources across space and time, providing some standardization of groups and categories to facilitate analysis, archiving the data, and publishing user-friendly documentation and online interfaces for interacting with and extracting data (Kugler & Fitch, 2018).

IPUMS NHGIS (National Historic Geographic Information System) is distinct from the other IPUMS data collections in that it does not provide microdata but provides historical U.S. Census summary data for every decennial census, all releases of the American Community Survey (ACS), and several other datasets. The U.S. Census Bureau does not focus on providing or maintaining historic data, so if you need census data prior to the 21st century the NHGIS will be the source for both the tabular data and GIS boundary files.

In this chapter, we will walk through the NHGIS interface for accessing data, but before we do we'll address a number of considerations that researchers face when working with historic data. Census questions change over time, new questions are added while others are removed, and various categories are revised and adjusted. Census geography, both legal and statistical, is also revised on an ongoing basis, which makes direct comparisons difficult the further back you go in time. The NHGIS provides nominal data for all time periods, meaning that the data is presented just as it was originally reported (although IPUMS does add value to its datasets by applying standardized codes to facilitate studying data across time periods). We will discuss the process of normalization, which is a technique for adjusting old data to fit the geographic boundaries of current data in order to make direct comparisons. The Diversity and Disparities Project at Brown University provides tools for normalizing census tract data and precompiled, normalized data from 1970 to the present. We will conclude with an overview of this resource before moving on to our second topic, microdata.

The Census Bureau's Public Use Microdata Samples (PUMS) are extracts of samples of individual responses to census questionnaires from the decennial census and the ACS, with personal identifying information removed to protect the confidentiality of respondents. The PUMS allows researchers to create their own cross tabulations that are not available for the summarized datasets. The Census Bureau also publishes a number of smaller sample surveys that it publishes microdata for, the most noteworthy being the Current Population Survey (CPS). The CPS is an ongoing, monthly survey that's jointly conducted by the Census Bureau and the Bureau of Labor Statistics (BLS) to constantly monitor key socioeconomic characteristics of the population and to occasionally capture data for special topics that are not captured in other datasets.

Working with microdata is fundamentally different from working with summary data, as you are working with records that represent individual responses to a questionnaire and not with data that's summarized to represent the entire population of an area. Researchers use the samples to generate estimates of total populations using special variables called weights. The Census Bureau publishes different weights for persons, households, and housing units, where the weight for that response indicates how many people in the population that record would represent. Given the size of the samples and the need to protect confidentiality, census microdata can only be used to create estimates for large geographic areas.

Given its utility and primary use as a microdata set, we'll provide an introduction to microdata using the CPS and will use the IPUMS CPS series to demonstrate how to create an extract and estimates using sample weights. Both the IPUMS interface and process for working with CPS microdata are similar to the IPUMS USA series, which contains PUMS for the decennial census and ACS. We'll briefly touch on the Census Bureau's own tools for exploring recent versions of the CPS and PUMS files.

To use any of the IPUMS resources at `https://www.ipums.org/`, you need to register and create an account. Registration is free, but use of the data is limited to noncommercial or educational use, and you must cite the IPUMS project in your work. You can visit any one of the sites in the series to create an account, and your account will be valid across all the data series. The Longitudinal Tract Database (LTDB) system at Brown University at `https://s4.ad.brown.edu/projects/diversity/Researcher/Bridging.htm` requires users to submit an email address when downloading any of the crosswalks or datasets, and they have similar license restrictions regarding acceptable use.

Since this is the final chapter of the book, we will conclude with some additional resources and technologies that you may wish to explore on your own.

## 12.2   HISTORICAL CENSUS DATA

While census data is remarkably consistent over time relative to other data sources, questions, categories, and geography do change to reflect broader changes in society. We'll explore these issues first, before proceeding to the NHGIS for accessing historic census data and the LTDB for obtaining normalized data.

### Historical Considerations

As discussed in Chapter 1, the questions that appear in the decennial census and the ACS have some basis in federal law or are requested by Congress for a specific purpose. Questions are added or dropped from the census forms as new laws are passed and old requirements fade in importance. For example, in the 2000s, questions were added on health care insurance and internet access as these issues grew in pertinence in society, and laws were passed mandating health insurance coverage and promoting internet connectivity. A question on whether homes have air conditioning that had been asked for several decades was removed in the 1990 census, as air conditioning had become more commonplace. When questions are added or removed, researchers often turn to administrative datasets to provide continuity and usually need to make compromises as these datasets are less geographically detailed.

The categories used for classifying people, housing units, and businesses also change to reflect changes in the economy and society. As we saw in Chapter 8, NAICS codes for classifying industries are updated every 5 years, and researchers must use concordances to create comparable categories. We discussed racial categories and how they have changed over time in Chapter 4. Two notable changes in the recent past include the addition of a Hispanic or Latino ethnicity question that was introduced in 1970 and became standardized in 1980, and the ability of respondents to select multiple races beginning in the year 2000. If the total population of a single race in a particular area grew or declined in 2000, some of that change might be due to actual population change, while some portion could be attributed to respondents' new ability to select multiple races. Studying these populations prior to the introduction of these questions is not straightforward. Possible approaches include looking at data for the first census year when questions for a group were introduced and comparing it with population totals for *other* groups in previous years to create an estimate of what the earlier population might have been, or to rely on other surveys or sources to create estimates. Another approach would be to study the individual responses of respondents, which become available 72 years after a survey is taken (see InfoBox 12.1).

Beyond changes in categories, changes in data collection methods and accuracy can also have an impact on historical comparisons. Recall from Chapter 5 the issues of differential undercounting of races in the decennial census and from Chapter 6 changes to sampling and weighting methodology in the ACS. The most fundamental change in data collection methods was the discontinuation of the decennial census long form in 2010 that coincided with the introduction of the ACS. To make historical comparisons, you would compare the basic demographic count data from the 2010 and 2020 decennial censuses with earlier 10-year counts while comparing the detailed socioeconomic variables from the ACS to previous decennial long form estimates from 2000 and back. Common practice is to use the 1-year ACS from 2010 or the 5-year 2008–2012 ACS for these comparisons, where 2010 in the 5-year ACS represents the midpoint year. The Census Bureau has published suggestions for making historical comparisons between the ACS and earlier decennial censuses at `https://www.census.gov/programs-surveys/acs/guidance.html`.

As discussed in Chapter 11, for money-related variables, the Census Bureau publishes data in nominal dollar values that reflect the value of money at the time the data was collected. If you are studying income, rent, home values, or any dollar-related variable over time, you need to adjust the values for inflation. Refer to Chapter 11 and the BLS's Consumer Price Index Inflation calculator at `https://www.bls.gov/data/inflation_calculator.htm`.

Changes in census geography present the biggest challenge in making comparisons over time. While changes in questions and categories are finite, changes in geography are universal from one decennial census to the next, and legal areas can change

> ## ✓ INFOBOX 12.1 HISTORIC CENSUS RECORDS FOR INDIVIDUALS
>
> The individual responses to the census questionnaires complete with names and addresses are released once 72 years have passed, so it becomes possible to get detailed data on individual people and households. The Census Bureau passes the documents over to the National Archives, which preserves and provides access to them. In the past, the forms were simply microfilmed and held in various libraries, but the Archives began making digital copies of newly released data available on the web. The 1940 census was released in April 2012 and can be explored at `https://1940census.archives.gov/`. Information on finding data from previous censuses is available at `https://www.archives.gov/research/census`.
>
> The enumeration sheets from 1940 were scanned and saved as high-resolution images. Since the data stored within the document can't be searched and the metadata is minimal, the only effective way to find information is by address. If you were looking for a specific person, you would need to know where they lived, then search through maps of enumeration districts to find that address, and then scan through a series of enumeration sheets to find the person you're looking for. Forms for individual households were not introduced until 1960, so these documents are ledgers where responses from many households were compiled on a single page. A sample of a 1940 form where some of my relatives lived in South Philadelphia is shown in Figure 12.1.
>
> These documents are a treasure trove for historical researchers and genealogists, and they form the backbone of datasets provided by genealogy companies like Ancestry.com who invest a lot of effort in capturing the data from these forms and making it searchable. If you are doing quantitative historical research, working with this data is challenging and time-consuming as it is not in a machine-readable format (delimited-text, spreadsheet, or database). Researchers have often turned to historic PUMS microdata files as an alternative.
>
> The 1950 census is next to be released in April 2022.

between one ACS and the next. At the highest level, census divisions, regions, and states are the most stable areas and have changed very little in the past 100 years (Alaska and Hawaii became states in 1959 but earlier data is published for them when they were territories).

Counties are frequently used for historical comparisons given the large amount of data that's available for them and the fact that they are the smallest unit of geography available for the entire country before the mid-20th century. The Census Bureau publishes all county-level changes from 1970 onward at `https://www.census.gov/programs-surveys/geography/technical-documentation/county-changes.html`. Many of these changes are minor and consist of adjustments to names or ID codes, but occasionally, these changes involve creation, dissolution, or modification of boundaries. You can adjust your data to

## FIGURE 12.1 ● A 1940 CENSUS ENUMERATION FORM FROM PHILADELPHIA

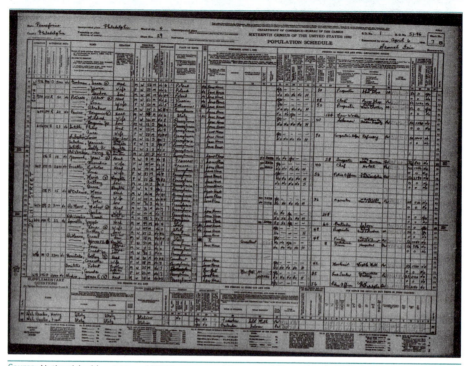

*Source:* National Archives https://1940census.archives.gov/. Pennsylvania, Philadelphia County, Philadelphia, ED 51-96, Image 14.

account for these changes by using apportionment or assignment techniques demonstrated in Chapter 11. As discussed in Chapter 3, Alaska and Virginia are the two states where counties often change over time. The definitions for metropolitan areas change on a frequent basis (several times each decade), but since they are county based, you can use county-level data to reconstruct data from the past to fit current definitions.

Census tracts are the smallest viable census geography used for measuring change over time below the county level. They were designed to be relatively permanent statistical areas defined by population, and to the extent possible, the Census Bureau minimizes changes to these areas (see Chapter 3). Boundaries are redrawn every 10 years, and between the 2000 and 2010 censuses, 69% of tracts either had no boundary changes or had minor changes that had no impact on the population of the tract (Logan et al., 2014). Of the tracts that did change, about 1.5% were simple consolidations (tracts that lost population were combined into larger areas), 17% were simple splits where one tract was split into one or many tracts (due to population growth), while 12% were involved in more complex boundary changes.

Given the consistency of the tract boundaries and numbering schemes, researchers often use normalized tract data when making historical comparisons. Normalization is the process of taking data published for boundaries in the past and modifying it to fit boundaries of the present. This process involves creating an apportionment or crosswalking scheme similar to what we discussed in Chapter 11, where you create a relational table to adjust the data from the past. If two tracts from the past are aggregated in the present, the data from the past is aggregated, whereas if a tract from the past was split into two tracts in the present, the past data is split proportionally based on either land area or population.

Researchers who are part of the Diversity and Disparity Project at Brown University have created a series of census tract crosswalks from 1970 to 2010 called the LTDB. You can download these tables to crosswalk your own data, or you can download precompiled tract data that's been normalized for a selection of the most common variables. The work for this project has been documented in a number of articles (Logan, Stults, & Xu, 2016; Logan, Xu, & Stults, 2014). We will explore this resource at the end of this section. An alternate source for prepublished normalized tract data is the Neighborhood Change Database published by the Geolytics company. It is a proprietary product that has been in the market for several decades, and many academic libraries have a subscription.

The 1970 census is the typical starting point for contemporary historical research, as data collection methods, subject categories, and the delineation of census geography as we know it began with that census. Tract-level data is available back to 1940, and unofficial tabulations for the largest cities is available back to 1910. An additional challenge to working with census tracts is that they have only covered the United States in its entirety since 1990 (together with a now extinct corollary called a block numbering area). In earlier decades, census tracts were only delineated within urbanized areas.

Historical research using other geographies is more challenging. Census blocks and block groups are completely renumbered following each decennial census, making a direct one-to-one relationship impossible. The Census Bureau does publish relational files to connect these geographies to the ones from the previous census, but given the large number of data points (at the block level in particular), relating these areas across time is difficult. Areas where tracts do not nest, such as incorporated places and Public Use Microdata Areas, are also difficult to work with. You would need to apply an apportionment scheme using tracts to create past estimates that fit modern boundaries. ZIP Code Tabulation Areas are a recent invention (2000 census), and since they are built from blocks and conform to no other boundaries they should be avoided for historical analysis.

## National Historic Geographic Information System

The Census Bureau does not specialize in providing historic data, nor does it focus on producing data tables for comparisons between one census and the next. There are a few exceptions, such as Tables CP02 through CP05 that compare two consecutive time periods for the ACS data profiles. Currently, you can retrieve the past two decennial censuses and all ACS data back to 2005 directly from the Census Bureau. Population estimates stretching back several decades are available on the Population Estimates Program page, and a few decades of business data from the Business Patterns and Economic Census are available on the individual program pages. The Missouri Census Data Center provides decennial census data back to 1980 and ACS data back to 2005, and as we have seen, they publish some comparative data for the recent past.

The IPUMS NHGIS is the main source for original, nonnormalized census data. They provide decennial data back to the first census in 1790, ACS data back to 2005, and the County Business Patterns back to 1970. They also archive a number of specialized datasets, including over 100 years of vital statistics from the Centers for Disease Control and Prevention. Most of the data provided by the NHGIS is nominal, published in the same manner as it was originally released. They do publish a select number of historical comparison tables, where comparable data for multiple decades can be downloaded in one extract. They provide nominal data with no adjustments for changes in categories or geography from 1970 to 2010 when possible, and for certain tables and variables, they provide normalized data from 1990 to 2010. The NHGIS is also the source for historical GIS boundary files, so if you need census tracts from 1980, or counties from 1880 this will be your source.

Let's walk through an example where we will download and map college graduates by census tract in 1970 for a given area. From the NHGIS page at https://www.nhgis.org/, click the Get Data button to Create an Extract. The NHGIS uses filtering options similar to **data.census.gov**, and we can follow the same search path we outlined back in Chapter 2, where we chose a geography, year, topic, and dataset. Click on Geographic Levels. Each of these filtering screens will look similar: The central portion of the screen contains a list of possible geographies, while the options on the left allow you to filter the geographies listed in the central portion. The Most Popular option is selected by default. Under each geography, there is a green circle with a plus symbol. You click the plus symbol to make a selection, which turns the circle to a check mark (Figure 12.2). The NHGIS does *not* give you the option to filter geographies, so we can't select all the tracts in Pennsylvania for example. We simply have to take them all.

**FIGURE 12.2** ● NHGIS GEOGRAPHY SELECTION MENU

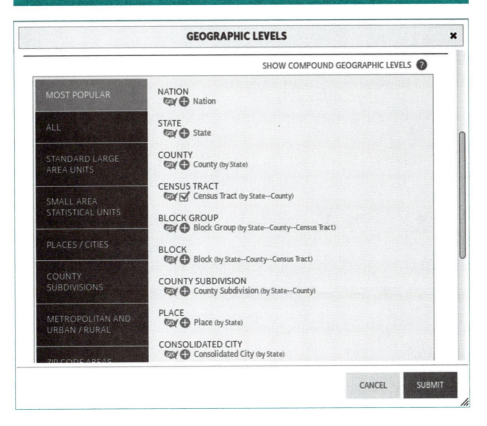

Click Submit. Back on the main search screen, a list of possible tables in the NHGIS database where data is available for tracts is displayed. Click on Years, check the box for 1970, and click Submit. The list of tables is narrowed down further. Click on the Topics filter, scroll down and under Population scroll further until you see Education, and select the first row for educational attainment. Click Submit, and we'll see that the tables have been filtered further.

The last filter for Datasets is something you should use only if you're familiar with the construction of the files for each era. Recall from Chapter 5 that the 2010 decennial census consisted of the public redistricting file PL 94-171 and two summary files, SF1 and SF2, that contain the 100% count and several extra race cross-tabulation tables, respectively. In the NHGIS, these files are further subdivided based on the smallest level of geography available. Older decennial censuses used a similar SF1 and SF2 structure, but the detailed one in six sample data for the socioeconomic characteristics of the population was stored in SF3, with detailed racial cross tabulations in SF4. The

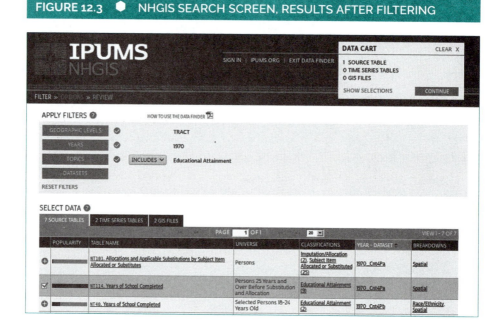

FIGURE 12.3 ● NHGIS SEARCH SCREEN, RESULTS AFTER FILTERING

NHGIS provides some description under the Datasets tab regarding what the files capture. We won't filter by datasets in this example.

At this stage, we have already filtered enough that we can see what tract-level educational attainment tables were available in 1970. Table NT114 Years of School Completed appears near the top, and a popularity ranking (in terms of downloads) is a clue that this is probably the table we're looking for (Figure 12.3). The Universe column (the population measured by this variable) tells us that it is for people aged 25 and above, in contrast to the table below it (NT40), which is for people aged 18 to 24.

Notice that each attribute has a link so you can get a description of the tables and the categories. Under Classifications, click the educational attainment link. You'll see the range of categories (columns) that are available in this table. There is a summary for people who completed 4 years of college (C06009) and another for people who completed 5 or more years of college (C06010). This question differs from the modern equivalent, which asks people if they have obtained an actual degree: associate's, bachelor's, or master's and above. These kinds of discrepancies are a fairly common obstacle when working with historic data. To gain more insight, we could consult the questionnaire and documentation for 1970, all of which are archived on the NHGIS website. We would have to assume that people who have 4 years of college finished their bachelor's degree (a more realistic assumption for that time vs. today) and that people with 5 or more years obtained their bachelor's and either pursued or obtained a graduate degree.

Close the description and return to the main menu. Click the green plus symbol beside the NT114 table to add it to our cart. Notice that this list of tables is presented on a tab titled Source Tables (Figure 12.3). There are additional tabs for time series tables and GIS files. Clicking on the time series tab reveals that a comparison table for this table from 1970 to 2010 is available; it's marked as a nominal (not normalized) table, which means the categories and geographies are reported "as is." The final tab let's you select GIS files that are relevant based on the filters. Click on this tab, and select the first file for 1970 census tracts to add it to the cart.

In the window in the upper right-hand corner, click Continue. This will bring you to an options screen where you can review your choices. If you didn't select a geography in the previous screen, you're given a second chance to do it here. Click Submit. On the final Review screen, you're asked to provide output formats; whether you want a CSV or a statistical package file, and whether you want a descriptive header row or not. Change the format to CSV. If your data file is destined for GIS or a database, you do *not* want to include the descriptive row option, don't select it. Click Submit. At this point, if you haven't logged into NHGIS, you'll be prompted to do so. You'll be shown an extracts history that displays all your requests, and once the data has been processed, links will appear for downloading the data tables and the GIS files.

When you download tables, they will be packaged in a ZIP file, where the files are named sequentially based on the extract number and source. Each file comes with a codebook, which correlates the names of the column headings with the variable names. Import the CSV into Calc, but on the import screen, be careful and designate the ID columns at the front of the table as text, to avoid losing leading zeros (Figure 12.4).

The unique identifier for the records is GISJOIN, which is a variant of the standard FIPS code. It begins with the letter "G," has extra zeros between the state and county codes, and (for tracts) does not include trailing zeros if the tract doesn't have decimals. GISJOIN is designed to match the unique IDs of all the GIS files that NHGIS publishes. The component geographic identifiers appear in separate columns. The AREANAME is the last identifier, and the actual variables follow it. The variable IDs and descriptions are provided in the codebook. Notice that this data file does not include a total count of the aged 25 and above population, nor does it include percentages. We would have to calculate these ourselves. To get this total, we can simply sum all the columns since there is no overlap between categories.

## FIGURE 12.4 ● NHGIS DATA EXTRACT, EDUCATIONAL ATTAINMENT BY TRACT 1970

| | A | B | C | D | E | F | I | K | O | P | Q | R | S | T | U |
|---|---|---|---|---|---|---|---|---|---|---|---|---|---|---|---|
| 1 | GISJOIN | YEAR | STATE | STATEA | COUNTY | COUNTYA | TRACTA | SMSAA | AREANAME | C06001 | C06002 | C06003 | C06004 | C06005 | C06006 |
| 2 | G01000300101 | 1970 | Alabama | 01 | Baldwin | 003 | 0101 | 5160 | Tract 101 | 100 | 242 | 198 | 103 | 178 | 360 |
| 3 | G01000300102 | 1970 | Alabama | 01 | Baldwin | 003 | 0102 | 5160 | Tract 102 | 21 | 66 | 145 | 93 | 77 | 235 |
| 4 | G01000300103 | 1970 | Alabama | 01 | Baldwin | 003 | 0103 | 5160 | Tract 103 | 38 | 114 | 164 | 66 | 140 | 241 |
| 5 | G01000300104 | 1970 | Alabama | 01 | Baldwin | 003 | 0104 | 5160 | Tract 104 | 31 | 143 | 162 | 98 | 147 | 229 |
| 6 | G01000300105 | 1970 | Alabama | 01 | Baldwin | 003 | 0105 | 5160 | Tract 105 | 25 | 72 | 109 | 105 | 123 | 409 |
| 7 | G01000300106 | 1970 | Alabama | 01 | Baldwin | 003 | 0106 | 5160 | Tract 106 | 36 | 100 | 152 | 57 | 99 | 219 |
| 8 | G01000300107 | 1970 | Alabama | 01 | Baldwin | 003 | 0107 | 5160 | Tract 107 | 60 | 233 | 206 | 166 | 211 | 615 |
| 9 | G01000300108 | 1970 | Alabama | 01 | Baldwin | 003 | 0108 | 5160 | Tract 108 | 24 | 46 | 171 | 35 | 83 | 259 |
| 10 | G01000300109 | 1970 | Alabama | 01 | Baldwin | 003 | 0109 | 5160 | Tract 109 | 85 | 308 | 501 | 248 | 520 | 947 |
| 11 | G01000300110 | 1970 | Alabama | 01 | Baldwin | 003 | 0110 | 5160 | Tract 110 | 20 | 66 | 92 | 100 | 86 | 169 |
| 12 | G01000300111 | 1970 | Alabama | 01 | Baldwin | 003 | 0111 | 5160 | Tract 111 | 33 | 50 | 130 | 117 | 212 | 343 |
| 13 | G01000300112 | 1970 | Alabama | 01 | Baldwin | 003 | 0112 | 5160 | Tract 112 | 53 | 97 | 166 | 101 | 189 | 552 |
| 14 | G01000300113 | 1970 | Alabama | 01 | Baldwin | 003 | 0113 | 5160 | Tract 113 | 8 | 35 | 68 | 77 | 110 | 206 |
| 15 | G01000300114 | 1970 | Alabama | 01 | Baldwin | 003 | 0114 | 5160 | Tract 114 | 72 | 172 | 343 | 319 | 382 | 978 |
| 16 | G01000300115 | 1970 | Alabama | 01 | Baldwin | 003 | 0115 | 5160 | Tract 115 | 35 | 105 | 158 | 119 | 208 | 351 |
| 17 | G01000300116 | 1970 | Alabama | 01 | Baldwin | 003 | 0116 | 5160 | Tract 116 | 21 | 55 | 163 | 87 | 223 | 406 |
| 18 | G01003300201 | 1970 | Alabama | 01 | Colbert | 033 | 0201 | | Tract 201 | 47 | 113 | 216 | 118 | 252 | 789 |
| 19 | G0100330020199 | 1970 | Alabama | 01 | Colbert | 033 | 020199 | | Tract 201.99 | 0 | 0 | 0 | 0 | 0 | 5 |
| 20 | G01003300202 | 1970 | Alabama | 01 | Colbert | 033 | 0202 | | Tract 202 | 12 | 45 | 108 | 76 | 154 | 399 |

Using the techniques we learned in Chapter 10, you can use the boundary file and this table to create a map in QGIS. First, you would add the tract shapefile to QGIS as a vector layer. The default coordinating reference system for all NHGIS layers is USA Contiguous Albers Equal Area, which is a common projected coordinate system for making maps of the United States. You could select all the tracts that fall within your state and county of interest using the Select by Attributes feature, and then you can export just those selected features as a new layer. During the export process, you can also transform the area to the local state plane zone. Once this new layer is added to the map, you can reset the window to match that file's CRS and remove the original layer.

Once you have modified the data table to include percent totals or other derivatives, you can save it in a Calc or Excel spreadsheet format, add it to your project, and join it to the shapefile using the join tab in the properties window. The style tab in the properties window can be used to create a graduated areas map. When creating maps of historical nonnormalized data, a common technique is to display the two time periods using the two different geographies side by side. It's important to adjust the classification schemes of the two maps to the same scheme, so that you can make an even comparison. You may also need to clip the boundaries of one layer by the other, in order to account for differences in how water features have been drawn over time.

To create such as map, you would return to NHGIS and download educational attainment data from the 2008–2012 ACS and 2010 census tract boundaries. In QGIS, you would add the 2010 boundaries and data to the same project as the 1970 layers. You can only view one period at a time in the main data screen, but in the map layout/design screen, you could add the 1970 map, lock it's features and symbols, return to the data view, turn off the 1970 features and turn on the 2010 features,

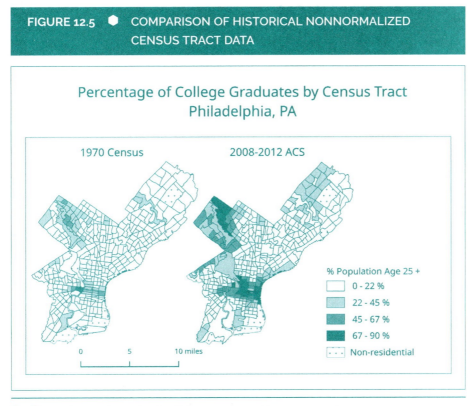

FIGURE 12.5  ⬡  COMPARISON OF HISTORICAL NONNORMALIZED CENSUS TRACT DATA

Percentage of College Graduates by Census Tract
Philadelphia, PA

1970 Census        2008-2012 ACS

% Population Age 25 +
☐ 0 - 22 %
▨ 22 - 45 %
▦ 45 - 67 %
▩ 67 - 90 %
⋯ Non-residential

0     5     10 miles

*Data Source:* IPUMS NHGIS, University of Minnesota, `https://www.nhgis.org/`

return to the layout, and add the 2010 map. Figure 12.5 is an example of a map comparing nonnormalized tract-level data for educational attainment in Philadelphia, created from NHGIS data. Read the online QGIS documentation for details on map layout.

NHGIS did provide a nonnormalized time-series table for this particular variable. These tables are useful if you know that you want to compare several decades of data between 1970 and 2010, as it saves you the time and trouble of downloading and modifying multiple tables. In a nonnormalized table, there is one record for each geography that existed in a given point in time, with different ID codes that indicate the period or periods in which the geography existed. This data can be used for making stand-alone maps for each decade.

## Normalization

To illustrate change over time using current geography in a single map, you would need to use normalized data. Unlike the map in Figure 12.5, with normalized data you'd be able to use just the recent set of tract boundaries to display data from both time periods. This allows for better, direct comparison of the data and the ability to calculate and depict change over time within census tracts. The NHGIS publishes a number of normalized time-series tables from 1990 to 2010. If you need to go back further in time, the LTDB at Brown University is your alternative for obtaining normalized data back to 1970 or for getting crosswalk tables to do your own normalization.

On the LTDB page at `https://s4.ad.brown.edu/Projects/Diversity/Researcher/LTDB.htm`, click on the link to access the download page. After submitting your email address and agreeing to the requirements, you are presented with a series of options that include downloading either normalized or nonnormalized data from the full (100% count) or sample (1 in 6) data for 1 year or all years, or downloading crosswalks in various file formats. There is a codebook that displays which variables are included in the precompiled data for a given decade. For our example, there is a variable for the number of people who completed a 4-year college degree.

Download the normalized sample table for 1970 and import the CSV in Calc. You'll see that there is one record for each 2010 census tract (Figure 12.6). Each of the variables is in a decimal format, as the project coordinators chose to display the precise outcome of the apportionment between tracts. To map this data, first we would need to calculate the percent total who completed college using the AGE25UP70 column and the COL70 column. We'd save the result as a spreadsheet, and then we would need to obtain a 2010-era tract file to join this data to. The unique identifiers in the LTDB are actual FIPS codes stored in the TRTID10 column, so it would be better to use one of the TIGER Line shapefiles instead of the NHGIS layers so that we have matching ID columns. To compute change over time, we could either download the sample data from 2010 and use VLOOKUP to tie it to the data from 1970 in the same spreadsheet or we could download a data table that contains all five decades and select just the years we want.

**FIGURE 12.6 ● LTDB DATA EXTRACT, NORMALIZED EDUCATIONAL ATTAINMENT BY TRACT 1970**

| | A | B | C | D | E | F | G | H | AC | AD | AE | AF |
|---|---|---|---|---|---|---|---|---|---|---|---|---|
| 1 | TRTID10 | state | county | tract | placefp10 | cbsa10 | metdiv10 | ccflag10 | AG25UP70 | HS70 | COL70 | CLF70 |
| 2 | 1001020500 | AL | Autauga County | Census Tract 205 | 62328 | 33860 | 99999 | 0 | 4.124946117 | 3.676666021 | 0.202976599 | 2.85610199 |
| 3 | 1003010100 | AL | Baldwin County | Census Tract 101 | 99999 | 19300 | 99999 | 0 | 1728 | 1612 | 68 | 1127 |
| 4 | 1003010200 | AL | Baldwin County | Census Tract 102 | 99999 | 19300 | 99999 | 0 | 980.7607231 | 934.0598211 | 15.22990914 | 640.0628239 |
| 5 | 1003010300 | AL | Baldwin County | Census Tract 103 | 99999 | 19300 | 99999 | 0 | 1743.480037 | 1621.714156 | 58.7802275 | 1335.939336 |
| 6 | 1003010400 | AL | Baldwin County | Census Tract 104 | 99999 | 19300 | 99999 | 0 | 1327.248937 | 1198.388204 | 72.00596842 | 966.8587595 |
| 7 | 1003010500 | AL | Baldwin County | Census Tract 105 | 4660 | 19300 | 99999 | 0 | 1647.232052 | 1300.550271 | 174.6706974 | 1239.600366 |
| 8 | 1003010600 | AL | Baldwin County | Census Tract 106 | 4660 | 19300 | 99999 | 0 | 840.5013847 | 762.4917822 | 48.31879944 | 738.6747091 |
| 9 | 1003010701 | AL | Baldwin County | Census Tract 107.01 | 71976 | 19300 | 99999 | 0 | 1333.862915 | 1071.435791 | 145.6982269 | 950.0205688 |
| 10 | 1003010703 | AL | Baldwin County | Census Tract 107.03 | 99999 | 19300 | 99999 | 0 | 1457.38005 | 1170.677319 | 159.1748846 | 1038.004301 |
| 11 | 1003010704 | AL | Baldwin County | Census Tract 107.04 | 19648 | 19300 | 99999 | 1 | 87.53885651 | 70.31626129 | 9.561893463 | 62.34801865 |
| 12 | 1003010705 | AL | Baldwin County | Census Tract 107.05 | 19648 | 19300 | 99999 | 1 | 177.2117157 | 142.3466949 | 19.35688591 | 126.21595 |

If the variables we are interested in didn't exist in the precompiled LTDB tables, we could use one of the crosswalks to normalize the data ourselves. On the LTDB download page, you would choose the data you wish to crosswalk, in this case 1970 to 2010, and download the Excel format. The table is constructed so that every row lists a 2010 tract ID, the ID of a tract in the source year that contributes to it, and the percentage of the source tract's population attributes that should be allocated to the 2010 tract. If there is an exact relationship between the source and 2010 tract, then there is only one row of data, otherwise there are as many rows as there are contributing tracts.

The crosswalk can be applied to the nominal, unadjusted historic data that's available on the LTDB page, or with nominal data from the NHGIS. If you're using data from the NHGIS, you will need to re-create the proper FIPS codes in order to associate the historic data with the crosswalk, as the NHGIS GISJOIN identifier is not an actual FIPS code. In a spreadsheet, you can make the adjustment like this:

=IF((LEN(T)=4),CONCATENATE(S,C,T,"00"),CONCATENATE(S,C,T))

where T is the cell that contains the census tract ID, S is the cell with the state ID, and C is the cell with the county ID. If the length of the tract ID is only four characters long, join the component FIPS and add two trailing zeros, otherwise just join the components. Concatenating these values is simpler than modifying the existing GISJOIN code. For this formula to work, it's important that you imported the CSV data into the spreadsheet correctly as text values. This operation will not work on numeric values, and any identifiers imported as numbers will lose leading zeros.

A database is better suited for crosswalking than a spreadsheet. Begin the process with a spreadsheet to make sure your ID codes are correct in your historic file, calculate totals, and eliminate columns that you don't need. Then in SQLite, import both the crosswalk and the historic tract table, join them using the 1970 tract ID, and do the weighting calculations in an SQL GROUP BY statement. The following statement illustrates part of the process:

```
SELECT cw.trtid10, cw.trtid70, cw.weight, c.C06009 AS col4yr,
c.C06010 AS col5yr, (c.C06009 + c.C06010) AS totcol,
ROUND(cw.weight*c.c06009 + cw.weight*c.c06010) as wgtcol
FROM crosswalk cw
INNER JOIN college1970 c ON (cw.trtid70=c.fips)
ORDER BY trtid10, trtid70;
```

The crosswalk table is joined to the historic table using the 1970 tract ID from the crosswalk and the 1970 FIPS code from the historic table. Each record represents a

## FIGURE 12.7 ● INITIAL SQL RESULT FOR NORMALIZING DATA

| | trtid10 | trtid70 | weight | col4yr | col5yr | totcol | wgtcol |
|---|---|---|---|---|---|---|---|
| 1 | 01001020500 | 01051010400 | 0.000961974380216139 | 123 | 81 | 204 | 0.0 |
| 2 | 01003010100 | 01003010100 | 0.999999990728862 | 59 | 5 | 64 | 64.0 |
| 3 | 01003010200 | 01003010100 | 0.0 | 59 | 5 | 64 | 0.0 |
| 4 | 01003010200 | 01003010200 | 0.966843049005554 | 5 | 0 | 5 | 5.0 |
| 5 | 01003010200 | 01003010300 | 1.77351955413484e-07 | 13 | 15 | 28 | 0.0 |
| 6 | 01003010200 | 01003010500 | 0.0488060537965405 | 129 | 68 | 197 | 10.0 |

portion of the 1970 tract that is in a 2010 tract. Figure 12.7 illustrates a portion of the query result. In the first record, the 2010 tract (205) only appears once, and only a small portion of a single 1970 tract falls within the 2010 tract. Presumably, the 2010 tract consists of an area that was largely unpopulated in 1970. In the second record, the relationship between the 2010 (101) and 1970 tract is essentially one to one, based on the large weight and the fact that this 2010 tract only appears once. The last four records are for one 2010 tract (102), and there are four tracts from 1970 that fall partially within it. The majority of 1970 Tract 200 (96.7%) falls inside it, along with small percentages of the other tracts (note that the value for 1970 Tract 300 ends with the scientific notation e-07, indicating that this is an infinitesimally small percentage and *not* a whole number of 1.77).

The fields for the number of people who completed 4 and 5 years of college and the sum of these values represents the total for the 1970 census tract. To calculate the percentage of this population that falls within the 2010 tract, we multiply the attributes (in this case just the total) by the weight. So for Record 1, there are 204 people who went to college in the 1970 tract, but since the weight is so small (there is little overlap between the 1970 and 2010 tract), the total number allocated to the 2010 tract is zero. In contrast, all 64 people from 1970 in Record 2 are allocated to the 2010 tract as there is complete overlap between them.

For Records 3 through 6, portions of the college population from several 1970 tracts are assigned to the one 2010 tract. The final step is to aggregate this proportional share of population for the pieces of the 1970 tracts back to the total for the 2010 tract, so each record represents a single 2010 tract. The following statement should be used instead of the previous one to complete all the actions in one step:

```
SELECT cw.trtid10,
ROUND(SUM(cw.weight*c.C06009) + SUM(cw.weight*c.C06010))
    AS col70
FROM crosswalk cw
INNER JOIN college1970 c ON (cw.trtid70=c.fips)
GROUP BY cw.trtid10
ORDER BY cw.trtid10;
```

Remember from Chapter 5, in a GROUP BY statement, you can only include identifiers that are being used for categorizing data and attributes that are part of an aggregate function. Here we want the data to be summarized by 2010 tracts, so that we only include the 2010 IDs in the SELECT and GROUP BY clauses. IDs for 1970 cannot be added, otherwise GROUP BY will perform the operation on the unique pairings of both IDs. We multiply the weight by the value for each record and sum them across rows where records are grouped.

If you are working within a specific geographic area, you can use the FIPS codes in a WHERE clause to select tracts within the states and counties that you are interested in. Once you have your normalized counts, you can insert them into a new table to permanently store them, and then you can create additional columns or views where you calculate percentages. Refer back to Chapter 5 for guidance.

While it's more cumbersome, you *could* use a spreadsheet to achieve the same ends by filtering or deleting records you don't want, using VLOOKUP to pull data from the historic table into the crosswalk, use formulas to do the weighting, and then use a pivot table to summarize and group the data by the modern tracts.

To compare and map the 1970 data to modern data, you would download the 2010 or 2008–2012 data from either the NHGIS or the LTDB, join it to the normalized 1970 data using the 2010 IDs, and then join the unified tables to the 2010 tract boundaries. As before, you could download the data from 1970 and 2010 separately and tie them together at the end, or you can download tables that contain data for all five decades and modify them to remove the decades and variables that you're not interested in.

## 12.3  MICRODATA

Microdata are datasets that consist of individual responses to surveys or questionnaires that have been cleaned and standardized in some way. Microdata sits inbetween raw data, which is survey or questionnaire data that has not been processed, and summary data, which has been aggregated by population groups and geography and subdivided into tables to provide counts or estimates for total populations.

The Census Bureau publishes a series of microdata sets that fall under the umbrella term *Public Use Microdata Sample* or *PUMS*. The PUMS files consist of samples of individual responses from both the decennial census and the ACS where personal identifying information from the respondents, such as names and addresses, have been removed. Each record contains values for all attributes for all the questions that were on the questionnaire. Some of the attributes such as age and income contain the specific value that was submitted, while other responses such as race or employment status are assigned a code that indicates what the response is.

Each record has a number of weighting variables that can be used for generating estimates for an entire population of persons, households, or housing units. The weight represents how many people in the general population a particular respondent represents. Microdata allows you to create cross tabulations that do not exist in the published summary tables and provides a different mechanism for creating derived values such as medians or ratios. It's also an accessible, machine-readable alternative to the full declassified census records for studying historical data. For example, one study examined the evolution of the nursing profession by race, sex, and marital status between 1900 and 1950 using IPUMS data (D'Antonio & Whelan, 2009). One of the limitations of using microdata is that estimates can only be produced for large geographic areas such as the nation, census regions and divisions, states, metropolitan areas, and in some cases Public Use Microdata Areas and counties. Data for other geographies can't be produced, partly to protect the confidentiality of respondents but also because the overall number of sample records isn't large enough to produce reliable estimates for either small geographies or large rural areas.

Beyond the decennial census and the ACS, the Census Bureau conducts a number of smaller sample surveys that focus on specific topics (see InfoBox 12.2). The Census Bureau produces microdata for these datasets as well, but unlike the PUMS, the microdata for these datasets contains records for all responses, not just a sample of them (although they are still referred to as samples, as the responses are taken from a sample of the population). The largest and the most widely used dataset of these surveys is the CPS.

In this section, we'll explore the CPS as a source for additional census data and as an example of working with microdata. We'll cover where to access sources for summarized CPS data and we'll also use IPUMS CPS to create an extract of samples that we'll use for generating estimates of the population. We'll conclude with additional sources for accessing microdata.

> ✔ **INFOBOX 12.2 OTHER CENSUS SURVEYS AND ESTIMATES**
>
> This book has focused on the largest datasets that appeal to the broadest array of researchers. The Census Bureau conducts a number of smaller sample surveys that are geared to specific topics, often in cooperation with other federal agencies. A list of all the Census Bureau's programs is available at `https://www.census.gov/programs-surveys/surveys-programs.html`. A selection of some of the major surveys is listed below. Summary and microdata are available for most of these programs.
>
> American Housing Survey: a biennial survey of housing units that collects detailed characteristics on the size and composition of the nation's housing inventory
>
> American Time Use Survey: an annual survey that measures how American's spend their time: working, sleeping, volunteering, socializing, attending school, caring for children, and more
>
> Building Permits: a monthly dataset on the number of new housing units authorized by building permits
>
> Commodity Flow Survey: a sample survey of 100k businesses conducted in Economic Census years that measures domestic freight shipments
>
> Small Area Health and Insurance Estimates: annual model-based estimates of health insurance coverage at the state and county levels
>
> Small Area Income and Poverty Estimates: annual model-based estimates of income and poverty at the state, county, and school-district levels
>
> Survey of Income and Program Participation: survey of households over a multiyear period for measuring economic well-being and family dynamics

## Current Population Survey

The CPS is a monthly sample survey conducted jointly by the Census Bureau and the BLS. Its origins date back to the Great Depression, when the government recognized the need for measuring unemployment on a regular basis in a standardized format, and it was one of the Bureau's first efforts at using sample surveys to generate statistics. As discussed in Chapter 8, it is the primary source for monitoring unemployment and labor force status in the nation.

The CPS samples 60,000 occupied households every month and includes respondents from all 50 states and the District of Columbia. It is unique among census surveys in that it is a longitudinal survey: The same households are surveyed for 4 consecutive months, are out of the survey for 8 months, and return to the survey for a final 4 months. The reference point for the questions for all activities is the week prior to the date the survey is taken, which is usually midmonth. Participants do not fill out and submit the survey themselves; census field representatives collect responses either in person or over the phone. As a result, the responses have a high degree of reliability and the response rate is high (more than 90%). The Census Bureau publishes detailed technical documentation for every aspect of the survey on its website: `https://www.census.gov/programs-surveys/cps.html`.

To be eligible to participate, individuals must be civilians 15 years of age or older and must not live in institutional group quarters facilities such as prisons, long-term care hospitals, or nursing homes. Generally, one person responds on behalf of all eligible members of the household. The questions capture basic socioeconomic and demographic characteristics of the population similar to the ACS, but the primary emphasis is to produce monthly labor force statistics (for a comparison of the differences, see Herman, 2008). Beyond the core questions asked every month are a number of supplemental questions that are asked once or twice a year. For example, the Annual Social and Economic Survey (ASEC) is collected each March and asks detailed questions on educational attainment, job status, earnings, and income. Questions on voting registration and participation are asked every 2 years in November during federal election years. Other supplemental surveys are conducted on a limited or as-needed basis, often at the request and with the cooperation of other federal agencies. Examples include public participation in the arts, households with or without bank accounts, volunteerism, fertility, tobacco use, and civic engagement.

Given the size of the sample and the fact that all responses are provided, estimates can only be generated for large areas: the nation, census regions and divisions, states, and the nation's largest metropolitan areas. Summarized estimates for the CPS are published throughout the Census Bureau's website, usually according to theme. The Census Bureau provides data on income, poverty, and health insurance coverage from the ASEC directly on the CPS website at `https://www.census.gov/programs-surveys/cps.html`. Supplemental data on voting is published on a dedicated page for voting: `https://www.census.gov/topics/public-sector/voting.html`. The monthly data that covers the basic, core part of the survey is published by the BLS at `https://www.bls.gov/cps/`. Data for supplemental topics is often summarized and published by the agency that commissioned the supplement. For example, the FDIC publishes the supplemental data for the unbanked population: `https://www.fdic.gov/householdsurvey/`.

## IPUMS Current Population Survey

For national- and state-level summaries of CPS data, consult the BLS, the Census Bureau's website (the CPS page or pages devoted to subject themes), or the agency that sponsored a supplement. If you want to create your own estimates or cross tabulations from the samples, visit the IPUMS CPS at `https://cps.ipums.org/cps/`. This is the simplest and most comprehensive source for creating extracts, and the website contains a wealth of technical documentation that will help you understand and explore the various samples.

Let's walk through an example where we'll create an extract of the CPS voting supplement and create estimates for census regions. From the IPUMS CPS homepage, select the option to create an extract. The extract page is designed for choosing specific variables from specific samples for specific months and years. Variables are separated based on whether they describe individual persons or entire households. Hover over the Person drop down, and you'll see different categories of variables: the core questions (asked every month), the ASEC, and the supplemental surveys. If you hover over one, additional subcategories will be displayed. Not all the supplements are immediately visible, including the voting supplement. We could choose our sample first and then the variables, or vice versa.

Let's choose the specific sample first. Click the Select Samples button. The samples menu is arranged into three tabs where you can select annual samples from the ASEC, basic monthly samples, and samples related to the supplemental measures. Samples from the past 10 years are selected by default. This is convenient for researchers who are doing large projects who either want to draw data from multiple samples to increase the sample size, or want to study change over time. In this case, the voting data is only captured once every 2 years in November, so we wouldn't want to select this large time frame. Check the All default samples box to turn it off. Click on the Supplement Topics tab, select the Voter tab, and select the box for 2016 Nov (Figure 12.8). Then at the top, click Submit Sample Selections. This returns us to the main screen. Now when we search for variables, our options will be limited to the November 2016 sample.

Hover over Person—Voter Supplement and choose Voter Supplement. This displays a chart that illustrates which voter variables are available (Figure 12.9). You can click on the link for any variable to get a detailed description that includes the codes that describe each response. Clicking on the little plus symbols adds the variable to your selection in the data cart. Choose VOTED (voted in the most recent November election), VOREG (registered for the most recent November election), and VOSUPPTWT (voter supplement weight). Whenever you download an extract, you will automatically get a standard person and household weight, but in some cases (like this one), a special weighting variable is provided.

Now let's select the basic demographic variables. Hover over the Person menu and choose Core, then Demographics. Most of these variables are included in every sample. Select Age, Sex, and Race (note that race does not include Hispanic or Latino

**FIGURE 12.8  ●  IPUMS CPS SAMPLE SELECTION**

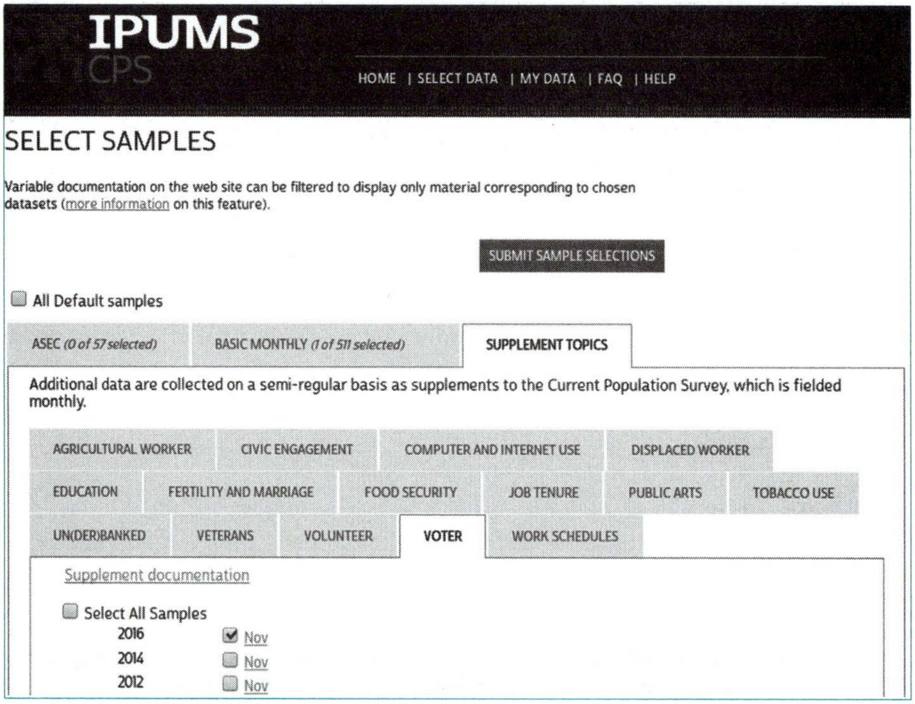

origin; this is a separate variable classified under Core—Ethnicity/Nativity). Then go to Household, Core, and Geographic, and choose Region.

In the upper right-hand corner, click the link to view the cart. This displays all the variables we've selected, plus variables that are included by default such as the survey month and year and the general person and household weights. Click the Create Data Extract button. On this last screen, we can change the data file format and how the data is structured. Change the data format from fixed width to CSV. Hit the Submit Extract button. Similar to NHGIS, this will display all the extracts you've requested, and once the processing is finished, you can download the data and the codebook.

Figure 12.10 shows this data imported into a spreadsheet. There are more than 131k responses in this particular sample. Values like Age are presented as the actual quantitative value, values for the regions use the standard geographic ID codes, while the other variables are coded. There are two sets of record identifiers in the data. CPSID is the identifier for the household in the survey, while CPSIDP is the identifier for the person, making it the unique identifier for the series. The PERNUM column identifies each person in the household with a sequential integer. For example, in Figure 12.10, the first household consists of two persons, while the second

FIGURE 12.9 ● VOTER SUPPLEMENT VARIABLES IN IPUMS CPS

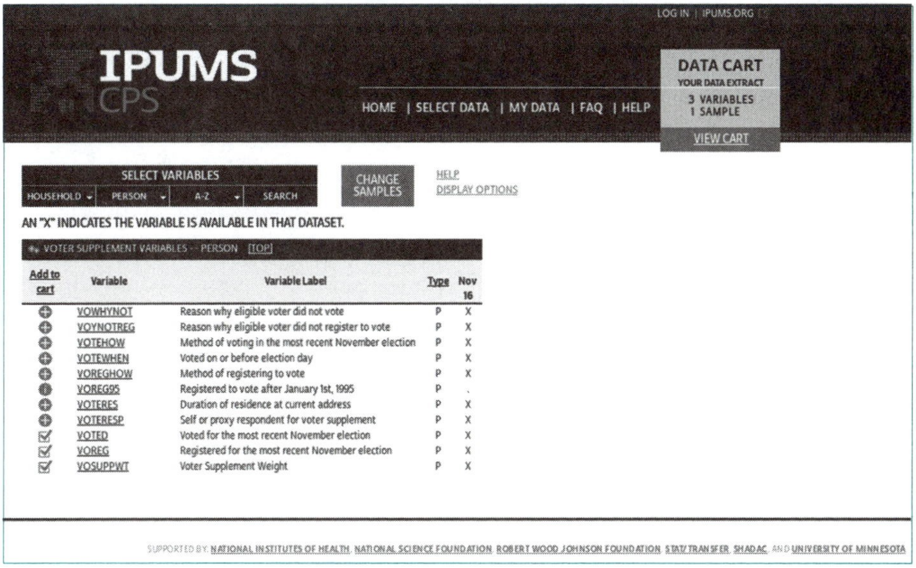

FIGURE 12.10 ● IPUMS CPS SAMPLE DATA EXTRACT

| | A | B | C | D | E | F | G | H | I | J | K | L | M | N | O |
|---|---|---|---|---|---|---|---|---|---|---|---|---|---|---|---|
| 1 | YEAR | SERIAL | MONTH | HWTFINL | CPSID | REGION | PERNUM | WTFINL | CPSIDP | AGE | SEX | RACE | VOTED | VOREG | VOSUPPWT |
| 2 | 2016 | 1 | 11 | 1519.4506 | 20161000000100 | 32 | 1 | 1878.9962 | 20161000000101 | 70 | 1 | 100 | 2 | 99 | 1878.9962 |
| 3 | 2016 | 1 | 11 | 1519.4506 | 20161000000100 | 32 | 2 | 1519.4506 | 20161000000102 | 63 | 2 | 100 | 1 | 1 | 1519.4506 |
| 4 | 2016 | 2 | 11 | 1674.5088 | 20161100000200 | 32 | 1 | 1674.5088 | 20161100000201 | 59 | 1 | 200 | 1 | 2 | 1674.5088 |
| 5 | 2016 | 2 | 11 | 1674.5088 | 20161100000200 | 32 | 2 | 1499.6532 | 20161100000202 | 79 | 2 | 200 | 1 | 1 | 1499.6532 |
| 6 | 2016 | 2 | 11 | 1674.5088 | 20161100000200 | 32 | 3 | 1413.0696 | 20161100000203 | 57 | 2 | 200 | 1 | 1 | 1413.0696 |
| 7 | 2016 | 3 | 11 | 1652.9364 | 20160900000300 | 32 | 1 | 1652.9364 | 20160900000301 | 34 | 2 | 100 | 98 | 98 | 1652.9364 |
| 8 | 2016 | 3 | 11 | 1652.9364 | 20160900000300 | 32 | 2 | 1499.0493 | 20160900000302 | 32 | 1 | 100 | 98 | 98 | 1499.0493 |
| 9 | 2016 | 5 | 11 | 1535.0338 | 20160900000700 | 32 | 1 | 1745.1453 | 20160900000701 | 80 | 1 | 100 | 2 | 99 | 1745.1453 |
| 10 | 2016 | 5 | 11 | 1535.0338 | 20160900000700 | 32 | 2 | 1535.0338 | 20160900000702 | 85 | 2 | 100 | 2 | 99 | 1535.0338 |
| 11 | 2016 | 5 | 11 | 1535.0338 | 20160900000700 | 32 | 3 | 1693.8964 | 20160900000703 | 47 | 1 | 100 | 1 | 1 | 1693.8964 |

Source: IPUMS Current Population Survey.

household consists of three. These identifiers also indicate the year and month the person entered the CPS. This information is invaluable for researchers who wish to study relationships within households across a survey period.

The weight variables represent how many persons in the total population would be represented by each individual record. There is a generic CPS weight for the household (HWTFINL) and person (WTFINL) and a specific weight that was generated for this supplement (VOSUPPWT). If we wished to aggregate and estimate person-level information such as age and race by region, we would use the generic person weight. Otherwise, if we want to summarize any of the data by the voting variables, we would use the special voting weight.

For example, the first record in the table is for a 70-year-old white male (according to the codebook, race code 100 is white, sex code 1 is male) who voted in the last November election, indicated by the VOTED value of 2. The VOREG registration value of 99 indicates that this person is not in the universe for that variable, which means he is not part of the population for that group. According to the documentation, the Census Bureau assumes that if a person voted, they must be registered, so the VOTED column counts all registered voters based on whether they voted or not, while the VOREG column only counts nonvoters. It's important to study the variable descriptions to ensure that you interpret the data properly. The voting weight for this record is approximately 1,879, which means that this person would represent this number of people in the total population for that variable.

To estimate the total population in each region that voted by sex, we would group and sum the weights by the division, sex, and voted codes. We can do this in the spreadsheet using a pivot table where region and sex are the row fields, VOTED and VOREG are the column fields, and the weighting variable VOSUPPWT is a data field that is summed. We can manipulate the results to calculate percentages for voter participation, but it's important to read the documentation and understand how the values are coded. If a person VOTED (2), then it is assumed they are registered and are not in the VOREG universe (99), whereas if a person did not vote (1), then they either did or did not register (VOREG 2 or 1). The universe for VOTED consists only of registered voters, while the VOREG universe consists of all citizens who are eligible to vote (U.S. citizens who are 18 years of age or older) but did not vote.

As in our previous example with the NHGIS, manipulating this data in a relational database provides additional flexibility in filtering and grouping results. If we import this data into SQLite, the following query would reproduce the same outcome from a pivot table:

```
SELECT region, sex, voted, ROUND(SUM(vosupptwt)) AS
population FROM cps_voting
GROUP BY region, sex, voted
ORDER BY region;
```

You could filter the results to select records that meet a certain criteria, such as just the estimates for people who voted, with a WHERE clause following FROM:

```
 WHERE voted='2'
```

SQL also allows you to write queries within queries (known as subqueries) and to join data by rows (as opposed to columns) using the UNION statement. To display two criteria individually and simultaneously, such as the number of people who did and did not vote, we can write two separate queries and union them together. The columns we add in each SELECT statement must be the same for the query to work.

**FIGURE 12.11 ● OUTCOME OF SQL QUERY WITH SUBQUERIES AND UNION**

| | REGION | SEX | status | population |
|---|---|---|---|---|
| 1 | 11 | 1 | notvote | 1065227.0 |
| 2 | 11 | 2 | notvote | 978866.0 |
| 3 | 11 | 1 | voted | 3347778.0 |
| 4 | 11 | 2 | voted | 3774616.0 |
| 5 | 12 | 1 | notvote | 3606392.0 |
| 6 | 12 | 2 | notvote | 3508538.0 |
| 7 | 12 | 1 | voted | 8054007.0 |
| 8 | 12 | 2 | voted | 9488008.0 |

We provide a different alias for the source table in each query, and create an alias for our criteria by adding static text in the SELECT statement, which is applied to the outcome of each individual query—that is, "notvote" as status for all results where the criterion is the person did not vote. The ORDER BY statement applies to the outcome of both queries (Figure 12.11):

```
SELECT n.region, n.sex, 'notvote' as status,
    ROUND(SUM(vosuppwt)) AS population
FROM cps_voting n
WHERE n.voted = '1'
GROUP BY n.region, n.sex
UNION
SELECT y.region, y.sex, 'voted' as status,
    ROUND(SUM(vosuppwt)) AS population
FROM cps_voting y
WHERE y.voted = '2'
GROUP BY y.region, y.sex
ORDER BY region, status;
```

The purpose of this section was to provide a crash course in understanding, downloading, and manipulating CPS data and microdata generally. Similar interfaces and principles apply for the decennial and ACS PUMS data that are available via IPUMS USA. One final point is that the estimates you create from the CPS are not precise but like the ACS are actually estimates with a margin of error. IPUMS provides a number of optional replicate weight columns that allow you to simulate several estimate scenarios and compute confidence intervals. This process is better suited to a statistical package and requires statistical knowledge that's beyond the scope of this book, but you can read about the details on the IPUMS website.

## Alternatives to IPUMS Extracts

### IPUMS Online Data Analyzer

In addition to the extraction tool, IPUMS has an online data analyzer for creating basic estimates and cross-tabulations. IPUMS USA contains microdata samples from all years of the ACS and from the decennial census from 1850 to present. The IPUMS CPS analyzer contains variables collected in the ASEC from 1962 to the present. Both analyzers use software developed by University of California, Berkeley's, Computer-Assisted Survey Methods Program.

The application screen is divided into two halves (Figure 12.12). On the left side of the screen are a series of drill-down menus that display the different variables that are included in the dataset. You can click on any variable to see its definition. In the middle of the screen, you provide inputs and filters. For example, if we wanted to know why people were unemployed by state, we provide statefips as the row and whyunemp (a variable under the Person—Work category) as the column. By default, all samples for all years are included, so if we want data for a specific year, we would add that as a selection filter, with the variable name followed by the filter in parentheses: year(2017). We can add multiple variables to the inputs or filters by separating them with a comma. To obtain data just for Minnesota and Wisconsin, we could add statefips(27,55) to the filter following the year. There are options for changing the weight, adding percentages, and displaying confidence intervals and standard errors. Checking the weighting box will sum the variables and present them as populations, as opposed to providing summaries of the sample records.

An example of the output is displayed in Figure 12.13. If selected on the previous screen, values are provided as percentages down the column first and across the row second. Confidence intervals are provided in parentheses below each percentage, and total estimates are displayed at the bottom. As before, we would need to verify what the universe for this variable is in order to understand who is not being included in the first category NIU; in this case, people who are either employed or are not part of the labor force are not in the universe. Values are color coded to indicate whether the expected values are smaller or larger than the general population.

## Census Bureau Sources

Naturally, the Census Bureau provides a number of tools for accessing CPS and PUMS microdata. Using the Census Bureau's FTP site is preferable to IPUMS if

| FIGURE 12.12 ● | IPUMS CPS DATA ANALYZER |
|---|---|

you want to access the most recent sample files in their entirety for individual sample months or years (as opposed to creating extracts for certain variables across several samples). Each individual program has a gateway page that groups the data with documentation and makes it easier to navigate:

ACS: `https://www.census.gov/programs-surveys/acs/data/pums.html`

CPS: `https://thedataweb.rm.census.gov/ftp/cps_ftp.html`

2010 Census: `https://www.census.gov/data/datasets/2010/dec/stateside-pums.html`

The DataFerret at `https://dataferrett.census.gov/` is a data analysis and extraction tool for creating customized spreadsheets for both summary data and microdata. It's a powerful tool that has been continuously developed for several decades. There's a learning curve for using it, but the Census Bureau provides ample documentation and it's primarily a matter of identifying and learning the specific aspects of the application that are of interest to you.

FIGURE 12.13 ● IPUMS CPS DATA ANALYZER OUTPUT

| Role | Name | Label | Range | MD | Dataset |
|------|------|-------|-------|-----|---------|
| Row | **statefip** | State (FIPS code) | 1-99 | | 1 |
| Column | **whyptly** | Reason for working part-time last year | 0-4 | | 1 |
| Weight | **sdawt** | Supplement Weight | -11,366.8100-44,423.8300 | | 1 |
| Filter | **statefip(27,55)** | State (FIPS code) | 1-99 | | 1 |
| Filter | **year(2017)** | Survey year | 1962-2017 | | 1 |

| Frequency Distribution | | | | | | |
|---|---|---|---|---|---|---|
| | | **whyptly** | | | | |
| Cells contain:<br>-**Column percent**<br>-Confidence intervals (95 percent)<br>-**Row percent**<br>-Confidence intervals (95 percent)<br>-Weighted N | | **0**<br>NIU | **1**<br>Could not find full time job | **2**<br>Wanted part time | **3**<br>Slack work | **4**<br>Other | **ROW TOTAL** |
| | 27: Minnesota | **48.8**<br>*(47.3-50.4)*<br>**83.4**<br>*(81.8-84.9)*<br>4,533,721.8 | **44.7**<br>*(32.3-57.7)*<br>**1.2**<br>*(0.9-1.8)*<br>67,147.8 | **49.8**<br>*(44.7-54.8)*<br>**8.4**<br>*(7.3-9.6)*<br>457,076.0 | **49.5**<br>*(40.3-58.8)*<br>**2.5**<br>*(2.0-3.3)*<br>137,730.8 | **42.3**<br>*(36.0-48.8)*<br>**4.4**<br>*(3.7-5.4)*<br>240,902.2 | **48.5**<br>*(47.1-50.0)*<br>**100.0**<br>—<br>5,436,578.6 |
| statefip | 55: Wisconsin | **51.2**<br>*(49.6-52.7)*<br>**82.4**<br>*(80.9-83.9)*<br>4,752,804.8 | **55.3**<br>*(42.3-67.7)*<br>**1.4**<br>*(1.0-2.0)*<br>83,220.2 | **50.2**<br>*(45.2-55.3)*<br>**8.0**<br>*(7.0-9.1)*<br>460,948.1 | **50.5**<br>*(41.2-59.7)*<br>**2.4**<br>*(1.9-3.1)*<br>140,310.0 | **57.7**<br>*(51.2-64.0)*<br>**5.7**<br>*(4.8-6.7)*<br>328,805.5 | **51.5**<br>*(50.0-52.9)*<br>**100.0**<br>—<br>5,766,088.6 |
| | **COL TOTAL** | **100.0**<br>—<br>**82.9**<br>*(81.8-83.9)*<br>9,286,526.6 | **100.0**<br>—<br>**1.3**<br>*(1.0-1.7)*<br>150,368.0 | **100.0**<br>—<br>**8.2**<br>*(7.4-9.0)*<br>918,024.1 | **100.0**<br>—<br>**2.5**<br>*(2.1-3.0)*<br>278,040.8 | **100.0**<br>—<br>**5.1**<br>*(4.5-5.8)*<br>569,707.8 | **100.0**<br>—<br>**100.0**<br>—<br>11,202,667.2 |

The Census Bureau has also developed a number of stand-alone tools for specific datasets. For example, it provides an application for creating simple extracts and estimates from the CPS such as the Current Population Survey Table Creator at https://www.census.gov/cps/data/cpstablecreator.html. Like the IPUMS Analyzer, this application allows you to create extracts from the ASEC.

## 12.4   IN CONCLUSION: WHAT NEXT?

This book has been your introductory guide to exploring U.S. Census data. We have covered the major concepts, datasets, and applications that will allow you to effectively access, process, and use this data in your research. Beyond delving into each of the datasets more fully and exploring more applications, what could you do next?

Whether you are working with large datasets on long and sustained research projects, or are constantly engaged in a series of short-term projects, learning a scripting language would provide many benefits. With a scripting language, you can access the Census Bureau's datasets directly through programs you write via the Census Bureau's application programming interface, without having to download any data (see InfoBox 12.3). Scripting languages can be used for looping through folders of files so that you can aggregate and process data. Repetitive tasks such as aggregating data, calculating margins of error, and creating derivatives can be automated. You can write programs to access SQL databases for importing and exporting data and running queries. You can visualize and analyze data, create graphs and charts, and generate new data files.

Python (`https://www.python.org/`) is a popular open source programming language that's been widely adopted in many fields, particularly within geography. It is commonly employed for data processing and analysis. It's relatively easy to learn, and thousands of developers have created third-party modules such as NUMPY, SCIPY, Pandas, and Matplotlib that extend its power and versatility. There are a countless number of other tutorials (e.g., `http://zetcode.com/lang/python/`) and books (Gries, Campbell, & Montojo, 2013; Sweigart, 2015) that can help you get started. There are also dedicated modules for working with census data, such as `https://github.com/datamade/census`.

If you are more statistically oriented, the R language for statistical computing is an alternative `https://www.r-project.org/`. It's also a popular open source language, and a number of modules have been created specifically for working with census data (Glenn, 2011). The tidycensus package is particularly popular: `https://walkerke.github.io/tidycensus/`. The decision of whether to use Python or R is largely a matter of preference and orientation, as both languages can be used for data processing, visualization, and analysis.

The concept of using shared, online notebooks for data-oriented projects is growing. Rather than manipulating data locally in a spreadsheet or writing linear code to complete a project from start to finish, notebooks allow researchers to write code in an iterative, modular fashion and to expose the entire process of working with their datasets to the wider research community. This transparency allows others to verify the outcomes and accuracy of your work and to build on it. Jupyter Notebooks (`https://jupyter.org/`) are a popular choice, and they can accommodate Python, R, and a number of other languages. By employing version control tools such as git and github, multiple researchers can collaborate on the same projects and notebooks without having to email results back and forth or constantly sync files from online storage.

✓ **INFOBOX 12.3 THE CENSUS BUREAU'S API**

The Census Bureau's API provides you with an alternative to downloading files or using the applications we covered in this book. By passing arguments to the API's base URL, you can access and retrieve data directly in a script. This Python-based example illustrates how to retrieve 2017 population estimates for all the counties in Rhode Island. You must request a key from the Census Bureau, store it in a text file, and read it into the script. Store the values as variables, and pass those variables into a string to create the proper URL. Send that URL as a request, and grab the resulting data. It's stored in a list, which you can subsequently manipulate. Visit `https://www.census.gov/developers/` to learn more.

```python
import requests
with open('census_key.txt') as key:
        api_key=key.read().strip()
year='2017'
dsource='pep'
dname='population'
cols='POP,GEONAME'
county='*'
state='44'
base_url = f'https://api.census.gov/data/{year}/{dsource}/
        {dname}'
data_url = f'{base_url}?get={cols}&for=county:{county}&in
        =state:{state}&key={api_key}'
response=requests.get(data_url)
print(response.text)

> > >
[["POP","GEONAME","state","county"],
["48912","Bristol County, Rhode Island","44","001"],
["163760","Kent County, Rhode Island","44","003"],
["83460","Newport County, Rhode Island","44","005"],
["637357","Providence County, Rhode Island","44","007"],
["126150","Washington County, Rhode Island","44","009"]]
```

If you intend to work on a large-scale project that involves storing and manipulating large datasets, or you want to provide several team members with simultaneous access, you'll want to consider using an enterprise-level relational database such as PostgreSQL (`https://www.postgresql.org/`), a long-standing open source project. While SQLite is suitable for storing moderate amounts of data for individual use or for embedding databases within applications, PostgreSQL can store large datasets and can be deployed over a network where multiple users can read and write to the database and can be assigned different levels of permission. It can also be installed locally for use by one person, which is worth doing if you need something powerful. PostgreSQL supports a much broader swath of the SQL standard, giving you access to additional functions and commands. The PostGIS module turns it into a spatial database for storing tabular data and geographic features and for performing geoprocessing and analysis that can supplement and even replace certain GIS tasks.

Beyond tools and technical considerations, one of the best things you can do is to gain additional subject knowledge. Use the methods introduced in this book as starting points for learning how to study places within your field. Use census data to supplement your understanding of different places and to study them, while keeping the limitations of the data in mind. Conduct background research, check your work, and verify your conclusions. Use census data to explore your town or the nation, but make sure to survey and read the work of others, and get out into the world and explore it in person.

## 12.5  REVIEW QUESTIONS AND PRACTICE EXERCISES

1.  Briefly summarize the different considerations that you need to take into account when studying historical census data.

2.  Describe the difference between nominal and normalized data, and explain how normalized data is created.

3.  Use NHGIS to download nominal data on Marital Status from the 1970 census at the census tract level. Use the LTDB crosswalk to create a normalized version of this data that fits 2010 tract boundaries.

4.  What is the difference between summary data and microdata? Describe how microdata can be used for creating estimates.

5.  Use the IPUMS CPS Online Analyzer to create estimates for a variable of your choice for two states for the most recent year for which data is available.

# REFERENCES

Abrams, R., & Gebeloff, R. (2018, May 3). A fast-food problem: Where have all the teenagers gone? *The New York Times.* Retrieved from https://nyti.ms/2FCKvXL.

Albrecht, J. (2007). *Key concepts and techniques in GIS.* Thousand Oaks, CA: SAGE.

Anderson, M. J. (2010). The census and the federal statistical system: Historical perspectives. *The ANNALS of the American Academy of Political and Social Science,* 631, 152–162.

Anderson, M. J. (2015). *The American Census: A social history* (2nd ed.). New Haven, CT: Yale University Press.

Aoyama, Y., Murphy, J. T., & Hanson, S. (2011). *Key conecpts in economic geography.* Thousand Oaks, CA: SAGE.

Apparicio, P., Abdelmajid, M., Riva, M., & Shearmur, R. (2008). Comparing alternative approaches to measuring the geographical accessibility of urban health services: Distance types and aggregation-error issues. *International Journal of Health Geographics,* 7(7), 1–14.

Aratani, L. (2018, April 3). Secret use of census info helped send Japanese Americans to internment camps in WWII. *The Washington Post.* Retrieved from https://wapo.st/2lqLZWT?tid=ss_tw&utm _term=.36da085f7e30.

Arias, E., Heron, M., & Xu, J. (2017, August). *United States life tables, 2014* (Vol. 66; National Vital Statistics Reports No. 4). Washington, DC: National Center for Health Statistics. Retrieved from https://www.cdc.gov/nchs/products/nvsr.htm.

Baffour, B., King, T., & Valente, P. (2013). The modern census: Evolution, examples, and evaluation. *International Statistical Review,* 81(3), 407–425.

Bauder, J. (2014). *The reference guide to data sources.* Chicago, IL: American Library Association.

Baumgaertner, E. (2018, March 26). Despite concerns, census will ask respondents if they are US citizens. *The New York Times.* Retrieved from https://nyti.ms/2pN40b5.

Bazuin, J. T., & Fraser, J. C. (2013). How the ACS gets it wrong: The story of the American Community Survey and a small, inner city neighborhood. *Applied Geography,* 45, 292–302.

Beaulac, J., Kristjansson, E., & Cummins, S. (2009). A systematic review of food deserts, 1966–2007. *Preventing Chronic Disease,* 6(3), Article 105. Retrieved from https://www.cdc.gov/pcd/issues/2009/jul/08_0163.htm.

Bellu, L. G., & Liberati, P. (2006, December). *Inequality analysis: The GINI coefficient* (EASYPol Analytical Tools, Module 040). Rome, Italy: Food and Agriculture Organization of the United Nations. Retrieved from http://www.fao.org/3/a-am352e.pdf.

Bishaw, A., & Benson, C. (2017, September). *Poverty: 2015 and 2016* (American Community Survey Briefs: ACSBR/16-01). Washington, DC: U.S. Census Bureau. Retrieved from https://www.census.gov/content/census/en/library/publications/2017/acs/acsbr16-01.html.

Boburg, S. (2017, May 31). How Jared Kushner built a luxury skyscraper using loans meant for job-starved areas. *The Washington Post,* p. A01. Retrieved from http://wapo.st/2qGLDSz.

Boscoe, F. P., Henry, K. A., & Zdeb, M. S. (2012). A nationwide comparison of driving distance versus straight-line distance to hospitals. *The Professional Geographer,* 64(2), 188–196.

Brennan Center for Justice. (2017, April 17). *Who draws the maps? Legislative and Congressional redistricting* (Tech. Rep.). New York, NY: Author. Retrieved from http://www.brennancenter.org/analysis/who-draws-maps-states-redrawing-congressional-and-state-district-lines.

Burnett, K. D. (2011, November). *Congressional apportionment* (2010 Census Briefs: C2010BR-08).

Washington, DC: U.S. Census Bureau. Retrieved from https://www.census.gov/library/publications/2011/dec/c2010br-08.html.

California State Data Center. (2016, April). *Re-calculating medians and their margin of errors for aggregated ACS data* (January 2011 Network News, revised 2016). Sacramento: California State Data Center, Demographic Research Unit. Retrieved from http://www.dof.ca.gov/Forecasting/Demographics/Census_Data_Center_Network/.

Chapman, J. (2017, September). *Migration in the Washington region: Trends between 2000 and 2015 and characteristics of recent migrants* (Tech. Rep.). Arlington, VA: The Stephen S. Fuller Institute, Schar School of Policy and Government, George Mason University. Retrieved from http://sfullerinstitute.gmu.edu/research/reports/migration-washington-region/.

Charreire, H., Casey, R., Salze, P., Simon, C., Chaix, B., Banos, A., ... Oppert, J.-M. (2009). Measuring the food environment using geographical information systems: A methodological review. *Public Health Nutrition*, *13*(11), 1773–1785.

Connerly, W., & Gonzalez, M. (2018, January 3). It's time the Census Bureau stops dividing America. *The Washington Post*. Retrieved from http://wapo.st/2CCT8Fa?tid=ss_tw&utm_term=.35a9257598b2.

Cook, T. M., Norwood, J. L., & Cork, D. L. (2011). *Change and the 2020 Census: Not whether but how*. Washington, DC: National Academies Press.

Coontz, S. (2010). Why American families need the census. *The ANNALS of the American Academy of Political and Social Science*, 631, 141–149.

Cope, M., & Elwood, S. (2009). *Qualitative GIS: A mixed methods approach*. Thousand Oaks, CA: SAGE.

Cunningham, J. (2015, September). Measuring wage inequality within and across US metropolitan areas, 2003–13. *Monthly Labor Review*. Retrieved from https://doi.org/10.21916/mlr.2015.35.

D'Antonio, P., & Whelan, J. C. (2009). Counting nurses: The power of historical census data. *Journal of Clinical Nursing*, *18*(19), 2717–2724.

Desmond, M. (2016). *Evicted: Poverty and profit in the American city*. New York, NY: Broadway Books.

Dickason, D. G. (2012). Census of population; "Panning for gold." In J. P. Stoltman (Ed.), *21st century geography: A reference handbook* (pp. 267–276). Thousand Oaks: SAGE.

Donnelly, F., Clark, A., & Billadello, J. (2018, February). *New Yorkers on the move: Recent migration trends for the city and metro area* (WCIB Occasional Papers Series No. 15). New York, NY: Weissman Center for International Business, Zicklin School of Business, Baruch College, City University of New York. Retrieved from https://zicklin.baruch.cuny.edu/faculty-research/centers-institutes/weissman-center-international-business/occasional-paper-series/.

Economics and Statistics Administration. (2015, April). *The value of the American Community Survey: Smart government, competitive businesses, and informed citizens* (Tech. Rep.). Washington, DC: U.S. Department of Commerce. Retrieved from https://www.commerce.gov/news/reports/2015/05/value-american-community-survey-smart-government-competitive-businesses-and.

Eichel, L., & Schmitt, M. (2016, July). *A portrait of Philadelphia's migration: Who is coming to the city—and who is leaving* (Philadelphia Research Initiative Issue Brief). Philadelphia, PA: Pew Charitable Trust. Retrieved from http://pew.org/29OhwCT.

Emigh, R. J., Riley, D., & Ahmed, P. (2016a). *Antecedents of censuses from medieval to nation states: How societies and states count*. New York, NY: Palgrave Macmillan.

Emigh, R. J., Riley, D., & Ahmed, P. (2016b). *Changes in censuses from imperialist to welfare states: How societies and states count*. New York, NY: Palgrave Macmillan.

Evergreen, S. D. (2017). *Effective data visualization: The right chart for the right data*. Thousand Oaks, CA: SAGE.

Executive Office of the President. (2017, January). *Statistical programs of the United States government fiscal year 2017* (Tech. Rep.). Washington, DC: Office of Management and Budget. Retrieved from https://obamawhitehouse.archives.gov/sites/default/files/

omb/assets/information_and_regulatory_affairs/statistical-programs-2017.pdf.

Fox, L. (2017, September). *The supplemental poverty measure: 2016* (Current Population Reports: P60-261 (RV)). Washington, DC: U.S. Census Bureau. Retrieved from https://www.census.gov/library/publications/2017/demo/p60-259.html.

Frey, W. H. (2018a). *Diversity explosion: How new racial demographics are remaking America* (2nd ed.). Washington, DC: Brookings Institution Press.

Frey, W. H. (2018b, March). *US population disperses to suburbs, exurbs, rural areas, and "middle of the country" metros* (The Avenue). Washington, DC: Brookings Institution Press. Retrieved from https://brook.gs/2l747ot.

Gebru, T., Krause, J., Wang, Y., Chen, D., Deng, J., Aiden, E. L., & Fei-Fei, L. (2017). Using deep learning and Google Street View to estimate the demographic makeup of neighborhoods across the United States. *Proceedings of the National Academy of Sciences of the United States of America, 114*(50), 13108–13113. Retrieved from http://www.pnas.org/content/114/50/13108.

Glassman, B. (2016, July). *Income inequality metrics and economic well-being in US metropolitan statistical areas* (SEHSD Working Paper 2016-19). Washington, DC: U.S. Census Bureau. Retrieved from https://www.census.gov/library/working-papers/2016/demo/SEHSD-WP2016-19.html.

Glenn, E. H. (2011). acs.R: An R package for neighborhood-level data from the U.S. census. *Computers in Urban Planning and Urban Management Conference*, 1–7.

Goldstein, B., & Dyson, L. (2013). *Beyond transparency: Open data and the future of civic innovation*. San Francisco, CA: Code for America.

Graser, A. (2016). *Learning QGIS* (3rd ed.). Birmingham, UK: Packt.

Graser, A., & Peterson, G. N. (2016). *QGIS map design*. Chugiak, AK: Locate Press.

Gries, P., Campbell, J., & Montojo, J. (2013). *Practical programming: An introduction to computer science using Python 3* (2nd ed.). Dallas, TX: Pragmatic Bookshelf.

Grubesic, T. H. (2008). ZIP codes and spatial analysis: Problems and prospects. *Socio-Economic Planning Sciences, 42*, 129–149.

Guzman, G. G. (2017, September). *Household income: 2016* (American Community Survey Briefs: ACSBR/16-02). Washington, DC: U.S. Census Bureau. Retrieved from https://www.census.gov/library/publications/2017/acs/acsbr16-02.html.

Hartnett, C. J., Sevetson, A. L., & Forte, E. J. (2016). *Fundamentals of government information* (2nd ed.). Chicago, IL: Neal-Schuman.

Harvey, F. (2015). *A primer of GIS: Fundametal geographic and cartographic concepts* (2nd ed.). New York, NY: Guilford Press.

Hayslett, M., & Kellam, L. (2010). The American Community Survey: Benefits and challenges. *IASSIST Quarterly*, Winter/Spring, 31–39.

Hayter, C. T. (2015). Adding a little ZIP to the mail: The development and growth of the ZIP code. *Documents to the People, 33*(3), 43–51.

Heimel, S. (2014, October). *American Community Survey fiscal year 2014 content review: Median county-level coefficients of variation of key estimates from ACS data* (Final Report). Washington, DC: U.S. Census Bureau. Retrieved from https://www.census.gov/programs-surveys/acs/operations-and-administration/2014-content-review/methods-and-results.html.

Hem, A. (2017, September 7). Facebook claims it can reach more young people than exist in UK, US and other countries. *The Guardian*. Retrieved from https://www.theguardian.com/technology/2017/sep/07/facebook-claims-it-can-reach-more-people-than-actually-exist-in-uk-us-and-other-countries.

Herman, E. (2008). The American Community Survey: An introduction to the basics. *Government Information Quarterly, 25*(2008), 504–519.

Hewko, J., Smoyer-Tomic, K. E., & Hodgson, M. J. (2002). Measuring neighbourhood spatial accessibility to urban amenities: Does aggregation error matter? *Environment and Planning A, 34*, 1185–1206.

Hobbs, F., & Stoops, N. (2002, November). *Demographic trends in the 20th century* (Census 2000 Special Reports: CENSR-4). Washington, DC: U.S. Census Bureau. Retrieved from https://www.census.gov/prod/2002pubs/censr-4.pdf.

Humes, K., & Hogan, H. (2009). Measurement of race and ethnicity in a changing, multicultural America. *Race and Social Problems*, 1, 111–131.

Humes, K., Jones, N. A., & Ramirez, R. R. (2011, March). *Overview of race and Hispanic origin: 2010* (2010 Census Briefs: C2010BR-02). Washington, DC: U.S. Census Bureau. Retrieved from https://www.census.gov/library/publications/2011/dec/c2010br-02.html.

Iceland, J. (2014). *A portrait of America: The demographic perspective*. Oakland: University of California Press.

Iceland, J., Weinberg, D. H., & Steinmetz, E. (2002, August). *Racial and ethnic residential segregation in the United States: 1980–2000* (Census 2000 Special Reports: CENSR-3). Washington, DC: U.S. Census Bureau. Retrieved from https://www.census.gov/hhes/www/housing/housing_patterns/pdftoc.html.

Ingraham, C. (2017, November 30). Scientists can now figure out detailed, accurate neighborhood demographics using Google Street View photos. *The Washington Post*. Retrieved from http://wapo.st/2AnuP9L.

International Association for Social Science Information Services & Technology. (2012). *Quick guide to data citations* (Special Interest Group on Data Citation). Retrieved from https://www.icpsr.umich.edu/files/ICPSR/enewsletters/iassist.html.

Jensen, J., & Kletzer, L. G. (2006). Tradable srvices: Understanding the scope and impact of services offshoring. In S. M. Collins & L. Brainard (Eds.), *Offshoring white-collar work* (pp. 75–116). Washington, DC: Brookings Institution Press.

Johnson, K. M. (2019, March). *Hispanic population of child-bearing age grows, but births diminish* (Data Snapshot). Durham: University of New Hampshire, Carsey School of Public Policy. Retrieved from https://carsey.unh.edu/publication/snapshot/hispanic-pop.

Johnson, T. P., & Tourangeau, R. (2018, January 23). Yes, the census should be tracking race and ethnicity.

*The Washington Post*. Retrieved from http://wapo.st/2n4GDau?tid=ss_tw&utm_term=.df0b40c25424.

Kallhoff, A. (2011). *Why democracy needs public goods*. New York, NY: Lexington Books.

Keith, T. (2018, March 27). Fact check: Has citizenship been a standard census question? *National Public Radio*. Retrieved from https://n.pr/2GdAVzL.

Kendall, B., & Adamy, J. (2019, February 15). Supreme court agrees to decide legality of census citizenship question. *The Wall Street Journal*. Retrieved from https://www.wsj.com/articles/supreme-court-agrees-to-decide-legality-of-census-citizenship-question-11550255991.

Kitchin, R. (2014). *The data revolution*. Thousand Oaks, CA: SAGE.

Klass, G. M. (2012). *Just plain data analysis* (2nd ed.). Lanham, MD: Rowman & Littlefield.

Klein, H. S. (2012). *A population history of the United States* (2nd ed.). New York, NY: Cambridge University Press.

Kochhar, R., & Cilluffo, A. (2018, July). *Income inequality in the U.S. is rising most rapidly among Asians* (Tech. Rep.). Washington, DC: Pew Research Center. Retrieved from https://pewrsr.ch/2NxhwcY.

Kreibich, J. A. (2010). *Using SQLite*. Sebastopol, CA: O'Reilly Media.

Krygier, J., & Wood, D. (2016). *Making maps: A visual guide to map design with GIS* (3rd ed.). New York, NY: Guilford Press.

Kugler, T. A., & Fitch, C. A. (2018). Interoperable and accessible census and survey data from IPUMS. *Scientific Data*, 5(180007). Retrieved from https://www.nature.com/articles/sdata20187.

Liptak, A. (2016, April 4). Supreme Court rejects challenge on "one person one vote". *The New York Times*. Retrieved from https://nyti.ms/2ooDh5b.

Livingston, G. (2019, May 22). *Is U.S. fertility at an all-time low? Two of three measures point to yes* (Fact Tank). Washington, DC: Pew Research Center. Retrieved from http://pewrsr.ch/2DhW0U2.

Logan, J. R., Stults, B. J., & Xu, Z. (2016). Validating population estimates for harmonized census tract data, 2000–2010. *Annals of the American Association of Geographers, 106*(5), 1013–1029.

Logan, J. R., Xu, Z., & Stults, B. J. (2014). Intepolating U.S. decennial census tract data from as early as 1970 to 2010: A longitudinal tract database. *The Professional Geographer, 66*(3), 412–421.

Mackun, P., & Wilson, S. (2011, March). *Population distribution and change: 2000 to 2010* (2010 Census Briefs: C2010BR-01). Washington, DC: U.S. Census Bureau. Retrieved from https://www.census.gov/library/publications/2011/dec/c2010br-01.html.

Maier, M. H., & Imazeki, J. (2013). *The data game: Controversies in social science statistics* (4th ed.). Armonk, NY: M.E. Sharpe.

Martin, J. A., Hamilton, B. E., Osterman, M. J., Driscoll, A. K., & Drake, P. (2018, January). *Births: Final data for 2016* (Vol. 67; National Vital Statistics Reports No. 1). Washington, DC: National Center for Health Statistics. Retrieved from https://www.cdc.gov/nchs/products/nvsr.htm.

Massey, D. S., & Denton, N. A. (1988). The dimensions of residential segregation. *Social Forces, 67*(2), 281–315.

Matthews, S. A., McCarthy, J. D., & Rafail, P. S. (2011). Using ZIP code business patterns data to measure alcohol outlet density. *Addictive Behaviors, 36*, 777–780.

Menke, K., Smith, R., Jr., Pirelli, L., & Van Hoesen, J. (2016). *Mastering QGIS* (2nd ed.). Birmingham, UK: Packt.

Micarelli, W. F. (1998). Evolution of the United States economic censuses: The nineteenth and twentieth centuries. *Government Information Quarterly, 15*(3), 335–377.

Monmonier, M. (2018). *How to lie with maps* (3rd ed.). Chicago, IL: University of Chicago Press.

MSU Land Policy Institute. (2014, October). *Northwest Michigan seasonal population analysis* (Networks Northwest). East Lansing: The Land Policy Institute at Michigan State University. Retrieved from http://www.canr.msu.edu/resources/northwest_michigan_seasonal_population_analysis.

Mule, T. (2012, May). *Census coverage measurement estimation report: Summary of estimates of coverage for persons in the United States* (DSSD 2010 Census Coverage Measurement Memorandum Series 2010-G-01). Washington, DC: U.S. Census Bureau. Retrieved from https://www.census.gov/coverage_measurement/post-enumeration_surveys/2010_results.html.

Muro, M., Rothwell, J., Andes, S., Fikri, K., & Kulkarni, S. (2015, February). *America's advanced industries: What they are, where they are, and why they matter* (Metropolitan Policy Program). Washington, DC: Brookings Institution. Retrieved from http://brook.gs/2bwynvV.

Murray, C., & Schuetz, J. (2018, June). *Housing in the US is too expensive, too cheap, and just right: It depends on where you live* (Metropolitan Policy Program). Washington, DC: Brookings Institution. Retrieved from https://brook.gs/2Mb3GM1.

National Research Council. (2007). *Using the American Community Survey: Benefits and challenges*. Washington, DC: National Academies Press.

Nesse, K., & Rahe, M. L. (2015). Conflicts in the use of the ACS by federal agencies between statutory requirements and survey methodology. *Population Research and Policy Review, 34*, 461–480.

New York City Comptroller's Office. (2017, April). *New York City neighborhood economic profiles* (2017 ed.) New York, NY: Author. Retrieved from https://comptroller.nyc.gov/reports/new-york-city-neighborhood-economic-profiles/.

Nicotera, N. (2007). Measuring neighborhood: A conundrum for human services researchers and practitioners. *American Journal of Community Psychology, 40*, 26–51.

O' hUallachain, B., & Leslie, T. F. (2013). Spatial pattern and order in Sunbelt retailing: Phoenix in the twenty-first century. *The Professional Geographer, 65*(3), 396–420.

Office of the Federal Register. (1997, October). *Revisions to the Standards for the Classification of Federal Data on Race and Ethnicity* (Federal Register, Vol. 62, Iss. 210; 62 FR 58782). Washington, DC: Author. Retrieved from https://www.gpo.gov/fdsys/granule/FR-1997-10-30/97-28653.

Office of the Federal Register. (2010, June). *2010 Standards for Delineating Metropolitan and Micropolitan Statistical Areas* (Federal Register, Vol. 75, Iss. 123; 75 FR 37245). Washington, DC: Author. Retrieved from https://www.gpo.gov/fdsys/granule/FR-2010-06-28/2010-15605.

Pew Research Center. (2015, September 3). *The whys and hows of generations research* (Tech. Rep.). Washington, DC: Author. Retrieved from http://www.people-press.org/2015/09/03/the-whys-and-hows-of-generations-research/.

Pew Research Center. (2018, February 5). *Social media fact sheet* (Tech. Rep.). Washington, DC: Author. Retrieved from http://www.pewinternet.org/fact-sheet/social-media/.

Pew Research Center. (2018, March). *Wide gender gap, growing educational divide in voter's party identification* (Survey Rep.) Washington, DC: Author. Retrieved from http://www.people-press.org/2018/03/20/wide-gender-gap-growing-educational-divide-in-voters-party-identification/.

Prewitt, K. (2013). *What is your race? The census and our flawed efforts to count Americans.* Princeton, NJ: Princeton University Press.

Pritzker, P., & Gutierrez, C. (2018, April 4). U.S. Census is not about citizenship. *Bloomberg.* Retrieved from https://www.bloomberg.com/view/articles/2018-04-04/u-s-census-is-not-about-citizenship.

Ratcliffe, M., Burd, C., Holder, K., & Fields, A. (2016, December). *Defining rural at the U.S. Census Bureau* (American Community Survey and Geography Brief: ACSGEO-1). Washington, DC: U.S. Census Bureau. Retrieved from https://www.census.gov/library/publications/2016/acs/acsgeo-1.html.

Reamer, A. (2017, August). *Counting for dollars 2020: The role of the decennial census in the geographic distribution of federal funds* (Initial analysis: Report No. 1). Washington, DC: George Washington Institute of Public Policy. Retrieved from https://gwipp.gwu.edu/counting-dollars-2020-initial-analysis.

Reamer, A. (2018, December). *Census-derived datasets used to distribute federal funds* (Counting for dollars 2020: Report No. 4). Washington, DC: George Washington Institute of Public Policy. Retrieved from https://gwipp.gwu.edu/counting-dollars-2020-role-decennial-census-geographic-distribution-federal-funds.

Reed, S. B. (2014, April). One hundred years of price change: The Consumer Price Index and the American inflation experience. *Monthly Labor Review.* Retrieved from https://doi.org/10.21916/mlr.2014.14.

Rogerson, P. A., & Plane, D. A. (2013). The Hoover Index of population and demographic components of change: An article in memory of Andy Isserman. *International Regional Science Review, 36*(1), 97–114.

Saenz, R., & Johnson, K. M. (2018, June). *White deaths exceed births in a majority of U.S. states* (Census Brief). Madison: Applied Population Lab, Department of Community and Environmental Sociology, University of Wisconsin-Madison. Retrieved from https://apl.wisc.edu/data-briefs/natural-decrease-18.

Salvo, J. J., & Lobo, A. P. (2010). The federal statistical system: The local government perspective. *The ANNALS of the American Academy of Political and Social Science, 631,* 75–88.

Salvo, J. J., Lobo, A. P., Willett, A. L., & Alvarez, J. A. (2007). *An evaulation of the quality and utility of ACS five year estimates for Bronx census tracts and neighborhoods* (Tech. Rep.). New York, NY: Population Division, New York City Department of City Planning. Retrieved from http://www1.nyc.gov/assets/planning/download/pdf/data-maps/nyc-population/eval_quality_utility_acs_five_year_estimates_bx.pdf.

Schlossberg, M. (2003). GIS, the US Census and neighbourhood scale analysis. *Planning, Practice, and Research, 18*(2–3), 213–217.

Schmidt, E. P. (2018, April). *Postsecondary enrollment before, during, and after the Great Recession* (Curent Population Reports: P20-580). Washington, DC: U.S. Census Bureau. Retrieved from https://www.census.gov/content/census/en/library/publications/2018/demo/p20-580.html.

Shaffer, J. (2016, April 20). *5 tips on designing colorblind-friendly visualizations* (Tech. Rep.). Tableau Blog.

Retrieved from https://www.tableau.com/about/blog/2016/4/examining-data-viz-rules-dont-use-red-green-together-53463.

Short, J. R., & Mussman, M. (2014). Population change in U.S. cities: Estimating and explaining the extent of decline and level of resurgence. *The Professional Geographer*, *66*(1), 112–123.

Smith, A. S., Holmberg, C., & Jones-Puthoff, M. (2012, September). *The emergency and transitional shelter population: 2010* (2010 Census Special Reports: C2010SR-02). Washington, DC: U.S. Census Bureau. Retrieved from https://www.census.gov/library/publications/2012/dec/c2010sr-02.html.

Smith, S. K., Tayman, J., & Swanson, D. A. (2013). *A practitioners guide to state and local population projections*. New York, NY: Springer.

Sperling, J. (2012). The tyranny of census geography: Small-area data and neighborhood statistics. *Cityscape: A Journal of Policy Development and Research*, *14*(2), 219–223. Retrieved from https://www.huduser.gov/portal/periodicals/cityscpe/vol14num2/ch11.html.

Spielman, S. E., Folch, D., & Nagle, N. (2014). Patterns and causes of uncertainty in the American Community Survey. *Applied Geography*, *46*, 147–157.

Stevens, N. (2006, June). *Changing postal ZIP code boundaries* (RL33488). Washington, DC: Congressional Research Service. Retrieved from https://fas.org/sgp/crs/misc/RL33488.pdf.

Storper, M., Kemeny, T., Makarem, N. P., & Osman, T. (2015). *The rise and fall of urban economies: Lessons from San Francisco and Los Angeles*. Stanford, CA: Stanford University Press.

Sun, M., & Wong, D. W. (2010). Incorporating data quality information in mapping American Community Survey data. *Cartography and Geographic Information Science*, *37*(4), 285–300.

Sunnucks, M. (2017, May 15). BBC: Forget Wall Street, Arizona leads US in finance, banking jobs. *Phoenix Business Journal*. Retrieved from https://www.bizjournals.com/phoenix/news/2017/05/15/bbc-forget-wall-street-arizona-leads-us-in-finance.html.

Swant, M. (2017, September 6). Facebook claims it reaches more people than the U.S. census data says exists. *Adweek*. Retrieved from http://www.adweek.com/digital/facebook-claims-it-reaches-more-people-than-the-u-s-census-data-says-exist/.

Sweigart, A. (2015). *Automate the boring stuff with Python*. San Francisco, CA: No Starch Press.

Talen, E. (2003). Neighborhoods as service providers: A methodology for evaluating pedestrian access. *Environment and Planning B: Planning and Design*, *30*(2), 181–200.

Teaford, J. (2006). *The metropolitan revolution: The rise of post-urban America*. New York, NY: Columbia University Press.

Terrazas, A. (2016, September). *The elusive truth on domestic migration: Comparing data sources on U.S. cross-county migration* (Tech. Rep.). Retrieved from https://www.zillow.com/research/comparing-migration-data-sources-13252/.

Terry, R. L., & Fond, M. (2013). Experimental U.S. Census Bureau race and Hispanic origin survey questions: Reactions from Spanish speakers. *Hispanic Journal of Behavioral Sciences*, *35*(4), 524–541.

The Economist. (2018, December 22). Less than the sum of their parts: Why American cities are so weirdly shaped. *The Economist*. Retrieved from https://www.economist.com/united-states/2018/12/22/why-american-cities-are-so-weirdly-shaped.

U.S. Census Bureau. (1994, November). *Geographic areas reference manual*. Washington, DC: Author. Retrieved from https://www.census.gov/geo/reference/garm.html.

U.S. Census Bureau. (2009). *Events in the chronological development of privacy and confidentiality at the US Census Bureau* (Tech. Rep.). Washington, DC: Author. Retrieved from https://www.census.gov/history/www/reference/privacy_confidentiality/privacy_and_confidentiality_2.html.

U.S. Census Bureau. (2010) *Table P1, total population* (2010 Decennial Census) [Data file] Washington, DC: Author. Retrieved from https://data.census.gov/.

U.S. Census Bureau. (2012a, September). *2010 census summary file 1: Technical documentation* (SF1/10-4(RV)). Washington, DC: Author. Retrieved from https://www.census.gov/prod/cen2010/doc/sf1.pdf.

U.S. Census Bureau. (2012b, February 12). *Stats in action: Target uses American Community Survey (ACS) data* (Tech. Rep.). Washington, DC: Author. Retrieved from https://www.census.gov/library/video/sia_target_uses.html.

U.S. Census Bureau. (2016a). *American Community Survey and Puerto Rico Community Survey 2016 subject definitions* (Tech. Rep.). Washington, DC: Author. Retrieved from https://www.census.gov/programs-surveys/acs/technical-documentation/code-lists.2016.html.

U.S. Census Bureau. (2016b, September 15). *Measuring same-sex couples, sexual orientation, and gender identity on Census Bureau and federal surveys* (Webinar for the National LGBTQ Task Force). Washington, DC: Author. Retrieved from https://www.census.gov/library/working-papers/2016/demo/file-01.html.

U.S. Census Bureau. (2017a, February 28). *2015 National Content Test: Race and ethnicity analysis report* (Tech. Rep.). Washington, DC: Author. Retrieved from https://www.census.gov/programs-surveys/decennial-census/2020-census/planning-management/final-analysis/2015nct-race-ethnicity-analysis.html.

U.S. Census Bureau. (2017b, September). *ACS summary file technical documentation* (2016 ACS 1-year and 2012-2016 ACS 5-year Data Releases). Washington, DC: Author. Retrieved from https://www.census.gov/programs-surveys/acs/technical-documentation/summary-file-documentation.2016.html.

U.S. Census Bureau. (2017c). *American Community Survey: Accuracy of the data (2016)* (Tech. Rep.). Washington, DC: Author. Retrieved from https://www.census.gov/programs-surveys/acs/technical-documentation/code-lists.html.

U.S. Census Bureau. (2017d). *American Community Survey: Multiyear accuracy of the data (5-year 2012-2016)* (Tech. Rep.). Washington, DC: Author. Retrieved from https://www.census.gov/programs-surveys/acs/technical-documentation/code-lists.html.

U.S. Census Bureau. (2017e, July). *Methodology for state and county total housing unit estimates* (Population and housing unit estimates vintage 2017). Washington, DC: Author. Retrieved from https://www.census.gov/programs-surveys/popest/technical-documentation/methodology.html.

U.S. Census Bureau. (2017f, July). *Methodology for the subcounty total resident population estimates* (Population and housing unit estimates vintage 2017). Washington, DC: Author. Retrieved from https://www.census.gov/programs-surveys/popest/technical-documentation/methodology.html.

U.S. Census Bureau. (2017g, July). *Methodology for the United States population estimates: Nation, states, counties, and Puerto Rico* (Population and housing unit estimates vintage 2017). Washington, DC: Author. Retrieved from https://www.census.gov/programs-surveys/popest/technical-documentation/methodology.html.

U.S. Census Bureau. (2017h, March). *Subjects planned for the 2020 Census and the American Community Survey* (Federal Legislative and Program Uses). Washington, DC: U.S. Census Bureau. Retrieved from https://www.census.gov/library/publications/2017/dec/planned-subjects-2020-acs.html.

U.S. Census Bureau. (2018a, March 2). *2020 Census operational plan executive summary* (version 2.0). Washington, DC: Author. Retrieved from https://www.census.gov/programs-surveys/decennial-census/2020-census/planning-management/planning-docs/exe-sum.html.

U.S. Census Bureau. (2018b, March 29). *Questions planned for the 2020 Census and American Community Survey* (Federal Legislative and Program Uses). Washington, DC: Author. Retrieved from https://census.gov/library/publications/2018/dec/planned-questions-2020-acs.html.

U.S. Census Bureau. (2018c, July). *Understanding and using American Community Survey data: What all data users need to know* (Tech. Rep.). Washington, DC: Author. Retrieved from https://www.census.gov/programs-surveys/acs/guidance/handbooks/general.html.

U.S. Government Accountability Office. (2009, December). *Formula grants: Funding for the largest federal assistance programs is based on census-related data and other factors* (Report to Congressional requesters No. GAO-10-263). Washington, DC: Author. Retrieved from https://www.gao.gov/products/GAO-10-263.

U.S. Government Accountability Office. (2016, September). *Community development block grants: Sources of data on community income are limited* (Report to Congressional requesters; GAO-16-734). Washington, DC: Author. Retrieved from https://www.gao.gov/products/GAO-16-734.

Van Auken, P. M., Hammer, R. B., Voss, P. R., & Veroff, D. L. (2006). The American Community Survey in counties with seasonal populations. *Population Research and Policy Review, 25*, 275–292.

Wang, F., & Luo, W. (2005). Assessing spatial and nonspatial factors for healthcare access: Towards an integrated approach to defining health professional shortage areas. *Health & Place, 11*, 131–146.

Wang, H. L. (2018a, April 3). 17 states, 7 cities sue to remove citizenship question from 2020 Census. *National Public Radio*. Retrieved from https://n.pr/2uJ4Ryj.

Wang, H. L. (2018b, February 8). 2020 Census to count deployed troops at home bases, prisoners at facilities. *National Public Radio*. Retrieved from https://n.pr/2FSsHZ5.

Wang, H. L. (2018c, January 26). 2020 Census to keep racial, ethnic categories used in 2010. *National Public Radio*. Retrieved from https://n.pr/2GhjoCY.

Wang, H. L. (2018d, March 30). 2020 Census will ask about same-sex relationships. *National Public Radio*. Retrieved from https://n.pr/2uy24Ie.

Wang, H. L. (2018e, March 13). 2020 Census will ask black people about their exact origins. *National Public Radio*. Retrieved from https://n.pr/2tJa8W1.

Wang, H. L. (2018f, February 1). 2020 Census will ask white people more about their ethnicities. *National Public Radio*. Retrieved from https://n.pr/2GAd1Ld.

Wang, H. L. (2018g, April 7). 2 More lawsuits join legal fight over 2020 Census citizenship question. *National Public Radio*. Retrieved from https://n.pr/2JU07cE.

Wang, H. L. (2018h, January 10). Adding citizenship question risks "bad count" for 2020 Census, experts warn. *National Public Radio*. Retrieved from https://n.pr/2EESQuO.

Wang, H. L. (2018i, January 29). No Middle Eastern or North African category on 2020 Census, Bureau says. *National Public Radio*. Retrieved from https://n.pr/2GqX9dT.

Wang, H. L. (2018j, March 29). U.S. census to leave sexual orientation, gender identity questions off new surveys. *National Public Radio*. Retrieved from https://n.pr/2njH5Rf.

Wang, H. L. (2019, February 15). Supreme court to decide whether 2020 Census will include citizenship question. *National Public Radio*. Retrieved from https://n.pr/2WIXy3s.

Wang, M., Kleit, R. G., Cover, J., & Fowler, C. S. (2012). Spatial variations in US poverty: Beyond metropolitan and non-metropolitan. *Urban Studies, 49*(3), 563–585.

Warshawer, G. (2013, January 25). Bronx's Little Italy tries to add new spice. *The Wall Street Journal*. Retrieved from https://www.wsj.com/articles/SB10001424127887323539804578261800609567478.

Wilson, R., Hasanali, S., Sheikh, M., Cramer, S., Weinberg, G., Firth, A., . . . Soskolne, C. (2017). Challenges to the census: International trends and a need to consider public health benefits. *Public Health, 151*, 87–97.

Wong, D. M. (2010). *The Wall Street Journal guide to information graphics*. New York, NY: W. W. Norton.

# INDEX